THE GREAT CALL-UP

Major General Frederick Funston, commander of the Southern Department, the key figure in the National Guard call-up and border service. Courtesy of the Kansas State Historical Society.

THE GREAT CALL-UP
The Guard, the Border, and the Mexican Revolution

Charles H. Harris III
and
Louis R. Sadler

University of Oklahoma Press : Norman

Library of Congress Cataloging-in-Publication Data

Harris, Charles H. (Charles Houston)
 The great call-up : the Guard, the border, and the Mexican Revolution / Charles H. Harris III and Louis R. Sadler.
   pages cm
 Includes bibliographical references and index.
 ISBN 978-0-8061-4645-4 (cloth)
 ISBN 978-0-8061-5592-0 (paper)
 1. Mexican-American Border Region—History, Military—20th century. 2. United States—National Guard—Mobilization—History—20th century. 3. Mexico—History—Revolution, 1910–1920—Influence. 4. United States—National Guard—History—20th century. 5. United States—Foreign relations—Mexico. 6. Mexico—Foreign relations—United States. I. Sadler, Louis R. II. Title.
   F786.H313 2015
   355.370973—dc23
                    2014023333

The paper in this book meets the guidelines for permanence and durability of the Committee on Production Guidelines for Book Longevity of the Council on Library Resources, Inc. ∞

Copyright © 2015 by the University of Oklahoma Press, Norman, Publishing Division of the University. Paperback published 2016. Manufactured in the U.S.A.

All rights reserved. No part of this publication may be reproduced, stored in a retrieval system, or transmitted, in any form or by any means, electronic, mechanical, photocopying, recording, or otherwise—except as permitted under Section 107 or 108 of the United States Copyright Act—without the prior written permission of the University of Oklahoma Press. To request permission to reproduce selections from this book, write to Permissions, University of Oklahoma Press, 2800 Venture Drive, Norman OK 73069, or email rights.oupress@ou.edu.

To Colonel Leonid E. Kondratiuk

Contents

List of Illustrations   ix
Acknowledgments   xi

Introduction   3

Part I: Border Problem

1. The Mexican Problem   11
2. The First Call-Up   21
3. The War Crisis   52
4. The Great Call-Up   66

Part II: Border Service

5. San Antonio   77
6. Corpus Christi   117
7. Brownsville and Llano Grande   136
8. McAllen, Mission, Pharr   174
9. More McAllen, Mission, Pharr   203
10. Laredo   242
11. Eagle Pass   267
12. The Big Bend   280
13. El Paso   290
14. More El Paso   314

Contents

15. Deming   343
16. Columbus   354
17. Douglas   374
18. Naco   399
19. Nogales   405
20. California   439

    Conclusion   451

    Appendix: National Guard Order of Battle   455

Notes   467
Bibliography   523
Index   537

Illustrations

Frontis: Major General Frederick Funston
General Funston and staff   221
Pharr, Texas, with New York National Guard encampment   221
Funeral in Pharr, Texas   222
2nd New York Field Artillery   222
Rifle pit on the Rio Grande, 23rd New York Infantry   223
23rd New York Infantry machine gun company   223
Lower Rio Grande Valley vegetation   224
23rd New York Infantry   224
Company I, 23rd New York Infantry, August 1916   225
23rd New York Infantry Post Exchange   226
2nd New York Field Artillery practice firing   226
Camp of the 4th South Dakota Infantry   227
Troop B, Texas Cavalry Squadron   228
Army YMCA in the Big Bend   229
Tractor train in the Big Bend   229
Football game in Ruidosa   230
Bird's-eye view of Camp Cotton   230
5th Massachusetts Infantry Band   231
Pennsylvania guardsmen establishing camp   231
Guardsmen on the "Big Hike" from El Paso to Las Cruces   232
Major General Charles M. Clement and Brigadier General George Bell, Jr.   232
8th Ohio Infantry Band   233
The Ohio-Pennsylvania Brigade   234
War-strength division parade in El Paso   235

Illustrations

Remount station at Fort Bliss, El Paso   236
Typical sandstorm at Fort Bliss   236
National guardsmen erecting tents at Deming, New Mexico   237
Camp of 1st Colorado Artillery   237
Detachment of the 1st New Mexico Infantry   238
2nd Montana Infantry guarding copper smelters   238
Officers of the 5th New Jersey Infantry at the international boundary marker   239
1st California Field Artillery, Nogales, Arizona   239
U.S.-Mexico boundary, Nogales   240
3rd Oregon Infantry on the move   241

Table

8.1. New York National Guard, June 18, 1916   176

Maps

Texas and the U.S.-Mexico border from Brownsville to El Paso   80
The U.S.-Mexico border from El Paso to San Diego   344

Acknowledgments

This book would not have been possible without the generous assistance we received from a number of institutions and individuals. Realizing the formidable research challenge we faced, we wrote to the adjutants general of the states requesting their assistance, and we received a gratifying amount of cooperation, whether from adjutants general themselves or from those to whom the adjutants general referred us. In addition, the personnel of various museums and historical societies went out of their way to support our endeavors, as did a number of librarians. To each of them we express our heartfelt thanks: Colonel Leonid E. Kondratiuk, director of Historical Services, Massachusetts National Guard Military Museum and Archives; Jim Gandy, assistant librarian/archivist, New York State Military Museum; 2nd Lieutenant Michael Anthony Rodriquez, historian, Public Affairs Office, California National Guard; Brigadier General James A. Adkins, adjutant general of Maryland; Captain Wayde R. Minam, command historian, Maryland National Guard; Joseph Balkoski, historian, Maryland National Guard; 1st Lieutenant Andy Thaggard, command historian, Mississippi National Guard; Darla Brock, archivist, Tennessee State Library and Archives; Michael W. Vogt, curator, Iowa Gold Star Military Museum; Gregory A. Moore, command historian, Florida National Guard; Steve C. Rucker, director, Arkansas National Guard Museum; Master Sergeant Brian J. Faltinson, command historian, Wisconsin Army National Guard; Staff Sergeant Joshua Mann, command historian, Ohio Army National Guard; Captain Chris Borders, Idaho Army National Guard; Mark Reaves, information specialist, State of Vermont Public Records; Richard N. Campbell, state military personnel officer, Utah National Guard; Deidre Forster and Bob Holmes, Wyoming Army National Guard; Staff

Acknowledgments

Sergeant Rita Tompkins, out of service records manager, Maine Army National Guard; Janet E. Roberts, Maine State Archives; Anthony Douin, archivist, Maine State Archives; Master Sergeant David R. Glidden, support service supervisor, Maine Army National Guard; Colonel Warren W. Aney, Oregon Army National Guard historian; Sergeant Gail E. Parnelle, History Office, Georgia National Guard; Wendy Goen, archivist, Arizona State Library; Lisa G. Sharik, deputy director, Texas Military Forces Museum; Rita Sanchez, executive assistant to the adjutant general of Texas; Donaly E. Brice, senior archivist, Texas State Library; John Anderson, photo archivist, Texas State Library; William B. Boehm, historian, National Guard Bureau; Cathleen Pearl, archivist, National Guard Association; Mark Millorn, colleague and computer whiz, New Mexico State University; Major Lori L. Hampa-Chamberlin, Montana National Guard; Tom Graham, historian, New Hampshire National Guard; Jim Hurst, historian, Las Cruces, New Mexico; Lieutenant Colonel Bob Vrana, public affairs officer, Nebraska National Guard; John Trowbridge, command historian, Kentucky National Guard; Lieutenant Colonel James B. McCabe, command historian, Illinois National Guard; Captain Tamara Spicer, public affairs officer, Missouri National Guard; Joseph G. Bilby, assistant curator, National Guard Militia Museum of New Jersey; Staff Sergeant Claudia L. Bullard, command historian, Oklahoma National Guard; Lori Pribble, assistant to the Oklahoma adjutant general; Major Scott Bell, South Carolina National Guard historian; Major General Steven R. Doohen, adjutant general of South Dakota; Mary Schaff, librarian, Washington State Library; Robert R. and Jean Gates, photo archivists, Texas Military Forces Museum; C. Sigrid Maitrejean and Teresa Leal, Pimería Alta Historical Society; Jivonna Stewart, librarian, New Mexico State University; Rosemary Loa, librarian, Corpus Christi Public Library; Amber Korb, librarian and archivist, California State Military Museum; E. G. "Buddy" Sturgis, Jr., director, South Carolina Military Museum; Don Williamson, archivist, Luna County Historical Society; Sergeant Roberto Digiovine, South Carolina Army National Guard; Rebekah Tabah, photo archivist and curator, Arizona Historical Society at Papago Park; Phyllis Kinnison, archivist, Museum of South Texas History; Nancy Sherbert, acquisitions archivist, Kansas State Historical Society; Tracy Thoennes, curator, Kathleen M. Daly, museum technician, and Brigadier General James B. Thayer, Oregon Military Museum; Laura Hoff, archivist, Arizona State Historical Society; Matthew T. Reitzel, archivist,

Acknowledgments

South Dakota State Archives; Shane Thomas, New Mexico State University, provided photographic assistance.

If we have inadvertently omitted anyone, we sincerely apologize. We thank our wives for their considerable assistance on this project and for putting up with us.

THE GREAT CALL-UP

Introduction

The Mexican border has become the topic of increasing concern and controversy in recent years. The current debate over border security takes place against a background of National Guard involvement. President George W. Bush in 2006, in Operation Jump Start, ordered 2,000 guardsmen to the border to deal with a peaceful invasion—the thousands of people flooding across the international boundary from Mexico, most of them in search of a better life. And in 2010, President Barack Obama ordered 1,200 guardsmen to the border to reinforce the 340 guard members already supporting the Border Patrol. But the National Guard's connection with the Mexican border did not begin just in the twenty-first century.

President Woodrow Wilson on June 18, 1916, took the unprecedented step of calling into federal service virtually the entire army National Guard of some 150,000 men to meet an armed threat from Mexico. Raids covertly sponsored by the Mexican government into the lower Rio Grande valley of Texas precipitated the call-up. About 110,000 guardsmen were rushed to the border as rapidly as rail transportation could be arranged.

This great peacetime mobilization has been neglected by historians for two reasons. First, it has been confused with the Punitive Expedition into Mexico led by General John J. Pershing against the Mexican revolutionary chieftain General Francisco "Pancho" Villa, who raided the New Mexico border hamlet of Columbus on March 9, 1916. The raiders killed eighteen soldiers and civilians and burned part of the town. Although President

The Great Call-Up

Wilson had been most reluctant to intervene in Mexico, a country in the throes of revolution since 1910, public opinion demanded retaliation. Hence the Punitive Expedition, which crossed into the state of Chihuahua on March 15, 1916. The expedition's strength fluctuated from eight thousand to twelve thousand troops, with a monthly average of about ten thousand.[1] Pershing and his men remained in Mexico until February 5, 1917. Their presence obviously precipitated a crisis in United States-Mexican relations. While the Punitive Expedition was able to defeat Pancho Villa's guerrillas, the real problem was Mexican president Venustiano Carranza's regulars, with whom the Punitive Expedition clashed on several occasions, one of them bringing the countries close to war.

The Punitive Expedition has projected an air of glamour as the last campaign of the U.S. Cavalry (and the last glorious cavalry charge against an enemy). The expedition was also characterized by the use of aircraft and by the forced mechanization of the U.S. Army, which occurred because the expedition was based on a false premise. Since Pancho Villa was the enemy of both the United States and President Carranza, Washington, D.C., rather naively assumed that Carranza would cooperate with the expedition, which was to be supplied by rail from El Paso. But the ultranationalistic Carranza denounced the expedition as a violation of Mexican sovereignty, demanded its immediate recall, and forbade entry into Mexican towns or the use of Mexican railroads. Pershing thus had to be supplied by hastily assembled truck convoys from his base camp in Columbus, New Mexico. Unfortunately the army was still committed to the traditional use of animals and had been most reluctant to adopt newfangled vehicles such as cars and trucks. Although the military had begun to mechanize, authorizing two truck companies in the wake of the Columbus raid, as of March 22, Pershing had a grand total of four operable trucks. In this crisis the chief of staff, General Hugh Scott, ordered $450,000 to be spent on trucks, without prior congressional authorization. The crash program resulted in the army purchasing nearly six hundred trucks in fiscal 1916.[2] By July 20, 1916, though, Carranza did permit the use of Mexican railroads to supply commodities such as forage to the Punitive Expedition. This was fortunate because the truck convoys were already strained to the limit.

The expedition has received considerable attention from professional historians, popular writers, and from the army itself.[3] This focus has overshadowed the National Guard call-up, which writers have tended to

INTRODUCTION

subsume into the Punitive Expedition. For example, William F. Howard's article "New Yorkers on the Southern Border,"[4] begins: "15,000 New York National Guardsmen went to the Mexican border in 1916 to defend America against Pancho Villa and his rebels." And a recent M.A. thesis purports to discuss Utah's role in the Punitive Expedition;[5] however, Utah had no role in the Punitive Expedition. As we shall see, some writers have the National Guard chasing Villa all over the place, even guard units that never got within six hundred miles of Villa.

To clear up this widespread misunderstanding it should be emphasized that the term "Punitive Expedition" refers to Pershing's command of regular army troops, which operated in the Mexican state of Chihuahua. The National Guard call-up was related to but was distinct from the Punitive Expedition. As Secretary of War Newton D. Baker stated, "This call for militia is wholly unrelated to General Pershing's expedition and contemplates no additional entry into Mexico, except as may be necessary to pursue bandits who attempt outrages on American soil."[6] In point of fact, only two National Guard infantry regiments, the 1st New Mexico and the 2nd Massachusetts, were assigned to the Punitive Expedition for administration, and neither unit saw action in Mexico; they only helped to guard the Columbus base camp.

The second reason the 1916 National Guard mobilization has been neglected is that it has been overshadowed by the entry of the United States into World War I in 1917. Despite its importance, even those writers who mention the call-up have tended to deal with it only in passing, in some cases devoting only a paragraph or two to the topic, focusing instead on the guard's performance in World War I. And much of what has been written has been from the army's point of view, which essentially disparages the National Guard. Ironically, however, the army held the National Guard to a standard that the army itself could not meet. Relations between the regulars and guardsmen were sometimes acrimonious, for the army reflected the professional's contempt for the amateur. There was considerable suspicion among guard officers that the army was using the mobilization in order to take control of the National Guard. The problem was that the National Guard historically had been organized by the states to deal primarily with domestic crises such as strikes, riots, and natural disasters. Thus there was a heavy concentration of infantry units and a lack of artillery, engineers, signal corps, and transport. "The National Guard's major problems had to do with the maintenance of unit strength and the inexperience of senior officers."[7] The National Guard was simply not organized to fight a major war. But then neither was the regular army.

The great call-up revealed not only the shortcomings of the National Guard—and they were many—but, as importantly, the shortcomings of the U.S. Army itself, which was under-strength and whose logistical structure was overwhelmed. In addition, the call-up placed an enormous strain on the nation's railroads, suddenly faced with having to provide hundreds of trains to rush guardsmen to the border. The call-up served as a dress rehearsal for World War I, revealing major weaknesses that urgently needed correction.

In discussing the 1916 call-up it is not enough to refer just to "the National Guard," for there were significant variations in proficiency, equipment, and leadership among units from the various states and sometimes even within the same state. At one end of the spectrum was New York, which fielded a well-equipped division of 18,500; at the other end was New Mexico, which had only become a state in 1912 and whose National Guard scraped along on an annual state appropriation of a mere $2,500. There were also significant differences between so-called elite "silk stocking" National Guard units composed of wealthy and socially prominent men and the much more numerous run-of-the-mill organizations. What characterized the guard and what caused the regulars to disdain it was first of all that many units resembled quasi-social clubs; moreover, the guard traditionally elected its officers and noncommissioned officers (NCOs), whose performance was uneven. On the other hand, the guard's strong suit was its political connections. Guardsmen were, after all, civilians in uniform, and their ability to appeal to their congressmen and senators continually upset regular officers, who were accustomed to observing the chain of command.

The nerve center of the mobilization was Fort Sam Houston in San Antonio, headquarters of the Southern Department. From there Major General Frederick Funston commanded not only the regulars in the border region and in the Punitive Expedition but also the concentration points of the National Guard: San Antonio, Corpus Christi, Brownsville, Llano Grande, the McAllen-Mission-Pharr triangle, Laredo, Eagle Pass, the Big Bend, El Paso, Deming, Columbus, Douglas, Naco, and Nogales.

Given the complexity of the subject, we decided against a strictly chronological treatment. Since the mobilization was state-based, we have opted to give the states their due by treating the guard in each of the major

Introduction

concentration points, beginning with San Antonio and Corpus Christi, then moving westward along the border from Brownsville to California.

As with differences in National Guard organizations, the experience of guardsmen on the border varied. Those in Brownsville got to endure a hurricane, while those in El Paso coped with blinding dust storms and the Southwest monsoon season. Despite these differences the call-up forced guardsmen to interact with men from other states, thus eroding regionalism and contributing to the concept of the United States as a melting pot, a concept that of course has since been replaced by diversity. Many guardsmen from the North and East experienced culture shock when they arrived on the border, and since most of the population was Hispanic many soldiers were uneasy about where the Hispanics' loyalty really lay.

The call-up had a significant economic impact on the border region, both in terms of army supply and construction, and in terms of businessmen eager to help the troops spend their pay. Besides pumping millions of dollars into the economy of the Southwest, the army used its considerable leverage to force the city fathers of various towns to improve hygiene and to combat prostitution and the liquor traffic, among other changes. Towns and cities in the border region vied with each other to cash in on the mobilization bonanza by having guardsmen stationed there, and they bitterly resented attempts by other localities to steal "their" guardsmen.

In examining the 1916 call-up the authors make no claim to be definitive, given the breadth of the topic. Rather, we attempt to synthesize the experiences of the men from forty-seven states (Nevada had no National Guard) and the District of Columbia. And we make no apologies for our extensive use of newspapers, for it is largely through this medium that the human story of the mobilization emerges. Finally, unlike almost all other American authors dealing with these events of 1916, we incorporate sources in Spanish.

For decades we have been engaged in a research project to analyze the impact of the Mexican Revolution (1910–20) on the border region.[8] The present book differs from our previous efforts. The great call-up was indeed motivated by the events of the Mexican Revolution, and the presence of thousands of guardsmen helped to convince the Mexicans that the United States was serious about protecting its border. In this sense the mobilization helped to preserve the peace between the United States and Mexico. Thus part I of the book is entitled "Border Problem." But by the time the guard was deployed to the border the crisis with Mexico had abated. To the great disappointment of the guardsmen who had come to fight Mexicans, the troops were kept on active duty. Thus part II of the book is entitled "Border Service." In some cases units were still in federal service when the United States entered World War I. And some of these remained on active duty for three years, going from camps in the United States to France and not returning home until the spring of 1919.

It is in connection with World War I that the significance of the great call-up emerges. Between June 1916 and April 1917 the guard received intensive field training. Units from different states were sometimes grouped into larger provisional organizations. Not only did the men become more proficient, but many officers gained invaluable experience in commanding large formations. At the same time, the guard was receiving badly needed equipment and supplies. The great call-up transformed the National Guard into a much more effective fighting force, for it was as close as the United States came to the large-scale military maneuvers in which European armies traditionally engaged.

PART I

Border Problem

Chapter 1

The Mexican Problem

Mexico was arguably the principal foreign policy problem for the United States from 1911 to 1916. Because of geographical proximity, developments in Mexico were automatically of concern to the United States, but from November 1910 to May 1920, Mexico was convulsed by revolution. Washington, D.C., was concerned not only with protecting American citizens and properties in Mexico but also with defending the border and controlling Mexican exile activity in the United States.

Having achieved independence in 1821, Mexico plunged into political instability for the next sixty years, lurching between monarchy, federal republic, and centralized republic, mainly through revolutions. Contributing to political instability were foreign invasions—notably by Spain in 1828, France in 1838–39, the United States in 1846–48, and France again in 1861–67. Political turmoil naturally had a devastating impact on the economy, and Mexican regimes were usually bankrupt.

All this began to change in 1876 with the seizure of power by General Porfirio Díaz, a hero of the 1861–67 war against the French. Díaz performed the seemingly impossible, transforming the country from instability and backwardness into a model for developing nations. First he imposed order, crushing banditry and insurrection while either eliminating or reaching accommodations with regional strongmen. Basically Díaz constructed a dictatorship behind a constitutional facade. Elections were held, but the government dictated the outcome. By imposing order and stability, he created a climate favorable to investment, and foreigners began to risk their money in Mexico. Since Díaz was careful to favor foreigners, their home governments had few complaints about him. Foreign investment fueled an economic boom that seemingly transformed the nation. Historically the axis of power in the country had been west to east, from Guadalajara through Mexico City to the gulf port of Veracruz. Thus from colonial times Mexico had been oriented toward Europe. Díaz, however, changed the axis to north–south, from Mexico City to the American border. He sponsored the building of three trunk rail lines linking the capital with Laredo, El Paso, and Nogales, tying the economy to that of the United States. The northern tier of states, sparsely populated and long wracked by Indian raids and drought, now developed rapidly, with American investment playing a key role. Reflecting these fundamental changes, the United States began deactivating the chain of forts built along the border in the nineteenth century.

Díaz had apparently found the key to governing. But as the decades passed and he was periodically reelected as president, his countrymen increasingly resented the preferential treatment of foreigners and foreign capital's domination of the economy. A growing feeling of nationalism was encapsulated in the slogan "Mexico for the Mexicans." Moreover, the younger generation was often frozen out of power, for Díaz usually relied on men of his own generation whose loyalty had been amply proven.

Beginning in 1900, an opposition movement emerged, led by a young intellectual, Ricardo Flores Magón, who became an anarchist dedicated to overthrowing the dictator and eliminating the capitalist system. Flores Magón and his followers, called *magonistas*, tried to launch a nationwide uprising in 1906 and 1908 but failed miserably. While urging his supporters to take up arms, Flores Magón himself remained safely at his headquarters in Los Angeles. (He was a thinker not a fighter.) Although the magonistas failed militarily they did have considerably greater success as propagandists, exposing the corruption and oppression of the regime and calling for social justice, thus helping to prepare the way for the Mexican Revolution. Another factor in this regard was Díaz's surprising announcement in 1908 that he did not plan to seek reelection in 1910.

Taking him at his word, political liberals began organizing for the 1910 presidential election. Among these liberals was a wealthy and idealistic young landowner from the border state of Coahuila, Francisco I. Madero. Although his family was closely connected to the regime and had benefited enormously by that connection, Madero felt that the nation's pressing social and economic problems, such as the concentration of land ownership, could not be resolved until there had first been political reform. When he announced his candidacy for the presidency in 1910, Madero's campaign slogan was "effective suffrage, no reelection."

Díaz had given the politically ambitious the opportunity to reveal themselves; he then announced that he planned to run for reelection in 1910 after all. But by 1910, Díaz was eighty years old and although still vigorous was using tactics that had worked in the past but were no longer as effective. For example, prior to the election he had Madero, the only opposition figure with the moral courage to challenge him for the presidency, arrested and jailed on a trumped-up charge of fomenting unrest. When the election was held, the government announced that Díaz had won overwhelmingly. This produced widespread outrage.

Meanwhile Madero, under arrest in the city of San Luis Potosí, faced a dilemma. He could either accept Díaz's reelection, make his peace with the dictator, and return to a life of luxury in Coahuila or he could try to lead a rebellion. Most reluctantly, Madero chose the latter course. One of the great ironies of the Mexican Revolution is that it was started by a man who was not a revolutionist and who took up arms only as a last resort. The movement he set on foot plunged Mexico into a decade of revolution, during which more than a million Mexicans died, out of a population of some fifteen million.

Madero escaped from San Luis Potosí in October 1910 and fled to the United States, where, like Flores Magón, he organized an opposition movement in exile. Establishing his headquarters in San Antonio, Texas, Madero set about fomenting a nationwide uprising against the dictator. Any self-respecting Mexican rebellion was accompanied by a "plan," a manifesto denouncing the incumbent and promising a glorious revolutionary future. Madero's movement was no exception, but, because of the neutrality laws of the United States prohibiting the use of American territory for attempting to overthrow a friendly government, such as that of Díaz, the manifesto could not be called the "Plan de San Antonio." Therefore it was backdated to October 19, the last day Madero had physically been in San Luis Potosí and was entitled the "Plan de San Luis Potosí." It was essentially political in nature, calling for a national uprising on November 20, 1910, naming Madero as provisional president, and promising effective suffrage and no reelection. (Mexico has achieved "no reelection" but the "effective suffrage" part is still a work in progress.)

Border Problem

Trying to organize a nationwide revolution in the space of six weeks was manifestly impossible, and, when November 20 came, nothing much happened. Madero's insurrection seemed even more futile than Flores Magón's attempts. Flores Magón, incidentally, denounced Madero as not being a real revolutionary and prohibited his followers from having anything to do with the Coahuilan rebel. Yet revolutionary spirit was stirring, especially in the border state of Chihuahua, where talented amateur guerrilla chieftains such as Pascual Orozco and Francisco "Pancho" Villa began defeating units of Díaz's army. With each victory more and more people became *maderistas*. By early 1911, Díaz was losing control of the largest state in the country. And by March 1911, in a related but independent movement, Emiliano Zapata emerged as the leader of agrarian revolutionists in the state of Morelos, which adjoined the Federal District. Adding to the dictator's troubles, the United States was losing confidence in his ability to retain power. As a precaution, in March 1911, the U.S. Army assembled a thirteen-thousand-man Maneuver Division at Fort Sam Houston in San Antonio to deal with any contingency.[1] The troop concentration also sent a powerful message—the United States now doubted Díaz's ability to contain the revolution.

Revolutionary momentum culminated on May 10, 1911, when Madero's forces unexpectedly captured the largest border town, Ciudad Juárez, across the Rio Grande from El Paso, Texas. The psychological impact was enormous—Díaz, the seemingly invulnerable strongman, was shown to be a paper tiger. Within two weeks his regime collapsed and he fled into exile in Paris, where he died in 1915. Improbably, the revolution had succeeded, but it succeeded too easily—Díaz was gone, but most of the Díaz structure remained in place.

Madero was the man of the hour. He made a triumphant entry into Mexico City to the wild acclaim of enormous crowds, whose expectations he had raised to unrealistic levels. Then in a laudable but politically naive move he resigned as provisional president to avoid the charge that he had shot his way into office. He planned to run for constitutional president in an election to be held in the fall of 1911. But until then he was just a private citizen who could only suggest and complain to the pro-Díaz provisional government he had agreed to. That regime, headed by Francisco León de la Barra, who had been Díaz's ambassador to the United States, did everything it could to undercut Madero and impede any revolutionary reform. So by the time Madero was duly elected president in October 1911, in the cleanest election yet, he was considerably weaker than in May at the height of his popularity.

The Mexican Problem

His presidential tenure was brief and unhappy. A succession of generals —Bernardo Reyes, Pascual Orozco, and Félix Díaz, the dictator's nephew— challenged him by leading rebellions. And in Morelos, Emiliano Zapata fought Madero as he had fought Díaz because Madero refused to implement immediate and widespread land reform. Madero favored land reform by due—and lengthy—legal process, something for which Zapata and his *campesino* followers had no patience. Although Madero managed to defeat the rebellious generals and to contain Zapata's forces, in the end he was overthrown in February 1913 by a military coup in Mexico City itself. On February 22, the plotters had Madero and the vice president shot as they were being transferred to prison.

Mexico's new strongman, General Victoriano Huerta, immediately began consolidating his power.[2] While many officials promptly acknowledged him as provisional president, Venustiano Carranza, governor of Coahuila, did not. Carranza, who would dominate the Mexican Revolution from 1913 to 1920, soon emerged as leader of a coalition of northerners fighting Huerta (Zapata fought Huerta independently).[3] A career politician, Carranza organized the Constitutionalist Army, whose very name reassured people that he was not some wild-eyed radical. And in a particularly shrewd move, Carranza did not proclaim himself provisional president since the powers of that office were constrained by the constitution. Rather, he proclaimed himself First Chief of the Constitutionalist Army, and his powers were whatever Carranza wanted them to be.

Huerta, popularly perceived as "the Usurper," relied on support from the regular army and traditionally conservative elements but was unable to stamp out rebellion. Under Carranza's leadership the Constitutionalist movement flourished, in large measure because of its strength in the border states. The Constitutionalists could secure weaponry, raise money, recruit manpower, market loot, and find refuge in the United States. As Carranza's subordinates, such as General Francisco "Pancho" Villa, won a string of impressive victories against the dispirited Huerta army, Zapata was threatening the Federal District, and by the spring of 1914, the Huerta regime was tottering. The United States gave it a final push. This country influenced the course of the Mexican Revolution in several important ways. First, the United States refused to accord diplomatic recognition to Huerta as the legitimate president of Mexico, which of course greatly encouraged his enemies. Second, the United States lifted the arms embargo on Mexico, enabling the Constitutionalists to acquire weaponry on a par with Huerta's forces. Third, the United States applied the neutrality laws selectively, harshly against Huerta's partisans while turning a blind eye to the activities of the Constitutionalists. And finally, the United States severed Huerta's crucial lifeline to Europe. Using the pretext of an alleged insult to the American flag, the United States bombarded and occupied the key port of Veracruz on April 21, 1914. General Frederick Funston was appointed military governor, and the United States did not withdraw its troops from the seaport until November.[4] By then, Huerta was no longer in the picture. Admitting defeat, he had fled into European exile.

The revolution had again triumphed, and during the struggle against Huerta much of the Díaz legacy had been destroyed. But now the victorious revolutionaries turned on each other in a ferocious power struggle. The revolution entered its bloodiest phase. Carranza retained his title of First Chief and demanded obedience from all Constitutionalists. But Pancho Villa had emerged as the most powerful general in Mexico and was becoming increasingly insubordinate.[5] The two were on a collision course. Carranza and his subordinate General Alvaro Obregón outmaneuvered Villa and Zapata, who had been blocked from occupying Mexico City as Huerta fell. Villa and Zapata became allies and rallied an anti-Carranza coalition, the Convention, whose military muscle Villa provided. In a period of desperate fighting in 1915, Obregón smashed Villa's hitherto invincible Division of the North, and Carranza prevailed. But he desperately needed U.S. diplomatic recognition; otherwise the United States retained the option of supporting Carranza's enemies.

While fighting for its life against Villa, the Carranza faction co-opted a visionary anarchist "plan" and put it to brilliant use. The Plan de San Diego, as it was called, came to light in January 1915 with the arrest of one Basilio Ramos in the south Texas town of McAllen. The authorities were dumbfounded for the manifesto called for nothing less than a Hispanic insurrection, the independence of the Southwest, and its possible annexation by Mexico. Most explosively, the plan called for the killing of all Anglo males over sixteen years of age.[6] The key figure in the plan was Agustín S. Garza, who was careful to remain in the background. Initially nothing happened, and the Anglo population not unnaturally regarded the plan as ludicrous. But in the summer of 1915, guerrilla warfare erupted, characterized by raids across the Rio Grande from Carranza-controlled territory into south Texas. The violence intensified, for the raids produced a massive Anglo backlash. The situation deteriorated to the point that a race war seemed imminent.

Although some have regarded the Plan de San Diego movement as a Hispanic liberation struggle, recent evidence indicates that the *carrancistas* were using the plan for their own purposes.[7] The only times the plan was important was when it received support from Mexico, and the only times it received support from Mexico was when it suited Carranza, whose forces controlled the Mexican side of the lower Rio Grande. On various occasions the raiders included Carranza troops in civilian clothing. Carranza had devised a sophisticated strategy for securing U.S. diplomatic recognition: covertly sponsor raids into Texas, assure Washington, D.C., that, if it recognized him diplomatically, he would put an end to the deplorable border violence and shut down the Plan de San Diego movement.

A series of raids from July into October convulsed the lower Rio Grande border. The most spectacular clash occurred on August 8, when raiders attacked the Norias subheadquarters of the enormous King Ranch, some seventy miles north of Brownsville. As was the case in most of these engagements, this raid was a defeat for the marauders—a scratch force of eight cavalrymen and a handful of civilians fought off some sixty Mexicans. The clash also produced a marked escalation in the Anglo backlash; besides the army bringing in reinforcements and the Texas Ranger force being increased, home guards and vigilantes sprang up everywhere. Being denounced as a "bad Meskin" was tantamount to a death sentence. In a larger sense, the troubles heightened Anglo suspicion of Hispanics in general, the concern being that their real allegiance was to Mexico rather than the United States, and thus they constituted a fifth column.

Despite the frequency of the raids, they accomplished little as far as the Plan de San Diego's stated objectives went, but the crisis they produced worked greatly to Carranza's benefit. Washington, D.C., not only permitted him to transport thousands of troops on United States railroads from Texas to Arizona to repel an offensive by Pancho Villa in Sonora, but the Wilson administration recognized him as the de facto president of Mexico on October 19, 1915; within a week the raids ended. The Plan de San Diego leaders hid in Mexico at Carranza's pleasure.

By the spring of 1916, Carranza's position was stronger than ever. Villa and Zapata were still fighting him but they had been reduced to regional figures. Villa might have been down but he was certainly not out. On the night of March 9, 1916, he attacked the New Mexico border hamlet of Columbus, burning and looting part of the town and killing eighteen soldiers and civilians.[8] Although President Woodrow Wilson had been most reluctant to intervene in Mexico, he had to respond. Since the army was already stretched thinly, there were calls to activate National Guard units to protect the border. However, on March 12, the secretary of war informed President Wilson that it was "most undesirable to call out militia until all [the] resources [of the] regular army are exhausted."[9]

Accordingly, on March 15, General John J. Pershing led the Punitive Expedition into Chihuahua. The State Department announced that his mission was to capture Villa,[10] but the army tasked Pershing with the much more realistic mission of dispersing Villa's guerrillas so they could no longer menace the American border. However, since the Punitive Expedition was predicated on the false assumption that Carranza would cooperate, Columbus, New Mexico, rather than El Paso necessarily became the base for the expedition, and the army embarked on a crash program of mechanization—truck convoys from Columbus, with civilian drivers, would be Pershing's logistical lifeline.

Once again the Mexican border preoccupied planners in the War Department. There were simply not enough regulars available to protect the border properly. Some areas were guarded only by small detachments. Manning one of these outposts, on the Rio Grande at the border village of Glenn Springs in the Big Bend region of Texas, were a sergeant and eight men of the 14th Cavalry. On the night of May 5, a force of several hundred mounted Mexicans forded the Rio Grande and swept into Glenn Springs. The cavalry troopers fought against overwhelming odds for several hours; three troopers were killed and two were wounded. After attacking the cavalry outpost the raiders looted and burned several buildings in Glenn Springs.[11] They then looted the store at the nearby settlement of Boquillas, killed a boy, took several prisoners (who later escaped), and disappeared across the Rio Grande. Glenn Springs was so isolated that it took some time for word of the raid to reach Southern Department headquarters in San Antonio. (The army embarked on strenuous efforts to improve communications in the Big Bend.)[12]

When news of the raid reached Marfa, the military headquarters in the Big Bend, two troops of the 14th Cavalry and a machine gun platoon started from Fort Clark, under the command of Colonel Frederick W. Sibley. Two troops of the 8th Cavalry from Fort Bliss in El Paso under Major George T. Langhorne, formerly military attaché in Berlin, likewise entrained for Marathon. From there the cavalry had an eighty-five mile ride to the scene of the attacks. A civilian posse of some fifty men also left Marathon for Glenn

The Mexican Problem

Springs. A Coast Artillery company provided security at Marathon, soon reinforced by two troops of the 6th U.S. Cavalry.[13]

What ensued was something the bandits probably had not envisioned—Major Langhorne's flying column pursuing them into the wilderness across from the Big Bend.[14] Trying to keep up with Langhorne was a convoy of three automobiles and two trucks loaded with food and forage, followed by a long line of pack animals with forage, machine guns, and ammunition. Colonel Sibley, with troops F and H of the 14th Cavalry and a machine gun troop, crossed the Rio Grande to reinforce Langhorne's column. Sibley's force, a miniature Punitive Expedition, penetrated more than a hundred miles into sparsely populated Mexican territory. To support Sibley, two troops of the 6th U.S. Cavalry were ordered from Marathon to Boquillas, but the order was countermanded, and on May 21 Sibley and Langhorne led their men back into Texas at Boquillas after ten days in Mexico. The cavalry had forced the bandits to release two captives but had outrun their supplies and communications. Moreover, Mexican troops were belatedly massing to confront the American forces. Sibley and Langhorne returned with their men to their normal stations, while the 6th Cavalry resumed its patrol of the Big Bend.[15]

Carranza declared that the Glenn Springs raid was another example of the work of the "common enemy" of the United States and Mexico. He blamed Mexican exiles, and he reiterated his demand for the withdrawal of American troops from Mexico.[16] Carranza vigorously protested against this new violation of Mexican sovereignty and territorial integrity. Relations between the two countries continued to sour as the American army poured thousands of reinforcements into the Southern Department from posts as far away as New York and Washington states.[17] On May 15, General Funston ordered guards to be stationed on every bridge on the Southern Pacific railroad between San Antonio and El Paso, since in the event of large-scale military operations the railroad would be indispensable. He also rushed seven companies of Coast Artillery to Del Rio, from where they were distributed westward along the Southern Pacific to guard bridges and provide garrisons for the small towns of Sanderson and Langtry.[18]

Minor raids from Mexico continued: two ranches near Presidio were the latest targets.[19] On May 14, a warning that a raid against Terlingua was imminent caused the twenty-five 14th Cavalry troopers stationed there hurriedly to construct earthworks and mount two machine guns. These preparations evidently prevented the attack, although the store of a Hispanic merchant was riddled by shots from across the Rio Grande. The man and his family survived by lying on the floor during the fusillade. Conditions at Terlingua were considered so dangerous that the county judge suspended the public schools and the sheriff wired the governor pleading for additional troops.[20]

On May 9, 1916, the chief of staff dispatched three regular regiments to the border. To reinforce the 12th Infantry at Douglas, Arizona, the 14th Infantry was ordered there, as were three batteries of the 6th Field Artillery; the garrison now numbered a brigade of nearly five thousand. In addition, the 1st Battalion of the 21st Infantry went to Nogales, where the 1st Cavalry was already stationed. On June 12, one thousand coast artillerymen and a battalion of engineers were ordered to the border.[21] But the army was rapidly running out of troops for border duty, the only available regulars being Coast Artillery units.

Besides ordering the above military dispositions, Major General Frederick Funston and Major General Hugh Scott, chief of staff of the U.S. Army, were negotiating in El Paso and Juárez with General Alvaro Obregón, Carranza's minister of War and Marine. Funston and Scott became convinced of the Mexicans' bad faith and sent an urgent joint telegram on May 8 to the War Department. They stressed that the army was stretched too thinly to protect the border and that the United States had no adequate reserves and that "we think the border should at once be supported by at least 150,000 additional troops." Therefore they urged that the National Guard of Arizona, New Mexico, and Texas be called into federal service at once to reinforce border defense, with the possibility of calling up additional National Guard if necessary. For the army it was a galling admission that it had to rely on the despised militia as the only available reserve. The generals' telegram produced a reaction that was, by Washington, D.C., standards, akin to the speed of light: by presidential order, the National Guard of the three states was called up the next day, May 9, 1916.[22]

Chapter 2

The First Call-Up

Arizona, New Mexico, and Texas were required to furnish four thousand guardsmen for border protection.[1] Nevertheless the administration remained uneasy about Mexican intentions, especially in light of Carranza's aggressive note of May 22 demanding the immediate withdrawal of the Punitive Expedition. Secretary of War Baker on May 29 felt it "desirable to increase the forces on the border at once, both as a safeguard against surprise and as a moral deterrent to aggression." He and General Scott agreed that if additional guardsmen were needed they should come from "southern States who are to some extent acclimated to the hot weather which will be experienced in Texas, and also not to rob the States of Militia in which there are large cities."[2]

As of May 9, the guardsmen activated from the three states numbered 4,191—Arizona: 984, New Mexico: 737, Texas: 2,470.[3] A major problem was that

> a large number of men were found physically disqualified, but in the absence of instructions from the War Department as to what disposition was to be made of them they were sent to the border with their organizations and later discharged on certificates of disability. This procedure was expensive to the government and a hardship to the individuals. . . . The experience gained by mustering the Militia into Federal service has taught that the various states have been very lax in making the physical examinations.[4]

In addition to the confusion surrounding physical disqualifications, the militias of the three states were not generally well organized. Arizona and New Mexico had somewhat similar problems, while the situation of Texas differed.

Arizona had only recently been admitted to the Union, in 1912. It was a relatively poor and sparsely populated state. Nevertheless, Arizona had duly organized a regiment, the 1st Arizona Infantry. The regiment's existence, however, was precarious. In 1914, the War Department had ordered that all government property be withdrawn from Companies C, D, and L, an order that effectively mustered out those units. The reason given for this drastic action was that the companies were understrength and their members were deficient in drill. The adjutant general of Arizona was warned that five other companies were on the verge of suffering a similar fate. Only four companies in the regiment met the government's minimum requirements. The adjutant general, Colonel Charles W. Harris, declared that the War Department was unfamiliar with conditions in Arizona, a state that faced many disadvantages in maintaining, let alone building up, a guard. He argued that unlike many eastern states, Arizona needed time to develop an effective organization.[5]

By the end of 1915, the 1st Arizona numbered 53 officers and 742 enlisted men. By the time it was mobilized on May 9, 1916, the regiment was in better shape, though far from being a crack outfit. Its nominal strength was 54 officers and 866 enlisted men, an increase of 1 officer and 124 men over 1915.[6] But at its last regular army inspection, no company was rated as "excellent" or "very good"; two were "good," five "fair," and five "poor."[7] The regiment lacked both a machine gun company and a supply company. Adjutant General Harris announced that the regiment could field 860 men immediately and could be recruited to its full wartime strength of 1,800 within five days if necessary. Moreover, "equipment for the full strength of the force is on hand."[8] These statements proved to be an exercise in optimism.

The mobilization site was originally the Whipple Barracks, near Prescott in central Arizona, but this was deemed impractical. Tucson asked to be the mobilization point because of the city's position as a railroad center, superior armory facilities, and accessibility to the border, but instead the authorities designated Camp Harry J. Jones, located a mile east of the border town of Douglas.[9] A campaign began immediately for recruits between eighteen and forty-five, at least five feet four inches tall, who could pass the army physical exam, swear to support the Arizona and United States constitutions, and agree to enlist in federal service if required. The two Tucson companies (E and K) drilled in their armory before an appreciative crowd of onlookers. Company E marched in a body to a restaurant on Congress Street for dinner, then marched back to the armory, where the troops slept pending orders to leave for Douglas.[10]

Douglas was a typical bleak and dusty border town, built around two copper smelters,[11] with its notable feature, the Gadsden Hotel, boasting a magnificent lobby graced by a sweeping staircase topped by large stained-glass windows. However, Douglas was in a state of considerable racial excitement, and the authorities were vigilant in preventing any street gatherings or quarrels between Anglos and Hispanics. The local guard company (Company G) had assembled at its armory and remained there, weapons at hand, ready for any emergency. Meanwhile, the chamber of commerce had arranged for a 160-acre site, with an ample water supply, near the local army camp to house the Arizona guard and the two battalions of the 14th U.S. Infantry being rushed to reinforce Douglas.[12] Presumably to their dismay, it fell to the local guardsmen to toil under the hot desert sun digging ditches for water pipelines and building latrines, preparing the campsite for the arrival of the remainder of the 1st Arizona Infantry.

Most of that organization traveled by a special train transporting 563 men, 140 of them the Tucson contingent of Companies E and K plus a medical unit of 16. The train's departure from Tucson was memorable. The regimental band played several selections for the more than 1,000 people who turned out to bid the troops farewell at the El Paso and Southwestern station, where each company had its picture taken. And "according to the custom of universities," the president of the University of Arizona promised that the 8 student guardsmen would not suffer because of the call-up. Final exams were only a week away, and those with passing grades would receive full credit without taking their exams. Those who were students at the Tempe and Flagstaff State Normal Schools received similar assurances. Besides the Tucson companies, the train carried 6 companies from Phoenix, Mesa, and other localities and arrived in Douglas on May 13. Company M, from Morenci, and Company B, from Safford, had reached Douglas the previous day. The Safford business community donated $75 and 8 boxes of cigars to their departing troops.[13]

The 1st Arizona Infantry that settled into its new quarters at Camp Harry J. Jones was both understrength and inexperienced. The regiment's

10 companies numbered 886 men, 29 fewer than the required peacetime strength and 1,029 under wartime strength. Only the company from Safford was at full war strength with 150 men. Moreover, only 12 men in the entire regiment had any prior military service.[14] Another feature of note of the 1st Arizona Infantry was its commander, Colonel A. M. Tuthill, who was a physician in private practice. His military career had begun as a private in the California militia. In 1903, he became a captain in the Arizona militia. During World War I he would be promoted to major general commanding the 40th Division, a National Guard outfit. For many years, he served as Arizona's adjutant general. "He is one of the few generals in army history who, although a doctor, served exclusively as a line officer."[15] Furthermore, discipline in the 1st Arizona Infantry was problematic. Colonel Tuthill got the nickname "Dobie Al" because he made his officers build a compound of "dobie" [adobe] bricks when the enlisted men refused to do it.[16]

Like their colonel, some of the 1st Arizona Infantry's units were unusual. Company F consisted of Pima, Papago, Hopi, Apache, and Mission Indian students from the Phoenix Indian School, prompting the Arizona press to boast that it was the only all-Indian unit in the United States. A recruiting officer even announced that on short notice Arizona could field two regiments of Indians for service.[17] Company L included fifteen Yuma Indians, while Company E was composed of Hispanics from Tucson who spoke Spanish almost exclusively.[18]

May 13 was a day of intense activity as the regiment erected tents and otherwise organized their encampment.[19] Brigadier General T. F. Davis, commanding the 6th U.S. Infantry Brigade at Douglas and the Arizona Military District, assigned several regular officers to assist the militia in setting up their camp, and he designated a mustering officer to handle the process of swearing the Arizonans into federal service. Davis detailed still other officers to instruct the state troops. Lending excitement and urgency to the activities was a report on the streets of Douglas that a detachment of the 1st U.S. Cavalry, patrolling the border west of town, had been fired on by a band of Mexicans trying to cross the border from Sonora in order to raid the outlying farms. Like many such rumors, this proved to be wildly exaggerated—a member of a 1st Cavalry patrol had fired twice at a Mexican who refused to halt when ordered to do so. The Mexican escaped across the border after tumbling into a pond and nearly drowning.[20]

The euphoria of going to the border to fight Mexicans quickly paled. There was no fighting, the boredom of camp life set in, and many men began to worry about their families, especially in those cases where the man was the sole breadwinner. To boost morale, residents of Phoenix organized "The Soldiers' Comfort Club" to send packages of fruit and other dainties to the Arizona soldiers. More importantly, the Ray Consolidated Copper Company, the Standard Oil Company, and the Ray Hercules Copper Company promised to continue paying the wages of their militia employees, at least temporarily.[21]

There was also the problem of recruiting enough men to bring the regiment up to the prescribed wartime strength. The campaign was producing only a trickle of recruits, and recruiting officers redoubled their efforts. In Tucson, for example, officers tried to "get recruits from transients passing through the city. A number of these are old army men and it is expected that many can be induced to join the National Guard." Not until each company reached a peacetime strength of sixty-five men could the unit be mustered into federal service.[22] A big part of the problem, according to the *Arizona Daily Star*, was the attitude of Governor George W. P. Hunt, who publicly defined patriotism as "the faithful and ardent exercise of the duties of citizenship." The newspaper excoriated Hunt, pointing out that "the difficulty which faces the recruiting officers here in Arizona—too deep for them to fathom—doubtless lies in the fact that, to quote the governor, 'precedence is being given to the importance of having a patriotic spirit permeate everyday business and professional life, instead of finding its chief expression in a ready response to a call for military volunteers when war clouds hover low.'" The editorial continued sarcastically: "So let those who will enlist in the National Guard and report to the National Guard mobilization camp at Douglas, but let him not sneer at or point the finger of scorn at those who stay behind in order not to miss the opportunity of 'faithfully and ardently' voting in the election this fall, mayhap for the governor himself, who will offer to do his bit for the country by occupying the gubernatorial chair for a third term."[23]

With a governor who actively discouraged enlistment, it was no wonder the Arizona militia struggled. It was May 26 before the first unit—Company A—was mustered into federal service. "It was admitted by officers of the regiment today that a number of members had failed to respond to the call for duty on the border. How many men will be in danger of prosecution for desertion under the provisions of the federal army bill was not stated, although the belief was expressed that they would be arrested and court-martialed."[24] The regiment's muster report contained the names of 355 men who failed to report for duty. Although the War Department ordered that all slackers who had not reported for duty by July 1 were to be tried for desertion, ultimately no adverse action was taken against them.[25]

Colonel Tuthill did request the Tucson authorities to arrest Private Taylor of Company K for failure to report at the mobilization camp, but Taylor belatedly made an appearance and all was forgiven.[26] This was not the case regarding Company K's Private P. A. Zorn, who engaged in some kind of disruptive activity at the mobilization camp and was packed off to Tucson. There he harangued a crowd in the Southern Pacific yards, telling them that he had been kicked out of the guard at Douglas, denouncing the guard and individual officers, and complaining that he had not even been furnished transportation back to Tucson. It turned out that he had sold his railroad ticket. The belligerent Zorn was charged with mutiny and disrespect toward a superior officer, and he was promptly arrested and court-martialed at Nogales, receiving thirty days in jail and a fine of two-thirds of a month's pay (ten dollars).[27] Unfortunately, Zorn's case of dereliction would not be unique.[28] By June 20 all the Arizona units had been mustered into federal service, but desertion remained a problem. In June, two deserters from Company E were arrested in Tucson on a charge of disorderly conduct and seditious language after they hurled insults at the Tucson home guard. They were sentenced to thirty days in the city jail. One was made a trusty, escaped, but was quickly recaptured.[29]

Governor Hunt inspected and addressed the 1st Arizona Infantry in camp at Douglas on June 17.[30] Since the governor had gone on record as not supporting the National Guard mobilization, presumably his visit did little to raise the troops' morale. In fact, despite continued recruiting, the regiment's strength declined while it was stationed on the border. The regiment settled into a routine, with a company assigned to guard each of the two smelters in Douglas while detachments patrolled the border.[31]

Like Arizona, New Mexico had only been admitted as a state in 1912. And like Arizona, New Mexico was poor and sparsely populated. On March 11, Governor McDonald notified the secretary of war that the New Mexico militia (61 officers and 877 enlisted men) was ready for service on short notice but that the state appropriation was not sufficient to enable it to do anything without federal assistance.[32] In response to a query from the chief of the Militia Bureau, the New Mexico adjutant general reported in

January that there were twelve Jews in the state's militia, three of them officers. The query evidently stemmed from allegations that the New York Guard deliberately excluded Jews.[33]

The New Mexico National Guard's main component was the 1st Infantry regiment, Colonel Edmund C. Abbott commanding. The regiment lacked a machine gun company. Companies D of Silver City and H of Las Vegas had been mustered out of the service for failure to maintain the required standard of efficiency, and Companies D of Las Cruces and H of Silver City were then recognized as companies of the New Mexico organization.[34] Interestingly, the 1st Missouri Infantry's captain commanding the machine gun company—made up of two officers, fifty-two enlisted men, and four machine guns—which had not been called up, wrote a confidential letter to the New Mexico adjutant general stating that his unit would like to serve with the New Mexico regiment if this could be arranged.[35] It could not. Besides the 1st Infantry, the New Mexico guard included Battery A, Field Artillery, and a field hospital, a total of 67 officers and 867 enlisted men, a net increase of 23 men over 1915. The last regular army inspection had rated three companies of the 1st New Mexico as "very good," three as "good," four as "fair," and two as "poor."[36] Between March 20 and April 10, the state adjutant general, Harry T. Herring, made an inspection trip throughout southern New Mexico to gauge the level of apprehension among the population regarding future Mexican incursions and reported no danger as long as due precautions were taken. Among the precautions was that of guarding the armories in the southern part of the state. Further, he assured the governor that should the United States decide to intervene in Mexico, "I can promise you one regiment of infantry and one battery of field artillery at full war strength, and after being given thirty days' training, competent to do the work required of them. I am of the further opinion that if volunteers should be called for I can easily organize another regiment of infantry in the southwest."[37]

Despite Herring's confident promises, the reality was that a number of New Mexico guardsmen had three or less years' service, the organization was short of equipment, and it limped along on a miniscule $2,500 annual state appropriation. It was frankly admitted that nothing could be done without federal help.[38] As the state adjutant general later put it: "The mobilization of the Guard in May, 1916, demonstrated the lack of foresight on the part of the Legislature in not giving us the necessary amount of funds with which to carry on the National Guard work, and placed the members of the Guard in the embarrassing position of having to do their duty under great handicaps."[39] As in the case of Arizona, the mobilization point was changed when the New Mexicans were called into federal service on May 9. Mobilization was originally scheduled at Las Vegas, in the northern part of the state, but it was logically changed to a location on the border itself—Camp Furlong at Columbus, the base camp for the Punitive Expedition.[40]

By May 11, the guard was on its way.[41] The *Albuquerque Morning Journal* worried that "the danger to the National Guardsmen who have been sent to the border will come, not so much from Mexican bullets as from Mexican disease."[42] The *Santa Fe New Mexican* gushed that the men "are acclimated to the deserts and high altitudes, their upbringing in this country has accustomed them more or less to the plains and the woods and their familiarity with the Spanish language will be a big advantage. Even better than Texans or Arizonans they are equipped to discharge the responsibilities assigned to them, and they will give a splendid account of themselves."[43] This proved not to be the case.

On May 12, a total of 779 officers and enlisted men reported for duty at Columbus, in a blinding dust storm.[44] Eight officers and nineteen men had been left behind on recruiting duty. But because of the rigid physical examinations by regular medical officers, New Mexico had a rejection rate of about 35 percent for physical defects, including Colonel S. A. Milliken, surgeon general of the state.[45] Because the New Mexico legislature had rejected a modern military code at its last session in 1915, the antiquated code remained, which required no physical examination of officers and men. Physical examinations were not conducted until the men reached Camp Furlong, and the army medical corps was not ready to begin such examination until May 15. The New Mexico field hospital was also rejected, and its thirty-three men were transferred to other units. After consulting with General Funston during a hurried trip to San Antonio, Adjutant General Herring was able to obtain a waiver on certain minor defects. "As a result of this rigid examination, we had accepted about sixty five percent, whereas the percentage of acceptance of applicants for the army is some fifteen per cent.... The total number rejected so far is approximately 300, mainly for reasons which the examiners have not disclosed in detail."[46] The regular inspector-instructor for New Mexico later reported that roughly one thousand men had been accepted and five hundred rejected.[47]

The First Call-Up

The 1st New Mexico Infantry was a skeleton regiment. The army reported:

> The personnel of the New Mexico regiment was [*sic*] weak and the organization was unstable. It almost went to pieces when the physical standards were applied. There was urgent need for the services of this regiment. As finally mustered in, its enlisted membership included at least 40 per cent of men who would not have been acceptable for the Regular Army. The main efforts of the organizers had been directed to obtaining 65 men for each company, and the dragnet had brought in many that were manifestly unfit. The result was an organization of the required strength on paper, but with the weakness of a mere paper organization.[48]

For example, although Company E, the Hispanic company from Santa Fe, exceeded the peacetime strength requirement of sixty-five men (it had eighty-three), the other Santa Fe unit, Company F, had only thirty. Adjutant General Herring's goal of delivering 1,000 to 1,200 troops to the government was a long way off.[49]

Still, what the regiment lacked in numbers it made up for in initial enthusiasm. On May 12 at Santa Fe the twenty-eight-man regimental band played martial airs as the troops marched through the plaza to the Santa Fe railroad depot amid the cheers of the citizenry. When the seven-coach special train reached Albuquerque, nearly one thousand citizens and almost every automobile in town were at the Santa Fe station to cheer the arrivals and to bid farewell to the Albuquerque contingent (Companies G and L). Being an officer was, as always, definitely more pleasant than being an enlisted man: the officers traveled in Pullmans, the troops in day coaches; at Albuquerque the officers dined at the elegant Alvarado Hotel by the depot, the troops got sandwiches and coffee in their coaches. The train continued south to Las Cruces, picking up Companies A and D (Las Cruces), then proceeded to El Paso, where the soldiers transferred to the El Paso and Southwestern railroad for the last leg westward to Columbus. By May 13, guardsmen from Roswell (Battery A, Field Artillery), Carlsbad (Company B), Artesia (Company C), Deming (Company I), Silver City (Company H), Portales (Company M), and Clovis (Company K) arrived by train to join them.[50] Their departure proved a serious hardship in many small New Mexico communities, for the units included many locally prominent businessmen and professionals.

By May 14, the 1st New Mexico had assembled at Columbus, population about five hundred. Being stationed at Columbus was hardly a prime assignment but one regular officer, a certain Lieutenant Zell, carried his disappointment to extremes. He alighted from the train, looked around, cried out, "Great God! Is this Columbus, New Mexico?" and proceeded to blow his brains out.[51]

Whatever their disappointment may have been, the New Mexico troops adjusted to life in Columbus. The men found the post in a heightened state of readiness, the direct result of the Glenn Springs raid a week earlier and a threatened Mexican attack on May 10 against Laredo. Although no attack on Columbus was anticipated the army took no chances, throwing up entrenchments around the military reservation and strengthening the detachments of guards.[52] Two weeks later, a private in the 20th U.S. Infantry was shot and killed while drinking with several disreputable people. To the dismay of the troops, the sheriff closed the red-light district on the fringe of the camp and warned the scores of prostitutes to leave town. He also closed down ten so-called social clubs, whose function was to ply the soldiers with liquor. Yet other clubs were soon incorporated.[53] To provide more wholesome entertainment, the YMCA opened a building containing a piano, phonograph, writing materials, games, and so forth. Thousands of troops patronized this establishment.[54]

As the logistical base for Pershing's Punitive Expedition, the Columbus cantonment was habitually in a frenzy of activity, with hundreds of trucks in row after row, either having returned from Mexico or preparing to go there. The trucks were the result of the crash program of mechanization. Between March 20 and July 31, 1916, seventeen truck companies, of twenty-seven vehicles each, were formed and based in Columbus. Army officers commanded these units, whose drivers and mechanics were civilians. In addition, extensive repair shops and warehouses were a prominent feature of this expanding army installation. And by July, the army owned 588 trucks, 10 machine-shop trucks, and 6 wreckers.[55]

A correspondent for the Chicago *News*, for one, was quite unimpressed by what he saw of the New Mexico National Guard at Columbus. He described their arrival, with some in bowler hats and white collars while "others carried suit cases like a troupe of barnstormers, some were coatless, with shirts of varied hue, others were in uniform or part uniform, but they all belonged to the regiment." He mentioned that "the first delegation to arrive were [*sic*] 100 youths whom the state had refused to bring. They came on their own responsibility." The midwestern reporter demonstrated his own provincialism by observing that "half of the New Mexican militia are dark skinned. They chatter and the corner of the big camp where they have called theirs seemed as if it were a Mexican camp. Three companies and the band of the New Mexico regiment asked that army regulations be amended because 25% of their number couldn't speak English."[56] The reporter allowed, though, that the army did have loyal soldiers even though they spoke in tongues other than English.

The newspaperman made a valid point when he commented that: "One of the fictions of the national defense, so far as state forces are concerned, is that each one is as completely equipped as is the regular army. They have plenty of equipment but not always of the most practical kind. Topping a pile of camp supplies was a mattress of feather bed proportions for some soft muscled militia officer. The outfitting of the regiment showed in the same uncertain way as that of the men."[57] Refutation was immediate:

> The allegations of a writer in the New York *Tribune* that some of the New Mexico National Guards showed up at the border in tennis slippers and that the regiment included men with wooden legs and glass eyes, as well as hobos and drunkards, is strongly resented by Captain James I. Seligman, Santa Fe postmaster, who served for a month with the Guard at Columbus. Captain Seligman pointed out that the mobilization of the New Mexico Guard in three days is a record which has not been approached by any other state. Seligman declares that recruits may have arrived in tennis shoes or even barefoot, as this is the privilege of a recruit, but emphatically denies that any enlisted men arrived to answer to the call without good marching shoes.[58]

Many New Mexico units lacked uniforms for all their members, and no unit had government-issued shoes because they had not yet been ordered.[59]

And the New Mexicans were pitifully naive. When they arrived one officer informed the army quartermaster that his men would be ready to cook dinner by noon the next day and he expected the regulars to feed them from their mess kitchens until then. The quartermaster officer replied that they had better start putting up ovens and building fires or they would go hungry: "We'll help them all we can, but we don't intend to pet them. No one is going to wait on them and they might as well start taking care of themselves."[60] The regulars did furnish trucks to haul the New Mexicans' "queer assortment of baggage" from the railroad station to their assigned campsite, one that had fresh water piped to within a few feet of the mess tents. The newcomers had considerable difficulty erecting the tents, and darkness fell before they were all up. A newspaper correspondent characterized the New Mexicans as ready to fight but far from ready: "They presented a reeling appearance, far different from the usual straight lines of a company street. There were as many varieties of tents as there were companies."[61]

The men were assigned to the southern extremity of the sprawling Columbus military encampment, near the ditch the *villistas* had used to attack the town back in March. Their efforts to make their camp habitable involved building a kitchen and mess hall for each company, but the troops suffered from the blistering heat and the dust from the spring windstorms blowing in from Arizona; the wind was so fierce that they had to hold their tents down to keep them from blowing away. Goggles became a prized item of equipment. Yet the troops' morale remained high, no doubt bolstered by the seven, later eight, bands in the Columbus camp. Nightly between six thirty and twilight one of the bands played in the grandstand.[62]

All was not well, however. The men wrote to the folks back home that unless the 1st New Mexico Infantry could be mustered into the army at peacetime strength of at least 65 men per company, the entire regiment might be sent home.[63] One of the men even wrote a poem entitled "Just So They Don't Send Us Back Home."[64] The crisis involved not just the number of men needed but also the quality of those men—for instance, the field artillery battery from Roswell, generally considered the best New Mexico unit, had 33 of its 151 men fail their army physical not for physical disabilities but because they were under age. In addition, 5 men deserted.[65]

Still, Major General Albert L. Mills, the army's chief of militia affairs, wrote to the New Mexico adjutant general praising the Roswell battery.[66] The state's adjutant general was extremely concerned. He was pleased with the mobilization process itself; for example, Colonel Edmund C. Abbott, who was the judge of the First District Court of New Mexico, had been holding court at Santa Fe when the mobilization order came. He immediately adjourned court and reported for duty.[67] But the adjutant general was disappointed at the strength of several companies: "I thought that the people of this state—a border state—would have shown more interest and have enlisted in the Guard."[68]

When the New Mexico militia was mobilized it was thought that it might be necessary to send them into Mexico to help protect the Punitive Expedition's lines of communication. Since the army air corps was barely

The First Call-Up

visible to the naked eye, it occurred to Adjutant General Herring that it would be quite useful for the New Mexicans to have an aircraft for scouting purposes. He contacted the Aero Club of America, who replied that if New Mexico could guarantee $2,500 they would contribute the rest and deliver an aircraft. Herring raised enough private money to meet the terms, and the Aero Club provided the remaining $6,000 and supplied a top-of-the-line Curtis R-2 twin engine airplane that had broken all American speed records. The plane arrived at Columbus on June 1; by June 10 it had been checked out, had made two test flights, and was ready for service. But when Herring offered the craft to the War Department, that agency refused to let the New Mexico National Guard operate the machine and finally refused to accept it for federal service. The law specified that all militia units had to be organized according to the regulations governing similar units in the regular army. No army unit had Curtis R-2 twin-engine airplanes, thus the rejection. Although the Aero Club appealed directly to the secretary of war, on November 8 the club's president informed Herring that the War Department was adamant and suggested that he have the airplane crated up and returned to the Curtis Company at Buffalo.[69] This was but the first instance of the War Department refusing to allow the militia either to operate equipment or to accept it for federal service. However, the Commonwealth of Massachusetts received two airplanes for use by the Massachusetts Naval Militia. The Aero Club of New England presented one and Eben S. Draper the other. The airplanes were stationed at Newburyport and Marblehead.[70]

The government's rejection of the aircraft was a bitter blow to Herring, who certainly could not be faulted for lack of vision; he arranged in July to send an officer to the Martin Aviation School in Los Angeles to train as a pilot, and if funds could be secured he planned to send several more candidates, for he hoped that with private subscriptions to purchase two or three more airplanes he could form a New Mexico aero squadron.[71]

Besides the fact that many New Mexico soldiers at Columbus were failing their physicals, they caused the army some concern on another score. On May 18: "A number of New Mexico National Guardsmen were brought back to camp here today under guard after having caused the American border patrol at the gate three miles south, as well as the Carranza customs guards there some alarm. The approach of the men who were on a sight-seeing trip made the Mexican officials believe a new body of troops was about to cross the frontier. The two patrol forces mounted and stopped the Guardsmen just as they unknowingly crossed the border." The ten who had crossed the wrong barbed wire fence and "invaded" Mexico received a dressing down and one day's police duty.[72]

In the best tradition of the American soldier, the men had no lack of complaints, and not just about the wind, the scorching days, and freezing nights. For one thing, Columbus was bone dry—there wasn't a single saloon in town.[73] Moreover, unscrupulous merchants were bent on fleecing the troops, a practice in which even some legitimate businessmen engaged. A soldier wrote that "one real treat is the ice-cold shower bath. Soap is advanced to $2 a cake, with no buyers in sight."[74] Fortunately there were plenty of shower baths available.

Some of the troops were avid souvenir hunters, scavenging for items from Villa's raid on Columbus such as buttons, teeth, and other things retrieved from the charred remains of raiders, whose bodies had been burned as a public health measure after the clash. Some souvenirs were more gruesome than others—a member of Company B sent to his friends in Carlsbad a hand that was taken from a pile of ashes and placed in a jar and pickled.[75]

Life for the state troops was improving—the regiment received one thousand cots. And when they were mustered into federal service, the men could look forward to being issued the army shoe, "which is a dandy." Sanitary conditions were excellent, removing one source of concern. Each company had an incinerator, and refuse was burned immediately. The garbage can from each company street was emptied each morning and was disinfected by burning straw and oil in it.[76] And the troops were not forgotten by those they were protecting; the Red Cross chapter at Deming, thirty miles north of Columbus, sent "soldier's housewife" kits that included needles, thread, and buttons and were patterned on those used by the regulars. They also sent confections, talcum powder, and cold cream.[77] The residents of Silver City sent their Company H two truckloads of apples, chocolate, cigars, tablets, envelopes, chewing tobacco, Bull Durham tobacco, cigarette papers, Camel cigarettes, ice cream, oranges, preserves, chicken salad, and homemade cakes and cookies.[78] On Memorial Day Battery A fired a twenty-one-gun salute at noon. Since it was the last day of the month, the 1st New Mexico was inspected. And on June 5, General Pershing himself arrived in Columbus on an inspection tour.[79]

By May 20, the 1st New Mexico was deemed sufficiently proficient to take over guard duty from some of the regulars, who were badly needed to protect Pershing's truck convoys in Mexico.[80] However, this did not change the fact that by June 5 only 707 out of 1,152 New Mexicans had passed their physical exams; fewer than half of the contingent from Santa Fe passed. Unless the regiment could produce 12 companies of at least 65 men each (780 men in all) who could pass the physical and be mustered into the army, the regimental staff officers and the colonel could not be mustered in. In that case, the companies would have to be mustered in by battalions of four companies each, commanded by a major.[81] It was expected that only two infantry battalions and the field artillery battery would meet the requirement. The situation was so serious that Adjutant General Herring even traveled to San Antonio to ask General Funston to have the physical exam standards reduced.[82] Funston refused and suggested that recruiting officers tour by automobile the six New Mexico counties they had not yet visited.[83]

There was a note of desperation in Adjutant General Herring's actions. He telegraphed to the governor that at least three hundred physically fit recruits were needed immediately because the honor of New Mexico was at stake. Herring even suggested that the state's sheriffs be enlisted in securing recruits. In Herring's words: "We cannot afford to fail as a border state. If our own public won't help when opportunity is afforded we cannot call on others."[84] Employing the slogan "For the Honor of New Mexico" did have some effect in stimulating recruitment but not enough.[85] The distraught adjutant general conferred with the governor and declared that "New Mexico is supposed to furnish a regiment of Infantry and a battery of Field Artillery for military service on the border. If we fail to do so it will be the most humiliating thing that has ever occurred in this or any other state."[86] He added:

> We are a border state. For three years, at least, we have been howling our heads off about the protection of our border, and have been bombarding Governor McDonald and President Wilson with requests to be allowed to protect it. And now, when called upon to make good we are falling down. . . . It is almost inconceivable that New Mexico, a state whose territory has been invaded and whose citizens have been massacred by Mexican raiders, is not ready to put a regiment of war strength in the field.[87]

Herring pointed out that, according to War Department figures, fifty-five thousand men between eighteen and forty-five were available in New Mexico for military service. Of this number, he believed that thirty thousand would fail their physicals, but this left twenty thousand young men who could readily volunteer for the militia. He blamed those with "cold feet" or "because they are not willing to get out of range of the saloons and the pool halls and the movie theaters. And I blame the mothers and fathers who take the stand that they didn't raise their boys to be soldiers and all others advising our youth to stay home."[88]

The adjutant general declared that there was a law on the books giving the governor the power to draft men for service at the call of the president, and unless volunteers appeared in the next few days, he favored having the governor exercise that power. However, the New Mexico attorney general ruled that any draft would have to be preceded by enrolling all the "reserve militia," that is, all male citizens between eighteen and forty-five years of age. This would be an expensive proposition, for which no funds were available. Furthermore, the state law governing drafting applied only to cities and towns, which had already furnished most of the troops at Columbus. The governor felt that additional recruits should come from rural communities.[89] In the meantime, eight recruiting officers were scouring the state for warm bodies, assisted by the sheriffs. The adjutant of the 1st New Mexico put the matter in some perspective when he wrote, "As a matter of fact few companies or batteries of the regular army on border duty are up to the minimum number required for our mustering and it is a matter of news in the public press as to the extremely slow rate of recruiting the 20,000 additional men in the army recently provided for by Congress. This latter has not been emblazoned in heavy headlines however."[90]

The *Santa Fe New Mexican* put the recruiting crisis into a broader context. In an editorial entitled "An Injustice," it took issue with a number of eastern newspapers, such as the New York *Sun*, that had assumed that New Mexico's poor showing was due to the fact that militiamen had refused to answer the call. Instead, the editorial declared, New Mexico should have prepared the militia long before the call came; it should have been vigorously recruited to full strength. The blame lay at the feet of the legislature, which had virtually ignored the militia. Thus the real issue was one of unpreparedness, not dereliction of duty by guardsmen.[91]

A subsequent editorial blamed an incompetent national government, arguing that it was the system that was at fault—"Americans will not stand for an un-American English snob military system." Americans would not "stand for a system where shoulder straps make a gentleman and a private's uniform makes an inferior. The creation of social caste by military rank

The First Call-Up

must be absolutely abolished from the American system before many men will enlist. It is inconceivable that a social equal may become a pariah by donning a suit of clothes."[92] The newspaper later viewed New Mexico's role from a different perspective. In an editorial entitled "A National Affair," it stressed that not just New Mexico but the United States had been invaded by Pancho Villa. Thus it was just as much the duty of, say, New York or Maine to defend the United States as it was of New Mexico.[93]

The entire New Mexico guard assembled for inspection at Columbus on May 31. The New Mexicans continued to inch toward meeting the army's requirements. Not until June 9 was the first unit—Battery A, New Mexico Field Artillery—mustered into federal service. It was transferred to El Paso on June 18. Battery A, from Roswell, was by far the best unit in New Mexico. Its commander, Captain Charles De Bremond, was a former Swiss artillery officer. In March 1917, Governor Lindsay offered him the post of adjutant general of New Mexico, but De Bremond declined the offer. He said he preferred to remain in the field in El Paso with his battery.[94]

As of June 14, four companies had been mustered in, and six others would be enrolled shortly.[95] When mustered in, units received regular army equipment—two woolen blankets, a field cot, a bed-tick mattress, and eating utensils. The men were also issued hats, shirts, trousers, two sets of underwear, shoes, and six pairs of socks.[96] The men got in a lot of training in handling their weapons, which had to be disassembled and cleaned after each of the frequent sandstorms. They began performing guard duty, and in June they began target practice.[97]

But the sad reality continued to be the struggle to fill out the 1st New Mexico Infantry so it could be mustered into federal service. If the current recruiting drive was unsuccessful, the unpalatable alternatives seemed to be either to adopt conscription or, even worse, to try to recruit Texans. New Mexico finally had to swallow its pride and recruit a bunch of Texans in order to be able to take the field.[98]

Texas theoretically presented a fertile field for recruitment because it was much larger, much more prosperous, and much more populous than its New Mexico neighbor. The Texas National Guard was considerably larger, better trained, and better equipped than its Arizona and New Mexico counterparts, but it was in the War Department's doghouse, still reeling from a major scandal.[99]

In April, 1915, the regular army inspector-instructor of the Texas Guard sent a confidential report to the War Department detailing the illegal sale of rifles, ammunition, tents, uniforms, saddles, and other equipment the army had issued to the Texas guard, some $90,000 worth. The War Department immediately ordered the commanding general of the Southern Department to make a full investigation and report. The Department of Justice also began looking into the prosecution of the guilty parties.[100] Secretary of War Lindley M. Garrison wrote to Texas governor James E. Ferguson on April 28 informing him of the investigation. Ferguson was dumbfounded.

On July 1, Garrison sent Ferguson a detailed account of the scandal. Lieutenant Colonel Emmett E. Walker, the veteran assistant quartermaster, was the principal culprit, along with his partner in crime Captain George J. Head, commander of the guard company in Brownsville. On March 2, 1914, Walker, using the name "Emmett George," had shipped—from storage in the basement of the capitol in Austin—to Head a boxcar load of uniforms, which Head sold to the Mexican garrison in Matamoros, across the Rio Grande from Brownsville. Walker also sold government property to army surplus dealers, including the firm of Cal Hirsh and Sons in St. Louis, Missouri. Moreover, Walker sold a considerable amount of federal property to officers and men of the Texas Guard, and he himself stole a sizeable amount, which he hid in his residence.[101] Walker had utilized his position as quartermaster to cover up the thefts by the technique of "surveying"—filling out the requisite paperwork certifying that the items were no longer serviceable.

Walker was dishonorably discharged effective April 15, 1915.[102] Both he and Head fled to Mexico when their scheme was uncovered, but they eventually returned to Austin and threw themselves on the mercy of the court. The government prosecutors were determined to show them no mercy— they brought the inspector-instructor all the way back from his current duty station in the Philippines to testify. In the face of overwhelming evidence, Walker and Head were found guilty in June 1916 and were sentenced to three years and one day in the federal penitentiary at Leavenworth and were fined five hundred dollars.[103] Head's sentence was subsequently reduced, and he was released in February 1918. His fine was also remitted.

All this was bad enough, but the investigation further tarnished the reputation of the Texas Guard. The secretary of war's report to the governor of Texas revealed that thefts from militia armories were widespread and long standing. The Texas Rangers, who had frequently been called in to investigate these thefts, had been ineffectual, and the state adjutant general since 1911, Brigadier General Henry Hutchings, was incompetent. The secretary concluded his letter by stating that "the general efficiency of the National Guard of Texas has reached a very low point."[104]

Governor Ferguson was understandably upset at having to answer not only for the misappropriations during his administration but also for those of his predecessors from 1900 on. He immediately ordered the rangers to locate as much of the missing equipment as possible. Among the many items the rangers retrieved was a tent that enterprising prostitutes at Corpus Christi were using as a portable brothel on the beach. But what really worried Ferguson was the army inspector general's recommendation that $91,136.44 be charged against the federal government's annual allotment of $100,000 for the Texas guard. It was the prospect of having to reimburse the U.S. government that concerned Ferguson because the finances of the Texas state government were chronically precarious. Therefore he took the unprecedented step of canceling the 1915 National Guard summer camp. The two-week annual encampment training under the supervision of regular officers was the only real training the men received.[105] Thus when the Texas guard was activated on May 9, 1916, the organization was not as well prepared as it otherwise could have been.

As early as May 1, the Texans were placed on alert for possible border duty. Secretary of War Baker, at President Wilson's behest, sent a confidential telegram to Governor Ferguson advising him of the possibility.[106] In his reply Ferguson had outlined the measures he had taken and promised the speedy response of Texas in the event of a call-up. Efforts were made to equip the units, and nearly all of them had been recruited up to the required minimum strength. On May 2, Brigadier General John A. Hulen was removed from the retired list and placed in command of the brigade. Hulen had won a Silver Star citation during the Philippine campaign, had served as adjutant general of Texas from June 1, 1903, to January 23, 1907. He would go on to organize, train, and command the 72nd Brigade in France during World War I and command the 36th Division from May 2, 1923, until his retirement on September 9, 1935.[107] Hulen immediately traveled to Austin to confer with the governor and the adjutant general. On May 5, Secretary Baker thanked the governor effusively for complying with the president's instructions and assuring him that "what seemed to be a near crisis, calling for an increased number of troops on the border, appears to have passed."[108] Ironically, that same day, May 5, the Glenn Springs raid occurred, precipitating the first call-up.[109]

The New York newspapers had a field day sneering at the Texans. The New York *Sun*, for example, wrote:

> The disquieting thing about the Texas Guard is that its nominal strength is only one twenty-eighth of 1 per cent of the population, and that its numbers have suffered an actual reduction in the last year, during which the opportunity for active service was constantly imminent. It would have seemed safe to predict that when the situation on the border became acute that the state and its citizens would bring their Guard to the highest plane of efficiency, in preparation for eventualities, but this natural precaution was neglected, and consequently the organized military forces of the state now cut an unimpressive figure.[110]

The New York *World* was much nastier:

> We must say that Texas is a disappointment. For many years that noble state has assured us that it was able to settle the Mexican question single-handed. Nothing restrained it but the refusal of the national government to say the word. We have trusted Texas in the belief that, no matter what disaster might overtake the federal forces on the border, the avenging citizenry of the Lone Star commonwealth would prove equal to the emergency.
>
> Not many presidents have ventured to invoke the military power of Texas, but Mr. Wilson has taken the awful responsibility, and what does he find? A powerful National Guard equipped to the last button? A fierce and seasoned body of warriors thirsting for gore? Hardly. What he sees is an organization, nominally embracing 3,381 men, and enjoying the distinguished honor of standing at the bottom of the list of states in efficiency at the latest inspection of the war department.
>
> It appears, therefore, that in depending upon Texas we have leaned upon a reed or a lath. It has been face to face with danger; it has talked terribly; and yet when the tocsin sounds we find that the fighting force of the greatest of states is only an awkward squad and that part of the equipment supplied it of late by the national government has been corruptly sold to Mexicans across the boundary.
>
> Alas for Texas and alas for the Americans who have felt secure in the presence of its sword and buckler. For our second line of defense

on the Rio Grande we now nominate the organized militia of Iowa and Minnesota, most of whose members never saw a Mexican.[111]

The Texas *Alpine Avalanche* was quick to respond to the insults of the snotty New York newspaper:

> It would be better for the *World* to forget a part of history that has, and always will be, a blot on the manhood of the State of New York. Texas troops may not have been as well equipped nor as well drilled as those of New York when the call came for them to enter the Federal army, but there is one thing the *World* may rest assured of, and that is, that no Texas regiment ever has or ever will lay down in the face of an enemy while a negro regiment has to charge over their cowering bodies to repel an attack. Can the *World* point to a like record for its New York Guard?[112]

The incident referred to was the battle of the Crater, at Petersburg, Virginia, during the Civil War.

In terms of the ratio of militia to total state population, Arizona was fourth and New Mexico fifth among the states, while Texas was at the very bottom, with only .28 of 1 percent of the population in the guard.[113] Still, the Texas organization was larger than those of Arizona and New Mexico combined.

Like some other states, the Texas guard included a political component—the governor's personal staff, authorized by state law. The staff consisted of twelve of the governor's closest political cronies, who were commissioned as lieutenant colonels in the militia. (This was how Colonel Edward M. House, Woodrow Wilson's closest confidant, became a colonel.)[114] They performed no military duties but did get to strut around in their dress uniforms at civic and social functions. In December 1916, the War Department ordered an end to governors' personal staffs, but on January 12, 1917, Secretary of War Baker ruled that governors' staffs could continue to wear their uniforms.[115]

The Texas guard was organized as a reinforced brigade, which as of May 31, 1916, numbered 3,847 men:[116] the 2nd, 3rd, and 4th Infantry regiments, having among them one machine gun company and no supply company; the 1st Cavalry Squadron (Troop A—Houston, Troop B—Amarillo, Troop C—San Antonio, Troop D—Corsicana); Battery A, 1st Field Artillery (Dallas) and Field Hospital No. 1. However, the "Hospital Corps Detachment not having been recognized by Federal Government cannot be accepted under present call." (The field hospital company was finally recognized on November 11, 1916.)[117] The units were to be recruited to war strength: 150 men per infantry company, 171 per field artillery battery, and 100 per troop of cavalry.[118] Governor Ferguson wanted to recruit the Texas cavalry squadron to a full regiment, and staff work had begun.[119] Texas Adjutant General Henry Hutchings announced on May 13 that a new Texas National Guard at full war strength of 7,000 men would immediately be organized to replace that just called into federal service. But the secretary of war decided not to authorize the raising of a brigade of cavalry at the present time.[120]

The last federal inspection had ranked one Texas company as "excellent," six were "very good," eight were "good," nine were "fair," fourteen were "poor," and one was "no drills." Between 1914 and 1915, there had been an actual decrease of 47 officers and 640 enlisted men. The inspector-instructor, Captain John D. Long, 3rd U.S. Cavalry, had inspected the 1st Cavalry Squadron in April and reported that Troops A and B were "very good," while Troop D had deficiencies.[121]

When the guard was activated on May 9, there was in progress at Camp Mabry in Austin[122] a school for all infantry officers and selected noncoms. The school was immediately disbanded and everyone hurried to their home stations to muster the companies pending notification of the mobilization point, which the War Department designated as San Antonio, the logical choice since Fort Sam Houston and the headquarters of the Southern Department were located there.[123] All units were notified, "directing them to report at San Antonio on trains arriving Thursday, May 11, in the forenoon if possible, with available officers and entire enlisted strength, but in no event with less than the prescribed minimum."[124] Some unit departures were tumultuous. In Amarillo, more than ten thousand people thronged the railroad station to send off Troop B, 1st Cavalry Squadron. In El Paso, thousands cheered as a military band led Company K, 4th Infantry, to the railroad station.[125]

By May 14, 3,730 men had reported to Camp Wilson, the 1,280-acre addition northeast of Fort Sam Houston.[126] Additional men continued to trickle in, at their own expense, from out of state and even from the Punitive Expedition, where they had been working in civilian capacities. Referring to the guard's mobilization, General Funston reported to the adjutant general of the army that its "promptness of movement was commendable." On May 16, the process of mustering the Texans into federal service began.[127]

The First Call-Up

Mobilization triggered a surge of patriotism in Texas, producing a flood of applications to enlist in both the Texas Rangers and the National Guard. For example, the governor was in New Braunfels addressing the state volunteer firemen's association when he received Secretary Baker's telegram. Ferguson informed the firemen of the call-up, and they all—more than 1,500—volunteered on the spot for military service. The El Paso chamber of commerce decided to buy four machine guns and present them to the Guard.[128] In San Antonio the members of Company B, 2nd Texas, had been mustered into the Guard in November 1915 but had not yet received their equipment. They had nevertheless been meeting regularly for drill. Since they had no equipment, the army inspector-instructor had recommended they be mustered out. But since no orders to that effect had been issued, when the May call-up came Company B mobilized at the armory—three officers and ninety-seven enlisted men. "Equipped with wooden axes borrowed from the Woodmen of the World, they drilled last night on Alamo Plaza, while the Mexicans of the neighborhood looked on and wondered what kind of military this could be, uniformed in band suits, palm beaches, overalls and a few here and there in the regulation khaki, their private property. Yet they are ready to go to the border, with equipment, if their status in the Guard is properly settled, but without equipment if necessary."[129] At San Benito, thirty miles north of Brownsville, Hispanics planned to organize three companies of infantry. Applications for enlistment in the guard poured into Adjutant General Hutchings's department in Austin, causing him to declare that there would be little difficulty in recruiting up to war strength.[130]

General Hulen took active command of the Texas brigade on May 12 at Camp Wilson, which was the scene of intense activity. Hundreds of men were drilling but still in their civilian clothes, for uniforms had not yet been issued. The troops waited to take their physicals and be vaccinated against smallpox and typhus, after which the brigade would be mustered into federal service.[131] There was a carnival atmosphere at the encampment. Visitors by the thousands on foot, in autos, carriages, and even a few on horseback flocked to inspect the tent city. It became necessary for the officers to station guards in the road and request motorists not to drive down the company streets. The soldiers seemed to enjoy being the center of attention from the throngs of citizens. "It was like a vast picnic ground, orderly, yet with a carefree note throughout." There were periodic band concerts, with the crowds cheering the military airs. Several companies went through the manual of arms for a delighted audience. And the sightseers even watched with apparent relish as the soldiers ate their meals. The citizens of San Antonio further expressed their appreciation for the militia's presence by hosting an elaborate dinner at the St. Anthony Hotel for regular and guard officers. A dance for the latter was also held at the hotel's roof garden. But it was not all fun and games; the men got down to serious drilling as of May 15.[132]

Within six days of arriving at Camp Wilson, the brigade was sworn in to federal service during a rainstorm that converted their camp into an ocean of sticky black mud and flooded the tents. But 116 men did not sign the muster roll, some 40 to 45 of them belonging to Company L, 3rd Infantry, from the town of Lott. The War Department took under advisement whether to court-martial them.[133] It was decided to give the errant 116 a second chance, and many of them quickly took it; it turned out that some of them had simply been away from their company stations when the call-up occurred. By May 28, only 41 were left against whom charges might be filed.[134] The charge could be desertion, a more serious offense than failure to report for muster as required by the Dick Act. A court-martial was scheduled for June 6, but, as it happened, no trials were held because by then all the recalcitrant militiamen had been mustered in.[135] Recruiting officers were ordered to investigate militiamen who had refused to report for mobilization at their home stations. The officers were to determine whether there were extenuating circumstances. There apparently were, because the Texas congressional delegation was deluged with requests from Texas guardsmen and their relatives asking them to use their influence to get the men discharged.[136]

While waiting for their border assignments, the troops repaired the damage from the heavy rains and drilled in the mud, the largest formation being by company.[137] The next item on the brigade agenda was giving the men their physical exams, with all available medical officers on hand to complete the process as quickly as possible.[138] Few men failed their physicals because the companies had been "weeded" of the physically unfit at their home stations. The few who failed did so because of diseases contracted since the previous inspection or because they were under age. On May 19, the entire brigade was inoculated for typhoid.

By May 21, the infantry regiments were pronounced "fully equipped." Most of the equipment was issued from Texas stocks, except for tents and some other items needed so badly that they were issued from the army depot at Fort Sam Houston. The 2nd and 3rd Infantry regiments each organized a machine gun company. The 4th Infantry already had such a unit. Moreover, each regiment now had a medical detachment of sixteen enlisted men and three officers, a doctor with the rank of major commanding each one. Their duty was to maintain sanitary conditions, employing methods such as vector control and oiling pools where mosquitoes were likely to breed. One of the striking features of the 1916 call-up was the remarkable improvement in the sick rate and mortality rates over the mobilization camps during the Spanish-American War in 1898.[139]

General Funston was desperate for more troops to deploy along the Rio Grande. On May 17, he had ordered the seven Coast Artillery companies stationed at San Antonio to Del Rio to protect railroad bridges between El Paso and Del Rio. But what Funston really needed was cavalry to patrol the border (he had even considered mounting two thousand infantrymen on Texas ponies straight off the range—not a good idea).[140] So Troop C, 1st Texas Cavalry Squadron, which had recently been organized in San Antonio, was hurriedly mustered into federal service, although it was currently at minimum strength.[141] This brought the squadron up to four full troops. Yet neither the cavalry nor the artillery was "fully equipped." They did sport their distinguishing hat cords—red for artillery, yellow for cavalry—but they lacked horses and some other equipment. This other equipment would not include sabers, or "cheese knives" as the cavalrymen referred to them. Sabers were deemed useless for border duty, so saber drill was eliminated.[142] The artillery and cavalry remained at Camp Wilson pending the arrival of their horses. In the meantime, Funston ordered the cavalry squadron to the rifle range at Leon Springs, some twenty-three miles from San Antonio, for target practice because he wanted them to get as much firing experience as possible.[143]

Funston also conducted a test of the army's newly acquired trucks. He had the 850 men of the 30th U.S. Infantry at Fort Sam Houston loaded into trucks, driven about eight miles over rough country roads, unloaded and deployed in extended order, reloaded, and returned to camp, all in less than two hours. Funston and his staff observed the exercise and declared that the use of trucks ushered in a new era in the transportation of troops.[144]

Governor Ferguson decided to visit the guard encampment together with his close associate and member of his personal staff Lieutenant Colonel Francisco A. Chapa, a prominent San Antonio druggist and politician. A sentry stopped their car at the entrance and informed them that civilian motor vehicles were prohibited. "But this is Governor Ferguson and party," protested Colonel Chapa. "I don't care if it's Governor Ferguson or Teddy Roosevelt, you can't drive that car in here," insisted the sentry. "You'll have to get out and walk." The governor did just that, after complimenting the soldier for following orders.[145]

General Funston decided to station the 4th Texas Infantry in that traditional trouble spot, the Big Bend region of Texas.[146] Funston reported that "this district is a long one, being about 500 miles in length. The distances from the railroad to [the] border vary from twenty-five to ninety miles.... It has been a difficult task to patrol the border and supply the troops."[147] Few soldiers wished to be stationed there. Although a desolately beautiful area of mountains and desert, it was hot, isolated, sparsely populated, and subject to raids from across the Rio Grande, some by the notorious Mexican bandit Chico Cano.[148] Of particular concern was the strategic Pecos High Bridge, an engineering marvel located only five miles from the Rio Grande on the Southern Pacific main line. This spectacular structure was 2,180 feet long and 321 feet high, and it was quite vulnerable to sabotage.[149] Most of the population in the Big Bend lived along the Southern Pacific railroad in the towns of Marfa, Alpine, and Marathon; those residing in Presidio or on the scattered ranches and hamlets near the Rio Grande such as Terlingua and Lajitas were most at risk.

The center of military activity was Marfa, headquarters of the Big Bend District. On the south side of town the army built what was officially named the "Camp U.S. Troops, Marfa, Texas" but was commonly called Camp Marfa. It evolved into the most important installation between Forts Clark and Bliss. Because of its location on the railroad, supplies could be brought in easily and in bulk to the large quartermaster warehouses. From Marfa supplies were distributed to army detachments along the river by mule pack train, wagon train, truck convoy, and later by tractor train.[150]

Much of the Big Bend was a logistical nightmare. It was advisable to station troops at Terlingua, where the Chisos Mining Company of Chicago produced strategically important mercury, the fulminate of which was used in explosives.[151] Howard E. Perry, who owned the Chisos Mining Company, was receiving nearly fifty thousand dollars a month from his mining operations by March 1917. Because of World War I, the price of mercury soared from $45 to $80 per 75-pound flask. The property that Perry had originally taken in settlement of a $200 debt had produced $3 million worth of mercury.[152] There were other, and smaller, quicksilver mines around Terlingua, and they too operated at capacity.[153] Perry used all the political influence he could muster to have the Chisos Mining Company protected.[154] Nor was he alone; the superintendent of the Presidio Mining Company at Shafter, forty-five miles south of Marfa and only twenty-two miles north of the Rio Grande, asked Governor Ferguson for protection from possible raids coming from the Ruidosa area, pointing out that the company had eight hundred or nine hundred Hispanic workers and only forty Anglos. The army had only a sixteen-man detachment detailed to protect the installation.[155]

Terlingua was eighty-five miles south of the railroad at Alpine and supplied by a rough unpaved track across mountain and desert. Escort wagons or trucks could get through in dry weather but were useless for days after heavy rains. Fifty escort wagon loads were required to supply a troop of cavalry for a month, and it took eight days for a wagon to make a round trip between Alpine and Terlingua. In order to rest the animals properly, a wagon could make only three trips a month. Under good conditions a truck could make the round trip in two days, barring the frequent breakdowns and accidents. But at Alpine the army had only two escort wagons and one truck in the fall of 1915, increased to three trucks by January 1916. To maintain the small detachment at Glenn Springs, supplies had to come either from Alpine, 120 miles away, or from Marathon, a mere eighty-five miles distant.[156]

The army immediately took several steps to meet the crisis in the Big Bend arising from the Glenn Springs raid. One was to transfer Battery E of the 5th U.S. Field Artillery from Fort Sill, Oklahoma, to Fort Bliss. The battery was equipped with 4.7" howitzers, the largest in the army inventory. Its presence had a salutary effect on the Mexican garrison in Ciudad Juárez, especially since the army displayed the artillery prominently in maneuvers and in a Preparedness Day parade of three thousand troops in El Paso. The units from Fort Bliss participating in the parade included the 7th and 23rd U.S. Infantry, a battalion of the 20th U.S. Infantry, batteries A and E of the 5th U.S. Field Artillery, the 8th U.S. Cavalry, motor ambulances, wagon trains, seven bands, a provisional company of motorcyclists, and two companies of Coast Artillery. The 2nd Battalion of the 20th Infantry was later transferred from Columbus to El Paso.[157] Moreover, the army built a telegraph line from Marathon to the border, improving to some degree the primitive communications in the region.[158] And General Funston on May 21 recalled the 6th U.S. Cavalry from the Punitive Expedition and assigned it to the Big Bend. Colonel Joseph Gaston of the 6th Cavalry established his headquarters at Presidio.[159] On May 28, the 4th Texas Infantry arrived from San Antonio instead of the additional Coast Artillery companies Funston had requested for static defense and had been denied. On May 23, Major General Tasker Bliss, chief of the Mobile Army Division, wrote to the chief of staff: "I concur with the Chief of Coast Artillery in his views as to the undesirability of removing any more companies of coast artillery troops from the fortifications. If the fortifications are further stripped of their present insufficient manning details it will probably cause serious public criticism which will be hard to meet."[160] There were only some fifteen thousand Coast Artillery in the country, and more than one thousand of them were already on the border.

Nevertheless, on June 12 the army ordered to the border eleven more companies of Coast Artillery: two from Portland, Maine, two from Boston, two from Narragansett Bay, two from the five forts on Long Island Sound, one from Fort Totten, one from Fort Hamilton, and one from Fort Hancock at Sandy Hook.[161] Small detachments of Coast Artillery guarded the railroad bridges from Del Rio to Laredo and from Laredo to San Antonio. The War Department felt that more could not be spared without jeopardizing the organization's mission.[162] Thus the 4th Texas Infantry would be deployed instead, helping to guard the towns and strategic railroad bridges from Sanderson to Sierra Blanca and the territory south to the Rio Grande.[163] In addition, Funston now had the 6th U.S. Cavalry and the Texas cavalry squadron, plus the eight companies of Coast Artillery, with which to defend this exposed section of the Texas border.[164] Funston assigned Captain James M. Love, who had been the inspector-instructor of the Texas guard up until the mobilization, to inspect the guard units in the Big Bend.[165]

The 4th Texas Infantry was dispersed all over the Big Bend. Its 1st Battalion headquarters and Companies C and D were stationed at Sierra Blanca, while Company A was at Hot Wells and Company B at Lobo.[166] The regiment's 2nd Battalion's headquarters and Companies E and G were at Marfa, with Company F at Valentine and H at Presidio. The 3rd Battalion headquarters and Company I were at Marathon with Company L at Sanderson and Company M at Alpine. (Company M relieved Troop A of the 14th U.S. Cavalry, which went to Del Rio. Company M was ordered to Presidio in July, being relieved by Company L, from Sanderson.) Company K was transported by truck from Marathon to Terlingua to guard the mining installations.[167]

As an example of conditions in the Big Bend, upon arriving at Terlingua, Company K had to pitch their tents on a tennis court, the only level piece of ground in the town, which was built on a hillside with no trees and very little vegetation. The men complained bitterly about the heat, claiming the temperature reached 120 degrees in the shade. The only water for drinking and cooking came in a mining company tank truck from a well two and a half miles away. In order to wash or bathe, the men had to hike to pools six miles from camp. This served to toughen them up for the routine of twelve-mile route marches, later increased to fifteen miles. One positive aspect of their time at Terlingua was that cordial relations existed with Troop C of the 6th U.S. Cavalry, who patrolled the Terlingua area.[168]

While duty in the Big Bend certainly had its drawbacks, there were some amenities. Company M, for instance, was the envy not just of the regiment but of the regulars at Camp Alpine, for they had brought with them two black cooks.[169] And residents of the Big Bend did what they could to show their appreciation for the militia's presence. For example, the good ladies of Sanderson surprised Company L by sending them cakes and salads for supper.[170] And one of the soldiers whiled away his time by drawing humorous cartoons about his service in the Big Bend.[171]

Most of the Texas infantry had it a lot better than the 4th Texas, for they were stationed in the lower Rio Grande Valley. Initially the 1st Cavalry Squadron was at Laredo. The 2nd and 3rd Texas Infantry were assigned to the Brownsville Military District, which encompassed the Rio Grande from its mouth to Rio Grande City and inland for twenty to forty miles. They were deployed from Harlingen to Roma, while Battery A Field Artillery was sent to Rio Grande City.[172] Headquarters and Companies F and H of the 2nd Texas Infantry were at Mission. Initially the machine gun company did not even have pistols, much less machine guns. They received two Vickers Maxim guns, but nobody knew how to fire them until regulars from Fort Ringgold taught them. Company F was subsequently transferred to Roma, sixty miles from Mission.[173] Company I was at Rio Grande City at Fort Ringgold, Company E at Sam Fordyce, Companies G, K, L, and M at Pharr, and Companies A, B, and D at Donna. Headquarters and the 1st Battalion of the 3rd Texas were at Harlingen, the 2nd Battalion at Mercedes, and the 3rd Battalion at San Benito.[174]

The Brownsville District was the area of greatest concern because it was more heavily populated than other border districts, and the events of 1915 had shown that the thick brush made pursuit of Mexican raiders extremely difficult.[175] Commanding the Brownsville District was Brigadier General James Parker, a tough, no-nonsense officer who took over on May 20. Through an automobile tour he quickly familiarized himself with his district, preparing to reorganize regular patrols and militia detachments. On June 3, he issued an order establishing the ground rules for the guard units in his jurisdiction. Until further notice, those camps would be regarded as separate stations from those of nearby regular units. For the present, guard units would not be used for border protection; rather, they would be training under their brigade commander, General Hulen.[176] Regulars would facilitate the all-important duty of instruction, taking a friendly interest in the progress of the guard and whenever possible supplying whatever was needed. At the guard's request, regular officers would be detailed as inspectors, advisers, commanders or to give theoretical or practical instruction. And when asked, the regulars would also provide noncoms as drill instructors. Parker stressed that "these matters must be managed with tact, and it is the desire of the district commander that the most friendly relations shall exist." In case of military emergency, the guard would be used in a supporting role.[177]

Parker put the Texas troops through the mill. After visiting the battalions stationed at San Benito, Harlingen, and Mercedes, he announced that the Texas regiments would engage in six to eight hours of drill daily, until they became "full-fledged American soldiers," and then they would undergo a course of target practice. "General Parker said the Texas soldiers are rapidly getting their camps whipped into shape and are ready and anxious to begin this training. While the long drilling hours may seem strenuous, he says the men evidenced their desire to undertake it."[178]

The program of rigorous drilling produced results, for the two regiments were rapidly being hardened. Within ten days they were making marches of six to twelve miles a day. It was anticipated that when their target practice was completed they would be ready for active service.[179] The sense of urgency in seasoning the troops was certainly shared by Lieutenant Colonel John M. Hoover, commanding the 3rd Battalion, 3rd Texas Infantry at San Benito. He announced that there would be no "off duty" time for any member of his command, for they must be ready to respond at a moment's notice. Furthermore, his men were prohibited from even entering any of the several saloons in San Benito.[180] Besides garrisoning San Benito, Hoover's troops were parceled out among various smaller towns, and he ordered that "isolated detachments guarding points should not be smaller than twenty men; in a few cases where they are stationed in a good-sized community, on which an attack by Mexican bandits would be unlikely and are used merely for moral effect, their size may be reduced to ten men."[181]

Mexicans caused just enough excitement to keep the men alert. Three days after leaving Camp Wilson, a patrol of Company L, 3rd Battalion, 3rd Texas at San Benito, was fired on at three o'clock in the morning. The soldiers replied by firing fourteen rounds but did not hit anyone. A twenty-man detachment immediately came to their assistance. Their attackers were probably horse thieves, for earlier that evening Texas Rangers had reported a band of Mexican rustlers in the vicinity, and an extra guard had been posted.[182] This clash was in sharp contrast to the other case of shots being fired in anger—a private in Company C, 2nd Texas, was accidentally shot and killed at Donna by another private who was shooting at a corporal in the same company. The shooter was immediately arrested and charged with negligent homicide.[183]

There soon arose the probability of a great many shots being fired in anger, for a new threat from Mexico menaced the Texas border. One response by the Southern Department was to order the Texas cavalry squadron to Laredo on June 10. (The squadron was later sent to Ruidosa in the Big Bend.) The urgency of reinforcing the Laredo garrison was so great that the squadron left Camp Wilson without its horses, which would be shipped later.[184] And in the Brownsville district all available troops, including the 2nd and 3rd Texas regiments, were hurriedly massed at Brownsville fully equipped for field service.[185] It appeared that the United States was on the brink of war with Mexico, something that many Texas guardsmen looked forward to. The Texas adjutant general wrote on May 26, 1916, that "Texas could whip Mexico if she had to."[186] This was not entirely bombast, for Texas had indeed "whipped Mexico" to become independent in 1836.

The atmosphere was perhaps best captured in a newspaper recruiting advertisement for the Texas National Guard that appeared on June 18 and ended with "Remember the Alamo!"[187]

Chapter 3

The War Crisis

President Venustiano Carranza had embarked on a policy of brinksmanship. His dilemma was how to get the Punitive Expedition out of Mexico in order to burnish his image as the nationalist champion of Mexican sovereignty. He had at least to match Villa's popular image of the leader fighting to expel Pershing's forces. When Carranza had shut down the Plan de San Diego in October 1915, he had prudently kept the cadre available. The ostensible leaders, Luis de la Rosa and Aniceto Pizaña, were given sanctuary in Mexico; each had a one-thousand-dollar price on his head in Texas. Carranza now reactivated de la Rosa, who began to rebuild his forces. By April 1916, the American government was receiving confirmed reports that de la Rosa was openly recruiting followers in Ciudad Victoria, the capital of Tamaulipas state, and in Monterrey, the capital of Nuevo León. More disturbingly, the federal Bureau of Investigation reported that de la Rosa intended to invade Texas between May 10 and 15. There were also rumors of an imminent Hispanic uprising in the lower Rio Grande Valley in support of de la Rosa's incursion.

The Mexican secret agent who had been organizing Hispanics for the uprising was one José M. Morín. In April and May, using the alias of J. M. Leal, he had been busily recruiting followers in the area from San Antonio south to the border. Morín professed to be a villista, and the date for his proposed uprising was May 10. Among other things, he issued commissions to those who would lead the "army of liberation" he was organizing.

Unfortunately for Morín, his principal associate, Colonel Viviano Saldívar Cervantes, was an informant who kept the Bureau of Investigation apprised of Morín's activities. On May 10, as Morín traveled by train from San Antonio to Kingsville, the bureau arrested him, as well as his associate Victoriano Ponce. The Texas Rangers then conducted a roundup of Morín's followers in Kingsville. When interrogated, Morín revealed that he wasn't a villista after all—he had become a general in Carranza's army in 1914. Morín and Ponce were turned over to the Texas Rangers, in whose custody they "evaporated." The rangers simply executed them, buried the bodies, and claimed that the prisoners had escaped.[1] Without Morín the proposed Hispanic rebellion collapsed.

May 15 passed without any raids by de la Rosa, but he and Pizaña were operating openly in the vicinity of Matamoros, and both de la Rosa's guerrillas and units of the Carranza army were massing along the border.

The Carranza regime labored under the delusion that the United States was so weak militarily that Mexico could launch surprise attacks to annihilate the Punitive Expedition and to overrun Laredo before the United States could react. Evidently not much thought was given to what would happen next, since such a Mexican attack would precipitate a full-scale war. Given the disparity between the two countries—the United States had more men of military age than the entire population of Mexico; the American army could invade northern Mexico; the U.S. Navy could blockade both coasts of Mexico; Mexico was dependent on the United States for almost all of her munitions—unless the United States sued for peace, a most unlikely possibility, the war would be an unmitigated catastrophe for Mexico.

Carranza sent the United States a strongly worded note on May 22 demanding the withdrawal of the Punitive Expedition. He also massed some thirty thousand troops in northern Mexico. According to historian Arthur S. Link, "Carranza had in fact already decided to run the risk of war to force withdrawal of the Punitive Expedition."[2]

Many American officials refused to believe that the Mexicans were serious. According to information obtained by U.S. intelligence, the invasion had been postponed until June 10 at the latest. On June 2, Mexico sent a diplomatic note to Washington, D.C., bluntly demanding the immediate withdrawal of the Punitive Expedition. This ultimatum set the stage for implementing the grand design—a revival of the Plan de San Diego together with an invasion of south Texas.

Border Problem

On June 1, the American consul at Nuevo Laredo reported that the Mexicans were rebuilding an abandoned branch railroad line from La Jarita station, about twenty miles southwest of Nuevo Laredo, to the Rio Grande, in order to move troops rapidly to the border. The consul stated that the invasion rumors and reports were in fact true. The Bureau of Investigation learned that de la Rosa was in close contact with a shadowy individual named Esteban E. Fierros and that the pair had recently traveled to Mexico City to confer with General Pablo González, who commanded the Army Corps of the East, in effect all of eastern Mexico. According to the report, González had conferred with Carranza, who ordered that de la Rosa's invasion of Texas not take place until the conclusion of the talks at El Paso and Ciudad Juárez between Generals Scott and Funston and General Alvaro Obregón, Carranza's secretary of war and marine. Since their conference, which began on April 28, had ended in stalemate on May 11, this precondition had already been met.

General González, Carranza's favorite and most loyal general, supervised the border operation from his headquarters in Cuernavaca. He had sent a secret agent to the border in the person of General Juan Antonio Acosta, who gathered intelligence on the American army and served as the conduit between González and disaffected Hispanics in Texas. More importantly, González selected Esteban Fierros to direct the invasion. Fierros was a native of Laredo and a member of a prominent Hispanic family in that city. In 1916 he was a colonel in the Army Corps of the East, who had served in various staff capacities involving the Constitutionalist railroads. When González selected him for the mission Fierros was superintendent of the Tampico railroad terminal. Fierros's familial connections on the border and his administrative and railroad experience would be invaluable for the operation, which involved rebuilding a railroad line.

As relations between the United States and Mexico continued to deteriorate, Fierros was promoted to the rank of brevet general and placed in command of a brigade that was quietly being assembled in Monterrey—the Fierros Brigade. One of the three other generals whom Fierros commanded was none other than Luis de la Rosa himself. To reinforce the Plan de San Diego veneer on this carrancista operation, Fierros was duly commissioned as a brigadier general in the "Liberating Army of Races and Peoples in America," the military arm of the nebulous "Revolutionary Congress of San Diego." The commission was supposedly issued at San Diego, Texas, on May 30, 1916, by the general in chief, Agustín S. Garza, a.k.a. "León Caballo," although in fact it was issued in Monterrey.

The War Crisis

Fierros's credentials were considerably more impressive than the motley brigade he commanded. Like many other military contingents during the revolutionary decade, it was top heavy—four generals, plus a corresponding proportion of subordinate officers through the rank of sublieutenant, for a brigade whose strength was 450 men. The majority of the men were raw recruits, along with militant Plan de San Diego refugees from Texas, and a cadre of carrancista regulars. The latter included forty men from the Railroad Corps, who were to rebuild the line to La Jarita station, which had been chosen as Fierros's base. Interestingly, the Fierros Brigade had six Japanese, who were apparently ordnance experts. A military train was provided to Fierros, who also controlled the brigade's funds. This ensured that Fierros's principal associate, Luis de la Rosa, would operate under strict carrancista control.

By June 8, the brigade at La Jarita was ready for action, and Fierros held a formal review. On June 9, he sent a status report to General González: the brigade numbered 143 infantry and 310 cavalry. But not all of these were at La Jarita because Fierros had been infiltrating three or four men across the Rio Grande at night to reconnoiter the terrain and serve as guides for the remainder of the brigade. Fierros assured González that the brigade would enter Texas shortly, just as soon as he arranged some final details with carrancista general Fortunato Zuazua. In translation, Fierros added:

> Most of the cavalry have crossed into Texas to penetrate the interior of the State, disguised as vaqueros, and to date we have had no difficulty in crossing in parties of 25 and 30 men, dividing them into bands of 20 [dispersed] in different directions, designating Kennedy [sic], Texas as the assembly point. The Coup should break out tonight after midnight [June 10]. I expect we will soon have very good news to communicate to you. I leave on Monday to put myself at the head of my troops, depending on the orders that [General] Fortunato [Zuazua] gives me. I send you a strong abrazo. [I am] expecting you to telegraph me the latest on the International situation.
>
> [signed] Esteban E. Fierros
>
> The lady who will deliver this to you is an intimate friend who has all my confidence, who has just returned from Laredo, Texas where I sent her on a mission.[3]

Mexican preparations included an orchestrated anti-American campaign, both in the government newspapers and in street demonstrations, the concentration of troops in Sonora and Chihuahua to attack the Punitive

Expedition, and the projected invasion of the lower Texas border. The plan reportedly involved a combined operation between the Fierros Brigade, using de la Rosa and the Plan de San Diego as cover, and carrancista regular units such as General Fortunato Zuazua's brigade. Crossing the Rio Grande above and below Laredo, columns would isolate that city and attack in conjunction with the garrison of Nuevo Laredo.[4] To keep the American army off balance, simultaneous diversionary raids would be launched from Matamoros, where Fierros's infiltrators would wage guerrilla warfare, and by Plan de San Diego militants, who would rise in arms.

However feasible this complex and ambitious operation may have appeared on paper, it was never implemented. "Precisely how the decision was reached remains unclear, but the realization that the Americans had uncovered the invasion plan and took an exceedingly dim view of it undoubtedly had a sobering effect; the Americans knew the invasion date, the location and strength of the Fierros Brigade, and that De la Rosa was being aided and abetted by Carranza officials. Accordingly, what took place on June 10 was not an invasion but the frantic postponement of the operation."[5]

The man on the spot was General Alfredo Ricaut, who commanded Mexican forces along the Rio Grande from Piedras Negras to Matamoros. Ricaut, who happened to be Carranza's nephew, rushed to Nuevo Laredo and met with Brigadier General W. A. Mann, who commanded American troops in the Laredo District. When they conferred on the international bridge, Ricaut informed Mann that he had just learned that the men at La Jarita were in fact bandits and that they'd been rebuilding the railroad for some nefarious purpose. (The camp at La Jarita, some twenty miles from Nuevo Laredo, was in plain sight of anyone passing along the main rail line from Nuevo Laredo to Mexico City.) He assured General Mann that he had immediately dispatched troops to deal with them. However, the press reported on June 12 that:

> General Alfredo Ricaut, Carrancista commander at Matamoros, today admitted that he was tricked by a ruse of De la Rosa's into furnishing a special train to bring his precious command of bandits from Monterrey to La Jarita, where they detrained and spread up and down the river. Ricaut was made to believe through false telegrams a la Villa [a reference to the ruse Pancho Villa had used to capture Ciudad Juárez in November, 1913] that 500 or 600 men were waiting to go north from Monterrey for railroad repair work.[6]

The War Crisis

This was an exceedingly lame story, especially since the U.S. Army knew that Ricaut conferred with de la Rosa at La Jarita on June 11 or 12 and had not arrested the guerrilla chieftain then.[7] Were one to believe Ricaut, he had also been blissfully unaware that de la Rosa had been recruiting in Monterrey and that the Fierros Brigade had been organized in that city. Either Ricaut was incompetently oblivious or he was in on the plot and his assurances to General Mann were a verbal smokescreen.

Although the invasion plan had been shelved, the Mexican government planned to exert pressure on the United States in a less dangerous way—by the proven 1915 strategy of raids into South Texas: covertly sponsor raids into south Texas but ensure that none was so serious as to provoke massive American military retaliation and imply to Washington, D.C., that if the Punitive Expedition were withdrawn the raids would immediately cease. Carranza revived the Plan de San Diego.

The movement's leaders had been hiding in Mexico ever since Carranza had shut down the plan in October 1915. Although presumably resenting Carranza's having cynically sacrificed their movement for his own designs, they had little choice but to dance to Carranza's tune. If they returned to Texas they were dead men. The Punitive Expedition crisis unexpectedly afforded them the opportunity to resume their struggle, and they eagerly seized the chance. For the next several months they openly recruited followers in Mexico, with the approval and assistance of the Carranza authorities. Repeated American demands that Carranza curtail these activities were met with soothing assurances that the Mexican government was moving energetically against these malefactors. Several hundred raiders, both Plan de San Diego militants and Carranza soldiers in civilian clothing, assembled along the lower Rio Grande. Supporting them was the Fierros Brigade.

The new strategy was quickly implemented. A series of raids under the aegis of the Plan de San Diego once again plunged the lower Texas border into turmoil.[8] On June 12, Secretary of State Lansing was notified that "a small party of armed Mexicans invaded Texas last night with a red flag and a can of kerosene oil."[9] The report referred to a party of Mexicans who had tried to cut the telegraph wires and burn the railroad trestle at Webb Station, some twenty miles north of Laredo. The group carried a red flag with a diagonal white stripe bearing the legend "Liberty, Equality, and Independence." However, before they could carry out their mission a Hispanic cowboy spotted them and raised the alarm. A running fight ensued between the raiders and a posse of ranchers reinforced by an army detachment. Three of the Mexicans were killed and three were captured.[10] One of the raiders killed was the leader of the group, a Lieutenant Colonel Villarreal, in full carrancista uniform. And one of those captured, Norberto Pezzar, wrote an indignant letter to the secretary of war in Mexico City stressing that he was not a bandit as the Americans claimed but was a lieutenant in the Carranza army who had simply been following orders. Accordingly, Pezzar demanded assistance. This incident increased American skepticism regarding reports that General Ricaut was vigorously combating de la Rosa's minions and even an official notice from the Mexican Foreign Office that de la Rosa had been captured.

American skepticism regarding Mexican intentions increased markedly when on the night of June 15 another band attacked a cavalry unit encamped at San Ignacio, thirty miles downriver from Laredo. Some sixty men led by Colonel Isabel de los Santos, one of de la Rosa's followers and a member of the Fierros Brigade, launched what they expected to be a surprise attack against the American unit. The raiders carried a red flag, and the men had been told they were invading Texas to carry out the Plan de San Diego. Unbeknownst to them their plan had been discovered and the American unit had been reinforced. Moreover, they just had plain bad luck—the burro carrying their homemade bombs fell while crossing the Rio Grande, and the bombs got wet and were useless. As the raiders neared the American camp, sentries detected them, and a furious firefight erupted. Three American soldiers were killed and six were wounded. Eight of the raiders, including a carrancista major and a Japanese man, were killed, several were captured, and the survivors fled back across the Rio Grande. One of the captured raiders was a twelve-year-old boy, who complained that one of the grownups had made off with his rifle. The San Ignacio raiders were so wretchedly equipped that the American commander later testified: "I do not wish to convey the idea that this force that crossed the river and attacked my camp was a military organization."[11]

An intriguing aspect to the Fierros Brigade's campaign is what happened to the men who had been infiltrating Texas. On June 20, a party of ten Mexicans dragged two Hispanics from their homes some fifteen miles west of San Antonio, forcing them to act as guides. For the next several days the raiders dodged posses, one of them composed of fifty men—deputy sheriffs, citizens, Bureau of Investigation agents, and city detectives from San Antonio. On one occasion they engaged in a brief skirmish with their pursuers, but in the end the Mexicans managed to disperse and escape. One

The War Crisis

of their captives later told the authorities that the marauders were trying "to capture Texas and restore it to the Mexicans."[12] Yet as far as can be determined, this band was the only group trying to conduct guerrilla warfare in the interior of the state. Most of Fierros's infiltrators apparently were not at all prepared to die for the cause, and they quietly merged into the Hispanic population or slipped back across the Rio Grande.

A few, however, showed greater commitment. On June 14, one Abel Sandoval, a Plan de San Diego militant, gathered about twenty men determined to strike a blow for the revolution in Texas. They crossed the Rio Grande near Brownsville on June 16 with a threefold objective: to assassinate Hispanics opposed to the Plan de San Diego, to wreck trains on the line running north from Brownsville, and to ambush U.S. Army patrols. Unfortunately for the Mexicans, this raid had unintended consequences. The guerrillas were routed and fled back across the river, but this time they were pursued by the U.S. Cavalry, who the next day were reinforced by infantry units.

The American incursion put General Ricaut on the spot, for Carranza had issued explicit orders to his commanders in northern Mexico. General Jacinto Treviño in Chihuahua informed General Pershing that the Punitive Expedition would be attacked if it moved in any direction except back to the border. And General Ricaut had orders to combat any American troops entering Mexico. Ricaut had no intention of fighting; in fact he evacuated Matamoros. To cover himself, he reported that the sorry state of his men's horses had prevented him from driving the American invaders back across the river. Meanwhile Ricaut assured the Americans that he would deal energetically with the raiders. The American troops, having made their point, withdrew back to Texas the next day.

Referring to this Plan de San Diego raid and the crossing of American troops near Matamoros, the distinguished historian Arthur Link writes that: "This was the incident that set war machinery in motion on both sides."[13]

Historian Joseph A. Stout asks, "How close did the two countries come to war in 1916? Some historians assume that war was imminent. I argue that the nations were not on the brink of war in 1916, but that Wilson and Carranza were sparring for diplomatic and political advantage in their respective countries."[14] However, this interpretation does not hold up under examination.

In discussing the 1916 war crisis, it perhaps takes a conscious effort to remember that the United States was not the superpower it is today. The army's authorized strength on June 30, 1916, was 127,711. Its actual strength was only 101,856, of whom 71,032 were in the United States and the Punitive Expedition; the rest were stationed in Alaska, Hawaii, Puerto Rico, the Canal Zone, the Philippines, Guam, and China. (The Philippine Scouts numbered 5,785.) The understrength army experienced considerable difficulty in attracting recruits due to the current demand for labor and consequently high civilian wages. Some 56,000 postmasters were authorized to act as army recruiting agents.[15] And the army's efforts to create a reserve were met with profound indifference. Thus the generals enthusiastically promoted the idea of universal military training, which presumably would eliminate, or at least significantly reduce, the need for a National Guard. The National Guard's reaction was predictable.

Ever since the Columbus raid on March 9, 1916, the army had been committing more and more troops to cope with the Mexican problem. Besides dispatching the Punitive Expedition into northern Mexico, the War Department had been transferring additional units to reinforce the Southern Department. Two companies of the 19th U.S. Infantry were rushed by special train from Fort Sill, Oklahoma, to Fort Clark at Bracketville, Texas, on May 7. In addition, elements of Company E Signal Corps, were transferred from Fort Shafter, Hawaii, to Fort Sam Houston.[16] At Funston's request, three field hospitals and their corresponding ambulance companies from Fort Ethan Allen, Vermont, Fort D. A. Russell, Wyoming, and the Presidio at Monterey, California, were ordered to Fort Sam Houston, Fort Bliss, and Douglas, Arizona. And Funston requested fifteen more junior medical officers for border duty.[17] One of Funston's greatest concerns was a critical lack of cavalry. With the exception of three squadrons, all the rest of the U.S Cavalry units were already either in the Southern Department or in the Punitive Expedition.[18] The call-up of the Arizona, New Mexico, and Texas National Guard on May 9 had provided some help but not much.

Three regular infantry regiments from Plattsburg, Watertown, and Oswego, New York, Vancouver Barracks, and Fort Lawton, Washington, were ordered to the Southern Department. The Pacific Coast was virtually depleted of mobile units, with only two troops of the 1st U.S. Cavalry and a battalion of the 21st Infantry at Calexico, a battalion of the 14th Infantry in Alaska, a company of engineers and a field hospital remaining. Almost every regular infantryman in the United States was either in the Punitive Expedition, on the border, or on his way there.

The War Crisis

The last available regulars were Coast Artillery. A total of 20 percent of its officers (80) and 22 percent of its enlisted men (2,912) had already been detached for border service.[19] Companies from stations such as Pensacola, Florida, Charleston, South Carolina, and Fort Oglethorpe, Georgia, had been sent to Texas as infantry in static defense of railroad bridges and other strategic installations. Coast Artillery command argued that no more of its troops could be sent to the border without impairing its mission. (By the end of September, all Coast Artillery units had been returned to their regular stations.)

Funston's command had been increased by about eleven thousand regulars, but he still considered this number insufficient. To support the infantry, five batteries of the 5th U.S. Field Artillery at Fort Sill and three batteries of the 3rd Field Artillery at Tobyhanna, Pennsylvania, were alerted for border service. (The battalion from Tobyhanna would join the other battalion of the 3rd Field Artillery, which had been stationed at Fort Sam Houston for the last nine years.)

Besides rushing units to the border, the army took other measures. The service schools at Fort Leavenworth, the Mounted Service School at Fort Riley, the School of Fire and the School of Musketry at Fort Sill were all closed on May 10, and the classes graduated as of that date. Students and instructors were immediately sent to join their regiments on the border. Even officers whose regiments were stationed in the Philippines or Hawaii were ordered to the border for special assignment.[20] Serious consideration was even given to graduating the senior class at West Point early, commissioning them as second lieutenants, and assigning them to border duty. General Tasker H. Bliss, the assistant chief of staff, spent a week advocating the matter at West Point, whose Academic Board finally persuaded him to abandon the idea.[21]

In reaction to the latest Plan de San Diego raid and to reinforce the regular army, the War Department had the president on June 18 take the unprecedented step of calling up in peacetime virtually the entire army National Guard, some 150,000 men. This momentous development will be discussed in the next chapter, but suffice it to say here that by July 31, there were 110,957 guardsmen on the border and another 40,139 still in state mobilization camps.

In this connection it might be mentioned that one of the easiest jobs around was to be a Mexican spy. All that was really needed was to be able to read English and to subscribe to the *New York Times*, which maintained comprehensive coverage of U.S.-Mexican relations and of course covered the war crisis in considerable detail. On June 19, for instance, the *Times* published a listing of the National Guard units called up in each state, including unit strength and place of mobilization. Then on June 20, the newspaper published the complete order of battle of the U.S. Army on the border, including the locations of the units and their strengths.

The war crisis may have forced the regular army to rely on the National Guard, but the regulars were certainly not impressed by the guard, writing condescendingly:

> The National Guard may be likened to the volunteer fire departments so popular years ago in our large towns. They were composed of the elite of the young men of the town, whose generous public spirit in so giving their services in extinguishing fires cannot be too strongly commended. When a fire broke out, whether by day or night, the members of the department, no matter in what engaged, dropped their occupations and rushed to the scene of action—often at considerable personal inconvenience and loss. But even with this sacrifice the desired end was frequently not attained, for even with the most strenuous efforts, before the fire brigade could assemble and get to work the conflagration would have reached a point beyond control.[22]

Even as the guardsmen were mobilizing, the crisis moved to a climax which brought the United States and Mexico perilously close to full-scale war. On June 19, the United States prudently, if belatedly, suspended all shipments of munitions to Mexico.[23] Responding to General Treviño's threat, Pershing announced that his troops would move wherever he chose to send them. And on June 21, he sent two troops (three officers and eighty-one men) of the black 10th U.S. Cavalry eastward to the hamlet of Carrizal, Chihuahua. There they confronted a force of some three hundred carrancista regulars under General Félix U. Gómez, who barred their entry into the town. The American commander, Captain Charles Boyd, attempted to force his way in, leading a charge across open ground into devastating machine gun fire. In the fierce firefight both he and General Gómez were killed, and the Americans were soundly defeated, suffering fourteen dead and twenty-five captured; the survivors who were not captured ran for their lives.[24] The American prisoners were marched off to the state prison in the city of Chihuahua.

The War Crisis

The clash at Carrizal seemed to mark the beginning of hostilities. Pershing was ready to take the offensive, having some days previously requested permission to seize the city of Chihuahua, a request the War Department rejected on the grounds that it was impractical at present and that "no overt act must be committed in [the] absence of specific orders from Washington."[25] On June 21, Secretary of State Lansing sent a "personal and confidential" letter to President Wilson beginning with: "As there appears to be an increasing probability that the Mexican situation may develop into a state of war."[26] On June 22, General Hugh Scott, chief of staff of the U.S. Army, was quoted as stating that "war may be declared at any moment."[27] On June 22 President Wilson wrote that "the break seems to have come in Mexico; and all my patience seems to have gone for nothing. I am infinitely sad about it."[28]

Even as the Army War College completed a plan of campaign in the event of war with Mexico, pontoons were being stockpiled at strategic points along the Rio Grande, for it was assumed that the Mexican Army would blow the international bridges. The American war plan called for the quick seizure of Mexican border towns, with three columns striking south from El Paso, Laredo, and Brownsville, occupying the area down to Torreón, the major railroad center in northern Mexico.[29]

On June 22 Secretary of War Baker sent the adjutant general a coded memorandum outlining the plan of campaign in the event of war. Basically it called for American occupation of northern Mexico. The force would consist of 30,000 regulars and 120,000 guardsmen. (Note the army's dependence on the guard.) Pershing would be reinforced up to 20,000 troops, 30,000 would concentrate at Brownsville, 30,000 at El Paso, 10,000 at Nogales, and 30,000 guarding the border between these concentration points. Baker originally considered sending 5,000 troops with the navy to occupy the port of Tampico and another 5,000 to Guaymas, but this component of the plan was dropped.[30]

The war plans did call for blockading both coasts of Mexico under the pretext of stationing warships to evacuate American citizens if necessary. The navy already had vessels off Gulf ports of Mexico: the battleship *Nebraska* at Veracruz, the gunboats *Machias* and *Marietta* at Tampico, and the *Wheeling* at El Carmen. On the Pacific coast were the cruiser *Cleveland* at Guaymas, the supply ship *Glacier* and the cruiser *Albany* at Manzanillo, and the transport *Buffalo* at Mazatlán. The navy dispatched seven destroyers and nine other small craft to join the units off the Mexican coasts.[31]

On June 20, three cruisers of the Pacific fleet left San Diego for Mexican ports: the *Denver* for Salina Cruz, the *Chattanooga* for Acapulco, and the *San Diego* for either Guaymas or Manzanillo. That same day the *Maryland* sailed south from Bremerton, Washington; the *South Dakota* soon followed. By June 21, units of the Pacific fleet were off San José del Cabo, La Paz, Guaymas, Topolobampo, Mazatlán, Manzanillo, Acapulco, and Salina Cruz. The navy also issued a nationwide call for volunteers to man additional vessels should a blockade of Mexican ports become necessary.[32]

Then on June 25, the United States sent Carranza what amounted to an ultimatum, demanding that he repudiate the attack at Carrizal and immediately return the American corpses, prisoners, and all U.S. government property captured with them.[33]

President Wilson evidently believed there was a war crisis. Although he had steadfastly refused to use the word "intervention" in the affairs of Mexico, on June 26, he drafted a speech and a resolution to a joint session of Congress. The draft was couched in fine distinctions, requesting neither a declaration of war nor an intervention. Instead, he requested merely

> that the President be and is hereby authorized and empowered to use the military and naval forces of the United States in any way that may be necessary to guard the southern frontier of the United States most effectively, if necessary to enter on Mexican soil and there require the entire suspension in the Mexican states which touch and border upon our own, of all military activities of every kind on the part of the Mexican authorities and people until by the establishment of a responsible and effective political authority among themselves they are prepared to resume and meet their full obligations towards us as a neighboring and friendly state.[34]

The Mexicans would probably have considered armed U.S. suppression of all Mexican military activities in the northern tier of Mexican states a rather warlike act.

Carranza's exercise in brinksmanship had brought his nation to the verge of a disastrous war, and, in the face of the ultimatum reinforced by the military buildup, Carranza folded—he agreed to the American demands. He also shut down the Plan de San Diego, this time for good. Not only did he prohibit further raids into Texas, but he also had de la Rosa arrested, to the distress of General Pablo González, who had wired the president on June 24: "Please tell me if this was Your Excellency's order and if said individual could be liberated so that he can proceed into the interior of the United States to continue carrying out the mission that he has in conjunction with Fierros."[35] The war crisis abated, and the differences between the United States and Mexico would be addressed by diplomacy rather than on the battlefield. A six-man joint U.S.-Mexican commission was created to discuss the controversies outstanding.[36]

Chapter 4

The Great Call-Up

The National Guard call-up on June 18, 1916,[1] sent a powerful message to the Mexican government that the United States was deadly serious about protecting its border. The army had figuratively scraped the bottom of the barrel insofar as manpower was concerned. Therefore, the high command had no alternative but to take the extremely distasteful step of recommending that the rest of the National Guard be called up, deploying them to protect the border, and reinforcing the regular army if an invasion of Mexico became necessary.

It has been stated that the call-up occurred in response to Carranza's commander in Chihuahua, General Jacinto B. Treviño, having notified Pershing on June 16 that the Punitive Expedition would be attacked if the American forces moved in any direction except back to the border.[2] This interpretation is questionable given the secretary of war's comments in a letter on October 4 to Colonel Clenard McLaughlin of the Oregon National Guard:

> When the National Guard was called into the service of the Federal Government, the lives of men, women and children along the southern frontier were in grave danger *owing to the formidable bandit raids from the Mexican side of the boundary* [emphasis added, an obvious reference to Plan de San Diego raids along the lower Rio Grande]. It is not too much to say that had these raids continued, there was

danger of international war. From the time of the arrival of the units of the National Guard on the border, the raids ceased and the tension between the two countries began to relax. It is the hope and belief of the Government that the presence of the units of the National Guard, together with the units of the Regular Army, on the border and in Mexico, has made possible a peaceful solution of a difficult and threatening problem.[3]

The army's general staff was less than enthusiastic about the call-up. Ever since 1914 the National Guard had theoretically been organized into twelve tactical divisions, but the program was unfinished because some states were unable or unwilling to provide the necessary auxiliary units and because of deficiencies in artillery, engineers, and transport. The army's mobilization plan called for assembling the National Guard at the respective state concentration points, where deficiencies in organization could be remedied, the units could recruit up to war strength, and the formidable task of training and fully equipping them could be undertaken. Then the guardsmen would be transported in an orderly manner to army posts vacated by regulars already sent to the border. Since these posts were functioning entities, where encampments did not have to be created from scratch, the guardsmen could devote themselves to becoming more effective soldiers, a "seasoning" process. Only then would they be deployed to the border.[4]

But the war crisis disrupted plans for the orderly mobilization of the guard, which had an excess of infantry regiments and a serious lack of field artillery, cavalry, engineers, and auxiliary units, primarily medical.[5] The War Department sent the states a quota of units to be activated, and the governors selected the units. National Guard units were ordered immediately to recruit up to war strength. In some cases governors expressed concerns about needing guardsmen at home in case of emergencies; in other instances governors, motivated by state pride, complained because more of their guardsmen were not called up. An official report claimed that "it is known that many discharges from the National Guard were issued by governors of States or State officials in the interval between the date of the call and the actual date of muster in, but the number so discharged cannot now be ascertained with any certainty."[6]

Rushing as many guardsmen to the border as rapidly as possible became the order of the day. On June 25, the secretary of war sent the following "urgent and confidential" telegram to the commanding generals of the Eastern, Central, and Western Departments: "A note has been sent to Mexican government demanding an answer within a few hours period. The probable reply makes rushing of troops to border an imperative military necessity period. Commanders on border can do nothing further without reinforcements period. Everything depends now on what you can do in expediting movement period."[7] The only reinforcements available were of course the National Guard, and on that same day the secretary of war sent another telegram to the commanding generals: "Grave necessity for additional troops on border period. Various requests are being made to delay movement of State organizations until the larger tactical units are organized at State camps period. Organization of these units will be perfected on border period. Meanwhile Secretary War repeats previous order that organizations move as soon as each is ready regardless of additional recruits which will follow organization to border."[8]

The National Guard had two major generals and twenty-four brigadier generals. Forty-four regular officers were now commissioned in the guard with the rank of brigadier general (3), colonel (10), lieutenant colonel (27), and major (40). As of June 30, 1916, National Guard strength was 18,195 enlisted men below its authorized peacetime strength. As of July 31, there were 110,957 guardsmen on the border.[9]

Inevitably, the great call-up produced significant confusion and problems, compounded because the war crisis and mobilization came at a particularly awkward time. The secretary of war, Newton D. Baker, was the pacifist former mayor of Cleveland. His job was certainly not dull. Baker had assumed his new office only on March 6 and was still settling in when Pancho Villa raided Columbus on March 9.[10] From then on, the Punitive Expedition and border security figured prominently on Baker's agenda. On May 9, the first National Guard call-up was ordered. Then on June 3 the National Defense Act was passed, representing the first comprehensive legislation for national defense. It established four classes of soldiers: first the regular army, second the National Guard, third the enlisted reserve, all of which existed in peacetime, and fourth the volunteer army, raised only in wartime. To enhance the guard's effectiveness, the act established three new companies for infantry and cavalry regiments: headquarters, supply, and machine gun. The act required three, not just the current two, field artillery regiments per infantry division and added headquarters and supply companies to field artillery regiments. The National Guard was to be federalized, a provision that hopefully would produce a guard of 17,000 officers and 440,000 enlisted men. The enlistment contract for guardsmen was now three years, with another three years in the reserve, and they had to swear an oath of allegiance both to their state and to the United States. This proved controversial; some men flatly refused to swear the dual oath, in some cases because they did not understand it. They were particularly concerned because the act empowered the president not only to call up guardsmen but also to draft them.[11] Finally, Secretary Baker's stress level increased markedly when the great call-up occurred on June 18. Trying to implement the National Defense Act in the midst of a mobilization proved to be a formidable challenge indeed.[12]

Reluctance to serve was quickly made manifest. Reportedly 21,884 guardsmen in federal service failed to take the oath called for under the National Defense Act, there were numerous applications for discharge from federal service, about 480 Guard officers resigned, and there was considerable difficulty in recruiting men for federal service. An active nationwide recruiting campaign from July 1 to October 31 produced about 15,000, but this was insufficient to fill vacancies caused by discharge and casualties occurring during the same period.[13]

Another major source of concern was the physical condition of the guardsmen. As the surgeon general of the army reported: "The large percentage of rejections at the muster-in physical examination in some of the State camps appears to the department surgeon as the most disappointing and discreditable feature of the mobilization, indicating that the enlistment examinations had been nominal and superficial."[14]

A significant failure of the mobilization was that the army's logistical system was overwhelmed, and the army admitted as much: "As rapidly as possible, all National Guard troops mustered into the service of the United States are being equipped with arms and accouterments identical with those furnished the Regular Army. The delays have been due to lack of reserve supplies kept on hand for the purpose."[15] The Central Department, for instance, reported on July 14 that all troops were being "equipped with arms and accouterments required by Army Regulations except machine guns for Colorado, Illinois, Indiana, Nebraska, 1st Kansas Infantry, 33rd Michigan Infantry, and one Ohio regiment."[16]

The prominent correspondent Floyd Gibbons, who covered the mobilization extensively, especially in the Brownsville District, wrote that "the absence of prearranged plans in the border mobilization devolved the biggest burden upon the regular army staffs in the border districts, which were suddenly called upon to mother a hundred thousand comparatively inexperienced officers and men who were eager and willing to help themselves but, in view of their admitted amateurishness and handicaps of equipment, became largely dependent upon the regulars. . . . Regiment after regiment of regulars was stripped of officers who were detailed to advise, instruct, and train the militiamen."[17] Regular officers not only advised the guard units but also conducted classes in Spanish for guard officers and "assisted the troop commanders and the supply department in solving the farcical mysteries of the requisition formulae, by which a week's mathematical computation and reams of documentation are necessary before a size seven shoe can be changed for a pair of elevens. This red tape was the despair of the militia. . . . The absence of blank forms frequently impeded this work for days."[18] There was not only a shortage of blank forms but also a shortage of the forms needed to requisition the blank forms. The army recognized the problem.[19]

The War Department managed the mobilization through the army's geographic military commands: the Eastern, Central, Western, and Southern Departments. The overriding problem was that while mobilization was decentralized through the departments, the army's logistical system was highly centralized: the Quartermaster Corps operated only two supply depots, at Philadelphia (for all units east of the Mississippi River) and St. Louis. "Inability to equip the Guard promptly was the Army's greatest failure during the Mexican Border incident."[20] As the army reported: "Under present regulations the equipment needed to cover the difference between peace and war footing is supposedly shipped automatically to the various National Guard organizations at their designated mobilization camps. Practically, however, this does not work. The stores should be available at the armory or mobilization camp at all times."[21] The Philadelphia depot

> had been converted recently into a multifunction facility, holding equipment that belonged to several bureaus. No single bureau chief controlled the depot any longer; instead, it responded directly to the orders of the Chief of Staff. The Chief of Staff's involvement, however, was overlooked by the General Staff in the initial excitement of the mobilization, and the depot was neither notified nor given guidance for the first three days. The depot commander exercised commendable but misplaced initiative and distributed the supplies, using a remarkably accurate Associated Press dispatch that gave mobilization

The Great Call-Up

locations. His problems were compounded by the unexpected speed of unit concentrations.[22]

The National Guard blamed the army for the deficiencies, and the army blamed Congress. Although rifles and ammunition were readily available, there was a critical shortage of machine guns, for which the army specifically blamed Congress for refusing to appropriate the necessary funds. The Philadelphia and St. Louis quartermaster depots lacked shoes, khaki uniforms, tentage, and blankets. Sidearms were also lacking, and some units received antiquated revolvers. The army pointed out that, with regard to shoes, guardsmen had been issued regulation footwear but in many cases had worn out their shoes in civilian pursuits; hence, there was a shortage at mobilization and it was the National Guard's fault. The St. Louis depot provided all the clothing and tentage for the Central and Southern Departments. Items such as khaki uniforms had been going to regular units already on the border, so there was a shortage when the guard was called up. Guardsmen from the Midwest wore woolen uniforms because of the climate, but Congress had failed to appropriate money to build up a reserve of khakis. Thus guardsmen arrived on the border in woolen uniforms in the middle of summer. By contrast, the Rock Island Arsenal performed efficiently. By June 27, it had shipped ordnance equipment necessary for war strength to mobilization points in Ohio, Indiana, Illinois, Michigan, Wisconsin, Minnesota, Iowa, Missouri, North Dakota, South Dakota, Kansas, Nebraska, Colorado, and Wyoming.[23]

Another source of confusion concerned the designated mobilization points. The War Department had designated these sites, but when the call-up occurred some of these mobilization points were found to be unsuitable and/or were changed. Kentucky was a case in point. The original mobilization point was Fort Thomas, but this was changed to Earlington, then back to Fort Thomas. These changes caused a delay of about five days in mobilizing the Kentucky National Guard. The site in Maryland was changed from Halethorpe to Laurel, that of West Virginia from Terra Alta to Charleston, that of Nebraska from Lincoln to Fort Crook.[24] Sometimes supplies and equipment were shipped to one location, but the troops had mobilized at another.

Then there was the matter of transportation. The call-up put an enormous strain on the nation's railroads, on which the army absolutely depended. The first 100,000 guardsmen who were rushed to the border traveled on

350 troop trains. Perhaps the greatest complaint by the guard was the lack of tourist sleepers to transport the troops. But about 3,000 such cars would have been required, and the Pullman Company owned only 750, of which 623 were supplied for the border movement. A great proportion of the troops had to be transported in day coaches, to their considerable inconvenience.[25] But the general staff developed no plan for coordinating railroad service in the event of national necessity. For its part, the Quartermaster Corps believed that its plan of cooperation with the railroads, a plan that had been adopted, demonstrated that rail congestion, which had been a major problem in the 1898 mobilization, had been eliminated.[26] Nevertheless, congestion was not entirely eliminated. An additional complication was that on several occasions railroad employees threatened a nationwide strike, jeopardizing the army's supply lines to the Southern Department. But on the whole the railroads performed quite capably. As of December 19, 1916, 156,414 guardsmen had been transported to the border and 47,707 had been returned for muster out.[27]

The great call-up painfully demonstrated that the system for mobilization was sadly deficient. As a result there were recommendations "that permanent mobilization sites and equipment depots be prepared for each National Guard division and that periodic practice call-ups be held to test the mobilization plans." Although the quartermaster general supported the concept, the general staff rejected it "on the grounds that another full mobilization was unlikely and that sufficient facilities existed to sustain incremental call-ups. It appeared that one of the major lessons to be learned from the 1916 mobilization had been rejected even before it was fully developed."[28] The lesson thus had to be relearned in April 1917.

A major source of concern for many guardsmen was their families, who in many cases faced destitution because the breadwinner was now in federal service. Patriotic and civic organizations attempted to alleviate the financial plight of these families but the scope of the problem was monumental. Therefore, on August 29, Congress appropriated $2 million for the support of the dependents of regular army and National Guard enlisted men. No family would receive more than $50 a month. (Subsequent appropriations increased the amount to $8.25 million.) These funds assisted 4,397 regular army families ($477,611.47) and 20,883 families of guardsmen ($4,399,660.28).[29]

The guard units were inspected once they had deployed to the border region. Between July 14 and August 15, the assistant chief of staff, Major

General Tasker H. Bliss, made a general inspection of all National Guard camps on the border.[30] Later the Inspector General's Department conducted a systematic inspection,[31] and what the regular inspectors reported to the inspector general was troubling:

> Most of the units barely had met their muster strength, and many of the men on hand were in process of receiving compassionate discharges. On the whole, inspectors felt that the social nature of many Guard units attracted older enlisted men with family and financial obligations that made them unsuitable for extended military service. Although a few units were filled with over-qualified college men, the personnel of most were comparable to those of the average regular unit. Nevertheless, inspectors considered the overall Guard personnel system to be flawed, a criticism that extended to the officers. The inspectors classified most of the Guard officers as willing and eager to learn, but on the average they were too inexperienced to fulfill the role of instructors that was expected of them in a mobilization.

But "not all the problems were unique to the National Guard units."[32] Reporting on regular units, the inspectors noted the low level of discipline, low levels of training overall, and, not surprisingly, lack of experience in the younger officers.

About 43 to 45 percent of guardsmen were without former service or training when the National Guard was at peacetime strength. When hurriedly recruited up to war strength after June 18, the guard consisted of about 75 percent of untrained men commanded by officers of very limited experience.[33] Regular inspectors replied to the question "'Present degree of readiness and fitness for field service of the organization;' the answer in 89 percent of the reports was either 'fair,' 'poor,' 'unfitted,' 'not ready,' 'wholly unprepared,' or some reply the equivalent of this." Reports were on the order of: "Under most favorable conditions, assuming that recruits and equipment for war strength were made available on call, the regiment might be made efficient for field service against an inferior enemy in six months; against trained troops, it will require two years."[34] Inspectors concluded that most units would require at least six months' intensive training under regular officers before being ready for the field.

A great learning experience was about to begin.

PART II

Border Service

Chapter 5

San Antonio

As of 1916, the army had divided the United States into four geographical departments: Eastern, Central, Western, and Southern. The Western Department had jurisdiction for the California border with Mexico. Baja California was a revolutionary backwater. The trouble spots were along the Arizona, New Mexico, and Texas borders with Mexico, and this area was under the jurisdiction of the Southern Department, which had been created on February 15, 1913. By placing most of the international boundary under a single command, the army could deploy units rapidly to meet any threat. The headquarters for the Southern Department were at Fort Sam Houston, which dated back to 1876. Its commander was Major General Frederick Funston.

Funston was the outstanding figure in the National Guard mobilization. He was a bantam rooster of a man, who stood only five feet four inches tall but had the heart of a lion, as shown by his having won the Congressional Medal of Honor. Born on November 9, 1865, in New Carlisle, Ohio, Funston at age two moved with his family to Iola, Kansas. An adventurous youth, he applied in 1884 to the U.S. Military Academy at West Point but failed both the entrance exam and the height requirement. Funston then attended Kansas University from 1885 to 1888 but did not graduate. He held a variety of jobs—surveyor, railroad ticket collector, newspaper reporter, and botanist for the Department of Agriculture. He also worked as a botanist in Alaska and selected land in Mexico for a coffee plantation.

His military career began in 1896 in rather unorthodox fashion. Inspired by a speech he heard in New York City in support of Cuban insurgents fighting for independence from Spain, Funston enlisted as an artillery officer in the insurgent forces although he was completely inexperienced. During his Cuban adventure Funston participated in twenty-two battles, had seventeen horses shot out from under him, rose in rank from lieutenant to lieutenant colonel, survived being shot through the lungs and a near-fatal bout of malaria, was captured by Spanish troops and court-martialed. Fortunately, the Spaniards decided to release him rather than shoot him.

During the Spanish-American War the governor of Kansas commissioned Funston on May 13, 1898, as colonel of the 20th Kansas Infantry, a militia unit. The war ended before the 20th Kansas saw action, but the regiment was among the units assigned to suppress the Philippine insurrection led by Emilio Aguinaldo in February, 1899. While the 20th Kansas waited in San Francisco to ship out, Funston whipped the regiment into shape. Under his leadership the 20th Kansas distinguished itself in the counterinsurgency campaign, but Funston later became controversial by stating publicly that he had personally hanged thirty-five Filipinos without trial. Funston, along with two privates, won the Medal of Honor on February 14, 1900, for swimming across a river under intense fire and tying ropes that enabled the regiment to cross by towed rafts and successfully storm insurgent positions on April 27, 1899. After the 20th Kansas was back in the United States, Funston returned to the Philippines with the rank of brigadier general of volunteers and performed the most spectacular feat of his career—by a ruse he captured the rebel leader, Emilio Aguinaldo. Funston came home a national hero.

In recognition of his capture of Aguinaldo, Funston was commissioned as a brigadier general in the regular army and was assigned to command the Department of California. He commanded the troops coping with the 1906 San Francisco earthquake, being hailed as "the man that saved San Francisco."

Funston's military involvement with Mexico began in 1914, when he was assigned as commander of American troops massing in Texas in response to revolutionary conditions in Mexico. He then commanded some five thousand troops occupying the strategic Mexican port of Veracruz, which the United States had bombarded and seized on April 21, 1914. His title was that of military governor, and he again demonstrated considerable ability as an administrator. In recognition of his achievements in Veracruz, Funston was promoted on November 17, 1914, to major general, the highest rank in the U.S. Army at the time.[1]

As commander of the Southern Department since 1915, Funston operated from Fort Sam Houston in San Antonio, the nerve center for border defense and for the National Guard mobilization.[2] He was the man on the spot, and on June 20, 1916, he sent an urgent request to the War Department for the National Guard to be rushed to the border. It was.

The deployment of the National Guard represented not just added border security but an economic bonanza for cities and towns in the border region. The city of Houston made strenuous efforts to use political pressure to become the National Guard's principal concentration point. Secretary of War Newton Baker left the matter up to General Funston, who opted for several major concentration points.[3] Nevertheless, the *San Antonio Express* triumphantly announced on July 2 that the city would contain about fifteen thousand troops—more than it had in 1898 or in 1911 during the Maneuver Division. In addition to the facilities being built there, thousands of guardsmen would pass through the city en route to the border. Not only would business boom, but the importance of "San Antonio, the great military town," would be recognized throughout the country.[4]

The troops at Camp Wilson constituted a strategic reserve. But when the great call-up occurred on June 18, 1916, Camp Wilson was largely vacant. The 2nd and 3rd Texas had been transferred to the Brownsville district on May 24 and 25, and the 4th Texas to the Big Bend on May 26. This left only Battery A, 1st Texas Field Artillery and the 1st Texas Cavalry Squadron. Because of the threat from de la Rosa's irregulars, on June 10 the Texas cavalry had been rushed to reinforce Laredo. Such was the urgency that the troopers left without their horses, and it was a week before the animals began to be issued to them at Fort McIntosh outside Laredo. On June 23, Battery A entrained for Brownsville.

But even as Camp Wilson was being emptied of Texans, crews of workmen were busy preparing facilities for the tidal wave of guardsmen on the way. During the first two weeks of July, fifty thousand passed through San Antonio.[5] A steady procession of special trains—on July 1 alone between twenty and thirty—arrived transporting other units to the border. Between June 28 and 30 the Missouri, Kansas, and Texas Railroad (the Katy) handled fifteen troop trains through McAlister, Oklahoma, and the Rock Island Railroad another five. The Katy had a contract to run ninety

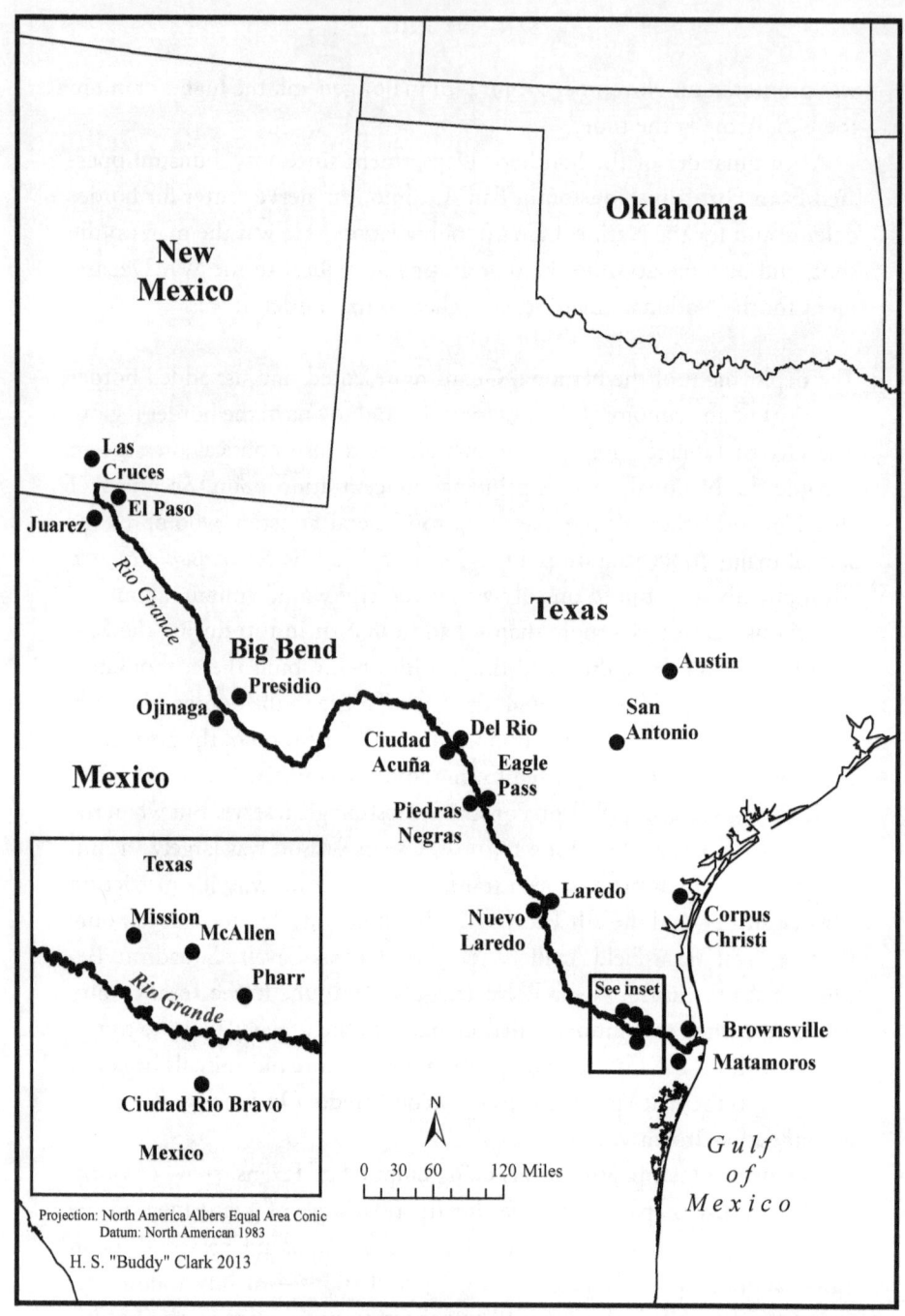

Texas and the U.S.-Mexico border from Brownsville to El Paso. Map by Harold "Buddy" Clark.

additional troop trains from St. Louis to San Antonio and Brownsville, which it fulfilled as quickly as rolling stock could be assembled. The Rock Island expected to handle about twenty-five additional troop trains from Memphis to El Paso in the first week of July.[6] Complicating the movement of troops to the border was that sometimes units reaching San Antonio had to transfer to another railroad for the remainder of their journey. For instance, the Missouri National Guard, who arrived on the Katy, marched through town and boarded the International & Great Northern Railroad for Laredo.

The procession of troop trains through San Antonio seemed interminable. As happened in other cities, the Red Cross and the good ladies of San Antonio quickly organized to provide the passing guardsmen with snacks, even though the devoted women had to arrive at the railroad stations early in the morning and stay until late at night, earning the fulsome praise of the grateful soldiers. The 1st Maryland Infantry, bound for Eagle Pass, reached San Antonio after ten o'clock at night, to be met by a score of women distributing soft drinks, sandwiches, and fruit. When the 4th Maryland Infantry arrived at six forty-five in the morning they were fed breakfast.[7] Although the movement of troop trains captured the popular interest, there was another movement of vital importance centered on San Antonio. As the press reported, "San Antonio is the hub of a preparedness movement such as this country has never seen before."[8] Hundreds of trained clerks were rapidly assembling at Fort Sam Houston to handle the mountains of paperwork involved in the mobilization, and impressive amounts of office equipment were also headed for the fort, which was now an army headquarters second only to that in Washington, D.C. This was not all—four hundred nurses had been ordered to report to Fort Sam Houston for assignment to army hospitals along the border. Besides stockpiling supplies and assembling personnel, the government was purchasing on a crash basis thousands of horses and mules for the border army. In the finest tradition of military contractors, a number of inferior horses were offered for sale to the government at exorbitant prices.[9]

The scale and speed of the military buildup initiated important changes. For instance, ten new regiments of regulars were to be formed in the Southern Department, four of them at Fort Sam Houston.[10] At that installation the government built a four-track siding from the Katy and Southern Pacific yards through the very center of bustling Camp Wilson. These tracks and hundreds of trucks made it possible to surmount the enormous logistical problem the National Guard influx caused. A huge supply tent was erected in the quadrangle at Fort Sam Houston, the post's storerooms were overflowing, and leased storage facilities in downtown San Antonio were full, as was the arsenal. Furthermore, there was a steady stream of mules and horses coming to the auxiliary remount depot at the fort.[11]

More importantly, at his own request, Major General Funston was relieved of responsibility for the entire border. The War Department reorganized border commands in accordance with recommendations that Funston had made, with a view to creating three field armies commanded by major generals and giving these commanders time to organize their staffs and be prepared for any eventuality. Under this plan Funston would continue to command the Southern Department, whose boundary would end east of El Paso. Major General J. Franklin Bell, commanding the Western Department, would transfer his headquarters from San Francisco to Douglas, Arizona, much closer to the scene of action. The middle border, between El Paso and Douglas and extending northward to the Colorado state line, would become the Department of New Mexico. This entity would have jurisdiction over the Punitive Expedition, and the departmental commander would be Brigadier General Pershing, who would be promoted to major general and whose headquarters would be in El Paso.[12] The War Department subsequently abandoned the scheme and decided to maintain unity of command, leaving Funston in charge of the entire Southern Department.

The majority of the 15,000 militia who would call Camp Wilson home consisted of men from Illinois and Wisconsin. When the mobilization order came, the Illinois National Guard was, like other militia organizations, scattered throughout the state. Illinois would contribute a grand total of 10,245 men for border service.[13] One battalion of the 1st Illinois Infantry was staging a Civil War battle for the movies, and the men were unaware of the mobilization until they arrived by train in Chicago. Their morale soared as they marched to their armory beside sidewalks crowded with cheering civilians. Their armory, on Sixteenth Street, was large enough for the entire regiment to parade. In less than a week, the Illinois guardsmen had massed in Springfield, the mobilization point. The 1st Cavalry regiment, the 1st Field Artillery regiment, Company A Engineers, Company A Signal Corps, and Field Hospitals Numbers 1 and 2 assembled at Camp Lincoln. The two Illinois infantry brigades were less fortunate, for they were assigned across town to the state fairgrounds, renamed Camp Dunne in honor of the governor: the 1st Infantry camped in the horse stalls, the 2st in the cow barns, the 3rd and 4th in the pigsties, the 7th in Machinery Hall, and the 8th (Colored) in the sheep pens. The old fairgrounds were littered with trash and debris and had to be thoroughly cleaned, which involved removing literally tons of trash, dirt, and manure. The adjutant general's staff directed scores of carpenters, plumbers, teamsters, and day laborers, who worked around the clock to make the exhibition halls for animals at least marginally fit for humans. Hay was scattered in the stables and stalls, bathhouses were erected, latrines dug, commissary and quartermaster supplies purchased and stockpiled in both camps, fuel was hauled in, tools and other necessities were acquired. The day before the regiments began arriving—their arrival delayed for two days by the above frantic preparations—the mess details began setting up their field kitchens and mess tents.

Adding to mobilization problems, the national government had provided nothing in the way of supplies and equipment at the mobilization camps, although army regulations stipulated that the Quartermaster Corps would supply everything needed. Chicago businessmen raised $25,000 to buy twenty machine guns for the Illinois National Guard, but the project had to be abandoned and the money returned to the donors because European countries had contracted for almost the entire output of machine guns from American factories.[14] Thus the state of Illinois had to assume the entire burden of equipping its National Guard, which it did in exemplary fashion. A serious problem was the double ownership of property. In peacetime the state had furnished blankets, uniforms, and so on, but once in federal service the U.S. government was supposed to furnish these items. Thus every item of state property had to be inventoried and priced so the government could reimburse Illinois. This went on even as the state's supply of arms, uniforms, and blankets was being issued to recruits. Another problem was that some of the men refused to take the federal oath. The army's response was that anyone refusing to be mustered in and to take the oath was to be jerked out of line and placed under arrest pending court-martial. The tactic worked. For example, in the 1st Illinois Infantry only one man still refused to be mustered in. He was arrested on the spot but quickly reconsidered and took the oath.

When a unit had been mustered in, the men underwent their physical examination. In an assembly line procedure lasting about two minutes, one army doctor noted height, weight, and chest measurements, a second checked heart and lungs with his stethoscope, a third tapped the knees to check reflexes, a fourth checked for rupture and disease, a fifth examined teeth and whispered in both ears to check hearing, and the sixth checked eyesight. Few men were disqualified because regimental surgeons had already conducted rigorous physical exams. For officers, the government waived physical disqualifications provided the officer waived any pension rights that might result from these physical deficiencies.

While this was going on, the guardsmen underwent a program of intensive squad and company drills as well as bayonet practice. They took their work seriously, for the army's Central Department had on June 28 ordered the immediate movement to the border of those Illinois, Missouri, Kansas, and Wisconsin units that were "reasonably ready."[15] The men at Camp Dunne understood that the first regiment to be mustered in would be the first to leave for the border. Rivalry was intense, and the winner was the 1st Illinois, from Chicago. With a mixture of pride and apprehension the regiment marched through a densely packed crowd of wildly cheering soldiers and civilians to board their troop trains for an undisclosed location on the border.

Transporting a regiment necessitated three special trains, one per battalion. Rations for ten days were issued, equipment was cleaned, packed, and loaded in the freight cars ahead of the coaches carrying the troops. Additionally, a freight car was equipped as a rudimentary kitchen, with a stove and with fuel and food piled to the roof. Unfortunately, the springs on the makeshift kitchen car, which was placed in the middle of the train to facilitate feeding the men, were terrible, and the contents bounced around throughout the thousand-mile journey to Texas. Some food spoiled for lack of refrigeration. Nevertheless, the mess detail performed heroically and managed to keep the troops fed. The freight-car kitchens were the worst aspect of the entire trip, not just for Illinois but for many other guard organizations. Complaints about food were numerous, but when the army investigated it reported that the complaints were either unfounded or resulted from the inexperience of National Guard cooks.[16]

But enlivening the trip were the ovations the regiment received at every large city along the way. At one stop, admirers placed almost a thousand pies aboard the trains.[17] The 1st Illinois Infantry,[18] considered the crack regiment of Chicago and including many prominent men of that city, was more fortunate than many other National Guard organizations because they were assigned tourist sleepers for all the men and a standard Pullman car for the officers and the accompanying newspaper reporters. Many other units had to ride in day coaches, some of them museum pieces, because of the shortage of rolling stock; the railroads' passenger equipment was stretched to the limit by the mobilization combined with the Fourth of July travel crunch. With the military being determined not to repeat the disaster of the Spanish-American War mobilization, the health of the troops was of paramount importance. Each troop train had a doctor and a few medics, who conducted sick call every morning and evening. Besides vaccinating everyone against smallpox, they monitored the men's health, constantly checked for cleanliness, and inspected the food before every meal.

The officers ensured that the time on the train was employed usefully. While they and the noncommissioned officers studied military problems, the enlisted men received lectures on the use and care of their rifles and other equipment. There was a sense of urgency, for many of the recruits had never handled firearms. (Of the regiment's 1,212 men, 250 were raw recruits.)[19] There were also lectures on military discipline and courtesy. On the whole the officers of the 1st Illinois Infantry genuinely cared about their men's welfare. For instance, a major asked one of his lieutenants to double up with another officer so that a sick sergeant could have a single berth. When the lieutenant grumbled, the major ordered him to sleep in the major's berth while the major sat up all night so the sergeant could have a berth. On another occasion the major commanding the second section of the special trains halted the train and refused to continue until the railroad furnished a more experienced and considerate engineer. Concern for their men meant that few guardsmen in the 1st Illinois threatened that their company officers would be the first men killed in battle, as did many men from other regiments (shades of Vietnam!).

Illinois claimed to be "the first to land her troops, fully equipped for field service, on the Mexican border and was highly commended for her promptness, equipment, general appearance and high standard of efficiency maintained."[20] The army stated that "the first militia organization of the call of June 18 to reach the border was the First Illinois Infantry."[21] Wearing heavy woolen uniforms, the two Illinois infantry brigades (1st Brigade: 1st, 2nd, 7th Infantry; 2nd Brigade: 3rd, 4th, 8th Infantry) arrived at Camp Wilson between June 30 and July 7. The 1st Cavalry regiment and Field Hospital No. 1 had merely passed through San Antonio on July 4, for they were assigned to the Brownsville District, at Harlingen. The state's 1st Field Artillery Regiment (five batteries), Company A 1st Engineers, Company A Signal Corps, and Field Hospital No. 2 reached Camp Wilson by the following week. Regarding the field artillery regiment, only one battery had even fired a shot. And a month later when the regiment went to Leon Springs for maneuvers and practice, regular instructors harshly criticized the organization, stating that it would be useless in the field because of its slowness in changing positions and handling its guns. Yet the batteries were restricted to only a few shells with which to improve.[22]

Joseph Medill Patterson, one of the Chicago *Tribune*'s publishers, and Hopewell Rogers, business manager of the Chicago *Daily News*, were among the sweating artillerymen unloading gun carriages from railroad cars.[23] The 2nd Battalion of the 1st Illinois Artillery was the "college battalion"—Batteries D and E consisted of college students from all over the country, while Battery F was exclusively a University of Illinois outfit. The two battalions were merged into a regimental formation; they had never before been combined tactically. A major commanded each battalion, and the War Department authorized the appointment of Captain Frank M. Allen, a retired regular artillery officer, as colonel and Lieutenant Louis R. Dougherty, the instructor-inspector of the Illinois artillery, as lieutenant colonel of the regiment.[24] Ironically, reducing the regiment's effectiveness was something as mundane as horseshoes. After weeks of requisitions, the 1st Illinois Artillery received some horseshoes but only enough to shoe the front hooves of the insufficient number of horses the unit had. Compounding the problem was the scarcity of tools and horseshoeing outfits.[25]

Some governors were concerned that most of their National Guard units had been mobilized. Illustrating this concern was when five companies of the 6th Illinois Infantry, which had been left behind, were called out on July 13 to suppress strike riots at La Salle and Oglesby. The guard continued to perform this kind of duty between May and August 1917.[26]

In the meantime the Wisconsin National Guard began making its appearance. This organization, which had mustered at Camp Douglas, Wisconsin, consisted of an infantry brigade (1st, 2nd, and 3rd Infantry), Troop A Cavalry (Troop B was mobilized on July 24), Battery A Field Artillery, and Field Hospital No. 1. Commanding the infantry brigade was Brigadier General Lorrain Thompson Richardson, an 1895 graduate of West Point. In 1916 he was a regular captain, serving as the inspector-instructor of the Wisconsin National Guard. With the approval of the War Department the governor borrowed Richardson and commissioned him as a temporary brigadier general to command the brigade. (The other candidate for this position, incidentally, was Captain Billy Mitchell.)

It has been stated that "the Wisconsin National Guard was perhaps the best prepared of any state in the union to meet a real emergency."[27] The army considered the Wisconsin troops probably the best trained at the time of mustering.[28] But at Camp Douglas 50 percent of all companies lacked complete uniforms and other equipment, and Battery A had only enough horses for one platoon. There were delays resulting from confusion in the physical exams—only five regular army doctors were available, and they frequently reversed themselves, accepting some men they later rejected and rejecting some men they later accepted. The confusion prolonged the process of issuing supplies for at least two days.[29] One man had refused to take the oath or sign the muster roll. The men in his company stripped him of his uniform, dressed him in overalls, tied yellow ribbons all over him, and marched him from regiment to regiment with a tin can tied to his pants. There had been a few other recalcitrants, but after a few hours in the guardhouse they decided to sign the muster roll.[30] By June 30 the entire Wisconsin guard was mustered into federal service after a delay caused in part by a shortage of muster blanks. The guard numbered 4,288, or 69 percent of its wartime strength.[31] Two separate infantry companies were retained in Wisconsin in case of emergencies. The rest of the guard boarded troop trains for San Antonio to the acclaim of thousands of civilians—some 9,000 had visited Camp Douglas on Sundays.

The guardsmen's patriotic fervor began to cool when they saw the railroad transportation that had been arranged for them—ancient wooden coaches instead of Pullmans, with three men sharing two seats. In fact, the departure of the cavalry and field artillery was delayed for four hours because the officers refused to subject their men to these "old, unsanitary, ill-equipped and unsafe" day coaches. The artillery captain protested that "the cars are old and rotten. I will not order my men aboard them. They are not fit for cattle. Remember, these men must live in those cars for four days and nights." The War Department quickly pointed out that the Milwaukee Railroad was doing the best it could and ordered the units to entrain forthwith. The order was obeyed. But upon reaching Milwaukee there was a delightful surprise. The cavalry and artillery were transferred to a new train of twenty cars, including nine sleepers, a baggage car containing a military kitchen, a stock car, two boxcars, and seven flatcars for artillery pieces, tents, and other equipment. The sleepers were not the most modern but the officer pronounced them satisfactory. The troops' morale soared; the sleepers made the difference. The men had bitterly resented the governor's statement that day coaches were good enough for the Wisconsin National Guard to travel in to the border.[32]

The 1st Wisconsin Infantry reached Camp Wilson on July 12, followed by the 2nd on July 15 and the 3rd on July 16. The 2nd Wisconsin, incidentally, was the largest National Guard unit present, numbering 1,400 men.[33]

In *Report on Mobilization*, the Illinois and Wisconsin guards were compared: "The two Illinois brigades are reported backward in this respect, being entirely without animals, and some lack even the guns. Some companies [are] just being organized, and instruction [has] not yet begun. In the Wisconsin brigade all companies are organized and have their guns but no animals."[34]

As the men settled into their new environment, they immediately noticed the heat—Texas summers were scorchers, and the guardsmen were in olive drab woolen uniforms; some even had on woolen underwear. Prolonging the misery were the red tape and inexperience involved in requisitioning shoes and khaki uniforms. However, by July 17 things began to improve. The 1st Illinois had the distinction of being the first regiment to be fully equipped with clothing—five suits of underwear, two pairs of shoes, two khaki uniforms, several pairs of socks, and so forth.[35]

Besides trying to stay cool, the guardsmen kept a wary eye out for the menaces lurking all around them. The natives talked funny, but they seemed friendly enough. They solemnly apprised the newcomers of the perils on every hand: rattlesnakes, copperheads, water moccasins, scorpions, tarantulas, and—most fearsome of all, they said—chiggers. Some members of the 3rd Wisconsin decided to take no chances. Their officers making bed checks were puzzled to find the tents empty but finally located the men, sleeping in rows on the roofs of their company bathhouses, safe from any attack by those nasty tarantulas.[36] To add to their discomfort, the Wisconsin troops lacked their beer allotment. Beer was an integral part of their life. Back at Camp Douglas in Wisconsin each man was issued several bottles of beer a day, but no beer was permitted on a federal reservation such as Fort Sam Houston, and none was allowed to be sold within a certain distance of a reservation. The men were left with their memories and had to make do with the ice cream cones and soft drinks that itinerant vendors provided.[37]

Camp Wilson quickly blossomed into a vast tent city, the rows of tents laid out with mathematical precision, the men brightening the ground around their tents with cactus and small whitewashed rocks. The camp underwent continual improvement. The road through the Illinois Infantry area was graded and topped with gravel, making a blessedly mudless drive the entire length of the two brigades, about a mile and a quarter. Further road improvements were imminent, for the hundreds of heavy trucks had cut up the roads badly. Loading platforms were going up alongside four recently built railroad sidings. At the northwest corner of Camp Wilson a large work force had laid water pipes and driven stakes to mark tent lines for the Wisconsin National Guard.[38] And the YMCA was active, building four large structures where the troops could relax and watch movies, among other amenities.[39]

One of the salient features of the camp, and of the whole mobilization, was the focus on hygiene. The surgeon general of the army stated that "the National Guard [were] proving themselves apt pupils, equaling as a rule and frequently excelling the Regular troops with whom they were closely associated in maintaining an exceptionally low sick rate."[40] Even before the influx of guardsmen the army had built bathhouses and latrines and installed water pipes to connect with the city network. Shortly after the guardsmen settled in they were put to work digging trenches to drain the camp, the trenches feeding into a sewer main that carried off the water. And there was water to be carried off: two days after the first Illinois troops arrived torrential rains deluged Camp Wilson, changing it into a swamp of sticky black mud—the "gumbo" that the troops instantly learned to hate. Another phase of the sanitary program required every company street to dig incinerators eight feet long, four wide, and two deep, lined with brick or stones, into which all refuse and dishwater were deposited and burned, to eliminate flies. The Medical Corps examined the incinerators on a daily basis, and periodically the stones or bricks were removed and crude oil poured in and ignited to destroy fly larvae. Perhaps no single aspect of camp life was so unrelentingly emphasized as this war against the fly. General Funston obtained $534,000 from the War Department to build screened kitchens and mess halls for all units stationed from San Antonio to the border. Flypaper was used by the wagonload, each company had an incinerator, tents and company streets were ditched to carry off rainwater, the areas around bathhouses were drained, and bedding and equipment were exposed to the sun for two hours a day, weather permitting. The troops were inoculated against typhoid fever and smallpox, and all personnel were required to bathe at least twice weekly.[41]

To protect the troops' health even further, the local police force and health department cooperated with the camp authorities in preventing objectionable characters from hanging around the vicinity of Camp Wilson, in taking measures to suppress prostitution, and in prohibiting solicitation. Plainclothes policemen made frequent rounds to enforce these measures.[42]

It might also be mentioned that for the first time in its history the army assembled a hospital train. This thirteen-car mobile hospital ran between San Antonio and the border to bring sick and injured soldiers to the Fort Sam Houston base hospital.[43] The army was justly proud of this advance in medical care. What took some of the luster off, however, was the fact that in 1914, when Pancho Villa had been the most powerful general in Mexico, he had had a hospital train, although admittedly not as fancy.

Besides complaining about "gumbo," the troops grumbled about some of the army's deficiencies. For example, there were no requisition blanks for drawing rations for the 1st Illinois, and for several days the troops had to continue eating the rations left over from their trip. When food began to be issued, they received bread but no butter, coffee but no sugar, unseasoned potatoes and meat. There were also shortages of blankets, cots, tents, pistols, and other items. Some of the troops were not issued blankets for a month. Yet the greatest complaint the men had was that they would not get to fight the Mexicans. Not only was the war crisis abating, but the National Guard units stationed at Camp Wilson constituted a strategic reserve and thus could not even anticipate being stationed along the international boundary and perhaps engaging in the occasional skirmish with Mexicans.

The only war news coming out of Camp Wilson was that emanating from the press. On June 24, the War Department issued permission for correspondents to accompany, at their own expense, guard organizations to the border.[44] The National Guard's activities were reported in detail by an active press corps, which included representatives of the International News Service, the Associated Press, the *New York Times*, the *Los Angeles Examiner*, seven Chicago newspapers, and four from Milwaukee. Competition among these journalists was fierce, with everyone trying to scoop his colleagues. But sometimes this desire to be first got way out of hand. Gene Morgan of the *Chicago Daily News* indeed produced a sensational scoop with a detailed and lurid account of a battle. The story was splashed across the paper's front page on July 14. Morgan reported that Mexican snipers had made repeated attacks on Camp Wilson for twenty-four hours straight, and that troops of the 1st Illinois Infantry were sent into the mesquite thickets south of the camp to flush them out. The snipers, moreover, were trained marksmen, not mere amateurs. Other Chicago papers also ran the story on their front pages under banner headlines. Two Chicago correspondents at Camp Wilson, from the *Record-Herald* and the *Tribune*, did not report the story and were chastised by their editors for getting scooped. Predictably, the story caused great alarm among the folks back in Chicago. The only problem was that the battle was a figment of reporter Morgan's fertile imagination. When General Funston was shown the *Daily News* story, he remarked dryly: "Well, I wish I had known about it. I would liked to have seen the battle." Upon investigation, it turned out that the "Mexican snipers" were a couple of American soldiers hunting jackrabbits in the mesquite thickets. Funston, who was "altogether displeased" with the newspaper story, not only branded it a fake but threatened to bar the offending reporters from the military reservation.[45]

There would continue to be problems with the press. Many hometown newspapers, unable to afford sending correspondents to the border, relied heavily on guardsmen's letters, and these not infrequently contained exaggerated or biased accounts. Funston expressed his anger in a wire to the adjutant general, calling the War Department's attention to what he termed "the carnival of lying" by many of the correspondents who had accompanied the militia to the border. Nothing in Funston's experience approached it for "sheer maliciousness and shamelessness." He had endured "these pests" as long as he could and would now bar them from the camps and from accompanying troops on the march.[46]

The great National Guard call-up took a breather on July 17, 1916. The War Department announced that henceforth units would be dispatched to the border only after they had been thoroughly organized and equipped, and department commanding generals were ordered to delay further transportation of incomplete units. The new orders affected about twenty-five thousand men still in state mobilization camps and revoked a ruling that had waived certain requirements made when the Mexican situation appeared acute. Some one hundred thousand guardsmen were already on the international boundary, and it was felt that they, combined with the fifty thousand regulars on the border and in the Punitive Expedition, constituted a force sufficient to make unnecessary the hurried dispatch of any more inadequately equipped National Guard units.[47]

The guardsmen underwent a rigorous training schedule, for General Funston had no intention of coddling them. He announced that they would have two days after their arrival to become acclimated before starting the training.[48] The 1st Illinois's training day began with roll call, immediately after which the men did brisk calisthenics for fifteen minutes then fell out for breakfast. After that they policed the camp, picking up all the trash. Around seven in the morning the regiment formed for its morning route march lasting between one and two hours; this exercise was conducted in heavy marching order, the men carrying their weapons and packs. By nine o'clock the troops got a few minutes to rest and change their sweat-soaked clothing. At ten o'clock they engaged in squad, platoon, and company drill until eleven forty-five. Drilling resumed at around two o'clock in the afternoon and lasted until four thirty or five. Then the troops got busy washing their clothes and cleaning their equipment.

But all was not well at Camp Wilson. One of the units in the 2nd Illinois Brigade, the 8th Illinois Infantry, was an all-black outfit, including the officers. This regiment caused the high command at Fort Sam Houston some nervousness.[49] Ever since Reconstruction the Democratic Party had done its work well in creating out of the old Confederacy the "Solid South," a region characterized by Democratic political domination, Jim Crow segregation, discrimination, exploitation, and the not-infrequent lynching of African Americans. Racist white southern Democrats were able to maintain the Solid South until the civil rights movement of the 1960s. Texas was a proud component of the Solid South, and Texans expected African Americans to know—and keep—their place. Black soldiers did not always do that, and Texans despised them. Over the years a series of incidents involving black troops had reinforced that antipathy.[50]

As an indication of what they could expect, when the 8th Illinois rolled through Muskogee, Oklahoma, on the train, the local newspaper jovially described them as "the 'Chicago Tar Babies,' Illinois' far-famed negro regiment."[51] The 8th Illinois had been instructed to adhere to the racial customs of the South. Although there existed the real possibility of friction with the locals when they reached San Antonio, there seemed to be no problems for the 8th Illinois at Camp Wilson. They soon gained a reputation as "the happiest regiment in camp," going about their duties with unfailing cheerfulness. And eight of the men "failed to pass the physical examination after being brought here without being mustered in. They are held at the hospital and there they twang banjos, do the plantation shuffle and other blithesome features for the soldiers."[52]

On July 24 there occurred a deplorable incident involving members of the 8th Illinois Infantry. Around six o'clock in the evening, Herbert G. Hebbe, a merchant and lawyer from New Braunfels, was being driven by his chauffeur back to New Braunfels. As they passed Fort Sam Houston and a number of rowdy black militiamen returning from town, one of the soldiers threw a large rock at Hebbe's car. Hebbe later stated that he then ordered his chauffeur to stop, and "I got out and started back a few feet with the intention of punishing the negro as every Texas man feels he should have been punished." But as he left the car, he said that other black troops, noticing that Hebbe was unarmed, started toward him, one of them brandishing a knife. Hebbe promptly fled into a nearby saloon, his chauffeur into the Cook and Baker's School on post, and somebody phoned the provost guard.

By the time the guard arrived, in the persons of a sergeant and six men of Company M, 19th U.S. Infantry, a crowd of several hundred black soldiers had gathered. One of their officers was trying to order them back to camp, with little success. Instead, the soldiers retreated about seventy-five feet and began to stone the provost guard. "An order was given to fire at the men who seemed to be in the thickest of the affray." The guards were ordered to shoot low; they fired five shots, of which three hit their marks in the legs. No one was killed, for the provost guard's regulation Springfield rifles were loaded with "guard cartridges," which had a reduced powder charge and a smaller bullet. The black soldiers ran back to camp, and the wounded were carried off to the post hospital. The *Brownsville Daily Herald* published an editorial entitled "The Negro Soldier Still Runs Amock."[53]

The post commander's report of the incident blamed it on "drunken soldiers," and the ringleaders of the affray were arrested and placed in the guardhouse. Despite the incident, the colonel commanding the 8th Illinois announced that he would not change his practice of issuing passes for three men per company per day. Unfortunately, the incident confirmed in the minds of many locals why black troops were undesirable. Reinforcing this view was another incident the same night, when some 8th Illinois soldiers boarded a streetcar downtown to return to camp. The seats in the rear, which were reserved for African Americans, were soon filled, so some of the men sat in the white section up front. Whites were outraged and protested to the conductor, who called a policeman, who started "to put the negroes in their place" but "discovered that the other passengers became disgusted with the proceeding." The policeman left, and the motorman started the streetcar, the African Americans having broken the color barrier.[54] A couple of days later there occurred yet another incident when a merchant filed a police report alleging that black soldiers had broken several windows and show cases by throwing rocks into his store around two thirty in the morning.[55] Prejudice against black soldiers was not confined to civilians: several white enlisted men complained bitterly because some of the courts-martial that tried them included black officers from the 8th Illinois.[56]

General Funston took measures to ensure better discipline. Since there were thousands of soldiers on the streets of San Antonio every night, a provost guard of 150 regulars from the 19th and 37th U.S. Infantries was stationed in the city, working in two shifts: from six o'clock to nine o'clock at night and from nine o'clock to midnight. Their headquarters were in the Central Fire and Police Station. The provost guard was divided into squads of eight men under a sergeant and were deployed not only downtown but also at the railroad stations, the arsenal, and other government installations, being transported in trucks. The military stressed that the action was not taken because of the 8th Illinois riot.[57] Despite denials to the contrary by the authorities at Fort Sam Houston, the cumulative effect of these incidents was a decision to keep the 8th Illinois confined to the post for reasons racial and disciplinary. White Texans' animosity toward black soldiers was powerfully reinforced on the night of August 23, 1917, when there occurred a serious riot in Houston in which twelve white men were killed. Martial law was declared, and the black troops were immediately withdrawn from Texas. Sixty-three black soldiers were tried by court-martial, forty-one of them being sentenced to life imprisonment and thirteen being hanged.[58]

Like the other militia infantry regiments, the troops from Illinois had been undergoing a routine of close-order drill, the manual of arms, and short practice marches of three or four miles designed to toughen them up. But a number of men fell from the ranks during these short marches, and General Funston felt they needed considerably more toughening up. He therefore ordered the 1st Illinois Brigade, 3,500 strong, to make a long route march. Many companies began practicing marching songs for the hike. They should have been practicing marching. The troops were baffled by the unfathomable ways of the army. Before leaving camp the Illinois guardsmen had to fill up every trench and leave the campground as smooth as a pool table, and upon their return they had to dig the trenches out again. Their destination was the Leon Springs military reservation, twenty-five miles from San Antonio. Two days were allotted for the exercise—a twelve-mile march the first day, the remainder the second day. The brigade started at seven o'clock in the morning in company formation, with about two hundred yards between companies. Each regiment had fifteen wagons (four for baggage, two transporting one day's rations, five loaded with ammunition, and the rest carrying additional rations).

Things did not go well at all.[59] The first day was the hottest day of summer, and men dropped out along the way at an appalling rate—the 1st Illinois Infantry alone had more than 250 collapse by the wayside. More than 20 men fell out from fatigue before the column was out of the city, or at least scarcely beyond the last houses. Many stragglers made themselves comfortable in shady spots along the road waiting for trucks to pick them up. The horse-drawn ambulances were filled to capacity, and for the last few miles every clump of bushes had its complement of exhausted guardsmen. In some cases entire squads fell out. Some of the men were so weak that they lay face up in the sun, lacking the energy to roll over. Their hardier comrades paused just long enough to put their packs under their heads and leave them for the Medical Corps to attend to. In short, the 1st Illinois Brigade made an abominable showing. As one of its officers ruefully commented, "It was certainly the first proof that no group of civilians would be worth a tinker's dam [sic] in a real emergency."[60] General Funston, who had unobtrusively watched the Illinois contingent march by, emphatically agreed. He subsequently announced "backbone drills," such as he had employed as commander of the 20th Kansas Infantry in the Philippines—a great deal of extra drill conditioning for the weaklings—commenting that "the extra drills soon build up their resistance to indisposition."[61]

On the second day of the march the three regiments started at five thirty in the morning and reached the Leon Springs destination by one o'clock in the afternoon. And but a handful of men had dropped out during the march: only two or three men at any one time had to be carried in the trucks, and then only for a short distance before resuming marching. Immediately upon arrival the brigade made camp, for they were to spend the next seven to ten days on the rifle range. Funston personally inspected the three regiments and observed them at target practice. He declared himself pleased, commenting that the men would become hardened during their stay at Leon Springs. Their work on the rifle range would put them in better condition to make the return march without incident.[62]

The press corps had a field day with this exercise. Toward the end of the first day's march, a reporter and a motion picture cameraman from the *Chicago Tribune* asked the colonel of the 1st Illinois Infantry to halt the advance guard so the rest of the regiment could close up and they could film it. The colonel of course refused, and the newsmen sulked. The correspondent retaliated by writing a blistering article criticizing everybody involved in the route march, from the Southern Department down to the wimpy guardsmen. As a final insult the article denigrated the climate in San Antonio. The Chicago newspaper used the article as the basis for a caustic editorial. These journalistic endeavors angered just about everybody. Funston was furious; an Illinois officer commented: "The people and press of San Antonio fairly raved that their climate should be so misrepresented (for San Antonio is a city that lives not by the sweat of its brow, but by sweating the tourist, and I heard one reputable citizen say that that he had no doubt that this adverse publicity cost the city one hundred thousand dollars)." The 1st Illinois Brigade held a special summary court-martial at which the reporter was called on to answer for his libelous statements. Nevertheless, the offending correspondent remained attached to the Illinois troops for the remainder of their stay at Camp Wilson.[63]

In evaluating this initial route march, one of the Illinois officers gave the following reasons for the brigade's wretched showing: the march took place on the hottest day of summer; the first two hours of the march were over pavement, which was twice as hard to walk on as a dirt road; the men were novices and did not know how to conserve their strength; contrary to orders, the men drained their canteens early in the march; when some men dropped out to rest, their example became contagious; the officers were so considerate of their men that discipline was relaxed and they lost control of their units. However, valuable lessons were learned from the debacle. Thereafter the troops hoarded their water, conserved their strength, helped their comrades having difficulty, and kept up their spirits by singing and good-natured banter. Furthermore, officers prided themselves on bringing their commands into camp without losing a single man. Oftentimes field grade officers marched the entire distance as an example to the men. Eventually the brigade was able to take seventeen-mile marches in stride. These long route marches tested not only the troops' physical condition but their character as well. Each soldier was allowed only one canteen of water. This was perhaps the hardest element of discipline to enforce, for many men used every subterfuge they could think of to evade the regulation. Besides water discipline, foot inspections took place as soon as a unit reached a new campsite.[64]

The Leon Springs military reservation was admirably suited for the guardsmen to learn the art of war. The reservation consisted of thousands of acres of hills, plains, and woods. It lacked only a river, so the troops were unable to practice the difficult maneuver of an opposed river crossing. But there were pistol, rifle, machine gun, and artillery ranges. It was at Leon Springs that the Illinois recruits had their first opportunity to fire the Springfield rifle.

One of the greatest weaknesses of the 1st Illinois Brigade was its lack of machine guns. When the organization arrived at Camp Wilson there were two machine guns per infantry regiment. The 1st Illinois's two machine guns had been at the Rock Island arsenal for a year awaiting repairs, and the army would not issue the two additional weapons authorized until the first two had been repaired and sent to the 1st Illinois. Consequently, the regiment was at Camp Wilson for a month before it had any machine guns at all.[65]

The Wisconsin National Guard, by contrast, was one of the few militia organizations with a machine gun company, of four guns, per infantry regiment. The guns were French-made Benet-Merciers, set on a one-foot tripod and operated by a two-man crew. They fired a thirty-round magazine of .30 ammunition in 2¼ seconds, could fire 600 to 800 rounds per minute, and had a range of 1.3 miles.[66] But they were delicate and had a tendency to jam unless the magazine was inserted with exquisite precision.

Fighting on the Western Front in France had chillingly demonstrated the effectiveness of machine guns, and the secretary of war fully realized their importance: "Perhaps no invention has more profoundly modified the art of war than the machine gun. In the European war this arm has been brought into very great prominence."[67] It was imperative to equip the army and National Guard with an adequate number of these weapons, but this proved quite difficult. As mentioned earlier, in June, patriotic Chicago businessmen had raised $25,000 to buy twenty machine guns for the Illinois National Guard but had to abandon the plan and refund the money because the Allies controlled practically the entire output of American machine gun production.[68] But in July, the United States persuaded the British to relinquish three hundred Lewis machine guns and six million rounds of ammunition for which they had contracted with the Savage

Arms Company. The Allies called the Lewis gun the "Belgian rattlesnake" because the Belgians had been the first to use it. A retired U.S. Army officer had invented the gun, but the War Department had rejected it. Two hundred fifty of the guns and a corresponding amount of ammunition were rushed to the San Antonio arsenal. The weapons began to be distributed, mainly to National Guard units, and noncommissioned officers of the machine gun companies soon learned their use.[69]

The army now tried to provide each infantry regiment with a machine gun company of four guns and five light Ford trucks to transport them. Five hundred modified Ford trucks were being issued to regular and National Guard units.[70] Hampering this process as far as the National Guard was concerned was the nationwide shortage of machine guns and because regular units had first priority. Complicating the matter was the fact that the army was still dithering over what kind of machine gun to adopt. The Benet-Mercier was currently the standard gun, but now the army was issuing Lewis guns and was still testing other types.

General Funston and his aides went to Leon Springs to observe Illinois troops firing Lewis guns with their distinctive circular magazine holding forty-seven cartridges. Lewises were lighter than the Benet-Mercier, were fired by a single soldier, fired four hundred rounds per minute, and could be cleared quickly if they jammed. But a big disadvantage was that the cartridges were larger than the .30 standard in the U.S. Army.[71] Like the regulars, the National Guard benefited from the growing emphasis in Washington, D.C., on preparedness. The Senate appropriated, over and above the House ordnance appropriation for machine guns, for regulars from $3.6 million to $7.725 million and for the National Guard, from $2 million to $6.586 million and for field artillery for the National Guard from $8 million to $14 million.[72] In addition, the Senate voted to add foreign duty pay to the National Guard and the regulars serving on the border—a 20 percent increase for enlisted men, 10 percent for officers. Furthermore, the Senate appropriated $250,000 for tent floors and screens for the troops on the border.[73] On December 17, Secretary of War Baker formally condemned the Lewis gun and directed that the bitter dispute among army officers concerning the gun cease. Two days later the War Department let contracts for four thousand Vickers guns and accessories, contracts worth $5.5 million.[74]

Besides engaging in firing practice, the Illinois artillery proceeded to draw its horses—the regiment needed close to one thousand—from the remount station at Leon Springs as rapidly as possible. Funston had established the remount station on June 1. As of July 27, the station had processed some thirteen thousand horses and mules.[75] Delaying the process of equipping the Illinois units was the fact that many of the horses were straight off the range, and Illinois collegians and professional men suddenly found themselves in the unaccustomed, distasteful, and frequently dangerous role of bronco busters.[76] Throughout the mobilization, unbroken horses being handled by untrained men remained a serious problem.

While the 1st Illinois Brigade was completing its training on the rifle range, the 2nd Illinois Brigade made a route march to Landa Park in New Braunfels. It was announced that since there were camping facilities at Landa Park for only two regiments, the 8th Illinois would not be making the march at this time and would instead remain in Camp Wilson. However, the 1st Brigade's three regiments had camped at Landa Park quite comfortably.[77] These arrangements lead one to speculate that the 8th Illinois was deliberately confined to Camp Wilson as punishment.

An unusual feature of all this was that there were 148 Illinois guardsmen from Chicago living in limbo. The government had rejected them for active duty because of physical disabilities before they had left the Illinois mobilization camp in Springfield for Texas on June 28, but they had been told they would quickly receive honorable discharges. Instead they had fallen through the bureaucratic cracks and had been living as "boarders" with their regiments. They desperately wanted to be sent home but no orders to that effect were forthcoming until July 29, when they were finally discharged.[78]

As for the two regiments of the 2nd Illinois Brigade, they left Camp Wilson on July 29 for Landa Park. The march took two days—after fourteen miles the troops camped for the night and traveled the remaining seventeen miles the next day. The brigade had about as many wagons as had the 1st Brigade on its march to Leon Springs. There existed a rivalry between the two Illinois contingents, and the men of the 2nd Brigade were determined to outdo their colleagues in the 1st. Spurring them on to greater effort was the presence of General Funston himself, who followed them for a way in his staff car. Accordingly, when men seemed about to drop from fatigue, their comrades supported them and kept on marching. Only about a half dozen fell out in the entire brigade, and ambulances carried only two or three to Landa Park. Funston pronounced himself well pleased. Despite having to march on muddy roads, the brigade reached its destination with colors flying, and the people of New Braunfels turned out to give them a rousing welcome. Compared with Camp Wilson, Landa Park was paradise. It was a resort, and its owner, Harry Landa, had patriotically loaned the park to the army. The Illinois encampment was on top of a wooded hill overlooking a lake where the weary troops could go swimming. When the guardsmen saw their new surroundings they uttered a lusty cheer and set about erecting their tents, which had already arrived by truck.[79]

The 1st Wisconsin Brigade (1st, 2nd, and 3rd Wisconsin Infantry) underwent weekly inspections, and the troops began preparing for their route marches by making hikes of nine to ten miles every morning in heavy marching order. They took great pride in the fact that only a very few men fell out, although most had impressive blisters when their feet were examined at the conclusion of the hikes.[80] Adding to the troops' discomfort was another violent rainstorm, which blew down tents. Although no one was injured, the men had to re-erect the tents in the midst of rain and mud. The rain ruined a scheduled open-air mass, which had to be conducted in one of the tents of the field hospital. Few visitors braved the storm to interact with the troops, and the jitneys—the taxis—that ordinarily ran through Camp Wilson had to be discontinued because the road was impassable. Still, the little soft drink stands, restaurants, and fruit stands on the fringes of the camp managed to do a brisk business.[81]

The troops continually complained about the extortionate prices the drivers charged—as much as one dollar. When military authorities tried to persuade the drivers to charge uniform—and reasonable—fares, they refused. General Funston then announced that troops going to and from town would be able to ride free in army trucks to and from the end of the streetcar line. Thus there was no need to bar jitney drivers from Camp Wilson because there was now no reason to patronize the jitneys. The jitney drivers promptly had a "sudden change of heart," agreeing to charge only five cents to the end of the streetcar line and ten cents for a trip all the way into town. Army trucks would not be needed after all.[82] As had others before them, the jitney drivers learned that Funston was not a man with whom to trifle.

Funston was also involved in the religious life of his soldiers. Religion played an important role in the lives of the guardsmen. Hundreds of them, along with civilians, regularly attended field worship services at Camp Wilson; on occasion the number exceeded one thousand.[83] Services were for both Protestants and Catholics. In addition to the usual worship services, Catholics attended a military Thanksgiving mass at the San Fernando cathedral in San Antonio and an open-air midnight mass in camp on Christmas Eve.[84] Several organizations were active in supplying the troops with Bibles.[85] Perhaps the most innovative was the American Bible Society, which in collaboration with the YMCA sent its "gospel jitney" on a two-thousand-mile tour of military camps along the border and the Punitive Expedition to distribute Bibles.[86] The "Bible Car" carried four thousand khaki-covered New Testaments as Christmas gifts for the men in San Antonio and the vicinity.[87]

The most contentious aspect of religion at Camp Wilson and Fort Sam Houston was the controversy between General Funston and the Baptists. Funston resented the view that soldiers were lost sinners, and he rejected the request of the Texas Baptist Convention to conduct religious revivals among the troops.[88] The Baptists argued that soldiers should hear the same gospel as civilians, and they took great exception to Funston's order.[89] Dr. J. B. Gambrell, corresponding secretary of the executive board of the Baptist General Convention of Texas, announced that Baptists would grudgingly abide by Funston's order but "they will go to the ends of the earth to set it aside."[90] Several Baptist associations promptly passed resolutions opposing Funston's view. Alabama Baptists even demanded a congressional investigation of the general, declaring that such military censorship violated the Constitution and was an invasion of religious liberty. Funston declined comment, considering the incident closed.[91]

Funston received support from some of the army chaplains at Camp Wilson: eight of them sent him a letter complimenting him for his stand against revivals.[92] And the chaplain of the 2nd Minnesota Infantry defended the general at the annual Gulf Conference of the Methodist Episcopal Church, meeting in DeRidder, Louisiana.[93] In an effort to end the controversy, Funston wrote a long letter to Dr. Gambrell, explaining his reasons from a soldier's standpoint for banning revivals.[94] The gambit failed. Gambrell, while declining to reveal the contents of the letter, indicated that he might talk with the president, for the issue was whether Funston could prescribe the creed that soldiers would be allowed to hear.[95] In New York City the Reverend Frank M. Goodchild, pastor of the Central Baptist Church, delivered a sermon criticizing the government and accusing Funston of discriminating against Baptists. Goodchild stated that he had advised any member of his congregation who was in the army to resign.

Most Baptist pastors disagreed with Goodchild's remarks.[96] Nevertheless, Reverend Gambrell and his associates continued their crusade, sending a delegation to Washington, D.C. Secretary of War Baker was thoroughly exasperated by their importunities.[97] In January 1917, a group of Baptists called on President Wilson to complain about Funston, to no avail.[98]

Interestingly, although Funston had banned revivals, interdenominational YMCA-sponsored evangelistic services were held almost nightly in border posts. And a report of YMCA activities on the border up to November 1 sent to Secretary Baker made a point of mentioning "the generous treatment we have received at the hands of General Funston."[99]

The army also encouraged athletics, and perhaps the most popular sport was football, at least in terms of spectators. When the University of Texas team traveled to San Antonio to play Oklahoma A&M, five hundred Wisconsin guardsmen attended the game to cheer the new Texas coach, Conrad Eugene Van Gent, who had been a three-sport star at the University of Wisconsin, playing halfback and tackle on that football team. Texas, incidentally, won the game 14 to 6.[100] But this encounter was the exception. Most games involved the National Guard and regular units competing in the Army Post Football Tournament. Some sample scores were:

> 3rd Wisconsin Infantry 6, 1st Mississippi Infantry 0
> 3rd Illinois Infantry 19, 2nd Wisconsin Infantry 6
> Virginia Field Artillery 19, 3rd Wisconsin Infantry 0
> 2nd West Virginia Infantry 6, 3rd District of Columbia Infantry 0
> 4th Illinois Infantry 24, 1st Texas Engineers 0
> 1st Wisconsin Infantry 21, 16th U.S. Cavalry 0
> 3rd Illinois Infantry 14, 4th Illinois Infantry 0 (a game played before some twenty thousand spectators)[101]

The anticipation level at Camp Wilson rose markedly when the 2nd Texas Infantry came to town from Corpus Christi to play a picked team from the Virginia Field Artillery. The *San Antonio Express* ran large ads announcing that tickets were on sale in three San Antonio drug stores, and box seat tickets were available in the lobby of the Gunter hotel. The Texans came in a special train accompanied by the regimental band and hundreds of their fellow guardsmen. They had a pleasant outing, for they obliterated the Virginians 52 to 0.[102] A new strategy was devised in San Antonio—to assemble a team of all stars from both Camp Wilson and Fort Sam Houston to take on the supremely confident Texans. It seemed like a good idea, but it just did not work. The game took place in Austin on January 16, 1917, amid considerable fanfare and publicity. The Katy Railroad even ran two special trains from San Antonio (the round trip fare was $1.50) to accommodate the fans. About all the all stars managed to do was to slow the Texan juggernaut, losing by a score of 34 to 6.[103] At least the all stars managed to score.

Then on January 20, the Texans met the undefeated 1st New York Cavalry, who were accompanied by some 1,400 of their military and civilian fans from McAllen. Their trip proved to be an exercise in futility—the Texans crushed the New Yorkers 69 to 0. This was the culmination of the Texans' unbelievable season; the team was disbanded at the conclusion of the game.[104]

The number of troops arriving in San Antonio by train had decreased dramatically, but the patriotic ladies continued to provide refreshments at the stations. One contingent consisted of one hundred regulars going to Fort Sam Houston; another of the 1st North Dakota Infantry, who passed through San Antonio on July 27. Only one unit was headed for Camp Wilson—a company of Texas Engineers, who arrived there on July 28 and pitched their tents next to the Illinois Engineer company.[105] The engineer units at Camp Wilson were being beefed up because the army on the border was being reorganized on a tactical basis.

Since the guard had been rushed to the border piecemeal, the original divisional plan never materialized. It was necessary to regroup the organizations on the border into provisional divisions and brigades. Accordingly, the War Department on August 4, 1916, ordered General Funston to create ten provisional divisions and six separate brigades.[106] Regular brigadier generals would command the provisional divisions and some of the separate brigades. In San Antonio, the army purchased ten Hudson super-six automobiles for use as staff cars by the brigadier generals on the border.[107] This reorganization gave the army significantly tighter control over the National Guard.[108] The National Guard's function would continue to be the defense of the border, for the army's judge advocate general had ruled that the guard could not be sent into Mexico unless and until the guardsmen were drafted.[109]

On September 3, 1916, General Funston changed the name of Camp Wilson to Camp Cecil A. Lyon, late commander of the Texas National Guard, following the army custom of naming camps after deceased persons.

Camp Wilson had been the name given to the post office substation when the Texas guardsmen were mobilized in May. At that time the camp was a militia camp and was not governed by army customs. However, the War Department ruled that the name would remain Camp Wilson. Funston announced on September 9: "The War Department has said so. That settles it." He refused further comment.[110]

The War Department's action settled a friendly rivalry between Funston and Postmaster George D. Armistead that had been going on since the postmaster had first named the substation that was established when the Texas National Guard was mobilized. The Post Office Department used the name "Camp Wilson." The Southern Department and the War Department officially used the name "Concentration Camp of the Texas Militia," while the Texas National Guard occupied the facility. When they left for border duty, a Civilians' Training Camp was held on the same site. There was no question but that the Civilians' Training Camp was under the sole control of the War Department, so Funston named it "Camp Cecil Lyon." The Post Office still called it "Camp Wilson." As the Civilians' Training Camp completed its course and the trainees returned to civilian life, the Illinois and Wisconsin guardsmen had poured into the facility.

There matters stood until September 3, when Funston announced that the name "Camp Wilson" was a violation of army regulations, since President Wilson was alive, and the name must be changed together with several other camps along the border, such as one near El Paso that had been designed "Camp Funston." He therefore ordered the name change. When Postmaster Armistead was informed of Funston's action, he declared that "Camp Wilson" would not be changed without positive instructions from the Post Office Department, and he reported the matter to the postmaster general. Funston had already made his official report to the War Department.[111] During World War I, Camp Wilson was again renamed, in accordance with army regulations—Camp Travis, after Colonel William B. Travis, defender of the Alamo.

In September 1916, for the first time a large body of troops in the United States—the two thousand men of the 1st and 2nd Kansas Infantry—were transported a distance of 183 miles by trucks, from Eagle Pass to San Antonio. The experimental operation involved four truck companies of thirty-three vehicles each, besides tank trucks, machine shop trucks, and other auxiliary vehicles. Two truck companies were dispatched from Fort Sam

San Antonio

Houston to join the two companies stationed at Eagle Pass. The trip was scheduled to take three days; the convoy left Eagle Pass on September 6 and arrived in San Antonio on September 8.

The Kansas regiments were ordered to Camp Wilson to complete the 12th Provisional Division, Brigadier General Henry A. Greene commanding. Together with the 7th Illinois Infantry, the Kansans formed the division's 1st Brigade. (The 1st and 2nd Illinois Infantry were scheduled to return home and be mustered out.) The experiment was a great success, the movement being accomplished in less than forty-eight hours. It demonstrated that, given halfway decent roads, infantry could move faster than cavalry. It would have required two weeks for the men to have made the trip on foot, and one week for cavalry to have covered the same distance.

The Kansans' arrival created a sensation in San Antonio. As the long convoy rolled through the business district, citizens thronged the route and the Kansans unfurled their colors and struck up their regimental bands. General Funston himself had gone outside the city to meet the convoy, and he expressed his pleasure at the troops' smart appearance, especially that of the 2nd Kansas, known as "Funston's Own" because when it was the 20th Kansas Infantry he had commanded the regiment in the Philippine campaign.[112]

A couple of nights after their arrival at Camp Wilson some of the Kansans experienced a sensation of their own. Company I, 2nd Kansas Infantry had as a mascot an eight-foot-long snake, which was customarily tied to a stake in the mess tent. Somehow the creature got loose and went visiting in the tents, even crawling in bed with one unfortunate soldier. The resulting commotion may be imagined. Eventually the snake was recaptured.[113]

On October 2–4, the 1st Battalion Virginia Field Artillery entrained at Camp Stuart in Richmond for San Antonio. On October 16, orders came for Company A Engineers, Company A Signal Corps, and Field Hospital No. 1 to do likewise. The field artillery included the Norfolk Blues battery, whose socially prominent members settled comfortably into their new quarters in Camp Wilson. On December 31, they enjoyed a sumptuous banquet at the Gunter Hotel, a banquet paid for by a substantial check from the citizens of Norfolk. The banquet was judged to be the liveliest ever held by the National Guard in San Antonio.[114]

Troop A District of Columbia Cavalry arrived in the first week of October. The 3rd District of Columbia Infantry, which since the call-up had been in camp at Fort Myer, Virginia, outside of Washington, D.C., arrived on October 10 and occupied the camp of the 8th Illinois. The following day they had their first drill and maneuver and did well, according to the regular officers who supervised them. All the District of Columbia's officers marched to General Greene's headquarters to pay their respects. As for the enlisted men, numbers of them engaged in frequent brawls with other guardsmen, who derisively called them "White House pets." The colonel of the 3rd District of Columbia had to issue an order strictly prohibiting fighting, and because of their good behavior on the trip to San Antonio he paroled the twenty-odd men of the regiment who were in the guardhouse for brawling.[115]

The next organization to arrive at Camp Wilson was the 2nd West Virginia Infantry. West Virginia was required to contribute an infantry regiment; the state had two, the 1st and 2nd. Although the governor urged that both be mobilized, the War Department decided to mobilize only the 2nd because the 1st had suffered the disbanding of two companies and the regimental band for failure to maintain the required standard of efficiency. The 2nd West Virginia mobilized on June 23 at Kanawha City, near Charleston. About 275 men, or about 30 percent of the 2nd Infantry, refused to be mustered into federal service.[116] The regiment was not ready for border service and began an intensive training program. However, on August 10, serious floods occurred, and the 2nd West Virginia was on flood relief duty for nearly two weeks. Not until October 17 and 18 did the regiment, 1,182 strong, depart for Camp Wilson. They paraded through the streets of Texarkana during a layover, arriving in San Antonio on October 21 and being assigned to the 12th Division's 1st Brigade.[117] They occupied the camp of the 2nd Kansas, which was about to depart for home.[118]

The climax of the National Guard's experience at Camp Wilson came when the 12th Provisional Division made a tactical march to Austin in September.[119] This was the largest body of troops to move overland since the Civil War—fourteen thousand men, five thousand horses, and a full divisional train of more than two hundred trucks and wagons. It was imperative that nothing go wrong, and to that end Company A Illinois Engineers deployed three working parties to prepare detailed maps of the route between San Antonio and Austin. And the divisional quartermaster and his staff traveled to Austin to arrange with the city authorities for an adequate water supply when the division reached its destination at Camp Mabry outside

Austin,[120] which was making its own preparations to welcome the troops. The most prominent citizens, complete with brass band, would greet them, and the governor himself would review the division. A contingent of Civil War veterans prepared to pay their respects.[121]

The division (including the all-black 8th Illinois Infantry) began its eighty-four-mile march from San Antonio on September 16. The plan was to take seven days on the road, then rest for three days in Austin, and be back in Camp Wilson by October 3. With the division absent, the provost guard at Fort Sam Houston was reduced to six men.[122] On the way to Austin the division halted near Landa Park to conduct a maneuver between "Red" and "Blue" armies, then resumed its march. There was no sympathy for stragglers—those men who fell out were considered as being AWOL. Some indeed were AWOL: eleven enlisted men got tired of marching, dropped out of the column, and hopped a freight train to Austin. They were promptly arrested, jailed, and returned to San Antonio. General Funston and his staff reviewed the troops as they marched through Austin, whose residents turned out en masse to greet the column. Governor Ferguson, Texas adjutant general Henry Hutchings, and other state officials, plus the Wisconsin governor's staff, also reviewed the troops, at Camp Mabry. The footsore soldiers got a day's leave to relax and visit Austin. Tragically, a sergeant in the 8th Illinois drowned while swimming in Lake Austin. The men's stay in Austin was enlivened by a severe electrical storm accompanied by two inches of rain. Rested and refreshed, the division marched straight through back to San Antonio, arriving as scheduled on October 3, just in time to march in a grand parade the next day.[123]

The city fathers of San Antonio officially designated October 4 as "Military Day" to show appreciation for everything the army and National Guard had done for the city, which was quite a bit. San Antonio went all out to honor the military. The governors of Wisconsin, Illinois, Kansas, and Texas were invited to review the troops. Committees of citizens arranged the parade route and other details. October 4 was proclaimed a legal holiday, and tens of thousands, both San Antonians and people from surrounding communities, enthusiastically watched the great parade, which began promptly at eight o'clock in the morning and included all the troops at Camp Wilson and Fort Sam Houston—a ten-mile-long column of some fifteen thousand men. General Greene, commander of the 12th Provisional Division, led the column. After the parade a gala banquet honored Funston, Greene, and four other generals. Texas adjutant general Henry Hutchings was in attendance, and Lieutenant Governor William P. Hobby represented Governor Ferguson.[124]

The 1st Mississippi Infantry arrived at Camp Wilson in mid-October. It was not a crack outfit. For one thing, the regiment had just been organized from three independent battalions upon receipt of the president's June 18 call-up. The state's adjutant general, Brigadier General Erie C. Scales, frankly admitted the guard's shortcomings: "It is only to be a source of humiliation to know that the State of Mississippi does less toward the maintenance of her National Guard (for the number of troops organized) than any State in the Union. To those persons who are enough interested to inquire, it is a cause of wonder that the young men of the State remain in the Guard when a greater part of the expense comes from their individual purses."[125]

Corroborating his evaluation was the report on May 27, 1916, of Lieutenant R. R. Pickering, the regular inspector-instructor: "The Mississippi National Guard is quite deficient in training. As to equipment . . . it is my opinion you will find the State just about equipped for its minimum strength with very little reserve on hand to raise the organization to war strength in case they were called out. As regards equipment, the officers as a whole are quite deficient." They had to furnish their own uniforms and equipment, whereas in some states this was furnished. "The care of equipment is not satisfactory, though improvement was shown. No company in the State has satisfactory means for properly caring for the equipment." The practice was to let the men take equipment home, resulting in the loss of thousands of dollars in supplies. Finally, a large percentage of the enlisted men had not attended even the minimum twenty-four drills per year.[126]

When called up on June 18, the 1st Mississippi numbered 45 officers and 1,292 enlisted men. The regiment immediately began recruiting to war strength; between June 18 and 24, 527 men were recruited, bringing the regiment up to 56 officers and 1,819 enlisted men. Sixty-six men refused to take the new federal oath. On June 24 the 1st Mississippi received orders to report to the state mobilization camp, but as the state had no mobilization camp the troops assembled on city property in Jackson. On October 17, the regiment received orders to entrain for San Antonio.[127]

Company A New Hampshire Signal Corps, arrived on October 25, completing the National Guard units in the 12th Provisional Division. On

November 18, Company F 1st U.S. Engineers arrived from Eagle Pass to join the division.[128]

To toughen the newly arrived regiments, a provisional infantry brigade consisting of the 1st Mississippi, the 2nd West Virginia, and the 3rd District of Columbia made a two-day march to Landa Park, in heavy marching order and with their combat (ammunition) wagons. The object of the exercise was to accustom the men to marching under Texas conditions. The troops performed well, even engaging in a competition to determine which regiment would have the fewest men in ambulances at the end of a day's march. The same units went to Leon Springs on December 4 for target practice. This proved to be an exercise in realism, for the five thousand guardsmen used ball ammunition as they charged across the field. The two weeks of target practice included surprise marches in heavy marching order ending in the firing of twenty rounds per man at olive drab silhouette targets. Incidentally, some of the men took the opportunity to gather mistletoe and send it back home, where it was prohibitively expensive.[129]

Marching and target practice were not the only exercises for the troops. The 1st Brigade of the 12th Division (1st Mississippi, 2nd West Virginia, and 7th Illinois) received instruction in trench warfare. At the southeast corner of Camp Wilson they dug an elaborate complex of trenches and then practiced attacking and defending them.[130] Increasingly, training was being shaped by the prospect of American involvement in World War I.

Dwight Eisenhower served with the 7th Illinois as a young lieutenant.[131] Though most guard regiments were untrained and indifferently equipped, they exhibited some semblance of organization. Eisenhower left the post to live in a camp where he became an inspector-instructor of the guard regiment, responsible for handling administrative problems and for supervising training. "I enjoyed the work." His assignment was to the 7th Illinois Infantry, Colonel Daniel Moriarity commanding. Practically the entire regiment was composed of Chicago Irish, and the officer of the day reports were filled with fights and all kinds of disputes, not surprising since the regiment called themselves the "Fighting Irish." "A night without serious disturbance was the exception." Eisenhower described Colonel Moriarity as "a fine old fellow who didn't like to bother much with the details of training and administration. Although he was jealous of his subordinates, he was happy to have me, as an instructor, take over in effect the running of his regiment." Writing all the orders, preparing reports and other papers for the colonel's signature, Eisenhower said he became "the power behind the Irishman's throne."[132] Eisenhower's instruction included teaching the 7th Illinois the principles of trench warfare. He supervised the construction of the trench complex at Camp Wilson, and he was reportedly "popular with officers and men alike."[133]

The War Department purchased enough turkey and "trimmings" to provide Thanksgiving and Christmas feasts for all 150,000 soldiers stationed on the border and in the Punitive Expedition.[134] But the Rotary Club of San Antonio wanted to do something more, and they came up with the idea of having the citizenry bake enough pies for Thanksgiving to supply all the troops at Camp Wilson and Fort Sam Houston. They needed four thousand pies. A vigorous pie campaign ensued, with the mayor urging housewives to bake pies and proclaiming November 27 and 28 as "Pie Days." Despite some apprehension when as of November 26 the Rotary Club had collected only three thousand pies, the mayor's appeal succeeded. The last-minute push produced the necessary number, with pies cooked to many recipes by the cosmopolitan population of San Antonio. One housewife baked fifty-five pies, and even children participated; one five-year-old girl delivered a five-inch pie to the Rotarians.[135]

The pie campaign demonstrated the citizens' regard for the military, but it also demonstrated something else—the army's apparent unconcern with security. The *San Antonio Express* not only ran a daily column of "Latest Army Orders" listing promotions, transfers, and so on, but it also carried daily stories on the doings at Camp Wilson and Fort Sam Houston. And on September 29, the *Express* ran a big article on the pie campaign, listing the complete order of battle of the 12th Provisional Division at Camp Wilson and the regulars at Fort Sam Houston together with their strength, and specifying how many pies each unit was to receive.

The first National Guard units to return home were those that had been at Camp Wilson the longest. The 1st and 2nd Illinois Infantry and Battery F (the University of Illinois battery) departed in September for Springfield.[136] Their departure was not without controversy, however. General Funston telegraphed the War Department asking that the quartermasters of the 1st and 2nd Illinois be ordered to return to Fort Sam Houston to account for fifty-five government horses and mules, valued at $15,000, which they had failed to turn in before departure. The quartermaster captains returned to

Fort Sam Houston and stoutly maintained that very few animals were unaccounted for. An investigation determined that most of the missing animals were either in the remount depot or scattered around Camp Wilson. The officers were exonerated.[137]

The Illinois National Guard caused further controversy. The 1st Illinois Cavalry was stationed in Brownsville, and the War Department decided to send half of the regiment home. A number of Chicago notables immediately protested to Washington, D.C., against dividing the regiment. Much newspaper space was filled with interviews with Illinois personages who conjectured about the order and denounced it.[138]

General Funston had something to say about the 1st Illinois Field Artillery. He telegraphed his recommendation to General Scott for five National Guard regiments to be returned from the border, one of them being the Illinois artillery. In a personal letter to Scott he subsequently explained that, like several other units, the 1st Illinois Artillery had too many men "who imagine that they are too important to be doing duty as soldiers." Their attitude produced considerable discontent in the unit and tended to demoralize other organizations.[139]

What happened once the Illinois units reached home merits some mention. Governor Dunne telegraphed the War Department on September 15 requesting a ten-day furlough for the entire 1st and 2nd Illinois in camp at Springfield. He stated that the men were suffering from cold, having only one blanket each and not enough clothing. The temperature at Springfield had fallen to forty-three degrees the previous night.[140] And when the men were transferred to Fort Sheridan outside Chicago to be mustered out, they suffered from the icy winds blowing off Lake Michigan because they were still in summer uniforms. To make matters even worse, they were shivering in tents because the War Department, on a technicality, refused to let the guardsmen occupy the vacant barracks at Fort Sheridan. Sixty-six men of the 1st Illinois Artillery left camp in disgust without permission. They included members of Battery C, the "millionaire battery," containing the scions of prominent Chicago families. Faced with growing insubordination, Secretary of War Baker personally investigated the matter and cut through the War Department red tape, the result being that the guardsmen were allowed to occupy the comfortable and well-heated barracks.[141] As for the men who had gone AWOL, the military tacitly admitted they had a point, because they were just lined up, questioned, and sentenced to assist the incoming 1st Illinois Cavalry, who had also protested against freezing in tents while the barracks remained vacant.[142] The Chicago newspapers covered these events in their usual lurid and sensational fashion.

The troubles of the Illinois National Guard continued. The problem was the new oath under the National Defense Act, requiring three years in the National Guard and three years in the reserve. Many guardsmen simply refused to take this oath. In Battery C 1st Illinois Artillery, the "millionaire battery," only a dozen of the 110 men were willing to take the oath. And of the eighteen commissioned officers in the entire artillery regiment, only eight took the oath. The 1st Illinois Artillery fell apart. And only 6 of the 1,200 enlisted men in the 1st Illinois Cavalry took the oath; 15 commissioned officers refused to take the oath, and 5 resigned.[143]

Then there were the bureaucratic glitches. For instance, eighteen men of Company M 8th Illinois Infantry fell through the cracks. They had enlisted in San Antonio, their hometown, but they were mustered out at Fort Sheridan with the rest of the regiment and found themselves temporarily stranded without transportation back to their homes.[144]

A final commentary on Illinois guardsmen is that at their Chicago homecoming, Field Hospital Company No. 1 paraded and buried a coffin containing the mock remains of "Texas, without regret." The *San Antonio Express* was indignant: "It is a pity indeed that such a spoiling, poor-spirited abuse of many fair considerations as the 'mock burial' of Texas in Chicago should be permitted to intrude."[145] The field hospital's sentiments were presumably shared by the 8th Illinois. The black regiment left Camp Wilson on October 7; the troops could not wait to leave (one battalion broke all records in loading aboard their trains) and San Antonians could not wait for them to leave. The other Illinois units seem to have appreciated the warm hospitality they received in San Antonio, and some, such as the 7th Illinois, received an affectionate and enthusiastic sendoff. The regiment had not had a single death or a contagious disease case during its stay at Camp Wilson.[146] A private in the 2nd Illinois's machine gun company died in the base hospital from a fractured skull after being kicked by a mule. In Company K, 1st Illinois, a sergeant died in the base hospital of peritonitis.

Eleanor Hannah in her study of the Illinois National Guard, which covers 1870–1917, devotes all of three pages to the Mexican border service and by way of conclusion makes the ridiculous statement that "if guardsmen made one small contribution to the preparation of the United States, it may have been their long experience with providing popular entertainments and competitive events for their members."[147]

The Reverend Wesley Peacock, president of the Peacock Military College in San Antonio, wrote to Funston complaining about the violations of the law by the proprietor of the Horn Palace Saloon on Houston Street, "whose so-called restaurant upstairs is frequented by soldiers in great numbers both day and night and by notorious prostitutes with whom they drink and carouse." This was occurring despite a provost guard stationed in front of the saloon. Peacock had complained to the sheriff and the police commissioner, to no avail. He enclosed a copy of a letter he wrote to the state comptroller. The problem, according to Peacock, was that in Bexar County for many years saloon men had controlled the grand jury, which refused to indict any saloon man for any kind of law violation. The reverend was writing to Funston because "nothing so frightens our city administration as a threat from the War Department."[148] Funston sent the reverend a confidential reply enumerating the steps he had taken and was taking to enforce the laws against prostitution and illegal liquor sales. He had obtained the services of a federal Bureau of Investigation agent to investigate alleged white slave cases "in which it is believed that members of the National Guard brought women to this town."[149] And Funston subsequently stated that if additional troops were to be trained in San Antonio, "I shall take it upon myself to read the riot act to the people here, and tell them that they can take their choice between the prostitutes and the soldiers; that they cannot have both." He felt that giving the chamber of commerce a good scare would be more effective than continuing to deal with the municipal authorities. But as Funston himself recognized, this was an empty threat given the enormous investment the federal government had in the military in San Antonio.[150]

The troops at Camp Wilson made elaborate preparations to celebrate Christmas. The YMCA and YWCA provided an entire week of parties and celebrations.[151] Besides the traditional turkey dinner with all the trimmings, many of the men received gifts from home. The citizens of Marshfield, Wisconsin, not only sent gifts but a tree to their neighbors in the 2nd Wisconsin. The choir of St. Mark's Episcopal Church sang carols for the patients in the base hospital.[152]

Several noteworthy events occurred in the Minnesota camp in January 1917. A prosperous department store owner in Minnesota, L. S. Donaldson, known to his employees as "Daddy," traveled all the way to Camp Wilson to visit his "boys"—his twenty-five employees in the National Guard. And the Minneapolis Symphony Orchestra designated January 29 as "Military Day" and played for the Minnesota troops at Camp Wilson, who attended in a body.[153]

Chief of Staff Scott wrote to Funston expressing his great interest in what Funston had to say about the training of the National Guard and its results. It corroborated what Scott had said to Congress and other people. Germany took two years to make a soldier, and Scott did not see how the United States could expect to train one in just a few months. Thus it was clear to Scott that American soldiers must be trained for at least two years before they would be capable of fighting Europeans who had had at least the same training.[154]

To keep the 12th Provisional Division up to strength, the 1st Minnesota Infantry had been transferred to Camp Wilson from Llano Grande in December to occupy the camp vacated by the returning 1st Wisconsin. The regiment paraded on January 14, 1917, for a visiting delegation of bankers from Minneapolis. According to a San Antonio newspaper, the men found the local weather most congenial compared with that of Minnesota.[155] A less cheerful report came in March, when Private Paul I. Scharfenberg of Company L 1st Minnesota was sentenced by a court-martial to five years at Leavenworth for furnishing military information to Germany. Scharfenberg, a native of Germany, had written to his mother an incriminating letter, which had been intercepted.[156]

The return of the guard from the border accelerated as a result of several factors. First, there was growing pressure from governors and other personages to bring the boys home since the crisis with Mexico had passed. Second, the United States was moving closer to war with Germany. But the return home did not proceed smoothly. There were shortages of railroad rolling stock. And orders to transport units home by rail were issued, suspended, and reissued as the threat of a nationwide railroad strike loomed and then passed.[157]

But in a lateral move, the 4th Texas Infantry, which for the last eight months had been performing its unenviable duty in the rugged Big Bend, was ordered back to Camp Wilson. As the news spread from regimental headquarters in Marfa, the troops were wild with joy that their purgatory was ending. On February 12, 1917, the 1,100 jubilant guardsmen pitched their tents in Camp Wilson, occupying the site recently vacated by the 3rd Illinois. Since the 4th Texas had been dispersed to guard a number of locations in the Big Bend, many of the men spent the first day renewing acquaintances and swapping stories.[158]

Breaking the routine of camp life was an invitation a month later: "The officers and men of the Fourth Texas Infantry have been invited to the exhibition of American paintings at the Carnegie Library Sunday afternoon as the guests of the San Antonio Art League. The exhibition hall will be open from 2 to 5 o'clock for the soldiers, and a committee headed by Mrs. H. P. Drought, president of the Art League, will be at the hall to receive the men and guide them through the exhibit."[159] It would be interesting to learn just how many art lovers there were in the 4th Texas.

As of February 18, 1917, the 12th Provisional Division at Camp Wilson still contained about eight thousand guardsmen: the 4th Texas Infantry, 1st Alabama Cavalry, 4th Illinois Infantry, 3rd District of Columbia Infantry, 1st Mississippi Infantry, 2nd West Virginia Infantry, 1st Minnesota Infantry, four batteries Virginia Field Artillery, one battery New Hampshire Field Artillery, Troop B Wisconsin Cavalry, Troop A District of Columbia Cavalry, Engineer Companies A Virginia and A and B Texas, Signal Corps Companies A Virginia and B New Hampshire, Florida Field Hospital No. 1, Virginia Field Hospital No. 1, and Oklahoma Ambulance Company No. 1.[160] The 126-wagon New York supply train, which had marched overland from McAllen, arrived on February 28, stopping over before proceeding home by rail on March 9. Pershing and his staff watched it pass in review.[161] In a surprising development, when the 1st Alabama Cavalry received orders to entrain on March 25 for home, it requested that it be allowed to remain in federal service for two more months. The request was refused.[162] Preparing for departure on March 21, the Alabamans went out in style; the officers gave a splendid dance for some three hundred guests.[163] Some examples of departures were: 3rd Illinois Infantry and brigade headquarters departed for Fort Sheridan on January 27, 1917,[164] New Hampshire Signal Corps, Virginia Field Hospital No. 1, Companies A Engineers and Signal Corps departed on March 13, 1917,[165] 2nd West Virginia returned to Huntington in March 1917 and was mustered out on March 24.[166]

The focus of attention on the departure of National Guard units for home was overshadowed by the sudden death of General Frederick Funston, who suffered a massive heart attack at nine o'clock at night on February 19 while seated on a sofa in the St. Anthony Hotel chatting with a group of friends. Dignitaries from President Wilson on down sent messages of

Border Service

condolence. San Antonians were shocked by the death of the popular general and paid extraordinary tribute to Funston, whose body lay in state in the Alamo while thousands filed by to pay their last respects. The body was transported by special train to San Francisco for burial, with soldiers and civilians paying tribute at every railroad station along the way. In San Francisco Funston's body lay in state in the rotunda of city hall; again thousands paid tribute. Major General John J. Pershing, whose Punitive Expedition had just finished crossing back into Columbus, New Mexico, on February 5, assumed command of the Southern Department, arriving in San Antonio on February 23. Pershing was the principal speaker at a memorial service for Funston.[167] Funston's death was arguably the luckiest break in Pershing's career. Had he lived, Funston, not Pershing, might well have commanded the American Expeditionary Force in France.

The 1st Texas Cavalry, which had been patrolling the Big Bend for the last ten months, were tired but jubilant when they reached Camp Wilson on March 16, having broken camp at Ruidosa on the Rio Grande and ridden seventy-five miles to the railroad at Marfa. The happiest of the five hundred cavalrymen were those of Troop C, from San Antonio, whose womenfolk had anxiously awaited their arrival since early morning. Evidencing the squadron's hard duty in the Big Bend, both the men's uniforms and their equipment were alkali-whitened.[168]

Most of the 4th Texas was mustered out at Camp Wilson on March 24, 1917.[169] Three companies of the 4th Texas were mustered out at Fort Worth.[170] The 2nd Texas was mustered out at Camp Scurry on March 23, 1917, Texas Field Hospital Company No. 1 and Battery A Texas Field Artillery on March 24,[171] and the 3rd Texas on March 26, 1917.[172] Company B Texas Engineers reached Dallas to a delirious welcome on March 22.[173]

All Texas organizations had been mustered out of federal service by the end of March 1917. However, they were called back into federal service on April 1, 1917.[174] Camp Wilson again blossomed during World War I, under its new name, Camp Travis.

Chapter 6

Corpus Christi

Perhaps the most fortunate National Guard units in the Southern Department were the 2nd and 3rd Texas Infantry, for they ended up in Corpus Christi, one of the leading summer resorts on the Texas Gulf Coast, built beside a large and lovely bay. Corpus Christi formed part of the Brownsville District under Brigadier General James Parker; the district stretched along the Rio Grande from Rio Grande City 120 miles downriver to Point Isabel on the Gulf Coast. For months Mayor Roy Miller and the Commercial Club had felt deeply aggrieved because in their view Corpus Christi was not receiving its fair share of the militia bonanza—although the city boasted four railroads, had an enviable climate, and was within striking distance of the border.[1] As one newspaper reported, "Many towns have asked for a few regiments. In fact, it is declared practically every town in South Texas is anxious to obtain a contingent."[2] Corpus Christi badly needed an economic boost, for a year-long drought had significantly depressed business activity.

Mayor Miller thought he had his opportunity when, in July, there was a rumor that because of unsatisfactory health conditions General Funston planned to transfer the five National Guard regiments from Laredo to Corpus Christi. However, the good citizens of Laredo feverishly set about improving conditions, with the result that Funston left the troops where they were. But he telephoned Mayor Miller and in a lengthy conversation expressed a favorable opinion of Corpus Christi and promised to assign troops there should the opportunity present itself. Mayor Miller assured the general that the city would do whatever was necessary to provide a suitable encampment "with water drainage and all other comforts and conveniences."[3] And he further assured General Parker that Corpus Christi "would go to the limit" in providing a camp.

The mayor's dream came true in August 1916, when Funston ordered the immediate transfer to Corpus Christi of the 2nd and 3rd Texas Infantries, plus the Texas Brigade headquarters. In ordering the two regiments to Corpus Christi, Funston explained that there were still ample troops to protect the Brownsville area. As the Corpus Christi newspaper excitedly reported, "The order means that approximately 3,500 Texans, who are serving in the Federalized militia are to remain in camp at Corpus Christi for possibly several months. It not only means a material gain to the city from the commercial viewpoint, but that the strategic advantages of Corpus Christi as a military camp will be more strongly emphasized."[4] Optimistically looking to the possibility of a permanent army post, the city began preparing a two-hundred-acre site capable of housing ten thousand troops. The camp was located on South Bluff, one block east of Corpus Christi Bay and extended west to Staples Street, a distance of six blocks. It was bounded on the north by Elizabeth Street, the terminus of a streetcar line, and extended south for nearly three-fourths of a mile.[5] A work force of more than 350 immediately began clearing the brush and mesquite, laying water mains to the property, digging drainage ditches to carry rainwater into the bay, stringing electric lights, erecting telephone poles, and grading and covering with a layer of crushed seashells several dirt streets traversing the site. The principal street would later be paved. In addition, a trolley line was extended into the camp, where forty buildings were going up, including twenty-four screened company mess halls, each twenty-by-eighty feet. Adjoining the railroad tracks three warehouses were leased for use by the camp quartermaster, who requisitioned 150,000 rations from Fort Sam Houston.[6]

The city fathers were determined to make the camp a model installation, and the citizens were determined to make the soldiers feel at home. To that end, more than one hundred women volunteered to serve as waitresses to welcome the troops with four thousand bottles of iced soft drinks and five hundred homemade pies. And numerous social functions were planned for the militia officers and their wives. Mayor Miller announced that the city council would not tolerate local merchants raising their prices for merchandise sold to the guardsmen.[7] Nothing was going to spoil the developing love feast between the military and the city. The local newspaper observed that "Thirty-five hundred troops will mean a great deal to Corpus Christi in a commercial and social way, and it will also mean a great deal to the soldiers, offering them, as it does, a chance for recreation and all the advantages of city life, heretofore lacking."[8]

The 3rd Texas Infantry, Colonel George P. Rains commanding, was the vanguard of the troop movement. The regiment began arriving from Harlingen on September 7. (The 2nd Texas Infantry was concentrating at Pharr in preparation for its journey to Corpus Christi.)[9] The citizens found the 3rd Texas Infantry's arrival quite impressive, as it came in on two special trains totaling eighteen chair cars, followed by a freight train of twenty-two cars carrying camp equipment, 130 mules, twenty-seven wagons, four ambulances, a water sprinkler, and a water wagon. Brigadier General John A. Hulen and his staff accompanied the 3rd Infantry as the regiment, 1,190 strong minus the machine gun company and the field hospital, which were coming later, marched through town to its new encampment. As a courtesy to the locals, Company C, the Corpus Christi Musketeers, had the honor of leading the line of march, just behind the regimental band. The 2nd Texas Infantry's arrival was less impressive. It came in two phases, seven companies arriving early on the morning of September 7 and the remaining five the next night. The regiment had had to accommodate itself to the overburdened Gulf Coast Lines railroad's schedule. During its tour of duty in Corpus Christi, the 2nd Texas rounded out its Table of Organization and Equipment by adding a supply company as well as its existing machine gun company and headquarters company.[10]

The Texans' workload eased with the arrival of trucks. Thirty-three Packard 1 1/2-ton trucks fresh from the factory came on September 8 in a special train that included two chair cars for the thirty-three civilian drivers under military discipline. The vehicles, designated as Truck Company 31, were immediately put to work hauling supplies and equipment from the two regiments' eighty freight cars to the tentatively named Alta Vista Army Camp a mile from the railroad station. The camp had telephones at the brigade and regimental headquarters, and the tents had electric lights, wooden floors, and were screened. The camp covered six hundred acres of tableland thirty feet above sea level, and brigade headquarters had a splendid view of Corpus Christi Bay, a hundred yards away.[11]

Camp Alta Vista was quickly replaced as the name of the National Guard encampment. There were suggestions that it be named Camp Roy Miller, in honor of the mayor, but General Hulen pointed out that army regulations prohibited naming an installation after a living person, so it was named Camp Scurry, "after Texas patriot and Civil War Gen. W. R. Scurry, who bled to death while cheering his men on at the battle of Jenkins Ferry in 1864."[12]

Things went splendidly from both the militia's and the citizens' point of view. General Hulen issued a detailed order to the entire brigade requiring all enlisted men to present a smart military appearance whenever they left the camp.[13] To minimize friction with the locals, a twenty-five man Military Police unit, composed of one man from each company in the two regiments, was installed on the third floor of the city hall. The men carried sidearms and a club and wore a band with "MP" on their right arm. The Military Police had orders to arrest any soldiers who did not have permission in writing from brigade headquarters to wear civilian clothes and/or be in certain districts of the city, mainly the red light district. "The district mentioned in the above order applies to certain sections occupied almost exclusively by Mexicans and negroes."[14]

A branch post office with one clerk was authorized for Camp Scurry and began doing a thriving business. Local merchants also immediately experienced a most gratifying increase in commercial activity. Occupancy at the Nueces Hotel, Corpus Christi's best, was 50 percent above that of the previous September because many of the officers were registered there, and a number of them had installed their families for the duration. Emphasizing the city's interest in the soldiers, the *Corpus Christi Caller* ran a daily column entitled "Along the Troop Streets of Texas Brigade Camp" containing news and personal items. In addition, the newspaper published the rosters of the 2nd and 3rd Infantry and ran daily feature stories about National Guard units and individuals.[15] For the two regiments, a welcome item of news was that the monthly payroll, amounting to approximately $60,000, would be disbursed within a few days of their arrival. Privates received $15 a month, privates first class $18, corporals $21, sergeants $30, top sergeants $45, second lieutenants $141, first lieutenants $166.67, and captains $200.[16] By October, the monthly payroll approximated $65,000, of which at least 75 percent was spent in Corpus Christi.[17]

Life was good. To make it even better, a female friend of one guardsman mailed him from San Antonio two sofa pillows, each containing a bottle of bourbon. Unfortunately one broke in transit, which alerted the authorities. Most recreation was of a more wholesome nature. A popular pastime was "blanketing," in which eight or nine men would hold on to a blanket and toss one of their comrades into the air, trying for a record height, at times reaching some fifteen feet. When no human was available they would toss a stray dog or two. "Blanketing" reportedly used to be the initiation in the regular army but had gone out of fashion.[18]

Some other forms of recreation had greater cultural value. The commander of Company M 3rd Infantry purchased a Victrola and a supply of phonograph records. Each night after the "Retreat" ceremony he set up the machine in the company street and the boys would gather around for a musical evening. Besides the records, Corporal Vernon Bolleter, who claimed to have been a major in the Mexican federal army, would sing songs in Spanish in his deep baritone voice, and the Company M quartette would contribute selections in English. Not only did Company M appreciate music, but the men had an unusual mascot, an albino raccoon, which would solemnly take its place in the chow line.[19] Company mascots were all the rage and included armadillos, snakes, a wildcat, goats, parrots, and a wide variety of dogs, both pedigreed and mutts. The troops spent a great deal of their leisure time constructing a spacious wooden YMCA building near the brigade headquarters. Dedicated on October 6, it provided a club room, a library, newspapers and periodicals, games, stationery, as well as religious services several times a week.[20] Each regiment had a canteen, which did a brisk business and was a godsend to many soldiers. If one were broke he could ask his commanding officer to issue a canteen coupon book representing up to one-third of his monthly pay. With the coupons he could purchase items such as tobacco, toiletries, soft drinks, and so on. At the end of the month the canteen's profits were divided among the units in the regiment and were usually applied to the mess fund.[21]

If life was pleasant for the enlisted men, it was, as usual, much better for the officers, who were feted by organizations such as the Elks and the Rotary Club.[22] Many officers were also the guests of Mayor Miller and his family at their home for a lengthy serenade by the 2nd Infantry band, who were rewarded for their performance with refreshments and sandwiches. Officers and enlisted men made up most of the 120 men who attended a gala banquet on September 19 at the Nueces Hotel for students and alumni of the University of Texas and Texas A&M College. The occasion further cemented relations between the guardsmen and the locals, for many prominent Corpus Christians had attended these institutions.[23] Another kind of banquet also mingled officers and enlisted men. For the third annual banquet of Company M 3rd Infantry, from Beaumont, also known as the "Governor's Guards," 132 officers and enlisted men gathered at the Nueces Hotel for an evening of dining, rousing speeches, and good fellowship.[24] This National Guard custom for officers and men to fraternize was not approved of by the regulars, who viewed it as further evidence that the guardsmen were amateur soldiers. A guard officer might find it awkward, for instance, to order his hometown drinking buddy to charge a machine gun nest.

There were parades and exhibition drills to demonstrate to the public the two regiments' military proficiency, and every evening large and enthusiastic crowds went out to Camp Scurry to witness these exercises, which General Parker had mandated throughout his command. The crowds were especially large whenever there were parades, both regiments passing in review with flags flying and bands playing; Corpus Christians turned out in droves by streetcar, automobile, buggy, and on foot.[25]

But most of the time was not devoted to spit and polish. Corpus Christi Bay was a major attraction, for swimming, fishing, and boating. Not only did the Texans enjoy these amenities, but on weekends many New York, Virginia, and Minnesota guardsmen stationed in the lower Rio Grande Valley took advantage of railroad excursion rates to enjoy Corpus Christi, much to the delight of the local merchants.[26] Some of the Texas militiamen found interesting outlets for their energies. The 3rd Infantry band decided to construct a nineteen-foot sailboat, complete with a twenty-horsepower engine for emergency power, with chief musician John Belardi as captain and a group of bandsmen as the novice sailors. Not to be outdone, the 2nd Infantry built out of scrap lumber a pier extending far out into the bay. At the end of the pier was a small locker room for changing clothes. About one hundred yards farther out into the bay they built a floating platform complete with diving board. At the entrance to the pier was a sign generously reading "Second Texas Infantry Pier. Welcome to All."[27]

The two regiments also engaged in athletics. The 3rd Infantry's pride and joy was its baseball team, organized while the unit was still stationed at Harlingen. The team usually won. The 2nd Infantry, on the other hand, focused on football. Its team was not just any football team. It included nine stars from the University of Texas, three from Texas A&M College, two from Baylor University, and one from Southwestern. This was by far the most formidable football team in the entire National Guard and one of the very best teams ever to play in the state of Texas.[28]

The city of Corpus Christi did what it could to facilitate the military's athletic endeavors. A two-hundred-acre tract immediately northwest of Camp Scurry and within one block of a streetcar line was cleared and fenced as the site for the second annual Gulf Coast Exposition, to be held November 20–25. As soon as the site had been cleared a grandstand was built "so that the grounds can be used as football and baseball grounds and field for the athletic features of the Texas Brigade." Temporary frame buildings were erected later for the exposition.[29]

The troops had a rude reminder that they were still in the army, not on vacation, when Captain James Love, the inspector-instructor of the Texas National Guard, inspected the brigade on September 23. Every unit marched to the parade ground with all its equipment for an inspection that lasted all day.[30] Underlining the fact that the boys were in the army now was the announcement that the next day, September 24, the entire Texas Brigade would make a twelve-mile march, the first route march since they had been activated back in May. Not only that, but they would be in heavy marching order: every man would carry his blanket roll containing a blanket, a poncho, a shelter half, pins and pole, one extra suit of underwear, soap, towels, brushes, and two pair of socks; plus a pack containing a mess kit, knife, fork, spoon, and cup; plus a canteen full of water; plus a rifle; plus a belt with ninety rounds of ammunition; plus a bayonet; plus entrenching tools (a small spade and pick), and a first aid kit. Even the regimental bands were included, although without their instruments. Only the camp guards and the cooks were excused.

The object of the exercise was to test the Texans' endurance while they carried out a tactical problem. Those who fell out would be picked up by ambulances stationed along the route. The public was invited to witness the march, for "it will be a grand sight to the citizens of Corpus Christi to view the movements of the soldiers in the field under such conditions."[31] Conditions could have been better. The guardsmen marched out of Camp Scurry at seven o'clock in the morning in high spirits, singing songs and cheering. When they had gone about four miles a heavy downpour began, but the men were ordered not to break out their ponchos as this would necessitate undoing their blanket rolls. Drenched to the skin, they gamely marched on along roads that quickly became quagmires. When they reached their destination, all the ball ammunition they carried was taken up so no one would accidentally get killed as they went into their combat maneuver, the 2nd Infantry going on the offensive against the defensive perimeter of the 3rd Infantry. The regiments completed their assigned exercise and returned to Camp Scurry still in high spirits and still singing. The men were soaked to the skin but at least their ponchos were dry. General Hulen declared himself well pleased with their performance, for only a handful of soldiers had fallen out during the march, and none had fallen out from the regimental bands, whose previous marching experience had been restricted to the parade ground. Hulen gave the men the afternoon off, and many of them promptly headed for the bay.[32]

Much less pleasant was the experience of some machine gunners. The army had purchased mules from the King Ranch to carry machine guns, but the mules bolted, wrecking some tents and escaping into the thick chaparral around Camp Scurry. For days, cursing soldiers thrashed through the brush chasing the mules and recovering scattered machine guns.[33]

Stressing the advantages that Corpus Christi offered, Mayor Miller and the Commercial Club were indefatigable in their efforts to make Camp Scurry a permanent post. In September the mayor led a delegation to San Antonio to lobby General Funston. Miller enlisted the considerable help of John Nance Garner, congressman of the Fifteenth Congressional District in Texas. Miller also extended a cordial invitation to General Funston to visit Corpus Christi, since the general was unacquainted with the city. Meanwhile the city fathers continued to raise money to improve Camp Scurry, the entire cost of the camp being borne by the city, by Nueces County, and by popular subscription.[34]

To Mayor Miller's intense gratification, General Funston agreed to visit the city on October 1, accompanied by General Parker, and to inspect the troops at Camp Scurry the following day. The mayor, together with General Hulen and his staff, met Funston's party at the railroad station and escorted them to their lodgings at the Nueces Hotel.[35] On the whole, Funston's visit was a success. In the morning he took the salute as the two Texas regiments passed in review. The general then inspected Camp Scurry, and in the afternoon Mayor Miller gave him a guided tour of the city. There was one unfortunate incident, however. As the newspaper reported, "Probably for the first time in his life, Major General Funston Monday faced an enemy from whom he ran." It seems the general and his entourage were enjoying a relaxing swim in the bay after a hard day of official duties when they were attacked by a swarm of jellyfish, who put the personages to frantic flight. Offsetting this, that evening Funston was the guest of honor at a nine-course banquet in the Nueces Hotel attended by everyone who was anyone. Mayor Miller, who introduced the general, "said that citizens of Corpus Christi had gathered to pay tribute to General Funston, not through any ulterior motive, but for his sterling worth as a man and as the commander of the Southern Department of the United States Army." The statement was heartily cheered. Funston graciously thanked the citizens for their hospitality and expressed his satisfaction with Camp Scurry and the Texas National Guard.[36] He said nothing about a permanent army camp.

The Texas guardsmen, however, felt that they might be on permanent duty at Camp Scurry. Morale took a dip when the War Department announced in late September that ten thousand guardsmen would be ordered home, and the Texans were not among them. The scuttlebutt was that the Arizona, New Mexico, and Texas National Guards would remain on the border indefinitely. Ominously, olive drab woolen uniforms began to be issued to the troops at Camp Scurry.[37] The men stoically went through the routine of drills, exercises, and parades while hoping for the best. One whose morale was just fine was Captain J. L. King, commanding officer of Company C 3rd Infantry. He had just purchased a red Cadillac roadster, which became the talk of Camp Scurry as the captain roared along at sixty-five miles an hour between the camp and city.[38] Less fashionable was the 3rd Infantry's quartermaster captain, who, the newspaper wrote, "is the proud possessor of an army regulation 'buck-board' vehicle, which arrived yesterday from Fort Sam Houston. It is drawn by two large mules and is one of the first means of transportation of its kind to be used by the National Guard. Captain Heckwald stated that it beats a 'flivver' for making time."[39]

Sunday was a day of rest at Camp Scurry. Many of the soldiers went into town to attend church services, while many of the locals took advantage of Sunday being "visitor's day" to wander around Camp Scurry. The brigade had a cordial standing invitation for Corpus Christians to inspect "the most model military camp in the entire southwest, which distinction was given to the Texas troops by General Funston on his recent tour of inspection."[40]

The process of improving the camp was a continual one. A complex of corrals and sheds for the brigade's horses and mules was completed in October. In November, Texas Hospital Company No. 1 arrived from Fort Sam Houston by truck.[41]

Border Service

The process of strengthening relations with the townspeople was ongoing. The entire Texas Brigade, led by the two regimental bands and with its equipment and vehicles, paraded through downtown Corpus Christi on October 11 in honor of the visiting members of the Order of the Eastern Star, who were having their convention in the city. The five-mile-long column, the largest in the city's history, passed before General Hulen, whose reviewing stand was at the Nueces Hotel. Not content with this impressive parade, that afternoon the 3rd Infantry held another parade at Camp Scurry for the visiting ladies, who were then treated to an exhibition drill by the regiment's machine gun company, which was equipped with Lewis guns and a Ford light truck. When the Daughters of the Confederacy held their convention in Corpus Christi, many of the ladies turned out to witness the brigade pass in review.[42]

So the troops would not lose their edge, there was a schedule of battalion drills in the mornings, during which the guardsmen worked out tactical problems under the supervision of regular officers. Regimental reviews were a weekly feature. A three-day march was scheduled for the entire brigade, which was to travel in heavy marching order, bivouac in their pup tents, and return. To the men's delight, however, the march was postponed because of inclement weather.[43] On Saturdays there were no drills; instead, there was a general policing of the camp followed by an inspection of equipment and quarters, and those soldiers who chose to do so got the opportunity to wash their clothes. Sometimes Saturday afternoon was enlivened by a Field Day, in which the men competed in a number of events such as races, tent-pitching contests, manual of arms competitions, and so forth, while the regimental bands kept up morale. The public was cordially invited.[44]

Morale declined as it became increasingly clear that there was no immediate prospect of the Texas militia being recalled from the border, as was indicated by the taking of measurements for overcoats and other winter clothing and the issuance of Sibley camp stoves to warm their tents. The large pyramidal tents themselves were framed, floored, and boarded up to a height of about four feet and fitted with doors. Many of the companies subsequently installed metal hoods and spark arresters on the tent tops to prevent fires, always a concern when hundreds of tents were packed into a relatively close area.[45] The tents were so well winterized that the local newspaper gushed that they were "as cozy as a hunting lodge and well-nigh as cheerful."[46]

The newspaper probably overestimated the degree of cheerfulness among the men. Yet they had little time to sit around brooding about their situation, for on October 14, General Parker issued a detailed program of strenuous training for the troops in the Brownsville District. Infantry companies, battalions, and regiments would conduct a series of marches and combat exercises and be graded on their performance.[47] The units responded enthusiastically, for the officers were at pains to explain to their men the importance of this training and to instill a spirit of competition among them.[48] A further focusing on military matters came on October 20 when the War Department stopped furloughs and the next day announced that no more guardsmen would be withdrawn from the border for the present.[49]

When drill was over, there was no lack of amusements, such as attending musical programs and movies at the camp YMCA or attending a dance for enlisted men at the Nueces Hotel. The YMCA offered nighttime classes in Spanish, arithmetic, English grammar, penmanship, and shorthand for those wishing to improve themselves.[50] Most of the men were not that ambitious, contenting themselves with pastimes such as shooting craps—not prohibited by army regulations—with the many civilian gamblers who had infiltrated the military reservation assuming they were immune from the civil authorities. They were shocked when the sheriff announced his intention of arresting them one and all.[51]

The soldiers at Camp Scurry did not commit much serious crime. A guardsman was arrested for burglary in January 1917. In February, an artilleryman from Battery A shot a Company D 2nd Infantry sergeant through the arm during an altercation. And that same month several soldiers robbed a taxi driver who had come to Camp Scurry to pick them up. A few days later two MPs left for San Antonio to bring back four men who had deserted from Camp Scurry.[52] As for petty offenses, some were dealt with extralegally, at least in the case of Company A 3rd Infantry, which maintained a "kangaroo court," whose proceedings were based largely on the Texas criminal code.[53]

More serious offenses against the army's code of military justice sent the offender into the large new guardhouse, whose population averaged some fifty to sixty inmates. To prevent escapes, the guardhouse was surrounded by an electrically charged barbed wire stockade with arc lights at each corner of the enclosure. The facility was considered escape-proof. Therefore the prisoners did not try to escape—they just burned the guardhouse down, on the night of November 8. The jailbirds were quickly rounded up and transferred to the city and county jails in Corpus Christi until a new guardhouse could be built. The score of military prisoners lodged in a large cell in the county jail became unruly for a prolonged period. The chief deputy sheriff finally lost patience and turned a fire hose on them. The troops were tough, withstanding the blast for about half an hour before finally promising to be good. But they again became obstreperous and had to be given a second dose of the water cure. This time they behaved themselves and spent their energies shivering and pleading for dry clothing.[54]

A popular off-duty pastime was duck hunting along Corpus Christi Bay. The sport was not limited to the guardsmen, though; General Funston and his aide met General Hulen and Mayor Miller for a two-day duck hunt in October. They were the guests of Robert and Caesar Kleberg of the enormous King Ranch, and Funston accepted the Klebergs' invitation to return for a deer hunt on the ranch. In January, Funston, Miller, and Hulen enjoyed another duck hunt.[55] Funston was not the only dignitary to visit Corpus Christi. Governor Ferguson attended a Democratic Party luncheon at the Nueces Hotel; the mayor, General Hulen, and Robert Kleberg sat at the governor's table. That afternoon the entire Texas Brigade passed in review before the governor.[56]

The brigade got to make a more extended march beginning on November 8. In fact, it was to be the longest march yet—forty-eight miles, over four days in heavy marching order (each man carried approximately sixty-five pounds of equipment). En route they would engage in repeated tactical exercises under the personal command of General Hulen. The two regimental canteens accompanied the column. But after covering a distance of thirty-eight miles in two days, the brigade returned to camp, the rest of the maneuver having been canceled because a wet norther blew in at night, dropping the temperature forty degrees and playing havoc with the troops and blowing down their pup tents. This was the beginning of the coldest November in the history of Corpus Christi. Despite the curtailed maneuver, Hulen declared himself pleased with the brigade's performance, for only a handful of men had fallen out during the exercise. He soon announced that the brigade would make the four-day march and maneuver as planned, beginning November 16. The brigade marched out of Camp Scurry with colors flying. General Parker then ordered that the exercise be extended to ten days.[57] Not only were the troops dismayed, but so was Mayor Miller, for the brigade would be away during Gulf Coast Exposition week, when its presence would constitute a considerable part of the celebration. He promptly phoned headquarters in Brownsville and argued the case for Corpus Christi. Within half an hour the order was canceled, and the army obligingly ordered the brigade back to Corpus Christi. The troops triumphantly marched through the city on November 20, the opening day of the exposition.[58]

Perhaps the most formidable component of the Texas Brigade was the 2nd Texas Infantry's football team. The team had originally been scheduled to open its season by traveling to College Station to play Texas A&M College, but the game was canceled at the last minute. Although disappointed, the 2nd Texas prepared to play other National Guard teams.[59] The men were excused from many duties so they could practice daily, and they ate at a separate mess. Their first game was on November 20 against the 3rd Missouri Artillery at the exposition grounds, where a two thousand–seat grandstand had been erected. The grandstand was filled to capacity by civilians and Texas guardsmen as well as a trainload of Missouri guardsmen who came from Laredo for the game, the biggest ever played south of San Antonio. The 2nd Texas Infantry crushed the 3rd Missouri Artillery by a score of 33 to 0.[60] And that was only the beginning. The Texans practiced twice a day in preparation for meeting the 1st Wisconsin Infantry team from San Antonio. Some 2,500 spectators witnessed this second football game of the exposition week, in which the Texans demolished the 1st Wisconsin 60 to 0.[61] This was an even bigger crowd pleaser than the Texas Brigade's formal review, which was one of the featured events of the exposition. The fans eagerly anticipated the 2nd Texas Infantry's next game, against the 1st Illinois Infantry on December 10 at the exposition grounds.[62]

The city of Austin went all out to welcome those Texas guardsmen going there on a four-day furlough for Thanksgiving to witness the game between the University of Texas and Texas A&M College, the fiercest rivalry in the state. From Corpus Christi members of Companies E and F of the 2nd Texas Infantry went to Austin. University of Texas students composed virtually all of Company F. They were met by a brass band, welcomed by the governor and the mayor, and treated to a sumptuous Thanksgiving feast.[63] For those remaining in Camp Scurry the army provided each with a pound of turkey for Thanksgiving dinner with all the trimmings. The local housewives contributed 385 home-baked cakes for the festive occasion. And a representative of the Chicago *Tribune* even filmed Company A 3rd Texas Infantry (the Houston Light Guards) as they ate.[64]

Corpus Christi began preparing a further demonstration of its appreciation for the soldiers. Mayor Miller came up with the idea of distributing presents to the troops at a large community Christmas tree. With the enthusiastic cooperation of various civic organizations he contacted the mayors of all towns represented in the Texas Brigade, asking them to send boxes of goodies for the men. The mayors and General Hulen thought this was a splendid idea. The fertile mind of Mayor Miller also conceived the idea of making Christmas week "Homecoming Week," urging the families of the guardsmen to come to Corpus Christi and spend a few days—and a few dollars—with their loved ones. The Commercial Club sent out three thousand invitations.[65]

The pace of life at Camp Scurry became even more relaxed. It was announced on December 10 that brigade headquarters would be closed on all holidays and Sundays as well as Saturday afternoons from one o'clock in the afternoon except for absolutely necessary business. Headquarters of the 2nd and 3rd Texas adopted a similar schedule, except that the 2nd's headquarters would stay open on Saturdays until four o'clock.[66] Hopefully any emergencies would occur only during office hours.

Athletics continued to form an important part of life at Camp Scurry. On December 5 the public was invited to a brigade field day at the exposition grounds. The men competed for prizes such as forty-eight-, thirty-six-, and twenty-four-hour passes, as well as wristwatches donated by the officers. Before a large and enthusiastic audience, the men ran the 100-, 220-, and 440-yard dashes and competed in the hammer throw, shot put, high jump, broad jump, the manual of arms, and a sack race. The honors went to the 2nd Infantry, which racked up 47 points to the 3rd Infantry's 31.[67]

Many of the troops participated in athletics vicariously. After the 2nd Infantry's fearsome football team demolished the 1st Illinois Infantry, the Texas team traveled to Laredo to play the 1st Missouri Infantry. A special trainload of fanatical fans, both guardsmen and civilians, accompanied them from Camp Scurry. The Missourians were massacred. As the press stated, "Throughout Texas football circles it is generally recognized that the Second Texas team can defeat any team in the state, either of civilian or militia lineup." The team's next game was at Camp Wilson in San Antonio, where their victims were the 1st Virginia Artillery, whom they routed 52 to 0.[68] Then the 4th Nebraska Infantry, complete with brass band and hundreds of supporters, came to Corpus Christi from the National Guard encampments at Llano Grande west of Brownsville to take on the Texans. The latter were disconcerted by General Parker's order, issued just before the game, that no commissioned officer could engage in football as a member of any regular team. Some of the 2nd Texas's best players thus had to sit out the game. No matter—the embarrassed Nebraskans went home after enduring a 68 to 0 thrashing.[69] The 2nd Texas's football team had become the pride of the brigade.

As Christmas approached, the pace of assembling presents for the troops increased. On behalf of the brigade General Hulen formally accepted Corpus Christi's invitation to participate in the Christmas Eve festivities at the municipal Christmas tree. And what a festive occasion it was. Every train brought a load of gifts for the troops, contributed from around the state. The mountain of presents, the elaborate Christmas dinner the next day at Camp Scurry, the influx of visiting relatives, and a week of light duty were making 1916 end on a decidedly high note.[70]

There were more troops than usual at Camp Scurry as 1917 began. Battery A Texas Field Artillery, armed with four 3" guns, had been stationed since June at Fort Ringgold outside Rio Grande City, a town of two thousand, 90 percent of whom were Hispanic, and twenty-five miles from the nearest railroad.[71] Its transfer to Corpus Christi was announced on December 20 but was delayed, perhaps in part because the citizens of Rio Grande City protested mightily against the removal of "their" guardsmen. Nevertheless, the unit, 207 strong and practically all from Dallas, was ordered to march overland to Harlingen, where it entrained for Corpus Christi, arriving there on January 2.[72] Delighted to be in Corpus Christi and busily setting up their camp, the artillerymen missed witnessing the 2nd Texas obliterate the 74th New York Infantry on New Year's day by the truly astounding score of 102 to 0 (fifteen touchdowns and twelve field goals) before a wildly cheering crowd of three thousand at the exposition grounds.[73] As had been the case after earlier Texas victories, their guardsmen supporters celebrated by exuberantly marching into town.

From their camp just north of the 2nd Infantry cantonment, the Texas artillerymen did get to witness something astounding—a mass demonstration on the evening of January 5 by soldiers of the 2nd Texas, who were yelling, "We are going home." What apparently touched off the outbreak by several hundred men was the news that recruiting stations for the Texas National Guard would close on January 10. They construed this to mean that the guard was about to be mustered out, and for an hour or more they marched into Corpus Christi loudly, and with considerable hilarity, voicing their intention of going home. Some panic-stricken observers thought that a near-riot was in progress, and the rumor spread that the demonstrators were marching on the railroad station to board the northbound train, which was simply not the case. Most observers considered the whole incident to be merely a harmless prank. Nevertheless, the officers took an exceedingly dim view of the matter, considering it not only a breach of military discipline but a reflection on the Texas National Guard. The provost guard was ordered to round up the malcontents, and details of troops from the 3rd Infantry with loaded rifles and fixed bayonets were deployed to comb the city. Within two hours every soldier from both regiments had been returned to camp, and the entire 2nd Infantry was confined to quarters under technical arrest. General Hulen immediately ordered an investigation of the whole affair, an investigation which resulted in the participants being denied passes to leave the post for thirty days.[74]

The unruly demonstration came at a particularly awkward time, for General Parker was to arrive the next day for a previously scheduled inspection of the Texas Brigade, formally designated as the 6th Separate Brigade and attached to Parker's 13th Provisional Division. During his daylong visit, Parker observed a tactical exercise several miles south of Camp Scurry in which a "Brown" invading force composed of the 2nd Infantry and two sections of Battery A Field Artillery had landed on the coast and was attempting to capture the city of Corpus Christi from a "White" defending force, composed of the 3rd Infantry and the other two sections of Battery A. During the engagement some ten thousand rounds of blank ammunition were expended and the "invaders" were repulsed and forced to retreat. Both Parker and Hulen pronounced themselves quite pleased with the brigade's performance. After all units had returned to Camp Scurry, General Parker took the salute as the brigade passed in review: the 2nd and 3rd Texas Infantry, Battery A, and Field Hospital No. 1, a total of 3,018 men.[75]

Shortly after these events, which constituted the climax of the National Guard's experience in Corpus Christi, tragedy struck—the brigade suffered its first fatality. Four enlisted men from the 2nd Infantry took out a small sailboat for a leisurely nighttime cruise around the bay. Four miles from shore the craft capsized. The men clung to the overturned boat in hopes of being rescued. When, by three o'clock in the morning, it became apparent that help was not forthcoming, two of them, both strong swimmers, decided to make for the shore. They had swum for about an hour when one of them became utterly exhausted. He said good-bye to his companion and sank beneath the waves. His companion struggled on and after four hours reached the shore and sent help to rescue the two soldiers still clinging to the boat. Two weeks later the drowned private's body was recovered. He was buried in his home town with full military honors.[76] And in February, a private in the 3rd Infantry was killed when he was struck by a train near Houston.[77] Compared with the other National Guard cantonments, the loss of life at Camp Scurry was remarkably low.

With the need for guardsmen on the border decreasing, the troops at Camp Scurry now considered themselves short-timers, and there was much speculation as to when the Texas National Guard would be mustered out of service. Texas politicians were urging Secretary of War Baker to demobilize the Texas National Guard immediately.[78] General Parker inquired as to how many Texas guardsmen would remain in the service for border protection provided they were given the alternative of being discharged. General Hulen replied that it was difficult to estimate, but thought that probably 50 percent of his two regiments would request discharges, although a much greater proportion of officers would elect to stay. Nevertheless, some would have to resign for business reasons—including Hulen himself.[79]

In the meantime, football was the center of interest in Corpus Christi, with the undefeated 2nd Texas Infantry being lionized by civic groups, who organized luncheons in their honor. The team continued to dominate its opponents, the most recent being the 12th Division All-Stars from San Antonio, coached by Lieutenant Dwight Eisenhower. The All-Stars lost 34 to 6 in Austin but had the consolation of at least scoring against the Texans, perhaps because the 2nd Texas was resting its starters for the season finale to be held in San Antonio four days later. The fans in Corpus Christi eagerly anticipated the team's next massacre, against the 1st New York Cavalry—a team composed of picked men from eastern colleges, of which thirty-three were lettermen and seven All-Americans from Yale, Harvard, and Princeton—at Camp Wilson.[80] Before six thousand screaming spectators, the Texans destroyed the New Yorkers 69 to 0.[81] As a reward, the entire team received a thirty-day leave.[82] (There was considerable enthusiasm for organizing a Camp Scurry baseball team, not the least attraction being that the players would be relieved of duty in the afternoons.)[83] The 2nd Texas Infantry had won all seven of its games by an astounding cumulative score of 432 to 6.[84]

Overshadowing the brigade's pride in the football team was the electrifying news received on February 17, 1917, that General Funston had ordered all National Guard units returned to their home stations for demobilization no later than March 7. Coming as it did after months of conflicting rumors, the news sent morale sky high. The troops were especially sharp when General Parker arrived for a routine inspection of the brigade the next day.[85]

On February 19, Corpus Christi was thrown into shock at the news that General Funston had suddenly collapsed and died in a San Antonio hotel. Mayor Miller, who had become an intimate friend of Funston's, was a member of the general's party.[86]

The new Southern Department commander, Major General John J. Pershing, arrived as part of his inspection tour of the forty thousand troops in the Brownsville District. Pershing reviewed the Texas Brigade on March 4, had lunch at the Nueces Hotel, then departed by automobile for the King Ranch, accompanied by Robert J. Kleberg.[87]

Yet the big news in Corpus Christi was the impending loss of the Texas Brigade. The newspaper declared: "The people of Corpus Christi received the news with mingled feelings. Everybody of course is glad that the boys are going home because the boys yearn to return to the native heath, and there is not a real Corpus Christian who would have them remain here a minute longer than their duties require. But there is no denying the fact that the stationing of the two regiments and other units here for the past six months has been a real 'life saver,' the boys arriving at a time when business conditions here were unusual, caused by the drought that has prevailed for more than a year."[88]

The troops had been a "life saver" indeed. The military had been pumping about $95,000 a month into the Corpus Christi economy. The payroll for the Texas Brigade was around $70,000 a month, and in addition the government spent some $25,000 per month for local merchandise.[89]

Jubilation reigned at Camp Scurry at the War Department's order that all National Guard units must be away from the border by the end of March. On March 12, the guardsmen received their pay for February and March—about $100,000.[90] A farewell eight-course dinner was held at the Nueces Hotel on March 22 for the Texas Brigade's officers. Three hundred attended, Mayor Miller was toastmaster, and General Hulen was presented with a silver loving cup as a token of Corpus Christi's appreciation.[91] By March 26, the 2nd and 3rd Infantry, Battery A, and Field Hospital Company No. 1 were mustered out and had departed from Corpus Christi. Company K of the 26th U.S. Infantry arrived from Kingsville to guard the government property and buildings at Camp Scurry.[92]

On the whole, Camp Scurry had been a model National Guard camp. Although Corpus Christi ultimately failed in its efforts to have the camp designated as a permanent post,[93] the city benefited enormously by the presence of the guardsmen, most of whom had thoroughly enjoyed themselves.

Chapter 7

Brownsville and Llano Grande

San Antonio may have been the nerve center of border defense but Brownsville was the area of greatest concern. During the war crisis Americans braced for further raids, while the Mexican Army in Matamoros braced for what they believed was imminent American invasion. In this highly charged atmosphere the Mexicans' apprehension was well founded for General Funston's orders were that in the event of armed conflict resulting from Mexican aggression he was authorized to seize the international bridges and all Mexican border towns.[1] In anticipation of a clash, reporters began rushing to Brownsville, among them Basil Dillon Woon of the New York *World* and Arthur Constantine of the International News Service.[2]

General Parker's Brownsville District was based at Fort Brown[3] and stretched from Rio Grande City 120 miles downriver beyond Brownsville to Point Isabel on the Gulf Coast. It eventually had the greatest concentration of United States troops of any military district on the border—some fifty thousand men, the equivalent of a reinforced army corps. As we have seen, the militia units originally assigned to this district were the 2nd Texas Infantry under Colonel B. F. Delameter and the 3rd Texas Infantry under Colonel George P. Rains.[4] The men were eager and willing, but Parker felt that these regiments were not yet ready for frontline duty, so he kept them as a reserve while putting them through a rigorous course of training.[5] Battery A of the Texas National Guard was assigned to Rio Grande City, reinforcing Troops I and K of the 3rd U.S. Cavalry and Headquarters 2nd

Battalion and Company I of the 2nd Texas Infantry. On June 22, three hundred men of the 28th U.S. Infantry, including a machine gun company, were rushed from Mission to Fort Ringgold at Rio Grande City, following reports that Mexican bandits were threatening the town of two thousand, mostly Hispanic, inhabitants. Battery A's arrival in Rio Grande City on June 24 caused the Mexican troops across the Rio Grande at Camargo abruptly to halt digging a complex of trenches.[6] Troop M of the 3rd U.S. Cavalry was stationed at the nearby town of Roma.

To protect Brownsville, General Parker had Troops E, F, G, and H of the 3rd U.S. Cavalry; Battery D of the 4th U.S. Field Artillery; and the 4th U.S. Infantry less Company M. This force proved adequate, especially since a battery of heavy artillery from the 5th Field Artillery was on its way to Brownsville from Fort Sill, Oklahoma.[7] The general must have breathed much easier when the powerful New York National Guard arrived in early July and took up station west of Brownsville, as will be discussed in the next chapter. Although the New York division was a separate command, it was still within Parker's jurisdiction, and it constituted a formidable deterrent to the Mexican troops across the river. The deterrent factor increased exponentially as National Guard units from Colorado, Illinois, Indiana, Iowa, Louisiana, Kansas, Minnesota, Nebraska, New Hampshire, North Dakota, South Dakota, Oklahoma, and Virginia poured into the Brownsville military district.[8]

An enormous logistical problem existed because there was only a single-track railroad line into Brownsville from San Antonio. During July alone, 106 special trains (consisting of 1,216 passenger cars and 1,201 freight cars) plus 680 cars of army supplies rolled into Brownsville and had to return along the same track.[9]

Parker's headquarters were at Fort Brown in Brownsville, population 13,163. The city went into high gear to prepare campsites, which regular officers selected, for the additional units scheduled to arrive shortly. The artillery occupied a site two miles east of the city, while the first National Guard reinforcement, the 1st Illinois Cavalry, set up shop three miles from Brownsville in the suburb of West Brownsville.

The Brownsville business community was initially outraged that only the 1st Illinois Cavalry was assigned there. On July 8, James H. Wells, the most powerful political boss in South Texas, and A. A. Browne, the mayor of Brownsville, telegraphed their congressman, John Nance Garner, protesting because Brownsville had gotten only one National Guard regiment and bitterly complaining because towns not as important as Brownsville had received large numbers of guardsmen. Congressman Garner duly forwarded the telegram to the War Department, which declared that the matter was up to General Funston.[10] In the meantime, the Brownville city manager supervised 225 laborers hurriedly clearing the ground of brush and installing water pipes. By July 6 they had cleared 140 acres and had laid nearly 40,000 feet of additional water mains.[11] A most unusual feature of the preparations was the creation of an artificial lake—half a mile long and nearly as wide, five to six feet deep, made by piping water into the basin of a dry lake bed next to the 1st Illinois Cavalry's camp—as part of an elaborate program of entertainment for the guardsmen, who could now disport themselves by frolicking in the lake.

Moreover, the Brownsville Board of City Development decided to raise immediately a fund of more than $5,000 with which to make border life enjoyable for the militia coming from the North and East. The plan included a downtown restroom for the troops. The sum was quickly raised, $1,500 of it within the first hour and a half. The shrewd business community frankly admitted they hoped a moderate investment would provide big returns. The board undertook to prepare campsites for six thousand more soldiers, calculating that in the very near future Brownsville would have twelve thousand troops, whose monthly payroll would exceed $200,000. "Besides the money released in paying the troops, large revenues will come to the Brownsville merchants in money spent by members of the National Guard who are independent of the salary paid by the war department." The board asked the citizenry to contribute another $5,000.[12] The army was well aware of the amount of cash involved in payrolls, and it took no chances. It leased a vault, which at times contained several million dollars for general expenses, including the payroll, in the First National Bank. To safeguard these funds a detachment of troops was deployed around the bank.[13]

On payday the troops feasted in their thousands. Brownsville restaurants were overwhelmed with one proprietor reporting that he had fed over a thousand people in one day. Several restaurants had to close because they ran out of food, and the city's bakeries were stripped clean. The hotels and boarding houses were jammed, and accommodations fetched a premium. A federal Bureau of Investigation agent reported on "the lack of suitable accommodation in the hotels along the border which are crowded to overflowing by the officers of the army. Rooms occupied by two to four, no tables, no privacy, no conveniences." Competing for accommodations were the numerous businessmen anxious to get their share of the bonanza. Those selling cigarettes did extremely well, for by August an estimated ten million cigarettes had been sold in the lower Rio Grande border since the coming of the state troops, and the Chesterfield brand sent its crack sales crew to Brownsville to inaugurate a sales campaign along the border. Business at the post office more than quadrupled.[14] The Board of City Development's investment was returning handsome dividends, and the city's vision expanded as it began making preparations to house thirty thousand troops.

With semipermanent frame buildings such as mess halls and YMCAs going up in the various camps, to say nothing of the large dancing pavilion surrounded by a broad, screened veranda being built at Fort Brown, carpenters were in great demand. The Southwestern Telegraph & Telephone Company was doubling its telephone system. In a rather euphoric editorial the *Brownsville Daily Herald* even anticipated an influx of what are today's "snowbirds," speculating that a horde of visitors would descend on Brownsville during the winter because European travel had been interdicted by World War I and because many of the visitors would be coming to see their guardsmen.[15] Tourism was a great potential source of revenue.

The immediate beneficiaries of the city's largesse were the soldiers of the 1st Illinois Cavalry from Chicago. Fortune smiled on this regiment, which was considered the cream of the state's National Guard and included many veterans. It also included men such as Major Robert R. McCormick, president of the Chicago *Tribune* company and editor of the *Tribune*. He was a leader of society, as was his wife, who was active in the Red Cross. The regiment's departure from Chicago had been delayed a day because Colonel Milton J. Foreman had adamantly refused to let his men be transported in chair cars; twelve Pullmans were then provided. The cavalry began arriving in Brownsville on July 4, "rested and exuberant."[16] The regiment brought with it a twenty-piece band, an English terrier mascot, and "Villa," an opossum one of the men had picked up during a stop in San Marcos, Texas.

Heartened by the refreshments and friendly crowds at stations along the route in Texas, especially in San Antonio and San Marcos, the new arrivals had no complaints about their reception in Brownsville, being welcomed by the mayor himself. They unloaded their equipment and proceeded in heavy marching order from the railroad station to their camp. Filming the whole spectacle for Pathe's weekly news service was the company's Brownsville representative. And writing about it for the home folks was the corps of newspaper correspondents accompanying the troops: reporters from the Chicago *Tribune*, *Evening Post*, *News*, *Examiner*, and *American*. The Board of City Development gladly made room for them at the press facilities it had already provided at its office opposite the Miller Hotel for newsmen from the International News Service, the Associated Press, the New York *World*, and the *Saturday Evening Post*. The Associated Press, incidentally, had sent correspondents to every important point on the border.[17] The city also provided quarters in the city hall for the Military Police detachment, who worked out for an hour every day at the punching bag and by boxing, in order to be in shape to take on any miscreants. As it happened, they should have been practicing firearms safety—one MP accidentally shot his sergeant in the jaw.[18] The eighteen-man detachment slept, fitfully, in one room. Eventually, the heat and humidity in Brownsville got to the MPs and they asked for a fan.[19]

The 1st Illinois Cavalry differed from some other guard organizations in several respects. First, it had three wagon-borne camp kitchens, one for each squadron. Major Robert McCormick had seen the German Army's field kitchens and thought they were just the thing for the Illinois cavalry. The army did not get around to trying out field kitchens until September 1916, when five different types went to Fort Sam Houston for testing.[20]

Another difference with the Illinois cavalry was its five machine guns, all purchased by private subscription. When the regiment had decided to outfit itself with these weapons, the War Department had not even reached a decision about whether to issue machine guns to the National Guard. In June, Chicago businessmen raised $25,000 to purchase machine guns but had to abandon the plan and return the money to the donors because, as mentioned earlier, the Allies controlled practically the entire output of American machine gun production. But the regiment subsequently acquired five.[21]

Major McCormick was the moving spirit in acquiring both the kitchens and the machine guns. The Illinois cavalry had a real sugar daddy in the person of J. Ogden Armour, the Chicago meatpacking magnate who also owned the Armour Grain Elevator Company, easily the largest company of its kind in the country. Many of the cavalrymen were Armour employees and continued receiving their full salary while on active duty. In addition, before the regiment left Chicago, Armour gave the cavalry $2,500 in cash and instructed the quartermaster to draw on him any additional funds needed.[22] It was good to have benefactors. Throughout the great call-up, funds from private donors and from public subscriptions served to alleviate in part the army's inability to supply guard units adequately.[23]

In addition to the huge artificial swimming pool, in short order the Illinois camp, named Camp Parker, had a large frame YMCA hall, paid for by private subscription. The camp was also equipped with a well-stocked canteen providing ice cream, cold drinks, fruit, candies, and cakes. There were also shower baths, a barber shop, and an open-air skating rink. The insects that had initially pestered the troops had practically disappeared, thanks to sprinkling the ground with crude oil and creosote and the use of pots of burning tar and oil. The work of installing flooring and screens on the colonel's tent had been completed, and the same improvements were being performed on the other officers' tents as rapidly as possible.[24]

Even as the 1st Illinois Cavalry was making itself at home and preparing to take on a team from Fort Brown in polo, the next militia contingent arrived. The 1st Virginia Infantry was considered that state's best, and its Company D claimed to be the oldest militia organization in the United States, tracing its ancestry back to the American Revolution as the Monticello Guard and being in continuous existence under several names ever since, having served in the Mexican War, the Civil War, and the Spanish-American War. The Virginians' trip to Brownsville had been eventful. They had spent five miserable days on the road, riding in day coaches and had been delayed by storms from Richmond to New Orleans, where they had finally been furnished with Pullmans. The first two battalions arrived in Brownsville closely together because through an error one had been sent initially to Mercedes. When the third battalion arrived shortly thereafter, the regiment, which included a hospital company, a regimental band, and a machine gun company, was complete. And the next day the 2nd Virginia Infantry made its appearance, in the midst of a terrific rainstorm. Both regiments went into camp outside the city on the road to Point Isabel.[25] A squadron of Virginia cavalry, the Richmond Blues, "the dandy National Guard organization of Virginia," was an independent cavalry squadron composed of wealthy and aristocratic Virginians who had outfitted and equipped themselves. Formerly the organization had been an independent infantry battalion. This unit arrived in August and occupied a camp immediately beyond that of the 2nd Virginia Infantry.[26]

The Iowa Brigade (1st, 2nd, and 3rd Infantry), the 1st Cavalry Squadron, the 1st Field Artillery Battalion, and Ambulance Company No. 1 came to Brownsville from Camp Dodge, a small National Guard encampment northwest of Des Moines, where they had spent about thirty days of training and conditioning. The units lacked some equipment because of a great increase in enlistments, but it was felt that they could be equipped on the border as easily as at Camp Dodge, while they were being acclimated to the border.[27] All Iowa units were assigned to Brownsville except for the cavalry squadron, which went to Donna.[28] The Iowans immediately moved off to their campground near that of the 5th U.S. Artillery. Their assigned area had a four-inch main connecting it to the city water supply but had not been entirely cleared of cactus and chaparral. The men went to work with a will, refreshed by the constant sea breeze from the gulf, comparing the local climate favorably with that back home. They were astute enough to leave a number of mesquite and huisache trees for shade.[29] The Iowans had machine gun companies, regimental bands, and, a real novelty, instead of a horse-drawn ambulance the regiment's ambulance company had a motorized vehicle. The 1st Iowa Infantry had the distinction of being composed almost entirely of marksmen.[30]

On November 31, armed guardsmen crossed the Rio Grande several miles below Fort Brown. This caused hysteria in Matamoros, whose residents thought they were being invaded. In fact, it was a search party looking for the body of a corporal in the 3rd Iowa Infantry who had drowned while swimming in the river.[31] Accompanying the brigade were two newspaper reporters, from the Des Moines *Capital* and *Register and Leader*.[32] It might also be mentioned that the 2nd Iowa Infantry was the first to arrive in Brownsville with an automobile for use by officers. One of the lieutenants sported a handsome touring car, which he had had painted khaki color before leaving for the border. The vehicle caused considerable interest on the streets of Brownsville.[33]

A glaring deficiency was machine guns. When General Bliss inspected the units stationed in the Brownsville district, only five of the twenty-two organizations had these weapons.[34]

Northwest of Brownsville, at San Benito, a town of five thousand, were stationed the 3rd Battalion 3rd Texas Infantry and Companies A, F, and H of the 26th U.S. Infantry under Colonel Robert L. Bullard.[35] He now commanded the provisional 1st Separate Brigade, composed of the 26th U.S. Infantry, the 4th South Dakota Infantry, the 1st Louisiana Infantry, and the 1st Oklahoma Infantry.[36] The Oklahomans arrived on July 21.

The Oklahoma National Guard, consisting of the 1st Infantry, Cavalry Troops A and B, Field Hospital No. 1, Ambulance Company No.1, and Company A Engineers, had experienced a series of delays regarding their mobilization point. The delays, centering on confusion as to the mobilization point, had created an adverse impression that Oklahoma was slow to respond to the president's call. First, Oklahoma City offered the use of the state fairgrounds, offering to provide water, electricity, toilet facilities, and three stables. Camp Bob Williams opened on a temporary basis, with some of the guardsmen camped on the fairgrounds racetrack. Then, the town of McAlester was suggested. That same day Secretary of War Baker designated Chandler as the mobilization site. An inspection team went to Chandler and found a mess. The rifle range was flooded and covered with weeds and mud, and recent rains had washed out the bridges. There had been hog pens between the rifle range and the proposed campsite, and the pigs' filth covered the area. Many residents of Chandler used open privies, and when the wind was right the stench at the proposed campsite was nauseating. Finally, the water supply was inadequate. In view of all this, the War Department finally changed the mobilization point to Fort Sill, Oklahoma.[37]

Upon its arrival in San Benito the Oklahoma regiment was quarantined when a case of measles was discovered. The patient was removed, and within a week so was the quarantine.[38] But the regiment was hardly combat ready. One company commander stated that his men only theoretically knew how to insert a cartridge into the chamber of their rifles. They had received no ammunition and had not engaged in target practice since the 1915 state encampment. About 50 percent of the regiment consisted of recruits, so some men had never even fired a weapon.[39]

In addition to the 1st Louisiana Infantry at San Benito, that state's National Guard consisted of the 1st Separate Troop (Troop A) of Cavalry, the Washington Artillery Battery (organized in New Orleans on September 7, 1838), and Field Hospital Company No. 1. The Louisiana guard numbered 1,619 and had mobilized at Camp Stafford near Alexandria. Troop A and the Washington Battery were stationed at Donna and Field Hospital No. 1 at Brownsville.[40] The 1st Louisiana Infantry's border experience was relatively brief, and their departure was not without incident. As they were boarding their trains, a drunken cook slashed a captain on the left jaw, severing a facial artery, and a sergeant was stabbed in the neck during the melee.[41] The 1st Separate Troop left Donna on October 2 to return to the Louisiana mobilization camp. They were replaced by a troop of Kansas cavalry.[42]

The 4th South Dakota Infantry reached San Benito on August 5, coming from their mobilization point, Camp Hagman, near Redfield, South Dakota. The one thousand men were mustered into federal service on July 15 and had remained in camp for intensive training until July 31, when they left for the border with huge crowds seeing them off. Coming from a predominantly rural state, many of the men were homesteaders who feared losing their land while serving on the border. However, Congress passed a resolution protecting them.[43] They traveled in comfort, in twenty-one tourist sleepers for the men and three Pullmans for the officers. At Fort Worth and Kingsville, Texas, they even got to take baths.[44] The South Dakotans encountered inclement weather and had to set up their camp in a rainstorm, and on August 18 a hurricane wrecked their encampment.

The 4th South Dakota Infantry was a rather well-equipped outfit, lacking only cots and summer uniforms. They sweated in their woolens until September, when they were finally issued khakis. Equally welcome, they were one of the first units to receive a complete new field issue, principally a new field pack, which was much more comfortable than their current blanket-roll. The South Dakotans' machine gun company had Colt guns, transported on pack mules. The crews serving these weapons were particularly proficient—they were able to unload the machine guns from the mules and start firing within one minute after receiving the order. Rigorous drilling kept the men in good physical shape, and on occasion they got a break from the monotony of camp life by guarding several ranches as well as irrigation pumping stations.[45] Since the South Dakotans spent most of their time in camp, they made it as comfortable as possible, building tennis courts, a polo field, and renting the San Benito baseball field for $110 for four months. Their regimental baseball team won twelve of its fifteen games.

Their relations with the locals were turbulent. They found the Hispanics to be generally friendly, and a number of soldiers even took Spanish classes at night in the high school. No doubt some of them wanted to improve their communication skills in the saloons and the red-light district, where business boomed on paydays. Some of the citizens complained about soldiers' misconduct and swearing on the streets. The soldiers, in turn, complained bitterly about price gouging and poor treatment by store clerks and about the school board not allowing female teachers to attend military dances. Their colleagues from North Dakota heartily concurred in complaining about price gouging.[46] The situation reached the point in December that the troops threatened to boycott the stores in San Benito. The boycott was averted when officers met with the businessmen, who promised to treat the men fairly. The school board, however, adamantly refused to change its policy. Many of the men spent their leaves out of town, in places such as Brownsville, Point Isabel, or Corpus Christi; the railroad ran weekend excursions to Corpus Christi for $4.15 for the round trip.[47]

The 4th South Dakota Infantry was fortunate for it recorded only one death while on the border—a wagon driver in Company B who was thrown from his wagon, which ran over him with a wheel crushing his skull. Another member of the regiment was wounded in a rather bizarre fashion. The captain of Company K was seriously wounded in the abdomen by a charge of birdshot fired by a mentally unbalanced woman who made a habit of shooting at soldiers. The captain was rushed to the base hospital in Brownsville and eventually recovered.[48]

At Harlingen were the Headquarters and Companies B, D, E, G, and I of the 26th U.S. Infantry. The town was also the headquarters of the 1st Texas Brigade and Headquarters and the 1st battalion of the 3rd Texas Infantry. Companies rotated tours of duty at Point Isabel guarding the U.S. naval radio station there. This was a choice assignment. Their camp was on a high bluff overlooking the Gulf, with cool nights offsetting the hot daytime winds. The men had abundant rations, and when not on duty they could relax at Padre Island three miles from camp, swimming in the Gulf. Their idyllic existence was shattered at three o'clock in the morning on July 17 by a volley of rifle fire; their position was under attack. The guardsmen reacted well—in less than five minutes they were in their trenches ready to fight; the machine gun squad set a precedent, for in less than two minutes they had their gun mounted and were ready to fire. But it was all a drill. The sentries had been ordered to fire the volley, and not until the bugler blew "Cease Fire" did the men realize it was only an exercise.[49]

At Donna, in Hidalgo County, fifty-five miles west of Brownsville, were stationed Companies A and C of the 28th U.S. Infantry; Troop B of the 3rd U.S. Cavalry; Companies A, B, C, and D of the 2nd Texas Infantry, the 1st Separate Troop Louisiana Cavalry, and the Washington Battery Louisiana Artillery.[50] Later the 1st Iowa Cavalry Squadron was also assigned to Donna. The one-hundred-acre encampment was favorably located on relatively high ground not subject to flooding, and the camp had an ample water supply through six-inch mains and four-inch laterals, providing 250,000 gallons every twelve hours.[51]

Mission was where Headquarters and Companies I and K of the 28th U.S. Infantry were stationed, along with Troop D of the 3rd U.S. Cavalry and Headquarters and Companies F and H of the 2nd Texas Infantry. At nearby Pharr were assigned Companies G, K, L, and M of the 2nd Texas Infantry, along with Company H of the 28th U.S. Infantry.[52] Sam Fordyce, on the Rio Grande, was garrisoned by Company M, 28th U.S. Infantry; Troop L, 3rd U.S. Cavalry; and Company E, 2nd Texas Infantry.[53] Mercedes was home to Company L, 26th U.S. Infantry; Headquarters and Troop C, 3rd U.S. Cavalry; and the 2nd Battalion, 3rd Texas Infantry.[54] The Texas infantry units were transferred to Corpus Christi in September.

By far the largest concentration of new National Guard units was just west of Mercedes, on a large tract known as the Llano Grande (the Big Prairie). The advantage of Llano Grande, besides providing an expanse of land for camps, was that it was adjacent to the railroad and abundantly supplied with water (unfortunately some of it in the form of torrential rainstorms). Some considered the Llano Grande the most attractive campsite in the Lower Valley, an opinion reiterated by the citizens of Mercedes, who enthusiastically assisted the army in preparing campsites covering several hundred acres. Brigadier General Edward H. Plummer, formerly colonel of the 28th U.S. Infantry, was assigned to command a provisional division of National Guard troops rapidly assembling at Llano Grande and Mercedes.[55]

Among them was the contingent from Nebraska. On June 19, the Nebraskans had assembled at their armories, and on June 21 the 4th and 5th Infantry began moving to the state fairgrounds in Lincoln, the mobilization point. The army pointed out that Nebraska's mobilization plan designated Camp Ashland as the mobilization point, and this could not be changed without consulting the War Department. But since most of the troops were already in Lincoln, the army did not press the point. By June 24, Camp Morehead (named for the governor) had been established, with the 4th Infantry camped south of the grandstand and the 5th by the racetrack. The transportation section was by the horse barns. The guardsmen remodeled the dairy building into a commissary and the textile building into a hospital, built bathhouses, and began training under regular army instructors. Civilians, estimated at some 35,000, flocked to Camp Morehead to visit the troops. In addition, the citizens of Omaha provided 30,000 cigarettes, crates of fruits, a bushel of smoking tobacco, and 170 cherry pies.

Physical examinations for the 4th and 5th Infantry took place on June 26. Out of 2,212 men, 270 were rejected for medical reasons. By comparison, the Ohio National Guard had 5,000 out of 13,000 rejected, and Kentucky

580 out of 1,100. Sanitary conditions at the camp were excellent, and Colonel George K. Hunter, inspector general of the Central Department, so reported. However, there was a critical shortage of regulation shoes. Colonel Hunter requisitioned shoes and other items of equipment through the War Department, with disappointing results. More than two thousand pairs of new shoes arrived from the St. Louis depot on July 6, but Hunter returned the entire shipment because they were of inferior quality. And he rejected a shipment of blankets because they were "insufficiently light." He immediately resubmitted his request, and new equipment arrived on the next train from St. Louis, along with two thousand model 1903 Springfield rifles. The 4th Infantry, a medical detachment, the band, and Company A Signal Corps departed for the border in three trains of antique day coaches on July 7. The 5th Infantry left on July 9. The citizens of Nebraska expressed concern as to how the state would be able to deal with emergencies without the National Guard.[56]

At Llano Grande the Nebraskans along with formations from other states had to build their camp from scratch, only then could serious training begin. The 4th and 5th Nebraska Infantry, Company A Signal Corps, and Field Hospital Company No. 1 were combined with the 1st, 2nd, and 3rd Indiana Infantry, a battalion of Indiana field artillery,[57] the 1st and 3rd Minnesota Infantry, the 1st Minnesota Field Artillery (battery F was composed of University of Minnesota students), the 1st North Dakota Infantry, a squadron of Iowa cavalry, and two troops of the 1st Oklahoma Cavalry into a provisional National Guard division at Llano Grande. As might be imagined, integrating this agglomeration of units would be a challenge.

Not surprisingly, this provisional division suffered some casualties. On October 16, a private in Battery E, Minnesota Field Artillery was found unconscious on the railroad track north of San Benito. A railroad motor car had passed over him, inflicting injuries that proved fatal. It was undetermined whether this was a case of murder or whether he was just drunk. In November, a homesick Minnesota soldier drank poison in the Harlingen baseball park and died.[58]

The 1st North Dakota Infantry, numbering 641 enlisted men, had mobilized under General Orders No. 9, issued on June 19 over the signature of Adjutant General Thomas H. Tharalson, directing all guardsmen to report to their home stations by nine o'clock that evening. However, the guard remained at their home stations for the next week. Almost all companies had to recruit men hurriedly before reporting to the mobilization camp, and the lack of reserve stocks of equipment, uniforms, and weapons delayed mobilization.

The War Department designated Fort Lincoln, an abandoned army post two miles south of Bismarck, as the 1st North Dakota Infantry's assembly point. Having to restore utilities to the post further delayed matters. When the 1st North Dakota left for Texas on July 22, it had increased to a little over one thousand officers and enlisted men, barely above peacetime strength. However, half of the privates were raw recruits, while a fifth of the NCOs had less than one year's service.[59]

The 1st North Dakota Infantry (twelve companies) plus a machine gun company, a band, and a medical detachment—reached the border on July 26 after a four-day rail journey and detrained at Mercedes in a driving rain. The North Dakotans outnumbered the residents of Mercedes, and their campsite outside the town was disappointing. The army had not prepared the site, which was the town dump, covered with chaparral, mesquite, and trash. The men set to work with a will and, despite frequent rainstorms during the next six weeks, managed to clean up the site and dig a system of drainage ditches. As with other state organizations, the North Dakotans were quickly integrated into General Parker's program of intensive training. And by late September, the 3rd Battalion traded the boredom of camp life for a three-week tour of patrol duty along the Rio Grande, while the machine gun company went to Harlingen in December for two weeks of instruction.[60]

The Indiana National Guard numbered 2,537 on June 18 and had assembled at Fort Benjamin Harrison.[61] The governor appointed Lieutenant Colonel Edward M. Lewis, a regular officer, as brigadier general commanding the infantry brigade (1st, 2nd, 3rd Infantry). Although short of horses the 1st Battalion Field Artillery departed for the border on July 6, and the infantry regiments began leaving the next day.[62] Company I, 1st Indiana Infantry, was composed of University of Indiana students. The 1st Battalion Indiana Field Artillery also contained an unusual unit: Battery B was composed of Purdue University faculty and students and its captain was a Purdue graduate. Battery B received orders on September 9 to be discharged as soon as possible. Battery D did not arrive at Llano Grande until October 2.[63] Generals Bliss, Plummer, and Lewis complimented the Indiana field artillery battalion for having the best camp in the whole sixty-mile district.[64]

A group of Indianapolis businessmen, who were considering what to buy with funds raised for the Indianans in Texas, were dumbfounded when a sergeant in the 2nd Indiana wrote that the best thing they could buy for the boys would be cold cream.[65] On July 22, Major General Tasker Bliss on an inspection tour found eight companies of the 3rd Indiana Infantry still in pup tents. Conical tents for the regiment quickly arrived by express.[66] The wretched troops had been enduring frequent torrential rains, and although some men had been able to purchase cots from private funds, almost half of them had been sleeping on the ground, or more precisely, in the mud.[67] Like some other state organizations the Indianans published, at Mercedes, a newspaper, *The Hoosier Guard*, for their units at Llano Grande.[68]

The pace of training was depressingly slow.[69] It took six weeks for arrangements to be made for the men to begin target practice. And even so, practice was conducted on a miniature scale, the size and range of the targets being reduced to suit cramped accommodations: targets were located only one hundred feet from the firing line, a rather unrealistic distance under battlefield conditions. The Minnesota field artillery had had only subcaliber practice—aiming a field piece and firing a blank pistol cartridge. Moreover, the Minnesotans could not move their guns because of the discrepancy between the size of the horses' necks and the sizes of the army steel collars. The collars just did not fit and could not be adjusted to fit. All units suffered from a lack of the authorized number of horses and mules. This deficiency particularly hurt the artillery organizations, in some cases virtually immobilizing them. The Indiana field artillery battalion finally received horses after six weeks, but had no horseshoes for the animals, which were straight off the range. Thus mounted practice was out of the question and the troops were reduced to stationary firing drills. And none of the men from Indiana had fired a shot in more than a year, not to mention that some of the recruits had never even heard a cannon fired.

Further reducing the efficiency of the National Guard organizations at Llano Grande was the lack of uniformity both in equipment and in the military appearance of the guardsmen. Some had new-model packs, while others still used the old shoulder roll pack. Some had the new bottle canteens, while others still had the old circular version. Uniforms were of different shades of khaki, and leggings were of different vintages. Some had the 1911 regulation .45-caliber automatic pistol, while others still used the old .38-caliber revolver.[70] And so forth.

Besides the National Guard, there were detachments of regulars stationed at a number of other localities in the region:

Kingsville	Companies K and M, 26th U.S. Infantry
Lyford	Company C, 26th U.S. Infantry
Madero	Company F, 28th U.S. Infantry
McAllen	Company G, 28th U.S. Infantry
Olmito	Company M, 4th U.S. Infantry
Peñitas	Company I, 28th U.S. Infantry
Progreso	Company B, 28th U.S. Infantry
Rabb's ranch	Troop A, 3rd U.S. Cavalry
San Juan	Companies D and E, 28th U.S. Infantry[71]

The 1st Illinois Cavalry led the way for the guard in getting down to business. The machine gun troop was certainly ready, having received five hundred thousand rounds of ammunition. The regiment developed a plan to repel any surprise attack on its camp—the third squadron and the machine gun troop formed the main line of resistance. Behind them the first squadron was in support, while the second squadron, mounted, was held in reserve to pursue when the attacking force had been repelled. As a signal honor, Troop A, the senior troop, reportedly became the first National Guard unit since the June 18 call-up to be assigned a sector of the Rio Grande to patrol—from the regiment's camp to a point six miles downriver.[72] Considerable excitement occurred on the night of July 30, when there was an attempt to raid the regiment's picket line. Sentries and patrols repelled the would-be raiders, and for the rest of the night there was sporadic gunfire, with some rounds whistling through the camp and soldiers diving for cover in their tents.[73]

On July 2, the War Department announced that all National Guard units would receive machine guns. The army had only 1,077 of these weapons, none having been acquired during the preceding three years pending a decision on which type to adopt. Ordnance Department boards had approved Vickers-Maxim guns tested in 1913 and 1914, but nothing had come of their recommendations. The Lewis gun was also tested and issued, but it was ultimately rejected, its rejection becoming the subject of controversy not only in the War Department and Congress but also in the press, since the British were employing the weapon successfully.[74] The army also tested the "best of all machine guns," the Browning but would not adopt it until 1917.[75] In Pershing's memoirs he discusses how the shortage of machine guns remained a major problem well into America's involvement in World War I.[76]

Regular units would receive Maxims, while National Guard units would be issued Lewis guns. Since the design and manufacture of pack outfits for these guns would have required a considerable time, five light Ford trucks per regiment were issued to transport the weapons.[77] The army's standard weapon was the Benet-Mercier, which had replaced the multibarreled Gatling gun in 1909. Unfortunately the Benet-Mercier was a temperamental weapon, difficult to use, and prone to jamming.[78] A shipment of the air-cooled Lewis guns arrived at Harlingen, and an officer and a noncom from the 2nd Virginia Infantry, the 1st, 2nd, and 3rd Indiana Infantry, the 1st Louisiana Infantry, and the 1st Oklahoma Infantry received instruction in their use.[79] In September, the secretary of war ordered the establishment of a temporary machine gun school at Harlingen. The machine gun company of each regiment was to receive two weeks of instruction. Complicating matters from a repair and ammunition supply standpoint, some regiments had Benet-Merciers, some had Lewis, and a couple had Maxim guns:[80]

Benet-Mercier	*Lewis*	*Maxim*
2nd Texas Infantry	3rd Texas Infantry	1st Illinois Cavalry
26th U.S. Infantry	1st Oklahoma Infantry	3rd U.S. Cavalry
7th New York Infantry	1st Indiana Infantry	
1st New York Cavalry	4th Nebraska Infantry	
1st Minnesota Infantry	2nd New York Infantry	
36th U.S. Infantry	1st Virginia Infantry	
1st Iowa Infantry	1st North Dakota Infantry	
2nd Minnesota Infantry	2nd Indiana Infantry	
4th South Dakota Infantry[81]	12th New York Infantry	
2nd Iowa Infantry	23rd New York Infantry	
3rd Minnesota Infantry	2nd Virginia Infantry	
3rd Iowa Infantry	5th Nebraska Infantry	
4th U.S. Infantry	3rd Indiana Infantry	
28th U.S. Infantry		

The army also made changes in command assignments. On July 26 it was announced at Fort Brown that General E. M. Lewis, formerly a lieutenant colonel in the U.S. Infantry and recently appointed a brigadier general in command of the Indiana Brigade, would command the camps at Llano Grande and the militia at Donna and Mercedes, except the 3rd Texas Infantry, still under Brigadier General John A. Hulen. In addition, Colonel A. P. Blocksom of the 3rd U.S. Cavalry was detailed to command the Nebraska and North Dakota regiments at Llano Grande and the North Dakota regiment at Mercedes.[82]

As was the case in San Antonio and elsewhere, the military had to contend with alarmist and even fabricated newspaper stories emanating from the press corps on the border. Many of these stories dealt with health conditions in the militia camps, a subject of considerable interest to the readers back home. For instance, a Chicago paper reported that an epidemic of dengue fever was raging in the 1st Illinois Cavalry. According to the Brownsville medical officer, there had been only one case of dengue at the camp, involving not a guardsman but a newspaper correspondent, and it was an exceedingly mild form. Another article asserted that thirty-six members of the Minnesota National Guard at Llano Grande were being treated for ptomaine poisoning, allegedly from eating canned tomatoes brought from Minnesota. Army officers denied the report. And a dispatch in the New York *Herald* alleged discontent among the militia at McAllen and unsatisfactory conditions in the base hospital at Brownsville. Stories of this kind led the army to threaten to impose censorship. Even the federal Bureau of Investigation resented having to waste considerable time and effort investigating groundless complaints from politicians who had read sensational stories in the press.[83]

What particularly irked the military was that extraordinary measures were in fact being taken to protect the men's health. Besides what the army and National Guard were doing, the city of Brownsville was spraying oil on mosquito-breeding surfaces, and the Public Health Service was implementing a plan to protect the troops against tropical diseases coming from Mexico. As part of this program, a modern fumigation plant was being built at the international ferry between Brownsville and Matamoros, and everyone entering from Mexico had to show proof of vaccination.[84]

In August, Fort Brown was elevated to the status of a division post. There were now in the Brownsville military district some fifty thousand regular and National Guard troops, more than any other section of the border. The army was engaged in organizing these units on a tactical basis, except the New York division stationed at McAllen, Mission, and Pharr.[85]

Two provisional brigades were formed in Brownsville:

***1st Provisional Brigade*, Colonel E. E. Hatch, 4th U.S. Infantry, commanding:**
4th and 36th U.S. Infantry; Companies A, B, F of the 1st Regiment of U.S. Engineers; a squadron of the 3rd U.S. Cavalry; Battery D of the 4th U.S. Field Artillery and Battery F of the 5th U.S. Field Artillery, organized as a provisional battalion; the 1st Illinois Cavalry; the 1st and 2nd Virginia Infantry; 1st Iowa Field Artillery Battalion; Iowa Field Hospital No. 1, Ambulance, and Engineer companies; U.S. Field Hospital No. 5; and Texas Field Hospital No. 1. Louisiana Field Hospital No. 1 (including many Tulane University medical students) was subsequently assigned to the 1st Provisional Brigade.

***2nd Provisional Brigade*, Iowa National Guard Brigadier H. A. Allen commanding:**
The Iowa Brigade (1st, 2nd, 3rd Iowa Infantry)[86]

Although only a brigadier general, Parker not only commanded the Brownsville District but had overall command of what amounted to an army corps: the two provisional brigades in Brownsville, one in San Benito, the Texas Brigade at Harlingen (and later at Corpus Christi), and the 13th Provisional Division composed of the Llano Grande units. (The New York and Pennsylvania divisions had their own commanding generals.) However the 13th was really a paper division. Brigadier General Lewis of the National Guard remained in command of these troops, and Parker would supersede him only in the event of an invasion of Mexico, which was now unlikely.[87]

On August 4, with the 4th U.S. Infantry band playing martial airs, the two Brownsville provisional infantry brigades, some seven thousand troops, passed in review before General Parker. (Only two men fainted while standing at attention in ranks waiting for the review to begin.) With the band again playing, the brigades then paraded through Brownsville. Thousands of civilians witnessed the event, and cameramen from several newsreel companies recorded it for posterity.[88] Three days later Parker conducted a mounted review—of all cavalry, artillery, trucks, ambulances, and motorcycles stationed in Brownsville.[89] Again, thousands of civilians witnessed this five-mile-long display of military might.

General Parker's training program for the militia eventually involved 90 regular officers and 162 noncoms as instructors.[90] The program included something unusual—an exercise to protect Brownsville from invasion by sea through Point Isabel.[91] The units involved were the 1st and 2nd Virginia Infantry, and the original plan was for them to march to Point Isabel, but they were transported in fifty trucks, accompanied by General Parker. Besides giving the Virginians field experience in target practice, the exercise was the first test of Fort Brown's truck transportation, and it proved successful.[92] The Virginians duly repelled the imaginary invader. The second phase of the maneuver involved transporting the Virginians, now transformed into the seaborne invaders, by truck to seize the rail junction at San Benito. To repel this "attack" the entire provisional National Guard brigade stationed at San Benito took the field. The exercise involved some five thousand militia, sweating under the critical eyes of army umpires. The weary Virginians were then driven back to their camps in Brownsville.[93]

In Brownsville, a tragic footnote occurred when a few days later Corporal James L. Clement, Company C, 2nd Virginia Infantry, gallantly answered a call for help from a sixteen-year-old Hispanic girl who was being assaulted by a drunken quartermaster corporal, who insisted that she marry him. He shot and killed Clement and critically wounded the girl.[94]

The San Benito Provisional Brigade published a weekly newspaper, awkwardly titled *The Oklasoda*—combining parts of the names of its three infantry regiments: Oklahoma, Louisiana, and South Dakota. The newspaper had little use for military "slackers," characterizing them as being worse than cowards. It was the second National Guard newspaper in the district, the first being the 1st Illinois Cavalry's light-hearted and appropriately titled *The Illinois Cavalryman*, which had a circulation of five thousand and was edited by a score of Chicago newspapermen serving in the regiment.[95] Several other militia newspapers appeared in subsequent months, among them *The Border Virginian* and *The Iowa Guardsman*.[96]

The 1st Illinois Cavalry engaged in an exercise with an eye to what was happening on the Western Front in France—trench warfare. They dug an intricate complex of trenches and connecting trenches, topped by breastworks, near the regiment's camp, having to use ordinary spades because as cavalry they were not issued entrenching tools. The following day they fought a prolonged sham battle, expending large quantities of blank ammunition and having a great time doing so.[97]

An important aspect of the National Guard experience was the entertainment program Parker formulated: a regimental baseball league; frequent band concerts in camp and in town; whenever possible, movies; weekly military dances; a polo tournament with weekly games in the larger towns; tennis; field days and gymkhanas at each camp or regiment.[98] The first field day took place on August 16 at the various camps, with competitors from both the army and National Guard representing virtually every battery, troop, and company. The events included the 100- and 220-yard dash, broad and high jump, horseshoe pitching, wall scaling by squads over an eight-foot wall, boxing, and wrestling, with prizes for the winners. Several weeks later a water field day was held at Fort Brown, the competitions including swimming, bareback horse riding, and boat combats. The boats, incidentally, were wagons with their canvas tops wrapped around them, a technique that Parker had developed during his earlier career.[99] There was also of course the time-honored army sport of polo, played enthusiastically by officers. But there was also an anomaly—at the Harlingen camps, not only did officers engage in polo but, and this was startling, enlisted men got to play a game: a team from the 26th U.S. Infantry took on one from the San Benito militia brigade and lost, 4 to 2.[100]

Entertainment included visiting personages. The most distinguished military visitor in 1916 was Major General Frederick Funston, who arrived in his private railroad car. Parker and his entourage met Funston at the station and escorted him to Fort Brown for lunch. Immediately thereafter, Funston inspected the Iowa and Virginia encampments, then presided from General Parker's front porch at an equipment review parade of all wagon trains and army trucks at Fort Brown. Leading the parade were three companies of three-ton trucks; these ninety-nine vehicles were capable of transporting three complete regiments with their tents and equipment. There followed a long line of wagons drawn by massive army mules, then the ambulances of the field hospitals, and the kitchen and mess wagons, led by the 1st Illinois Cavalry's three portable kitchens. Funston declared himself pleased with what he saw during the hour-long review. The general followed this by reviewing the 1st Illinois Cavalry, which passed by flashing sabers at the salute, and the 2nd Iowa Infantry. Following a reception at the Fort Brown officers' pavilion Funston retired to his private car and left the next morning to inspect other National Guard camps in the lower Rio Grande Valley before returning to San Antonio.[101]

The most distinguished civilian visitor was Governor Edward F. Dunne of Illinois. After visiting the Illinois troops at Camp Wilson in San Antonio, the governor, his wife, and his staff were met by General Parker at the depot. The 3rd Squadron of the Illinois Cavalry escorted the visitors to Fort Brown, where a seventeen-gun salute greeted the governor. He then reviewed the 1st Illinois Cavalry and enjoyed a luncheon that Parker hosted in his honor. That evening the governor and his party were guests of honor at a banquet and reception at the 1st Illinois Cavalry camp. Governor Dunne spent most of the next day conducting a detailed inspection of the camp and gathering information for a report to his constituents. Dunne expressed his great satisfaction with the troops' condition. That night Major McCormick of the Illinois regiment and his wife were the hosts at the local country club for the visiting delegation and about one hundred officers and their guests.[102]

Governor Dunne and his party got to experience one of the facts of life on the Gulf Coast—hurricanes. One blew into Brownsville during the late afternoon of August 18. The weather was so menacing that General Parker issued an order to all commanding officers specifying how units might have to take temporary shelter in the town of Brownsville: "The regiments will march equipped for the field and carry two days' cooked rations and receptacles for making coffee; candles and lamps will be taken."[103] Fortunately the hurricane was not a devastating one, and Brownsville escaped the brunt of it. Although hit with fifty- to sixty-mile-an-hour winds and torrential rains, the city suffered only moderate damage, mainly to fences, trees, and roofs. Luckily nothing critical occurred, and the worst blow the military suffered was that the telephone and telegraph lines went down, cutting Brownsville off from the outside world for a week. At the military camps damage was largely confined to tents blown down and their contents drenched. The 36th U.S. Infantry and the Iowa brigade were the worst sufferers. The Virginia camp fared better, while the Illinois cavalry encampment escaped major damage. It was the only camp not blown down because the tents had been floored and framed by private subscription raised by the regiment's colonel after Secretary of War Baker had refused local commanders' request for lumber.[104] Public buildings and churches in Brownsville were opened as shelters for temporarily homeless troops. General Parker inspected the Virginia and Iowa camps east of the city and announced that he was quite pleased with the troops' conduct during the hurricane and with the energetic way they had repaired the damage.[105]

The storm delayed a five-regiment exercise in which the 1st and 2nd Virginia Infantry defended an irrigation canal outside Brownsville against an attack by the Iowa brigade. Supporting the maneuver were Battery F of the 5th U.S. Field Artillery with its heavy guns and Battery D of the 4th U.S. Field Artillery, which had pack howitzers. And the 1st Illinois Cavalry's machine gun troop engaged in maneuvers for the first time—a nine-mile march followed by target practice. Twenty-eight pack mules carried the unit's guns and equipment.[106]

On the night of August 30, Company A of the 1st Minnesota Infantry was stationed at the Mercedes pumping station. Four shots were fired at their position from the Mexican bank of the Rio Grande. This resulted in a general exchange of fire with about 150 rounds being fired. There were no American casualties; Mexican casualties were unknown.[107]

On August 30, General Funston ordered the Texas Brigade (Brigadier General John Hulen, his headquarters, and the 2nd and 3rd Texas Infantry) transferred from Harlingen to Corpus Christi, but the brigade remained under Parker's jurisdiction.[108] Company G, 2nd Virginia Infantry, relieved the company of the 3rd Texas Infantry that had been guarding the navy's radio station at Point Isabel. The 28th U.S. Infantry at Fort Ringgold in Rio Grande City relieved the companies of the 2nd Texas Infantry stationed at Roma, Sam Fordyce, and Peñitas because the regiment was concentrating at Harlingen for its move to Corpus Christi.[109]

General Parker conducted his initial inspection of the 13th Provisional Division on September 6. That organization was far from combat ready. For instance, the Indiana Field Artillery had only recently received its horses. Furthermore, Battery B, 1st Indiana Field Artillery, and Battery F, 1st Minnesota Field Artillery, both composed of college students, would be returning to their mobilization camps to be mustered out. The 2nd Battalion, 1st Minnesota Field Artillery, had had a narrow escape on July 23 on its way to Brownsville. The seven hundred men were asleep while their train was taking on water. Another train rammed into it at thirty miles an hour, injuring eight men.[110] The 1st Louisiana Infantry at San Benito had already departed for Alexandria, Louisiana, to be mustered out. After spending three days at Llano Grande, Parker's evaluation was that the division, and especially the officers, still had much to learn.[111]

Parker's program of rigorous training for the National Guard continued. Bugles blasted the 1st Iowa Brigade awake at midnight on September 8. By twelve thirty the entire brigade had assembled and began marching to Fort Brown, and at one o'clock the Iowans reported at district headquarters at the fort. They then marched back to their camp, and by two o'clock the four thousand soldiers were asleep again. The exercise was pronounced a success.[112] The same type of problem was posed a few nights later on a larger scale—how quickly could infantry regiments turn out at night making as little noise as possible and report to a brigade commander at a concentration point a mile or so away fully armed and ready to go into action? The organization involved was the 1st Provisional Brigade (4th and 36th U.S. Infantry and the 1st and 2nd Virginia Infantry). Bugles roused all four camps at eleven o'clock. The 1st Virginia Infantry excelled, marching with its complete equipment in pitch darkness over a muddy road in a torrential downpour and arriving at the concentration point in exactly one hour, followed by the 4th U.S., the 2nd Virginia, and the 36th U.S. The four regiments had reached their objective within a span of sixteen minutes.[113]

The 1st Illinois Cavalry attempted three practice marches with its horses:

> Only one squadron could ride at a time, because to put one squadron on horse left the other two squadrons on the ground. The horses walked about eighteen miles on each of the two days. They marched at a rate less than two and a quarter miles per hour, which is also less than the infantry rate. These marches so exhausted the horses that the third squadron never had its march. . . . After two months' presence on the border this regiment, when ordered to move twenty-six miles to Point Isabel for maneuvers, had to send a large number of its men on motor trucks.[114]

The guardsmen spent eight days at Point Isabel training under the direction of the regular inspector-instructor. Although it was now September, not all of the authorized horses had been issued; those lacking horses, as well as the hospital company, traveled in trucks. The regiment took its water wagons, portable field kitchens, and so forth. Only two or three men fell out and one horse died on the way. Immediately upon arrival, the colonel prudently ordered all saloons in Point Isabel closed for the duration.[115] Besides a correspondent from the Chicago *Daily News* the Illini brought with them a cameraman from Chicago to film their daily drills and maneuvers to be shown in Chicago and other Illinois cities. In reporting this story, the *Brownsville Daily Herald* enthusiastically noted that the film would advertise the tourist attractions of Point Isabel.[116] The regiment had a difficult trip back to Camp Parker due to flooding from the Rio Grande, which was at its highest stage in four years. Slogging their way through the overflow, about ten miles from the coast they encountered three feet of water on the road for about half a mile, forcing them to leave the portable kitchens and some of the trucks until conditions improved. Still, their colonel and the regular inspector-instructor pronounced themselves quite pleased with the way the exercise had gone.[117]

The 1st Illinois Cavalry operated under another disadvantage—a shortage of saddles. Urgent appeals to Southern Department headquarters in San Antonio finally resulted in a partial shipment of saddles, but they were less than top quality. The cases in which they came were marked "1898," the leather was beginning to disintegrate, and the saddles were impregnated with salt for the cases had been salvaged from Galveston harbor after the great 1900 hurricane.[118]

Despite these handicaps the 1st Illinois Cavalry conducted a novel maneuver—an all-night "hide-and-seek" exercise. The object was for the 1st and 3rd Squadrons to locate and attack the 2nd Squadron and for the 2nd either to elude or repel the attackers. The 2nd left Camp Parker early in the morning to take cover in the brush somewhere within an eight-mile radius of the camp. Camp kitchens, hospital troops, and supply wagons all participated in the maneuver. Patrols from the 1st and 3rd Squadrons searched all night but failed to locate the 2nd. The latter's camp, on the San Benito road, was finally revealed early the next day by a 1st Squadron scout, who had been "wounded and captured" by an outpost of the 2nd Squadron and had escaped after being left on the field for "dead." It turned out that the 2nd Squadron had protected itself so well with outposts that enemy scouts could not approach within five miles of the camp—45 percent of the 2nd Squadron had been placed on outpost duty.[119]

Some National Guard officers received training on an individual basis. For instance, a lieutenant of the 3rd Iowa Infantry was assigned to command a regular truck company, composed of thirty-three 1 1/2-ton Packard trucks sent to Brownsville, and from there transferred to Laredo. These were light trucks compared with the heavy 3-ton Peerless trucks that had been used in the city for the past two months. Unfortunately, the Peerless trucks had torn up the pavement so badly that they were now used only to transport freight between the railroad station and the quartermaster depot. Another Peerless truck company came overland from Fort Sam Houston to be used for the same purpose. Two more light truck companies were also coming, making a total of fifteen companies (495 trucks) in the Brownsville military district.[120] One of these had been the first truck company sent into Mexico with the Punitive Expedition. It was transferred to San Benito.[121]

BORDER SERVICE

While training and the routine of camp life occupied most of the men's time, there were enough shooting incidents to make the troops take their training seriously. About 175 men had been left back at the 1st Illinois Cavalry's camp while the rest of the regiment was at Point Isabel. On the night of September 16, horse thieves tried to raid the picket line. Sentries fired eight to ten rounds at them, but the thieves escaped into the brush.[122] And a few days earlier a lieutenant of the 3rd Iowa Infantry on outpost duty at the Naranjos ranch, twelve miles downriver from Brownsville, was standing on the riverbank when two rounds whizzed by him from the Mexican side of the Rio Grande. He fired back once with his pistol at several forms running through the brush but without result. Several times during the past few months shots had been fired from across the river at this point.[123]

The military's impact on Brownsville was profound. For one thing, the army forced the city to institute some reforms, however reluctantly. The municipal market, especially the meat market, was cleaned up when the army placed an embargo on it, and to emphasize the point an MP guard was placed at the entrance. The deficiencies were rapidly corrected, the embargo was lifted, and the city health officer began prosecuting violations of the municipal sanitary code.[124] The state pure food inspector found great improvement since his first visit three years earlier.

In addition, the post commander at Fort Brown issued an order prohibiting enlisted men as of October 4 from entering any saloon or place where intoxicants were sold. The MPs enforced the order, issued because of flagrant violations of the liquor laws at beer joints that flourished at night on the outskirts of Brownsville. A subsequent crackdown on gambling involved the MPs gathering most of the evidence to close down roulette, poker, and other games that had proliferated in the business and outlying districts of Brownsville for the last several months.[125]

The army also pumped tens of thousands of dollars into the local economy by way of construction. Four entire blocks near downtown became the site of a base army vehicle repair facility, and sites were secured for the building of large supply warehouses. The military, furthermore, had an indirect effect on construction—a large amount of track was laid to store dozens of tank cars for military use.[126]

But the army's most immediate impact was through its payroll. On September 12, it amounted to $175,000.[127] As we have seen, Brownsville really lit up on payday. The arriving trains were loaded with soldiers on weekend leave. All available rooms were occupied, and the city placed cots in the spacious corporation courtroom in city hall to provide free accommodation for those unable to obtain lodging. The local newspaper ran an editorial urging its readers not to gouge the visitors: "The business houses of Brownsville, the restaurants, confectionary stores and curio stores have thrived and flourished as a result of the soldier trade. . . . While the army was not sent here for the purpose of enriching the merchants of this section, no reasonable person could nor will complain on that score." The paper also commented on the shortage of rental cottages in Brownsville and encouraged investment in this type of property.[128]

Reflecting the military impact were the deposits in the local banks: "The banking and financial situation in Brownsville is declared to be exceptionally good." In the first published statements since the troops' arrival, the Merchants' National Bank broke all records, showing total assets in excess of $2 million for the quarter ending September 2, an increase of $200,000 over the previous quarter. The total deposits in Brownsville banks were $600,000 over those for the quarter ending in June. The First National Bank reported a $300,000 increase, with total deposits of nearly $1 million. The merchants' total deposits approached $1.5 million.[129] Brownsville had never had it so good.

The surrounding towns also basked in unaccustomed affluence. The local newspaper reported, for instance, that San Benito had been "hard hit with prosperity," as reflected by the deposits in local banks on November 17, 1916, as compared with the same date a year earlier. The San Benito Bank & Trust had gone from $113,369 to $222,589, an increase of $109,220; the Farmers' State Guaranty Bank from $109,144 to $176,666, an increase of $67,522; and the First State Bank of Rio Hondo from $9,828 to $15,294, an increase of $5,466.[130]

By the end of September what was on most of the troops' mind was whether their unit would be recalled for mustering out. An article in the *Illinois Cavalryman*, commenting on a current rumor, was entitled "One Consolation, We're Going Back." The Illini were just homesick and were heartily sick of Texas.[131] And the Iowans were getting rambunctious. One night two hundred of them paraded through the business district of Brownsville, led by the regimental band and dressed in pajamas, shouting at the top of their lungs and cutting boyish capers in the streets. Neither the MPs nor the municipal police interfered.[132] Partly to keep the soldiers' minds on their work and partly to advertise to the public the level of proficiency they had reached, General Parker instituted a policy of daily regimental parades.[133]

There was also a parade and an exhibition drill at Fort Brown on September 23 by the 2nd Squadron of the 3rd U.S. Cavalry. The spectacle involved a saber drill, a parade at a march, trot, and gallop, and for the climax machine guns and cavalrymen in action. This involved a spectacular charge against the machine gun troop in which three troops of cavalry attacked brandishing their pistols. A second charge followed in which machine guns met charging troops with rapid fire. The horsemen dismounted at once, formed a skirmish line, and sent their horses to the rear at a gallop, every fourth man taking his and three others' horses. After a sharp engagement, the horses were brought to the front, the troopers mounted and galloped to the rear. The salient feature of this exercise was the rapidity with which machine guns were taken from pack horses and placed in position and again dismantled and repacked and the rapidity with which the cavalry dismounted and remounted and got their horses to the rear out of machine gun range, then returning them to the front.[134]

No doubt this exhibition thrilled the many spectators, but it also demonstrated that the army had learned absolutely nothing from the clash with the Mexicans at Carrizal in June, not to mention developments on the Western Front. Cavalry charges might be glamorous, but in actual warfare troopers charging into machine gun fire with pistol in hand were liable to be dead meat, as the Carrizal affair had already shown. The army's love affair with the horse lasted long after the relative uselessness of horse cavalry in modern warfare had been conclusively demonstrated. Not until February 1943 did the 1st Cavalry Division at Fort Bliss reluctantly turn in their mounts and become infantrymen.

The 1st Illinois Cavalry participated in a midnight "surprise attack" exercise in which the regiment stormed the city of Brownsville and captured it. Within an hour other National Guard units had mobilized to expel the attackers. Eventually some eleven thousand troops, including cavalry, infantry, artillery, machine gun companies, and hospital companies swarmed through the streets of the city in what was described as one of the most comprehensive military maneuvers ever held in Brownsville. "The civilian population, accustomed to border excitement, was given an unusual thrill."[135]

People near San Benito also experienced some excitement on the night of October 5, when four heavily armed Mexicans crossed the river at Scott's ranch and attacked field hands. A detachment of eight Oklahoma infantrymen as well as some soldiers from the 4th South Dakota set out from San Benito in pursuit. As a precaution, the army reinforced the guards along the railroad between Brownsville and Harlingen and placed a detail aboard a passenger train heading for Brownsville.[136]

This excitement could not compare with that at Camp Parker when word reached the 1st Illinois Cavalry that they were going home after three and a half months of border service. It will be remembered that they were the first National Guard organization to arrive in Brownsville in July. The ecstatic cavalrymen began loading their trains in preparation for their journey on October 16 via Houston and New Orleans to Fort Sheridan, Illinois, and mustering out. But the War Department decided to send only half of the 1st Illinois Cavalry home, keeping the rest of the regiment in Brownsville.[137]

Replacing the Illinois regiment in its camp was a provisional cavalry regiment composed of Troops A, B, and C of Colorado cavalry, the 1st Squadron 1st Virginia Cavalry (the aristocratic Richmond Blues), and Troop A New Hampshire Cavalry.[138]

Some eleven thousand men paraded on November 1 for General Parker at the historic Mexican War battlefield of Resaca de la Palma, four miles from Brownsville, where General Zachary Taylor had defeated a Mexican army. Parker ordered the review in honor of Major General Arthur Murray, chairman of the executive committee of the American Red Cross Society, retired Brigadier General W. P. Hall, and Brigadier General William G. Rosier from Fort Sam Houston. This was the only review of all the regular and National Guard troops stationed in the Brownsville vicinity.[139] The big news, however, was that Parker was planning a massive maneuver to repel an imaginary invasion.[140]

The Iowa and Virginia guardsmen stationed in Brownsville since early in the summer were probably griping about the sultry weather when they had their first experience with a real Texas norther, on November 13. The wind came up suddenly out of the northwest accompanied by a drenching rain, dropping the temperature by dusk to thirty-five degrees. The twenty-five-mile-an-hour wind and the rain lasted only a few minutes, but a number of tents at the camps were blown over. The unusually frigid weather forced a brief postponement of the large-scale maneuver Parker had ordered.[141]

On November 16 the maneuver, which represented the climax of the National Guard experience in the Brownsville District, got under way. It involved some twenty-three thousand regulars and guardsmen, was scheduled to last twelve days, and was called the most elaborate exercise yet attempted by the army in peacetime. Parker served as the chief umpire, assisted by the two regular officers handling militia instruction in the Brownsville District and a host of regular and National Guard umpires in the field. The exercise had three objectives: to serve as a test for the new troops, to prepare the new troops, and to discover deficiencies and determine to what extent this component of the military was fit for wartime service.

The scenario supposed that a foreign nation was intervening in Mexico and its army, the "Browns," had invaded the United States at Point Isabel and was encamped at Olmito, eight miles north of Brownsville, with the intention of attacking the next day the advance guard (one brigade) of the defending "White" army at San Benito and forcing it across the Arroyo Colorado. The script then called for the invaders to encounter a large force of the "White" army and be driven back to the vicinity of Point Isabel. The maneuver would continue day and night, exactly as in real warfare, and would range across the flat lower Rio Grande valley, intersected by numerous irrigation canals and ditches, with the western limit covered by mesquite and chaparral and the eastern part by the coast. The exercise not only provided officers with badly needed experience in commanding large formations but also practical experience in solving logistical problems such as supplying water to the huge number of men and animals. Transportation included four truck companies, field and combat wagons, wagon trains, and three pack trains.

Brigadier General E. H. Lewis of the Indiana National Guard commanded the "White" army of more than ten thousand regulars and guardsmen from camps at Donna, Mercedes, Llano Grande, Harlingen, and San Benito:

Indiana Infantry Brigade
Minnesota Infantry Brigade
Nebraska–North Dakota Infantry Brigade
Oklahoma–South Dakota–26th U.S. Infantry Brigade
Provisional Artillery Brigade
2nd Provisional Cavalry Brigade
Provisional Cavalry Regiment

Commanding the "Brown" maneuver division was Brigadier General Hubert A. Allen of the Iowa National Guard, assisted by regular officers as chief and assistant chief of staff. The "Brown" army consisted of some eleven thousand troops stationed at Brownsville:

Iowa Brigade
Virginia Brigade
1st Provisional Cavalry Regiment (Virginia, New Hampshire, Colorado cavalry, and one squadron from the 3rd U.S. Cavalry)
Two U.S. field artillery battalions
Engineer companies
Signal Corps companies
Field Hospital companies[142]

The "Brown" army captured San Benito, sweeping the advance brigade of the "Whites" before them but not until the "Brown" cavalry regiment was almost annihilated by heavy "White" machine gun fire. The "Whites" wore white bandages around their arm and were posted on the tops of buildings throughout the town. When the "Browns" entered San Benito their adversaries scattered and many were captured. No rifle firing was allowed. Occasional machine gun fire with blank cartridges was permitted in defense of bridges, three of which were theoretically destroyed by the retreating troops. As the "Whites" retreated from San Benito they received powerful reinforcements from a brigade of artillery and a cavalry regiment who made a notable thirty-mile forced march from Llano Grande. This came as a complete surprise to the "Brown" army, who had believed that such reinforcement could not arrive for at least another day.[143]

On November 20, the war game came to an abrupt truce when both commanders claimed to have scored a decisive victory. The "Browns" unleashed an envelopment movement on the San Benito–Harlingen road and claimed to have captured virtually the entire "White" army; at the same time the "Whites" attacked the "Brown" center and claimed to have captured their headquarters. Both sides appealed to Parker for a decision, which turned out to be the aforementioned temporary truce, a declaration that neither army had been victorious, and a resumption of the maneuver the following day, the "Browns" retreating toward Brownsville with the "Whites" pursuing.[144]

The "Browns" established a seven-mile defensive position north and east of Brownsville, while the "Whites" prepared to cut the enemy's line of communications with their base at Point Isabel. However, the "Browns" advanced to attack the "Whites" and in doing so on November 23 reoccupied the 1846 Mexican War battlefield of Palo Alto. The "Browns" claimed a decisive victory as a result of outmaneuvering and surrounding their adversaries. The gigantic exercise concluded with a bang on November 24 at another Mexican War battlefield, Resaca de la Palma, where the two armies expended more than three hundred thousand rounds of blank ammunition.[145]

Parker expressed great satisfaction with the entire war game, commenting that the maneuvers had hardened the guardsmen to the extent that they could now stand almost any kind of military work. Three months ago, he added, few guardsmen could have endured the nine days' strenuous work in the field. Evidence of the men's conditioning was that of the twenty-three thousand, fewer than four hundred had reported sick, and most of these had quickly returned to duty. The exercise had also provided guard officers with an invaluable opportunity to command and maneuver large formations.

The following morning, November 25, Parker reviewed the contending armies at the Resaca de la Palma battlefield, a review witnessed by thousands of civilians who came from throughout the Lower Valley. From the reviewing stand Parker telegraphed to President Wilson: "After a course of strenuous training, lasting for five months, and culminating in a marching maneuver of eight days duration, 23,000 men, massed in review on the historic battlefield of Resaca De La Palma, salute you."[146]

The next day the men were given a day's leave in Brownsville (to the delight of the local merchants). The twenty-three thousand troops thronged the streets, nearly doubling the city's usual population. Restaurants, confectionaries, and motion picture theaters were forced to close their doors to keep out the crowds. After the day's relaxation, the "Whites" returned to their camps at Llano Grande, San Benito, Harlingen, and Mercedes.[147] Some of those marching to Llano Grande went through Harlingen: "About six thousand troops which are stationed at Llano Grande are spending the night in Harlingen on their return hike from Brownsville, where they took part in the field maneuvers and parade. Restaurants and confectionaries are overtaxed tonight."[148] To add to the soldiers' pleasure, there arrived twenty-five thousand pounds of turkey for the Thanksgiving dinners of those in the Brownsville District.[149]

Best of all, General Funston announced that some guard units would be returning home and would not be replaced. Among them were the 3rd Indiana Infantry and the 3rd Minnesota Infantry at Llano Grande. They would leave as soon as rail transportation could be arranged. Both regiments had formed part of the "White" army. Immediately upon the conclusion of the maneuver they were returned by truck to Llano Grande, where they boarded trains for home.[150] On December 8 it was announced that the 1st Iowa Infantry and the 1st Iowa Field Artillery Battalion[151] would be returning home from Brownsville.

Fort Brown announced on December 19 that as quickly as rail transportation could be arranged, units would be going home in three groups: in the first group were Company A Iowa Engineers; Company A Indiana Signal Corps, Indiana Ambulance Company No. 1, 1st Indiana Artillery Battalion less Battery D, and 4th Nebraska Infantry. The 4th Nebraska left Brownsville on December 27 with 777 men and 53 officers. It arrived in Omaha on New Year's Eve. Several companies of the 4th Nebraska, mustered out at Fort Crook, Nebraska, on January 15, 1917, were so incensed by a War Department order to turn their uniforms in to the state that they destroyed them, arguing that they had purchased the uniforms themselves.[152] The 5th Nebraska returned from the border on February 9 and was demobilized at Fort Crook on February 22.[153]

In group two was the 1st Virginia Infantry. In group three Indiana Field Hospital No. 3, Minnesota brigade headquarters, 2nd Minnesota Infantry, and 1st North Dakota Infantry.[154] The 1st Virginia Infantry had endeared itself to the citizens of Brownsville. When the regiment left on January 2, 1917, to parade in New Orleans on the way home to be mustered out at Richmond, the *Brownsville Daily Herald* ran an editorial entitled "Bon Voyage, Virginians."[155]

But not all traffic was homeward bound. Fort Brown announced that an Indiana ambulance company had been ordered to the border. It had just been mustered in at Indianapolis and was en route to Llano Grande to replace a sister unit. The 1st Minnesota Infantry left Llano Grande but not for home; it was transferred to Camp Wilson in San Antonio to replace a departing regiment in the 12th Provisional Division.[156]

There was also a novel arrival at Fort Brown—an armored car built at the government arsenal at Rock Island, Illinois. It was of the same type as that recently sent to the Big Bend from Fort Sam Houston. The vehicle sported solid rubber tires, was as long as an ordinary seven-passenger touring car, was ten feet high from the ground to the top of the turret, traveled at twenty to twenty-five miles an hour on fairly good roads, and had a three-man crew (driver, gunner, loader). Three machine guns were included in the car's equipment, but only one gun could be mounted at any one time. The armored car was assigned to the lieutenant commanding the motorcycle detachment of the 4th U.S. Infantry and would be field tested at some later date.[157]

An unusual unit at Fort Brown was a light pontoon outfit, commanded by a captain, that had been at the engineers' camp for several months. It was transferred in December to Fort Ringgold in Rio Grande City. The pontoon wagons were towed by army trucks the eighty-five miles to their new destination, and an engineer detachment was stationed at Ringgold to instruct the garrison in the use of pontoons. A heavy pontoon outfit brought to Fort Brown a few weeks earlier remained in Brownsville, just in case the heavy artillery ever needed to cross the Rio Grande.[158]

Once Major General John O'Ryan of the New York National Guard left to return home, Parker became the highest-ranking officer in the Brownsville military district and as such automatically assumed command of the remaining New York Guard units in the district. For example, he reviewed the 2nd New York Infantry at McAllen.[159]

The Southern Department then ordered a complete reorganization of the National Guard in the Brownsville District effective January 10, 1917, a measure that involved transferring some units to a new station in order to facilitate administration.[160]

The 13th Provisional Division, consisting of three infantry brigades, one cavalry brigade, one artillery brigade, engineers, signal corps, and division trains, was retained. In addition, there were the 2nd and 6th Separate Brigades:

13th Provisional Division: **Brigadier General James Parker commanding. Headquarters: Brownsville** (The entire staff was transferred from Llano Grande.)[161]

1st Infantry Brigade: Brigadier General E. M. Lewis, Indiana National Guard, commanding. Headquarters: Llano Grande
   1st Indiana Infantry
   2nd Indiana Infantry
   5th Nebraska Infantry

2nd Infantry Brigade: Brigadier General James W. Lester, New York National Guard, commanding. Headquarters: McAllen
   12th New York Infantry
   69th New York Infantry
   74th New York Infantry

Brownsville and Llano Grande

3rd Infantry Brigade: Colonel Robert L. Bullard, 26th U.S. Infantry, commanding. Headquarters: San Benito
  3rd Tennessee Infantry
  1st Oklahoma Infantry
  4th South Dakota Infantry

Artillery Brigade: Brigadier General William S. McNair, New York National Guard, commanding. Headquarters: McAllen
  3rd New York Field Artillery (4.7" howitzers)—McAllen
  1st Minnesota Field Artillery, less Battery F—Llano Grande
  1st Louisiana Field Artillery Battalion—McAllen
  Battery D Indiana Field Artillery—Llano Grande
  Battery A Texas Field Artillery—Corpus Christi

Cavalry Brigade: Colonel A. P. Blocksom, 3rd U.S. Cavalry, commanding. Headquarters: McAllen
  1st New York Cavalry—McAllen
  1st Squadron 1st Iowa Cavalry—Llano Grande
  Troop A 1st Kansas Cavalry—Llano Grande
  Troops A and B 1st Oklahoma Cavalry—Llano Grande
  1st Squadron 1st Colorado Cavalry—Brownsville
  1st Squadron 1st Virginia Cavalry—Brownsville
  Troop A 1st New Hampshire Cavalry—Brownsville

Engineers
  Company A Oklahoma Engineers—Llano Grande

Signal Corps
  Company A Nebraska Signal Corps—Llano Grande

Division Trains
  MEDICAL
  New York Ambulance Company No. 4—McAllen
  New York Field Hospital No. 4—McAllen
  Indiana Ambulance Company No. 2—Llano Grande
  Indiana Field Hospital Company No. 2—Llano Grande
  Nebraska Field Hospital Company No. 1—Llano Grande
  Louisiana Field Hospital Company No. 1—Brownsville
  Iowa Ambulance Company No. 1—Brownsville
  Iowa Field Hospital Company No. 1—Brownsville
  Texas Field Hospital Company No. 1—Corpus Christi
  Oklahoma Field Hospital Company No. 1—San Benito

SUPPLY
>   New York Field Bakery—McAllen
>   New York Supply Train—McAllen

1st Separate Brigade: abolished

2nd Separate Brigade: Brigadier General H. A. Allen, Iowa National Guard, commanding. Headquarters: Brownsville.
>   2nd Iowa Infantry—Brownsville
>   3rd Iowa Infantry—Brownsville
>   2nd Virginia Infantry—Brownsville

6th Separate Brigade: Brigadier General John A. Hulen, Texas National Guard, commanding. Headquarters: Corpus Christi
>   2nd Texas Infantry—Corpus Christi
>   3rd Texas Infantry—Corpus Christi
>   4th Texas Infantry—Big Bend
>   1st Texas Cavalry Squadron—Big Bend

The 2nd and 6th Separate Brigades were attached to the 13th Provisional Division for court-martial purposes, administration, and instruction.[162]

The regular troops in the Brownsville District were also formed into a provisional brigade, Colonel E. E. Hatch, 4th U.S. Infantry commanding:

> 1st U.S. Engineer Regiment, less Companies C, D, E, F
> 2nd U.S. Signal Corps Field Battalion
> 2nd Squadron, 3rd U.S. Cavalry
> Battery D, 4th U.S. Field Artillery
> Battery F, 5th U.S. Field Artillery
> 4th U.S. Infantry
> 36th U.S. Infantry
> U.S. Field Hospital No. 5
> U.S. Ambulance Company No. 5
> U.S. Pack Train No. 17[163]

Under the reorganization the most heterogeneous organization was the provisional National Guard cavalry brigade, with units from New York, Iowa, Kansas, Oklahoma, and Colorado.[164] General Parker not only reviewed the brigade but found work for it to do. There was unrest in the vicinity of Zapata County, at the western edge of the Brownsville District, as a result of filibuster activity. Groups of conservative Mexican exiles opposed to the Carranza regime were slipping across the Rio Grande into Mexico. Parker assigned the 1st New York Cavalry to patrol the river from McAllen upriver across a portion of Hidalgo County, across Starr County, and nearly halfway across Zapata County, to the district boundary. While the New Yorkers had frequently patrolled the river in Hidalgo County, this was the first time that they had been assigned such an extensive territory. Their mission was to enforce the neutrality laws and to guard against bandit raids from Mexico. Troop B Virginia Cavalry was detailed to patrol another twenty-mile stretch of the river.

Parker also assigned the infantry units at McAllen, Llano Grande, and San Benito to patrol their sectors of the river.[165] Company A 2nd Iowa Infantry went to Point Isabel to guard the naval radio station and Company B of the same regiment had outpost duty at Brulay's ranch, both assignments lasting a week. The 3rd New York Artillery came to Brownsville for target practice at the Loma Alta range.[166]

But the big news from January 1917 on was about the units going home. General Parker was quite concerned about his ability to protect the border without the National Guard. He currently had twenty-four detachments guarding fords and patrolling along 150 miles of the Rio Grande as well as numerous troops deployed along the railroad. The guard's absence would necessitate a major redeployment of the insufficient regular units.[167] The guard's withdrawal also sparked renewed rivalry among some towns to have the remaining regular units stationed in their localities. San Benito requested that General Funston transfer the 26th U.S. Infantry from Harlingen to San Benito, emphasizing that no matter what Harlingen offered San Benito would beat it. Harlingen boosters promptly asserted that they were not asking to retain the 26th, the ordnance headquarters, and the quartermaster depot just to make money out of the army but because Harlingen was the logical location because of its facilities. Besides, the troops liked being stationed in Harlingen.[168]

General Parker apprised General Funston of his plans for breaking up the 13th Division as the guard left the Brownsville District and, in view of the imminence of war with Germany, for establishing a training cantonment in Brownsville in the camps vacated by the Iowa and Virginia brigades. Parker recommended an immediate halt to the dismantling of the National Guard camps, for, as was the case the summer before, almost a month of training was lost by the establishment of new encampments. That month of training might be infinitely precious as involvement in World

War I loomed. He recommended that the cantonment be built by cheap Mexican labor. Not only would this save money, but "soldiers don't like to be laborers."[169]

Marring the departure of the guard was the reprehensible conduct of a handful of guardsmen who "sold" camp frame buildings to unsuspecting Hispanics as the camps were being vacated. A member of the Iowa Brigade sold the YMCA building for seven dollars, another Hispanic bought a considerable number of camp structures for six dollars, and so on. Several Hispanics who had "bought" structures started to haul them away and were dumbfounded to learn that they had been had.[170]

The evacuation of the guard camps proceeded fitfully, due in part to conflicting orders coming from Southern Department headquarters as to the sequence in which units would leave. In part these changes resulted from changes in the availability of rail transportation, in part to the threat of a nationwide railroad strike, and finally because of the imminence of war with Germany. Some units left on schedule: Company A Iowa Engineers (December 23, 1916), 4th Nebraska Infantry (December 26, 1916), 1st Virginia Infantry (January 2, 1917).[171] The 1st North Dakota left on January 23 for Fort Snelling, Minnesota, to be mustered out. The regiment had shrunk during its border service; it arrived with 1,011 officers and men and departed with only 850. As with many other National Guard organizations, when it had become evident that the guard was not going to invade Mexico, whip the Mexicans, and go home, recruitment had suffered.[172]

Some units, such as the 2nd Virginia Infantry, were not fortunate enough to depart on schedule. On January 2, 1917, it was announced that the Virginians would be among the units leaving in the next seven to ten days.[173] They were not. Then on February 5, Funston canceled the movement order, including the 2nd Virginia. On February 9, a new order for departure listed the 2nd Virginia as leaving on February 15.[174] The very next day yet another order changed the departure date to February 11. To the Virginians' great relief they actually departed for home on February 11.[175] The 4th South Dakota was mustered out at Fort Cook, Nebraska, on March 3.[176] Troop A New Hampshire Cavalry departed from Brownsville on March 12. On March 16, the last National Guard unit left the lower Rio Grande border—the 1st Squadron Colorado Cavalry, headed for Fort D. A. Russell, Wyoming, to be mustered out.[177]

Tragedy marred the departure of the 1st Iowa Field Artillery Battalion. Private William Brady, of Battery C, while en route home with his unit on December 14, stuck his head out of the railroad coach window to get a last look at Brownsville. A bridge girder decapitated him.[178] The battalion had further bad luck. Three sleepers on a mixed train carrying Battery A derailed on December 16 near Palestine, Texas. A brakeman was severely injured, the conductor and eight soldiers were badly bruised. A lieutenant in one of the cars beat out a fire with his bare hands. The troops on the train helped to clear the wreckage.[179]

Brownsville merchants certainly missed the National Guard. In April, 1917, a federal Bureau of Investigation operative wrote: "It is a conceded fact that almost all the grocers or merchants of this city [Brownsville] and those adjoining the border doubled their capital when the National Guard was performing duties along the frontier. Now, at the present time their trade has greatly depressed, as a result of the withdrawal of the military forces, and, hence they are circulating news that tend to alarm the people, their object being to have the Militia brought back, that they may continue to profit thereby."[180]

Alas, the National Guard did not return, but its presence in the lower Rio Grande Valley had been instrumental in cooling the martial ardor of the Mexican Army across the river. The degree to which relations between the United States and Mexico had improved was epitomized in March 1917, when Major General John J. Pershing, on an inspection tour of the area, invited Colonel Tirso González, the commander at Matamoros, to attend a reception at Fort Brown in Pershing's honor. González readily accepted, but this renewal of exchanging military courtesies between the two armies nearly ended in disaster. González and his staff were enjoying themselves at the reception when they were informed that federal officers were about to arrest the colonel on a charge of having conspired to violate the neutrality laws. González had forgotten that there was an outstanding warrant for his arrest. While federal agents were telegraphing the U.S. attorney's office in Houston for instructions, the colonel and his entourage were quickly bundled into an automobile and rushed across the international bridge to safety. Despite this embarrassing incident, González reciprocated by inviting Pershing to visit Matamoros. Accompanied by General Parker and other officers, Pershing drove over the international bridge, and were met by Colonel González and his staff. There followed a sumptuous banquet for more than one hundred dignitaries, an event that concluded with the playing of the two countries' national anthems and a number of flowery speeches pledging eternal friendship and goodwill.[181]

Chapter 8

McAllen, Mission, Pharr

Anchoring the most dangerous sector of the border—the Brownsville District—was the best guard organization in the country—the New York National Guard, commanded by Major General John F. O'Ryan. He was a former major in the 1st New York Field Artillery, was appointed major general and division commander on May 1, 1912, and was the first National Guard officer to graduate from the Army War College (class of 1914).[1] The New Yorkers all by themselves could have put a sizeable dent in the Mexican Army.

Secretary of War Baker required New York to provide one division, consisting of the following:

three infantry brigades of three regiments each
one regiment, one squadron, and one machine gun troop of cavalry
two regiments of field artillery
two battalions of engineers
one signal corps battalion
three field hospital companies
four ambulance companies[2]

New York could not only see Baker's call, it could raise him a brigade—the New York National Guard had thirteen infantry regiments as well as three Coast Defense regiments. In short, New York could easily put an infantry division in the field:[3]

Infantry:	(1st Brigade)—7th, 12th, 69th, 71st (Manhattan)
	(2nd Brigade)—14th, 23rd, 47th (Brooklyn)
	(3rd Brigade)—1st, 2nd (Troy) 10th (Rochester)
	(4th Brigade)—3rd, 65th, 74th (Buffalo)
Cavalry:	1st Cavalry (12 troops, mainly Brooklyn)
	Squadron A (New York City)
	Mounted Machine Gun Troop (an independent organization, New York City)
Field Artillery:	1st Field Artillery (Manhattan)
	2nd Field Artillery (Brooklyn)
Signal Corps:	1st Signal Corps Battalion
Engineers:	22nd Engineers (one pioneer battalion, one pontoon battalion)
Hospitals:	Field Hospital Company No. 1 (New York City)
	Field Hospital Company No. 2 (Albany)
Ambulance:	Ambulance Company No. 1 (New York City)
	Ambulance Company No. 2 (Binghampton)
	Ambulance Company No. 3 (Rochester)
	Ambulance Company No. 4 (Syracuse)

Division Field Train

As of June 18, the New York National Guard's strength is summarized in table 8.1.

Both New York and Pennsylvania had National Guard divisions, although as of June 30 both were deficient in auxiliary units. And the most striking deficiency in both divisions was in machine guns. New York had only eight of the forty authorized, while Pennsylvania had none. And there was in both cases a serious lack of trained personnel to operate the weapons.[4]

On the other hand, the New York National Guard included several unique units. The Division Field Train was the only complete division train of its kind in the U.S. military since the Civil War. The army had other supply trains of equal size and equipment, such as the one that accompanied the Punitive Expedition, which was even larger, but these were merely long trains of wagons, whose numbers fluctuated according to the number of troops they supported. They were not a specially organized supply train for a division of troops. What New York could field was a unit divided into pack, supply, and ammunition trains, which consisted of 126 wagons, 602 mules, 182 enlisted men, 3 officers, 10 saddle horses, a train of 61 pack mules, and 25 draft mules. The Division Field Train's commander was a

Table 8.1. New York National Guard, June 18, 1916

	Officers	Enlisted Men
Division Headquarters	20	0
1st Brigade Headquarters	9	2
2nd Brigade Headquarters	6	2
3rd Brigade Headquarters	9	2
4th Brigade Headquarters	10	2
Quartermaster Corps	13	7
1st Battalion Signal Corps	9	149
22nd Engineers	30	562
1st Cavalry	55	904
Squadron A Cavalry	13	206
Machine Gun Troop Cavalry	2	63
1st Field Artillery	35	755
2nd Field Artillery	38	627
65th Infantry (later became 3rd Field Artillery)	39	646
1st Armored Motor Battery	4	78
1st Infantry	53	951
2nd Infantry	55	1,197
3rd Infantry	51	986
7th Infantry	52	869
10th Infantry	54	891
12th Infantry	37	673
14th Infantry	43	646
23rd Infantry	39	661
47th Infantry	47	560
69th Infantry	45	872
71st Infantry	45	649
Field Hospital No. 1	5	62
Field Hospital No. 2	3	56
Field Hospital No. 3	1	67
Ambulance Company No. 1	4	79
Ambulance Company No. 2	4	63
Ambulance Company No. 3	4	76
Ambulance Company No. 4	2	72
Field Bakery	1	6
Total	837	13,441
Grand Total	14,278*	

Annual Report . . . New York, 1916, 53; the *Annual Report* erroneously gives the total as 15,289.

quartermaster major, assisted by a captain, who was a medical officer, and a lieutenant, who was a veterinarian.[5]

In addition, New York shamed the hidebound army by having the first armored unit in U.S. military history—the 1st New York Armored Motor Battery. The unit's headquarters were in the armory of the 22nd New York Engineers in New York City. It had seven armored cars of the latest design and sixty motorcycles. Several of the armored cars already had their machine guns mounted, and the rest were expected shortly. The cars had 3/8-inch steel armor. They were a gift to the state of New York from captains of industry such as Judge Elbert H. Gary and Henry Clay Frick, as well as several prominent bankers. (The armored cars would be most useful in case of strikes.) The battery's personnel were scions of New York City's most prominent families. In addition, a wealthy citizen planned to equip the guard with an entire company of the latest-model motorcycles with a machine gun mounted in the sidecar.[6]

New York was even creating its own air force: the 1st Aero Company of the New York National Guard. Organized in the fall of 1915 under the auspices of the Aero Club of America, the company boasted four late-model aircraft and had been training thirty-five men, twelve of whom were now ready to take their exams for pilots' licenses. In June 1916 the Aero Club of America contributed $7,500 to the guard to purchase an additional Curtis airplane.[7] The 1st Aero Company was given federal recognition in June 1916 as Aero Squadron C, and plans were made to send it to the border with the rest of the New York National Guard.[8]

Mrs. Cornelius Vanderbilt donated an entire ambulance train, costing $25,000. It consisted of a tractor pulling a train of six trailers, five of them equipped as ambulances that were capable of carrying a total of twenty-four soldiers on stretchers; the sixth held medical supplies.[9] She was the wife of Cornelius Vanderbilt, the multimillionaire railroad builder and operator who was prominent in the high society of two continents. Cornelius Vanderbilt, with the rank of major, was inspector general of the New York National Guard. In December 1916 Governor Charles S. Whitman commissioned Vanderbilt as colonel of the 22nd New York Engineer Regiment.[10]

The formidable Mrs. Vanderbilt[11] was also the chair of the newly organized Active Service Auxiliary, whose mission was the care of mobilized guardsmen's families, many of whom had been left destitute by the call-up of the breadwinner. She organized a variety of fund-raising events, one of which enlisted several hundred showgirls to sell tickets in the financial district of New York City. Complementing the auxiliary's efforts, the United Synagogues of America resolved to cooperate with the military branch of the Young Men's Hebrew Association to aid the dependents of the five thousand Jews in the National Guard who had been ordered to the border.[12] The New York National Guard would have eight base hospitals in the event of war with Mexico, each hospital with five hundred beds and fifty surgeons. The New York Red Cross was raising the funds, and some sizeable donations were coming in, such as $50,000 from attorney Edward B. Close.[13] In March 1917, Mrs. John W. Markay and her son Clarence H. Markay presented the government with a military hospital of three hundred beds.[14] Obviously, one of the New York National Guard's greatest strengths was the support it received from wealthy benefactors.

New York's mobilization was impressive. On May 20, 1916, the state legislature appropriated an unprecedented $500,000 for mobilization expenses.[15] And within twenty-four hours of Governor Charles S. Whitman telephoning General O'Ryan the order to mobilize, 15,289 guardsmen were assembled and ready for duty.[16] Because the War Department ordered all guard units to be recruited up to war strength as rapidly as possible, New York would have to build up its division to twenty-two thousand men. Should there be insufficient volunteers, Governor Whitman had the power to conscript. Presumably this would not be necessary, for volunteers were streaming in, including many former guardsmen.[17] Among them was Congressman W. R. Oglesby, who declared that he was ready to resign his office and rejoin his old regiment, the 71st New York Infantry, as a private,[18] and Judge Emory A. Chase of the state Court of Criminal Appeals, who, although sixty-two years old, volunteered to join the 10th New York Infantry.[19] Conversely, U.S. senator from New York James W. Wadsworth resigned as first lieutenant of Troop M 1st New York Cavalry, citing the pressure of his duties in Washington, D.C.[20] As is the case whenever troops are about to march off to war, there was a rush of marriages. Even society women "have already shown a patriotic spirit by urging their sons to enlist and by marrying off their daughters hastily so that the bridegrooms may answer the call to the colors."[21] When the fashionable 7th New York Infantry and Squadron A New York Cavalry went to the Mexican border, the fiancées, wives, and parents of many of the men went to be with them for the rest of the summer, thus depleting high society back in New York City.[22] Amateur athletics also suffered. The 71st Infantry, which had recently won the military championship, contained more athletes than any of its sister organizations. The 69th Infantry, by contrast, had only two prominent athletes in its ranks.[23]

Division headquarters were established in the Municipal Building in New York City in order to be in close contact with Major General Leonard Wood's Eastern Department headquarters at Governors Island. General O'Ryan had high praise for the department commander:

> During the period of activity which followed, many apparently unsurmountable [sic] obstacles afforded by federal rules and regulations were removed solely through the willingness of General Wood to assume responsibility to ignore them.... It may be said in connection with this mobilization, so far at least as the New York Division was concerned, that practically all of the delays and shortcomings which followed were directly attributable to the War Department and its methods—none to the state or to the authority of the Eastern Department commander.[24]

For the previous two years O'Ryan had urged the War Department to stockpile the necessary supplies and equipment for the division somewhere in New York State where they would be readily available. General Wood had recommended the plan be approved, but the War Department had failed to act. When the call-up came, the Philadelphia depot, where much of the division's equipment was stored, had to ship property to other states besides New York, and under emergency conditions the result was confusion, inefficiency, and delay. O'Ryan also had nothing good to say about the army's regulations for physical examinations, and "regulations to many elderly professional soldiers are like the laws of the Medes and Persians. The military crustaceans complained of by Colonel Theodore Roosevelt at the outbreak of the Spanish War were in evidence again."[25]

As the mobilization plan proceeded, one Manhattan infantry regiment was left behind to care for National Guard property and to handle recruitment. Since the state camp at Peekskill could accommodate only about one-eighth of the division, other sites had been considered. Of the various sites proposed, the 825-acre State Industrial Farm at Beekman, in Dutchess County, was chosen and was designated as "Camp Whitman." The units assembled at their armories and prepared to converge on the mobilization point. An unfortunate incident occurred on the day of muster involving First Lieutenant Samuel S. Rapp of the 23rd Infantry, who "collapsed in abject terror at the thought of taking the field in campaign, thereby bringing disgrace to the service. Charged with cowardice in refusing to march with his company, he was allowed to resign his commission on July 12th 1916."[26]

Since the guard had already been planning to mobilize at Camp Whitman on July 9, arrangements were partially completed. There were en route 1,200 horses purchased in Oklahoma for the artillery and 500 Missouri mules for the quartermaster. And the New York division had just purchased one complete motor truck train.[27] Still, there was the inevitable confusion. In the 2nd New York Infantry some of the men reported in civilian clothes because all the khaki uniforms had already been issued, and some men reported in threadbare uniforms. "Ten militiamen who were nominally mounted troopers marched afoot, with their spurs clanking. One hundred of them were without guns. A recently organized machine gun company of fifty-eight men marched as infantry, because it had not a single article of special machine gun equipment. This company has been notified . . . that its status will be that of infantry for an indefinite period." Militia officers were outspoken and bitter at the War Department's failure to provide the equipment to bring units up to war strength.[28]

The logistics involved in mobilizing the New York guard at Camp Whitman were impressive. Some 320,000 gallons of water for man and beast were required daily to flow through the additional wells being dug and the seven miles of distribution pipes being hastily laid to cope with the influx. Initially, some troops had to wait in line for hours for a drink.[29] As for foodstuffs, just for a two-week period the following were required:

150,000 pounds of beef
200,000 pounds of flour
150,000 pounds of potatoes
35,000 pounds of sugar
20,000 dozen eggs
40,000 pounds of bacon
40,000 pounds of ham
30,000 pounds of mutton
12,000 pounds of butter
12,000 pounds of beans
10,000 pounds of dried fish
25,000 pounds of onions

The field bakeries produced 15,000 pounds of bread daily. The approximately 5,500 horses and mules required 840,000 pounds of oats; 800,000 pounds of hay; and 12,000 pounds of rock salt.[30] Besides training and equipment, logistical capability constituted one of the greatest disparities between the American and Mexican armies.

Perhaps the most elite unit in the New York National Guard was cavalry Squadron A, which boasted a sprinkling of millionaires. When the call-up came, the unit was already at peacetime strength. As one of the members recalled:

> [Our] departure for the front had been delayed by the necessity of securing a full complement of horses. However, on July 5th, everything was ready: all men sworn in, examined, and mustered; a horse, such as he was, for every man, and mules for every wagon and machine gun pack. Moreover, generous relatives and friends had supplied each troop with a 1½-ton motor truck (absolutely invaluable throughout our service), and a delegation of former squadron members and other friends had presented two motor cars for the use of squadron headquarters.[31]

The New York aero company and the motor battery experienced different fates. The 1st Aero Company, the first militia military aviation squadron to be organized in the United States, was mustered into federal service at Garden City on July 13, 1916. The unit had four aircraft, but two of them had worn out in the training of pilots, and the government would have to replace them. There was now also a 2nd New York Aero Company, organized in Buffalo, which the government had recognized and which went to New York City to be mustered into federal service.[32]

By contrast, the 1st Armored Motor Battery, the first armored formation to be organized in the United States, was initially rejected. The unit owned three armored cars, three "heavy and powerful machines adjustable to armor," seventy motorcycles, and "a score of automobiles for scout purposes." This equipment, valued at $40,000, had largely been the gift of wealthy benefactors. To the consternation of the battery's members, the War Department informed them that they could not be mustered into federal service because army regulations prohibited enrolling any organization for which there was not a counterpart in the army, and the army did not have an armored unit and would not until June 1916 when it acquired its first armored car, built at the government's Rock Island, Illinois, arsenal. The vehicle was built on a Jeffery "Quad" chassis, weighed about twelve thousand pounds when fully equipped, had two revolving turrets, each fitted with a Benet-Mercier machine gun, and had a crew of at least five men. The vehicle was shipped to Fort Sam Houston for testing.[33]

The best the War Department could do was to suggest that the 1st Armored Motor Battery personnel join the 47th New York Infantry, assuring them that they would receive "considerate treatment," but the socially prominent young guardsmen could not see themselves as infantry, marching and digging trenches and so on. They suggested that perhaps the regulations could be circumvented by simply attaching the 1st Armored Motor Battery as an entity to some larger unit. The army appointed an ordnance board to decide the matter. As far as the 1st Armored Motor Battery was concerned, the real trouble was petty jealousy on the army's part.[34] But to the guardsmen's joy, the army finally mustered in the unit.[35]

The 69th Infantry was the first contingent to leave for Camp Whitman, on June 20. The regiment had been formed by Irish immigrants in 1851 and was characterized by intense Irish nationalism; in 1860, for example, they had refused to parade for the visiting prince of Wales. During the Civil War, an admiring General Robert E. Lee had called this crack Union regiment "the Fighting 69th," a nickname in which the organization took great pride.[36] Having been blessed by the archbishop, the regiment marched out of its armory in New York City before admiring crowds, paraded through downtown, and boarded special trains for the mobilization camp. Other infantry regiments assembled at their armories, while the artillery and cavalry massed in Van Cortland Park in New York City awaiting further orders.[37] General O'Ryan was determined to phase the units into Camp Whitman[38] as smoothly as possible, thus avoiding the congestion and blunders that had characterized the 1898 militia mobilization.

But the 69th Infantry soon learned that the honor of being the first regiment to reach Camp Whitman had a down side. They had to march a mile and a half in the rain along muddy roads from the railroad to camp. Once there, they were immediately put to work digging drainage ditches around their tents. Furthermore, the draft horses did not arrive together with the troops, who had to haul by hand the regimental wagons loaded with equipment.[39] The 69th considered themselves fighters, not laborers, and when the 22nd Engineers, who had also gone to Camp Whitman on June 20, needed them to build roads and work on the camp's water supply, only a few men responded, and they reported late. The engineers thereafter drafted their work crews from the 2nd New York Infantry.[40]

The Carrizal clash on June 21 of course jeopardized O'Ryan's plan of phasing units methodically into the mobilization camp and assembling the full division. With General Funston urgently demanding troops, the War Department's policy now became that of speeding National Guard units to the border piecemeal as quickly as possible.[41] O'Ryan, however, was adamantly opposed to fragmenting the New York division and scattering its components along the border. He discussed the matter with General Wood, who notified General Funston of O'Ryan's objections and recommended that the New York National Guard be kept intact as a division.[42] On June 30, a vastly relieved General O'Ryan was able to announce that the division would indeed be kept intact on the border.[43] O'Ryan's stance would be emulated in 1917–18 by General Pershing, who successfully resisted British and French pressure to feed the American Expeditionary Force piecemeal into their beleaguered lines.

When the war crisis reached its climax on June 25, General Wood lent weight to the American ultimatum to Carranza by ordering some seventeen thousand National Guard troops from six states to start for the border within twenty-four hours. The New York units were the 7th, 14th, 47th, and 71st Infantry regiments, the 1st Cavalry, the 22nd Engineers, one field artillery regiment, the signal corps battalion, one field hospital, and one ambulance company. Governor Whitman selected the infantry and cavalry regiments. He also recommended that a number of regular officers be appointed to New York guard units.[44] While the guardsmen proceeded to take the federal oath, the New York legislature appropriated $600,000 (to be reimbursed by the federal government) to defray the expense of sending the guard to the border.[45] Their departure was delayed for a day by a shortage of railroad rolling stock. As General O'Ryan explained, "There are plenty of Pullmans for the officers . . . but not near enough tourist cars [sleepers] available for the enlisted men."[46] The railroads stoutly denied they were to blame for delays, asserting that troop trains were ready as ordered and blaming the delays on the army. And at New York National Guard headquarters it was stated that one of the reasons for delays was the lack of equipment that the War Department was supposed to have already furnished.[47]

By June 27, the vanguard of the New York division, 6,337 men and their equipment, entrained for the border.[48] Wishing them Godspeed, Governor Whitman addressed the officers of the 7th New York Infantry in their massive armory.[49] The regiment had 1,267 officers and men, of whom 1,070 served during the entire tour of duty.[50] By June 28, the 7th, 14th, and 71st New York Infantry and the second battalion of the 1st New York Field Artillery were en route to the border, reveling in the fact that at every station there were huge crowds to cheer them on. The 7th Infantry traveled in two sections totaling forty-nine tourist sleepers, three baggage cars with ammunition, seven gondolas with equipment, and three stock cars with horses.[51] Its sister regiment in New York City, the 71st Infantry, numbering 1,305 men, occupied four special trains of fifteen cars each. W. A. Davenport, special war correspondent for the New York *American*, traveled with the 71st, enjoying the privileges of a second lieutenant.

The matter of food during the journey to the border was of great concern to guard units across the board. One explanation for the reported food shortages on troop trains was that supplies of foodstuffs were insufficient, the diet was distasteful, and the supplies available were poorly managed.[52] At San Antonio, for instance, immediately upon arrival the tired, hungry, thirsty, and testy soldiers of the 7th and 71st New York poured out of the trains and ate and drank everything they could find at the station and vicinity. They cleaned out fruit stands in short order: they bought bananas by the bunch, oranges by the box, and purchased every watermelon they could find. They even bought a large box of avocados, not knowing what they were but confident that they must be some kind of fruit. They gulped down milk, buttermilk, and butter. One delighted bartender quickly filled an order for forty mint juleps. The satiated soldiers then boarded their new trains, as both units were transferred to the St. Louis, Brownsville & Mexico Railroad for the last leg of their trip to Brownsville.[53]

The 12th New York Infantry followed on June 29.[54] While one of the troop trains stopped over in Dallas, Private Harry A. Cuffier was ordered not to allow anyone to leave the train. He was descending the steps of the coach when he slipped and fell on his rifle's bayonet, suffering a serious chest wound. By the time the 12th reached McAllen, the men had exhausted their rations and were known as "the hungry 12th." They had followed the route of country stores already cleaned out by foraging parties from 71st and 7th New York.[55]

The 12th New York had been substituted for the 47th, originally scheduled for border duty, because the 47th had been found wanting when physical examinations were conducted. Many men were rejected just because they wore glasses. With regard to physical examinations, the 14th New York Infantry came out on top, with no officers and just 2 percent of the men failing. The 7th, 14th, 71st, and the 1st Field Artillery came next, with a 6 percent failure rate. But the 47th New York Infantry had the worst record of all. Its failure rate, which included some officers, was not made public, but it was much greater than any other regiment. This was due in large measure to its crumbling Brooklyn armory, where the men had been under arms for ten days. The armory was in such a deplorable condition that many men had developed colds and pulmonary problems. The building was probably going to have to be demolished. So instead of going to the border, the 47th was dispatched to the training camp at Peekskill to recuperate and await further orders.[56] Later there were conflicting accounts of noisy protest demonstrations and of desertions in the 47th.[57] The regiment was transferred to Camp Whitman, and its recent difficulties were attributed to the inexperience of its raw recruits.[58] There were also allegations that the adjutant general was using trained men of the 10th New York Infantry, still stationed at Camp Whitman, to fill vacancies in the regiments already on the border. And there were charges that the troops still at Camp Whitman, particularly the 10th New York Infantry, suffered from a lack of supplies and equipment.[59]

There was another change in guard units. The 65th New York Infantry, from Buffalo, was converted into the 3rd Field Artillery (howitzer) with 4.7" guns. This gave the New York National Guard the first regiment of heavy field artillery equipped exclusively with howitzers.[60] Captain Daniel W. Hand, who for the last year had been the inspector-instructor of New York's field artillery, was, with the War Department's consent, commissioned as colonel of the regiment.[61] General O'Ryan recommended to the War Department that Lieutenant Colonel W. S. McNair, formerly a major in the Inspector General's Department, be promoted to brigadier general commanding what was now a three-regiment brigade of New York field artillery.[62]

In addition to the 12th New York Infantry, other units departed on June 29: four troops of the 1st Cavalry and the second battalion of the 1st Field Artillery. Five more infantry regiments and the remainder of the field artillery and cavalry were preparing to leave, as were the division's support units. The remainder of the cavalry departed on July 2.[63] The division also shipped to Texas 3,377 horses and mules.[64]

Belatedly, the War Department's press censor, a certain Major Douglas MacArthur, ordered the railroads to cease all news of troop movements.[65] The War Department also placed the Red Cross's movements under the same news blackout. Three Mexicans were arrested in Parsons, Kansas, on July 1 shortly before a troop train passed through. It was alleged that they tried to throw a switch and wreck the train. Regulars guarded the rail line between San Antonio and Brownsville, and reportedly on at least one occasion a troop train ran at night with lights extinguished and the locomotive headlight muffled.[66] Military censorship did not really matter, because the newspapers kept the public well informed.

With military traffic having priority, the units moved on several railroads and were in a jubilant mood as they began their journey in elderly day coaches. The 7th Infantry's spirits soared as the troop trains were cheered while passing through New Jersey and Pennsylvania by crowds and by workers leaning out of the windows of factories draped with American flags. The men of the 7th New York were exuberant; from their troop trains they sang, to the tune of "Tipperary":

> It's a long, long way to capture Villa;
> It's a long way to go;
> It's a long way across the border
> Where the dirty greasers grow;
> So it's good-by to dear old Broadway,
> Hello, Mexico;
> It's a long, long way to capture Villa,
> But that's where we'll go.[67]

During the stopover at Erie, Pennsylvania, the men of the 1st New York Cavalry, who had not been able to bathe in seventy-two hours and were rather ripe, got a chance to do so, being sprayed by a fire hose in the railroad freight yard.[68] An especially welcome stop for the 7th New York Infantry was in Harrisburg, Pennsylvania, where groups of girls came to the headquarters train and distributed five hundred packages of cigarettes and tobacco.[69] At St. Louis a tobacco firm gave each man in the 71st New York Infantry a big box of cigarettes and smoking tobacco.[70] Also at St. Louis a Presbyterian minister distributed Bibles to men of the 14th New York Infantry, causing some to grumble that they would have preferred cigarettes. The Sons of the Revolution in New York State sent the guardsmen a gift of ten thousand briar pipes, fifty-five thousand packages of smoking tobacco, and one hundred thousand cigarettes.[71]

At least for the men of the 71st New York Infantry an unpleasant aspect of their trip was that from St. Louis southward, storekeepers were reaping an unscrupulous harvest at their expense, leading to complaints such as: "So far there has been only one shopman who did not raise his prices at the sight of khaki, and his action was due to the fact that he had sold out his stock. Everything from a cup of coffee to stationery has soared."[72] At Sedalia, Missouri, soldiers were being gouged so outrageously that a concerned citizen appealed to the mayor, who rushed to the railroad station and declared that he would take immediate action to halt profiteering.[73] In another case, when Squadron A New York Cavalry had a five-hour layover in Houston, several of the men had to pay $2.50 each to use the bathroom in a hotel, and the taxi drivers raised their rates by 100 percent.[74]

But then some New Yorkers hardly endeared themselves to merchants they encountered en route. The press reported that at Cleveland on July 13, about seven hundred guardsmen, both recruits and veterans from the 14th and 20th [sic] New York Infantry and the 1st New York Cavalry took advantage of a railroad layover to dash up the street to the business district and "to raid nearby groceries and commission houses, taking food and merchandise and destroying what they did not carry away."[75] They raided the market district of Cleveland, taking "200 watermelons, several hams, twenty packages of chewing tobacco, a box of stogies, and keg of ale, and considerable other booty." Police, including reserves and the riot squad, rushed to the scene. The major commanding the train deployed a squad of twenty armed soldiers who drove the looters back to the train. In attempting to justify their rampage some of the rioters said they had been cooped up in day coaches and claimed they had not eaten in thirty-six hours. Outraged Cleveland merchants were preparing loss statements to send to the War Department.[76] Some of those involved in the Cleveland affair indignantly denied to the press that they had been without food for thirty-six hours. The train had a kitchen box car and the meals prepared there were served regularly and were of sufficient quantity.[77]

The next day at Erie, Pennsylvania, a battalion of the 71st New York Infantry, saying they had not eaten since the day before, at ten o'clock in the morning, took advantage of their train's layover to raid a baker's wagon, a fruit stand, and a bakery before their officers detailed armed troops to get them peacefully rounded up and back on the train. The men claimed they had not been fed since they left Camp Whitman. The local police were of course called. In this instance, though, the soldiers paid for practically everything they had taken.[78] An embarrassed New York National Guard declared that the recruits who had left New York City had been issued ten days' rations—regular army rations of hard tack and canned meat, which in the absence of kitchen cars were supplied to all troops en route to distant points. In addition, the government provided an allowance of twenty cents a day per man for coffee or tea. General Leonard Wood declared that the trouble had been due to a lack of discipline, and Generals Funston or O'Ryan would have to deal with the matter.

Most New York units made it to Texas without engaging in hooliganism. The high spirits of the 71st New York Infantry waned as the days passed and they endured the tedium of riding in uncomfortable and antiquated day coaches, three men to two seats.[79] Those who traveled in real style were the 12th New York Infantry—every soldier and officer had a Pullman berth of his own the entire way.[80] New York Ambulance Company No. 4, from Syracuse, had an innovative approach to comfort. Upon arriving at Buffalo the unit learned they had been assigned day coaches instead of the promised Pullmans. The disgruntled soldiers boarded the cars, but en route to Cleveland the captain commanding the unit telegraphed the New York Central Railroad to have Pullmans waiting there or the ambulance unit would camp on the railroad's tracks in their pup tents until their demand was met. Five Pullmans were waiting for them at Cleveland.[81] The southbound troop trains did halt periodically to let the men stretch their legs, and in some cases even go swimming. The New York division suffered its first casualties on one of these swimming breaks—at Jerome, Missouri, two privates in the 14th New York Infantry drowned while swimming in the river.[82]

As one of the New York regiments reached Chickasha, Oklahoma, a group of Mexicans working on the railroad were imprudent enough to hoist a Mexican flag on their tent and yell "Viva Mexico" as the troop train stopped. The outraged guardsmen poured out of their coaches, ripped down the flag, and chased the Mexicans into the brush.[83]

Even as the New Yorkers were racing toward the border, General Parker was selecting sites for the division's encampments. They were a few miles north of the Rio Grande some sixty miles west of Brownsville, between the towns of Pharr, McAllen, and Mission, the camps being about five miles apart.[84]

The 7th New York Infantry won the race to the border, beating its sister regiment, the 71st, by a few hours.[85] But the 7th almost arrived at its destination without its commanding officer. Like the other units, the regiment changed trains in San Antonio. The colonel and his staff were on the platform watching the loading of field rations into the kitchen car when the conductor, anxious to keep his schedule, gave the signal for the train to depart, leaving the officers dumbfounded on the platform. There ensued a Hollywood-style chase by the colonel and his staff in a hastily commandeered locomotive and caboose. Sixteen miles down the track they finally caught up with the train, persuaded the conductor to halt and return to the station, and completed loading the errant train.[86]

Winning the race to the border enhanced the self-image of the 7th, for it was considered the "silk stocking" regiment of the New York National Guard. "The Seventh had always been particular in the men it recruited. It was almost as difficult to get into the Seventh to play soldier as it was to get into the upper echelons of Manhattan society."[87] The regiment's armory, opened in 1881 on Park Avenue in the heart of Manhattan, could only be described as sumptuous.[88] The 7th was the first regiment to be completely organized and equipped, and it was designated to be the first to leave for the border. But as usual the procedure did not go smoothly, prompting a denunciation of the army:

> Although sleeping cars had been promised by the Quartermaster Department of the Army, who had had a whole week to arrange for them, only ordinary day coaches had been provided. With two men in every seat there was not sufficient accommodation on the trains for the Regiment. The Army quartermaster who should have been in charge was conspicuous by his absence, and Colonel [Willard C.] Fisk took matters in his own hands and commandeered some extra cars which he had the railway officials, in spite of their objections, attach to the trains so the entire Regiment could have accommodations. . . . Numerous telegrams from Colonel Fisk to the War Department and high railroad officials has brought the information that proper sleeping cars would be in waiting on the arrival of the Regiment at Indianapolis. . . . The entire handling of the troop movements throughout the mobilization seemed to have been bungled wherever possible and to show great inefficiency and lack of knowledge of its work on the part of the Quartermaster Department of the Army.[89]

The 7th established its camp at McAllen. "The ground was flat and ankle deep in dust, with a scattered clump of small cactus and mesquite bushes. When the work of clearing the ground began it was found that what vegetation there was contained all kinds of animal life, small prairie dogs, horned toads and snakes, scorpions, tarantulas and centipedes. In clearing the ground sixteen rattlesnakes alone were killed—to say nothing of other vermin. Every bit of growth that might harbor animal life was finally cleared and the camp pitched."[90] If the regiment's camp ground was not much, neither was McAllen, a town of about one thousand residents. The local business community was ecstatic. "It was estimated that over $10,000 a day was being spent by militia units and off-duty soldiers when in town."[91]

The 3nd New York was based at Mission, a town divided into an Anglo section of some one thousand residents and a Hispanic barrio of about three thousand. Mission had only one bank but boasted ten saloons.[92]

Major General O'Ryan and his staff left New York City on July 2 aboard Governor Whitman's private car in a special train to take field command of what was formally designated as the 6th Division.[93] His headquarters were to be in McAllen. O'Ryan was entitled to a division chief of staff, and he selected Captain William D. A. Anderson, an engineer officer who was an honor graduate of West Point and who had been an inspector-instructor of the New York National Guard. Anderson's new rank was that of colonel.[94] After some initial shifting around of regiments, one brigade was stationed at Pharr, another at McAllen, and the third at Mission. The 1st Squadron of the 1st New York Cavalry encamped just west of Mission.[95]

The troops arrived wearing heavy winter uniforms and woolen underwear, and General O'Ryan declared that the delays in equipping the militia were due to an obsolete army system, "which had gone to pieces under pressure."[96] Evidence of this was the following press report from 6th Division headquarters at McAllen on July 8:

> Although much is said about millions of rounds of ammunition being available at Brownsville, there is certainly very little of it in camp. There are twelve three-inch guns of the First Field Artillery in camp, but there is not a single shell here.
>
> Officers admitted that there was a shortage, but said that if ammunition were needed it could be got to McAllen from Brownsville in time. This is equivalent to saying that shells and cartridges could be loaded on a train at Brownsville, rushed here, a distance of sixty miles, and unloaded and distributed before a Mexican force could cross the Rio Grande and ride eight miles into the camps.
>
> As it now stands, there are very few of the privates who have 210 rounds of ammunition, the required quota. Most of them have fewer

than 100 rounds, while the officers, as a rule, have only two clips, fourteen shots, of ammunition for their magazine pistols. Not a few of the officers never have fired automatic pistols, and one in going through the camps often hears their speculation about their own marksmanship.

General O'Ryan said that a few weeks before the order came to mobilize he had scented trouble, and urged on Adjutant [General] Stotesbury the need for more ammunition. He said that General Stotesbury had purchased 1,000,000 rounds with State money.[97]

O'Ryan, in an article in the *Seventh Regiment Gazette*, warmly defended the New York guard's mobilization and its subsequent service along the Rio Grande.[98] Luckily, the critical shortage of ammunition was remedied in a timely fashion. By July 16 a general order required that all combat wagons be kept loaded with ammunition and litters as if the regiments were immediately to go into action.[99] A good part of the problem had been that the single-track St. Louis, Brownsville & Mexico Railroad's branch line between the army depot in Brownsville and McAllen had simply been overwhelmed by the enormous volume of men, supplies, and equipment it was now having to handle.[100]

As for the demoralizing wearing of heavy olive drab uniforms, khakis were quickly requisitioned, but in the meantime, to keep the men from suffering unduly, there was no work between ten thirty in the morning and four o'clock in the afternoon. The soldiers gratefully took to this "siesta" period, for "it daily becomes more evident that the troops cannot work under a Texas sun. The least violent exercise when the heat is at its height causes the weaker men to wilt by the score."[101] One guardsman described the heat most succinctly: "Heat. If you take your hat off, you die."[102] It was so hot that the heat split the woodwinds of the 23rd's regimental band.[103] Working conditions became more tolerable as by July 18, khaki uniforms began to be issued. Woolen underwear was also being replaced, although in one regiment a carload of lightweight underwear turned out to be boys' sizes (which made for a really tight fit) sent by mistake. The mistake was corrected.[104] The men not only had to adjust to their semitropical environment but were understandably edgy, not knowing if the local Hispanics were friendly or if the Mexicans across the Rio Grande would attack.

Then there were the constantly circulating rumors that served to enliven camp life. For instance, in the 7th New York word was passed along the company street for the cook details to "go and get your meat." By the time the word reached Company K, a few hundred yards down the street, wild cheering erupted—the order had been garbled into "We're going home next week."[105]

It was against this background that the 71st New York Infantry had the honor of firing the first shot in anger. One night a sentry spotted a shadowy shape moving in the brush, gave the password, and, when the countersign was not forthcoming, fired a fatal shot at the intruder. It turned out that the deceased could not possibly have given the countersign—he was a burro.[106] Two weeks later, sentries of the 1st New York Field Artillery opened fire on Mexicans who were trying to steal horses from one of their corrals at night. The would-be thieves fled unscathed in a hail of gunfire. The division suffered its first loss on the border when on July 3 the quartermaster sergeant of the 14th New York Infantry died of a heart attack at Mission.[107]

While the New York guard was streaming into its border cantonments[108] all was not well back at Camp Whitman, the mobilization point. Much of the problem was the 69th New York Infantry, composed of feisty Irishmen. The most famous member of the regiment would be William J. "Wild Bill" Donovan. When the call-up occurred, Donovan, who was captain of Troop I, 1st Cavalry, from Buffalo, was in Berlin representing the Rockefeller Commission for the Relief of Poland. Ordered to join his unit, he left on the first steamship he could find.[109] Donovan became the colonel of the 69th in 1917, distinguished himself in World War I, winning the Congressional Medal of Honor. In World War II, Donovan, by then a major general, commanded the Office of Strategic Services, the predecessor of the CIA.

Because Pancho Villa is the only Mexican revolutionist some writers dealing with the events of 1916 have ever heard of, they have "Wild Bill" Donovan chasing Villa all over the place. Peter Grose[110] states that Allen Dulles's "career thus diverged from the career of another New Yorker who did go to the Mexican campaign, William J. Donovan, nicknamed 'Wild Bill' for his exploits against Pancho Villa." Since Donovan never got within six hundred miles of Villa, his "exploits" occurred only in Grose's imagination. Anthony Cave Brown[111] has Donovan as a member of the Punitive Expedition, chasing Villa and his Doratos [sic] along the Rio Grande. And Joseph E. Persico[112] says, "In 1916, Donovan's Silk Stocking Boys were called to active duty under General John 'Black Jack' Pershing to help capture the Mexican revolutionary General Pancho Villa. The expedition never caught Villa, but Donovan had the time of his life, driving his men and himself mercilessly, sitting around the campfire at night, singing and swapping tales." The Donovan misinformation has also been repeated in Britain: "Donovan was nicknamed Wild Bill when fighting against Pancho Villa with General Pershing's expedition to Mexico in 1916."[113] The most recent Donovan biography devotes fewer than two paragraphs to Donovan's border service, but the author manages to repeat the error.[114] These examples illustrate how the 1916 National Guard call-up has been confused with and subsumed into the more glamorous Punitive Expedition.

The other outstanding personality in the 69th was the regimental chaplain, the redoubtable Father Francis P. Duffy. The archbishop had reportedly banished him in 1912 to the small Bronx parish of Our Savior because he was too liberal. Biographies of Duffy range from the simplistic[115] to the scholarly.[116] Duffy published his World War I memoirs.[117]

The 69th had been the first unit to reach Camp Whitman and was still there although other regiments were being sent to the border. Spoiling for a fight, the 69th was becoming restive. They were particularly incensed when the 23rd Infantry was ordered south although it had not yet been mobilized and was still in its Brooklyn armory. That regiment traveled in antiquated and unsanitary day coaches, three men to two seats, "the remaining seat being overloaded with heavy field equipment." Not until they reached Oklahoma did the 23rd finally receive tourist sleepers.[118] There were rumblings of political favoritism by the governor in selecting units for the border. The frustration of the 69th Infantry was also felt by other units at Camp Whitman. To express their dissatisfaction, the field artillery batteries omitted firing the customary eighteen-gun salute when Governor Whitman visited the camp on July 3.[119] The governor evidently got the message, for he quickly announced that the 69th and other formations, amounting to half the troops still in camp, would be on their way to the border within a week. Governor Whitman also announced that he planned to form a new National Guard infantry division of 12,681 men to take the place of the one now on the Mexican border. The announcement was greeted with enthusiastic cheers.[120]

The 69th finally left on July 10. Looking on the bright side, its officers declared that the delay had resulted in the 69th being much better equipped than those regiments preceding it southward.[121] But the regiment was thunderstruck when General Leonard Wood announced that he was relieving the revered colonel of the 69th, Lewis S. Conley, because he was physically unfit to command, as was the regimental executive officer, Lieutenant Colonel John J. Phelan. New York congressmen were furious and immediately protested to Secretary of War Baker, demanding the repeal of Wood's order. General O'Ryan stated that he regretted that the two officers had failed their physical exams and expressed his confidence that politics had played no part in their rejection by army surgeons. The *New York Times* also expressed its regret but observed that Conley and Phelan had been held to the same standard as applied to regular officers, and General Wood was being attacked for simply doing his job. The newspaper sneeringly described the 69th as "a sort of social club of which its Colonel is the most important and best liked member" and added that if Conley were reinstated it would set a most unfortunate precedent, showing that politics rather than military discipline prevailed.[122] The affair became a cause célèbre, reaching all the way to President Wilson, who took a personal interest. After conferring with the president, Secretary Baker directed Major General Hugh Scott, chief of the Army General Staff, to conduct a thorough investigation. Some of Wilson's friends hated Wood, in part because he had been mentioned as a possible Republican presidential candidate, and they would welcome any adverse finding. Furthermore, there existed the suspicion in the National Guard and its supporters that the army was plotting to place regular officers in command of the militia on the border, and the removal of Colonel Conley was evidence of this nefarious campaign.[123]

Senator O'Gorman of New York led the political charge to reinstate Conley and Phelan. He conferred with President Wilson, afterward expressing his confidence that Wood's order would be rescinded. Wood, for his part, prepared a report, as did the army's surgeon general, whose opinion was that Phelan had a hernia that was operable but that Conley's cardiac problems—he was too stout—would imperil both his life and the lives of his men.[124] The reports were submitted to General Scott. Wood also pointed out that forty-six other National Guard officers besides Conley had been retired because of physical disabilities as diagnosed by army surgeons. And five regular colonels, four of them regimental commanders on the border and in the Punitive Expedition, were being retired for the same reason.

Colonel Conley not only appealed Wood's order but accompanied and remained in command of the 69th on its journey to Texas. When the regiment arrived on July 18, Conley relinquished command, bade farewell to the men he had led for more than six years, and returned to New York, to be discharged effective July 26. Secretary Baker upheld Conley's retirement. Yet New York politicians continued to call for Conley's reinstatement and a review of the other National Guard officers who had been involuntarily retired. However, President Wilson upheld Colonel Conley's dismissal.[125]

Governor Whitman commissioned as the new colonel of the 69th Captain William N. Haskell, a West Point graduate who was an inspector-instructor for the New York National Guard and who had been nominated by the commander of the 1st Brigade and endorsed by General O'Ryan. Fortunately, Haskell was popular with the prickly 69th. Almost every staff officer, company officer, and NCO who served under Haskell went overseas with the regiment in World War I.[126] The 69th loved to fight; if it couldn't fight Mexicans, it took on whoever was handy. On August 11 it engaged in a brawl with men of the 2nd New York Infantry, for considerable animosity existed between the two regiments.[127]

Yet the Irishmen were rather sentimental. When the regimental mascot, Mike the Irish terrier, wandered off during a railroad stopover in Prescott, Arkansas, and was left behind, the regiment wrote an urgent appeal to the local newspaper asking that a search be made for the errant mascot. As a result, Mike was found and dispatched by express to a relieved 69th.[128]

The 6th Division created a problem for General Frederick Funston. The division was assigned to the Brownsville District, Brigadier General James Parker commanding, but Major General John O'Ryan of New York outranked Parker. To resolve this awkward situation Funston made New York a separate divisional command reporting directly to him.[129]

The New Yorkers soon established sprawling cities of conical tents at Camps McAllen, Pharr, and Mission. Division headquarters, the 2nd Brigade (7th, 12th, and 71st Infantry), and many support units were at McAllen, whose camp consisted of more than 10,000 men and 3,500 animals. The 3rd Brigade (3rd, 23rd, and 74th Infantry) was at Pharr and the 1st Brigade (2nd, 14th, and 69th Infantry) at Mission. General Funston had selected the sites for their strategic value in protecting vital crossings of the Rio Grande from raids,[130] rather than for the comfort of the troops. "The First New York cavalry and its fashionable satellite, Squadron A, brought most of their horses with them to McAllen, where they were placed in camp with a twenty-acre swamp on one side of them and the brigade dump on the other side. The swamp contributed mosquitoes and the dump incubated flies and gnats."[131] New York's divisional cavalry was unique in having its full quota of horses, perhaps because one of its officers had been detailed to the horse-purchasing board in San Antonio, the result being that "his regiment was probably the first and possibly the only completely mounted militia cavalry unit on the border."[132] The principal equipment needs of the New York division were cots, flooring, and mosquito netting. At first the government refused to approve the repeated requisitions for lumber for tent flooring. Only after the guardsmen had spent considerable sums of their own money for lumber was the policy changed and lumber provided.[133]

As General O'Ryan recalled:

> Preparation of these camps was under way when we arrived. Some of the errors in their preparation illustrated the complete unfamiliarity of the average army officer, accustomed to handling small units such as companies and battalions, with the requirements of a relatively large body of troops. For example, we found that the water system would not furnish water to more than half the camp at McAllen. No adequate allowance had been made in the pipe installation for the carrying of water sufficient for the units near the source, plus an excess sufficient to pass on to all units to the end of the system.

However, the New York division included a variety of talented officers, among them the chief engineer of the New York City water system, as well as other officers who were hydraulic engineers and specialists in constructing water systems. "These officers soon designed and installed an adequate system at a minimum of cost to the government."[134] But Squadron A had a somewhat different view:

> The official camp water system, which never produced more than a gentle perspiration, was replaced by our own well, pump, tank, and pipe lines, the gift of a member of Troop B, anonymous but ever blessed. Watering troughs for the horses and shower baths for the men appeared. Water flowed freely. No longer was it necessary to buy White Rock with which to shave. Not to us applied the daily order which came down from headquarters that "owing to the scarcity of water," baths would be permitted only between the hours of 2:00 and 2:05 A.M.[135]

A radio installation at McAllen operated by the New York Signal Corps and with a radius of thirty miles provided effective communications among the camps. The station on occasion was even able to communicate with

Fort Sam Houston, 240 miles away. The signal corps not only ran telephone lines to the various outposts and participated in field maneuvers but also furnished election results and news of baseball and football games, including the World Series and a play-by-play account of the Princeton-Yale football game.[136]

On the fringes of the National Guard camps were the long lines of tethered horses and mules, and alongside the open-air stables were the rows of wagons and motor vehicles. Although trucks were being assigned to the guard, the division was still quite dependent on its animals. Each camp had a rifle range, and there was an artillery and rifle range at La Gloria, twenty-three miles from McAllen. Other facilities, including frame YMCA buildings,[137] were under construction, as was an impressive network of drainage ditches. With time, clubhouses, shower baths, and a movie tent made life more agreeable, as did cigarettes: on July 20, for instance, five hundred thousand cigarettes were rushed from Brownsville to Mission. The 7th New York Infantry even began publishing an official monthly bulletin, *The Seventh Regiment Gazette*, with articles written primarily by noncoms. The division also published a newspaper, the *Rio Grande Rattler*, which gained "a reputation unequaled by any other service journal of a like nature."[138]

The troops arrived on the border eager for action: "Unless we can go to Mexico to fight we want to go home is the opinion of every man, officer and private, but there is also determination to fulfill the obligations of the oath of allegiance."[139] The New York division was to constitute a striking force in the event of an invasion of Mexico. But as the war crisis passed, the men increasingly realized that their stay on the Mexican border was likely to be an extended one. If any doubts remained, General O'Ryan laid them to rest by announcing that the New Yorkers would be spending Christmas and New Year's on the border and would remain there indefinitely in 1917.[140]

General O'Ryan was concerned by the

> large number of saloons, cafes and other places where strong liquor was sold. I felt that such conditions in connection with the almost intolerable heat of that region would make desirable the total abstinence of officers and men from the use of liquor. Venereal disease has ever been the curse of armies, and such disease and the use of liquor have been intimately related. It was felt that by prohibiting the use of liquor effective measures might be adopted to keep down the venereal rate. Accordingly, the order which became somewhat famous, known

as G[eneral] O[rders] 7, was issued prohibiting officers and men of the New York Division from using intoxicating liquors in any form during their service on the border, or entering houses of prostitution or establishments where liquor was sold. Military Police enforced the order.[141]

O'Ryan claimed that this order and the high standard of conduct that accompanied it produced the most unparalleled health record in the history of the army for any comparable organization. Venereal disease was practically nonexistent in the division, and the same comment applied to typhoid fever.[142] The general's comments about typhoid fever were rather optimistic, as we shall see. And regarding prostitution and the liquor traffic, General Funston observed that it had been easy for O'Ryan to control his men because they were stationed in small towns in "dry" territory, whose residents were rather upstanding citizens.[143]

The division embarked on an intensive training program, but one that took a certain toll. A company of the 71st New York Infantry, one of the 7th' and one from the 12th, conducted a thirty-seven-mile route march in heavy marching order, taking five days' rations. A private in the 12th died during the march, which allegedly took place in 114-degree heat and resulted in 75 of the 350 men involved falling by the wayside from heat prostration. An investigation ensued amid charges that the 12th had brought physically unfit men to the border. The brigade commander stated that everyone had a physical exam but conceded that because of the war crisis the exams had been cursory. An army investigation determined that the dead private had indeed collapsed from heat prostration but that he had actually died from tuberculosis.[144]

A court-martial was established at McAllen with Lieutenant Colonel William S. Beekman, 71st New York, as president. In the case of Private Henry Scheiner, Battery D, 1st Field Artillery, charged with attempting to escape from the guardhouse, assaulting a corporal, taking his pistol, and biting his hand when the corporal tried to restrain him, the guilty verdict resulted in a sentence of dishonorable discharge, forfeiture of all pay and allowances, and a year at hard labor at Leavenworth. General O'Ryan approved the sentence, and General Funston selected the place of confinement. A much lesser punishment was meted out to a private of Battery D, also from the 1st Field Artillery, charged with sleeping on sentry duty. He lost two months' pay and allowances.[145]

Despite a drum roll of complaints by militiamen and by politicians back home about the heat, the food, the transportation, the health care, and the equipment,[146] Major General Tasker H. Bliss, assistant chief of staff, inspected the New York division and pronounced it a first-class organization with high morale, a judgment with which General O'Ryan of course heartily concurred. General Parker inspected the encampment at McAllen and declared that the New Yorkers were unquestionably the best-outfitted division ever mustered in the army, which was high praise indeed.[147] They even had insect bags: "Eighteen hundred 'insect bags' designed to protect the troops from fleas which infest many of the camps along the Mexican border were forwarded today [August 6] to the soldiers of the Twelfth infantry, New York national guard, at McAllen Texas, by the women of the army and navy supply committee of the American Defense Society. The bags are filled with naphthalene and are made to fit over a man's shoulders, one end suspended down his chest and the other down his back. The committee plans to supply other New York Guardsmen with the bags."[148]

The praise heaped on the New York National Guard seemed to be borne out when a surprise exercise was conducted on July 24, the first real test of the division's readiness. At seven o'clock in the morning buglers simultaneously blew the call to arms, to repel an imaginary attack from the north. The eighteen thousand men in the New York camps responded promptly and efficiently, forming up in the company streets ready for battle. They deployed around the complex of camps. The only real failure in this two-hour exercise was that the mules bringing up ammunition for several of the machine guns did not move fast enough to keep the guns, capable of firing six hundred rounds a minute, adequately supplied.[149] Both as a courtesy and to impress on him what he would be up against in the event of war, General O'Ryan invited the Mexican commander at Reynosa, the closest Mexican town to the New York division, for dinner and to review the 7th Infantry and tour the McAllen camp.[150]

A rite of passage occurred on July 11 when a provisional troop of sixty-five men chosen from the 2nd and 3rd Squadrons of the 1st Cavalry left McAllen for the riverside hamlet of Hidalgo to begin patrolling some thirty to forty miles of the most dangerous section of the lower Rio Grande. This was the first detachment of New York troops given a tactical assignment, and they must have felt that at last they were real soldiers. The detachment contained many junior officers and noncoms, whose experience would be shared with future patrols. The 1st Squadron of the regiment was still en route, having enjoyed the hospitality of the people of St. Louis, who opened the YMCA swimming pool for them, but when it arrived in camp it too would send out a provisional troop on patrol.[151] Troop I of the 1st Cavalry was considered a "silk stocking" unit, composed of the elite of Buffalo. The troop's captain was attorney William J. Donovan. In 1916, he was nicknamed "Galloping Bill" by his men for his hard-charging style of leadership. According to Father Duffy, Donovan was the best-known captain in the division.[152]

As of July 1916, it had not rained in Hidalgo County for eighteen months. Ranchers had watched helplessly as most of their cattle had starved to death. To cope with the searing heat, soldiers of the 74th Infantry sometimes made themselves a bit too comfortable, to the distress of nearby residents. Their complaints resulted in the 3rd Brigade commander issuing an order: "On account of numerous complaints from citizens living near this camp, that men indecently expose themselves, the Commanding Officers are directed to issue orders that no officer or man shall leave his company street unclothed, and shall further direct their guards to arrest anyone disobeying this order. Particular attention is called to men going back and forth to latrines, bath houses, and to bathing in pools of water in or near camp. The latter must not be done unless bathing suits are worn."[153]

But the New York troops soon got a respite from the heat and drought—they found themselves awash from torrential rains: sixteen showers in twenty-four hours on July 31. The network of drainage ditches proved ineffectual, as the terrain was practically level. Conditions at the 12th New York Infantry's camp were so bad that moving the regiment a quarter of a mile to slightly higher ground was seriously considered. The entire division was sodden and miserable, and it was a week before the rains permitted the training schedule to be resumed.[154] But not for long. A hurricane swept in from the Gulf of Mexico on the night of August 5, pounding the militia camps with wind and rain and turning the area once again into a huge lake. The soldiers spent much of the night grimly holding on to their tent ropes, and even as so many tents were blown over, so was Lizzie, the 7th Infantry's pet mule.[155] Worse was to follow. On August 18, a hurricane packing eighty-mile-an-hour winds blasted the lower Rio Grande Valley. McAllen was battered for six hours, getting 4 1/2 inches of rain. Half of the tents in the New York camps were blown down, along with some semipermanent buildings. The 3rd New York even had to abandon its camp at Mission. These guardsmen along with the rest of the thirty thousand troops in the area, both

National Guard and regulars, had to seek what shelter they could, many of them taking refuge in public buildings. The good news was that no one was seriously injured.[156]

Even as the extensive storm damage was being repaired, the New York regiments prepared for their most ambitious undertaking. The exercise was postponed a few days so that the eighteen thousand men could be paid for the period between mobilization and their muster into federal service. This came to about $150,000, to the delight of the local businessmen.[157] The plan was to have all nine infantry regiments travel in heavy marching order and engage in maneuvers while making a twelve-day swing around an eighty-four-mile circle that General O'Ryan had already reconnoitered with Squadron A.[158] One infantry regiment from each brigade—the 2nd, 7th, and 23rd—would set out first, then be followed the next day by the 3rd, 14th, and 71st. It was finally decided not to have the remaining three infantry regiments follow the day after that because of the scarcity of waterholes. The 23rd, for example, broke camp at two or three o'clock in the morning, marched until ten o'clock, then took shelter for the rest of the day. The men often had to hack their way through semitropical jungles to avoid the "glue-like adobe muck encountered in the trails of lower levels."[159]

When the infantry returned, the two field artillery regiments marched and engaged in several days of target practice. Then the cavalry rode the circuit. The troops made their night camps at the headquarters of some of the large ranches in Hidalgo County. One of these was the Sterling ranch at Monte Christo [sic], northwest of Mission. One officer of the 23rd, Rutherford Ireland, was not impressed: "A scattered settlement called Monte Christi [sic] presents still another misnomer"—the area was flat as a plate—"and I venture to say that Christ never dwelt in such a hell hole."[160] Rupert Hughes of the 69th wrote an interesting first-hand account of the exercise, entitled "The Big Hike."[161] Rancher (and future Texas Ranger captain and adjutant general of Texas) William W. Sterling reminisced about the cordial relations his family enjoyed with General O'Ryan and hundreds of other New Yorkers, among them Cornelius Vanderbilt, William Donovan, and Rupert Hughes. The ranch had a canteen and a branch of the YMCA. More importantly, the ranch had two deep wells, much appreciated by the parched New York troops. And Sterling had fashioned a ten-inch perforated pipe long enough for an entire company to enjoy a shower bath at one time.[162] But "in his memoirs, Sterling neglected to mention that he charged visiting soldiers twenty-five cents each for a one-minute bath."[163]

The second phase of the exercise a week later involved the remaining three regiments making the route march; the maneuver pitted the 12th New York and Cavalry Squadron A trying to capture division headquarters, being defended by the 7th New York and the 1st Cavalry. Regular officers acted as umpires.[164] The men began the exercise in high spirits. Not only had they just gotten paid, but they looked forward to twelve days in the field breaking the tedium of camp life. There was more singing as the columns set out than there had been since the last hope of fighting Mexicans had vanished.[165] However, things did not go as well as had been expected. In some places the leading units had to hack out a road through the mesquite thickets and cactus, the wagons carrying food and water had great difficulty in keeping up with the marching columns, and the heat was terrible. In the 71st, some two hundred men dropped by the roadside from the heat. The 14th spent the last day of the march without food and short of water. One company simply sat down in the road and refused to proceed farther. Desperate for water, some men drank from puddles and even filled their canteens with the brackish liquid until their officers put a halt to this unhealthy practice.[166] Their border experience had become even more miserable.

Chapter 9

More McAllen, Mission, Pharr

New Yorkers' spirits soared as the result of a threatened nationwide railroad strike. The New York division, like other National Guard organizations, had been gathering data on its men with railroad experience in case the military had to help operate the trains. On August 31 the War Department announced that fifteen thousand guardsmen from states with large railroad terminals would be recalled from the border to protect government property and maintain law and order. Included in the order were three New York regiments—the 3rd, 14th, and 71st—scheduled for return to Camp Whitman.[1] Although the strike crisis passed by September 2, the movement order was not rescinded and the New York units were ordered to prepare for departure. The men cheered wildly. They became positively ecstatic when they learned a few days later that the three regiments were to be mustered out.[2]

But all was not well. The division's sick rate had been excellent, under 2 percent, a source of great pride for General O'Ryan.[3] A prominent war correspondent, Floyd Gibbons, presented a less favorable assessment. He wrote that initially at McAllen the sick lay on the ground, and sometimes in the mud, in open, unfloored tents. The only hospital was a field hospital, which in theory was little more than a mobile first aid station, but of necessity it functioned as an evacuation or base hospital. Fortunately the hospital was upgraded with cots and with tents having floors and sides. Moreover, a base hospital costing $25,000 was built at McAllen boasting a number of wooden structures. This new installation grew out of complaints by the New Yorkers over their treatment at the base hospital at Fort Brown in Brownsville.[4]

But now a number of paratyphoid fever cases had appeared, reaching a peak of 120 in August, mainly at Mission.[5] The disease was apparently contracted during the field exercises and was thought to have originated in the 7th New York Infantry. By September 6 there were sixty-two cases, with the 2nd New York Infantry reporting the greatest number of new cases. Sixty patients, including those with paratyphoid, were sent to the base hospital at Fort Sam Houston.[6] For whatever reason, many of the soldiers had not been inoculated.[7] The 71st's regimental surgeon tried to secure vaccine from Fort Sam Houston before the 71st left camp for home, but it was unavailable. He then telegraphed the New York state health commissioner, who promised to supply vaccine so the regiment could be inoculated as soon as it reached Camp Whitman.[8]

The 71st broke camp, which was considered the most attractive in the division, on September 5, leaving behind the headquarters detachment, the supply company to guard the wagons and other equipment, and two soldiers suspected of having typhoid. The next day the regiment boarded a passenger train consisting of Pullmans for the officers and tourist sleepers for the men, who luxuriated in amenities such as sheets and pillow cases on the trip home.[9] The 71st's journey home was quite pleasant. When the regiment reached Indianapolis the men paraded through the city, passing in review before the mayor, who conferred the liberty of the city on them.[10] The 71st arrived back at Camp Whitman complete with their mascots, including an armadillo and a raccoon, on September 11 but was immediately quarantined. Visitors were prohibited from kissing the troops or even shaking hands with them.[11] When the 3rd and 14th New York Infantry arrived, they too were placed under strict quarantine. The 14th, incidentally, arrived with several burros and a goat they were taking to the folks back home in Brooklyn. Some of these troops complained loudly about the heat, the lack of water, and the mud in Texas, besides griping that Texans treated the guardsmen with contempt and a total lack of hospitality.[12] About 4,500 troops were under quarantine—the 71st, the 3rd, and the 14th, plus the 2nd Brigade commanding general and his staff. Twenty-two doctors conducted a program of vaccinations for everyone.[13] A sprinkling of new paratyphoid cases appeared, but by the end of September the 14th and 71st Infantry were released and returned to New York City.[14]

More McAllen, Mission, Pharr

Some New Yorkers never returned home. On August 26 the entire 12th Infantry went swimming in an irrigation canal, sergeants acting as lifeguards for the one thousand–odd swimmers. When the regiment reformed on the bank, there was one unclaimed uniform. Twenty-six-year-old Sergeant Arthur Lockwood had dived into the canal, had landed headfirst in mud, and had drowned.[15] That same day a private in the 7th Infantry, an attorney in civilian life, died in the base hospital at McAllen of intestinal fever.[16] Two days later, the first sergeant of Company H, 7th Infantry, an architect in civilian life, died in the hospital at McAllen of dysentery.[17] Another New York death occurred on September 13. A private in Ambulance Company No. 1 accidentally shot himself while playing with a pistol in camp at McAllen.[18]

The press also reported that dysentery claimed the life on September 8 of the sixty-four-year-old commanding officer of the 74th New York, Colonel Nathaniel. B. Thurston, who had been in the National Guard since 1877 and who had been deputy New York City police commissioner in 1902.[19] It turned out, however, that the report was wrong. The colonel was seriously ill, but he vehemently denied that he was dead. This story was an example of how "18,000 men, who have little to do but dig ditches and drill, work their imaginations long after taps has sounded."[20] The colonel was evacuated to New York City to recuperate. On November 11, he returned to Pharr to resume his command. The regiment welcomed him joyfully. A coach drawn by four gray mules, with outriders blowing bugles, went to the Pharr railroad station to meet their colonel. The officers rode into town on horses to greet him. When Thurston reached the 74th's camp the men lustily cheered him. That evening a reception was held for him. It was all very gratifying.[21] Unfortunately, on January 16, 1917, Colonel Thurston died in camp at McAllen of a stroke, and this time the press report was correct.[22] He was accorded full military honors, which included a cortege more than two miles long composed of more than five thousand New York guardsmen, who marched in a drizzling rain. The 74th led the procession to the railroad station; his coffin was sent to New York for burial.[23]

Although the return of the 3rd, 14th, and 73rd marked the beginning of the end of the division's border duty, General O'Ryan continued his program of route marches and field exercises. He announced a schedule lasting into October that required every remaining regiment to make another fifty-mile march lasting twelve days. And the 22nd Engineers continued working on building new windmills and a storage tank to provide a better water supply. September was considered the hottest month in that part of Texas. Company I of the engineers also set a record in the division by marching more than twenty-one miles in less than seven hours. Of 103 men in the company, only three fell out, one from a sprained ankle.[24] The two field artillery regiments conducted two-day route marches on their way to the range at La Gloria for firing practice. Squadron A was divided into two groups for daily combat exercises.[25]

As for the paratyphoid epidemic, only six new cases were reported, and the medical officers believed the outbreak was nearly over.[26] At its height, the epidemic had sent ninety New Yorkers to the hospital, and more than three hundred more were confined for observation with undetermined fevers. The epidemic was the worst aspect of camp life for the division. The unofficial bulletin of the 7th Infantry, the *7th Regiment Gazette*, observed that conditions in the camps in and around McAllen were not nearly as gloomy as some reports from Texas would lead the man on the street back home to believe. Many of the stories of hardship emanating from McAllen were concocted out of whole cloth.[27]

Some redeployment of units occurred when a line of detached posts was established along the military road from Madero to San Juan Hacienda.[28] For instance, in early September a company of the 7th was dispatched by truck to the riverside hamlet of Madero, seven miles southwest of McAllen, to occupy a post just evacuated by the 2nd Texas Infantry. Guarding the vital irrigation pumping stations at Madero was the first real border service for any of the New York infantry.[29] General Parker also deployed part of the 1st Cavalry on patrol duty above Rio Grande City. General Funston considered the 1st Cavalry an excellent regiment.[30]

Another New York unit was chafing for border service. Back home the 3rd Field Artillery regiment (formerly the 65th Infantry) was in excellent shape and ready to leave for the border. General O'Ryan announced that he intended to bring to Texas this heavy (4.7" howitzer) field artillery unit[31] and the divisional subsidiary units—the aero company, the ammunition train, Field Hospital No. 3, and the supply train.

The 1st Aero Company, based at Mineola, New York, never went to the border. However, while at Mineola, there were occasional disciplinary incidents. Private Frank Gorey was convicted by a general court-martial of "conduct to the prejudice of good order and military discipline" for giving a newspaper interview in which he criticized the officers. Gorey was sentenced to six months' hard labor and forfeiture of two-thirds of his pay for three months. Higher headquarters approved the sentence but remitted it.[32] The company was mustered out at Mineola on May 12, 1917. Its officers resigned their commissions, but a number of the enlisted men decided to remain in the National Guard.[33]

General O'Ryan wanted to have the only field artillery brigade (three regiments) not just in the National Guard but in the U.S. Army. But two months after arriving on the border, the brigade only had horses enough for one and a half regiments.[34] And the infantry regiments left behind in New York—the 1st (Binghampton), 10th (Albany),[35] and 47th (Brooklyn)—were now being viewed as the nucleus of a second National Guard division. Toward that end, a regiment of black soldiers was organized in New York City—the 15th Infantry. Before a crowd numbering thousands, the regiment received its colors and was reviewed by Governor Whitman on November 1, 1916.[36]

The pattern for the division in Texas in September was for additional units to be ordered home—the 2nd Infantry, now commanded by Colonel James M. Andrews, a West Point graduate, being the first—while the remaining formations continued to train.[37] There were now only five of the original nine infantry regiments, three of them commanded by regular officers, left in the division. Nevertheless, the largest maneuvers yet undertaken occurred in September, centered around the village of Hidalgo on the Rio Grande. The 2nd Infantry Brigade (7th, 12th, and 69th Infantry), a reinforced squadron of cavalry, and a battery of artillery comprising a "Blue" army opened a two-day exercise against a "Red" or imaginary villista force that had driven an imaginary Mexican federal army out of the border state of Tamaulipas. The 4,500–5,000 men of the "Blue" army advanced toward the Rio Grande to confront the invading "Red" army consisting of an infantry brigade, a company of the 22nd Engineers, a signal corps company, Ambulance Company No. 3, Squadron A, and a field artillery battery. Aiding the "villistas" were regular units: a company of the 28th U.S. Infantry, a squadron of the 3rd U.S. Cavalry, and a squadron of the 1st U.S. Cavalry.[38]

Although briefly delayed by rain, the exercise attracted a large and appreciative Mexican audience, who viewed it as an entertainment thoughtfully put on for their enjoyment:

> While half the Mexican population of the Mexican city [of] Reynosa, about a half mile from Hidalgo, gathered along the river bank to

watch the "Blue" or "American" army annihilate the advance party of an invading force of 10,000, the entire Mexican population of Hidalgo stood on the porches of tumbledown cafes or at the doors of straw and willow shacks and shouted "Bravo,! Bravo!" when "Blue" cavalrymen, charging through the streets, gave invading "Red" infantrymen lusty strokes with the flats of sabers. . . .

Mexico enjoyed the battle until, as a final part of the exercise, the Seventh, the Twelfth, and the Sixty-ninth infantry regiments suddenly advanced to the edge of the river bank, set up their machine guns and flopped down as if to fire upon the "Red" force in the corn fields on the other side of the river.

The spectators thought they saw trouble in the barrels of these 3,000 rifles and there was a wild scramble for burros and phaetons. The cloud of dust traveled the mile to Reynosa in remarkably short time.[39]

In the final phase of the exercise the "Blue" army conducted a fighting retreat back to its base at McAllen while fending off repeated cavalry charges by the "Reds." The troops had been ordered to exchange their ball ammunition for blanks before the exercise began, but not all did so. When a detachment of the 3rd U.S. Cavalry fired on a section of the "Blue" wagon train, one of the teamsters was shot in the arm and a mule was shot through the nose. An investigation was ordered. The other casualty was an infantryman, who, unable to get out of the way in time, was ridden down by a cavalry charge, suffering a broken arm and two broken ribs but being extremely lucky to be alive.[40]

At the conclusion of this extensive maneuver, the New Yorkers concentrated on refurbishing their equipment and preparing for the inspection visit of General Parker. On September 22, some eight thousand men passed in review before Parker at McAllen, the 7th New York as the senior regiment leading the parade. Following the 7th were the 12th and 69th. Behind the infantry brigade came the divisional pack train of sixty animals, Field Hospitals Nos. 1 and 2, Ambulance Companies Nos. 1, 2, and 4, the 22nd Engineers, the 1st and 2nd Field Artillery regiments, the 1st Cavalry, and Squadron A. Men who had been in the National Guard for decades described it as the greatest spectacle the New York regiments had presented since the Civil War. The New Yorkers, lean and tanned by their border experience, now considered themselves veterans and marched with a confident step. Following the review Battery E, 2nd Field Artillery, marched to the railroad station accompanying the coffin of a comrade who had died of injuries received in the performance of his duty.[41]

More marching was in store. On October 1, General Funston, who was touring the militia camps in the Brownsville District, reviewed the New York division accompanied by General Parker. In addition to the review the men had a field day on the parade ground, a highlight of which was the cavalry demonstrating "Roman riding" and other tricks of horsemanship. Publicly Funston was pleased by what he saw, expressing his satisfaction with the condition, morale, and discipline of the division and commenting especially on the horsemanship displayed. Some three thousand New Yorkers attended the free horse show of the 1st U.S. Cavalry at McAllen on October 7, at which nearly five hundred military mounts, artillery horses, and army mules were displayed.[42]

Although Funston publicly praised the New York division, privately he had reservations about several of its units. He recommended that Squadron A be returned from the border, the problem being the same as with the 7th New York and the 1st Illinois Field Artillery: too many of their members imagined that they were too important to be performing military duty. The result was considerable discontent in these organizations, which tended to demoralize other units. Funston commented that when he had inspected the New York division six weeks earlier, General O'Ryan told him that he wished he could get rid of the 7th New York as their continual bellyaching was making other organizations discontented. Furthermore, while O'Ryan did not specifically refer to Squadron A, Funston learned from other sources that the same condition largely obtained in that unit. Funston's assessment was:

> There is no getting around the fact that a great many men in some of those so-called crack city regiments are men of very much importance in the business life of their respective communities, and there is further no doubt of the fact that they do suffer more loss than men in other organizations who, as a rule, come from somewhat different walks of life. As a matter of fact, those men had no business going into the National Guard to start with, as they, like a good many other people, overlooked the obligations that they would be under if the federal service needed their services. I still believe it would be a good idea to get rid of Squadron A, but if it cannot be done without embarrassment because of the apparent favoritism shown, I think the matter had better be dropped.[43]

Morale improved when the War Department announced that an additional ten thousand guardsmen would be relieved from border duty and be replaced by eight thousand men currently in mobilization camps. The 1st Field Artillery, Ambulance Company No. 1, the 1st Battalion of the 22nd Engineers, and Field Hospital No. 1 were among those units going home. The 368-man engineer battalion traveled home comfortably in Pullmans, and upon reaching New York City proudly marched up Broadway to the cheers of an estimated ten thousand people.[44]

On September 17, the 3rd Tennessee Infantry, which had been at its mobilization camp at Nashville since June 27, entrained for the border, arriving in Pharr on September 20. The Tennesseans were brigaded with the 23rd and 74th New York.[45]

For the troops still in Texas there were periodic reminders that the border was dangerous. On the night of October 2 all New York units on detached duty guarding pumping stations and other outposts along the Rio Grande were ordered to take extra precautions by doubling guards and issuing sixty rounds of ball ammunition to every man. Bands of armed Mexicans had been spotted across the river. These, however, proved to be only reinforced patrols of Carranza troops and nothing untoward happened.[46] Ten days later there occurred an incident involving the 69th Infantry. A squad from Company E of that regiment was guarding the pumping station at Madero, and shortly after midnight one of the sentries thought he saw a boat pulling away from a sandbar on the Mexican side of the Rio Grande and then heard a gunshot. Believing himself under fire, he shot back, using up all his ammunition. Awakened by the shooting, the rest of the squad rushed to the riverbank and began firing. They were certain they saw boats crossing the river. Up and down the river, sentries, alarmed by the fusillade, opened fire on the enemy. Some seventy soldiers from the 69th ultimately got involved. One of the officers on the scene telephoned the signal corps at Mission that Mexicans crossing the river had fired on the 69th and that fire had been returned. The troops remained under arms the rest of the night but there was no further excitement and certainly no incoming fire. At dawn an abandoned boat was discovered on the American side of the river in a position that one sentry claimed it had not occupied the day before. The Mexican garrison across the river stoutly denied that any of its men had been involved. Only smugglers would be crossing from the Mexican bank, and it was unlikely that they would have chosen a crossing so well protected. In short, what was apparently one sentry's nervousness had triggered a panic among his companions.

Whether there had in fact been an attempted Mexican crossing or not, General O'Ryan and his staff began working on a plan for New York infantry companies permanently to cover fords, ferries, and pumping stations on the Rio Grande, giving some of the men experience in patrolling under conditions more like those they would encounter in wartime. The division received orders on October 14 to establish the following outposts along the Rio Grande:

7th—at Madero
12th—at Granjeño Ranch
69th—at Hidalgo
23rd—at Capote Ranch
74th—at San Juan Hacienda

A line of observation was expanded to cover fifty-two miles along the Rio Grande, reinforced by a main line of resistance twenty-eight miles long on the military road paralleling the river that General Zachary Taylor had built in 1847 during the Mexican War. Manning these outposts were alternating battalions of the regiments, each performing a weekly tour of duty in the trenches.[47] Besides strengthening border defense, patrolling broke the dull routine of camp life. Companies not on patrol received training in map reading, reconnaissance, and tactical problems.[48]

The plan was implemented on November 1.[49] Some two thousand New Yorkers (six battalions of infantry and a cavalry squadron) patrolled fifty miles of the Rio Grande, divided into twelve sectors, in coordination with detachments of the 28th U.S. Infantry and 3rd U.S. Cavalry, as well as guardsmen from Iowa, Nebraska, Minnesota, and South Dakota based at Llano Grande. The New York Signal Battalion and the 22nd Engineers maintained roads and telephone lines; the artillery was studying the fords and crossings on the river in order to be ready to support the infantry and cavalry in an emergency. This arrangement proved temporary, though. In late November the New Yorkers were relieved of patrol duty so they could receive intensified individual training. Regular army units took over their river patrols.[50]

Back in Albany, Governor Whitman echoed the sentiments of many other New Yorkers when he wrote to President Wilson on September 20 inquiring whether additional National Guard units from that state could be ordered home. Whitman pointed out that New York still had some twelve thousand guardsmen in federal service. They had been on active duty for more than three months, the war crisis with Mexico had seemingly passed, and the men were suffering as far as their families, employment, and business interests were concerned. Wilson replied by listing the New York units already demobilized and emphasized that the emergency that had produced the guard call-up "unhappily still exists." The president added that conditions in northern Mexico were improving and that it would probably be possible "in the near future" to do more to relieve the militia.[51]

Thus for the short run at least it was business as usual for the New York division. General O'Ryan decided to give the 1st Cavalry a workout by ordering them to make a 125-mile route march, to Brownsville and back, making it the longest march by any regiment on the border. Traveling partly on the old military road, it took the troopers three days to reach Brownsville. On October 23, General Parker reviewed them on the parade ground at Fort Brown, following which officers from Squadron A took on a team from the 3rd Cavalry in polo, losing the match. And the next day the New York cavalry left Brownsville for Point Isabel, twenty miles away on the Gulf Coast, so the troopers could swim in the surf and fish for tarpon.[52]

O'Ryan had also planned to have the 7th New York make the march to Brownsville but abandoned the idea, at least temporarily, because the 7th had already seen more than its share of field duty. Still, this remained an option not just for the 7th but for the other infantry regiments. In the meantime, the infantry brigade underwent two days of maneuvers: the 69th blocked the military road near Hidalgo against successive assaults by the 7th and 12th Infantry. On the second day of the maneuver the 7th defended the brigade camp against an attack by the 12th.[53]

The weary infantrymen could only envy the 2nd battalion, 1st Field Artillery, which started for home on October 27. "Thin, but tanned and vigorous" the five hundred officers and men of the battalion arrived back in New York City on November 4.[54] And on November 16, the War Department announced that six thousand more guardsmen would be going home. The 7th New York Infantry was one of those fortunate units.[55] On November 21, "as the last note of the general bugle call was sounded in the camp of the Seventh Regiment this afternoon every tent was struck. Where the minute before had been a city of conicals [tents] was now only a flat, brown waste, with a thousand happy soldiers in uniforms dancing about and cheering."[56] The 7th left the next day, seen off by the officers and bands of three other regiments and all the young Anglo women of the countryside, an eight-hour farewell extravaganza.

On reaching New York City the regiment, including ex-members, made the obligatory parade up Fifth Avenue behind its fife and drum corps, passing in review before Governor Whitman. The regiment was mustered out of federal service on December 2, 1916.[57] Sadly, shortly after returning home a guardsman from the 7th received a note from his fiancée saying she was marrying another. The devastated suitor dressed himself meticulously in his uniform, went into the kitchen, stuck his head in the oven, and gassed himself.[58]

The men of the 7th had perhaps marched more smartly than usual on November 16 in what was their final parade, for Governor Whitman had come to McAllen to visit his guardsmen on November 15–16, and the officers had received him in great style.[59] Of the nearly 20,000 New Yorkers who had seen border service, only about 9,500 were still in Texas. Whitman not only watched 8,000 of them pass in review, which he described as a "magnificent military spectacle," but he visited the various camps, the base hospital, and even the outposts on the Rio Grande. Before returning to Albany, the governor and Mrs. Whitman were guests at the King Ranch. When Whitman was inaugurated for his second term on January 1, 1917, a detachment of the 7th was his escort of honor.[60]

A major flap had occurred at McAllen on November 29. Colonel Gordon Johnston, formerly a captain in the 11th U.S. Cavalry and an aide to Major General Leonard Wood and now detailed to command the 12th, tendered his resignation, as did forty of his officers. Officers of the 12th New York Infantry, by now compressed into two battalions, claimed that General O'Ryan had insulted the regiment during a parade for Senator James W. Wadsworth of New York and a major in the Mexican Army. The alleged insult was that the unit had passed the reviewing stand with the U.S. flag furled, whereupon O'Ryan ordered them to march by again but led the dignitaries off the reviewing stand before the 12th made its reappearance. Johnston stated that the reason for keeping the flag furled was that it was so tattered there was fear the wind would whip it to pieces; a replacement flag had been requisitioned several weeks earlier but had not arrived. Although headquarters denied that any insult had been intended, the 12th's "officers say that after such an affront, given before a United States Senator from New York and an officer of a foreign government, the other regiments of the New York Division and several hundred spectators, they cannot serve conscientiously and loyally under the present divisional commander." They insisted that their letters of resignation be forwarded up the chain of command to the War Department. Regular officers in Washington, D.C., were indignant at the actions of the New Yorkers, stating that this reflected badly on military discipline.[61]

Colonel Johnston's resignation letter and his request for an investigation, as well as General O'Ryan's account of the incident, were sent to General Funston. At O'Ryan's request Funston promptly accepted Johnston's resignation, removed him from command, and ordered him to report to General Parker, who placed him on inactive duty at Fort Brown. Funston also ordered an investigation, "informed the officers of the regiment that no more resignations would be considered now," and appointed a regular officer in temporary command of the 12th New York. The forty officers of the 12th then withdrew their resignations.[62] On January 23, 1917, in a development that surprised many National Guard officers, Funston reinstated Colonel Johnson to his command. The 12th Infantry held a review for its returning commander. Funston reportedly took this action because he wanted an experienced regular officer leading the regiment.[63] When O'Ryan was asked his reaction, he merely replied that "General Funston . . . is my superior officer and I cannot discuss any action he may take in any matter."[64]

The affair was only of academic interest to the men of Squadron A, for on December 4 they received orders to return from border duty to be mustered out. They left McAllen on December 15 after a rousing sendoff by the 12th Infantry and the 1st Cavalry. "Bronzed and happy," they arrived back home after a week-long trip, bringing their horses, two burros, and a goat. As one of New York's premier units, they enjoyed an official reception, beginning with a review by Governor Whitman and other personages.[65] General O'Ryan received notification from Funston on December 7 that six thousand additional guardsmen were to be mustered out, including the divisional headquarters staff, Ambulance Company No. 2, Field Hospital No. 2, and the signal corps battalion, which arrived in New York City on December 20, 1916. The second battalion of the 22nd Engineers, 403 strong, arrived there on December 24 and marched up Fifth Avenue behind the regiment's new colonel, Cornelius Vanderbilt. Governor Whitman (who must have been getting tired of doing so) reviewed the troops.[66]

The exodus from the border accelerated. The War Department on December 18 announced that a total of 16,647 guardsmen would soon leave. This still left some 75,000 National Guard troops along the border. Among them were New York Ambulance Company No. 3, the 23rd Infantry, the 2nd Field Artillery, and Field Hospital No. 3. Because of a delay caused by a lack of railroad transportation, none of these units reached New York City before Christmas, to the bitter disappointment of the men. The 2nd Field Artillery finally left McAllen on December 29, the 23rd Infantry departing Pharr on January 2.[67]

After the 2nd Field Artillery regiment reached New York City there was a scandal. Six enlisted men were under arrest in the armory, one for desertion and the rest for minor offenses. When they refused to perform police duty as ordered, their lieutenant decreed that as punishment they be tied spread-eagled on the wheel of a gun carriage. Five of the offenders then agreed to police duty. The sixth, Private Max Kellerman, confined for being drunk, still refused, and was spread-eagled for an hour, in full view of the many visitors observing from the armory's gallery. General O'Ryan and Governor Whitman refused to take action, pointing out that the regiment had not yet been mustered out and was still in federal service. Some regular officers remarked that the punishment was certainly unusual but was not a violation of the Articles of War, which only prohibited flogging and branding. The weight of army opinion, however, was that tying men to gun carriages had not been practiced for years, besides which "cruel or unusual" punishment was prohibited. Furthermore, punishment could not be inflicted at the will of an officer but had to be imposed by a duly-constituted court-martial.[68]

The army began an investigation of the affair, which became messier when enlisted men came forward alleging that such punishment had occurred several times while the regiment was in Texas. They asserted that one man had been spread-eagled all night. They also complained about the food. The regiment was mustered out on January 12. The spread-eagled private and the other offenders received summary punishment and were transferred to Fort Hamilton in Brooklyn for a few days' confinement. Investigation revealed that "four others besides Kellerman were lashed to gun carriage wheels and for periods varying from one to two hours [and] they so remained on the drill floor in full view of other soldiers and of visitors to the armory." The two artillery officers involved were court-martialed.[69]

Yet the "wagon wheel treatment" continued to be employed during World War I in cases of men being AWOL.[70] In a development unrelated to the 2nd Field Artillery affair, the army conducted rigid inspections of the New York units that had returned from the border, the first inspection under the new National Defense Act.[71]

Upon General O'Ryan's departure the New York troops still on the border came under General Parker, commanding the Brownsville District.[72] They were given light duty during the week preceding Christmas, and on Christmas eve Father Duffy of the 69th said midnight mass, one of the many religious observances held.[73] Religion played a significant part in the lives of many guardsmen. According to a YMCA official who spent two months working among the troops, "There is more religion to the square inch among the troops on the Mexican border than there is to the square yard in New York."[74] To celebrate the New Year, the New Yorkers at McAllen had a parade down the brightly lit main street. An hour later an exuberant Texan shot out one of the street lights, whereupon the power company turned off the current to preclude further vandalism.

The week of rest in the camps of the 12th and 69th New York Infantry ended on January 1, and the regular training schedule resumed.[75] In early January there was a report that the 3rd Tennessee Infantry, which had occupied the camp vacated in McAllen when the 2nd New York returned home, would be transferred to San Benito. This was welcome news to the Military Police, for there had been constant trouble between the Tennesseans and the New Yorkers. Quite often fistfights had mushroomed into near-riots, and it was commonly believed that the transfer had been ordered in the interests of peace and tranquility. The other report current was that the 74th New York Infantry would be transferred to McAllen. General Parker came from his Brownsville headquarters to McAllen to observe the exhibition and drill of the 1st New York Cavalry.[76]

In a welcome but "better late than never" development, the New York Zoological Society announced that it was delivering to the surgeon general of the United States two hundred tubes of rattlesnake serum imported from Brazil for use among the troops on the Mexican border.[77]

The War Department ordered a further withdrawal of National Guard units from the border on January 20. The 25,243 men that General Funston selected reduced the border guard to between 55,000 and 60,000 regulars and guardsmen.[78] Among the units Funston chose were the 74th New York, Ambulance Company No. 4, the Field Bakery Company (the only one in the National Guard), and the Division Field Train.[79]

The situation changed dramatically when in February President Wilson broke diplomatic relations with Germany. As the United States moved toward war with the Central Powers, the return of guard regiments from the Mexican border was accelerated. The 3rd Tennessee, 1st Cavalry, and Field Hospital Company No. 1 were mustered out at Knoxville on March 14, 1917.[80]

Meanwhile, the entire New York National Guard and Naval Militia had been activated on February 3 by Governor Whitman after a conference with General O'Ryan. The National Guard was ordered to guard every arsenal, armory, and watershed in the state, while the Naval Militia guarded the bridges.[81] On February 17, the remaining National Guard units on the border were ordered home. The 12th and 69th New York Infantry, the 1st Cavalry, Field Hospital No. 4, and the 3rd Field Artillery, which left for Buffalo on March 6, 1917, jubilantly prepared to break camp.[82]

Whereas the other units returned by rail, the Division Field Train had left McAllen on February 11 for a three-hundred-mile, seventeen-day overland march via Laredo to San Antonio. The column of canvas-covered wagons sometimes marched at night and rested during the day; otherwise, hundreds of mules could have died. One mule was hit by an automobile. The injured animal was placed aboard the lead wagon, strapped in with its head sticking out the front, and rode like that the rest of the way to San Antonio. The novelty of this sight caused considerable comment, not the least from General Pershing and his staff, who on February 28 watched the column pass through the city to their temporary station at Camp Wilson. There the mules were turned in at the remount station, the wagons were dismantled and loaded on boxcars, and on March 9 the unit took the train for New York.[83]

The 12th and 69th were scheduled to return to New York City via Washington, D.C., for they were to participate in President Wilson's second inaugural parade.[84] Because of the imminence of war with Germany a somber mood characterized the inauguration, which was marked by the tightest security since Abraham Lincoln's first inauguration in 1861. Secret Service agents, regular troops, detectives, and police formed a hollow square around

Wilson as he drove in a carriage between the White House and the Capitol. In addition, marksmen were stationed on the roofs of buildings along the route. And, for the first time since Lincoln's second inauguration, a military guard was placed along the parade route; the 12th and 69th New York Infantry lined Pennsylvania Avenue twenty paces apart with their backs to the crowd. At intersections, the guardsmen faced the crowd as the president's carriage passed.

Following the inauguration, President Wilson reviewed the parade, which was essentially a military one. The New York contingents had a prominent role in the spectacle, of which Major General Hugh L. Scott, the army chief of staff, was the grand marshal. Governor Charles S. Whitman was mounted on a charger, escorted by Squadron A in elaborate dress uniforms and with sabers drawn. Behind the governor's staff marched the 69th, whose band played "The Harp That Once through Tara's Halls." The 12th New York came next, its band playing the less-inspired "Hail, Hail, the Gang's All Here." Then came a real crowd pleaser, the 1st Armored Motor Battery. Six men in khaki stood at rigid attention in each of the three khaki-colored armored cars. Each vehicle had two turrets mounting a machine gun apiece. A supply truck followed, then fifty soldiers on motorcycles, four of which had sidecars with machine guns. The remainder had rifles slung across the handlebars.[85] Tragically, the very day the 1st Armored Motor Battery returned to New York City, one of its privates died in a motorcycle accident on Fifth Avenue.[86]

Having performed their inaugural duties, the 12th and 69th reached New York City on March 6. For the 46 officers and 918 enlisted men of the 69th, who had been in federal service longer than any other New York outfit, it was a particularly memorable homecoming. Greeting them at Grand Central Station was a band playing "Garryowen." Both regiments were welcomed by their depot battalions and by Spanish-American War veterans. In addition, the 7th New York met the 69th and escorted them to their armory by way of returning the compliment; the 69th had escorted the 7th when that regiment left for the border. The new arrivals enjoyed the customary welcoming parade. One regiment marched up Fifth Avenue, the other down Fifth Avenue. Cheering spectators lined the sidewalks eight deep and filled the windows of hotels, clubs, and stores. The 69th's band played "The Rocky Road to Dublin." Governor Whitman, accompanied by General O'Ryan and other dignitaries, reviewed the parades, catching a bad cold as a result, for it was a frigid day. A group of prominent Roman Catholic clerics braved the wintry weather to watch the parades from the steps of Saint Patrick's Cathedral. Following the parades, the two regiments marched to their armories for a reception and joyful reunion with their friends and families. Ever the politician, Governor Whitman dropped by to deliver a brief welcoming speech. The men would not be mustered out for another seven to ten days but were allowed to go home and to report daily at the armories. Returning to civilian life, Father Duffy resumed his parochial duties at the church of Our Savior in the Bronx.[87]

A heartening development was that employment had been found for everyone in the 69th, and the officers of the 12th, in cooperation with the business community, were engaged in finding jobs for all their men.[88] A detachment of the 12th had one more ceremonial duty—to escort James W. Gerard, the former U.S. ambassador to Germany, when he arrived in New York City on March 16, 1917. Gerard had been a captain and adjutant of the 12th for years. The 1st Field Artillery band provided the music for the procession.[89]

With the arrival in New York City of the Division Field Train, Ambulance Company No. 4, and the 1st Cavalry, the state's National Guard experience on the border ended on March 14, 1917. The seven hundred cavalrymen got the traditional parade down Fifth Avenue and were reviewed by the mayor and General O'Ryan.[90]

Commemorating New York's border service was an event that the newspapermen and magazine writers who had been correspondents with the Punitive Expedition and on the border, together with a number of New York guardsmen, organized—a "Rio Grande Rally," a costume ball in New York City on March 29 at which everyone had to appear in Mexican, Texan, or military attire. A number of "military mascots"—burros, goats, and so on—brought back from the border were paraded. Professional dancers and the chorus of a current Broadway show performed before an appreciative audience. The evening's menu was Mexican food, but the Prohibitionists on the organizing committee succeeded in keeping that potent Mexican liquor pulque off the bill of fare. The highlight of the evening was when "Pancho Villa" appeared at thirty minutes after midnight. The proceeds from the highly successful event were donated to the Red Cross.[91]

The state of New York recognized the guard's border service by having the adjutant general commission a Mexican Border Service medal and ribbon for anyone who served there between June 18, 1916, and April 5, 1917. On the obverse of the medal was the Aztec war god Huitzilopochtli, and on the reverse the New York coat of arms and "Mexican Border Service, 1916–1917. Presented by the State of New York." "The colors of the ribbon will be red, blue, yellow, green (center), yellow, blue and red, in the order named."[92]

General Funston and staff on a tour of inspection of border posts. Courtesy of the El Paso Public Library, Horne Collection.

Pharr, Texas, with New York National Guard encampment in the background. Courtesy of Margaret H. McAllen Memorial Archives, Museum of South Texas History.

Funeral in Pharr for a 3rd Tennessee Infantry private who drowned. Courtesy of Margaret H. McAllen Memorial Archives, Museum of South Texas History.

The 2nd New York Field Artillery passing through Pharr. Courtesy of Margaret H. McAllen Memorial Archives, Museum of South Texas History.

Rifle pit on the Rio Grande, 23rd New York Infantry. Courtesy of Margaret H. McAllen Memorial Archives, Museum of South Texas History.

The 23rd New York Infantry machine gun company. Courtesy of Margaret H. McAllen Memorial Archives, Museum of South Texas History.

Example of Lower Rio Grande Valley vegetation with which troops had to contend. Courtesy of Margaret H. McAllen Memorial Archives, Museum of South Texas History.

The 23rd New York Infantry resting while on a 110-mile hike. Courtesy of Margaret H. McAllen Memorial Archives, Museum of South Texas History.

Company I, 23rd New York Infantry at Pharr, August 1916. In World War I, five of this unit were killed, three were wounded, one was taken prisoner, and two were missing in action. Courtesy of Margaret H. McAllen Memorial Archives, Museum of South Texas History.

The 23rd New York Infantry Post Exchange, Pharr, Texas. Courtesy of Margaret H. McAllen Memorial Archives, Museum of South Texas History.

The 2nd New York Field Artillery practice firing. Courtesy of Margaret H. McAllen Memorial Archives, Museum of South Texas History.

Camp of the 4th South Dakota Infantry at San Benito, Texas. Courtesy of the South Dakota State Historical Society.

Troop B, Texas Cavalry Squadron, on the Rio Grande at Ruidosa, Texas, in the Big Bend. Courtesy of the Texas Military Forces Museum.

Army YMCA in the Big Bend. Courtesy of the Texas Military Forces Museum.

Tractor train in the Big Bend. Courtesy of the Texas Military Forces Museum.

Football game in Ruidosa. Courtesy of the Texas Military Forces Museum.

Bird's-eye view of Camp Cotton, El Paso, Texas. Courtesy of the El Paso Public Library, Horne Collection.

The 5th Massachusetts Infantry Band at Camp Cotton. Courtesy of the El Paso Public Library, Aultman Collection.

Pennsylvania guardsmen establishing camp in El Paso. Courtesy of the El Paso Public Library, Horne Collection.

Twenty thousand guardsmen on the "Big Hike" from El Paso to Las Cruces, New Mexico. Courtesy of the El Paso Public Library, Horne Collection.

Major General Charles M. Clement (*center*), commander of the 7th (Pennsylvania) Division, and Brigadier General George Bell, Jr. (*left*), commander of the El Paso District, at a National Guard review. Courtesy of the El Paso Public Library, Aultman Collection.

The 8th Ohio Infantry Band in the parade of a war-strength division in El Paso. Courtesy of the El Paso Public Library, Horne Collection.

233

The Ohio-Pennsylvania Brigade in the parade of a war-strength division. Courtesy of the El Paso Public Library, Horne Collection.

The war-strength division parade in El Paso. Courtesy of the El Paso Public Library, Horne Collection.

Remount station at Fort Bliss, El Paso. Courtesy of the El Paso Public Library, Horne Collection.

Typical sandstorm at Fort Bliss. Courtesy of the El Paso Public Library, Horne Collection.

National guardsmen erecting tents at Deming, New Mexico. Courtesy of the El Paso Public Library, Horne Collection.

Camp of 1st Colorado Artillery, Deming. Courtesy of the Deming Luna County Museum Archives.

A detachment of the 1st New Mexico Infantry at Columbus, New Mexico. Courtesy of the Deming Luna County Museum Archives.

The 2nd Montana Infantry guarding the copper smelters at Douglas, Arizona. Courtesy of the Arizona Historical Society, Panoramic Photo Collection, Photo #26206.

Officers of the 5th New Jersey Infantry at the international boundary marker at Douglas. Mexican sentry box in the background. Courtesy of the Arizona Historical Society.

The 1st California Field Artillery at Nogales, Arizona. Courtesy of the California State Military Museum, 1st Battalion of Field Artillery, California National Guard, Battery C, Mexican Border Service, 19 June 1916 to 6 January 1917, Major General Otto Sandman Collection.

The U.S.-Mexico boundary running down the middle of the street in Nogales. Courtesy of Pimería Alta Historical Museum collections, Nogales, Arizona.

The 3rd Oregon Infantry on the move, California border. Courtesy, Oregon Military Museum, Camp Withycombe, Clackamas, Oregon.

Chapter 10

Laredo

Laredo was one of the most strategic points along the Rio Grande. Nuevo Laredo across the river had been repeatedly fought over during the Mexican Revolution, for it was one of the principal Mexican ports of entry. At Laredo the International & Great Northern Railroad connected with the Mexican National Railroad, one of the trunk lines running south to Mexico City. Elements in the Mexican Army entertained notions of capturing Laredo, whose principal defense was Fort McIntosh, situated in a military reservation that the city of Laredo had donated.[1]

The Laredo District extended for about a hundred miles along the Rio Grande—thirty-two miles northwest and sixty-seven miles southeast of town. As relations between the United States and Mexico deteriorated, conditions around Laredo were considered so threatening that many of the Anglo women in the town, including the families of army officers, were sent to San Antonio for safety.[2] Brigadier General William A. Mann arrived in Laredo on May 7, 1916, succeeding Brigadier General R. K. Evans as commander of the Laredo garrison and the 2nd Brigade, with headquarters at Fort McIntosh. Mann, who for some time had commanded the cavalry and artillery school of instruction at Fort Sill, Oklahoma, now divided his time between Fort McIntosh and the camp of the 9th U.S. Infantry regiment, the principal component of the Laredo garrison.[3] The battery of the 6th U.S. Field Artillery, stationed at the 9th Infantry camp adjoining Fort McIntosh, was ordered to Douglas, Arizona, where the 6th Field Artillery was being concentrated for possible action in Mexico. Batteries E and F and the headquarters of the 2nd Battalion of the 3rd U.S. Field Artillery arrived in Laredo as replacements. These units, the 9th Infantry, and a squadron of the 14th U.S. Cavalry, now constituted the reinforced garrison. (In July, Company C, U.S. Engineers, manning a large searchlight with a range of two miles, arrived at Fort McIntosh.)[4]

On June 10, the date of the proposed Mexican attack on Laredo, nothing untoward happened. Mann met his counterpart, General Alfredo Ricaut, on the international bridge to discuss the de la Rosa threat, and Ricaut assured the American general that he would crush de la Rosa or at least drive him away from the border.[5] Doubtless Ricaut's cooperative attitude stemmed from the fact that the United States had learned of the planned invasion and was taking steps to repel it. Besides strengthening the 14th Cavalry's patrols along the Rio Grande, Mann deployed an infantry company on the lawn of the federal building ready for any eventuality. Moreover, there had arrived at Fort McIntosh five large Packard trucks capable of moving troops rapidly wherever needed—two trucks could transport an infantry company. And still more reinforcements continued to arrive—two companies of coast artillery came by special train from New York and Boston to serve in static defense as infantry. By mid-July they were joined by eight more coast artillery companies, and the ten units were organized into a provisional regiment. The Texas National Guard—Troops A, B, C, and D of the 1st Texas Cavalry Squadron—arrived (minus their horses) by special train from San Antonio and were quartered at the 9th U.S. Infantry camp, along with the 3rd U.S. Field Artillery battalion and the coast artillery companies.[6] (On July 14, the Texas Cavalry Squadron left for their new station at Marfa, in the Big Bend.)[7] As a further precaution, under orders from Washington, D.C., the federal authorities seized all the arms and ammunition in Laredo. All this saber rattling made a considerable impression across the Rio Grande. On June 19, intense excitement prevailed in Nuevo Laredo, and all business houses were closed by official order, the direct effect of the National Guard call-up. Moreover, the garrison hurriedly evacuated the town on July 1, falling back along the rail line.[8]

As part of the military buildup in Laredo it was announced that the National Guard of Missouri, Maine, and New Hampshire had been ordered to the border city, and frantic preparations commenced for their reception. Besides Fort McIntosh and the adjoining 9th U.S. Infantry encampment, at a third campsite, outside of the military reservation, workmen hurriedly cleared brush and laid water mains, while a 9th Infantry officer supervised the placing of small placards designating where the guardsmen's tents and other facilities were to go.[9]

First to arrive was the 5,030-man 1st Missouri Brigade, Brigadier General Harvey C. Clark commanding. Coming from their mobilization camp at the state rifle range near Nevada, Missouri, they constituted the bulk of the arriving guardsmen. There had been a delay in mustering them into federal service because the army had provided only a single mustering officer. And after the mustering process was nearly completed, a telegram arrived from the War Department advising that no mustering in was necessary. And the War Department could not provide in a timely manner the equipment it was supposed to, causing further delay. A tragedy occurred on June 29, when the acting chief surgeon of the Missouri Guard, who had been working around the clock supervising physical examinations and camp sanitation, had a seizure and died instantly.[10] While in camp some men refused to take the federal oath. In one company the seven recalcitrants were treated roughly: "Their uniforms were taken from them, they were given fatigue clothes and told to leave camp. Their departure was something of an event since their late comrades formed behind them with tin wash basins, and 'drummed them out of camp' by marching along, thumping on the tin pans and chanting in loud unison, 'Yellow, yellow, yellow.'"[11] Despite the delays, General Clark was able to state that: "Missouri was the first state to report its mobilization completed and with one exception, a Connecticut regiment, our troops were the first to reach the Border."[12]

The 1st Missouri Infantry, whose commander, Colonel Arthur B. Donnelly, had been elected in 1914, was mustered into federal service on June 25 and left for Laredo on July 1.[13] The 1st Missouri reportedly had some excitement on their journey to Laredo, its officers claiming that on three occasions—once in Kansas and twice in Texas—attempts were made, presumably by Mexicans, to wreck the trains on which the guardsmen were traveling. On the night of June 19, a small railroad bridge thirty miles east of Laredo was burned by parties unknown. It was this kind of incident that impelled General Funston and Secretary of War Baker to impose censorship on military movements.[14]

By July 16, the Missouri brigade, consisting of the 1st, 2nd, 3rd, and 4th Infantry regiments and 1st Battalion (Batteries A [St. Louis], B [Kansas City], and C [Independence]) Field Artillery,[15] Company A Signal Corps, Troop B Cavalry, Field Hospital Company No. 1, Ambulance Company

No. 1, and a machine gun company, had reached Laredo safely and had settled into their new tent city on the northern outskirts of town.[16] Company F 2nd Missouri Infantry and the machine gun company were composed largely of college men; the machine gun company consisted of St. Louis University students. The officers of the three artillery batteries later decided to recruit up to a total of six batteries, and they immediately dispatched a recruiting officer back to Missouri. The additional batteries were not, however, organized during the period of border service.[17] The Missouri State Aeronautical Society arranged to present a fully equipped airplane to the Missouri National Guard.[18] To keep the home folks apprised of the guardsmen's activities, correspondents from the *St. Louis Star*, the *St. Louis Post-Dispatch*, and the *St. Louis Republic* began filing their stories. And by the end of July a post office substation was established at Camp Missouri to serve the five thousand guardsmen there.[19]

The campsite allocated to the Missouri Guard was certainly not to their liking. When the 2nd Missouri arrived on July 7, the

> regiment detrained and marched about two miles to the place selected for its permanent camp, which proved to have been at one time an isolation camp for contagious diseases, and was still the public dumping ground for trash from the city of Laredo, and located in a section of the city where the population was mostly of Mexican peons. While it was muddy when the regiment arrived, it did not remain that way long—soon dust storms filled the eyes and ears, and covered the tent floors in drifts. The ants were thick and a great annoyance, while lizards and tarantulas appeared to dispute the coming of the soldiers.[20]

And as General Clark recalled, part of the camp

> had been used as a public dumping ground and in the midst of the camp were the public pest houses of Laredo from which typhus, typhoid and small-pox patients had been discharged about a month prior to our arrival. The amount of ground available for camping purposes was so limited that the camp was very much crowded and the dry soil made it so dusty that the strong winds and the unsanitary surroundings due to the squalid Mexican population all about the camp, made sanitation a very difficult problem. The water supply was inadequate and the delivery of lumber to construct latrines was so slow that conditions were very bad for the first two weeks. . . . The

presence of the pest houses in the midst of the camp had a depressing effect upon the men who could not be made to believe that there was no danger of infection. . . . One of the highly objectionable features was the presence of dozens of mushroom saloons which were erected just across the road and facing the camp. However, be it said to the credit of the Missouri National Guard their discipline was such that we were able to keep them from entering these places.[21]

Some distance northwest of the Missourians, a fourth camp had appeared by July 4—that of the Maine National Guard, which sent 1,514 officers and men to the border. Called into federal service on June 19, the 2nd Maine Infantry, Colonel Frank M. Hume commanding, mobilized at Camp Keyes, Augusta, and was mustered in on June 28. The regiment entrained the next day for Laredo, its federal service lasting until October 25. (Maine also maintained a coast artillery corps of thirteen companies.)[22] Controversy developed over the role of Governor Oakley C. Curtis. Republican newspapers in the state, led by the *Portland Press*, accused Curtis, a Democrat, of neglecting the troops and their needs during the mobilization and journey to the border which his supporters denounced as being politically motivated and false.[23]

The 2nd Maine traveled uncomfortably to the border in day coaches with three men to a double seat for two days until they reached Kansas City, where they received tourist sleepers, "thus affording the men two good nights of sleep before reaching Laredo."[24] The regiment, complete with band, was in good spirits and pitched its tents with brisk efficiency upon arriving in Laredo on July 4. The band, incidentally, up to ten days earlier had been the University of Maine band—now the only college band in the U.S. Army. The Maine contingent was not only well equipped but boasted a large Reo truck of its own.

As the day of Maine's arrival was a holiday, many Laredoans flocked to watch the soldiers at their labors, and a committee of the local Red Cross arrived in the afternoon with ice cream, cakes, and other delicacies for the newcomers from Missouri and Maine. The Maine adjutant general would express concern over learning from the regimental medical officer that Laredoans "have been very lavish in furnishing you with ice cream, also that the Mexicans are allowed on the camp grounds selling watermelon, fruit, candy, etc. I do not wish to say too much but Captain Foster suggests that this is a matter which should be looked after very carefully. The men should not eat ice cream made down there and especially any of the fruit handled by those dirty Mexicans." That evening many of the troops went into town for what would become a daily ritual—promenading around the plazas or attending the movie theater. And on July 17, morale improved even more because the troops, still sweltering in their woolen uniforms, received "khaki clothing for use in the tropics."[25]

The Maine regiment settled in comfortably, a lieutenant colonel reporting on July 19 that:

> We reached Laredo the afternoon of July 4th, and since that time have been getting settled and now are about ready to begin to build an organization on the return of the Battalions from Patrol duty on which they have been sent. The heat here is something new to Maine men but there is no humidity and there have been no prostrations. And every day there is a cool breeze blowing, which offsets to a degree the heat of the sun. And the nights are the most delightful I have ever experienced. Our sickness so far is from minor ailments due to change of living and food, and we believe that we have not so much sickness as we would have in camp at Augusta. The food supply is ample and of excellent quality, and water is piped through the camp, with a tap at each kitchen, and an ample supply for bathing and watering streets about camp. The water is filtered but we are ordered to boil it before drinking, which of course takes time and causes some objection. . . . In relation to certain "Diamond Dick" or "Nick Carter" tales which have been related in certain State of Maine papers, in regard to stabbings, shootings and suicides, I would state that it has never been the experience of the Regiment to be quartered in a place where they were so well treated by the citizens as in the City of Laredo. We are welcomed here heartily and the Board of Trade has done everything in its power to make us comfortable and to make us feel at home.[26]

By late summer, there had developed in the 2nd Maine a steady flow of requests for discharges because of dependent families. There being no state law providing assistance, the cities and towns were trying to look after National Guard families.[27] Although many requests upon investigation were deemed fraudulent, enough men were leaving to be cause for concern. Compounding the problem, letters of complaint from the men were frequently published in Maine newspapers.[28] Shedding light on the matter of discharges, not just for Maine but for the guard in general, when

Congress passed an act providing that guardsmen with dependents could apply for discharge, a veritable stampede resulted. On July 6, Secretary Baker authorized the discharge of enlisted guardsmen who had one or more dependents and instructed recruiting officers not to enlist men with dependents.[29] This reportedly caused some commanders, worried that their units would be gutted, to come up with all sorts of obstructions to avoid processing discharges.[30]

The flow of new recruits from Maine slowed to a trickle, and the Maine Adjutant General, George McL. Presson, asked the colonel of the 2nd Maine for help in securing some nine hundred men to bring the regiment up to wartime strength: "What I want to ask of you is to send me pictures of companies, squads, patrols, also camp grounds. Send the most inviting pictures you have, not prairie or desert land but hills if you have any and streams and the best you can get that will appeal to the public."[31]

Between the Missouri and Maine cantonments a fifth military installation, the New Hampshire camp, appeared by the end of July. The New Hampshire National Guard consisted of the 1st Infantry, Troop A Cavalry, Battery A Field Artillery, Company A Signal Corps, and Field Hospital No. 1. (The army would distribute the New Hampshire National Guard widely: Troop A Cavalry, at Brownsville; Field Hospital No. 1, at Deming; Company A Signal Corps and Battery A Field Artillery, at San Antonio; 1st Infantry, at Laredo.)

New Hampshire adjutant general Charles W. Howard issued the mobilization order on June 19, Camp Spaulding at Concord being the mobilization point. As matters developed, the guardsmen remained at the camp until their full complement was recruited and adequately equipped. Some local newspapers stated that the New Hampshire National Guard was ready—no equipment was lacking and abundant supplies were stored at the camp arsenal.[32] But other newspapers reported that the 1st New Hampshire Infantry, Colonel M. J. Healey commanding, which was scheduled to leave for the border on June 29, was unfit for duty and lacked equipment.[33]

On June 26, Major General Leonard Wood, commander of the Eastern Department, ordered the 1st New Hampshire Infantry to entrain at once, it being among the National Guard regiments being rushed to the border. Yet the rigid physical examinations conducted by army physicians resulted in one-third of the regiment being rejected. A frantic recruiting drive ensued, and by July 11, the regiment finally reached peacetime strength and was deemed ready for the field. It was mustered into federal service, although a third of its personnel were raw recruits.[34]

Perhaps the most distinctive feature of the 1st New Hampshire Infantry was its Company A, "composed of French Canadians—a husky bunch, who hold the record for being the best drilled company in the entire East (at the last big militia encampment held in the East). It was first to achieve readiness when mobilization was ordered. All are tall, perfect specimens."[35]

On July 15, the 1st New Hampshire Infantry and the artillery battery marched through the streets of Concord to the cheers of thousands, escorted by veterans of the Civil War and the Spanish-American War and reviewed by Governor Roland H. Spaulding and other dignitaries. The cavalry troop, signal corps company, and field hospital company had not yet been mustered in, and with one thousand more men needed to put New Hampshire on a wartime footing, Camp Spaulding became a recruiting camp. There followed an uncomfortable six-day journey by rail, with makeshift kitchens placed in baggage cars. Making the trip memorable were delays, derailments, and mechanical breakdowns. The troops' spirits did rise as they traveled through Texas, where at every station they received a rousing welcome.

When the weary guardsmen reached Laredo on July 20, a large crowd cheered them as they marched from the railroad station to their new camp, located on level ground just north of the Missouri brigade headquarters and equipped with telephones, water, gas, and electric lights.[36] Their initial impression of Laredo was one of dust, heat, and no trees, subsequently modified by sand storms and electrical storms.

Colonel Healey was nearly the first New Hampshire casualty. It seems that a sentry going off duty at the Missouri headquarters one morning accidentally fired his rifle, the round passing through two tents, into the colonel's tent, through a pair of boots, a pair of riding pants, an overcoat, and finally lodging in some books in a footlocker. The colonel stormed into the Missouri headquarters and sarcastically asked General Clark, the brigade commander, if that was the morning gun, and if so, would they please elevate it. Clark genially informed Colonel Healey that it was a quaint western custom and the men from New Hampshire would doubtless grow accustomed to it. "Cordial relations were restored before the colonel departed." But the good feelings did not last. There was no love lost between New Hampshire and Missouri because on repeated occasions stray rounds from the Missouri camp whistled through that of New Hampshire.

A frustrated Colonel Healy finally complained to Laredo District headquarters, with the result that the Missouri sentries received orders to carry unloaded weapons.[37]

By August, Laredo boasted six military camps, all located within the city limits, almost adjoining each other, and equipped with telephones, electric lights, waterworks, gas, and so forth: Fort McIntosh (a squadron of the 14th U.S. Cavalry); the 9th U.S. Infantry camp (9th Infantry and 4th Provisional Coast Artillery Regiment); Camp Missouri (which boasted a post office substation and a weekly paper, *The Sentinel*); Camp Maine; Camp New Hampshire; and Heights Camp (Troop B, 1st Missouri Cavalry, and Batteries E and F, 3rd U.S. Field Artillery).[38] By late September, the camps' wooden mess halls and kitchens had replaced the original cook tents, and a veritable city of wood-framed tents had mushroomed in the abandoned onion fields of north Laredo.[39]

The vexing shortage of machine guns was not as great in Laredo as at some of the other concentration points: the army reported that "all regiments except Third Missouri equipped with guns, some companies just being organized; very little instruction as yet has been given."[40]

When it rained in Laredo it rained in torrents. On July 21, a storm blew down a number of tents, but this was only the beginning. On the evening of August 18, the worst storm on record—a small hurricane—struck the Laredo area with seventy-mile-an-hour wind, the fierce wind and torrential downpour continuing all night, blowing down many of the tents. The storm left six inches of water, blew down three-fourths of the New Hampshire tents, including the regimental infirmary, demolished a wooden mess hall, and scattered equipment and personal possessions over a wide area. The soldiers, exhausted from sitting in water throughout the night holding down their tents during the deluge, finished a thoroughly miserable night by sleeping in the rain wherever they could.[41] Then on September 13, three inches of rain flooded the National Guard tent city and produced a nine-inch rise in the Rio Grande.[42]

The military was not just more numerous, it was also significantly more mechanized. There were now a hundred army trucks in Laredo, virtually all of them with civilian drivers and mechanics since the army was way behind the curve in training its own personnel in these skills. But "one of the greatest nuisances Laredo residents have to suffer is the impudent, arrogant contempt for the comfort of the citizens shown by drivers of army trucks," who drove day and night with mufflers roaring and habitually sped through the city's narrow and congested streets. Since they were civilians, the only way the army could punish them was by firing them, which of course defeated the object of the exercise.[43]

General Funston daily received requests from small Texas towns, some of them a day's travel from the border, urging him to station large National Guard contingents in their localities. Everywhere the National Guard went it brought in a lot of money, and business boomed.[44] This generalization certainly applied to Laredo, population fourteen thousand. The influx of regulars and guardsmen rejuvenated the town. The military presence now exceeded ten thousand soldiers. When the guardsmen received their first pay, in August, it amounted to about $250,000, by far the largest payroll in the city's history. Although the men would remit about three-fourths of the sum to their families, at least $60,000 would be spent in Laredo itself, and this did not even include the pay of the two thousand regulars (some $50,000 monthly) or what the army was spending locally on supplies and maintenance (about $100,000 monthly). So, "many failing Laredo businesses are now booming."[45] Not surprisingly, the local newspaper commented that "the hardest blow Laredo could have received would be the withdrawal of the eight thousand or so militiamen from the city. They are a fine lot of young men and are becoming acclimated to the place. Their loss would also mean a financial loss of about $10,000 a day to Laredo."[46]

Panic struck the business community over the possibility of losing this bonanza. A committee of prominent Laredoans headed by the county judge telegraphed to their congressman, John Nance Garner, that there existed dangerously unsanitary conditions at the Missouri and Maine camps and that the water was contaminated. Although the committee's actions were a ploy to persuade the army to spend still more money on these encampments, there was some basis for their allegations. The committee urged that more buildings be erected, an improved sewage system be installed, and numerous other expensive improvements be made, improvements that would bring substantial additional sums to Laredo.[47] Congressman Garner sent the telegram to the War Department, which immediately demanded a reply from General Funston. The latter was furious both that Laredoans were using political pressure and that they had gone over his head in their complaint, so he called Laredo's bluff—announcing that if conditions were as dire as was claimed, why then he would just transfer all eight thousand guardsmen to healthier locales.[48]

Alarm and despondency gripped the city. As the local paper lamented, Funston had treated the subject sarcastically in the San Antonio newspapers, and he had hurt Laredo's feelings. So, the local movers and shakers quickly convened a mass meeting to repudiate the complaint committee and prepared to dispatch another committee to Fort Sam Houston to plead directly with Funston. To their enormous relief, when they appealed to Funston by telephone shortly before the committee was to leave, the general announced that the guardsmen would stay and he would detail an inspector to investigate conditions in Laredo.

The *Laredo Weekly Times* ran an indignant editorial that the recent reports that the National Guard would be removed from Laredo showed that "whatever our appreciation of their stay here, it is surpassed by the desire of other cities to have them located in their midst." No sooner did the rumors circulate than Corpus Christi and Eagle Pass each made a strenuous bid for the guardsmen. According to the editorial, Eagle Pass already had a large complement of National Guard and regular troops, while "Corpus hasn't had soldiers for so long they've forgotten what a soldier looks like." The newspaper reflected the citizens' outrage at the dastardly attempt by other cities to steal "their" guardsmen. The *Times* did allow that Laredo was hot and dusty but pointed out that it was a dry heat, which the National Guard undoubtedly preferred to the humidity of their home towns, adding that every effort was being made to cope with the considerable dust by frequent and copious sprinklings of water. "One thing that is missing to those who come from a heavily timbered country is shade. This can't be helped easily but by building shelters. But the same thing is true of Eagle Pass and Corpus despite their claims to superiority over Laredo."[49]

The *Laredo Times* also addressed stories in guardsmen's hometown newspapers such as the *St. Louis Globe Democrat* about "the awful conditions prevailing in the border camps," stressing that it was newspaper correspondents, not guardsmen, who were complaining. "But recent issues have contained articles which came direct from officers of the Missouri National Guard and which have been fair in every respect. Tales of horrible heat that prostrated Guardsmen have given way to articles telling of the magnificent condition of the Missouri Guard, as well as reprints of menus given the men by the officers." The editorial quoted one Missouri officer as saying: "If there are any companies that are dissatisfied with their rations, it is their own fault. The government allows each company 27 cents a day for each man, and the captain can buy whatever the men want with that money. I know my men are not grumbling about their meals." Colonel Arthur B. Donnelly, commanding the 1st Missouri Infantry, sent to the St. Louis papers for publication a sample menu:

Breakfast: bacon and gravy, German fried potatoes, syrup and coffee, sweetened with condensed milk.
Dinner: rice soup, roast beef and brown gravy, mashed potatoes, apple pie, bread and lemonade.
Supper: hamburger smothered with onions, brown gravy, boiled potatoes, bread, jam and iced tea.

"Can the average workingman eat like this?" the *Laredo Times* asked triumphantly.[50]

Yet conditions in Laredo did leave much to be desired. Lieutenant Colonel Edward Munson of the medical corps, whom Funston sent to make an inspection of Laredo, duly arrived, and despite the city fathers expecting a favorable report, he found the municipal hospital, located next to the militia camps, to be not just unsatisfactory but positively medieval, a veritable pest house. The chagrined mayor and city health officer reluctantly agreed that the entire establishment—two buildings and adjoining sheds—had to go. With considerable ceremony, on July 22 the local fire department burned the structures to the ground, a spectacle witnessed by thousands of appreciative troops. The onlookers included not only Brigadier General Mann and Brigadier General Harvey C. Clark, commanding the Missouri Brigade, but also Major General Tasker H. Bliss, who was on a tour of inspection of border camps. Bliss reported that conditions in Laredo were improving; fewer than 1 percent of the troops were hospitalized. The water, however, needed boiling before drinking. The Laredo authorities immediately improved purification, making boiling unnecessary.[51] In October, the city council voted to build a new hospital, a one-story brick structure twenty feet wide and sixty long equipped with all modern conveniences.[52]

This incident illustrates a significant but frequently overlooked aspect of the National Guard call-up—the army's role as a civilizing force in border towns; if these localities expected to make fabulous profits from the presence of the military they had to comply with the army's demands, whether it be improving sanitation, paving the streets, suppressing prostitution, controlling the sale of alcohol, or whatever.

But what neither Laredo nor other Texas towns wanted was black soldiers, whether National Guard or regulars. A rumor, unfounded as it proved to be, that the black 8th Illinois Infantry was coming to Laredo produced a strongly worded editorial entitled "A Negro Outrage," recapitulating the 8th Illinois's riot in San Antonio and commenting that "most of the so-called race troubles begin with the negroes. They are apt to go about with a chip on their shoulder, looking for someone who denies that they are as good as the white folks. Naturally this sort of conduct is irritating, and when one of the negroes oversteps the line he is apt to suffer."[53]

One reason thousands of soldiers got to witness the hospital conflagration was because General Mann, at least initially, was a much more lenient taskmaster than was General Parker in the Brownsville District. Whereas Parker implemented a rigorous training regimen, the troops under Mann had a lot more free time: "The work of the men isn't arduous. They have plenty of spare time for study and recreation; every third day they can come to town and enjoy themselves. Their afternoons are not devoted to drill or work of any kind, and they have longer hours of sleep than the average man is given. They also get better medical attention than the average working-man."[54] This pleasant state of affairs resulted in swarms of soldiers strolling through the streets of Laredo and congregating on Jarvis Plaza in the afternoons. As the local paper reported, "Last night some 1,500–2,000 Maine, Missouri and New Hampshire militiamen congregated on Jarvis Plaza to hear a band concert by a military band (9th Infantry, Maine, and Missouri bands combined). The lawn of the plaza was literally covered with soldiers lying on the grass, while many families likewise rested themselves while listening to the music. Several medleys were played. When one containing 'Dixie' was played the air resounded with acclaim from the Missourians."[55]

Jarvis Plaza was not the only attraction in town; men attended the churches, especially the Catholic churches, by the thousands, as they did the Royal Theater to watch movies. In fact, demand for movies was so great that a second theater was under construction. The men also kept the folks back home apprised of their new environment: "Thousands of postcards showing Laredo & some showing scenes of Mexico are going out every day, sent by the National Guard."[56] And the guardsmen spent thousands of dollars on presents for the home folks, such as Mexican table cloths, doilies, handkerchiefs, toys, pottery, and fancy leather goods.[57] Some of the troops spent their leisure time in the red-light district of town. To keep things under control, the only soldiers who could carry arms in the district were the provost guard, who not only patrolled the area but at eleven o'clock at night cleared the streets of soldiers; those found after eleven thirty were arrested, as was anyone found to be armed. A general order stipulated that each regiment and independent command furnish a noncom and two privates, who reported to the commander of the provost guard and escorted back to camp the soldiers whom the guard had arrested. The Laredo District strictly enforced this policy.[58]

Some of the guardsmen were shocked by the appalling poverty of many Hispanics, especially the Mexican refugees:

> After the final meal of the day at Camp Missouri, or the 9th Infantry Camp, a bread line of about 50 Mexican women and little children were there to get the scraps left on the soldiers' plates, pleading for something to eat. Cook was sympathetic, as were several soldiers who passed food down the line. It is not a custom to establish a "bread line" in the United States army, but there will be one hereafter at Camp Missouri, if the good-hearted soldiers of that camp can benefit suffering humanity by giving them the little things that are left over after a meal and then adding a little bit more to make the morsel really worth while. And other people could do likewise and help some of the unfortunates who are feeling the pangs of starvation.[59]

Not only did the guardsmen from Missouri, New Hampshire, and Maine share their rations, but their medical officers did what they could to alleviate suffering.

Yet the troops were by no means just on vacation or engaging in good works. Like guardsmen elsewhere, they had come to the border to fight Mexicans, and when it became apparent that this was not going to happen, they became restive and wanted to go home:

> The presence of the guardsmen, of course, has given the border people a feeling of security, and at the same time it served notice on the lawless element of Mexico that no further raids must be attempted. But there is a distinct feeling on the part of the guardsmen that they have been fooled; that there was nothing to require their presence in the first place, and still less to keep them here all these months. There are few of them who will not welcome an order to return to their home stations, while they regret that they are going back without the chance of striking at least one blow at the enemy.[60]

The solution was to keep the troops busy. The 1st New Hampshire Infantry received an innovative course of instruction—on urban warfare. They learned how to occupy a Latin American city, using Laredo as the training ground. "As a result of this practical experience, theoretical studies and individual views, some interesting facts were gleaned as to the methods to be employed in the capture and occupation of Latin American cities." The urban warfare training incorporated lessons learned from the U.S. seizure of Veracruz in 1914.[61] But mainly the National Guard units experienced the routine of drill and target practice, with route marches to toughen the troops. There were daily regimental parades, in which the units marched from their camps in north Laredo, headed by their bands, to Fort McIntosh where they passed in review before General Mann.[62] The Maine band, composed of University of Maine students, rejoiced when on August 26, the War Department announced that all enlisted college students were to be discharged.[63]

There was also patrol duty, with troops stationed at intervals of 10 or 15 miles up and down the river, covering the entire district of 145 miles. At Zapata, San Ygnacio, Dolores, and Perrones Ranch, towns of three or four hundred, two companies were stationed. A platoon was stationed at a few points where there was nothing more than a ranch house. The general plan was to guard all of the crossings, although the river could be crossed just about anywhere. The signal corps maintained a telephone line connecting all of these stations with each other and with Laredo. All the posts were supplied by trucks from Laredo. Zapata, the farthest point south, was sixty-four miles from Laredo.[64] Guard units began to take over patrolling the Rio Grande, where at the very least they had to be alert for Mexican infiltrators.[65] Company A, 2nd Missouri Infantry, was detailed to Indio ford northwest of Laredo. Each man carried one hundred rounds of ammunition in his belt besides two bandoleers, each with sixty rounds. The company later manned an outpost at Ramireño in Zapata County, fifty miles downriver from Laredo, for six weeks.[66] The *Laredo Weekly Times* announced on July 23 that "all Ninth Infantry Regiment detachments or companies which had been detailed to patrol duty at places some distance from Laredo have returned to their camp here and are now enjoying a deserved rest. Their places have been taken by detachments from the Maine regiment of infantry."[67] And on August 27: "The Second Maine Infantry [which] has been absent from their camp here for the past thirty days, part of them at

San Ignacio and Zapata and other detachments at other places along the Rio Grande, will return to Camp Maine on Sunday, when the First Missouri will go out to take their places."[68] But torrential rains delayed the Maine troops' return for some days by making many creeks impassible.[69] The troops from Maine thus missed participating in the greatest spectacle in the history of Laredo—the divisional review—as did the 2nd Missouri Infantry, at the time on the target range, and Troop B Missouri Cavalry. These troopers were on patrol duty from August 26 to October 27 at Dolores Creek, twenty-three miles upriver from Laredo. They also patrolled at Bigford Ranch, likewise upriver, from October 28 to December 22, when the unit returned to Camp Missouri.[70]

On September 3 General Mann, commanding the 15th Provisional Division, reviewed the troops in Laredo. The 3rd Separate Brigade under Missouri Brigadier General Harvey Clark consisted of the 1st, 2nd, and 4th Missouri Infantry. The 3rd Provisional Brigade under Colonel Lyman Walter Vere Kennon included the 3rd Missouri Infantry, the 1st New Hampshire Infantry, the 2nd Maine Infantry, and the regular units, which consisted of the 9th U.S. Infantry, the squadron of the 14th U.S. Cavalry, the 4th Provisional Coast Artillery Regiment, Batteries E and F 3rd U.S. Field Artillery, and their supporting units. Several hundred people from out of town arrived for the event, most of the businesses closed their doors, and thousands of townspeople turned out to witness the longest parade Laredo had ever seen.[71] More than eight thousand soldiers passed in review before Mann and then paraded through town with their full equipment, artillery, and vehicles, a show of military might that not only advertised the proficiency that the National Guard had achieved but also served as a reality check for the Mexican garrison across the river.

What ensued thereafter was significant change in the troop strength in Laredo. The War Department announced that the coast artillery on the Texas border would be ordered back to their posts in the Eastern and Western Departments. An additional 10,000 National Guardsmen would go to the border to replace them.[72] The 1,200 men of the 4th Provisional Coast Artillery Regiment—eleven companies from Boston, New York, Long Island, and vicinity—departed from Laredo on September 7.[73] And General Funston began selecting National Guard units to return home, among them the 1st and 3rd Missouri Infantry, who left for their mobilization camp at Nevada, Missouri.[74]

Meanwhile, the training schedule continued.[75] The three Missouri artillery batteries spent much of their time at the target range, and the remainder of the Missouri brigade engaged in maneuvers. In the first of a series of tactical problems, the 4th Missouri Infantry carried out a mock attack against the 2nd Missouri near Dolores Creek. Marring the exercise, at Dolores a corporal of the guard attempted to arrest a drunken private, who shot him in the foot and was about to shoot his commanding officer, a lieutenant. The corporal shot and killed the private.[76]

The 1st New Hampshire Infantry began six weeks of outpost duty covering some 130 miles of the Rio Grande on November 22. The distance between outposts varied from twelve to sixty-five miles. The troops marched, often in stages, while truck convoys transported rations and forage. This assignment evidenced the degree of efficiency the regiment had reached and was a source of considerable pride.[77]

General Funston himself arrived in Laredo to inspect General Mann's command. The 1st New Hampshire Infantry, on patrol duty along the Rio Grande, made a forced march of thirty-eight miles, partly at night, in twenty-four hours in order to reach Laredo in time for Funston's inspection. The highlight of his visit was his review of the city's six thousand troops. Local dignitaries enthusiastically met with the general, to whom they owed so much, and gave him a lavish banquet at the Bender Hotel, Laredo's finest.[78]

As per Funston's dispositions, the 2nd Florida Infantry left for Laredo to replace the 2nd Maine Infantry, which returned to Augusta and was mustered out at Camp Keyes on October 25. The local newspaper gave Maine a glowing sendoff: "Laredo regrets to lose the Maine boys and their excellent college band. Since their coming here they have made an excellent reputation as gentlemen as well as soldiers and leave Laredo with a clean record, not a single one of their men having been arrested for any violation of the civil law while here. Laredo people have met and enjoyed the company of Maine officers and men; they have enjoyed the music rendered by the Maine University Band—hence Laredo people as a whole sincerely deplore the departure of the Second Maine Infantry."[79]

Among the few fatalities the Maine contingent suffered while in Laredo were a private, who drowned while swimming in the Rio Grande, and a corporal, who was shot in the back by a member of the provost guard while walking away eating peanuts. He died with a peanut between his teeth. The circumstances of this affair were murky, some of his comrades swearing he did nothing wrong, others claiming he resisted arrest. A military inquest failed to ascertain the truth.[80]

On the 2nd Maine Infantry's way home, there occurred an incident, in Hoxie, Arkansas, causing the town constable to write on October 15 to the secretary of war himself:

> Dear Sir: On the evening of the 9th inst. a portion of the Maine State National Guard, returning from the border en route home, stopped over at this place for an hour for rest and recreation. Not long after their departure it was discovered that old "Blue" the town dog and faithful guardian of the post office was gone. He was last seen giving the boys a warm and friendly welcome to this town, but now he is gone, and the hearts of our people are sad, they fear he will be mistreated, starved, beaten, bruised, kicked and cuffed and possibly be left to freeze this winter, all of which God forbid. It is the wish of old Blue's friends that you cause to be issued an order that they protect dear old Blue, give him all the comforts a faithful old dog should have, and that when he passes away, that he have a fitting burial, in the mean time, if his life be spared much longer, that he be placed on the pension list, that the wolf may never come to his door. Respectfully, [signed] Bill McCraw, Constable of Boas Township.[81]

The New Hampshire troops were not as law-abiding as their comrades from Maine. Four members of Company L, 1st New Hampshire, were arrested for burglarizing the Laredo Music & Jewelry Co. They each received two years in the penitentiary. On the other hand two regulars from the 9th Infantry were convicted of holding up and robbing a private in the 1st New Hampshire Infantry. They each received seven years in the penitentiary.[82]

New Hampshire had the distinction of conducting the first regimental funeral in Laredo. The entire regiment, with its colonel at the head, escorted to the railroad depot the coffin of a private who died of appendicitis. The regimental chaplain delivered the eulogy, and the playing of "Taps" and three rifle volleys concluded the ceremony.[83] Two months later, a private in the 1st New Hampshire Infantry on outpost duty at Zapata accidentally shot and killed himself when unloading his rifle. He too received a military funeral: the regimental band led the procession from the funeral parlor to the railroad station, playing a dirge. The casket was on a caisson, with an escort of men from his company.[84] The men of New Hampshire also performed an elegant gesture, building an attractive fountain for the city as a token of appreciation for the hospitality shown them. And the New Hampshire troops had another distinction. Members of Company L adopted a Texas boy whose parents had died while the guardsmen were in Laredo. They took the boy with them when they returned home.[85]

There was considerable excitement in Laredo on October 30 because of a rumor that a Mexican attack was imminent. The 2nd Missouri Infantry received orders to guard the post office, the municipal power plant, and other strategic buildings. Machine guns covered the main plaza, and both foot and cavalry patrols were constantly on the move. As it turned out, the rumor proved false, and things soon returned to normal.[86] Still, on the border anything was possible, and even probable.

On the same day as the false alarm, October 30, Brigadier General William A. Mann, who had been in command in Laredo since May, left for Washington, D.C., to begin his new assignment as chief of the Militia Bureau. As befitted his promotion, he received an escort of honor to the railroad station: the 4th Missouri Infantry and band, plus all of the other officers, regulars, and National Guard in Laredo. Succeeding Mann as interim commander of the Laredo District was Brigadier General Harvey C. Clark of the Missouri brigade. Then on November 7, a regular officer, Brigadier General John W. Ruckman, arrived from Eagle Pass and assumed command of the Laredo District.[87]

Replacing the 2nd Maine Infantry was the 2nd Florida Infantry, who together with Field Hospital Company No. 1, had been at their mobilization camp in Jacksonville since the June call-up.[88] They got off to a rocky start—354 enlisted men were discharged because they failed their physical examination. According to the state adjutant general: "154 were rejected as being underweight, and that the disabilities of about 50 more were of temporary character, contracted after enlistment, answerable to treatment, and not such as would have caused their discharge from the Regular Army." As of July 10 the 2nd Florida consisted of ten companies and a band. Four companies had recently been mustered out by the War Department because they had failed the annual federal inspection, and there were still two company vacancies when the call-up came. On that date the regiment numbered 44 officers and 635 enlisted men. Only 18 men declined to take the federal oath.[89] But the 2nd Florida persevered by intensive recruiting and by accepting volunteers from the 1st Florida, and by October 2, when they departed for Laredo, the regiment numbered 55 officers and 1,080 enlisted men.

Upon mobilization the 2nd Florida had equipment sufficient for peacetime strength except for shoes. As the adjutant general explained:

> The standard Army marching shoes have never been issued to the troops of this State; this because the funds for their purchase have not been available, and because no system or plan for their issue has been prescribed which would protect the Government against the use of shoes for other than military purposes and at the same time provide each soldier with the proper shoes for military duty. The difficulties involved are apparently understood at the War Department, for, so far, the states have not been positively required to provide shoes as a part of the equipment supplied by the Government.[90]

However, the state of Florida was prepared if necessary to use its own funds to purchase shoes in local markets.

The adjutant general continued:

> It was expected, of course, that the equipments and supplies for the personnel in excess of peace strength would be promptly supplied by the proper Federal agencies. . . . No Quartermaster's supplies were received for the Second Regiment Infantry until 9 days after its arrival in camp. Only a fraction of the needed supplies were received in the first shipments. . . . On July 25, or one month and three days after the regiment came into camp, the Regimental Commander advised this office of a long list of supplies still needed to complete his "Type C" field equipment of the regiment. . . . The arms and ordnance stores required for men in excess of peace strength came in within a day or two after the regiment arrived in camp, and, except for supplies of spare parts for arms and cleaning materials, all ordnance stores were promptly furnished. . . . From the above it will be seen that upon the arrival of the regiment in camp, on June 22, the several hundred men in excess of peace strength were without proper military clothing; without ponchos, cots, blankets and many other articles urgently needed for the protection of their health. . . . It must be perfectly apparent that the logical and proper system to employ is one which

would place with the states all arms, equipments and supplies which will be needed to equip and supply all National Guard organizations maintained.

In addition to the above, the army failed to supply the necessary books and blanks for regimental and company administration, which greatly handicapped the administration of regimental affairs since the army is a huge bureaucracy. "On July 25 none of the regimental or company books had been received, no A. G. O. forms, and very few other forms. For National Guard officers to suddenly be called upon to operate under a system of administration with which they are only partially familiar involves some difficulties, but these are materially increased when the proper books and forms are not supplied or cannot be obtained."[91]

Logistical shortcomings were instrumental in preventing the 2nd Florida from complying with a telegram from the department commanding general on June 25, at the height of the war crisis: "Can your regiment of infantry be ready to entrain tomorrow or not later then Tuesday equipped for field? . . . Troops needed at the border, wire tonight." The Florida adjutant general replied that since shoes were urgently needed and there were seven hundred to eight hundred untrained and unequipped recruits in camp, if "it is necessary to move [the] regiment within next few days it is recommended that partially trained peace strength be sent forward and authority be given to organize depot battalion to train recruits, who can be held here." On June 26, the Floridians received the following telegram: "Department Commander desires you send your regiment infantry, earliest possible moment to Texas border. Equipment 'C,' two hundred rounds ammunition per man, five days' travel rations, necessary sanitary personnel and supplies. . . . It is deemed better to send the regiment at minimum strength of trained troops than to attempt to have a larger regiment with uninstructed personnel. Recruits forwarded later when instructed." The regiment prepared to entrain for the border, but on July 27 it received a telegram postponing departure and informing that the Philadelphia Quartermaster Depot had been instructed to provide the necessary supplies.[92]

Not until October 8 did the 2nd Florida arrive in Laredo, fully equipped, including a band. The Floridians went into camp next to the New Hampshire regiment.[93] While the 2nd Florida was in Laredo the much-reduced 1st Florida Infantry back home was officially renamed the 1st Separate Battalion and assigned to guard railroads and bridges. The field hospital remained at the mobilization camp.[94] In December, the 2nd Florida was dispatched together with Battery F, 3rd U.S. Field Artillery, and the 2nd and 4th Missouri Infantry on a four-day maneuver down the Rio Grande.[95]

By the end of December the 2nd Missouri Infantry and most of the rest of the Missouri brigade had returned home.[96] Sadly, after telling friends that he preferred death to further border service, a mess sergeant in the 2nd Missouri home on leave at Joplin committed suicide by drinking poison.[97] In August, Company A Missouri Signal Corps was transferred to San Antonio and remained there until released from federal service at Fort Riley on January 5, 1917. The 1st Missouri Infantry was recalled on September 2 to the Nevada, Missouri, mobilization camp because of a threatened railroad strike, remaining there until September 25, when it was mustered out. The regiment returned to St. Louis, where the mayor declared a public holiday, and the 1st Missouri proudly paraded through downtown.[98]

The 3rd Missouri, from Kansas City, was also recalled on September 2 and was mustered out on September 26.[99] Batteries A, B, and C of the Field Artillery departed from Laredo between December 15 and 18 in eleven sleepers, eighteen flat cars, six stock cars, and three baggage cars, reaching Fort Riley on December 18. The army sent them to Fort Riley rather than to their mobilization camp at Nevada because the permanent barracks at Fort Riley were deemed more suitable for men who had just spent six months in the torrid Texas climate than would be the tents at the Missouri encampment. Battery A (the oldest military organization in Missouri) was mustered out on December 21 and arrived back in St. Louis two days later, Batteries B and C being mustered out on December 22. The 2nd Missouri departed from Laredo on December 28 for Fort Riley, to be mustered out on January 13, 1917. The 4th Missouri was mustered out on February 21, 1917.[100] Troop B Cavalry, Ambulance Company No. 1, and Field Hospital No. 1 also left for Fort Riley, Kansas, to be mustered out.[101]

In a disgusting development, as the 2nd Missouri, who proudly called themselves the "Houn' Dawg" regiment, prepared to leave, some unscrupulous enlisted men "sold" the buildings in their camp to innocent and trusting Hispanics. When the latter showed up to remove their property they were dismayed to learn that they had been scammed. "One of the Mexicans 'bought' the Y.M.C.A. building for $6, and he had a receipt to show for it, signed 'Sergt. Cheatem.' Others had 'purchased' mess halls, and even the latrines.... Some of the mess halls having been 'sold' to three or four different persons.... While the Second Missouri were merrily rolling on their way to their homes, the deceived Mexicans were preparing to remove their 'property' from the camp, and only by a show of force were some of them restrained from bodily carrying off the building material. Naturally this has harmed the prestige of the 2nd Missouri."[102] Indeed!

As the *Laredo Times* commented editorially, allegations that Laredo mistreated those in uniform were ridiculous.

> For many years we've had soldiers stationed here, e.g. the 14th Cavalry is rounding out a five-year station in Laredo. The 9th Infantry, if it stays here until next March, will have completed a three-year tour. They'll declare that no one discriminates against them. The majority of the troops have been well behaved. With the coming of the Guardsmen a change was observed. Not that all the Guardsmen—or even an appreciable number of them—were barred from social intercourse with the people of Laredo. But a certain element of the Guardsmen were aggressively discourteous, disposed to make trouble, and were so evidently unfitted for society that they were dropped from the list of those invited to the various functions. There are black sheep among all classes of American society, and the soldiers themselves are reluctantly forced to admit that the number of black sheep among the uniformed enlisted men is greater than that of the black sheep among the civilians. One need but walk through the streets at night to observe that the uniformed men are in the majority as for disorderly conduct, foul and abusive language, drunkenness and indecency.... Decent military are welcomed into Laredo society.[103]

Doubtless to the dismay of the business community, by the end of 1916 only about five thousand troops—regulars and National Guard—were left in Laredo. Of these, three thousand were the guardsmen of the 4th Missouri Infantry, the 1st New Hampshire Infantry, and the 2nd Florida Infantry.

In early February 1917, the 1st New Hampshire left for Greenfield, Massachusetts, near the New Hampshire border, from where the regiment dispersed to its home stations. The regiment sported a new stand of colors, the personal gift of the governor (by proxy) in September.[104] The 1st New Hampshire received a letter of commendation from Colonel Herbert J. Slocum, of Villa's Columbus raid fame, commanding the 3rd Brigade of the 15th Division at Laredo. As for the other New Hampshire units, the field hospital company arrived at Manchester on March 11, 1917, in the middle of the night, slept on their train, and early the next morning marched to their armory virtually unnoticed. The field artillery battery arrived the same day, but in the afternoon, by which time hundreds of citizens had gathered at the Union Station to welcome them home. The cavalry troop arrived on March 18, to the same kind of reception.[105] The New Hampshire legislature passed a bill not only recognizing the guard's border service but also compensating the men—$7 for each month on the border.[106]

It was the Floridians, the latecomers, who fired shots in anger. On the night of February 14, 1917, a patrol ten miles below Zapata encountered a party of eight mounted Mexicans, apparently bandits; the Mexicans began shooting, and a running fight along the U.S. bank of the Rio Grande ensued. The guardsmen captured one man and wounded several others, judging from bloodstains found on the ground. They also killed one Mexican horse and captured seven others and in addition seized "a lot of belongings of the bandits which were lost in the flight following the battle."[107] The Mexicans turned out to be followers of Pedro González, an anti-Carranza exile who unsuccessfully tried to mount several filibustering expeditions into Mexico. The jubilant Floridians delivered their captive to the county jail in Laredo.[108]

The Floridians were left as the sole National Guard representatives in Laredo when the 4th Missouri departed on February 20 in three sections on special trains. Then on March 9, the 1st Battalion of the 2nd Florida returning from patrol duty was relieved by two battalions of the 9th U.S. Infantry and a troop of the 14th U.S. Cavalry, who took over the patrol camps. When on March 9 the 2nd Florida left, ending the guard's presence in Laredo, the press reported that "quite a large number of Laredo people, both ladies and gentlemen, were on hand today to bid the Florida boys good by as they left on special trains for 'home, sweet home,' after an absence from the dear ones back in Florida of nearly ten months. Florida is making elaborate preparations for welcoming home her troops."[109] The *Laredo Weekly Times* proudly reported that a number of Floridians had received their discharges and planned to make Laredo their future home.[110]

As were other state adjutants general, J. Clifford R. Foster of Florida was outspoken regarding the call-up:

> It is a significant fact that only a few weeks had elapsed after the call of the President before the press of the country began to announce the failure of the National Guard system under the new Federal law

and to condemn the troops of the several states for alleged shortcomings and defects brought to light because of the mobilization. That these reports were inspired and that a deliberate attempt has been made to influence public opinion adversely to the National Guard is clearly demonstrated. The absurdity of attempting to estimate the operation of the militia provisions of the National Defense Act by a mobilization which occurred within fifteen days after the Act became a law and before any of its provisions had been put into effect by administrative action of the War Department will be at once apparent to any reasoning mind. It is true that the mobilization may not have been as complete a success, measured by the standards of true military efficiency, as could be desired, or as might reasonably be expected, but upon a full investigation of the facts it will be made plain that the chief defects are chargeable not to the National Guard but to those agencies of the War Department which completely failed to meet their responsibilities in the matter of equipping and transporting the troops, and to the unfavorable action of the Federal authorities with regard to recruitment. A careful investigation will result in establishing the fact that, on the whole, the National Guard has done well in the mobilization, and, when a true estimate of the situation is reached by the American people, the citizen soldiers will receive the full credit to which they are entitled.[111]

Chapter 11

Eagle Pass

The next concentration of National Guard troops was upriver at Eagle Pass, across from Piedras Negras. Brigadier General Henry A. Greene commanded the Eagle Pass District until August 18, 1916, when Brigadier General Frederick W. Sibley relieved him. On October 21, 1916, Brigadier General Francis H. French relieved Sibley.[1]

The buildup in Eagle Pass included the Maryland National Guard, whose principal home station was Baltimore and whose strength was as follows:

Staff Departments   11
Headquarters 1st Brigade   2

1st Infantry Brigade, Brigadier General Charles D. Gaither commanding
    1st Infantry   811
    4th Infantry   625
    5th Infantry   671

1st Separate Company
    Infantry (Colored)   68
    Troop A Cavalry   65
    Battery A Field Artillery   129

Field Hospital Company
    No. 1   37
    Ambulance Company No. 1   33

1st Company Coast
  Artillery Corps   68

Total 2,520

Some staff officers, the 1st Separate Company, and the 1st Company Coast Artillery Corps were not included in the call-up.[2]

The Maryland mobilization camp was established at Laurel, on the Baltimore and Ohio Railroad some twenty miles from Baltimore. In the two infantry regiments from Baltimore, only about half were native born, and many were of German descent. As with other state organizations, at Laurel a few guardsmen refused to take the federal oath. Several in Troop A did so, however, after their officers appealed to their patriotism. Peer pressure proved even more effective: three men in the 5th Maryland Infantry adamantly refused to swear, whereupon their comrades rushed out, bought a bolt of yellow ribbon, decorated the trio, stripped them of their uniforms, and sent them packing back to Baltimore in their underwear.[3] All units except Battery A arrived at Laurel by June 25. Battery A, delayed by the late delivery of equipment and supplies, arrived four days later. On June 30, the 1st Infantry entrained for the border, followed on July 5 by all the remaining units except for Battery A, which left on July 6 to train at the field artillery camp in Tobyhanna, Pennsylvania. An intensive recruitment drive resulted in a total of 3,382 men being mustered into federal service by July 5.[4]

Unlike many other National Guard units, the 1st Maryland Infantry (50 officers and 1,500 enlisted men) had a relatively pleasant trip to the border, traveling in sixteen tourist sleepers and five Pullmans. When they passed through San Antonio, scores of women provided the hot, tired, and sleepy guardsmen with soft drinks, sandwiches, and fruit.[5] Adjusting to life in Eagle Pass was another matter. A member of Troop A Cavalry wrote home describing the scorpions, centipedes, tarantulas, rattlesnakes, and ugly señoritas. Furthermore, he and his comrades were having a lot of trouble breaking their horses, which were mustangs straight off New Mexico ranges. Many of the troopers had been repeatedly thrown, including their captain, who had landed in cactus. Nevertheless, despite the intense heat they were having the time of their lives.[6]

The Marylanders settled in at Camp Ord in Eagle Pass. The weather did not cooperate. A storm in July obliterated the elaborate stone designs erected around their pyramidal tents in order to beautify their company streets. Another storm on August 17 collapsed the mess halls of two of the companies. Besides repairing storm damage, the men from Maryland spent much of their time drilling and going on practice marches designed to toughen them. They also pulled guard duty at the international railroad bridge between Eagle Pass and Piedras Negras. In October, they manned an outpost at the isolated Windmill Ranch, located in the desolate forty-mile stretch between Indio and the Blocker Ranch. Among the relatively few amusements available, shortly before the 5th Infantry returned to Baltimore in February 1917, the regiment's football team played a Tennessee team at Camp Ord for the championship of the Eagle Pass District.[7]

The buildup at Eagle Pass included the Kansas Brigade, whose peacetime strength was 2,268: the 1st Infantry (mainly from northeastern Kansas), 2nd Infantry (from smaller towns in central and western Kansas), Battery A Field Artillery, Company A Signal Corps, 2nd Separate Company (which became Troop A Cavalry on July 22 and left for the border on September 25). The Kansans mobilized at Fort Riley, Kansas, beginning on June 22. The state adjutant general had been stockpiling against such an eventuality, and the brigade was well supplied and equipped, both for the troops under arms and for recruits. Although well equipped, the brigade had its problems. For instance, of the nearly 400 men recruited for the 2nd Infantry, army doctors rejected 162 upon examining them at Fort Riley. But as has been observed, "In many cases, the Guard's mustering officers had not known what to look for in a recruit."[8]

By July 9 the Kansans had reached Eagle Pass and established camp amid the mesquite and cactus. Eager for action, they were bitterly disappointed. The closest they came to danger was when two squads of Company H, 1st Infantry, were detailed to guard an abandoned mine about five miles from Eagle Pass. They relieved a coast artillery detachment which had been guarding the mine ever since the army learned that a large quantity of dynamite was stored there.[9] Instead of fighting Mexicans, the Kansans found themselves going through a routine of drill and training. The 1st Infantry had a practice march each Saturday, beginning with short marches minus field packs and building up to marching some fifteen miles a day with full packs. General Funston declared that the 2nd Infantry was not just the best among the six regiments stationed at Eagle Pass in areas such as drill, discipline, appearance, and efficiency but was among the four best National Guard regiments on the border. The Kansans seemed to thrive in the arid climate of Eagle Pass; only 2 percent of them reported sick. The 2nd

Infantry, for instance, had one case each of measles, mumps, smallpox, and typhoid, all contracted prior to the mobilization.

The most exciting feature of their Eagle Pass experience was when the 2,500 men of the 1st and 2nd Infantry participated in the army's first experiment in transporting large bodies of troops and their equipment by truck and were hauled 183 miles from Eagle Pass to San Antonio.[10] But the most appreciated feature of their border experience involved pay. Members of Governor Arthur Copper's staff announced that the National Guard's pay was several months in arrears, and there were no funds in the treasury for this purpose. In a remarkable gesture, Governor Copper advanced the needed $12,000 out of his personal funds. Then in March, 1917, the Kansas legislature appropriated $172,000 to defray the difference between state and federal pay for the 2,800 men of the Kansas National Guard for their border service.[11]

In a bizarre footnote to the Kansas experience, one Henry Debord, a substitute mail carrier in Kansas City and former Kansas guardsman, was tried in January 1917 for rifling the U.S. mail. The judge ruled that the defendant's mind had been weakened by the injection of antityphoid serum by an army surgeon the previous July and by the heat of Eagle Pass, where Debord had been stationed. Since, according to the judge, Debord's condition was the government's fault, he imposed the lightest possible sentence—thirty days in jail.[12]

Like the National Guard of Maryland and Kansas, on June 18 that of Vermont received the official order to mobilize. Notification went out for units to assemble in their armories and await further orders. The designated mobilization site was the state reservation adjoining Fort Ethan Allen, at Colchester, where, on June 22, the 1st Infantry reported for duty, followed on June 24 by the 1st Cavalry Squadron, composed of the Norwich Cadets of Norwich University, the military college of the state of Vermont. As of June 30, the Vermont National Guard consisted of departmental staff (7 officers, 1 enlisted man), the 1st Infantry (55 officers, 884 enlisted men), and the 1st Cavalry Squadron (16 officers, 155 enlisted men), a total of 1,045.[13] The commander of the 1st Infantry, Colonel Ira L. Reeves, was president of Norwich University.[14] He had been elected colonel by the regiment's commissioned officers.

A history of the Vermont National Guard states: "The mobilization experience was one of frustration, confusion, and mismanagement from beginning to end."[15] Some of this was specific to Vermont, while some was applicable to the mobilization as a whole. Brigadier General Albert L. Mills, chief of the Militia Bureau, had assured the Vermont adjutant general on June 20 that the army would supply at the mobilization camp any deficiencies in equipment, obviating the need for requisitions. And on June 21, the Eastern Department adjutant general assured Vermont that arms, ammunition, clothing, and blank forms and instructions needed for mustering the guard into federal service would be sent by mail. They did not arrive. On June 24, General Leonard Wood requested that requisitions be submitted. They were immediately submitted to the Eastern Department by telegraph but were not filled as submitted: some articles were never furnished, while some articles not requested or needed were sent, such as 1,500 blankets, of which Vermont already had a sufficiency. Badly needed supplies, such as socks, shoes, cotton uniforms, and tents were not furnished until after the 1st Vermont had gone to the border. Supply problems continued to the end.

About the only bright spot was that very few Vermont guardsmen refused to take the federal oath. There was delay in mustering in the Vermonters because the requisite instructions and blank forms did not arrive on time from the War Department. Misdirected mail was the reason. Mail was going to the Colchester post office instead of the Fort Ethan Allen post office. Despite urgent and repeated notifications from Vermont officials, the mail continued to go to Colchester. There was also the problem of conflicting orders; some said the men should undergo thorough physical exams before leaving the mobilization camp; others ordered that physical exams and all nonessential preparations be disregarded and the units entrain for the border as soon as transportation was available. Yet because sufficient railroad rolling stock was not immediately available, the Vermonters were able to conduct physical examinations in an orderly manner after all.

The 1st Infantry departed on June 27 in a pouring rain for an uncomfortable ride to the border.[16] Tourist sleepers were not available, so the men had to ride in chair cars, three men to each double seat. To make the accommodation a bit more bearable, the commanding officer of the 1st Infantry, Colonel Reeves, exercised some Yankee ingenuity: "At the suggestion of the regimental commander the Adjutant General of the state secured a sufficient number of pine boards, 12 inches wide and three feet long, so as to provide three for each two seats in all passenger cars. By this arrangement the men were made fairly comfortable in sleeping at night by improvising bunks made up of the bottoms of the seats placed on top of the boards, which extended longitudinally along the sides of the cars and rested on the seat bases."[17] Presumably the troops were vastly relieved to get off the trains when they arrived at Eagle Pass on July 1. The cavalry squadron remained at the mobilization camp.[18]

When the 1st Infantry left Vermont,

> many who boarded the train for Texas left the Springfield armory with few or totally without necessary personal items such as toilet articles, pajamas, and stationery. They carried with them clothing and equipment issued for use in northern climates. Too many woolens and too few socks, shoes, and sets of underwear caused a good deal of discomfort during the first hot weeks outside Eagle Pass. The absence of rifle cases proved to be a considerable annoyance to soldiers suddenly introduced to the corrosive persistence of sand and wind storms. Hard rains in late July wracked [sic] havoc with tents and equipment and strained severely facilities for cleanliness and sanitation.[19]

The regiment had been in Eagle Pass for a month before their tents arrived. "Much of the ordnance received was of obsolete pattern. For instance, black leather horse equipment was received in part, and some 38 caliber revolvers with information that the supply of automatic 45 caliber pistols was exhausted." Furthermore, "such problems continued unabated, the needs of the Vermont troops and the actions of the Department of the Army seldom meshing. . . . One of the more bizarre examples involved the apparent assumption on the part of the Army Quartermaster that Vermonters had achieved an unprecedented uniformity in the size of their heads."[20]

Vermont claimed to have been the first National Guard regiment to arrive intact on the border.[21] The Vermonters received compliments on the way their camp was laid out, with special attention given to sanitary measures.[22] Even while getting settled, they began pulling their weight. The second day at their new station brought their first assignment; the 3rd Battalion manned outposts on the Rio Grande, facing Mexican cavalry on the opposite bank. Nothing untoward happened. The soldiers from Vermont also guarded the international bridge between Eagle Pass and Piedras Negras, and they rotated with regular units on outpost duty. By May, the 2nd Battalion furnished detached outposts at the Lehman Ranch, twenty miles upriver from Eagle Pass, at the Indio Ranch, thirty miles downriver from the town, at the Windmill Ranch, forty-two miles downriver, and at the Blocker Ranch, sixty-two miles downriver. The tour lasted for a month.

Company C, incidentally, was composed mainly of University of Vermont students. Less exciting was the routine of camp life with its route marches, target practice, and fatigue duties.[23] A distinctive feature of the Vermont experience was that, unlike guardsmen on the border from some states, they were able to cast absentee ballots, voting in the Vermont primary the second Tuesday of September 1916.[24] The Vermonters acquitted themselves quite well during their stay in Eagle Pass:

> The regiment participated in a number of practice marches and field maneuvers, notable among them being a three days' march during the early part of September, in which the regiment on the first day's march formed an advance guard of a provisional division. On the return march the cadence of the entire division was greatly increased and severely taxed the marching qualities of all the troops. The regiment in the lead of this march was a Regular army regiment. The First Vermont made a remarkable record by having a proportionately smaller number of men fall out because of fatigue or bad feet than any organization participating in it. In this march an actual distance of 12 and 3/10 miles was covered in three hours and twenty minutes, actual marching time.[25]

When General Bliss inspected the guard at Eagle Pass, he found the usual shortage of machine guns: "Two Maryland and one Kansas regiment supplied with neither guns nor equipment; the other three regiments had guns and equipment but no animals. All were being instructed by the personnel from the Regular organizations."[26] The officer from the army's Inspector General Department who inspected the 1st Vermont reported that "it is the best National Guard regiment at Eagle Pass in equipment and general efficiency. The Colonel is a Regular, a good executive and the regiment shows it. It will be fit for the field in about two months."[27] This was high praise indeed.

Still, the Vermonters could only ponder the ways of the army: "The 1st Cavalry Squadron of about 160 men had been mobilized but had not gone to the border with the 1st Infantry. The reason was because the squadron was composed of Norwich University, 'the Military College of the State of Vermont' cadets and thus fell in the army's category of 'student organizations.'" The War Department proved reluctant to send this unit to the border, giving a variety of excuses, although as we have seen, other units composed of students were in fact sent. The War Department solved the problem by disbanding the squadron and transferring its personnel to the 1st Infantry's headquarters company, supply company, band, and machine gun company, all of whom remained at the mobilization camp together with some 150 recruits.[28] The colonel commanding the Vermonters repeatedly urged the War Department to order these personnel to Eagle Pass in order to complete the regiment. After he assured the War Department that none of these units was predominantly composed of students, the army issued orders for these troops to join the regiment.

They left Fort Ethan Allen on August 30 and got as far as Brattleboro, Vermont, when on August 31 they received orders to return to Fort Ethan Allen, ostensibly because they were predominantly student organizations. This although the policy of discharging students had been rescinded on August 30. But according to the officers in charge, they returned because of a threatened railroad strike—the railroads could not guarantee getting them to the border before the time set for the strike.[29] The adjutant general of Vermont was convinced that the real reason for their return was because of somebody's influence with the War Department. After the regiment returned from the border Colonel Reeves resigned because of his duties at Norwich University, his resignation to be effective as soon as the regiment's commissioned officers elected his replacement.[30]

Compounding the confusion, just as the 1st Infantry received orders on September 18 to prepare to return home from Eagle Pass, the commander of the Eastern Department ordered that the units sent back to Fort Ethan Allen on August 31 proceed to Eagle Pass and join the regiment after all. As it happened, the Vermont adjutant general, Lee O. Tillotson, was in Eagle Pass at the time and enlightened the department commander, who countermanded his own order, thus preventing the two components of the Vermont National Guard from meeting—or passing each other—somewhere between Fort Ethan Allen and Eagle Pass. The 1st Infantry entrained on September 20 and arrived at Fort Ethan Allen on September 27. Between October 7 and 11, all units were mustered out of federal service.[31]

Marylanders began to leave Eagle Pass on September 26, the 4th Infantry leading the way, followed by Battery A on October 6, 1st Brigade Headquarters on November 3, the 1st Infantry on November 4, Troop A on December 23, Field Hospital No. 1 and Ambulance Company No. 1 on January 6, 1917, and the 5th Infantry on February 24. The Marylanders had suffered only one casualty while on the border, a private of Company C, 5th

Maryland, who drowned accidentally. Another type of casualty was Major Henry S. Barrett, 4th Maryland, who declared that he was disgusted with conditions on the border and intended resigning from the National Guard. He was tried by court-martial at Camp Stuart, Virginia, in October.[32]

In late October, 1916, other units began to be ordered home. The 1st Kansas Infantry was mustered out at Fort Riley on October 30, the 2nd Kansas a week later; Battery A Field Artillery in late December; Company A Signal Corps in mid-January 1917; and Troop A Cavalry in early March.[33]

By early March the 1st Tennessee Infantry had arrived in Eagle Pass, in keeping with War Department policy of capitalizing on the National Guard mobilization to give as many units as possible some border service. The Tennessee Guard consisted of some 1,800 men. Sent to the border directly from Knoxville were the 3rd Infantry, Cavalry Troops B, C, D, and Field Hospital No. 1.[34] Separate Company G (Colored) was not called up.[35] The Tennesseans had mobilized at Cumberland Park in Nashville, naming the camp Tom C. Rye for the governor, despite the mayor of Memphis making a bid for the troops from western Tennessee to mobilize in his city.[36] Although the War Department initially ordered that each unit be rushed to the border as quickly as it could be equipped, the Tennessee National Guard remained at their mobilization camp.[37]

In contrast to the experience of some other National Guard organizations, Tennessee had no complaints about the performance of the railroads: "The railroads carried out these schedules perfectly except that a majority of the trains arrived at the mobilization camp ahead of time. The cooperation of the railroads was splendid."[38] But there were major problems with equipping the troops. For instance, a supply of underwear arrived but unfortunately it was in boys' sizes.[39] (One wonders why an army depot would stock boys' size underwear in the first place.)

> The Supply Department of the Army failed to get supplies and equipment on the ground for weeks after the troops arrived. There were insufficient blankets and several hundred soldiers were without blankets for weeks; shoes were not fully supplied to the command for an inexcusably long time after mobilization; and, in fact, the Supply Department of the Government (Quartermaster Department) failed most ignominiously in connection with furnishing supplies for this State. The Ordnance Department and the Medical Department of

the Army had their supplies and equipment at the mobilization camp upon the arrival of troops. These Departments deserve great credit for this dispatch.[40]

A most welcome addition was the arrival of six Victrolas presented to the Nashville companies and eight to the Memphis contingent.[41]

The War Department had a different view of the equipment shortage. "A high staff officer" declared on June 26 that:

> if the state militiamen find themselves without sufficient equipment in the present emergency, it is their own fault and not the fault of the War Department. In proof of his statement, he showed the general laws touching on militia, ordering that sufficient equipment for minimum peace strength shall be kept by each state, and providing funds for this purpose. The law specifically states these commands shall not call upon the War Department for any shortage, for there must be no shortage. It was said today there has been some disinclination on the part of many states to lay in proper supplies, in view of the possibility that such things as shoes would be kept by the guardsmen instead of being held in storage in the armories. Then, again, some states find themselves with more men than they had anticipated, and hence not able to meet immediately their requirements. Shortage manifestly exists in some quarters. Lack of preparedness is more evident in southern states, though the northern states are not without their share of shortcomings. Taken all in all, however, army men say the equipment situation generally is satisfactory and that merely the matter of transporting supplies from central depots is the only difficulty confronting officials.[42]

General Leonard Wood weighed in, declaring that

> the present system, or rather lack of system, of equipping the state militia for active duty was the main reason for delay in the mobilization and sending of troops to the border. The militia is not permitted under existing laws to keep extra field equipment in their armories, and as a result when the call to arms came rifles, canteens, clothing, etc. had to be obtained from the nearest arsenal. There is no reserve supply of horses, necessitating purchase in the open market and their training before they can be used. . . . The result of the Mexican trouble, I believe, will be reconstruction of the system of equipping the

national guard. In the future I believe state organizations will have on hand in their armories their own equipment.[43]

Besides lack of equipment, the 1st Tennessee underwent considerable turmoil over the election of its officers, the process culminating in the election of the regiment's colonel. Most officers favored Captain W. N. Hughes, Jr., the regular instructor-inspector of the Tennessee guard, while some favored Thomas A. Halbart, a former colonel of the regiment. But a deadlock developed when Governor Rye declared that he would not commission Hughes if the latter were elected because Hughes was attached to the adjutant general's office and was not a resident of Tennessee. Rye said he feared that with Hughes the adjutant general's office would exercise undue influence over the regiment's officers. The officers elected Hughes anyway. Governor Rye reiterated that under the laws of Tennessee he could not issue a commission to Hughes. The officers then held a caucus to try to select someone. They finally elected Major Harry S. Berry of the Nashville battalion, a graduate of West Point and gentleman farmer, as their new colonel. The governor issued the commission.[44] The National Guard's practice of electing officers reinforced the regulars' disdain for the guard.

The Tennessee units received orders to remain in camp for an indeterminate period.[45] The guard launched a statewide recruiting campaign, the result of more than three hundred men having failed their physical examinations. A regular medical officer who conducted examinations while the Tennessee troops mustered in recalled that although the soldiers were already in state service, 23 percent were rejected for physical disqualifications, and a considerable number for illiteracy. "'I had to reject one man, a member of the National Guard, because he had no right arm' he said. 'And there were five or six belonging to the guard who had glass eyes. That wasn't the worst state, either.'"[46]

The 1st Tennessee added a machine gun company in August. By the middle of September, the Tennessee Guard had increased to 2,463 and was considered ready for border service. The 1st Tennessee departed from Camp Rye on September 16, the 3rd Tennessee the following day.[47] The 1st went to Eagle Pass, but while en route there the 3rd Tennessee's orders were changed from Eagle Pass to Pharr, in the lower Rio Grande Valley of Texas. Cavalry Troops B, C, and D, Ambulance Company No.1, and Field Hospital Company No. 1 were ordered to El Paso.

The 1st Tennessee was composed of men from west and middle Tennessee.[48] When the regiment arrived in Eagle Pass on September 20, they marched into the camp recently evacuated by the two Kansas regiments. "At Eagle Pass, families of many officers and men from various states lived in a section of newly constructed one-room houses affectionately known as 'Squaw Street.'"[49] For the troops, however, their stay in Eagle Pass was one of routine and boredom, punctuated by complaints about all kinds of things. "One Tennessee Guardsman credited the climate of the Southwest with his decision to switch his allegiance from the army to the navy when World War I came: 'Being stationed in such a god-forsaken dreary place in Texas—dry, parched, uninteresting, and infested with rattlesnakes, scorpions, and tarantulas—inspired me to join the navy.'"[50] Presumably many of his comrades shared this sentiment. The 1st Tennessee Infantry departed for Memphis on March 15, 1917. Together with Ambulance Company No. 1 it was mustered out at Memphis on March 24.[51]

Guardsmen who had been in Eagle Pass for months had adjusted better to their situation. For instance, early on Christmas Eve the 5th Maryland sponsored a Christmas tree—a gift from the city of Baltimore—on the courthouse lawn and distributed more than three thousand toys, donated by the citizens of Baltimore, to the children of Eagle Pass and Piedras Negras. The tree and the gifts had come to Eagle Pass in a boxcar supplied by the Baltimore and Ohio Railroad. Later that evening, regulars and guardsmen gathered in Our Lady of Refuge church and sang "Silent Night," reportedly in thirteen different languages. As a touching expression of international good will, at midnight a member of the choir of the Catholic church in Piedras Negras stood on the Mexican bank of the Rio Grande and sang the first verse of "Adeste Fidelis." A member of the choir of the Catholic church in Eagle Pass stood on the Texas bank and immediately sang the second verse. Alternating thus, they sang the entire hymn.[52]

Upriver, the town of Del Rio missed out on the National Guard bonanza, being guarded by regulars, but not always happily. Ever since October 1915, six companies of the 19th U.S. Infantry had been stationed there. In March 1916, one thousand Carranza troops reportedly massed within thirty miles of the border. To counter the move, two companies (some three hundred soldiers) of the 24th U.S. Infantry were dispatched to Del Rio. The problem was that the 24th was a black regiment, and like other Texas towns the residents of Del Rio did not want black soldiers. The citizens demanded that they be removed.[53] The War Department refused, but on April 10, some members of the 24th rioted, attacking a brothel in the red-light district.

During the disturbance a Texas Ranger killed one of the rioters, and the black soldiers riddled the brothel with gunfire before their officers regained control. On April 15, the army transferred the 24th contingent to Columbus, New Mexico.[54] But Del Rio remained well protected: during April and May 1916, eight companies of coast artillery and two additional companies of the 19th U.S. Infantry were sent there.[55]

On June 19, General Henry Greene, commanding the Eagle Pass District, rushed a battalion of the 3rd U.S. Infantry by truck from Eagle Pass to reinforce the Del Rio garrison in response to reports that 1,500 Mexican troops had concentrated forty miles below Del Rio and were moving toward the Rio Grande to attack the town. Colonel Frederick W. Sibley, commander of the Punitive Expedition that had crossed into Mexico at Boquillas following the Glenn Springs raid, was now in command of Del Rio and the adjacent river patrols. He had taken precautions and was confident of his ability to defend Del Rio. An attack never materialized.[56]

On July 15, 1916, the six companies of the 19th Infantry entrained for Fort Sam Houston, where the regiment was being concentrated. At the same time, three companies—the 41st, 69th, and 103rd—of the 5th Provisional Coast Artillery regiment were sent from El Paso to Del Rio, where the entire 5th Coast Artillery regiment assembled. In October, the 3rd Battalion, 3rd U.S. Infantry, arrived from Eagle Pass, also by truck. Despite the lack of National Guardsmen the Del Rio business community did well. In September, the three local banks had a combined $1,313,302.98 on deposit, the largest amount in the town's history, reflecting a steady gain in deposits over the last two years.[57]

Chapter 12

The Big Bend

The Big Bend was the most inhospitable region the National Guard encountered. The army continued to reinforce the Big Bend while working to improve communications in the region. From headquarters at Marfa, Colonel Joseph A. Gaston commanded the 6th U.S. Cavalry and, in his capacity as commander of the Big Bend District, the 4th Texas Infantry and Motor Truck Company No. 11 as well. Additional truck companies were scheduled to be stationed in Marfa, Alpine, and Marathon. The rugged terrain in the Big Bend gave the civilian truck drivers ample opportunity to enhance their reputation for recklessness. The cavalry mainly patrolled the Rio Grande. The 1st Texas Cavalry operated in the Presidio-Ruidosa area, while the 4th Texas Infantry was scattered from Sanderson to Sierra Blanca and southward to the Rio Grande.[1]

The men understandably resented the fact that their colleagues in the 2nd and 3rd Texas Infantries were disporting themselves at the beach in Corpus Christi while they sweltered in the searing heat of the Big Bend.[2] Private Joseph Harris of Company I found himself stationed at Marathon and later on outpost duty at Stilwell Crossing on the Rio Grande. He combated the heat and monotony by drawing cartoons chronicling his experiences.[3] Incidentally, Samuel T. Williams, an eighteen-year-old private in Company B, 4th Texas, made the army his career, becoming a much-decorated officer and retiring in 1960 with the rank of lieutenant general.[4]

The Big Bend

Because of persistent rumors of villistas and common bandits heading toward the Rio Grande opposite Presidio and Boquillas, the army took exceptional precautions. General Funston decided in mid-July to send in additional National Guard units. From the thousands of men concentrated in El Paso, the general selected a battalion from the 2nd Pennsylvania Infantry and one from the 10th Pennsylvania and rushed them by rail to Marathon. The Pennsylvanians sweltered in the Big Bend from July 13 to September 4. By July 15, a company of the 2nd Pennsylvania went to Boquillas by truck. The rest of the Pennsylvania battalion at Marathon was deployed to border points as quickly as transportation became available. A company of the 10th Pennsylvania as well as a troop of the 6th U.S. Cavalry reinforced the cavalry troop already stationed at Glenn Springs. Two companies of Pennsylvania infantry were stationed at Presidio, where the first rainstorm of the year was accompanied by a terrific wind that blew down a number of their tents. Compensating for this, the rainstorm cooled the atmosphere and settled the dust, for which the troops were truly grateful. A month later, the Presidio camps both of regulars and guardsmen boasted a network of water pipes supplying shower baths.[5]

What Funston really needed was more cavalry, so he transferred the four troops of the 1st Texas Cavalry Squadron from Laredo to Presidio. Part of the urgency stemmed from rumors that the seven-hundred-man Carranza garrison at Ojinaga, across the river from Presidio, might defect to Pancho Villa.[6] Funston's dispositions included deploying guardsmen along the river from Boquillas to Glenn Springs to reinforce detachments of the 6th Cavalry. Patrols on bandit watch from Glenn Springs covered some eighty miles of the Rio Grande. Protecting Boquillas were a company of the 4th Texas and one of the 10th Pennsylvania. In an innovative development, Funston hired twenty civilian scouts, men who were familiar with the country south of Marfa and Alpine, and attached them to army units in the area. By July 17, Funston had completed the realignment of his forces in the Big Bend.[7] Colonel Gaston was quite confident. In response to reports that some three hundred villistas were near the Rio Grande, he stated that "we wish they would attack us."[8] It turned out, however, that the "bandits" were actually some five hundred Carranza troops camped thirty miles south of Boquillas, but as the press reported, "Even the Regular troops of the United States border patrol may be pardoned for mistaking Carrancistas for bandits." The carrancistas' ostensible mission was to patrol the border.[9]

Adding to Funston's problems were the continual alarms emanating from the Big Bend. A report on August 26 claimed that Mexican raiders had driven horses and cattle across the border near Ruidosa and that detachments from the 6th Cavalry and 1st Pennsylvania were searching for the raiders. After investigating, army headquarters at Marfa announced the next day that the report was without foundation.[10] On August 29, units at Fort Bliss and neighboring Camp Stewart in El Paso were placed under arms following a report from Marathon that the day before Mexicans had raided and blown up a mine near Terlingua and that Troop C, 6th U.S. Cavalry, had killed seven of the raiders. Upon investigation, it turned out that a lieutenant and sixteen cavalrymen in Troop C had merely gone to the mine to quell a disturbance at a dance given by Mexican miners.[11]

But not all reports were wild exaggerations. At Alamito, about halfway between Marfa and Presidio, a small signal corps detachment repairing a field telephone line took sniper fire on August 4. Colonel Gaston immediately sent a platoon of the 4th Texas Infantry to investigate, but they failed to locate the culprits.[12] On the night of September 19, a band of about thirty Mexicans opened fire on a twenty-three-man patrol of 6th U.S. and 1st Texas Cavalries near San José, ten miles below Ruidosa. A lieutenant in the Texas cavalry, commanding the patrol scouting between Ruidosa and Presidio, ordered his men to return fire. There ensued a furious firefight lasting about forty-five minutes in pitch darkness across a Rio Grande swollen by recent rains, with each side firing at the others' muzzle flashes. The Americans suffered no casualties and returned to Ruidosa. Reportedly one Mexican was wounded. The lieutenant could not say whether his adversaries had been carrancistas or bandits. (An army investigation concluded that they were followers of the bandit Chico Cano, at the time in his checkered career a captain in the Carranza forces, that they were smuggling cattle, and that many of the bandits were in a state of belligerent inebriation.)[13]

On September 23, a patrol consisting of a corporal and seven privates from Troop B Texas Cavalry, crossed the Rio Grande at Ruidosa—against standing orders. They soon encountered about ten Mexican soldiers, who demanded that they return to Texas forthwith. The Texans opened fire, which was returned; one American horse was killed, and the Texans retreated back across the river. Colonel José Rojas, the Carranza commander at Ojinaga, formally protested against this invasion of Mexico. General Funston ordered Colonel Gaston to conduct an investigation, which resulted in the United States making a formal apology and the army court-martialing the corporal for disobeying orders.[14]

Some of the gunfire, however, had nothing to do with Mexicans. On July 14, near Presidio, several 6th U.S. Cavalry troopers were returning to camp, having rounded up some horses. As they neared a thicket they detected movement, called out, and fired several shots into the brush. A cavalry patrol hidden in the thicket mistook them for bandits and returned fire. A private was shot in the jaw; fortunately the wound was not serious.[15] This incident perhaps indicates the degree to which soldiers were on edge. Besides friendly fire incidents, there was just plain carelessness. A private in the 4th Texas while cleaning his pistol accidentally shot a comrade in the knee. The wounded private was taken to Marfa for treatment. Most improbably, a few days later another member of the same regiment while at target practice shot a comrade through both legs above the knee.[16]

But mainly service in the Big Bend was mind-numbingly monotonous. The good ladies of Alpine did what they could to brighten the lives of the soldiers stationed there. They showed their appreciation by baking, donating, and serving a complimentary supper of chicken pie, salad, cakes, and fruit pies to the troops. Despite having to dine in the midst of a sandstorm, the men were most appreciative, commenting that they were quite used to enduring sandstorms.[17]

In July, Lieutenant Colonel M. C. Butler, in command in Alpine, took the precaution of establishing a military patrol at night in the Hispanic part of town, a move that met with the hearty approval of the Anglo residents. A week later Harry J. Spanell in a jealous rage shot and killed his wife and Colonel Butler.[18] After sensational and prolonged judicial proceedings Spanell was acquitted of murder.

A guardsman identified only by the initials F. P. tried to express the rigors of duty in the Big Bend in a poem entitled "Militia Border Patrol":

It's off to the cactus lands for us—
    The militia border patrol.
We're off to a spot where it's doggone hot,
Where the worst you have is the best they've got.
The reward? A chance to get shot—get shot!
    For the militia border patrol.
What's the use of all this fuss
    For the militia border patrol?

There ain't any lack for our dry hardtack,
Marchin' and luggin' a sixty pound pack,
But doggone it all—we'll soon be back!
    The militia border patrol.
Far from the land of the june bug
    Is the militia border patrol.
Trampin' the sand to beat the band,
Hikin' until we can hardly stand—
God only knows just where we'll land!
    The militia border patrol.
What's the odds to the dough-boy cuss
    Of the militia border patrol?
'Taint any lark, at the Springfield's bark,
Makin' himself a Mexican's mark—
But we're keepin' you folks from those
Raids in the dark;
    The militia border patrol.[19]

With a raid from Mexico still a possibility, Major A. V. P. Anderson, commanding the garrison at Presidio, conferred with Colonel José Rojas, the commander at Ojinaga, about a report that Pancho Villa with two thousand followers was headed toward Ojinaga. The report proved unfounded, but Rojas prudently sent his wife to Presidio for safety, and he himself departed hurriedly for El Paso.[20]

At Terlingua, Company K, 4th Texas Infantry, had been taking precautions. The guardsmen were well aware of their potential vulnerability—not only from raids from across the Rio Grande, but they also had concerns about the local Hispanic population's loyalty. In 1915, the mining camp at Terlingua had a population of about one thousand, 95 percent of whom were Hispanic.[21] Troop C, 6th U.S. Cavalry, had constituted the garrison, but all except fifteen men had recently been transferred to Lajitas, seventeen miles downriver. Keenly aware that in the event of an emergency they were pretty much on their own, the guardsmen prepared as best they could. They laboriously dug a trench from their camp to "Fort Perry," a loopholed adobe house completely surrounded by a trench. In the event of an attack, the men would sprint from their camp to Fort Perry to make a stand. Moreover, they made arrangements to safeguard all the women and children in Terlingua. And to prepare a suitable reception for any raiders, Company K built a rifle range, and they all qualified as marksmen. As a change from digging trenches, one of the platoons from that company made a memorable route march in the blistering July sun. The men, in full field equipment (heavy marching order) covered the seventeen miles from Terlingua to Lajitas in three hours and forty-five minutes. Although life in Terlingua remained hard, morale improved. The local school house was converted into a YMCA recreation room with some amenities. And the supply line from Alpine had improved, with two truckloads of supplies and delicacies arriving in time for the Fourth of July. Supplementing these were periodic deliveries of letters and packages from home. What also raised morale was the fund started in El Paso to assist the families, some of them destitute, of the men of Company K.[22]

On July 24, Company A, 4th Texas, which had been stationed at Boquillas since May 29, arrived to reinforce the detachment at Terlingua.[23] There remained the menace of Mexican bandits; the twenty-six men of Company I, 4th Texas, entrenched on a hill protecting the wax factory at Stilwell Crossing, thirty miles below Boquillas, eyed the Rio Grande nervously when news reached them in late July that a large body of Mexicans was encamped across the river.[24] In August, Company K was transferred to Lajitas, which they considered a much better station than Terlingua. For one thing, it was much cooler, and their quarters were houses rather than tents. And there was a telephone line linking them with "civilization." The company watched all the fords on the Rio Grande for some fifteen miles above and below Lajitas, but there were also the daily drills and practice marches, relieved by walking ten miles to a swimming hole. In September, an El Paso firm presented the company with a Victrola and a number of records.[25] Company K now numbered 75, above the peacetime minimum requirement, but its captain hoped to build the unit to the wartime strength of 150.[26] Reports in September that some 300 bandits were headed for the border near Lajitas were of academic interest to Company K, which by that time had been transferred to the railroad town of Marathon after four months on the Rio Grande.[27] Company H, 4th Texas, was relieved at Presidio by Company G, 4th Texas. Company H was transferred to Shafter.[28]

Civilians tried to show their appreciation for the military presence. For instance, Colonel Gaston, in acknowledging a gift of "comfort bags" from the American Red Cross in Waco, stated that he had been in the army nearly forty years and this was the first time he had known of such a gift to regulars.²⁹ In response to urgent requests, El Pasoans sent cold cream, talcum powder, candy and dark goggles to the men of their Company K, 4th Texas. That unit also received a six-by-twelve-foot American flag, a gift of Everybody's department store in El Paso.³⁰ As Christmas approached, the *El Paso Morning Times* urged the citizenry to remember the boys of El Paso's Company K with gifts: "When the call of the president came early last May the officers and men of Company K donned their uniforms, shouldered their rifles and marched away. Little has been heard of them since. During the heat of the summer they performed patrol duty in the wilds of the Big Bend country where the temperature rivals that generally credited to the regions of the damned."³¹ And the ladies of El Paso responded on Christmas with pies, cakes, and "comfort bags" containing sixteen different articles. By Christmas, Company K was no longer patrolling the Rio Grande—half of the unit was at Marfa and the rest at Alpine.³²

Relations between the troops and the citizens of Marfa were evidently cordial, as newspaper accounts reported: "The Banquet and hop given at the Post Saturday evening was a grand success. It was largely attended and all report having a lovely time." Moreover, "Major S. L. Terrell, of the Fourth Texas infantry, delivered an address at the opera house on Tuesday evening. His experiences at the battle front in France was [sic] indeed wonderful and interesting to hear. Quite a large crowd attended to hear the address and appreciated greatly the talk the major made."³³ And a week later "the officers at the military camp gave an entertainment last Saturday night to the citizens of Marfa. The entertainment was enjoyed by all who attended and there was a large crowd."³⁴

For a few soldiers, duty in the Big Bend was just too much to bear. In October, the police in Fort Worth arrested two deserters from Company D, 4th Texas. One of them related quite an odyssey: claiming he had deserted because he had been treated badly, the man had walked eighty miles from his camp at Presidio to the railroad, catching a train to Kansas City, then traveling to Fort Worth. His next stop would be the stockade at Fort Sam Houston.³⁵ Regulars deserted too. At a ranch twenty-five miles from Presidio, two recruits who deserted from Troop L, 6th U.S. Cavalry, were apprehended.³⁶

In December some inhabitants of the Big Bend got to witness something unprecedented. Because of the rugged terrain in much of the region, the army decided to supplement transportation by trucks and wagons with a caterpillar train. A tracked prime mover towed four tracked trailers, which had a capacity of thirty thousand pounds of condensed cargo such as ammunition, the equivalent of what thirty 1 1/2-ton trucks could haul. Several types of engines were tested: eighteen horsepower, twenty-seven horsepower, and seventy-five horsepower. Not surprisingly, the army found the latter to be the most effective. The fully loaded caterpillar train of a tractor and four trailers chugged along at a decorous average speed of two miles an hour (as compared with trucks, which raced along at fifteen miles an hour). The inaugural run was from Marfa to Presidio. The army pronounced the test a success, and the experimental unit was designated as "Tractor Company No. 1."[37] The initial test run of the tractor train had been over a road "that is a road in name only." Further tests confirmed the effectiveness of the caterpillar train.[38] General Funston was said to be well pleased with the experiments.[39]

As with other sections of the border, the army's presence injected badly needed funds into the regional economy. In May a delegation from Alpine lobbied General Funston to have the town designated as a supply depot for the Big Bend, apparently unsuccessfully, for the quartermaster corps operated mainly out of Marfa and Marathon. Those facilities did provide employment for some lucky residents of Alpine, salaries starting at one hundred dollars a month and board, comparable to what a Texas Ranger captain made.[40] The army also constructed a base hospital for the Big Bend at Marfa. It was built to a standard plan; each wooden ward was one hundred feet long by twenty wide with eight-foot porches on all sides. The structure was screened and had electricity and running water. In the winter the building was weatherproofed and had stoves installed.[41] Designed to handle about five hundred patients, the first ward opened on August 16, 1916, with the Red Cross sponsoring a dinner and a dance. The authorities decided to move in at once because the temporary hospital, located in the Catholic school building, had to be discontinued before the school year started. Work on the other two wards of the new hospital was completed in September, at which time the Red Cross organized another "big supper and entertainment for all."[42]

The battalion of the 10th Pennsylvania was ordered back to El Paso in August. In September, the battalion of the 2nd Pennsylvania returned to El Paso after their long and unpleasant tour of duty in Presidio.[43]

On the night of September 14, elements of the 1st Texas Cavalry Squadron patrolling near Ruidosa surprised a band of Mexican rustlers heading for the Rio Grande with a herd of stolen cattle. About seventy-five rounds were exchanged without casualties on either side before the rustlers escaped into Mexico, abandoning the cattle. A few days later, soldiers again exchanged shots with Mexicans, this time with cattle smugglers bringing some twenty-five head into Texas at Candelaria without inspection. The smugglers fled back across the Rio Grande. Again there were no casualties from this skirmish.[44]

In August fifteen members of the 4th Texas stationed at Sanderson participated with the sheriff of Terrell County in searching for a Texas Ranger, an inspector for the Texas Cattle Raisers Association, and a young rancher. The trio was overdue on a search for cattle rustlers along the Rio Grande, and it was feared they had encountered bandits. However, they turned up safely.[45]

In what they no doubt considered an ominous development, in October the 4th Texas Infantry received an issue of overcoats and other items of winter clothing. The 4th Texas had few casualties during its tour in the Big Bend. Sergeant Harry F. Butler developed a brain tumor and was taken to the base hospital in El Paso, where he died on September 23. A private in Company B died in the Fort Bliss base hospital of pneumonia in January 1917.[46]

A newspaper dispatch from Fort Worth on December 4 reported that "Major Cal O. Elliott, former superintendent of the money order department of the Fort Worth post office, and a major in the 4th Texas Infantry, was arrested in Marfa Friday on a federal indictment charging embezzlement of post office funds. He was released on a $5,000 bond. Elliott arrived in Fort Worth in the custody of a deputy U.S. marshal from Marfa and was taken before the U.S. commissioner. Bond was posted. He was in uniform. He'll probably rejoin his regiment. His trial will probably be next week." The case was continued until the March term of court. In the meantime he rejoined his regiment.[47]

The 4th Texas may have admired General Funston, for the regiment's band played the "General Funston March," but the general most certainly did not admire the 4th Texas. He wrote: "I did not like to send the 34th Infantry into the Big Bend District, but I had to get the 4th Texas out of there, that regiment having become so demoralized because of lack of control of the company commanders by higher officers, the regiment being so widely scattered, that something had to be done. I have ordered the regiment brought here to Fort Sam Houston where we can give them some training, and possibly court-martial the rest of the officers that have not already been tried for one thing and another."[48] The 4th Texas Infantry's ordeal in the Big Bend lasted about six months. In early February 1917, the 34th U.S. Infantry from El Paso relieved the Texans, who eagerly set out for Camp Wilson in San Antonio.[49]

The 34th U.S. Infantry and the 6th U.S. Cavalry now had responsibility for the Big Bend. The 34th Infantry, Lieutenant Colonel William R. Semple commanding, was ordered from El Paso to the Big Bend on February 3, 1917. The regiment, with headquarters in Marfa, was split up into companies and deployed along the railroad and at strategic points along the Rio Grande. Trucks supplied the troops stationed along the river, using reasonably passable roads the army had constructed during the past year. Before then, roads were practically nonexistent south of Marfa, Marathon, and Alpine. In addition, the caterpillar train continued in operation, delivering supplies slowly but surely. The company of the 34th Infantry stationed in Terlingua was probably not impressed to learn that they now guarded the largest quicksilver mine in the world.[50]

The 4th Texas Infantry and the 1st Texas Cavalry Squadron were transferred to Camp Wilson in San Antonio. On March 8, 1917, the Southern Department announced that they would be mustered out there, the cavalry on March 15 and the infantry on March 25. The units were in fact mustered out on March 24. El Paso had a big celebration, including a dinner and dance, to welcome its Company K home.[51] The Texas National Guard, now numbering about five thousand, had been on duty for almost a year, longer than the troops of any other state. The *El Paso Morning Times* eulogized them: "For many months, while the Guardsmen of other states were being trained and equipped in their home mobilization camps, the Texas soldiers were doing border patrol duty at isolated points along the border. They were thrown into patrol work without any training and without proper equipment, but they went without whimpering or crying to 'go home,' and uncomplaining service has marked their conduct since they were called out by the president."[52]

Chapter 13

El Paso

El Paso was the principal National Guard concentration point on the border. While the Brownsville District contained more troops, some fifty thousand, they were distributed all the way from Brownsville through Llano Grande, the McAllen, Mission, Pharr triangle to Rio Grande City, a distance of 120 miles. By contrast, in and around El Paso were stationed more than forty thousand men. Brigadier General George Bell, Jr., commanded the El Paso District.

The city was the commercial hub of the Southwest besides being a major rail center. And Fort Bliss was the premier military installation on the international boundary.[1] On March 18, it housed the 8th U.S. Cavalry, less Troops I, K, and M; Batteries A and E, 5th U.S. Field Artillery; the 7th U.S. Infantry; Headquarters and Companies E, F, G, and H, 20th U.S. Infantry; and the 103rd Company U.S. Coast Artillery. At Camp Cotton in El Paso were the 23rd U.S. Infantry, Companies H, I, K, and L, 20th U.S. Infantry, and the 69th Company U.S. Coast Artillery. Troops were also stationed in localities downriver: at Ysleta, Troop I, 8th U.S. Cavalry; at Fabens, Troop K, 8th U.S. Cavalry, and the 41st Company U.S. Coast Artillery; at Dick Love's ranch Troop E, 6th U.S. Cavalry; at Hot Springs Troop F, 6th U.S. Cavalry.[2]

What loomed large in the army's thinking was the question of just how loyal the Hispanic population was. On June 18, bugle calls in Juárez summoned Mexicans to the colors. This produced a veritable stampede in south El Paso—"virtually every Mexican in south El Paso ran for street cars and jitney busses, climbing on much like firemen to a fire truck, and hurried to answer the call."[3] In addition, many Mexican exiles volunteered to fight for their country in the event of war. The U.S. Army not just in El Paso but all along the border thus had figuratively to keep looking over its shoulder against the possibility of Hispanic unrest.

The first National Guard unit reached Fort Bliss on June 18: Battery A New Mexico National Guard, which was transferred from Columbus. The battery had four 3" guns and it supplemented the two batteries of the 5th U.S. Field Artillery, equipped with 4.7" howitzers, sent from Fort Sill, Oklahoma.[4] But the real National Guard influx resulted from the War Department's order on June 25 for fifteen thousand guardsmen to entrain immediately for border service. Beginning on July 1, a steady procession of troop trains brought a significant number of them to El Paso. Among the first arrivals was Battery B New Jersey Field Artillery (four 3" field pieces, five officers, 168 enlisted men, 120 horses, and 16 mules), who detrained on July 1 and went into camp near Fort Bliss. However, the next morning just after breakfast the dumbfounded guardsmen received orders to break camp, get back on the train (which they accomplished by ten o'clock that morning), and proceed to Douglas, Arizona, because the army had changed its mind about stationing the New Jersey National Guard at El Paso.[5] To the disgusted New Jersey artillerymen this was what soldiers in World War II would have called a prime snafu. During the next few days the rest of the New Jersey Guard rolled through El Paso on their way to Douglas.

For those units stationed in El Paso, the process of establishing their camps went much more smoothly than in towns such as Brownsville or Laredo. A committee of city officials, chamber of commerce representatives, and army officers inspected all the possible sites for National Guard encampments and selected three: one an extension of Camp Cotton between Cotton Street and the Rio Grande, a second in Morningside Heights between Fort Bliss and Mount Franklin (Camp Pershing), and a third three miles farther out on the road to Alamogordo (Camp Stewart). Regular officers met each troop train and escorted the guardsmen to their assigned camps which had already been furnished with firewood, sanitary facilities, refuse pits, and a network of water pipes. The guardsmen just had to pitch their tents and cook their evening meal.[6]

The first substantial guard contingent arrived between July 1 and 3—the Massachusetts National Guard, Brigadier General E. Leroy Sweetser commanding. He had been a second lieutenant in the 5th Massachusetts Infantry in the Spanish-American War and was later elected a captain, major, and colonel of the 8th Massachusetts Infantry. Appointed as a brigadier general, he was the highest-ranking officer sent from Massachusetts in response to the president's call. In civilian life he was a district judge in Malden, Massachusetts. His law partner was Colonel Willis S. Stover, commander of the 5th Massachusetts Infantry.[7]

The contingent consisted of a reinforced infantry brigade: the 2nd Infantry Brigade (5th, 8th, 9th Infantry), 1st Field Artillery, 1st Signal Battalion, 1st Squadron Cavalry, Hospital Company No. 1, and Ambulance Company No. 1. The 2nd Massachusetts Infantry, it should be noted, continued on to Columbus, New Mexico, where it was stationed. Massachusetts initially sent 275 officers and 5,152 enlisted men to the border on June 27–28, followed by 7 officers and 1,949 men on July 10; additional reinforcements brought the total up to 296 officers and 7,777 men as of September 1.[8] However, initially between 500 and 800 men had refused to take the federal oath and faced court-martial proceedings, according to the Massachusetts adjutant general.[9]

The call-up produced considerable administrative confusion. The Massachusetts adjutant general later reported:

> Blank forms, which were required for from the Federal government, containing the Federal oath for signature of both officers and men, failed to materialize, and finally had to be prepared by this office and forwarded to the camp ground. . . .
>
> As the Massachusetts Militia had not at that time been transformed into the National Guard, an immense amount of confusion resulted and a mixing up of records which has not yet been straightened out. The sudden orders to entrain for the Texas Border, with directions to leave practically no men or officers behind, added to the confusion, and while as far as I can ascertain, Massachusetts officers and soldiers were not responsible for the above conditions, the confusion caused thereby has been a tremendous handicap to this office ever since. . . .

The failure of the War Department to co-operate with this office in furnishing records of the enlistments of men mustered directly into Federal service has occasioned serious inconvenience, and in many cases an inability to furnish information which has been continually sought. . . . The extreme haste manifested from start to finish of the mobilization undoubtedly accounted for most of the discrepancies to which the troops were subjected. . . . The haste in departure of troops from Framingham was deplorable, and future events proved there was no necessity for doing so. It was done against the protest of every army officer on duty with the State organizations. Another week's time would have allowed the movement to proceed in an orderly manner, and saved much loss of equipment and subsistence.[10]

In September, the adjutant general of Massachusetts had to dispatch several officers to El Paso to prepare an accurate muster roll of the state's guardsmen.[11]

The Massachusetts brigade had mobilized at Camp Whitney, at Framingham. About sixty thousand citizens in some five thousand automobiles flocked to the mobilization camp, where there occurred countless family gatherings and a number of weddings.[12] The men received a cursory medical examination, and Governor McCall not only reviewed the troops but gave each regiment a pep talk. Yet some units of the brigade were not ready to take the field. For example, Private Roger Batchelder, who had just finished his sophomore year at Harvard, recalled that his unit, the machine gun company of the 8th Massachusetts, had four 1908 model Benet-Mercier guns, for which there was almost no ammunition, which was perhaps just as well because the unit lacked the mules necessary for transporting the guns and equipment. To make matters worse, the men had almost no training in the use of the machine guns.[13] All but one of the Massachusetts regiments were equipped with the Benet-Mercier machine gun; the other regiment had the Colt gun.[14] This of course caused logistical problems. Moreover, although about 75 percent of the 8th Massachusetts qualified as marksmen, their rifles were no longer up to standard because of excessive use in practice. And only ten new rifles were allotted to a company at one time.[15] Hampering the mobilization process were delays in the issuance of clothing because the quartermaster depot in Philadelphia was overwhelmed by requisitions. The troops were in their heavy woolen uniforms, most unsuitable for border duty.

At Framingham a new unit was organized, Ambulance Company No. 2, and it too was included in the president's call.[16] Ambulance Company No. 2 and Field Hospital Company No. 2 were authorized by the governor's executive order on June 28. They were sent to the border on September 1.[17] Serious consideration was given to converting the 6th Massachusetts Infantry into an engineer regiment, but the officers of the 6th Massachusetts eventually decided against the reorganization.[18] Governor McCall appealed to the War Department to mobilize the 6th Massachusetts for border service but his request was denied. Members of the regiment then requested transfers to units that had already been called up.

Although further delayed in loading their equipment by a shortage of trucks, draft animals, and railroad cars, the Massachusetts units began entraining on June 26, with the 9th Massachusetts in the vanguard. Crowds, bands, and cheers sent them on their way. The 2,060 recruits in training at Framingham were ordered to the border forthwith. Their arrival brought the Massachusetts total to 7,100.[19]

Adding to the discomfort of traveling to El Paso for five days partly in day coaches, the guardsmen were inoculated for typhoid while en route. Card games played from morning to night helped to break the monotony of the trip. During a stopover at Mexico, Missouri, the men from Massachusetts saw their first real live Mexicans. The locals were taking no chances: Mexicans were prohibited from buying firearms and militia patrolled the streets with loaded rifles. Presumably the Massachusetts guardsmen heartily approved, for on sides of the railroad coaches "many minor inscriptions and pictures appeared. 'Get Villa'; 'We're after Villa'; 'To Hell with Mexico'; and 'The Only good Mexican is a dead one,' were the favorite mottoes."[20]

Upon arrival in El Paso the infantry were assigned to Camp Cotton, an area bounded by Paisano Drive on the north, Cotton Avenue on the west, Cordova "Island" on the east, and the Rio Grande on the south.[21] Cotton Avenue became a city of pyramidal tents. "Long rows of tents, set up in streets, appeared; the officers' tents were lined along the road, with the cook-tents in the rear; then the wide regimental street, with the company streets running perpendicularly toward it." From north to south were encamped the 5th, 8th, and 9th Massachusetts.[22] Camp Cotton offered some amenities such as an irrigation canal in which the troops bathed nightly, preferring it to the camp's inadequate shower baths. The cavalry squadron and other units went to Camp Pershing. These included the field artillery regiment, whose Battery A boasted a number of Harvard athletic stars.[23] Lack of adequate bathing facilities bothered the guardsmen at Camp Pershing more than anything else; they had to walk over to Fort Bliss for a shower.

But Camp Cotton was located dangerously near the international boundary, which was Cordova "Island," a section of Mexican territory located north of the Rio Grande as a result of the river channel having shifted. Surrounding the "Island" on three sides were encampments of American troops, which made for a tense situation. Mexican customs inspectors had recently shot and killed a sergeant of the 23rd U.S. Infantry who had inadvertently crossed the line.[24] General Sweetser took precautions. One infantry company per regiment had interior guard duty every day, and one company per regiment was also sent out alternately as a border patrol. Moreover, a machine gun platoon was held in readiness throughout the night. Two squads slept under arms—fully dressed, with loaded sidearms and a machine gun with 1,200 rounds of ammunition outside the tent.[25] Sweetser also deployed a line of sentries along the boundary and took measures to prevent any of his men from straying into Mexico.

Yet the Massachusetts troops at Camp Cotton soon learned about sniping from Mexico. Sniping across the boundary occurred nearly every day, the favorite targets being mounted customs inspectors or civilians but on occasion soldiers. On July 6, Private Worden Wood, a mounted scout of the 9th Massachusetts, was riding along the boundary near the "Island" when five shots narrowly missed him. Wood, who was unarmed, galloped back to camp and reported to his commanding officer and "was cautioned to carry his rifle with him in the future and to return the fire if fired upon." The next day a Mexican sniper took a shot at a private of the 3rd U.S. Cavalry near Camp Cotton. The bullet passed between the private's legs.[26] On July 18 and 23, outposts of Company L, 9th Massachusetts, and Mexican snipers exchanged some sixty shots. Several Mexican bullets passed through Massachusetts camps; one lodged in a wooden mess hall. The Mexican and American authorities disputed who was to blame. General Sweetser ordered an inquiry, but General Bell stated that "the sooner Mexicans learn they cannot snipe with impunity, the better it will be for both sides." The commander in Juárez, General Francisco González, decided to depopulate the "Island;" families living there were relocated to Juárez, and only Mexican military and customs officials were permitted to enter the area.[27] The "Island" might be calmer, but sniping continued elsewhere. Company M, 9th Massachusetts, on guard duty at the stockyards, took about sixteen rounds of incoming fire at dawn on July 27 before returning fire.[28]

On July 6, the city council of Las Cruces, New Mexico, some fifty miles north of El Paso, requested that troops be stationed there. Although away from the border, Las Crucens were uneasy because hundreds of ex-followers of Pancho Villa worked on farms and ranches in the surrounding Mesilla Valley. The town already had a home guard organization: seven companies of forty or more men each served in turn one night a week, and the entire force was held in readiness at all times.[29] A committee from Las Cruces together with Senator Albert B. Fall of New Mexico met on July 7 with General Bell, emphasizing that not only was the Mesilla Valley exposed to raids from Mexico but also that there was a heavy Hispanic population there. Bell promised to send three companies of infantry to the Mesilla Valley—one to Canutillo, one to Las Cruces, and one to Fort Selden.[30]

With the arrival in Las Cruces of Company H, 5th Massachusetts, on July 12, the home guards were discharged, and the Massachusetts guardsmen encamped at the fairgrounds. This was nice, but Las Cruces sent a delegation to El Paso to confer personally with General Bell in hopes of having at least one thousand guardsmen stationed there,[31] which of course would be a considerable boost to the local economy.

Las Cruces did not get anything like one thousand guardsmen, but the relieved citizens welcomed the Massachusetts guardsmen they did get, with a large kite bearing a canvas sign: "Welcome H Company." The newcomers quickly established rapport with the locals, among other things playing baseball against a picked home team. Las Cruces residents went out of their way to entertain "their" guardsmen, even taking them for automobile rides through the Mesilla Valley. After two weeks the company from the 5th Massachusetts was relieved by Company M, 8th Massachusetts, whose principal accomplishment was capturing three deserters from the 7th U.S. Infantry. Company G, 9th Massachusetts, served next. The Massachusetts guardsmen continued to enjoy cordial relations with the locals. In fact, men of the 9th Massachusetts Infantry hated to leave the Mesilla Valley because farmers had been showering them with gifts of fresh vegetables.[32]

The stationing of Massachusetts troops in Las Cruces was but part of a larger deployment. Companies manned outposts in El Paso at the smelter and the cement plant north of town, and at Las Cruces, Canutillo, Ysleta, Fabens, and Fort Hancock. Each company engaged in patrol duty for fifteen days, then rotated back to Camp Cotton.[33] Fort Hancock, ninety miles downriver from El Paso, where detachments from the 8th U.S. Cavalry and Massachusetts infantry were stationed, was the most troublesome point in this line of outposts. Yet on occasion there was unexpected cooperation between the U.S. and Mexican military. On July 31, a squad of Carranza troops crossed the river in response to an appeal for help from an American patrol engaged in a firefight with bandits. The bandits retreated, leaving two of their members dead, while American dead were a private in the 8th Cavalry and a civilian scout.[34] More common, though, were reports of Mexican raids. On August 1, a serious raid was reported east of Fort Hancock. Fort Bliss responded by immediately rushing through the night to Fort Hancock two troops of cavalry, a motorcycle detachment, and a company of the 23rd U.S. Infantry. However, it turned out that a sergeant at Fort Hancock had seen three ranchmen and sixteen cattle, which his overheated imagination had interpreted as a large body of Mexican raiders.[35] Despite false alarms such as this one, there was in the Fort Hancock area danger of incursions from Mexico. In August, a patrol of the 9th Massachusetts captured three raiders.[36]

While the Massachusetts troops settled in, their heavy woolen olive drab uniforms were replaced by lighter cotton khakis, each man receiving three complete sets, including underwear. This of course was most welcome, for the men continually complained about the heat, although the nights were cooler. All the guardsmen lived in tents. The camps boasted incinerators, which contributed significantly to the good health of the men by eliminating camp refuse. Rations were plentiful, including fresh meat, vegetables, and bread, as well as canned goods.[37]

But inevitably there were logistical problems. In most cases National Guard units were still using the old blanket roll, "which is extremely hot and undesirable in this climate," prompting General Funston to inform the adjutant general that the generals on the border urgently recommended that "Infantry Equipment model 1910" be issued. The army lacked enough equipment for all guardsmen, but Funston urged that all available stocks be shipped immediately to the Southern Department. But an adequate supply of this equipment could not be furnished to the National Guard for at least the next nine months because of limited army appropriations. For the present, where National Guard regiments were equipped with both the old and the new model of equipment, only the old equipment would be issued.[38]

Shortly after arriving in El Paso, the commander of Troop C, 1st Massachusetts Cavalry Squadron, wrote, "We are in a strange country with men none too well trained and with green horses."[39] This frustration with their horses extended to Troop A, known as the "National Lancers," who since 1836 had always acted on state occasions as the bodyguard for Massachusetts governors. "The organization is exclusive in the personnel of its membership."[40] The squadron received its horses within several weeks, but they were "all undersized, weak, poor in flesh, and in quarantine for shipping fever." Until September, the squadron's entire drill period was used in riding instruction, although it did perform some patrol duty. Outside the drill periods the squadron labored at distasteful tasks such as building mess halls, incinerators, latrines, shower baths, permanent picket lines, and constantly repairing the water system.[41]

The Massachusetts troops had no hesitation in using political influence to improve their situation. When Massachusetts officers complained about having too few cots and their complaints went unheeded, a captain telegraphed Senator Henry Cabot Lodge, asking him to investigate the report that several thousand army cots were recently sent from the Southern Department to Plattsburg, New York. The captain explained that about half of the Massachusetts troops were sleeping in the mud at Camp Cotton, and if there were any cots available in the United States, the Massachusetts guardsmen would appreciate it if some of them could be sent to El Paso. Massachusetts officers were promptly advised that cots would be immediately issued.[42] The guardsmen's access to their political representatives constituted the kind of end run out of channels that regular officers bitterly resented.

Regulars did not always respect guardsmen, but at least in the case of the 8th Massachusetts and the contiguous 23rd U.S. Infantry at Camp Cotton, "contrary to general opinion, their treatment of the Guard was very good."[43] But some regulars could not resist playing practical jokes on the newcomers. For instance, regulars solemnly warned the men from Massachusetts under no circumstances to go into town without their sidearms because the Mexicans were especially vicious downtown. Dozens of guardsmen heeded the warning, venturing warily into El Paso armed to the teeth and keeping a sharp lookout for Mexicans. To the soldiers' surprise and chagrin, the provost guard promptly rounded them up, disarmed them, and explained the situation to them.[44] Practical jokes such as this worsened relations between regulars and guardsmen.

The provost marshal had imposed a nine o'clock curfew, by which time all soldiers not on duty were to be back at their camps. The military police continually arrested violators, a record seventy-five, mostly guardsmen, on the night of July 12. The curfew was later extended to eleven o'clock. On the night of July 24, a brawl broke out on South El Paso Street. The police as well as military police were called out several times to quell such fights. The military police detachment later used a light truck as a patrol wagon. As more and more guardsmen poured into El Paso, the provost guard was more than doubled. From eighty regulars it was eventually increased by detailing six guardsmen from each of sixteen regiments. Reportedly, service in the provost guard was popular among both regulars and guardsmen.[45]

On the heels of the Massachusetts troops came those of Pennsylvania, between July 4 and 13. Commanding the Pennsylvanians was Major General Charles M. Clement, who had risen through the ranks of the state's National Guard, beginning as a private in the 8th Pennsylvania Infantry in 1877. He became a first sergeant that same year, was elected a first lieutenant in 1879, a captain in 1882, a major in 1896, and a lieutenant colonel in 1898, serving in the 12th Pennsylvania Infantry in the Spanish-American War. Clement was elected colonel of the 12th Pennsylvania in 1899, being reelected in 1904 and 1909. In 1910 he was commissioned as a brigadier general and on December 22, 1915, a major general. Mustered into federal service on July 5, 1916, Clement was assigned to command the 7th (Pennsylvania) division on July 10, 1916.[46] The 1st Infantry Brigade also had an experienced officer as commander—Brigadier General William G. Price, Jr., who had also begun as a private and had risen through the ranks of the Pennsylvania National Guard.[47]

Pennsylvania's division[48] at mobilization was 12,711 strong, consisting of: 1st Brigade (1st, 2nd, and 3rd Infantry), 2nd Brigade (4th, 6th, and 8th Infantry), 4th Brigade (10th, 16th, and 18th Infantry); 1st Cavalry; 1st Field Artillery (armed with the new 1915 model 3" field pieces manufactured in Bethlehem, Pennsylvania); 1st Battalion Signal Corps; Companies A and B, 1st Engineer Battalion; Hospital Companies Nos. 1 and 2; Ambulance Companies Nos. 1 and 2. The 9th and 13th Pennsylvania Infantry were not included in the call-up.[49] Governor M. G. Brumbaugh notified the War Department that the personnel in these regiments felt slighted, and he urged that these units be mobilized too. They were not included initially, although the 13th Pennsylvania eventually went to El Paso to replace the 2nd Pennsylvania, which was reorganized as an artillery regiment. The 9th Pennsylvania remained at Mount Gretna and was also converted into an artillery regiment. Company B Engineers was transferred from El Paso to

Nogales on July 18. Company F, 4th Pennsylvania, which had twenty-nine civil engineers, became Company C Pennsylvania Engineers. A new Company F was recruited. The 3rd Field Artillery arrived on October 5, and the 13th Pennsylvania on October 10.[50] The cost of mobilization, including transportation, was a cool $2.5 million. The Pennsylvania troops eventually totaled nearly fourteen thousand.[51] As an example of diversity, Companies E and G of the 4th Pennsylvania were composed of Pennsylvania Dutch, who got their commands in their native language instead of in English.[52]

The Pennsylvanians' trip to El Paso had not been without incident. Press dispatches published during the rail journey from the mobilization camp at Mount Gretna stated that during a layover in Kansas City, some of the troops claimed they were not being properly fed. Pennsylvania officers were puzzled as to the origin of these stories because the troop trains had more than enough food on board. The trains had improvised kitchens serving cooked rations and coffee every day. It turned out that many of the spirited young soldiers had developed the habit of writing their names and addresses on hardtack and passing it out to the pretty girls at railroad stations along the route. But there were more pretty girls than hardtack, and by the time the regiment reached Kansas City all the hardtack was gone, hence the complaints.[53]

Also along the train route, Mary Hainesey, a nineteen-year-old belle of Hobson, Pennsylvania, sacrificed her lips for her country. When the train transporting the 8th Pennsylvania stopped for water, Mary undertook to kiss every man in the regiment—all 971 of them. She would have succeeded, too, if the killjoy locomotive engineer had not insisted on sticking to his schedule and pulled the train out of town with sixty men still unkissed. The 8th Pennsylvania was thereafter derisively known by their comrades as the "Hobsons."[54]

The 1st Pennsylvania Cavalry experienced considerable delay in leaving Mount Gretna because of a lack of railroad coaches and freight cars. They finally departed on July 6, without their horses, which they would receive in El Paso. In sharp contrast to the inadequate rail accommodations endured by the Pennsylvania infantry units, the 1st Cavalry rode to the border in style, traveling in first-class cars that had been thoroughly cleaned and supplied with extra water tanks and washbasins and with only one man per seat. And they later transferred to Pullmans.[55] The regiment included the elite "First City Troop," so named by the Pennsylvania legislature in 1774. These Philadelphian cavalrymen, ninety-five enlisted men and four officers, were worth over $100 million, and they could easily have bought Fort Bliss. Some ten thousand of their comrades from Pennsylvania lined the tracks and cheered when the first section of the regiment arrived on July 11. The cavalrymen cheered back from train windows and platforms. The 1st Pennsylvania Cavalry also enjoyed support from back home; the residents of Sudbury raised $510 for Troop I to buy a truck for hauling water. The captain commanding the First City Troop bought a Ford truck for the troop, to haul supplies from El Paso. The socially prominent First City Troop suffered one casualty during its stay in El Paso; on October 27, a despondent trooper cut his throat.[56]

The Pennsylvania units detrained at the Union Depot, enjoyed the coffee, lemonade, sandwiches, and fruit provided by patriotic ladies' organizations and got back aboard for the short trip to Camp Pershing, where large numbers of Mexican laborers had been working for days to prepare campsites in the rocky ground. There the troops pitched their pup tents, sometimes under less than favorable conditions; when the 1st battalion of the 1st Pennsylvania arrived, for example, they were greeted by a terrific sandstorm and a thunderstorm. The incoming troops were required to spend several hours a day clearing cactus and brush from the areas where they were erecting squad tents in company streets. They removed cactus and large stones, filled in the smaller ravines with boulders and dirt, and generally leveled the inhospitable terrain. They also spent time collecting snakes, centipedes and tarantulas to pickle as souvenirs for the home folks.[57] To keep the home folks abreast of developments, Mrs. H. H. Fisher, special correspondent of the *Pittsburgh Post*, joined El Paso's growing community of special newspaper correspondents. And the *El Paso Morning Times* began publishing a one-page *Philadelphia North American: Camp Pershing and Fort Bliss Edition* beginning on July 12.[58]

The Pennsylvanians groused about conditions at Camp Pershing. They then groused even more about having to relocate to a new encampment, Camp Stewart, three miles farther north on the Alamogordo road, a movement completed by July 25. The principal officers' street extended the entire length of the camp and was called Pennsylvania Avenue.[59] The complaints made to General Stewart about the new camp for the Pennsylvania division were that it was hot and dusty in dry weather and subject to flooding in extreme wet weather, was far from a trolley line, and lacked a satisfactory water supply. However, water pipes were installed throughout the camp and, ameliorating the division's isolation, the El Paso and Southwestern

Railroad established an hourly shuttle train between Camp Stewart and El Paso beginning July 28. The fare was twenty-five cents for a round trip. The railroad also provided express service for packages.[60]

Like many other Guard organizations, initially the Pennsylvanians were deficient in machine guns. General Bliss reported that the division had neither guns nor equipment and that generally speaking, machine gun companies had not yet been organized.[61]

On July 12, one battalion of the 2nd Pennsylvania and one of the 10th were ordered to the Big Bend, to Marfa, Marathon, and points on the Rio Grande such as Boquillas.[62]

Whereas the 6th (New York) division anchored the buildup in the lower Rio Grande Valley, the 7th (Pennsylvania) division performed the same function in El Paso. And as with Major General John F. O'Ryan of New York outranking Brigadier General James Parker, the commander of the Brownsville District, Major General Charles M. Clement of Pennsylvania outranked Brigadier General George Bell, Jr., commander of the El Paso District. The army adopted the same solution to the command problem—Clement would head the 7th Division as a separate command, and Bell would command the remaining troops in the El Paso District, organized as a provisional infantry division, composed of both regulars and guardsmen.[63]

The next major National Guard contingent to arrive in El Paso was two-thirds of a brigade of Michigan infantry under Brigadier General John P. Kirk. They had mobilized at Grayling.[64] The 32nd Michigan Infantry caused quite a commotion on their way to El Paso. When they reached Muscatine, Iowa, they refused to continue on to the border unless they received better transportation—Pullmans instead of the uncomfortable day coaches in which they were traveling. In fact, they were so angry at what they considered the War Department's incompetence that an officer threatened to pitch their tents along the railroad right of way unless they got sleepers by nightfall. They were promised better accommodations.[65]

The 31st Michigan arrived on July 13 and the 32nd Michigan on July 18. (The 33rd Michigan did not arrive until October 7.) Batteries A and B of the Field Artillery reached El Paso on October 5. Field Hospital Company No. 1 arrived on October 14. Michigan also sent Company A of the Signal Corps, Companies A and B of the Engineers, Troops A and B of the Cavalry, and Ambulance Companies Nos. 1 and 2.[66] The Michigan troops were stationed at Camp Cotton. Two correspondents of the *Detroit Free Press* accompanied the regiments "and are now full-fledged members of El Paso's large and growing and welcome colony of special military correspondents."[67]

In Detroit, many auto workers had rushed to join the National Guard. Henry Ford would have none of it. He announced, in line with his pacifist policies, that any of the twenty-thousand-odd employees of the Ford Motor Company who already belonged to the Michigan National Guard would not be paid while on active duty and they would lose their jobs. Not only that, but any Ford employee who intended to enlist in the National Guard would likewise be fired.[68] Still, about 1,000 Detroiters tried to enlist in the Guard; 636 of them were instead recruited by the army to be civilian truck drivers, who were in critically short supply as the army belatedly and frantically began to mechanize. From March 20 to July 23, the Packard Motor Company received government orders for 716 vehicles. Packard's truck division operated twenty-four hours a day. During 1916, the War Department spent $34.5 million on trucks. Civilian drivers signed up for one year, at $100 a month (compared to an army private's $15 a month). When honorably discharged, even if the year was not up, they were guaranteed return transportation to Detroit.[69]

However, civilian truck drivers were most unpopular in El Paso, for they roared around with utter disregard for pedestrians and for their fellow motorists. Because of a deluge of complaints the provost marshal finally had to detail some of his men on motorcycles to enforce the traffic ordinances. The army finally decided, by January 1917, that soldiers instead of civilians would drive the trucks and serve as mechanics, just as soon as soldiers could be trained.[70]

The 31st Michigan Infantry was assigned to Camp Cotton, where canvas water bags hung in front of nearly every tent, the bags being more effective than ice water. It took some of the men a while to adjust to army life. Initially many of the troops slipped out of camp without passes to visit the nearest saloon. And when they did receive passes, some men overstayed them. On July 15, the commander took action, rounding up more than one hundred offenders and placing them in the guardhouse. The next morning they received a stern lecture and were allowed to return to their units. Thereafter men took army life much more seriously. What also contributed to a more focused approach was that not all of the Michigan guard duty assignments were in downtown El Paso. They included outpost duty at the viaduct at Hart's Mill on the bank of the Rio Grande (subsequently the site of the Hacienda restaurant). The men described this strategic point as "creepy" because of its isolation and its vulnerability to fire from the Mexican bank, for the river narrowed to less than a city block in width. The number of guards was doubled, and they had orders to shoot anyone seen prowling around.[71] Also contributing to guardsmen's uneasiness when on duty in this area and in nearby Smeltertown was "the presence of so many Mexicans on the American side" of the river which "renders it doubly precarious."[72]

When the 31st Michigan was called up, one of their members, Private Samuel I. Aker, was in Claflin, Kansas. He claimed that upon receiving the news he set out on July 11 to rejoin his regiment. Being short of money, he rode freight trains as far as Amarillo, Texas, where he learned where the 31st Michigan was stationed on the border. To finance the next leg of his journey, he gave diving and swimming exhibitions. After a journey of one thousand miles, Aker finally reached El Paso and reported for duty at regimental headquarters on September 25.[73]

The arrival on July 18 of the 32nd Michigan Infantry with colors flying doubled that state's presence in El Paso. The daily routine for the two regiments centered around drills, inspections, and route marches to toughen the troops. After a month of drill, the men engaged in a series of maneuvers.[74] The Michiganders became upset when they heard they were going to be relocated to Camp Pershing. Although Camp Cotton had some disadvantages, being located near the river and thus exposed to Mexican sniping, it was near downtown El Paso, which offered multiple attractions for soldiers. Fortunately, General Bell decided not to transfer the Michigan units, partly because water was not easily accessible on the mesa at Camp Pershing and partly because many improvements had been made at Camp Cotton.[75] The most terrific sandstorm of the season hit the Michigan camps on the night of July 25, and the troops were nearly smothered.[76] Despite the weather problems, possible operations in Mexico were not neglected as the Michigan regiments underwent a course of instruction on how to attack Mexican towns and how to combat guerrillas.[77]

Besides the contingents from Massachusetts, Pennsylvania, and Michigan, units from Rhode Island arrived in July. The Rhode Islanders enjoyed training in their magnificent castle-like armory in Providence, which was built in 1907 and occupied a city block.[78] They impressed their regular inspector-instructor: "I feel that it is due the officers and men of the National Guard of Rhode Island that I comment on the excellent discipline that was maintained during the whole camp. As far as I know, there were but two cases during the camp that called for even troop discipline, and no summary court was even appointed. In view of the fact that much liberty was given to the troops, this record seems to me to be most commendable."[79] Battery A Field Artillery arrived on July 6 and was assigned to Camp Pershing, where the men spent the first night sleeping on the ground. The battery had been on a practice march when the call-up came. They turned and marched three days to the mobilization point at Quonset Point. Battery A included more than fifty students from Brown University. It arrived at El Paso fully equipped and with eighty-five horses.[80] The battery claimed to be the only complete, fully enlisted, horsed, and equipped war-strength battery in the entire army. And Battery A would distinguish itself as the best artillery battery in the entire National Guard, as rated by the Militia Bureau on October 9, 1916.[81]

The 1st Rhode Island Cavalry Squadron and Ambulance Company No. 1 arrived on July 14. At mobilization Rhode Island had organized four independent troops of cavalry into a squadron with a major in command, but "some of the men are not up to the required standards of horsemanship, due to the scarcity of animals."[82] But they improved significantly. When regular officers inspected the provisional cavalry regiment at Camp Pershing in September, Troop M of the Rhode Island Cavalry received a rating of 82, second only to Troop C of the Massachusetts Squadron, which received a rating of 85.5.[83]

There was a considerable social whirl, especially for the officers. One resident recalled that "many young ladies of El Paso seemed to show a preference in dating the militiamen—to such an extent that the home-town boys felt neglected." This of course was not entirely the case. There were reported incidents of young ladies refusing to date a guardsman simply because he was a lowly enlisted man. To their chagrin, some of the girls later discovered that the soldiers they had disdained were millionaires.[84]

Some National Guard contingents also brought with them their controversies, such as an echo of an ongoing Massachusetts society war. The elites of Boston society resented those of Brookline, an upstart city a hundred years younger. When the NCOs of Battery A, Massachusetts Field Artillery, the "millionaire battery," chartered the roof garden of the upscale Paso del Norte hotel for a dance attended by the elite of El Paso, Colonel John H. Sherburne, commander of the artillery regiment, not only refused to attend but also prohibited his staff from attending. Sherburne stated that in the army, officers and NCOs did not mingle on the dance floor. However, a number of regular officers as well as General Sweetser and his staff attended and thoroughly enjoyed themselves. The affair caused a great deal of gossip, and it was generally felt that Sherburne was merely reflecting the disdain of Boston society toward that of Brookline.[85]

Colonel Sherburne was evidently an obstinate sort of fellow. When the Massachusetts adjutant general sent three officers to secure descriptive cards of all Massachusetts soldiers in order to complete his office records, Sherburne flatly refused to fill them out for his regiment, stating that it would require an immense amount of unnecessary work. General Bell had to step in and order Sherburne to furnish the cards. Instead, Sherburne left for Boston on a leave of absence, and Bell ordered the regiment's executive officer to have the cards prepared.[86] Regardless of Sherburne's prickly personality, his field artillery regiment was considered a crack unit with considerable social cachet.[87]

The Sherburne incident was not the only case of a dispute from back home making news in El Paso. Political controversy erupted in the 1st Pennsylvania Artillery. Battery commanders charged that their colonel, William B. McKee, state senator from Pittsburgh, had received his appointment as the result of a political deal in 1913, which involved a compromise between Pennsylvania adjutant general Stewart and the Pittsburgh delegation to the state legislature. Stewart had requested an $800,000 appropriation for armories, and allegedly McKee had held up the bill in committee until Stewart agreed to retain McKee in the National Guard with the rank of colonel. McKee, who had been the colonel of the 14th Pennsylvania Infantry, was left without a command when the 14th was abolished in a reorganization. Stewart appointed McKee as colonel of the 1st Pennsylvania Artillery, allegedly as a payoff. The disgruntled battery commanders asserted that McKee was an infantryman, who knew nothing about artillery and the same went for his staff. They claimed that "they are receiving no instruction, that the Quartermaster doesn't know how to draw rations for the men nor forage for the horses, that the NCO staff doesn't know a gun from a caisson, and the headquarters officers cannot tell a horse from a mule." They threatened to take their grievances to higher authority.[88]

Colonel McKee did not protest over the publication of these allegations, but the Pennsylvania division's headquarters and a number of subordinate officers took fierce exception to these charges, categorically denying that

Colonel McKee had traded for his commission and asserting that the story had been published in Pennsylvania newspapers for political reasons. They stressed that McKee had not even been a member of the legislature when the $800,000 armory appropriation bill had passed. As for his appointment to the artillery, when his infantry regiment was abolished McKee had offered to remain without a commission, but the adjutant general felt he was entitled to another command with the same rank. Prior to the reorganization, which occurred because Pennsylvania had an excess of infantry, there were three independent batteries of artillery. It was decided to create a full regiment. Two batteries were created out of the personnel of the 14th Infantry; other members of that regiment were formed into an ambulance company, and one company was transferred to the 18th Infantry. While it was true that McKee was a former infantry officer, the same was true for the majority of the line officers in the 1st Pennsylvania Artillery, which was only six months old. His superiors vouched for McKee's integrity and dedication. The regiment subsequently showed its confidence in McKee by giving a concert and dance in front of Colonel McKee's quarters in honor of army officers and citizens of El Paso.[89]

Continuing the reconfiguration of the Pennsylvania National Guard in order to increase its firepower and mobility, two Pennsylvania infantry regiments, the 2nd at El Paso, and 9th still at Mount Gretna, were converted into artillery regiments. The 2nd was to be heavy artillery, equipped with 4.7" howitzers. (The novice artillerymen adapted to their new role in exemplary fashion; in January 1917, they made an excellent showing at the Fort Bliss artillery range.)[90] It was planned to bring the 13th Pennsylvania Infantry to El Paso to replace the 2nd Pennsylvania. The 9th and 13th Pennsylvania were ordered to El Paso, but owing to the prevalence of poliomyelitis among the troops at Mount Gretna, the movement was suspended. Not until October 5 did the 3rd Pennsylvania Artillery arrive in El Paso.[91] This reorganization gave the 7th Division a full brigade of field artillery, like that of the New York division. Stretched out on the road in marching order the brigade covered some fifteen miles.[92]

The field artillery's horses and mules came from the remount station at Fort Bliss, the largest on the border. The government placed orders totaling seventy-three thousand animals from every state west of the Mississippi, with Missouri furnishing most of the mules. Twenty thousand animals were sent to El Paso and distributed throughout the district. On arrival, all horses were quarantined, inspected, and vaccinated. The remount station expanded into an enormous complex with each corral holding from fifty to seventy-five animals. Horses of the same color and weight were penned together. Although the army was attempting to mechanize, it was still heavily dependent on animals:

An infantry regiment needed:
 49 riding horses
 92 draft mules
 6 riding mules
 17 pack mules for the machine gun company
 1 pack mule for the sanitary detachment

A field artillery regiment needed:
 340 draft horses
 260 riding horses
 54 draft mules
 3 riding mules
 1 pack mule for the sanitary detachment

A cavalry regiment needed:
 1,030 horses
 194 draft animals
 3 riding mules
 11 pack mules for the machine gun platoon
 1 pack mule for the sanitary detachment

As with other border stations, the horses arrived straight off the range, and breaking them was a distasteful, and often hazardous, undertaking. In August, twenty-four Pennsylvania cavalrymen were in the hospital with broken arms or collar bones as a result of handling bucking outlaw horses. A Pennsylvania sergeant lost his eyesight from a kick by a mule. Yet he was comparatively lucky; a Rhode Island trooper died from a similar kick.[93] On the other hand, "Massachusetts cavalrymen have been taming their horses to stand fire by shooting pistols behind them. Some of the animals continued to dance around when the shots are fired suddenly behind them, while others have learned to go ahead munching alfalfa without batting an eye."[94]

A serious problem developed over arrears in the guardsmen's pay. In August, local merchants and the chamber of commerce telegraphed the U.S. senators from Texas urging an emergency appropriation by Congress to pay the state troops on the border. Some National Guard units had not been paid since their deployment. The Michigan units were paid on July 31.[95] Not so some Massachusetts units. The chaplain of the 8th Massachusetts, Captain H. B. Edwards, even arranged to borrow $18,000 at 6 percent interest from an El Paso bank, but fortunately it did not come to that. The Massachusetts brigade was finally paid before the end of August.[96]

Of course the soldiers did not spend all their time training. Off duty, some of them trained their mascots, which, besides the usual dogs and goats, included a gopher that answered mess call and a mule that prayed.[97] American soldiers have always been avid souvenir hunters, and El Paso offered a wide variety. One enterprising businessman urged guardsmen to buy a burro for only five to ten dollars and suggested that a regiment could purchase a whole carload. Guardsmen were prone to mail souvenirs such as horned toads and lizards back home, and the practice became so prevalent that the post office finally had to prohibit the traffic. General Funston reiterated the prohibition.[98] Most souvenirs were less exotic. "The post card and curio shops of course were heavily patronized. A 1,000-peso Pancho Villa bill made a most pleasing souvenir for the militia men to send to the folks back home, especially when it could be purchased for ten cents. Stores and restaurants were always busy, and the banks equally so, with long lines at every window."[99] But guardsmen complained that El Paso merchants gouged them. "With the arrival of the Guard prices went up in El Paso. This was especially true in the case of souvenirs and Mexican knick-knacks. An article which cost a dollar a month before was now priced at ten or fifteen. Hair-cuts advanced to thirty-five and fifty cents. And in every line of business it must be said that the merchants made the best of their opportunity. On pay-day the camp was thronged with peddlers, selling souvenirs of every kind at exorbitant prices. Truly the merchants of the Southwest are good business men!"[100]

While in camp a soldier could always patronize the canteen, which was "to the army post what the general store is to the country village. Here the soldier can obtain, at moderate prices, all the necessities and luxuries of his life." Canned goods, candy, crackers, ice cream, tonic, and 2 percent beer were the most popular items, but all kinds of toiletries, shoe polish, and a host of other indispensable articles were also available. Members of the companies operated the canteens, and profits went into the company fund. One of the attractions of the canteens was that they would extend a certain amount of credit until payday.[101]

BORDER SERVICE

Off-duty entertainments covered a wide range of activities. A favorite sport among the troops was to climb nearby Mount Franklin.[102] Regiments also employed whatever talent they had to produce occasional vaudeville shows. A stage was improvised and a few benches were constructed for the spectators. The regimental band opened the program with a lively tune. Quartets, solos, and skits followed to prolonged applause, and "The Star Spangled Banner" closed the performance. The problem was that these performances were infrequent and quickly exhausted the available regimental talent. Boxing exhibitions and baseball games provided a change of pace, as did athletic tournaments, and on at least one occasion a famous hypnotist performed at Camp Cotton. There were also polo matches between guardsmen and regular officers.[103] One of these matches provided the opportunity for a group of guardsmen to cross into Mexico. A team (a major and three lieutenants) from Pennsylvania's First City Troop traveled to the Punitive Expedition's headquarters to play that polo team, losing the match.[104] An innovation was that the polo teams in units such as Troop B of the Massachusetts Cavalry, included (wealthy) enlisted men, something regular officers had trouble accepting in what was traditionally a sport for officers. But something more reliable was needed to occupy the men.[105]

The answer proved to be the YMCA, which provided one of the greatest benefits available during off-duty hours. At Camp Cotton the YMCA maintained a recreation hall (as it did at Camps Pershing and Stewart).[106] At one end was a desk where stamps and postcards could be purchased and money orders cashed. The El Paso chamber of commerce had bought 10,000 postcards and writing paper. Free writing material was readily available to the guardsmen: the YMCA received 150,000 sheets, the Fort Bliss chaplain 25,000, the base hospital 2,000, the Knights of Columbus building at Camp Stewart 10,000, and the Travelers' Aid Society at the Union Depot 2,000. The chamber planned to distribute 300,000 sheets, with pictures of El Paso on the back.[107] At the opposite end of the building there was a piano, surrounded by tables equipped with sets of dominos and checkers. There was a bulletin board with notices, baseball scores, telegrams, and other items of general interest. Files contained New York and Boston newspapers. And the *El Paso Morning Times* included brief daily *Boston Globe* and *Boston Post* Camp Pershing and Camp Cotton editions as well as a Philadelphia *North American* Camp Pershing and Fort Bliss edition. Each night saw an overflow crowd using the YMCA facility.

The staff exercised a beneficial influence on the guardsmen. In the matter of profanity, to which soldiers are prone, no notices prohibited it; instead, the staff posted small notices reading, "If you must swear, put it in writing." This appealed to the men's sense of humor and produced the desired result. The YMCA organized basketball and baseball games. But perhaps the most popular thing the YMCA did was to show movies nightly. A frame was erected for the screen and the operator worked from a box ten feet off the ground. Regimental officers occupied benches at the front, while several hundred enlisted men stood behind them. The YMCA obtained the latest releases in El Paso and showed five reels a night, with comedies proving the most popular fare. The movies continued to be the chief form of amusement.[108] The YMCA allocated more than $20,000 to build forty-one wooden structures in twenty-one camps along the border, and evidencing the importance of El Paso, the YMCA established its border headquarters there.[109]

The Red Cross provided considerable support to guardsmen on the border, under President Wilson's proclamation that all supplies and comforts for the guardsmen must pass through the Red Cross. The society established receiving stations in cities throughout the country, appealing for items such as reading material, games, comfort bags, pajamas, cotton socks, towels, pipes, tobacco, cigarettes, electric fans for base hospitals, chewing gum, tinned chocolate, hard candies, coffee, and canned fruits.[110]

The city of El Paso also arranged a program of entertainment for the regulars and guardsmen. In addition, civic and fraternal organizations did what they could to brighten the soldiers' lives. The Knights of Columbus held smokers, on one occasion for 850 officers and enlisted men. The Moose lodge entertained their guardsmen colleagues with a barbeque lunch and a program.[111] Local doctors entertained regular and militia medical officers with food, Mexican music, and speeches.[112] Spanish-American War veterans gave a dance in honor of regulars and guardsmen. The University Club admitted college men in military service. There were also the movie theaters downtown, which in addition to Hollywood productions sometimes showed footage of military activities in the El Paso area.[113] For those seeking to improve themselves, the *El Paso Morning Times* organized Spanish classes at the National Guard camps. Some soldiers took a more informal approach by having Hispanic newsboys teach them Spanish.[114]

Besides these secular activities, religion played an important part in many soldiers' lives.[115] Not only did regiments hold services each Sunday but, whether out of conviction or merely to escape the routine of camp life for a time, hundreds of men attended services in El Paso churches and synagogues. There were also Sunday night programs of sacred music by military bands. Bible societies were extremely active, selling or giving away Bibles. Their agents were engaged in distributing forty thousand copies among the National Guard in El Paso. The American Bible Society bought a vehicle to distribute Bibles to the militia camps. Supporting the societies' efforts were the campaigns that several cities in Pennsylvania conducted to buy New Testaments for the troops.[116] Temple Sinai held a reception for Jewish guardsmen, which was attended by five hundred to six hundred militia and regulars.[117]

For the troops, cigarettes came just after rations and shelter as necessities of life. During the month ending on December 14, 1916, alone, the roughly 43,000 regulars and guardsmen in El Paso smoked some 6 million cigarettes, the average consumption being 4½ cigarettes daily per man. In addition, the men burned tens of thousands of packages of sack tobacco and cigars and masticated about a ton of chewing tobacco. Pipes were relatively uncommon, due to the inconvenience of carrying them while in uniform.[118] From today's health perspective some might display moral outrage at the prevalence of smoking and the government's role in making cigarettes available to the men.

For those interested in less wholesome pursuits, El Paso boasted 157 saloons (which contributed $26,000 in taxes). On August 7, lawmen raided a saloon at the suburb of Lynchville and found 250 soldiers. They arrested the owner and bartender for selling liquor on Sunday.[119] And of course there were the prostitutes, whose numbers increased to accommodate the massive influx of guardsmen. The city authorities periodically went through the motions of closing the red-light district and raided brothels and cribs in south El Paso, but the inmates simply found other locations from which to ply their trade.[120]

As fall approached, the National Guard units accelerated their efforts to make the camps as comfortable as possible. At Camp Cotton, a hospital with a capacity for 150 patients from the Michigan and Massachusetts units was established in five large tents. The Santa Fe Railroad provided huge quantities of cinders to reduce the dust in company streets. Screened wooden mess halls replaced mess tents. Pyramidal tents received wooden flooring. The electric light network was expanded. Additional shower baths were built. Wooden structures now housed regimental headquarters. About

130,000 feet of water pipes had been laid in the camps as of September. Whitewashed stones lined the walks around tents and structures. At Camp Stewart the principal street, Pennsylvania Avenue, was being beautified. At Camp Cotton, troops were digging drainage ditches, and a large storm drain connected with the city system to prevent a repetition of floods.

The guardsmen stoically prepared for an indefinite stay.

Chapter 14

More El Paso

The second wave of guardsmen reached El Paso beginning in August. Once the crisis with Mexico abated, the War Department had decided to hold additional National Guard units in their mobilization points until they could be properly recruited, examined, and equipped. Then the War Department ordered that the twenty-five thousand men still at mobilization camps be sent to the border as soon as practicable.[1] At El Paso, campgrounds for twenty additional regiments were prepared, and the city, especially the business community, anticipated having a total of fifty thousand stationed there, the greatest concentration of troops since the Civil War. Furthermore, El Pasoans confidently expected that their camps would be the healthiest in the history of the army.[2]

Leading the second wave was the South Carolina National Guard, which had mobilized at Styx, in Lexington County, across the river from Columbia, the state capital. They arrived in El Paso on August 11 and 14: the 1st and 2nd Infantry (the "Palmetto" regiment); Troop A Cavalry (the Charleston Light Dragoons); Company A Engineers; Hospital Company No. 1; and Ambulance Company No. 1.[3] Their camp was on the mesa between Camp Stewart and Mount Franklin. Company B, 2nd Infantry, was the Washington Light Infantry of Charleston, a militia unit dating back to 1807.[4] As Private Henry B. Reid of Company A, 2nd South Carolina, recalled, "At the time most of us looked upon our mobilization as a lark, . . .

a chance to have a good time and see some of the country." But then most surprisingly he added: "I served in France in 1917 and 1918, and I want to tell you that the training and conditions we experienced in Texas along the border were tougher than what we underwent in combat in France."[5]

Accompanying the arrival of the South Carolinians was a terrific rainstorm fanned by eighty-mile-an-hour winds. The storm played havoc with the army camps. Practically every tent in Camp Cotton was blown down or torn from its foundations. Where wooden floors had not yet been installed, water was two feet deep in tents. Mud was everywhere; vegetation, including gardens the enlisted men had planted and lovingly cultivated, washed away. Two men from Company D, 5th Massachusetts, were seriously injured when a wooden recreation pavilion collapsed on them.[6] A unique feature of this particular storm was that gallant Massachusetts cavalrymen rode to the rescue of chorus girls from a burlesque show at the open-air theater at Camp Cotton and carried them to shelter. Unfortunately, the supply of cavalrymen far exceeded the supply of willing girls.[7] A few days later another fierce nighttime storm formed lakes three feet deep in the roads near camps Cotton and Stewart, and guardsmen were driven from their tents by a wall of water rolling in from the hills. Yet another cloudburst and fierce windstorm on August 20 deluged the camps, washing out streets. A mess hall under construction—the largest building in Camp Cotton—blew over, injuring a Michigan private and narrowly missing several of his comrades.[8] The Southwest monsoon season had arrived with a vengeance.

Besides the violent weather, another major problem was a threatened nationwide strike on September 4 by four hundred thousand railroad workers. Since the army depended heavily on the railroads, such a paralysis of the nation's transportation system would be a catastrophe. While negotiations between railroad management and the unions proceeded, the War Department nervously watched developments, and at General Funston's request temporarily halted further National Guard movement to the border because of possible difficulties in supplying them. Meanwhile, National Guard units in El Paso compiled lists of railroad employees in their ranks, in case the army had to take over the operation of some trains. At least a strike would not cut off rations for the border army because the quartermaster depots at El Paso, Columbus, and San Antonio had ample supplies.[9] The strike was averted when the national government stepped in and forced a compromise.[10]

An epidemic of sleeping sickness seemed to have hit the sentries of the 31st Michigan. As of August 20, six members of Company E had been caught asleep on guard duty, most recently at the viaduct by Hart's Mill, where, on August 18, Private John A. Lind removed his belt and sidearm, laid his rifle on the ground, and made himself comfortable for a nice refreshing nap. A few days later, two NCOs from Company K were found asleep at a Michigan outpost, bringing the total of those charged with dereliction of duty to eight. They of course faced court-martial for such a serious offense. A soldier in the Punitive Expedition had recently been sentenced to nine years in Leavenworth in a similar case. But to the dismay of many at Camp Cotton, Lind and the other defendants received only a figurative slap on the wrist. A special court-martial assessed his punishment at five days' hard labor. The rest also received sentences that did not exceed fifteen days' hard labor. Michigan officers worried about the effect this would have on morale.[11]

While these sentences appear ridiculously mild, there was an instance of a sentence that appears ridiculously harsh. An enlisted man in the 1st Pennsylvania Infantry[12] wrote to the *El Paso Morning Times* complaining of inhumane treatment of an enlisted man in the 2nd Pennsylvania Infantry. The complaint resulted in an official investigation by the inspector general, the investigation verifying that the unfortunate soldier had been spread-eagled by his captain, staked to the ground in the company street to lie in agony from the blazing sun and from the ants crawling all over his body. His comrades were so outraged that they forced the colonel to free the man and consign him to the guardhouse. But as the newspaper reported, "The colonel yesterday morning was inclined to think the man had received the treatment he deserved. The colonel was also inclined to belittle the whole affair. He jocularly said the man ought to have been given 'a good beating.'"[13]

The Ohio National Guard, whose peacetime strength was 7,295, was the next major arrival, on September 3. Most of this organization was assigned to El Paso: the 1st Infantry Brigade (4th, 5th, and 8th Infantry); 2nd Infantry Brigade (2nd, 3rd, and 6th Infantry); Cavalry Squadron A; 1st Field Artillery Battalion; 1st Engineer Battalion; Company A Signal Corps; Field Hospital Companies Nos. 1, 2, and 3; and Ambulance Companies Nos. 1 and 2. The two ambulance companies arrived in El Paso between September 8 and 13. Despite an appeal from Governor Frank Willis to Secretary

Baker that the 1st Ohio Infantry also be mobilized, the 1st and 7th Ohio, the 9th Infantry Battalion (Colored), and a signal corps company were not called up and conducted their scheduled summer training.[14] One element of the Ohio guard had recently been activated for the kind of duty the National Guard sometimes performed—crowd control. Battery B of the Field Artillery had been mobilized in May to assist the police in Akron to control a crowd of some ten thousand gathered as the result of a disastrous building collapse.[15]

The Ohio National Guard is interesting for several reasons. First, the organization was the last to mobilize in the army's Central Department, which covered fourteen midwestern states. Barely beating Ohio by four days were Iowa, Minnesota, and South Dakota; Missouri and Wisconsin had mobilized nine days earlier. In the case of Ohio, neither the state administration nor the Central Department had met their responsibilities in preparing a mobilization site. "When the call to mobilize came on June 18, Ohio was almost completely unprepared."[16] A board of officers had declared in 1914 that Camp Perry, the National Guard camp on Lake Erie in northern Ohio, was unsuitable because of its location and small size. The board recommended a site near Columbus. Unfortunately, nothing further was done. Thus when the mobilization order came, Ohio adjutant general Benson W. Hough had to make some immediate and difficult decisions. He picked a site slightly northeast of Columbus for a semipermanent camp costing over $200,000. Camp Willis, the mobilization camp, was named for Governor Willis. The 9th Ohio Infantry Battalion, the state's only black unit, was detailed to build the camp, assisted by local workers and two hundred inmates of the state prison. By dint of frantic labor Camp Willis, consisting of dozens of temporary wooden buildings, was completed on June 27, but at a cost; the National Guard colonel in charge of it collapsed under the strain.[17] The War Department was furious that Ohio had spent $202,000 in constructing this camp without authorization—more so because once the troops left on September 9, Camp Willis was abandoned.[18]

The Ohio National Guard finished mobilizing by July 2. But all was not well at Camp Willis, where guards sometimes had gently to herd thousands of sightseers away: "The appallingly unsanitary conditions and the lack of facilities were evidence that the Guard had learned nothing from the 1898 mobilization." A number of men fell ill from ptomaine poisoning, and complaints about the food finally caused Governor Willis to visit the camp and initiate measures to improve the situation.[19] Having to construct its mobilization camp was the main reason for Ohio's delay and failure to comply with the War Department's order to move immediately to the border, and for this the army's adjutant general severely criticized Hough. Moreover, even while assembling, the Ohio Guard performed only perfunctory medical examinations; when the men were later examined by army medical officers, more than 25 percent were rejected, over four hundred in the 8th Ohio alone. This was also the worst showing in the Central Department, where the average National Guard rejection rate was 15.5 percent. Only on July 15 was the Ohio National Guard completely federalized—almost a month after the initial notification. As with other state organizations, the War Department had been unable to provide all the weapons, supplies, and equipment needed to bring the guard up to wartime strength.[20]

The army had rigorous physical standards. However, these standards were not absolute, providing that one knew the right people. A case in point is Emil Holmdahl, an American soldier of fortune in Mexico, who was convicted of violating the neutrality laws of the United States and sentenced to Leavenworth. Before beginning to serve his sentence, in 1917, he received a pardon on condition that he enlist in the army. But because of wounds suffered during his turbulent career as a mercenary he failed the army physical. In a most unusual development, the adjutant general of the army and the secretary of war intervened and ordered that he be enlisted. Holmdahl served honorably during World War I, ending with the rank of captain.[21]

Nor was this a unique instance of the army's physical standards being relaxed because of influence being brought to bear, which brings us to the second reason the Ohio National Guard was interesting: there were not only differences between guard units from different states, but there were also significant differences between guard units from the same state. Troop A, 1st Cavalry, was the elite Black Horse Troop, for many years known as the First City Troop of Cleveland. It was one of the National Guard's "silk stocking" units composed of the socially prominent. At a special luncheon at Cleveland's Union Club, the unit received a $2,000 check "for the comfort and enjoyment of the men." The cavalrymen left for the mobilization camp on July 4; the next day the Cleveland *Plain Dealer* ran a headline: "Society Weeps as Wealthy Sons Go Away as Soldiers." The troopers were appalled by the abysmal conditions at Camp Willis. The camp was poorly laid out, was unsanitary, and served unhealthy rations, all of which was made even more miserable by an extremely hot summer. But while the rest of the Ohio guard suffered, Troop A received privilege cards for Columbus's best hotels and private clubs. When the physical examinations were conducted, about half of Troop A were found to be overweight and too tall for cavalrymen.[22] As one of its members recalled

> Gloom descended on the command at Camp Willis. About half the Troop were over weight and over height for cavalrymen. Every effort, in the good old army way, was made to reject these splendid men, but Captain Norton telephoned Mr. Bascom Little, President of the Cleveland Chamber of Commerce, to take the matter up with the Secretary of War. Mr. James R. Garfield was of great assistance, and after General Scott, Chief of Staff, had referred the matter to General Barry in Chicago, the regulations were waived, and the suspense lifted. The feelings of these big fellows who, for the mistake of being too well developed, were expecting to be transferred to some infantry unit can well be imagined.[23]

The Ohio cavalry squadron entrained for El Paso on September 1, arriving at Camp Pershing five days later.

A key factor in the waiving of regulations may well have been because Private Paul Patterson was the law partner of Secretary of War Newton D. Baker: "Private Paul Patterson, in civil life the law partner of the Secretary of War, received no little publicity in the El Paso papers from the fact that being the heaviest man in the Troop he was detailed to drive the four mules on the Troop combat wagon [the ammunition wagon], which he learned to do like an expert."[24] Patterson indeed received attention from the El Paso press, which stated that despite being Baker's law partner he would have to go through army channels to communicate with Baker.[25] Regulations notwithstanding, a private with a direct pipeline to the secretary of war must have given regular officers severe heartburn.

There were other prominent men in the Ohio National Guard. For instance, Major Harold Montfort Bush, commanding the Ohio field artillery battalion, was a Cornell graduate and in civilian life had held various engineering and consulting positions. He was also the younger brother of Samuel Prescott Bush, whose son Prescott Sheldon Bush became a U.S. senator from Connecticut and was the father of President George Herbert Walker Bush. President George Walker Bush is the major's great-grandnephew.[26]

The 8th Ohio claimed to be the largest National Guard regiment in the country, with nearly 1,900 men. Before the regiment departed, the citizens of Alliance, the home of its commander, Lieutenant Colonel C. C. Weyrecht, presented the unit with three Ford trucks to transport baggage and supplies. James H. Langon, correspondent for the Cleveland *Plain Dealer*, and C. R. Wood, of the *Columbus News*, arrived on September 3 with the Ohio troops and registered at the Paso del Norte hotel.[27]

When the Black Horse Troop drew their mounts at the Fort Bliss remount station, "our Troop secured a full complement of the black horses, and so retained the historic color." But the horses were "a bunch of broncs," very small and very wild.[28] The entire 1st Ohio Cavalry Squadron initially received only 176 horses, which was but one-third of the number needed.[29] Like other guardsmen, those from Ohio had their problems with the animals. "Fractious horses and mules are creating more havoc in the Ohio camps than sickness." The men's health was remarkably good, but "the machine gun company of the 5th Ohio has about six men laid up from the effects of kicks, and the other regiments have the same story to tell. . . . Over 100 men have been disabled by kicks since the state troops first began coming to El Paso."[30]

Besides its delay in mobilizing, and one of its units receiving preferential treatment, the Ohio contingent was interesting because it was the only National Guard organization—in fact the only military organization in the United States—with a $100,000 observation balloon, a gift from the Goodyear Tire and Rubber Company of Akron. Operating the balloon was Battery B of the Ohio Field Artillery. The War Department allowed Ohio to keep the balloon, probably because the War Department had ordered several more like it for the regular army.[31] After several postponements the balloon made an exhibition ascent on September 25. It reached a height of two hundred feet and was towed along the mesa in preparation for an observation exercise. On a subsequent flight the observer, in a basket swinging underneath the balloon, took motion pictures of the army camps, experiencing some thrilling moments when the balloon hit air pockets.[32]

Like other newcomers, those from Ohio experienced culture shock. As one hometown newspaper reported, "A ballad description of the Rio Grande thirty years ago has been revived for the Rookie Soldiers now getting their first taste of border life. The author was an army bugler whose name appears to have been forgotten":

Hell on the Rio Grande
The devil, we're told, in hell was chained,
And a thousand years he there remained;
He never complained, nor did he groan,
But determined to start a hell of his own,
Where he could torment the souls of men
Without being chained in a prison pen.
So he asked the Lord if he had on hand
Anything left when He made the land.
The Lord said, "Yes, I had plenty on hand,
But I left it down on the Rio Grande;
The fact is, old boy, the stuff is so poor
I don't think you could use it in hell any more."
But the devil went down to look at the truck,
And said if it came as a gift he was struck;
For after examining it carefully and well,
He concluded the place was too dry for hell.
So in order to get it off his hands,
The Lord promised the devil to water the lands;
For He had some water, or rather some dregs,
A regular cathartic that smelled like bad eggs,
Hence the deal was closed and the deed was given,
And the Lord went back to his home in heaven;
And the devil then said, "I have all that is needed
To make a good hell," and hence he succeeded.
He began to put thorns on all the trees
And mixed the sand with millions of fleas;
He scattered tarantulas along all the roads;
Put thorns on the cacti and horns on the toads.
He lengthened the horns of the Texas steers,
And he put an addition to the jack rabbits' ears
And he put a little devil in the bronco steed,
And he poisoned the feet of the centipede.
The rattlesnake bites you, the scorpion stings,
The mosquito delights you with buzzing his wings;

The sand burrs prevail and so do the ants,
And those who sit down need half-soles on their pants.
The devil then said that through the land
He'd managed to keep the devil's own brand,
And all would be mavericks unless they bore
The marks of scratches and bites and thorns by the score.
The heat in the summer is a hundred and ten,
Too hot for the devil and too hot for men.
The wild boar roams through the black chaparral—
It's a hell of a place he has for a hell.
The red pepper grows upon the banks of the brooks;
The Mexicans use it in all that they cook.
Just dine with a greaser and then you will shout;
"I've hell on the inside as well as the out."[33]

The next arrivals were from Kentucky, whose National Guard mobilized at Fort Thomas on June 25 and contributed 2,394 men for border service.[34] There was a scare at Fort Thomas in July when smallpox was discovered in the camp. Sentries with bayoneted rifles were deployed around the installation to prevent anyone leaving or entering while the medical staff successfully dealt with the problem.[35] The Kentucky guardsmen arrived in El Paso on September 4 and 5: an infantry brigade (1st, 2nd, and 3rd Kentucky) under Brigadier General Roger Williams, Ambulance Company No. 1, Field Hospital Company No. 1, and Company A Signal Corps. The 1st Kentucky Infantry was organized in 1839 as the Louisville Legion and saw service in the Mexican War. It became the 1st Kentucky Infantry when the state guard was organized in 1878.[36] Commanding the 2nd Kentucky was Colonel Allan Guillon, who was a captain in the 20th U.S. Infantry before taking command of the regiment, which was noted for its crack shots: "Lanky mountaineers can hit moving targets due to squirrel hunting practice." The Kentucky units encamped on the mesa.[37] The infantry brigade received its full complement of horses and mules. Each of the three regiments got about one hundred mules for the combat and other wagons and about forty-five horses for the officers who did not bring their own mounts to the border. But the procedure did not go smoothly—all three regiments had to chase animals that had gotten loose; some horses ran for miles. Though dependent on animals, the Kentuckians did benefit from the mechanization program, for each regiment received four Lewis machine guns and four

Ford trucks to transport them. The machine gun companies began drilling and practicing immediately and soon engaged in target practice.[38]

On September 19, Troop B, 10th Tennessee Cavalry, Ambulance Company No. 1, and Field Hospital Company No. 1 came to El Paso.

The North Carolina National Guard mobilized at Camp Glenn, in Morehead City. Its infantry brigade (1st, 2nd, and 3rd Infantry) under Brigadier General L. W. Young arrived in the border city between September 28 and October 1, accompanied by Cavalry Troops A and B, Field Hospital Company No. 1, and Ambulance Company No. 1. Engineer Companies A and B arrived on October 23 and Field Hospital Company No. 2 on November 20.

On October 7, the trains transporting the 1st Battalion Georgia Field Artillery (Batteries A and C [Savannah] and Battery B [Atlanta]) pulled into El Paso's Union Depot, followed on October 27–28 by an infantry brigade (1st, 2nd, and 5th Regiments, the latter known as "Atlanta's Own"), Troop A 1st Cavalry Squadron, 2nd Cavalry Squadron, and Field Hospital Company No. 1. (The 3rd Separate Infantry Battalion remained in Georgia.) Mustered into federal service between July 2 and 31, as of July 31, Georgia numbered 4,192 men, of whom 3,892 went to the border. Issued ten days' rations, they made the four-day journey in ten trains.[39] The Reverend and Mrs. W. R. Foote of Washington, Georgia, had sent their only son, 2nd Lieutenant W. W. Foote, off to serve his country with the admonition to "live like a Christian and fight like a Southerner."[40]

The Georgia National Guard had suffered its first casualties while still at Camp Harris (named for the governor, Nat E. Harris), the mobilization camp at Macon. On July 18 during a thunderstorm a lightning bolt killed one soldier and seriously injured another. Then on August 25, a distraught woman fired twice with a small caliber revolver and killed Captain Edgar J. Spratling of Company F, 5th Georgia, in his tent. The deceased was a physician, who was prominent in Atlanta medical and social circles; the woman claimed he had molested her while she had been in his office for treatment. Spratling's fellow officers thought that she was mentally ill.[41]

The Georgians' brigade headquarters and the 1st, 2nd, and 5th Infantry set up shop at Camp Cotton, occupying the site of the Massachusetts brigade, which was leaving for home. They found Camp Cotton to be quite comfortable, for it had a sewage system, electric lights, large, screened mess halls, and tents whose sides and floors were planked. The 2nd Cavalry Squadron and the 1st Battalion Field Artillery were stationed at Fort Bliss. When the artillery unit was inspected between August 24 and September 8, it was still practically without horses. The same was true for the 2nd Cavalry Squadron, inspected between September 1 and 8. Life for the Georgians was made a little easier when women back home began furnishing that state's guardsmen with comfort bags, containing sewing kits, cards of buttons, thimbles, thread, and needles. The bags, of brightly colored cloth, were hung from tent poles.[42]

The Georgians were less than overjoyed to discover that a bunch of Yankees—the Michigan brigade—were encamped next to them. The railroad spur separating the camps became a kind of Mason-Dixon line. Initially there was considerable name-calling and a few fistfights, but a more serious clash occurred when state sensibilities were outraged. One evening a Michigan band marched through the Georgia encampment playing "Marching through Georgia." Furious Georgia guardsmen poured out of their tents, and what resulted was a massive brawl between the militiamen of the two states. Although no one got killed, hundreds were treated for their injuries. The animosities continued for the next few weeks, to the degree that officers kept the contingents separated and ordered that no band could play any selection that offended any region.[43] A more benign account of this incident attributes it to "when some Georgia militiamen walked through the Michigan camp whereupon the Michigan band, not knowing about the unpleasant associations attached to the tune, struck up 'Marching Through Georgia.' The infuriated Georgians, stomping on the drums and assaulting the bandsmen, caused a general riot. The next day two regimental hospitals were full and busy caring for the many fortunately minor injuries which resulted."[44]

Eventually the Michiganders and Georgians developed considerable mutual respect. One thing they had in common was the dust. "Due to the dust everywhere it was impossible to keep anything clean," recalled Lieutenant Albion Smith of the 2nd Battalion, 5th Georgia. However, an officer of the 5th Massachusetts passed along important classified information—at a nearby house on Magoffin Avenue a hot bath could be had for a reasonable fee. The Georgia officers zealously guarded this secret, and the hot baths greatly improved their quality of life.[45]

The final state contingent began arriving on October 14: Company A of the Colorado Signal Corps, followed on November 3 by Batteries B and C of the 1st Colorado Field Artillery Battalion. The batteries had been transferred from Deming, New Mexico, marching overland. They covered the eighty-five miles to El Paso in less than five days. Some of the unit's equipment was shipped by rail.

Upon their arrival the Colorado gunners were attached to the 5th U.S. Field Artillery for administration and training. The 5th and 8th U.S. Field Artillery regiments formed a brigade commanded by Brigadier General E. St. John Greble. After resting for a few days, the Colorado artillerymen began an intensive training program that lasted for the remainder of their stay in El Paso. Part of the training involved setting up firing positions on the mesa targeting some twenty-five prominent locations in Ciudad Juárez and its environs. The brigade command post was atop the Paso del Norte Hotel, the tallest building in El Paso.[46]

The Colorado National Guard had mobilized at the state rifle range in Golden, near Denver. The organization consisted of two infantry battalions, a cavalry squadron, two artillery batteries, two engineer companies, a signal company, and a field hospital company, a total of 1,860 men. In December, public subscription raised enough money to present the Colorado National Guard with an armored car.[47]

Battery A of the District of Columbia Field Artillery departed from El Paso February 25, 1917, but the authors have been unable to determine when it arrived there.

Major General Clement's 7th Division was no longer exclusively from Pennsylvania. Because some Pennsylvania infantry units had been rotated back to the mobilization point, Clement's 1st Infantry Brigade now consisted of the 1st, 2nd, and 3rd North Carolina Infantry.

Brigadier General Charles G. Morton arrived to take command of the 10th Division (Provisional)[48] organized on September 3 and located under canvas about two miles northeast of Fort Bliss, across the railroad tracks from the 7th (Pennsylvania) Division. Under the supervision of regular officers, Mexican laborers laid water pipes, constructed latrines, and generally prepared the camp for occupancy.[49] General Bell issued General Orders No. 43, officially naming the division's camp "Camp Owen Bierne," after a twenty-nine-year veteran sergeant who was a member of the provost guard and who while on duty had been shot and killed by a drunken Texas Ranger in a downtown saloon. This killing outraged Bell, who publicly declared that "I am going to see that justice is given my men if they stay on the border. Sergeant Bierne was a true, loyal soldier, and died in the performance of his duty. He was an example of the highest type of American soldier." The troops evidently shared Bell's outrage, for more than one thousand of them attended Bierne's funeral, as did many civilians.[50] The Texas Ranger, W. B. Sands, was tried for murder but the trial ended in a hung jury. Sands was fired from the rangers. As commanding general of the 10th Provisional Division, Morton was a strict disciplinarian. When the cavalry regiment failed to meet his standards he placed that whole command under arrest.[51]

Brigadier General George Bell, Jr., commanding the El Paso District, now commanded the 11th Division (Provisional)[52] as well as the regular units based at Fort Bliss.[53]

The entire Massachusetts brigade, more than 4,310 men, went on a practice march on September 13. The troops, fully equipped, covered ten miles in 4 1/2 hours. General Sweetser adroitly performed the difficult feat of turning the brigade and its sixty-six mule-drawn wagons around in the narrow road to Ysleta for its return march. On the whole the march went well. Only three men dropped out of the 9th Massachusetts, two from exhaustion and one because a mule stepped on his foot. The 8th Massachusetts, however, lost twenty-nine men from exhaustion or more properly, from hangovers, since the regiment had been paid the previous day. The 5th Massachusetts lost seven men from exhaustion. Ambulances picked up those who fell out.[54] Perhaps not coincidentally, on Mexican Independence day, September 16, the entire Pennsylvania division except the artillery conducted a large-scale maneuver that consumed five hundred thousand rounds of blank ammunition.[55]

The climax of the National Guard experience in El Paso came on September 21, when the biggest parade in the city's history was held. The mayor declared a holiday, the courts suspended their activities, merchants decorated their stores, and autos were prohibited at intersections along the parade route. The parade was unprecedented in the history of the U.S. Army—never before had a full war-strength division of twenty-two thousand men been assembled. It was the largest parade since the Union Army's victory parade down Pennsylvania Avenue in Washington in 1865. An area of twelve thousand by four hundred yards—one square mile—northeast of Fort Bliss was cleared of brush for assembly purposes. The two Michigan regiments were converted for the day into a war-strength regiment, as was the Kentucky brigade; the same was done with units from other states. The two South Carolina regiments were merged with three regiments of regular infantry to form a reinforced brigade. The division marched from its assembly area through downtown El Paso and back. Since the column was nearly twenty miles long, the leading units were back at Fort Bliss before the last units began their march. General Clement of Pennsylvania was the reviewing officer.

It should be noted that General Clement loaned some three thousand of his guardsmen to the regular units to bring them up to their authorized strength for the parade (an example of the regular army being unable to meet the standard it set for the National Guard).[56] The parade began at eight o'clock in the morning and continued for six hours, the troops being considerably bothered by the clouds of dust that preceding units generated. The column included forty bands, which among other selections played "My Old Kentucky Home" and "Dixie." As the parade wound through downtown at least one Mexican was observed busily taking notes.[57]

El Paso did not receive all of the fifty thousand National Guard troops it had hoped for. Because the Florida, Alabama, and Mississippi National Guards were sent elsewhere, only three instead of four National Guard divisions were stationed in El Paso. But the city certainly had no cause for complaint, since it had the largest concentration of force on the border, over forty thousand including guardsmen from eleven states. As of October 1916, Fort Bliss was the headquarters of what amounted to a National Guard army corps.[58]

When the National Guard arrived the men found pocket watches cumbersome and clamored for wristwatches. Soon local stocks were exhausted. Rush orders to factories replenished stocks, and local jewelers, druggists, clothing merchants, cigar dealers, stationery stores, and even fruit dealers displayed wristwatches in their windows. The soldiers bought most of the twenty-five thousand wristwatches sold during July and August.[59]

The scope of training accelerated, with emphasis now on exercises involving large units. On September 23, more than twelve thousand Pennsylvania guardsmen—infantry, cavalry, artillery, engineers, and signal corps—marched by the Ohio camps for over three hours as they set out on a four-day hike.⁶⁰ The 1st Infantry Brigade distinguished itself, marching one day for eighteen miles without a single man falling out.⁶¹ When the division reached the town of Anthony, on the New Mexico state line, the truck train with their supplies was unaccountably delayed. Facing the prospect of going to bed hungry, the men purchased everything edible in country stores. As the column trudged northward, more than one thousand exhausted guardsmen dropped out of line, most of them temporarily. Attending to the serious cases was the 215-man Pennsylvania field hospital company in the rear. On November 3, the 7th Division undertook another hike, but this one lasted for only two days.⁶²

On October 1, some eighteen thousand men of the 10th Provisional Division, composed of fifteen Ohio, Kentucky, Massachusetts, Michigan, and South Carolina regiments, set out on a fifty-eight-mile march up the Mesilla Valley to Fort Selden, New Mexico, in heavy marching order. The troops broke camp at three o'clock in the morning and began marching at eight thirty, with the 6th Ohio in the van. They toiled through sand four to six inches deep; those who fell out from exhaustion were picked up by ambulances.⁶³ The best account of this hike is by Private Roger Batchelder of the 8th Massachusetts, who dubbed it "the great hike" and described it as the "hardest and most trying days of our border service."⁶⁴

A Massachusetts infantry company went ahead to Anthony to establish a supply point for the column. The men only got a sandwich at noon, and they were rationed to one quart of water a day. At night they did get more water, although much of it came from oily tanks. The division made it another fifteen miles up the road to Las Cruces on the first day, hundreds of camp fires marking its bivouac. As the column passed through Anthony, the arrangements for supplying the division with water improved, as did the road to a slight extent. When on the fifth day the column reached the hamlet of Mesquite and a nearby irrigation ditch, "within fifteen minutes after our arrival this ditch was dotted with thousands of naked figures, splashing, swimming, and howling delightedly. For we had not had a bath for three days."⁶⁵ Making the hike more interesting, and arduous, was the fact that the guardsmen advanced as though engaged in an actual campaign, fighting an imaginary foe.⁶⁶ The column was so long that the leading elements would be in camp before the last units had left the previous camp.

Apparently because of the logistical problems involved in supplying so many troops, it was decided to end the march and maneuver at Las Cruces rather than continuing on to Fort Selden. The division encamped on the mesa and hills east of Las Cruces, a town of some three thousand. Private Batchelder recalled that:

> We started for Las Cruces at noon, passed Mesilla Park at three, and soon came within sight of our destination. High in the air, suspended by kites, there flew a banner bearing the legend, 'Welcome to Las Cruces.' The town was decorated with flags; the streets were filled with the inhabitants, who gave us such a demonstration as we had not received before. We passed through the town and reached the camping-ground. The large banner was now directly overhead. Suddenly some one shouted, "My God! The town dump." And so it proved. The ground, uneven and covered with thick bushes, was strewn with every variety of refuse. . . . It took an hour to put the grounds into proper shape. Many months' accumulation of tin cans, bottles, barrel-hoops, and rusty wire had to be cleared away; the remains of what appeared to have been a fox were gathered and buried without ceremony. The men then razed the bushes with their bolos and set up the tents.[67]

Las Cruces boasted five saloons, but to the frustration of the enlisted men, guards were placed around the saloons and only officers were permitted to enter. However, each enlisted man got a bottle of beer. Las Cruces teemed with guardsmen. "The barber-shops, baths, and stores were overcrowded; the bakeries sold their entire stock within a few hours. Las Cruces, with its few thousand people, had never seen such throngs within its borders."[68] The local newspaper reported that "the town is the mecca of the men and every place and corner of the streets are filled, every store and shop is packed to the doors. Sweets, fruit, cakes and soft drinks and ice cream were at first the most in demand, but tonight staples, eggs, meat, groceries are being sent to camp every hour."[69] A series of maneuvers was planned in which three brigades would engage an enemy force advancing from the nearby Organ Mountains.

The division began its return march on October 10, enduring frequent rainstorms that turned the road to ankle-deep mud and soaked the exhausted men as they tried to sleep in their pup tents.[70] It rained every night, and at one point the men slogged through rain, hail, and snow at the village of Canutillo. By October 14, the weary troops were back in camp. The entire maneuver was frustrating for the cavalry, who frequently had to march at the rear of the column in order to keep pace with the infantry and consequently ate a lot of dust. The city of Las Cruces—and especially its merchants—formally thanked General Morton for his troops' visit.[71]

With the approach of winter, which in 1916–17 was unusually windy, Camp Cotton became quite a cheerless place. Windstorms played havoc with the tents, sandstorms forced the men to wear handkerchiefs as masks, and the nights grew colder. No matter how tightly the tent flaps were battened down, the wind and cold penetrated. Small, conical Sibley stoves provided heat, and a long pipe passed through a vent in the top of the tent to carry away the smoke. Although the pipe had a spark arrester at its end, holes were frequently burned in the tents. And because of the strong draft the stoves burned hot for a short time and the tent once again became cold. During the evenings some men wrapped up in blankets and whiled away the hours playing poker. Others walked to Magoffin Avenue and for a five-cent fare caught a jitney, a ramshackle Ford touring car, into town. Jitneys passed every few minutes and never refused to take on a passenger. "Almost invariably it was necessary to sit in someone's lap or have them sit in yours."[72]

Mexican snipers kept the troops along the Rio Grande on their toes. On August 7, five rifle shots were fired near Camp Cotton. On August 10, two shots were fired at men of Battery B, 1st Pennsylvania Artillery, one of the rounds hitting a watering trough. On August 14, three shots were fired at an outpost of the 8th Massachusetts near the "Island." The captain who was sent to investigate was also fired on. A squad of Massachusetts marksmen was promptly dispatched to the river with orders to return any further fire. On September 4, an outpost of Company I, 9th Massachusetts, took incoming fire on three occasions. On September 15, three shots missed a detachment of the 31st Michigan machine gun company on guard at the smelter. On September 25, Company F, 31st Michigan, took sniper fire, but "a couple of volleys fired in the direction from whence came the shots frightened the snipers away." On October 9, snipers fired several times at the Michigan encampment at Camp Cotton.[73] Complicating matters was that besides genuine sniping incidents, some guardsmen on outpost duty at lonely or dangerous spots experienced what was called "shadowitis"— seeing imaginary enemies. When the company commander investigated a reported incident, often it proved nonexistent. This happened several times at Michigan outposts, and two Massachusetts privates "contend a riddled cactus plant is a band of Mexican smugglers."[74]

The sniping incidents culminated in what became known as the "Battle of Hart's Mill." On Christmas Eve a detachment of Company L, 3rd Kentucky Infantry, was on outpost duty at Hart's Mill. Without warning a fusillade of some twenty shots came from the Mexican bank of the Rio Grande. The Kentuckians were fed up with being sniped at, and they fired back with everything they had and suppressed the Mexican fire. Over three hundred rounds were exchanged during the bloodless firefight, one that produced panic in El Paso. Subsequent investigation by both Mexican and American officers cleared up the affair. The cause of all the trouble turned out to be large piles of slag at the nearby smelter. As the slag cooled in the freezing night it exploded. A Mexican outpost on the river thought the Americans had launched a surprise attack and fired back, along with other Mexican positions opening fire in support. This produced the furious response from the Kentuckians.[75]

Unpleasantness of a different sort occurred on Christmas day. A ferocious windstorm disrupted celebrations throughout the El Paso area. Clouds of sand blew over Christmas dinners at noon in mess halls and prevented many of the planned band concerts and outdoor celebrations from being held.[76]

An important aspect of the training program was to phase the more recently arrived contingents into outpost duty along the Las Cruces–Fort Hancock corridor. For example, Ohioans relieved the Michigan units doing the two-week tour of duty. Regarding the Ohio cavalry, "here the future officers of the 136th F.[ield] A.[rtillery] acquired, as enlisted men, the military experience which was to prove so valuable on the fields of France."[77] The 2nd Georgia Cavalry Squadron underwent a month of mounted training at Fort Bliss, then on December 1 marched the thirty-two miles to Fabens for field duty. The Georgians patrolled the border with the 1st Kentucky Infantry, and from December 16 with the 2nd Kentucky.[78]

Complementing the September parade, the grandest since 1865, was the artillery review held on January 27, 1917. It was the largest peacetime collection of field artillery in the history of the United States. The spectacle took place on the cavalry parade ground at Fort Bliss, with Brigadier General St. John Greble reviewing the equivalent of a division of artillery. All the units, both National Guard and regular, in El Paso assembled in a massed front a mile long. At precisely nine thirty that morning, they began rolling past the reviewing stand in battery formation, each regiment being preceded by its band. The division consisted of three brigades:

1st Brigade—5th U.S. Field Artillery with Battery A, New Mexico Field Artillery, and Batteries B and C, Colorado Field Artillery attached; 8th U.S. Field Artillery

2nd Brigade—3rd Pennsylvania Field Artillery and the provisional field artillery regiment of the 11th Division

3rd Brigade—2nd Pennsylvania Field Artillery and the provisional field artillery regiment of the 10th Division

The most striking feature of the review was Battery C, 5th U.S. Field Artillery, whose 4.7" guns were drawn by five armored caterpillar tractors. Each caterpillar weighed sixteen thousand pounds and handled a load of eighteen thousand pounds, consisting of one gun and its limber and one ammunition caisson and limber carrying fifty-six rounds of ammunition.[79]

Another impressive review occurred on March 6, 1917, when once again a war-strength division marched through El Paso, this time for the benefit of a cattlemen's convention. The fifteen-mile-long column of regulars and guardsmen took three hours to parade through downtown. The soldierly appearance of the guardsmen caused particular comment, and when a reporter "asked several regimental commanders yesterday as to the number of men who fell out of ranks during the review the commanders acted as though they were genuinely astonished at such a question."[80]

Ironically, when it came to unit strength, the army demanded that the National Guard meet a standard that the army itself was incapable of meeting. Four regular regiments were stationed at Fort Bliss, two of them—the 34th Infantry and the 17th Cavalry—having recently been activated at the post. But the army was having considerable difficulty in recruiting. In September, it informed guardsmen that they would be stationed in the South if they enlisted in the regular army. The results were disappointing. The army then launched a drive in November to bring the four regular regiments stationed in El Paso up at least to peacetime strength. Now guardsmen were offered a month's leave if they enlisted in the regular army. In January 1917, a recruiting office opened in El Paso. But in March, even Major General Leonard Wood had to admit that on the whole, army recruiting was "going slow."[81]

When a shipment of fifty-two Lewis guns arrived at Fort Bliss in August, the 7th Division received most of them.[82] The Lewis gun was widely distributed to National Guard units, but in December Secretary of War Baker officially condemned the weapon. The War Department let a contract for four thousand Vickers machine guns to be the army's standard. This news dismayed members of the National Guard machine gun companies in El Paso, as they were becoming very proficient in the use of the Lewis gun. Pennsylvania troops, for instance, took a three-day course in operating and dismantling the gun, and every fourth day they practiced firing on the Fort Bliss range.[83] Baker's decision produced considerable negative comment, centering around the secretary's ignorance about machine guns and consequently having to rely on the army's Ordnance Department, which was chastised for its incompetence.[84] Then in January 1917, word reached El Paso that the army planned to test on May 1 a new lightweight machine gun with an improved magazine, manufactured by the Marlin Company, and that the test would not affect the recent contract for four thousand Vickers.[85] While the army was trying to decide on a standard weapon, at Fort Bliss there was held on January 29 a grand review of the machine gun companies of fifteen guard and regular regiments. The companies passed in review before General Bell in their Ford trucks. In March, the machine gun school at Fort Bliss was discontinued because of the departure of the National Guard.[86]

The army's inability to select a standard machine gun continued to produce logistical problems. For instance, "The 33rd Michigan machine gun company is making a practice march to Columbus to test out the new machine gun automobiles with which that organization was recently supplied." The three automobiles were Studebakers, of the latest type and designed specifically for border patrol work. "Each car has bullet-proof shields on both the front and rear with attachments for machine guns. The cars are of the six cylinder type with high-powered motors and will carry eight men, including the driver. Compartments in the automobile body provide space for extra rations and water and will carry 20,000 rounds of ammunition. A gasoline supply for a 300-mile trip can be carried, in addition to automobile accessories." The machine gun company had fifty-five enlisted men, all of whom went on the trip, some of them in the Ford motor trucks used to transport machine guns and ammunition. Other long runs were planned to places such as Elephant Butte dam in New Mexico.[87] The arrival of these vehicles left the machine gun company with four Studebaker cars, one Reo armored car, and five Ford light trucks stripped down to transport members of the company instead of machine guns. The company had four Lewis guns and two Benet-Merciers.[88] The whole thing was a logistical nightmare.

Largely as a result of requirements by the Punitive Expedition, the army had embarked on a crash program to purchase trucks. As of March 1917, it boasted some two thousand.[89] One goal was to provide every infantry regiment with a company of twenty-seven trucks. In addition, the National Guard's horse-drawn ambulances were to be replaced by the motorized version. An innovation was that, as a result of the Punitive Expedition, trucks would be painted khaki color to match the sand, rather than the dark warship gray in which they had been coming from the factory.[90]

Despite the army's efforts to modernize, it still depended heavily on animals. In February 1917, the War Department increased the allotment of wagons to war-strength regiments:

Cavalry—from 27 (5 combat, 5 baggage, 17 rations and forage) to 37 (8 combat, 8 baggage, 21 rations)
Infantry—from 22 to 27 (11 combat, 11 rations, 5 baggage)

Since the National Guard regiments were turning in nearly all of their mules and wagons there were plenty, both at Fort Bliss and Fort Sam Houston, fully to equip all regular units.[91]

Large-scale exercises continued. The 1st Brigade of the 10th Division, composed of three Kentucky and one South Carolina regiments, conducted an exercise on January 26. The Kentuckians launched a raid that attempted to capture the depots at Fort Bliss, which the South Carolinians defended. "During the course of the raid a large number of the raiders were rendered 'hors du combat,' but the Kentuckians accounted for an equally large number of the defenders of the fort."[92]

While Ohio guardsmen chafed at the delays in leaving El Paso, they received a dose of culture.[93] On January 14, 1917, Madame Ernestine Schumnn-Heink sang a number of her favorite songs to an audience of officers and enlisted men at Camp Pershing. They presented her with a bouquet of flowers and a silver loving cup.[94]

Overall the troops' health had been excellent, the result of the army's determination to avoid the mistakes of the 1898 mobilization. Hygiene measures had been strictly enforced in the camps. The death rate for both regulars and guardsmen in El Paso was a mere 4.25 per 1,000 in 1916; among the National Guard, between July 1 and December 31, the death rate from disease alone was 1.36 per 1,000. Adding the deaths due to suicide and violence brought the death rate among the militiamen to about equal that among regulars. However, the incidence of pneumonia proved to be surprising to army medical officers. Even so, there were less than fifty pneumonia deaths on the entire border. This was the largest number of deaths from any specific disease.[95] By February 1917, the base hospital had a record number of patients—1,050. Except for the pneumonia cases, few were serious, but the army established an isolation camp to treat contagious diseases.[96] Medical officers had placed the Colorado signal company at Camp Stewart under quarantine and took preventive measures against typhus.[97] The measures were successful. An additional measure was General Bell's imposition of a two-week quarantine beginning on March 1 prohibiting all soldiers from visiting El Paso except on government business—such as a parade—and those personnel had to be back in camp by six thirty in the evening.[98] The unusually high incidence of pneumonia that winter continued to be a source of concern to the army. The quarantine was extended for a week, and there was a noticeable decrease in communicable diseases.[99] When it came to deaths, according to the *El Paso Morning Times* some state organizations were luckier than others, as shown in the list at the end of this chapter.

One death had caused a considerable stir. A rumor circulated among the Ohio National Guard that Private Rodney Lapp of the 8th Ohio had died of pneumonia after being placed in the guardhouse because he was too ill to participate in drill and that an officer involved had been arrested and was to be court-martialed. Some four hundred of Lapp's comrades in the 8th Ohio signed a "round robin," a petition protesting against camp conditions. The petition was intercepted en route to an Ohio newspaper and delivered to the regimental commander. General Bell had a major on his staff conduct a formal investigation of the matter. The investigation concluded that no officer was involved, that Lapp had simply died of pneumonia in the base hospital, that he had been properly cared for, and that no one was to blame for his demise. Furthermore, the investigating officer recommended that the twenty-odd NCOs who had signed the petition be demoted to the rank of private, that the privates not be punished because of "ignorance on their part," but that all the signers be lectured on the duties of soldiers and warned that their actions had been unmilitary, and that Private Richard Dixon, who had drafted the petition, be considered for court-martial. The NCOs involved stated they had signed the petition believing it was a correction to an article that had appeared in an Ohio newspaper. They kept their stripes. As for camp conditions, the investigation stated that all of the

8th Ohio's tents had wooden floors and walls, stoves, and ample fuel. The regiment was comfortably and adequately housed and the number of its sick was below average.[100] C. R. Wood of the Columbus *News*, one of the Ohio correspondents reporting on the National Guard in El Paso, asserted that the troops were getting a "square deal."[101] A summary court-martial sentenced Private Dixon to one month's detention and forfeiture of two-thirds of his pay for three months.[102] Another Ohio death, that of Private Harry L. Baker, Company B, 4th Ohio, was truly bizarre. He was fatally shot at Camp Owen Bierne a few days before his scheduled departure for home. Baker, who had just come off guard duty, was standing at attention in formation in the company street at the "Retreat" ceremony while the band played the national anthem. When the command "Order Arms" was given, a corporal's rifle discharged, killing Baker instantly. The corporal was immediately arrested because his rifle was supposed to be unloaded.[103]

The National Guard organizations began departing on September 20, 1916: Massachusetts Field Hospital Company No. 1, Rhode Island Ambulance Company No. 1, and Troop B of the Rhode Island Cavalry.[104] The Central Department decided that all National Guard units under its jurisdiction would not return to their mobilization points but would be mustered out at permanent posts in Illinois, Kansas, Michigan, and Indiana, which had facilities for large numbers of troops.[105] During October and November, departures were Massachusetts and Pennsylvania units plus the 1st South Carolina Infantry. In December, Massachusetts, Pennsylvania, and Michigan units entrained. The pace accelerated in January 1917, with mainly Pennsylvania organizations, plus some Michigan and Kentucky units. By February, a torrent of units—from South Carolina, Pennsylvania, Ohio, the District of Columbia, and Colorado—pulled out. The climax came in March, when an averted nationwide railroad strike enabled delayed National Guard units finally to leave for home. Accelerating their departure was the imminence of war with Germany. On March 23, Battery A of the New Mexico Field Artillery, the first National Guard unit to arrive, was the last to leave.

The difference that training on the border had made to the National Guard was illustrated by Lieutenant Albion Smith's recollections of the contrast between the 5th Georgia Infantry when it marched to the trains in July 1916 and when it detrained in Atlanta on March 29, 1917:

Then every man was dressed as he thought fit in queer fitting uniforms of many descriptions; some with sleeves rolled up and others with them down; packs unequal in size, and poorly adjusted to the backs; rifles at all angles; some were eating and others drinking; everybody left ranks at will to kiss any pretty girl he passed, and they liked it. These were Atlanta's darlings—they could do no wrong—they are our boys and we love them, everyone thought or said. To-night the people were expecting more of the same, and when they did not receive it they felt momentarily rebuffed. The long, solid column advanced down Peachtree Street heavier and browner than when they left ten months ago. With shoulders erect, eyes to the front, rifles at a correct angle, and presenting a businesslike attitude they advanced through the roaring welcome. They had left Atlanta with sympathy and love, they returned to find that love changed to a feeling of deep pride for a son now grown to manhood. Yes, Camp Cotton had done a good job.[106]

The big news in February had been the arrival of the Punitive Expedition, and more particularly the arrival of General John J. Pershing. Both Secretary of War Baker and General Funston commended him for a job well done.[107] El Paso went all out to welcome Pershing. A detachment of the 8th U.S. Cavalry escorted him between crowds of cheering citizens, the New Mexico Field Artillery battery fired a salute, and at a formal banquet Pershing received a silver punch service. He was accompanied by General Bell on February 6 to visit the army headquarters offices in the downtown Mills Building. Pershing resumed command of the El Paso District from Bell. (Not infrequently, writers have described Pershing as commandant at Fort Bliss. Pershing never commanded Fort Bliss—he commanded the El Paso District.) General Bell continued to command the 11th Provisional Division.[108] Pershing's tenure as commander of the El Paso District was brief. By the end of the month he was promoted to major general and succeeded the late General Funston as commander of the Southern Department. Pershing left for San Antonio, receiving a thirteen-gun salute upon arrival at Fort Sam Houston.[109] Bell resumed command of the El Paso District.

The fifty thousand regulars in the Southern Department were now responsible for border security. They were organized as a field army, with three provisional infantry divisions and a provisional cavalry division.[110]

Fort Bliss remained a major installation, being the headquarters of two of these divisions. Most units of the Punitive Expedition were now stationed there, occupying camps vacated by the National Guard. The 2nd Provisional Infantry Division was organized in March, commanded by General Bell:

1st Infantry Brigade:
  7th Infantry
  17th Infantry
  23rd Infantry
2nd Infantry Brigade:
  6th Infantry
  16th Infantry
  20th Infantry
3rd Infantry Brigade (at Columbus)
Divisional Cavalry (headquarters at Marfa)
Artillery Brigade:
  4th Field Artillery (less 2nd Battalion)
  5th Field Artillery (less Batteries D and F)
Engineers:
  2nd Engineers (less Companies E and F)[111]

And on February 12, the six regular cavalry regiments at Camp Stewart were formally organized into the 1st Provisional Cavalry Division under General Eben Swift:

1st Brigade—8th and 17th Cavalry
2nd Brigade—7th and 13th Cavalry (less one troop)
3rd Brigade—5th and 11th Cavalry[112]

The division conducted a grand review on March 9, a review in which General Bell's guest was General Francisco González, commander of the Juárez garrison. The six regiments first walked past the reviewing stand, then trotted by, then passed at a gallop. The grand finale was a charge by all six thousand cavalrymen toward the reviewing stand.[113] As was the similar spectacular held in Brownsville, massed cavalry charges were great theater but of rapidly decreasing value in modern warfare.

A portent of change was the arrival of two army aircraft that flew from Columbus to El Paso on March 9 in forty-five minutes.[114] And General John J. Pershing declared that for scouting purposes he would rather have one airplane than a regiment of cavalry. And indeed, in January it was announced that a squadron of twenty army aircraft would be stationed at Fort Bliss.[115]

With an eye to possible involvement in World War I, in February much attention focused on teaching the troops how to throw hand grenades. Detachments from three regular regiments received intensive instruction, instruction that did not always go as planned. On one occasion a grenade struck the side of a trench, wounding two soldiers, one of whom died. There was also emphasis on bayonet drill.[116]

Looking beyond the National Guard mobilization, El Paso confidently expected to maintain, and even improve, Fort Bliss's position as an outstanding military post.[117] In November 1916, a chamber of commerce committee began inspecting available property, as part of an effort to secure a permanent division post. Property values around Fort Bliss soon soared. And in February 1917, El Paso, San Antonio, and Brownsville entered bids for cantonments.[118]

General Funston was not enthusiastic. "There is no doubt in the world that the vicinity of a large town like San Antonio, or El Paso, especially along this border where there are so many Mexicans, is an undesirable station for young men in training."[119] And Secretary of War Baker had strict standards for localities where troops were stationed. He announced in October that the illegal sale of liquor to soldiers on border duty must stop at once; troops would be withdrawn from towns where the liquor laws were violated. "Army officers say the chief cause of complaint is the sale of whiskey in resorts and by bootleggers on the street which has caused numerous fights and cutting affrays. First, leave will be discontinued; then, troops will be withdrawn."[120] El Paso had a well-deserved reputation as a town where a soldier could have a really good time. Gambling was a problem, with the sheriff conducting raids against illegal slot machines.[121] A bigger problem was prostitution, and despite sporadic raids the city fathers made only half-hearted efforts to eliminate the practice. The area around Ninth and Mesa Streets was notorious.[122] General Funston had expressed his disappointment that General Bell had not been more successful in combating prostitution and the liquor traffic in El Paso: "I fear that he regarded it from the first as an almost hopeless proposition."[123] In an effort to provide an alternative to vice, the local YWCA operated a program designed to introduce guardsmen to decent girls by organizing social events in which YWCA members acted as hostesses.[124]

Border Service

Besides prostitution and the flourishing traffic in liquor, there was the traffic in narcotics.[125] As a result of Baker's edict, "the territories adjacent to the army posts became infested with saloons, 'soldiers' clubs,' and, where the sale of liquor was prohibited by civil statutes, dives and rum holes of the lowest order."[126] Yet El Paso was not wholly to blame; Ciudad Juárez was then, as to an extent it is now, wide open. Although standing orders forbade soldiers from crossing into Juárez, it was easy to ride the trolley over in civilian clothes, and in Juárez a soldier could find just about anything he was looking for. But occasionally the Military Police would employ a stratagem to apprehend a soldier on his way across the river. An MP would quietly enter a streetcar from the rear and suddenly yell "Attention!" Those soldiers whose conditioned reflexes caused them to leap to their feet at attention were promptly arrested.[127] Largely as a result of El Paso's reluctance to reform itself, coupled with the proximity of Juárez, Secretary Baker decided that the division cantonment would go to Deming, New Mexico, a small, isolated locality where the boys could not get in trouble as easily. The El Paso city fathers were devastated.

Appendix: National Guard Deaths in El Paso

MASSACHUSETTS
Officially, "there was only one death in the entire number of Massachusetts troops on the Border."[128] But according to the local newspaper, the following men lost their lives:

> Pvt., Troop F, 1st Cavalry Squadron—fall from a train near camp[129]
> Pvt., Co. I, 5th Massachusetts—base hospital, appendicitis[130]
> Pvt., 8th Massachusetts—base hospital, appendicitis[131]

RHODE ISLAND
> Pvt.—base hospital, scarlet fever[132]
> Pvt., Cavalry Squadron—kick from mule[133]
> Pvt., Cavalry Squadron—fall from horse[134]

PENNSYLVANIA
> Pvt., Company G, 6th Pennsylvania—base hospital, peritonitis[135]
> Pvt., 18th Pennsylvania—took nap in railroad car full of lumber, which fell on him[136]
> Pvt., Company H, 18th Pennsylvania—shot in head in quarrel[137]

More El Paso

Pvt., Company G, 4th Pennsylvania—base hospital, peritonitis[138]
Pvt., Company F, 13th Pennsylvania—base hospital, pneumonia[139]
Pvt., 8th Pennsylvania—unknown[140]

NORTH CAROLINA

Pvt., Troop A Cavalry—accidentally shot self with pistol[141]
Sgt., 3rd North Carolina—base hospital, unknown[142]
Cpl., 3rd North Carolina—base hospital, pneumonia, unknown[143]
2/Lt., 1st North Carolina—unknown[144]
Pvt., Engineers—base hospital[145]
Pvt., 2nd North Carolina—base hospital, pneumonia[146]
Pvt., Ambulance Company No. 1—unknown[147]
Cpl., 3rd North Carolina—base hospital, unknown[148]

SOUTH CAROLINA

Sgt., 1st South Carolina—base hospital, peritonitis[149]
Sgt., 2nd South Carolina—base hospital, pneumonia[150]
Pvt., 2nd South Carolina—base hospital, pneumonia & measles[151]

GEORGIA

Pvt., 5th Georgia—base hospital, meningitis[152]
Pvt., 8th Georgia—base hospital, meningitis[153]
Pvt., Cavalry—base hospital, meningitis[154]
Pvt., 5th Georgia—base hospital, unknown[155]
Pvt., 1st Georgia—base hospital, pneumonia[156]
Pvt., 1st Georgia—base hospital, unknown[157]

TENNESSEE

Cpl., Cavalry—base hospital, pneumonia[158]

MICHIGAN

Pvt., 31st Michigan—killed in fall from truck[159]
Cpl., 32nd Michigan—base hospital, amoebic dysentery[160]
Pvt., 32nd Michigan—base hospital, amoebic dysentery[161]
Pvt., 33nd Michigan—murdered[162]
Pvt., 32nd Michigan—base hospital, pneumonia[163]
Pvt., Field Artillery—base hospital, pneumonia[164]
Pvt., 33rd Michigan—base hospital, pneumonia[165]
Pvt., 33rd Michigan—base hospital, pneumonia[166]
Pvt., 33rd Michigan—base hospital, pneumonia[167]
Pvt., 32nd Michigan—base hospital, pneumonia[168]

Border Service

Sgt., 33rd Michigan—base hospital, heart trouble[169]
Sgt., 33rd Michigan—accidentally shot himself[170]
Sgt., 33rd Michigan—base hospital, diabetes[171]
Capt., 33rd Michigan—base hospital, complications after operation[172]

OHIO

Sgt., 8th Ohio—suicide[173]
Sgt., 4th Ohio—unknown[174]
Capt., 8th Ohio—base hospital, diabetes[175]
Pvt., 8th Ohio—base hospital, pneumonia[176]
Pvt., 8th Ohio—base hospital, pneumonia[177]
Unassigned recruit—base hospital, pneumonia[178]
Pvt., 4th Ohio—accidentally shot[179]
Sgt., 5th Ohio—killed when train hit truck[180]
Pvt., 5th Ohio—killed when train hit truck[181]
Pvt., 4th Ohio—base hospital, meningitis[182]
Unassigned recruit—base hospital, pneumonia & measles[183]
Pvt., 3rd Ohio—fatally stabbed in affray[184]
Pvt., 5th Ohio—base hospital, pneumonia[185]
Sgt., 6th Ohio—base hospital, pneumonia[186]
Pvt., 5th Ohio—unknown[187]

KENTUCKY

Lt., 3rd Kentucky—accidentally shot by fellow officer[188]
Pvt., 3rd Kentucky—base hospital, pneumonia[189]
Pvt., 1st Kentucky—base hospital, pneumonia[190]
Sgt., 3rd Kentucky—unknown[191]

Chapter 15

Deming

The arrival of the National Guard in July 1916 was the most exciting thing that had ever happened in Deming, New Mexico. The citizens, proud of their pure air and water and pleasant climate, lobbied intensively to have a large number of guardsmen stationed there, emphasizing that the town was on the Southern Pacific main line, providing excellent communications.[1] The citizens were electrified by reports in July that a huge camp site was being prepared for two brigades of cavalry, a battalion of artillery, a field ambulance company, and two truck companies, each with twenty-seven trucks. The camp would have a large base hospital and a number of other structures. In preparation for the National Guard the good ladies of Deming organized a chapter of the Red Cross.[2] Their hopes soared when they received word that a regiment of Delaware National Guard, mobilized at Newcastle, Delaware, was coming.

Furious preparations were under way at a New Mexico National Guard encampment, Camp Brooks, renamed Camp Deming. The campsite was about a mile and a half from town. Hundreds of latrines were ready and others were under construction; several units of shower baths had been completed. When Mexican laborers employed in building Camp Deming's headquarters at $1.30 for a nine-hour day went on strike, the mayor had the instigators arrested as vagrants. Work continued without interruption, as other workers immediately took their places. The quartermaster at El Paso was already employing drivers to go to Columbus in order to operate trucks

The U.S.-Mexico border from El Paso to San Diego. Map by Harold "Buddy" Clark.

between Columbus and the new camp at Deming. Fifty-two civilian drivers based in Deming handled the convoys, and the army planned to erect a large machine shop in Deming to repair the vehicles.[3]

The first contingent of Delaware troops had some excitement on the way to Deming. As their troop train neared a point west of Sierra Blanca, Texas, at one thirty in the morning on July 30, unknown parties threw stones and fired six shots through the windows of two of the cars. Fortunately there were no casualties. Lights were immediately extinguished and the train reached El Paso without further incident. After a brief layover the troops continued on to Deming. By August 1, the 1st Delaware Infantry, consisting of two separate battalions with a peacetime strength of 551, had arrived. The mayor issued a proclamation welcoming them, and the Deming Red Cross association served them lunch at the camp while a local band played. The citizens came in droves to welcome the National Guard; hundreds of automobiles were parked around the encampment.[4] In addition, the mayor and the chamber of commerce hosted an informal reception, followed by a banquet at the Harvey House by the railroad station for all of the commissioned officers at Camp Deming. Flowery speeches and expressions of goodwill were the order of the day, and the festivities ended with everyone toasting with Deming's famous water, advertised as being 99.99 percent pure.[5]

Camp Deming, whose commander was Brigadier General Granger Adams, got off to a promising start. Assistant chief of staff Major General Tasker H. Bliss and his entourage inspected the encampment on August 9 and pronounced themselves pleased with conditions. The guardsmen were settling in, fielding a baseball team to play against the locals, and the soldiers engaged in a refreshing water fight with the town fire department, a contest that ended in a draw and drew hundreds of admiring townspeople as spectators.[6]

The next contingent to arrive was from Arkansas. That state's National Guard had for years been fighting for its very existence, in large measure because businessmen refused to grant their employees leave to participate in guard activities.[7] The 1st and 2nd Arkansas Infantry regiments mobilized at Fort Logan H. Roots near Little Rock. Each lacked a machine gun company; the state arsenal boasted only two obsolete Gatling guns. But in March one machine gun company was being organized.[8] An alarming deficiency was that when the regular doctors performed physical examinations they rejected 922 men, including 19 commissioned officers. Reportedly more than 200 of the rejections resulted from excessive cigarette smoking. The result of this debacle was that the Arkansas guard was reorganized, the able-bodied men from the two regiments being consolidated into one[9]— the 2nd Infantry, commanded by a regular officer, Captain Albert B. Sloan, who was commissioned as a lieutenant colonel in the Arkansas guard. By July 1, the mobilization process was completed and the regiment was mustered into federal service.[10] A reconstituted 1st Arkansas was later mustered in and dispatched to Deming.

Patriotism ran deep in Arkansas. One Hiram Martin, age twenty, left the plow in the furrow at his farm when a passing rural postman shouted that troops were needed for the border. Martin walked twenty miles to Fort Smith and tried to enlist in the 1st Arkansas Infantry. To his dismay, he was five pounds underweight at his physical, due to his twenty-mile walk. But after resting and consuming a prodigious dinner he made the weight requirement and was duly enlisted.[11]

The Arkansans arrived in Deming on August 13 and pitched their tents in their assigned area. They reported having a comfortable and uneventful trip by rail with not a single man becoming ill in transit. During their brief stopover in El Paso the men had purchased large quantities of postcards to give the folks back home some idea of the Southwest. The Deming mayor promptly issued a proclamation welcoming them and invited them to a public reception arranged by the chamber of commerce, the Red Cross, and prominent citizens.[12]

The newcomers soon made their presence felt. On the evening of August 16, bullets whistled through Camp Deming. The call to arms rang out and detachments raced to the camp's boundaries to suppress the incoming fire. The presumed Mexican snipers, however, turned out to be a group of Arkansas guardsmen, who, unknown to their officers, had gone hunting in the desert and had fired promiscuously toward the Delaware end of Camp Deming. An angry Delaware patrol apprehended three of the clueless Arkansans, who were placed under guard pending an investigation of the incident by General Adams.[13]

A more welcome development was the visit to Camp Deming by the international secretary of the YMCA and his announcement that arrangements had been completed for erecting and equipping a building to serve the Delaware and Arkansas troops, as well as any others that might be stationed in Deming. The structure, having an auditorium holding four thousand, was dedicated on September 20.[14]

The first death at Camp Deming was a private in Company B, 2nd Arkansas, who died in the hospital. He was ill when he left Arkansas but was determined to go in the same company as his brother, who escorted the body back to their home in Fort Smith, Arkansas.[15] A lieutenant from Company G, 2nd Arkansas, mysteriously disappeared from Camp Deming. It was feared that he had been waylaid by Mexicans while walking into town. The fact that he was carrying considerable cash on his person at the time lent credence to the story. Armed troops searched Deming and vicinity, fearing he had met with foul play. However, a few days later he turned up in Little Rock, Arkansas, home of the bride he had married just before leaving for the border. The marriage had caused much comment at the time, for it was performed at the Arkansas mobilization camp on a high bluff called "Lover's Leap" and a large throng of soldiers and civilians had witnessed the ceremony. The lieutenant mailed his resignation from the National Guard to the commander at Deming.[16] Then it developed that he was wanted for bigamy as well as for being away without official leave—twice within the last two weeks he had left his unit at Deming and gone to Little Rock. Police in Little Rock arrested the slippery lieutenant and turned him over to the army. He was returned to Deming under guard to stand trial for desertion by a general court-martial. Convicted and transferred to Fort Bliss for safekeeping, he managed to escape but soon gave himself up.[17]

On September 20, General Adams announced that Camp Deming would no longer be known as headquarters of a provisional division, but merely as the 4th Separate Brigade, which consisted of the 1st Delaware Infantry (two battalions), 1st and 2nd Arkansas, 1st Wyoming Infantry (two battalions), New Hampshire Field Hospital Company No. 1, and Batteries B and C, 1st Separate Battalion Colorado Field Artillery.

On September 26, Deming suspended business and closed its schools in order to witness the inspection, parade, and review of the 4th Separate Brigade by General Adams. Unfortunately, during the review Major W. E. Lank of the Delaware regiment was thrown from his horse and seriously injured. Two nights later the officers of the brigade honored General Adams with a banquet on the day of his retirement because of age. Colonel Edwin F. Glenn of the 18th U.S. Infantry at Douglas assumed command at

Deming on September 29. Glenn had been chief of staff to Major General Leonard Wood, commanding the Department of the East, when he was transferred on July 15 to command the 18th U.S. Infantry. *Army Magazine* published a flattering article on Colonel Glenn.[18] On October 1, Adjutant General I. P. Wickersham of Delaware arrived from Wilmington to inspect his state's regiment.[19]

The Wyoming National Guard mobilized at Fort D. A. Russell, three miles from Cheyenne. One guardsman demonstrated a remarkable devotion to duty. William Smyth was a homesteader at Warren, Wyoming; when he heard of the call-up he rode fifty miles for his physical exam, disposed of his property at a loss of $600, and hired an auto to take him to the mobilization point. When the auto was stopped by a flooded river a fourth of a mile wide, he swam the river, then walked twenty-eight miles until he could hire a horse for the rest of the way to join his company.[20]

The Wyoming contingent, ordered to the border on September 23, consisted of the 1st Infantry (the 1st and 2nd Separate Battalions), Field Hospital No. 1, and several small detachments of auxiliary troops, as well as several carloads of horses. The 18th U.S. Infantry, currently stationed at Douglas, was also ordered to Camp Deming.[21]

Unlike some other guard organizations, the Colorado National Guard had recent field experience as strikebreakers, having been called up in 1903–1904 and again in 1913–14 to suppress strikes by miners in Cripple Creek and Ludlow.[22] The 1st Colorado Field Artillery Battalion had mobilized and been mustered into federal service at Golden by August 14. However, more than three-fourths of Battery A's personnel consisted of students from the State Agricultural College at Fort Collins, and under War Department orders they were mustered out on September 16 and the battery returned to its home station. Battalion headquarters and Batteries B ("Denver's Own") and C (from Colorado Springs) left Golden on September 30 and arrived in Deming on October 3. Theirs was the encampment farthest west of town. By October 26 their training had progressed to the point that they began a three-day route march and firing exercise under the critical eye of a regular major sent from Fort Bliss to inspect them. The night of their return to Camp Deming, October 28, they received orders to march immediately to Fort Bliss.

The Arkansas regiments suffered several additional casualties while at Camp Deming. On October 3, a sergeant in the 1st Arkansas died at the base hospital of wounds received when the supply sergeant of the machine gun company accidentally discharged a Lewis gun. The unfortunate sergeant was lying on his cot, watching a demonstration of the gun that was being given for some Wyoming officers, when a bullet shattered his leg. He received a military funeral. In addition, an Arkansas private died in the hospital of spinal meningitis in November, three died of pneumonia in December and two in January; that same month another private died from drinking poisoned whiskey sent to him as a Christmas gift. A buddy of his who luckily took only a few sips survived.[23]

Arkansas's efforts to recruit up to war strength were not uneventful. The governor on October 13 pardoned a man just beginning to serve a two-year prison sentence, apparently for statutory rape, on condition that he enlist in the National Guard. The man had taken the army physical when he was convicted. However, an army recruiting officer denounced the governor's action and demanded an investigation because the law stipulated that enlistees have a clean record.[24] On December 9, 1916, the Arkansas National Guard was ordered to recruit to full wartime strength, and a recruiting drive began.[25] On January 1, a major, a captain, and a first lieutenant of the 1st Arkansas resigned their commissions.[26]

New Hampshire Field Hospital Company No. 1 had left Concord on October 17, being assigned to Laredo and then transferred to Deming. The routine of its camp life continued until November 22, when the seventy-five men of the unit participated in the 4th Separate Brigade's route march to Fort Bayard near Silver City, New Mexico, which was used as an army sanitarium for tubercular patients. The march lasted twelve days and was a disaster. Originally scheduled for fifteen days, the march of these three thousand men was curtailed because of bitterly cold weather. A brutal cold front, combined with the troops marching to higher altitudes and a lack of blankets, made for a truly alarming situation. Temperatures dropped below zero during the night, but the New Hampshire men were more accustomed to cold than were some of their comrades. Company M, 1st Arkansas, suffered the worst, with one of its men freezing to death. The wretched column struggled into Fort Bayard and nearby Silver City, where the men rested, got warm for two days, and passed in review before Colonel Glenn and his staff. But with temperatures near zero and with sickness increasing, Glenn left the most serious cases at Fort Bayard and started back three days early. After a four-day march his men gratefully reached Camp Deming on November 18, "fully recovered from the effects of the recent cold wave which temporarily disorganized its personnel." Fifteen of their comrades had preceded them—they had deserted at Silver City and had taken the train back to Deming, where the provost guard promptly arrested them for being absent without official leave. A reinforced provost guard scoured the town searching for additional deserters. Following the Fort Bayard ordeal, the New Hampshire Field Hospital Company remained at Camp Deming until its return to Manchester on March 11, 1917.[27]

Matters at Camp Deming were generally uneventful. On November 23, there were a number of personnel changes at the 4th Separate Brigade headquarters.[28] To combat the boredom of camp life, a series of boxing matches pitting men from different units against each other proved to be a popular entertainment.[29] A well-equipped range for machine gun target practice was in operation by December, complete with targets, pits, and a telephone system. The machine gun companies of the 1st and 2nd Arkansas Infantry inaugurated the facility.[30]

In December a serious health problem developed in Camp Deming. A member of the supply company, 1st Arkansas Infantry, died of measles complicated with pneumonia. Two more similar cases ended fatally—one each from the 1st and 2nd Arkansas. And three more Arkansas guardsmen soon succumbed. By the end of the month, though, Colonel Glenn announced that sickness was well under control, this after the acting surgeon general of the army had conducted a thorough inspection of the camp and base hospital. Glenn declared that only one more case of measles had recently been reported, and twenty-five convalescents had returned to their units. Almost all the cases currently in the hospital were just simple colds. Only about thirty patients were absolutely unfit for duty out of the three thousand men in camp. The remainder of the patients could be returned to duty in case of an emergency. Two more men of the 1st Arkansas and one from the New Hampshire Field Hospital Company No. 1 died in the base hospital of pneumonia during January 1917.[31]

Colonel Glenn and his staff presided over an impressive ceremony on the afternoon of December 23. The troops assembled in parade formation, and the bands marched to a position facing the flagpole at brigade headquarters. As the consolidated bands played, a color guard escorted the American flag, and the senior color sergeants raised it while the regiments presented arms. Patriotic airs and the national anthem preceded a Retreat ceremony. The consolidated bands then marched to the west end of the 2nd Arkansas camp and were dismissed. Regimental commanders marched their units to their respective camps and dismissed the men.[32]

What the troops really enjoyed of course was not ceremony but Christmas. On Christmas Eve about one thousand men jubilantly paraded through the streets of Deming in their night shirts. The next day the troops enjoyed a big Christmas tree, an elaborate turkey dinner, and a program of music and short talks. Many of them also opened packages containing gifts from home. Perhaps more useful but certainly not as much fun, each man also received from his Uncle Sam a package containing one razor, one shaving brush, one hair brush, one toothbrush, one shoe brush, one comb, a box of shoe polish, two towels, one cake of soap, one whisk broom, and one "housewife" containing needles, thread, buttons, and so forth.[33]

The troops could have put these items to good use in preparing for the most important inspection yet. On January 12, 1917, Major General Frederick Funston arrived in Deming in his private railroad car to conduct a formal review of the 4th Separate Brigade. This occurred the next morning at the polo grounds, following which he was given a banquet at the Harvey House by the chamber of commerce. The general expressed himself as "highly satisfied" with the troops, stating that "some of the regiments are in better shape than others, but I think they would all be ready for active service if called on." Funston and his party then drove to Columbus to inspect the troops there.[34]

Camp Deming recorded several losses of personnel in January. Two deaths occurred on the 16th: a private in the 2nd Arkansas of pneumonia and a private of the 1st Wyoming of tuberculosis. The battalion sergeant major of the 1st Arkansas was commissioned a second lieutenant in the Philippine Scouts. And Major H. B. Scott and Capt. F. C. Burnett, 2nd Arkansas, resigned their commissions.[35]

Camp Deming's morale probably improved as a result of several developments reinforcing the view that the guard's deployment on the border was ending: the recruiting parties that the Arkansas regiments had sent back home received War Department instructions to return to Deming, and a truck train arrived from the Punitive Expedition carrying pumping and well-drilling machinery that had been used in Pershing's lines of communication.[36] These were welcome signs that the Punitive Expedition was winding down and the regulars would be resuming responsibility for protecting the border. Then a few days later electrifying news swept the camp—the 1st Arkansas and 1st Delaware were ordered home. The bands of the lucky units serenaded their camps with "Home, Sweet Home." And convalescents poured out of the base hospital to rejoin their units, almost emptying the facility.[37]

The Arkansas and Delaware contingents differed markedly in one respect. The 1st Arkansas lost a number of men to pneumonia, and in every case the patient's blood showed the presence of malarial bacteria. The high mortality rate was attributed to this fact and to complications with measles. Private Roy Fondern, of Company G, 2nd Arkansas, died at the base hospital in El Paso on February 5 of blood poisoning. His remains were shipped to his home in Clarkesville, Arkansas. The 1st Delaware, by contrast, lost not a single man either to disease or accident during its seven-month border service.[38]

Camp Deming received information that two regular cavalry regiments —the 11th and the 13th—now with the Punitive Expedition, would be stationed in Deming following the evacuation, but in February, those units were ordered to Fort Sam Houston.[39]

On February 2, 1917, the jubilant 1st Arkansas and the 1st Delaware boarded trains for the journey home. "Citizens gave the departing troops a noisy farewell."[40] It was generally believed in Deming that two villista spies observed all the details connected with the departure of the two regiments. The local police were convinced that the spies had made a careful survey of the town and a minute examination of the railroad facilities. The two suspects were believed to have gone to El Paso.

On a more cheerful note, the press reported on February 5 that General Funston had notified the 2nd Arkansas and New Hampshire Field Hospital that all officers and enlisted men at present absent on furloughs were to report to their home stations, turn in their government property, and be mustered out of the federal service.

There was a general exodus from Deming to Columbus on February 4 and 5 to witness the return of Pershing's Punitive Expedition from Mexico. All officers from Camp Deming who could be spared from duty made the journey, as did a third of Deming's school children.[41]

On February 19, Colonel Glenn received official notification that all the state troops of the 4th Separate Brigade would be sent home as soon as transportation could be arranged. The 2nd Arkansas would proceed to Little Rock, the Wyoming infantry to Fort D. A. Russell at Cheyenne, and the New Hampshire Field Hospital Company to Manchester, on March 7.[42] The New Hampshire unit had only one death while in border service. But first, Glenn, his staff, and the men of the 4th Separate Brigade stood in formation on February 21 at the railroad station to pay their respects as the special train carrying Major General Frederick Funston's body halted at Deming on its way to San Francisco. The troops stood at attention while the band played "Nearer, My God, to Thee."[43]

A few days later, trouble surfaced in the 2nd Arkansas Infantry. Twenty-eight of the regiment's fifty-three officers signed a petition to Arkansas governor Charles Brough demanding that seniority rules be strictly observed in promotions. The petition fell into the hands of Colonel Henry Stroupe, the regimental commander and never reached the governor. Stroupe's feelings were hurt, and he confined several of the signers to quarters. The petition's signers declared their loyalty to the colonel but said they wanted greater efficiency in the Arkansas National Guard and to eliminate politics in the appointment and promotion of officers. What had precipitated the petition was Colonel Stroupe's selection of Captain Almon Stroupe as temporary commander of the 1st Battalion during the absence of its regular commander.[44] The troubled regiment departed on March 2 for Fort Logan H. Roots at Little Rock to be mustered out.[45]

On March 1, 1917, the 1st Wyoming Infantry left Deming for Fort D. A. Russell to be mustered out of federal service.[46] When this last guard unit departed, the citizens of Deming no doubt regretted the loss of "their" guardsmen, but their spirits subsequently soared, when Deming was designated as a divisional cantonment during World War I.

Chapter 16

Columbus

Columbus, New Mexico, flourished as the logistical base for the Punitive Expedition, despite efforts by other New Mexico communities to cash in on the National Guard mobilization. The Albuquerque chamber of commerce asked that the city be designated as a training center for out-of-state guardsmen. At a mass meeting, the citizens of Alamogordo offered General Bell the use of Alamogordo and vicinity as a camping ground for his troops. A delegation from Lordsburg also tried to interest the army in using that town as a border mobilization and training camp.[1] These efforts were unavailing, although Las Cruces did succeed in having a few guardsmen stationed there.

The military presence produced a boom in Columbus, with a number of new businesses springing up virtually overnight. Landowners naturally tried to cash in by charging the government exorbitant prices for their property. However, the army purchased sections of land several miles north of Columbus and moved its camp there, checkmating the speculators and facilitating its control of the troops.[2] The army also established an airfield two miles east of the camp, which produced an oddity: "The Columbus post office is the only one in the United States that has an airplane rural free delivery, for first-class mail only, to Pershing's camp in Mexico. The rest is sent by truck. Before Villa's raid the post office was just a fourth-class one; Columbus had a population of 700. In less than a week after Pershing entered Chihuahua, the post office jumped to being a first-class facility."[3]

As of June 19, 1916, the New Mexico National Guard at Columbus numbered 56 officers, eleven companies of 65 men each, and a field artillery battery of 133. "We're about sixty men short," stated Adjutant General Herring, "but will have a complete regiment in a few days."[4] The news of Carrizal did produce an increase in recruiting, especially in Roswell, which also canceled its traditional Fourth of July fireworks display in order to use the $500 to assist families of guardsmen.[5] Recruits continued to trickle in, from Texas as well as New Mexico. As the 1st New Mexico Infantry was gradually being built up, recruiting officers made a final determined effort to enlist the needed sixty recruits. The principal difficulty was finding men who could pass the rigid physical examination. For example, Captain Carl Hinton, commander of Company H, was rejected by examining surgeons in Columbus. Despite Hinton's appealing his case personally in Washington, D.C., the rejection stood.[6] Colonel Edmund C. Abbott, commanding the 1st New Mexico, vigorously defended the morality and discipline of both regulars and guardsmen, this in reply to a New Mexico preacher who at a camp meeting had pronounced them immoral, presumably because recruiting officers had invaded the camp meeting and made off with nine recruits. While defending the military, Colonel Abbott nevertheless chastised the young men of New Mexico for not enlisting in greater numbers, declaring that "New Mexico is going to have a full regiment of clean, strong, sound, wholesome young men. She is going to do it in spite of the indifference of scores of young men in our cities who are injuring their health smoking cigarettes and drinking alcohol in the daytime and lounging around pool halls and saloons at night."[7] In desperation, a recruiting office was opened in El Paso. "New Mexico is going to have a regiment to be mustered into the U.S. army if it has to draw on the state of Texas for men," declared Colonel Abbott.[8]

Governor W. C. McDonald of New Mexico appealed to sheriffs and prominent citizens for help in enlisting. But sometimes the zeal to find recruits allegedly got a bit out of hand. Lieutenant Colonel W. C. Porterfield of the New Mexico National Guard, who was on recruiting duty, was charged with enlisting two men whom he knew to have prison records, General Funston announced on September 8. Porterfield was tried in El

Paso on September 29 by a court-martial, whose president was Brigadier General E. Leroy Sweetser, commander of the Massachusetts brigade.[9] Porterfield's defense was that the enlistees had previously been pardoned by the governor and that he, Porterfield, had merely recommended that they be enlisted, subject to the action of the mustering officer.[10]

The governor made it clear that no commissions for raising volunteer units would be issued until the 1st New Mexico Infantry and Battery A were at full strength.[11] But politics remained a factor. Protests were filed with the War Department against the governor and the adjutant general for having relieved Major E. P. Bujac of Carlsbad from his command on the date the New Mexico National Guard had been called up. Bujac had been placed on the unassigned list and Major Bernard Ruppe, of Albuquerque, appointed in his place. The protesters claimed that at the call-up the New Mexico Guard passed into federal control and thus the governor and the adjutant general had no authority for their action. Bujac may well have been relieved because on April 4, 1915, he had delivered a speech to the cadets of the New Mexico Military Institute criticizing the Wilson administration.[12]

Governor McDonald spent June 24 and 25 inspecting the New Mexico guardsmen at Columbus and expressed his pleasure at their progress.[13] By July 6, only some ten to twelve recruits were still needed. Ten companies of the 1st New Mexico had been mustered into federal service. Some employers guaranteed the jobs of any employee who joined the guard and even promised to look after their families. By July 17, New Mexico finally had a full regiment of twelve companies. Adjutant General Herring proudly announced that the task was completed and that the state had made good.[14]

Because the national government had so far refused to defray the expense of mobilization, the First National Bank of Santa Fe offered its resources and credit to tide the state over until Congress acted on the matter.[15] On the grounds that the men were recruited on orders from the War Department, Governor McDonald requested federal funds to pay the rejected New Mexico recruits whose expense claims had been rejected. They had enlisted after the mobilization was completed and afterward failed to pass the physical examination. The governor sent a strong plea to the War Department, emphasizing that the state lacked funds to pay the men.[16]

Tension along the New Mexico border increased in the "bootheel" area near Hachita, a village of some seven hundred inhabitants located at the junction of two copper mine railroads: from Morenci, Arizona, the Arizona and New Mexico joined the El Paso and Southwestern, which ran along the border from Douglas, Arizona, to El Paso.[17] On June 26, Mexicans crossed the boundary and murdered a young married couple, William Parker and his wife, at their ranch four miles from the border and eighteen miles from Hachita. A posse was formed, rode into Mexico, and captured an aged Hispanic couple as the suspected murderers. The posse reportedly executed the male, and outraged Anglo cowboys wreaked vengeance on Hispanics in the Hachita area.[18]

So, there was considerable satisfaction when four more of the Columbus raiders were hanged in the county jail in Deming on June 30. As a precaution, Adjutant General Herring brought Company D, 1st New Mexico Infantry, from Columbus to assist in case of emergency. None occurred.[19] But people in Deming remained nervous; a member of the home guard shot and killed an ice cream vendor near the county jail thinking he was reaching for a gun.[20]

On the night of June 30, an American patrol riding along the invisible international boundary across from the village of Palomas, three miles south of Columbus, challenged a group of Mexicans and was fired on. The Americans returned fire but to unknown effect. Colonel H. C. Sickles, commander of the army border patrol, issued strict orders to redouble vigilance to prevent groups of Mexicans from approaching the international boundary too closely.[21]

On July 3, New Mexico troops were rushed to guard Elephant Butte dam on the Rio Grande one hundred miles north of El Paso. The dam held an enormous body of water that provided irrigation for agriculture all the way to El Paso.[22]

Pershing assigned Lieutenant Colonel Charles Stewart Farnsworth, 16th U.S. Infantry stationed at Namiquipa, Chihuahua, to assume command of Camp Furlong at Columbus.[23] Farnsworth arrived there on June 19. The 1st Aero Squadron, the 2nd Battalion of the 17th U.S. Infantry, and the 1st New Mexico Infantry constituted the major units on the post, which also contained ordnance, engineer, and quartermaster depots, a signal corps detachment, a bakery company, and the bands of the 11th and 13th Cavalry and the 17th and 24th Infantry. As already mentioned, the 2nd Massachusetts arrived to reinforce the garrison.

Farnsworth was appalled by the condition of the 1st New Mexico, which as of June 19 consisted of only nine officers and 196 enlisted men mustered into federal service. Not until July 14, as a result of the frantic recruiting drive, was the 1st New Mexico finally mustered in as a unit. Farnsworth reported that "the regiment was poorly equipped and had little training, and was of little value as a military unit for a considerable period." Furthermore, he referred to the large number of rejections for physical disability (4 officers and 427 enlisted men) when the regiment was mustered in. "The regiment, as it was accepted into the Service, was practically a regiment of recruits. This probably explains the large number of trials by court-martial and the many desertions."[24] At no time did the 1st New Mexico exceed 752 men.

The colonels commanding the two National Guard regiments outranked Colonel Farnsworth, who theoretically commanded them. Therefore Farnsworth issued orders as the personal representative of General Pershing, "special efforts being made, before issuing orders, to learn the exact intention of the Commanding General in all cases." Fortunately this arrangement caused no friction. On July 15, on orders from General Funston, the 1st New Mexico was transferred to the New Mexico Border Patrol District, ceasing to be a part of the Punitive Expedition, and two companies were stationed at Hachita. However, on October 3, Funston returned the regiment to the Punitive Expedition and Farnsworth resumed command.[25]

The 1st New Mexico was used for extensive outpost and guard duty. In addition, for a time the 1st New Mexico operated a small Casual Camp for enlisted personnel traveling to and from the Punitive Expedition.[26] The regiment's performance was mediocre, and Farnsworth reorganized the camp, assigning its operation to the black 24th U.S. Infantry on October 10.[27] A major problem with the camp was a lack of authority in keeping track of the casuals passing through and their property. Farnsworth solved the problem by setting up a card system for every man at Camp Furlong, no matter how short his stay. He also brought order to the considerable problem of storing the excess equipment that units brought to Camp Furlong. Another headache for Farnsworth was the base remount depot, which had various commanders during the course of the Punitive Expedition. Nor was that all. In letters to his wife Farnsworth described the shack he was renting for five dollars a month, a shack lacking a porch, closet, running water, and toilet. One can imagine the living quarters of lower-ranking officers. Still, conditions were not unbearable, for Farnsworth described recreations such as hunting and tennis, and evidently the meals were quite acceptable.[28]

While the 1st New Mexico was attached to the Punitive Expedition, prior to the regiment's temporary transfer that lasted until October 3, detachments were helping to guard Pershing's line of communications in Chihuahua.[29] A press dispatch from Columbus on June 29 stated that: "For the first time, National Guardsmen crossed into Mexico on military service last night. Three motor trucks were loaded with New Mexico Guardsmen and dispatched down General Pershing's line of communication to help guard lines being cut. This action was taken following receipt of a report that the Carrancistas have been concentrating large forces of cavalry at or near Guzman on the Mexico Northwestern railroad."[30] Furthermore, according to the Silver City *Independent*'s correspondent at Columbus, a one-hundred-man detachment of New Mexicans left one afternoon in July for Palomas, Mexico, leading cavalry remounts being sent to Pershing's main base at Colonia Dublán, Chihuahua. Orders were to go only as far as Palomas and go into camp there for the night. Some hours after they had departed with the horses, word was received, probably by wireless, that a large force of Carranza troops, some 2,500 according to the report, was approaching Palomas. Immediately there was activity around headquarters. Attempts were made to warn the detachment but the buzzer line had been cut. Then the commander rushed to the camp of Company B, roused the men out of bed, loaded them into trucks and raced to reinforce the detachment. Investigation later developed that the detail with the cavalry mounts reached Palomas about sundown and went into camp, not bothering to post sentries. During the night, the carrancistas arrived, going into camp on the opposite side of a small creek. Doubtless they knew that the American soldiers were there but not knowing their strength, the Mexicans posted sentries and waited for daylight. However, shortly after midnight the American reinforcements arrived. The men with the cavalry mounts were apprised of their potential danger and all returned to Columbus with the horses, arriving shortly after six o'clock the next morning. The correspondent ended by stating that "it is not denied that a serious clash was narrowly averted."[31] The authors have been unable to verify this account.

As a result of the judge advocate general's ruling that guardsmen could not be used outside the limits of the United States unless they had first been drafted, it was announced that the 1st New Mexico would be employed only to patrol the border and guard New Mexico towns.[32] Interestingly, though, the press subsequently reported that: "For a tour of duty to command motor truck trains from Columbus to Colonia Dublan and El Valle nine lieutenants of the Pennsylvania division [at El Paso] have gone to Columbus. They will be in command of the trains and will have an opportunity to serve on foreign soil even if not in a hostile capacity."[33] The truck trains had civilian drivers, and they were a turbulent lot. On June 20, a number of them had been arrested for insubordination when, after arriving from the field in Chihuahua, they refused to return immediately with another shipment of supplies. They were soon released when they promised to obey orders.[34]

The National Guard presence in Columbus doubled with the arrival of the 2nd Massachusetts Infantry, Colonel W. C. Hayes commanding, on July 2. It was known as the "farmer regiment" because it was largely recruited from rural districts of Massachusetts. Unlike their colleagues from New Mexico, the Massachusetts unit was described as being splendidly equipped due to a generous state government, having good morale, and ready to begin target practice immediately.[35] When the regiment arrived in Columbus it numbered 52 officers and 921 enlisted men; the arrival of new recruits on July 16 increased the enlisted men to 1,458, and they roughly maintained this number for the remainder of their stay in their camp 2 1/2 miles northwest of Columbus.

The 1st New Mexico and the 2nd Massachusetts were unique in that they were the only National Guard regiments assigned to the Punitive Expedition and directly under the command of General Pershing.[36] The 2nd Massachusetts was a good outfit. Farnsworth reported that it was "well equipped and was composed of a very good class of men. The officers were intelligent and zealous and the regiment, of its own initiative, without urging by any officer of the regular Army, and led by its watchful and able colonel, rapidly improved in efficiency."[37] Furthermore, "this regiment has 20 side-carriage motorcycles, on which are to be carried men, [machine] guns, and supplies."[38]

The 2nd Massachusetts had passed through El Paso on its way to Columbus. "It was said that as the troop trains passed along the Rio Grande the commanding officer ordered his men not to expose themselves at the car windows lest they be spotted and fired on by Mexicans across the river. The soldiers all sat down on the floors and rode in that position for thirty-five miles until railroad personnel passed through the cars assuring the men there was no danger." And when the guardsmen arrived in Columbus, some of the regulars had fun with them by solemnly warning the newcomers never to let a Mexican get behind them. "The maneuvers of the Guardsmen to keep the Mexicans at Columbus in front of them is said to be about the most amusing sight to be seen at that place."[39] The Massachusetts guardsmen took the tricks played on them good naturedly. The *Santa Fe New Mexican* reported on July 27 that the Massachusetts men were fine specimens but that their credulity was amazing, commenting that the previous week many of them believed Villa had been captured and that they were to be sent into Mexico the next day to escort him to the border. Some were so sure of this that they stayed awake all night in order to make an early start.[40] And the press gleefully reported a "War Tragedy at Columbus"—a Massachusetts sentry on night duty spotted what he thought was a Mexican spy, who refused to halt after twice being challenged. The sentry fired, killing a calf, "which was entirely ignorant of military practices."[41]

Secretary of War Baker ordered that married guardsmen and others who had one or more relatives dependent on them for support be discharged upon application to their commanders. New Mexico adjutant general Herring immediately received a number of requests for discharge but lamented that this would cripple the state's National Guard, reducing it below peacetime strength. By contrast, Colonel W. C. Hayes, commanding the 2nd Massachusetts at Columbus, received no such requests.[42]

An El Paso newspaper reported on July 4 that "a field inspection of the New Mexico and Massachusetts National Guard regiments will be held 'somewhere along the border' this week by Major [*sic*] C. S. Farnsworth of the 16th U.S. Infantry. Owing to the rigid censorship the whereabouts of these troops is not allowed to be stated."[43] The army did maintain censorship at Columbus, but since both the 1st New Mexico and the 2nd Massachusetts were stationed there, newspaper readers would have little trouble in figuring out where the field inspection would be held.

Both regiments were subjected to a very strenuous daily routine, from breakfast to eleven thirty in the morning—drilling, bayonet exercise, manual of arms, marching, and target practice. In the afternoon, they had individual instruction, which was not quite as strenuous as the morning duties. In addition, the guardsmen furnished all the police for the town of Columbus as well as the camp. Luna County had a number of special deputies on duty in Columbus, but they had never gotten along well with the soldiers, since the latter resented taking orders from civilians. To guard against possible serious clashes, the military had assumed police duties.

Massachusetts troops patrolled the airfield, two miles east of Columbus's post headquarters. Airplanes for the new aero squadron arrived: eight

Curtis biplanes with 120 hp engines. Giant humidors (used for seasoning and preserving tobacco) were erected to keep wooden airplane propellers in proper condition, for New Mexico's dry climate played havoc with propellers. It was one of the pilots, incidentally, who thought of the humidors. The squadron was subsequently increased to twelve airplanes, equipped with automatic cameras. Captain Benjamin D. Foulois commanded the 1st Aero Squadron of twenty-four aviators. In August, work began to enlarge the airfield to three times its original size.[44]

On the night of July 31, Massachusetts soldiers had some excitement as Mexicans crossed the border and opened fire on the Massachusetts outposts. One bullet passed through the hat of Captain F. H. Locke, commanding the Americans, while four more rounds whipped over the guardsmen's heads. They returned fire, but the shooters escaped in the darkness. Their footprints were traced from the border north a few hundred feet, from where they had begun firing. And in another incident four rounds were fired by parties unknown. Later that morning sentries apprehended two Americans with hunting rifles. After an examination they were released. Responsibility for the firing was not determined.[45] And on August 18, Private P. R. Penniman, Company L, 2nd Massachusetts, was shot while on outpost duty, the bullet severing an artery in the private's leg and tearing away the muscles. Initially a Mexican sniper was blamed, but investigation determined that the weapon involved was a pistol, fired accidentally.[46]

U.S. senator Albert B. Fall of New Mexico visited that state's troops at Columbus, pronouncing himself quite satisfied with the condition of the 1st New Mexico and commenting that the men were anxious for active service.[47] Instead, the New Mexico troops were used to guard towns in the interior of the state and to patrol the border under the control of Colonel Sickles of the regular army border patrol.[48] Company I of the 1st New Mexico was detailed to guard the Luna County border. "The boys find it rather exciting at times during night patrol." The company's headquarters were at the international boundary gate between New Mexico and Mexico.[49]

The 1st battalion was stationed at the hamlet of Hachita, on the railroad forty miles west of Columbus. The battalion was on border patrol duty, the first repositioning of troops since the recent announcement that the New Mexico guard would relieve regulars at points along the New Mexico border. Companies A and B garrisoned Hachita, while Company C was assigned to border patrol duty at Animas. The guardsmen relieved a unit of regular cavalry at Hachita.[50] This was not a desirable duty station; three deserters from Troops K, L, and M of the 12th U.S. Cavalry, the units being relieved, said "the heat there was almost unbearable." The deserters had made it all the way north to Las Vegas, New Mexico, before being apprehended.[51]

Things got out of hand at Hachita. On August 11, General Funston forwarded to the governor of New Mexico a telegram from Lieutenant Colonel J. C. Waterman, commanding officer at Hachita:

> This evening between six thirty and eight o'clock two automobiles loaded with drunken civilians were running back and forth on road through camp yelling and otherwise creating a very serious disorder. A number of shots were fired by unknown parties. I went into the town to consult civil officers regarding the disorder. On speaking with deputy sheriff Jess Cook regarding the matter he and deputy sheriff J. C. Parks assaulted me, Parks striking me with his pistol and then cocked it and pointed it at me, both cursing and abusing me. The same lawless element has been abusing and otherwise maltreating peaceful Mexicans. Request that the matter be taken up with United States District Attorney of this district with a view of prosecuting them and with the governor of state with view of having commissions as deputy sheriffs cancelled. Situation quiet report by mail.

Funston requested that the governor investigate the matter, and if the facts were found to be as stated, that the governor take steps to bring to justice deputy sheriffs J. C. Parks and Jess Cook. The general also requested that he be informed as to the action taken in this case.[52]

Governor McDonald sent to Hachita a representative who reported on August 21 that he, Captain Louis Van Schaick (the intelligence officer at Columbus),[53] Assistant District Attorney J. S. Vaught, and Sheriff Herb McGrath met in Hachita and investigated both the Waterman affair and the jailing of three soldiers by the civil authorities. McDonald's man concluded that Colonel Waterman had become unduly excited, lost his head, and was abusive to Deputy Cook, who was attempting to do his duty. However, this in no way excused the unprovoked attack on the colonel by Deputies Cook and Parks. He recommended that Parks's commission be revoked and that Cook receive less severe disciplinary measures. Sheriff McGrath agreed to remove Parks from office. Regarding the three jailed Hispanic soldiers, there was no doubt that they had been drunk and disorderly and had disturbed the peace, "but on the other hand there was hardly a necessity for the Deputy Sheriff to club them as he did." According to the testimony of several men the arresting deputy, J. E. Schrimpser, made a habit of pistol-whipping unarmed men. The offending soldiers were tried before the justice of the peace and pleaded guilty. The recommendation in this case was that the deputy be admonished against pistol-whipping and warned that if this continued he would be removed from office. The sheriff agreed that in the future any disorderly soldiers would be delivered to their commanding officer, who would administer the necessary punishment.[54]

Speaking of punishment, Private Lewis G. Gardiner, 1st New Mexico Infantry, adamantly refused to take federal oath. His court-martial was scheduled for August 17. On July 29 he made public why he did not take the oath as his companions did. He was a cook by trade and said he was inveigled into enlisting in National Guard on the promise that he would receive forty-five dollars a month. At his first payday he realized he was making only fifty cents a day. He protested, to no avail. He refused to take the oath and was placed in the stockade. Gardiner further stated that he was the father of three children whom he was supporting. He declared that he would fight the case to the finish. A general court-martial found him guilty. The prosecution argued that a "not guilty" verdict would have a detrimental effect on future National Guard enlistments.[55] The verdict awaited the War Department's approval. Gardiner escaped from custody on September 2 while being conveyed from the stockade to mess.[56] President Wilson approved the court's verdict.[57]

Hugh Clark, a recruit in Company D 2nd Massachusetts, was placed in the stockade on August 3 for writing and sending to a hometown newspaper an article in which he accused his company commander of failing to ensure that the company mess was properly operated, of neglecting the men, and of appropriating company funds.[58] The article was printed in the Holyoke newspaper on July 29, whereupon the War Department sent the clipping to Columbus and ordered a strict investigation of the charges. After questioning Clark the officers of his regiment placed him under arrest on the charge of making false and misleading statements. They said he was given an opportunity to prove his allegations but failed to substantiate them. A general court-martial convened on August 4. A search of Clark's tent revealed a list of twenty-eight comrades who had signed a statement vouching for the truth of Clark's allegations. The signers belonged to Company D and claimed they had signed after learning that Clark had gotten himself into trouble, but they did so at Clark's solicitation. They apologized.[59] They were exonerated, but Clark still faced a general court-martial. On September 26, the court sentenced him to six months' hard labor in the disciplinary barracks at Fort Leavenworth plus a dishonorable discharge. The War Department approved the sentence.[60]

General Pershing ordered that effective immediately, guardsmen at Columbus were forbidden to act as newspaper correspondents. A number of New Mexico and Massachusetts guardsmen who were journalists in civilian life had been acting as correspondents for hometown newspapers and other publications.[61] The culmination of the Clark affair came on October 12: having been sentenced to prison in Leavenworth by court-martial at Columbus because of articles in the Holyoke newspaper, he was released. Although his prison sentence was remitted, Clark received a dishonorable discharge.[62]

Columbus being an isolated and uninspiring locale, the soldiers had limited choices for recreation. The two regiments organized a baseball league composed of ten clubs from each regiment. A schedule of fifty games was planned. The hometowns of the various companies were expected to furnish the baseball equipment. The men could also attend the military boxing matches, featuring fighters calling themselves names such as the "Insurrecto Kid," the "Iron Man of the United States Army," and the "Pride of the Punitive Expedition."[63] They could also attend performances at the Airdrome Theater, which had wooden seats and a wooden runway extending through the center of the house. Among its offerings were performances by guardsmen, such as the Company I, 2nd Massachusetts, quartet, "considered among the best on the border." The men also organized amateur theatricals, with a regimental band furnishing music for the performances.[64]

For those interested in racier entertainment there were the "clubs" that were a transparent front for liquor and gambling. Despite the efforts of the authorities, these establishments kept springing up like mushrooms. For example, the New Mexico Athletic Association of Columbus filed articles of incorporation. "The papers announce that dispensing liquor to its members is one of the objects." Authorized capital was $3,000, and the three incorporators were listed; it was just another Columbus "club."[65] Periodically, both the Luna County sheriff and the Military Police raided these shady establishments. However, gambling, alcohol, prostitution, and drugs remained a continual problem for the authorities.[66]

A recreation hall for the troops was lacking, and they appealed to the citizens of New Mexico to provide one by raising $1,000 through public subscription.[67] There was of course the consolation of religion, and many soldiers availed themselves of it. The chaplain of the 2nd Massachusetts was an Episcopal priest, while a Roman Catholic priest ministered to the men of that faith. As for the 1st New Mexico, Reverend T. I. Vincent, the Episcopal rector in Silver City, resigned his position in order to remain as the chaplain of that regiment, with the rank of captain.[68]

Columbus was a lonely place for soldiers, but at least the bachelor officers devised a novel solution. Through several El Paso society girls, acquaintances of these officers, a list of names of a dozen El Paso girls was delivered to the commanding officer at Columbus. A dance was organized, and from this list of names each officer gambled on a name chosen as his partner. One girl called it one of the biggest blind dates ever. Since good roads and automobiles were scarce, the officers decided for the first dance to pool their resources and hire a Pullman car to bring the El Paso girls and their chaperones. It took a month's salary for each officer to pay for the dance and the Pullman. One of the girls recalled that on arriving they enjoyed a lovely dinner, accompanied by the fun of becoming acquainted with their dates and later preparing for the dance. "It was a crowded and busy time with fifteen or more girls in the two Pullman dressing rooms endeavoring to comb their long hair (not short bobs at that time); but everything was going fine until suddenly all the lights in the car went out. For the next hour it was darkness and confusion, but no one seemed to care that we arrived at the dance with unkempt hair and make-up all awry." The party was a smashing success, although thereafter the officers did not hire the expensive Pullman for the weekends. "We were their guests often again and made numerous trips to Columbus, staying at the homes of the wives at the camp or at the Clark Hotel in Columbus. We were always chaperoned by prominent El Paso matrons."[69]

Since 1916 was a presidential election year, with Republican Charles Evans Hughes running against President Wilson, politics became an issue involving the guard. The New Mexico attorney general ruled that guardsmen could vote on November 7 if they were still in Columbus; they would be considered residents of Luna County, nearly doubling that county's voting strength.[70] Not coincidentally, a few days later Robert Bacon, former secretary of state and ambassador to France, arrived in Columbus. Although he maintained that his visit was purely personal in nature, Bacon was evidently an emissary of candidate Hughes. Bacon stated that he was investigating how the guard had been handled and what populations along the border thought of President Wilson. The press commented that "the significance is the fact that practically every National Guard organization ordered to the border has been from a Republican state."[71] Incidentally, on November 1, the New Mexico attorney general reversed himself and ruled that the guardsmen at Columbus could not vote unless they returned to their homes to cast their ballots. But on November 4, he reversed himself yet again and ruled that they could vote in Columbus after all.[72]

The other personages who visited Columbus were all generals. On August 11, Brigadier General Granger Adams, commander of the National Guard brigade at Deming, arrived to conduct an inspection and to confer with Lieutenant Colonel Farnsworth regarding ordnance supplies.[73] On September 1, General Pershing came "to review the Regulars stationed at this point and to inspect the new camp site of the Massachusetts National Guard." He remained for several days. Pershing had driven from his field headquarters in Chihuahua in less than fifteen hours.[74] Then on January 17, 1917, General Frederick Funston, returning from his visit to the Punitive Expedition headquarters, reviewed the troops in Columbus and continued on to his headquarters in San Antonio.[75]

The 1st New Mexico Infantry was finally becoming a better regiment. The press reported that "military men at Columbus expressed enthusiasm over the spirit and loyalty of Hispanic Guardsmen from New Mexico." One-third of the 1st New Mexico were Hispanic, some of them of Mexican birth. Three companies (A, E, and I) were entirely Hispanic, from various walks of life, including a few college graduates. "James Baca, of Company E, Santa Fe, himself a Spanish-American, says: 'There are 66 Spanish-Americans in my company. Give me 66 plugs of chewing tobacco and 66 canteens of water, leave out the 'grub,' and together we'll march 100 miles without a whimper.' Seventy percent of the regiment speak Spanish. Hispanics are as proud of their American citizenship as are the men of the 2nd Massachusetts Infantry encamped at their side. Col. Abbott praised them as among the first to fall into the ranks and shoulder rifles."[76] As of October 7, they had to shoulder their rifles alone because the 2nd Massachusetts departed for home.

Phil McLaughlin, the Associated Press correspondent in Columbus, declared in December that the New Mexicans were among the best guardsmen on the border and were fast approaching the efficiency standards of the regular army.

> Recently the New Mexico regiment has been attached to the Punitive Expedition, being the only [sic] National Guard regiment directly under command of Major General Pershing and it is now doing a considerable share of the outpost duty and guard duty about the base of communications. Another honor which has fallen to the lot of the New Mexicans is the selection of several of their officers to command truck trains running between Columbus and the headquarters of the Punitive Expedition in Mexico, Captain Arthur Stock and Lieutenant Frank Newkirk being recently assigned to this responsible work.[77]

Responding to stories that the guardsmen were inadequately fed, Colonel Abbot submitted menus to prove that these stories were not only not based on fact, but that the fare was better than what many of the men ate at home.[78] Reinforcing this view, Captain J. H. Toulouse, Company G, 1st New Mexico, on October 28 painted a rosy picture when he informed the Red Cross on the condition of the New Mexico guardsmen. There had been little sickness among the troops, two of whom had been accidentally shot, one case being serious. "The duties of the men while not hard, are monotonous. At present, duties are divided between outpost guard, interior guard, and camp guard. On outpost the men go on duty each night for a week. On interior guard they go on duty every other day, and on camp guard every eight days, so the time for duty will average 24 hours out of each 48." The men were properly clothed and housed. They had cots, plenty of blankets, and would soon be furnished with tent stoves. Sweaters and overcoats had been issued. Rations were more than adequate; "nothing more can be desired in the way of food." The troops ate in dining halls. Toulouse had requested permission to convert Company G's mess hall into a reading room, but good reading material, especially books, was needed. He also wanted a gramophone or Victrola with a selection of records. Through the regimental Post Exchange, the companies had received enough funds to provide any needed "extras." Although conditions were satisfactory, "there is some dissatisfaction among the men because they are still on duty, while other Guard organizations are being sent home."[79]

However, a less rosy picture of the 1st New Mexico's condition appeared in the *Santa Fe New Mexican* two weeks later, stating that the New Mexico guardsmen, now the only guard regiment left at Columbus, got the worst of it at the camp, lacking stoves and suffering other hardships. The New Mexicans were doing all the guard duty around the entire camp working in shifts of twenty-four hours out of every forty-eight, and the time they were supposed to be at liberty was largely taken up with policing their camp, cleaning their clothes and equipment, and getting ready for another twenty-four-hour tour on guard. They had to march the 2 1/2 miles back and forth between their camp and Columbus when they went on guard, "and in a word they are wearing the martyr's crown all the time." Finally, they were forgotten by the folks back home.[80]

The last was not entirely true. The Silver City chapter of the American Red Cross planned to remember the New Mexico guardsmen at Columbus at Thanksgiving and Christmas, besides sending them magazines, games, and writing paper and pencils. The Red Cross staged a big cabaret ball on November 23, with the proceeds going to the chapter's treasury. The band of the 11th U.S. Cavalry, currently stationed at Fort Bayard, provided the music. The Silver City Red Cross chapter was one of the largest and most active in the state.[81] Major Ludwig William Ilfeld of the New Mexico guard started a movement to have New Mexicans send the boys at Columbus at least one thousand Christmas packages. "The response has been general and immediate and it is expected a 'Santa Claus Car' may be needed to carry the remembrances."[82] And Adjutant General Herring announced that he would pay the express charges on all Christmas packages sent to the regiment from Albuquerque, Las Vegas, Silver City, and Roswell.[83]

The 1st New Mexico might be improving as a unit, but the New Mexico National Guard continued to have problems with Washington, D.C. The Militia Bureau demanded that New Mexico reimburse the government for $3,841.12 worth of quartermaster and signal corps property found to be missing as a result of a report of survey. The Militia Bureau stressed that: "You are informed that unless prompt and satisfactory adjustment of this matter is made, the War Department will be obliged to debar the State from further participation in any or all appropriations for the National Guard until such adjustment is made." Adjutant General Herring replied that first of all, the state had no funds for that expenditure, and second, the records of the adjutant general's office had been in disarray when Herring assumed that office, and the property had evidently been lost prior to 1911, and, lastly, the War Department's appropriation for fiscal year 1917 contained a provision allowing the secretary of war to relieve a state from further accountability for property lost or destroyed prior to 1911.[84]

With the exception of Pancho Villa's raid, the most exciting thing that ever happened in Columbus was the return of General Pershing's Punitive Expedition, whose rearguard crossed back into the United States on February 5, 1917.[85] A committee of the El Paso chamber of commerce arrived on February 1 to invite the general and his staff to a banquet in El Paso. Not to be outdone, the New Mexico legislature passed a joint resolution inviting guard officers to join Pershing at a banquet in his honor in Santa Fe on February 22, at which the general would formally receive the thanks of New Mexico. But because of General Frederick Funston's death, Pershing was unable to travel to Santa Fe.[86] Not only were the citizens of Columbus wild with excitement at the arrival of the Punitive Expedition, but the army post overflowed, at least temporarily, with Pershing's troops. Most of the units continued on to Fort Bliss in El Paso, but the black 24th U.S. Infantry at war strength remained in Columbus as part of the garrison, replacing the 2nd Massachusetts Infantry.

Moreover, 2,700 refugees—Mexicans, American Mormons, and Chinese—accompanied the Punitive Expedition as it entered Columbus. The army quickly established a refugee camp, examined these wretched people, and undertook to find them work.[87] Most of the refugees were Mexicans, who had either collaborated with the Punitive Expedition or were simply trying to keep from starving. Many of them found work in the Chino Copper Company's mines near Silver City, some sixty miles north of Columbus.[88] By February 19, the only refugees left were the 527 Chinese who came with their household goods and farm implements, and they constituted a particular problem. They could not be returned to Chihuahua because Pancho Villa, a vicious racist, delighted in massacring Chinese. But they could not stay in the United States because of the Exclusion Act, and accordingly they remained under guard. A few Chinese returned to China at that government's expense, a few others settled in Baja California, but 427 were still on the War Department's hands. A temporary solution was to have them work for the quartermaster at Fort Sam Houston, and later at other military installations in the Southwest. Finally, in 1922, Congress enacted legislation enabling them to reside permanently in the United States. A number of the Chinese settled in San Antonio.[89]

Despite the garrison's reinforcement by the 24th U.S. Infantry, Columbus residents were quite nervous over the possibility of another raid. A band of some thirty villistas was spotted encamped at Palomas. "Unconfirmed rumors that a Villa band would attack Columbus last night caused many women and children to be sent to Deming and other nearby towns for the night. The army in Columbus took precautions while discounting the rumors."[90] The Columbus garrison, composed of the 1st New Mexico Infantry, the 24th U.S. Infantry, and a squadron of the 12th U.S. Cavalry, went on alert. But on February 20, the villistas evacuated Palomas, and the next day a force of 150 Carranza troops occupied the town.[91] Then a 400-man force of Carranza cavalry was sighted below Hachita.[92] These troops caused considerable excitement when they "rode rapidly from the south in apparent battle array up to the international line as if to make an attack on Columbus. The American troops were quickly rushed to the front to give them battle when they discovered the Mexicans were Carrancistas. The American officer in command sharply reprimanded the Mexican officers and told them never to repeat such a thing again, as it was impossible for our men to distinguish them from the Villistas in the distance." [93]

Refugees, the Punitive Expedition, and rumors were soon overshadowed by more sensational news. On February 13, Mexican raiders crossed the international boundary at the Corner Ranch in the New Mexico bootheel, carrying back into Chihuahua livestock, supplies, and three captured Mormon cowboys. Three miles across the boundary, the Mexicans murdered the unfortunate trio. Three Mexicans were subsequently jailed at Deming accused of the Corner Ranch massacre.[94] These events caused General Funston to order the dispatch of 1st New Mexico units on February 17 to reinforce the Hachita district, where Colonel Waterman was still in command. Duty at Hachita could prove painful: "Three Regulars stationed at Hachita pleaded guilty to unlawfully killing a cow. A district judge sentenced each to serve 18–24 months in state penitentiary. One had to serve his sentence; sentences of the other two were remitted on condition they work 90 days on county roads."[95]

Two troops of the 12th U.S. Cavalry had been patrolling the bootheel, and two more were now rushed to the scene. Patrols were now conducted both day and night instead of just in daytime.[96] Companies A and B of the 1st New Mexico were already at Hachita; Company C went by truck convoy to Campbell's Wells; Company D to the Corner Ranch; Company G to Gibson's ranch; Company L to Las Ciénegas; Company I was at the border gate near Columbus with a detachment at Mimbres, 9 miles east; Companies E, F, and H remained at Columbus awaiting orders along with regimental headquarters, band, and medical detachment.[97]

On March 15, the plant of the *Columbus Courier* was completely destroyed by fire, which started in an adjoining lunch room and also destroyed a real estate office nearby. Cartridges exploding in the fire, which occurred before daylight, made the jittery residents of Columbus think at first that another raid was under way.[98]

Columbus recorded few casualties among the guardsmen. On October 9, Second Lieutenant Antonio J. Luna of the 1st New Mexico, at the time attached to the 20th U.S. Infantry, died in the Fort Bliss hospital.[99] And on December 4, a private in Company K, 1st New Mexico, died after he was accidentally thrown from the seat of a truck and run over.[100] Unlike some other National Guard concentration points, Columbus had virtually no cases of disease. In January 1917, a case of smallpox was discovered in the stockade, and Colonel Farnsworth immediately placed the stockade under quarantine and had the entire garrison vaccinated. Also, two cases of measles were reported in the 1st New Mexico's camp. The patients were immediately isolated.[101]

By January 1917, the New Mexicans were heartily sick of fatigue duties and seemingly endless patrols along the border. They desperately wanted to go home. For example, in autumn the men of Battery A had wanted to go home and attend to their crops. "New Mexico boys believe they should be allowed to see to the welfare of their families, since the emergency is past."[102] And hometown newspapers wanted them home. The *Albuquerque Morning Journal* published an editorial entitled "Recall the Guardsmen."[103] In the ensuing weeks the men's hopes rose when, on February 17, the demobilization was ordered of the entire National Guard, leaving the regulars to guard the border.[104] Finally, the New Mexicans received a War Department order on March 26 that they were to be mustered out. The regiment joyfully broke camp and loaded their equipment on railroad cars when, at eleven thirty on the morning of March 27, a telegram ordered them to remain on active duty after all. Although bitterly disappointed, the New Mexicans reestablished their camp and gamely soldiered on. Finally, word came that demobilization would occur on April 10.[105] To the guardsmen's intense joy, however, "The 1st New Mexico Infantry was mustered out of federal service at Columbus on April 5, 1917, after ten months and 26 days of continuous service on the border. The total strength of the New Mexico National Guard on that date was 52 officers and 732 enlisted men."[106] Governor Lindsey appealed to the citizenry to show their patriotism by manifesting their appreciation of the guard's service.[107]

Not all New Mexicans appreciated the National Guard. State senator Baird of Otero County introduced a bill in the legislature to abolish the New Mexico Guard, arguing that the guard was a useless expense and a failure. Advocates of the senate bill claimed that this would save the state $38,000, that it was impossible to get recruits for the guard, that many present guardsmen would leave the state when they were mustered out, that the New Mexico Guard could not qualify under the National Defense Act, and, finally, that a volunteer regiment could always be raised.[108] The guard's status remained in doubt. It was in the service of the state of New Mexico but had no federal standing, in the view of Adjutant General Herring.[109]

This soon became a moot point. "When the New Mexico Guard was again called into federal service on April 21, 1917, the total strength of its units—1st New Mexico Infantry, Battery A New Mexico Field Artillery, and a medical detachment, was 49 officers and 39 enlisted men. During the intervening sixteen days all officers and men who failed to comply with the provisions of the National Defense Act of June 3, 1916, had been given a discharge from state service."[110]

Chapter 17

Douglas

Located on a bleak expanse of Arizona desert, Douglas was a strategic point, for it was the main headquarters for both the Phelps Dodge Company and the Copper Queen Consolidated Copper Company, two of the greatest industrial organizations in the Southwest.[1] The invisible international boundary separated Douglas from its Mexican counterpart, Agua Prieta, Sonora. The two towns were separated by a narrow strip of vacant land marked by a wire fence.

The citizens of Douglas were understandably apprehensive about their own security, having witnessed in October 1915 Constitutionalist troops under General Plutarco Elías Calles successfully resist a ferocious assault against Agua Prieta by the forces of Pancho Villa. Thus when the June 1916, war crisis erupted, they were reassured because Douglas was well protected by some 4,500 regulars at Camp Harry J. Jones a mile east of town. The camp was named in honor of a private killed by a Mexican sniper while on guard duty. The regulars consisted of headquarters and a squadron (plus machine gun troop) of the 1st U.S. Cavalry; headquarters and Batteries A, E, and F, 6th U.S. Field Artillery; the 11th U.S. Infantry (less Companies C and F); the 18th U.S. Infantry; the 22nd U.S. Infantry; Companies G and H and the 3rd Battalion, 14th U.S. Infantry.[2] Facing them under the command of General Calles, military governor of Sonora, was a Mexican force composed mainly of some eight thousand untrained volunteers.[3] The civilian population of Agua Prieta evidently had little confidence in Calles's ability to protect them in case of war; they evacuated the town. Not until the war crisis had passed did they return to their homes.

Arizonans also had little confidence in their own governor. Many were disgusted with Governor Hunt, not only because of his apparent contempt for the National Guard but more recently because of his warm friendship with the Mexican Socialist and agitator Lázaro Gutiérrez de Lara, who had strongly supported Hunt during a miners' strike in Clifton in 1915. The state also had financial problems: "With a balance of but $17.11, the general fund of the state of Arizona is the lowest in history. The depletion of the general fund, it is said, is due largely to the extra expense caused by the mobilization of the National Guard at the time of the Clifton strike and also to the amount of money loaned by the state to the various counties for the construction of bridges. The counties are required to pay the loans back in installments."[4] Gutiérrez de Lara was in Phoenix after a tour of mining towns in Arizona, conferring with Hunt before departing for Los Angeles, and he openly expressed his satisfaction at the killing of the black American troopers at Carrizal. The press quoted him as stating that "there never have been any niggers in Mexico, and no American niggers will be tolerated there."[5]

Anti-Mexican feeling ran strongly, but compared with what had been happening in Texas and New Mexico, the Arizona border remained quiet. Although the Mexicans had practically evacuated Agua Prieta, the U.S. Army had to spend considerable time and energy investigating the spate of wild rumors: peace officers killed while checking conditions near Naco; U.S. troops fighting a Mexican detachment at Forrest Station, ten miles west of Douglas; Fort Huachuca being attacked and captured; the residents of the San Pedro valley being driven from their homes, and so forth.[6]

Brigadier General Thomas F. Davis, commanding the Arizona District, issued the following statement on June 19: "On account of the raids and the resulting pursuit of bandits occurring along the Rio Grande, uneasiness over the situation is apparent among the Mexican population of border towns in the United States. Trouble has been and is conspicuously absent along the Sonora-Arizona border and no occasion has arisen here for any change in the prevailing quiet and order. Mexicans residing or working in Douglas and vicinity need not be alarmed, they will not be molested by United States troops unless they give cause for such action."[7]

Nevertheless, the border population remained nervous. In Douglas hundreds of people rushed into the streets on the night of June 19 when the rumor spread that a Mexican Army airplane was reconnoitering over the city. It turned out that the "airplane" was a large box kite sent up in the course of an experiment by the signal corps at Camp Harry J. Jones.[8] The clash at Carrizal of course raised the level of apprehension markedly.

The 1st Arizona Infantry had arrived by train at Camp Harry J. Jones on May 12 and 13. The regiment was understrength, with 49 officers and 837 enlisted men, 29 men short of peacetime strength and 1,029 under wartime strength. On June 21 the 1st Arizona was deployed to relieve detachments of the 1st U.S. Cavalry. The 3rd battalion (Companies I, K, L, and M) of the 1st Arizona was alerted for action. In less than an hour the battalion was under arms in marching order. These troops and a battalion of the 14th U.S. Infantry were rushed by special train from Douglas to Camp Stephen A. Little outside Nogales, Arizona. Company A of the 1st Arizona was dispatched to Slaughter's Ranch eighteen miles east of Douglas and Company D to the Forrest Ranch on the El Paso and Southwestern Railroad, twelve miles east of Naco.[9] Colonel Tuthill of the 1st Arizona had detailed a sergeant and two corporals to work in plainclothes under the local federal Bureau of Investigation agent to conduct surveillance on suspected ammunition smugglers. The arrangement ended when the regiment's headquarters moved to Naco.

General Davis usually responded to appeals for troops by area ranchers by stating that he did not consider it a good policy to divide his troops at Douglas into detachments at various points.[10] Davis, on orders from the War Department, did send the 22nd U.S. Infantry from Douglas to Bisbee, 30 miles to the northwest, to forestall a rumored Mexican raid on the copper installations there. But the 22nd's principal assignment was to guard the border west of Douglas.[11]

Back at Douglas, General Davis was preparing for the arrival of several more regiments of National Guard troops. Sites were selected and about fifty acres northwest of town were leased from a mining company. Davis stated that an unlimited expanse of adjoining land could be secured if necessary to accommodate any number of guardsmen. The new camp was located across town from that of the regular units stationed in Douglas. It was close to the city water plant and the smelters, near Pirtleville, a working-class Hispanic settlement northwest of Douglas. As soon as the leases were secured, workmen began laying a water pipeline to the site.[12]

While awaiting the imminent influx of National Guard units from out of state, the citizens of Douglas were increasingly apprehensive because some five hundred Mexicans residing in Douglas and vicinity had crossed the border to volunteer to fight for Mexico in case of war. Immigration officers refused to readmit them to the United States because American civil and military authorities had given guarantees of safety to law-abiding Mexicans, and their departure despite these guarantees indicated their personal hostility toward the United States. Reports of Mexican Army units moving toward the border also kept the inhabitants of Douglas in a state of nervous tension. At Camp Harry J. Jones, surprise nighttime drills kept the troops alert.[13]

At Tucson, the citizens focused on defending themselves. They were so jittery about the Mexican situation that even the customary Fourth of July celebrations were canceled. The sheriff's office received a report that about 250 Carranza soldiers were near Sasabe, on the border sixty miles from Tucson. That city took no chances when it came to defense. Supplementing a large force of home guards was a unit of home guard cavalry, a rifle club battalion, and an auxiliary automobile corps to transport guards rapidly wherever needed. Tucson boasted of having more defense units than any other city in the border region.[14] In Phoenix, forty police reserves armed with rifles began weekly drills at the local armory.

The Phoenix chapter of the Red Cross supplied substantial amounts of cantaloupes, milk, and bread to National Guard units passing through Tucson on their way to the border.[15] And the people of Tucson did not ignore the welfare of their own guardsmen. The local newspaper, which had already announced payment or partial payment of salaries to its employees in the National Guard, organized a fund-raising effort to provide comforts and delicacies for the Tucson companies (K at Nogales and E at Douglas) as well as the medical detachment, which had been organized in Tucson and was divided equally between Nogales and Douglas. The troops were quick to express their appreciation. Captain Sidney Mashbir of Company K, who would become an intelligence officer in World War II, thanked the newspaper for his unit's share of the mess fund, explaining that most companies of regulars had a balance of $500 or more in their mess funds, whereas Company K had no such fund. Other residents of Tucson also contributed to the welfare of the local guardsmen. A judge sent the boys two crates of melons on ice, the Variety Smoke Shop contributed pipes, tobacco, and cigarettes, and the Bull Durham company donated "2000 Sweet Caporal cigarettes for the enjoyment of the Tucson soldier boys."[16]

Someone who could have used some comforts and delicacies was Private William Dockery of Company B at Douglas:

> The private, a recent recruit, it was said at militia headquarters, was placed on guard at the international line yesterday with the instructions to walk to the east until he met the sentry he was to relieve. In some manner Dockery missed the sentry, officers stated today. He kept walking until finally last night he met a patrol on guard at Slaughter's ranch, eighteen miles east of the camp. "Dockery certainly obeyed instructions," an officer remarked, "but it is a good thing he met that patrol or he probably would have walked to El Paso."[17]

Dockery's adherence to orders was commendable, in contrast to those Arizona guardsmen who still refused to report for duty. The state adjutant general, making an inspection of the troops on the border, announced that the War Department had ordered him to submit a list of those absent. All the slackers who had not reported for duty by July 1 would be tried by court-martial for desertion.[18]

On July 5 there was some excitement in Douglas. Private Edward Stone, who had deserted from the Arizona National Guard, was being held at the 1st Arizona's guardhouse, which was only a short distance from the international boundary. Stone managed to escape, and he sprinted for the town of Agua Prieta across the line. A number of guardsmen pursued him, and as he crossed the border army regulars who were on patrol joined the chase. A number of shots were fired at Stone, who was captured after he had penetrated approximately five hundred yards into Sonora. Although the shooting caused some excitement on both sides of the border for several minutes, fortunately no international incident resulted, and Stone was returned to the guardhouse.[19]

Private Stone's insubordination perhaps reflected what the press reported on July 14 as growing discontent among the Arizona guardsmen at Douglas:

> According to an arrival from Douglas yesterday, deplorable conditions are evident in the National Guard camps there because of a lack of equipment. In the Arizona guard many men mustered into the national service a month or more ago have not received uniforms, proceeding about military duties in civilian clothing. Many of them

are without suitable shoes, their footwear having been worn out in service and not replaced with new ones. An officer is quoted as saying that he had loaned $150 among his men to buy uniforms. He purchased his own uniform and was wearing the same shoes he had on when he left home.[20]

Perhaps not coincidentally, further 1st Arizona deployments immediately took place, on July 14–15: regimental headquarters and the 1st Battalion left for Naco on July 15, and Company M moved to Roosevelt on the Salt River to guard Roosevelt Dam. (Farmers in the Salt River Valley were outraged because Governor Hunt had refused to send National Guardsmen to protect this important dam immediately after the Columbus raid.)[21] The 2nd Battalion (four companies) was transferred from Douglas to Fort Huachuca, relieving regular units for service with the Punitive Expedition.[22] As of August, two companies of Arizona guardsmen were stationed at Fort Huachuca, and there was talk of stationing an additional five thousand to ten thousand guardsmen there, provided an adequate water supply could be developed.[23] Fort Huachuca, which in 1910 had been the only occupied post between El Paso and San Diego had but a small garrison with less than one hundred regulars. The commander had been understandably nervous about Mexican intentions, and on June 24 had ordered that the 150 Mexican laborers on the military reservation and its vicinity be disarmed, and that the 40 Anglos living near the fort be issued arms and ammunition.[24] The arrival of the Arizona battalion presumably reassured the Anglos.[25] Meanwhile, Companies A and D of the 1st Battalion, which had been on duty at Slaughter's and Forrest Ranches were recalled to Douglas to complete that battalion.

The first contingent of guardsmen from out of state reached Douglas on July 2: Battery B of the New Jersey Field Artillery and a New Jersey field hospital and ambulance company. These units, plus a signal corps company, had originally been designated for Fort Bliss in El Paso, but shortly after the men had detrained and had begun setting up camp the army in its wisdom had them break camp, get back on troop trains, and go to Douglas instead.[26] The New Jersey National Guard had mobilized 4,288 men: an infantry brigade (1st Infantry [Newark], 4th [Jersey City], and 5th [Paterson]), 1st Cavalry Squadron, Batteries A and B of the Field Artillery Battalion, Company A Signal Corps, Field Hospital Company No. 1, and Ambulance Company No. 1. These units assembled at Camp Fielder, at Sea

Girt. Battery C, Field Artillery, was subsequently called up and was mustered in at the field artillery camp at Tobyhanna, Pennsylvania.[27]

However, the 2nd New Jersey, from Trenton, and the 3rd New Jersey, from Camden, were not mobilized, and their officers complained bitterly to the state adjutant general.[28] These two regiments were not called up because it was necessary to strip them of their equipment in order to issue it to recruits. When the 1st New Jersey marched to the railroad station, three hundred recruits in civilian clothes but with rifles and other equipment marched at the rear of the column. More than one thousand recruits lacked uniforms, few had rifles, and they had shelter halves only because the 2nd and 3rd New Jersey had been plundered. The War Department had hardly been a model of efficiency, and New Jersey officers were bitter at Washington, D.C.'s, failure to provide the equipment to bring the National Guard up to wartime strength, which was what the War Department had ordered. Moreover, medical inspection blanks had been slow to arrive from Washington, D.C., which had temporarily halted New Jersey physical examinations. Regarding these examinations, many men had been rejected because the government had raised the standards. A private from Newark, for instance, complained that he had served a three-year enlistment in the regular army and six years in the New Jersey National Guard but was rejected because several of his teeth were missing. About one hundred married men were excused from active duty upon presentation of their marriage certificates.[29]

The government had been able only to provide shoes, socks, underwear, and fifty tents. New Jersey adjutant general Wilbur F. Sadler, Jr., asked for and received permission to buy locally five thousand blankets, for which he promptly placed an order. Troops B and C of the New Jersey Cavalry, had insufficient horses, saddles, and mess kits.[30] In response to New Jersey's complaints, General Leonard Wood, commanding the Eastern Department, gave assurances that needed supplies and equipment would be shipped beginning on June 29. Washington, D.C., officials admitted that there had been delays, expressed their regrets at any inconvenience, and promised to do better. Meanwhile, lack of equipment alone had delayed the New Jersey brigade from entraining for the border. While the army's logistical system was in chaos, a wealthy citizen of New Jersey, George Brensinger, donated an armored truck to the 4th New Jersey.[31]

A tragic aspect of the New Jersey call-up was the death at the age of forty-five of Adjutant General Sadler at his brother's home in Carlisle, Pennsylvania, on November 11. Sadler, who had been appointed adjutant general in 1909, had literally worked himself to death. During the mobilization he worked day and night with practically no sleep, suffering a breakdown from which he never recovered.[32]

One recent recruit did not accompany the 2nd New Jersey Infantry to the border. He was Allen Dulles, future director of the Central Intelligence Agency, who with some of his Princeton classmates had enlisted in Trenton. Dulles had taken the Foreign Service exam and was notified on May 18 that he had been appointed as a Class 5 secretary of embassy or legation. He was to report to the State Department. Dulles later said that he resolved the dilemma by leaving it up to the National Guard as to whether they needed him or not but would not use the Foreign Service as an excuse to avoid serving. The National Guard notified him to proceed to Washington, D.C., and the Foreign Service. James Srodes states that Dulles enlisted in "the 16th [sic] Regiment of the New Jersey National Guard."[33] Peter Grose states that Dulles's "National Guard unit was ordered to the Rio Grande to combat a band of marauding Mexican irregulars led by Pancho Villa."[34] Of course the New Jersey National Guard neither went to the Rio Grande nor took on Pancho Villa.

Other guardsmen were less passive about going to the border. A drummer in the 5th New Jersey fatally slashed his throat at the mobilization camp. It was said he "had been greatly excited over the order to move." Another private in the same regiment deserted and hid in his mother's house in Paterson until a party of soldiers and police broke down the door and hauled him off to the guardhouse and court-martial. At the mobilization camp some men refused to take the federal oath, whereupon their officers stripped them of their uniforms and equipment and told them to get home the best way they could. Eighteen members of Ambulance Company No. 1 were among the recalcitrant. They were drummed out of camp and sneaked back to their homes in Red Bank late at night. A few had overalls, several huddled in blankets; one was clad only in his underwear and a sweater. All were barefoot and without hats. One had only a coat over his underwear. He went into a saloon near the railroad station, but a crowd of jolly patrons ripped his coat off and drove him out in a shower of beer. Some of these wretched slackers appeared downtown early the next morning, only to be greeted with catcalls and jeers.[35]

Then there was the band of the 5th New Jersey—twenty-seven of the twenty-nine bandsmen were dismissed from the mobilization camp, and from the National Guard, when they delivered an ultimatum demanding their union wage of thirty-four dollars a week each for their services, threatening to quit if their demand was not met. Colonel Albert A. Van Walraven, commanding the 5th New Jersey, was outraged, informing them that "you're the worst lot of yellow curs I ever heard of" and "you're a disgrace to the Guard." He dismissed them, provided transportation, ordered them to turn in their equipment at the armory in Paterson by six o'clock the next evening or an arrest warrant would be issued. Further, the colonel decreed that the name "Fifth Regiment Band" must be erased from the drumhead and the designation must never be used again. One of these miscreants soon apologized, was forgiven, and was mustered in. The Cadet Band of Paterson volunteered to replace the dismissed band. Twenty-seven of twenty-nine were accepted, passed their physical exams, and left with the regiment for the border.[36]

When the 4th and 5th New Jersey entrained, some 1,500 recruits accompanied the regiments. The troops from New Jersey traveled in day coaches with five days' rations and cook stoves in cars for each section. Camp Fielder, the mobilization camp, then officially closed, for it was anticipated that if the 2nd and 3rd New Jersey were called up they would mobilize in their armories.[37] With regard to the 2nd New Jersey, at an officers' dinner a captain caused a sensation by sharply criticizing the New Jersey adjutant general, Wilbur F. Sadler, and charging that under state control there was more political and social influence in the New Jersey guard than efficiency. The captain then tendered his resignation. It was accepted.[38]

The Essex Troop (Troop A) of the New Jersey Cavalry began loading its horses on June 27. However, there occurred a snafu: several of the cattle cars supplied were double-decked sheep cars.[39] And a trooper wrote to his mother that for its journey to the border instead of horse cars the unit got chicken and hog cars, which had to be extensively modified. Moreover, the men had to travel in day coaches, and one day all they got was one small meal. Fortunately, they got refreshments from patriotic ladies at the stations.[40]

Upon arriving in Douglas beginning on July 2, the New Jersey brigade, Brigadier General Edwin W. Hine commanding, began unloading their equipment and making camp at the site prepared for them the previous week. They were pleasantly surprised when regulars delivered large quantities of provisions for men and horses to the National Guard camp. Both General Davis and Mayor W. M. Adamson officially welcomed the New Jersey vanguard. By July 6, the rest of the New Jersey brigade joined them at Camp Frederick Funston on the outskirts of Douglas.[41]

Laundrymen did a land-office business, as did purveyors of ice and the proprietors of several ice cream and soft drinks wagons, easing the guardsmen's discomfort from days of travel in antiquated day coaches. Moreover, most guardsmen and regulars got the Fourth of July off. As for the guardsmen, "most of the soldiers expressed a desire to see Mexican soldiers; a few inquired concerning Indians." Many guardsmen spent the holiday in Douglas, inspecting the town and avidly listening to the locals' accounts of battles in Mexico and along the border. They also inspected the town of Agua Prieta from a distance.[42] The New Jersey brigade encamped two miles west of Douglas and learned mundane skills such as how to make adobe bricks to line their tent floors and how to fit pipes for drinking water and showers.[43]

To keep the guardsmen occupied, the army prescribed close-order drill and school-of-the-soldier training from five o'clock to ten o'clock in the morning and three o'clock to five o'clock on afternoons. Between drills, the troops policed the camp and worked on their equipment, while the officers conducted inspections and received training of their own. As a change of pace, the New Jersey brigade made route marches, including the cavalry since their horses had not arrived. These day hikes were usually to local ranches such as Slaughter's, which was eighteen miles from camp; Hunt's at eight miles; and McDonald's at twelve miles. The 5th New Jersey also made a five-day sixty-five-mile route march to Fort Huachuca.[44]

On July 6, the 2nd Montana Infantry and Troop A 1st Montana Cavalry arrived and began setting up their camp adjoining that of New Jersey. Commanding the 2nd Montana was Colonel Dan J. Donohue, nicknamed "Dynamite Dan" for his exploits in the Spanish-American War. The 2nd Montana had mobilized at Fort William Henry Harrison, with supplies being transferred from the state arsenal nearby. Because of severe flooding, the railroads were out of service, delaying the arrival of some outlying companies. Between June 23 and July 1 the regiment drew equipment and transferred property from state to federal ownership. On July 1, those men physically fit were mustered in. Their salary was fifty cents a day, doubled to one dollar a day upon entering federal service. The 2nd Montana departed by rail in three sections on July 2 in a storm that left eighteen inches of snow on the ground. The Montanans "were all husky in build and appeared to be accustomed to outdoor activities." This was good, because on the way to the border the regiment paraded through downtown Denver on July 4 in a driving snowstorm.[45]

How the Montanans came to be stationed in Douglas is interesting. They were initially ordered to Nogales, but W. A. Clark, one of Montana's "copper kings," owned the Calumet smelter outside of Douglas. Clark used his influence with Montana senator Thomas J. Walsh, Chairman of the Committee of Mines and Mining, and Walsh persuaded Secretary of War Newton Baker to reassign the Montanans on June 28 to Douglas in order to protect the Calumet and Phelps Dodge smelters. Along with units from New Jersey, who shared the protection duties, the Montanans established their camp near the smelters, about three miles from town and half a mile from the border. When they detrained at the way station of Calumet, the Montanans were perhaps dismayed when they first saw their campsite, which regulars had already laid out. Nevertheless, the guardsmen set to work with bayonets and a few axes and by nightfall had cleared the site of brush and cactus. Orderly rows of pyramidal tents soon went up in Camp Harry Clark.[46]

The Montanans arrived just two days before the rainy season began. They immediately dug a system of open drains, which proved to be an inspired action, for the next day torrential rains turned the camps of other organizations into a sea of mud and blew down a number of tents. The Montanans "were snug and dry, and able to give their fellow-sufferers the laugh." A lack of lumber and other material delayed the construction and screening of mess halls, bathhouses, latrines, and other buildings. The men experienced "discomfort" when inoculated against typhoid and smallpox and subsequently against paratyphoid. During July, a machine gun company was organized, with four Lewis guns and trucks to transport them.[47]

Like the Coloradoans, Montana guardsmen had recent experience as strikebreakers, enforcing martial law against striking miners in Butte in 1914. And like other National Guard units, the Montanans plunged into the "hardening process" the War Department had ordered. Drill began on the third day after their arrival: an early-morning two-mile hike without arms, much of it at double time, followed by breakfast. At seven o'clock in the morning, they started drill, which lasted until ten o'clock. They had leisure time until three o'clock, except for NCOs, who had to attend NCO school. Between three and four thirty, they had more drill, followed by free time until Retreat at sundown. Twice a week there were practice marches of ten to twenty miles in light marching order: rifle, ammunition, and field equipment. Their equipment left a lot to be desired—it was condemned surplus from the Spanish-American War. The rifles were heavy Krag-Jorgensens and sidearms were .38 Smith & Wesson revolvers. Each man carried a bayonet, plus the obsolete canvas ammunition belt and round tin canteen. Perhaps the hardest part of the "hardening process" was that the Montanans went through it in their winter woolen uniforms and woolen underwear—in temperatures often reaching 115 degrees in the shade. Two carloads of overcoats arrived on July 18, reportedly the first of a considerable consignment for the National Guard at Douglas.[48] At first glance issuing overcoats might seem odd, but it got very cold in the desert at night.

Following the "hardening process" schedule, the Montanans could anticipate guard duty along the border east and west of Douglas. Guard duty had its hazards: on July 30, Mexican snipers fired five shots at a sentry of the 2nd Montana. The Americans did not return the fire. Sniping became almost a nightly nuisance.[49] After two days without sniping, Mexicans lying in the brush two miles west of Agua Prieta and several hundred yards south of the international boundary fired a number of rounds at a patrol of the 2nd Montana on the night of August 2. Being unable to locate the snipers, the guardsmen did not return fire. Then on August 14, a Mexican fired six shots at Montana sentries at the regimental camp two miles west of Douglas. The Americans watched through field glasses as the Mexican, evidently an officer, rode out of Agua Prieta followed by his orderly, halted about eleven hundred yards south of the border, dismounted, took a rifle from his orderly, adjusted the sights, and calmly fired the six rounds at the Americans. He then mounted and galloped off. Fortunately he was a lousy shot and all the rounds fell short. The American sentries did not bother to reply.[50]

The federal Bureau of Investigation made arrangements for a New Jersey lieutenant and a sergeant to conduct surveillance on suspected ammunition smugglers in Douglas.[51] Smuggling ammunition was a major aspect of criminal activity, but other commodities figured as well. On August 1, a soldier on border guard duty plunged his bayonet into a can of lard, one of four being shipped from Douglas to Nacozari, Sonora. The bayonet broke a bottle of liquor, and it turned out that each can contained a case of whiskey packed in flour to prevent breakage and topped with a layer of lard. The army confiscated the shipment.[52]

By mid-July there were 12,500 regulars and guardsmen in Douglas, but there was trouble in the National Guard encampments. A lack of essential equipment, particularly clothing, caused a great deal of discontent and adverse comment among the New Jersey and Montana guardsmen.[53] As we have seen, the Montanans' woolen uniforms were not exactly suited to the Douglas climate. Not until mid-September was the army able to issue cotton uniforms. At the same time, the men had to turn in two of their three blankets.[54]

"Rules for the camp were not stringent" in Douglas, and many viewed their service as "a summer camp on a large scale."[55] Some soldiers, such as the elite Essex Troop of New Jersey cavalry, had a rather enjoyable time of it. Every evening numbers of them gathered at the Gadsden Hotel, making it their unofficial headquarters. "It became so after a time that the dining room of that hostelry could almost have been called the Essex Troop Club." There were some complaints against enlisted men dining at the Gadsden but the proprietor ignored them. And when the commanding general ordered that no men would be permitted in Douglas in the evening, "this ruling nearly caused a revolt among the troopers, but was soon rescinded."[56] As for the majority of the troops, the tedium of camp life began to tell. The YMCA and the YMHA provided a range of services such as refreshments and writing paper (consumed at the rate of 2,500–3,000 sheets daily). Baseball teams and horseshoe tournaments provided some interest. A number of the guardsmen acquired pets and mascots. Still, some soldiers sought less savory entertainment such as gambling and visits to the red-light district.[57]

New Jersey and Montana troops were becoming increasingly restless.[58] Some of the discontent became desertion. Because their pay was in arrears, a number of New Jersey guardsmen deserted. They just walked away from camp. However, the army quickly tracked them down and as punishment subjected them to forced marches across the desert. The 2nd Montana too was losing men. Many of the troops came from farming families, and as harvest season neared the desire to go home increased. Furthermore, university students were anxious to get home for the fall semester. Complicating the situation, Montana governor Sam V. Stewart, a Democrat, was up for reelection, and Republicans and some Democrats put him on the spot by assuring worried parents that the governor could get their sons home.[59]

Colonel Donohue was also worried. He wrote to the governor on August 10 that he was nine hundred men short of Montana's quota and recruits were not arriving fast enough to offset losses due to discharge. He had had five desertions to date; three of the deserters had been caught in El Paso and were being court-martialed. Donohue had at present twenty-five applications for discharge because of dependent relatives, and most were fraudulent. The colonel is reported to have said, "this dependent relatives thing makes me sick," adding that only about one in four applications was genuine. He also resented the way men complained to their congressmen in hopes of getting discharged. Despite stating that "it is a most discouraging situation," Donohue was proud of his command: "The men here are magnificent. You would not know it for the same outfit that left home. We have the finest laid out and planned camp on the border. Discipline is excellent and the spirits of the men fine. Of course there are a few afflicted with the hook worm, but we are even curing that. There are a few officers who will have to walk the plank soon for the good of the service. Two of them have resigned already and two or possibly three more will have to go, the others are doing fine."[60] To the colonel's disgust, two more of his men deserted in September. Mexican authorities finally located them in Cananea, Sonora, looking for work in the copper mines.[61]

Adding to the guardsmen's misery, nature in the form of a ferocious storm with wind gusts in excess of one hundred miles an hour hit on the night of July 22–23. The newcomers were taken aback by the Southwest "monsoon" season. Those who fared the worst were the New Jersey brigade. The storm demolished company streets, ripping more than one hundred tents from their moorings and smashing wooden structures such as the forty-foot by one-hundred-foot building the YMCA had finished only a week earlier, hurling the structures across the road into the ditches between the camp and the railroad tracks. Twenty combat wagons weighing 1,800 pounds apiece were overturned. Tons of uncovered quartermaster supplies were ruined, and telephone and telegraph lines were severed. Mercifully, only two men were injured.[62] The Montanans fared much better. They had dug trenches around each tent and section of their camp, these trenches draining into a large trench that carried the rainwater away. Although the men had complained loudly at the time that digging trenches was just more stupid army busywork, when the cloudburst hit they could have a good laugh as the adjoining unprepared New Jersey camp was virtually washed away. The guardsmen began to realize that wind, rain, and sandstorms were a fact of life on the border.[63]

As if this were not bad enough, in late July an epidemic of dysentery broke out in the National Guard camps. The 2nd Montana was particularly hard hit.[64] A private died of dysentery at Douglas and another soon after the regiment returned home. (In addition, a corporal died after an appendicitis operation.)[65] A New Jersey artilleryman in Battery A also died in the base hospital of dysentery. Doctors blamed lack of screened mess halls for the problem; flies carried the disease from latrines to the mess area. A contributing factor was poor water facilities.[66]

On the morning of August 30, a serious situation developed in the camp of the 4th New Jersey Infantry, from Hoboken. Company M turned out armed with bayonets and refused to drill, on the ground that their regimental commander, Lieutenant Colonel George T. Vickers, was trying to force them to elect First Lieutenant Hugh M. Gillespie, commander of Company C, as their captain. The men wanted to elect their own first lieutenant, Arthur H. Easterly, to the vacancy, which was caused when the company commander, Captain William M. Kroog, left that day for his home on thirty days' leave pending his resignation. The soldiers stated they were prevented from electing Easterly by an official request from Colonel Vickers that they elect Lieutenant Gillespie. They refused to hold the election until they could elect their own choice. After the men refused to drill, a lieutenant was assigned as temporary company commander, but the men still refused until their own Lieutenant Easterly pleaded with them. The insubordinate company then laid down their bayonets and consented to drill under the temporary commander. That night the men of Company M paraded through the streets of the camp brandishing a placard on a pole saying "We Want Easterly for Captain." The officer of the day confiscated the placard. The men yelled and sang songs improvising verses consigning Lieutenant Gillespie to hell and declaring that they would hang him to a sour apple tree.

Adding to Colonel Vickers's problems, Company B refused to elect First Sergeant August Urbansky of Company C, whom Colonel Vickers had appointed second lieutenant; they wanted Sergeant Major Harry H. Young. And other companies also refused at first to elect the officers the colonel chose. They finally acceded, however. Lieutenant Easterly wrote and prepared to tender his resignation because he was not promoted in regular order. Many of the men alleged that Colonel Vickers's appointments were illegal, but he had apparently acted on the advice of regular officers, and he declared that the men appointed would serve whether the companies elected them or not. A few days later, another New Jersey company, angry about what they considered inadequate rations, refused to go on a route march.[67]

General Funston announced on September 2, 1916, without elaborating, that he was ordering the 1st and 4th New Jersey Infantry home.[68] Three trains left Douglas on September 4. "Some of the militiamen at El Paso have been watching with longing eyes the long trains of sleepers loaded with homeward bound New Jersey National Guardsmen which have been passing through the city for the past two days. The New Jerseyites were in a jovial mood as they passed through the business part of El Paso. They shouted, tooted their bugles, tossed hardtack at the pretty girls on the sidewalks and generally comported themselves boyishly."[69] The heavy baggage of the 1st and 4th New Jersey regiments was shipped in a special train of twenty-seven cars.[70]

To their delight, the New Jersey cavalry and artillery also received orders to return to their home stations. But Company A, Signal Corps, was ordered to march to Nogales, its new station, whereupon on October 2, the officers tendered their resignations. Colonel Van Walraven, commanding the 5th New Jersey Infantry, accepted the resignations and forwarded them to General Funston.[71] The army punished the offending unit by ordering them to care for the 192 horses that the New Jersey artillery and cavalry had left behind in Douglas and to take good care of these ten carloads of horses on their long journey home.[72]

October saw the bulk of the New Jersey guard return home and be mustered out. The major commanding the 1st Cavalry Squadron rejected his men's appeal that their troop train halt in Fort Worth en route home so they could watch the returns of the World Series. The major pointed out reasonably enough that it was more important to adhere to the railroad schedule.[73] The 4th New Jersey arrived back at the Sea Girt mobilization camp on September 10 accompanied by General Hine and his staff. Some thirteen thousand civilians visited the camp, where the 4th began mustering out on September 11. The 1st New Jersey arrived home in Newark and on October 2 paraded before cheering crowds with General Hine and the regimental band in the van. The mayor and city council reviewed the regiment, commenting on how sharp the troops looked.[74] The 5th New Jersey left Douglas on October 27 for Sea Girt. The regiment returned to Paterson from Sea Girt on November 3, being welcomed by some twenty thousand citizens. The city was decorated with flags, and the extensive silk mills closed for the afternoon so that the workers too could watch the regiment parade through downtown.[75] Battery C of the Field Artillery was the last unit to leave Douglas, on March 8, 1917. It too received a delirious welcome from the home folks when it paraded in Orange on March 14.[76]

The 2nd Montana Infantry also received orders to break camp and return home. Their tour of duty in Douglas had not been particularly enjoyable, but the *Douglas Dispatch* gave them fulsome praise and was particularly complimentary of Colonel Donohue.[77] Unfortunately their ordeal was not over.

The regiment left on October 11 by rail, arriving back at Fort Benjamin Harrison on October 16. But the army ordered the Montanans to pitch their tents and remain on post until they were mustered out, even though they were wearing their summer uniforms and had only one wool blanket each—in minus-twelve-degree temperature. This even though the nearby barracks had excellent stoves. The Montanans were not allowed to sleep in the barracks and had to make do in their Sibley tents, which did have stoves but necessitated the men staying up half the night scrounging for wood. It was almost impossible to sleep because of the cold, which in a way was fortunate, because in their efforts to keep warm the men overheated some of the small stoves and burned several of the tents down. After enduring these abominable conditions for nearly two weeks, the 2nd Montana was finally mustered out on November 3.[78] The guardsmen had little use for the army.

Even as some New Jersey units departed from Douglas, other National Guard contingents were arriving. Battery B, District of Columbia Field Artillery, and District of Columbia Field Hospital Company No. 1 arrived on October 2 and occupied the camp vacated by the 1st New Jersey Infantry. On November 16, the battery left for Fort Huachuca on a practice march. They camped two nights on the road, spent two days at Huachuca, whose principal attraction was that it boasted the only swimming pool in the region. The troops then spent two nights on the road back to Douglas.[79]

An important redeployment of troops occurred on October 30 when two battalions of the 18th U.S. Infantry were moved from Camp Harry J. Jones, east of Douglas, to Camp Frederick Funston, the National Guard camp west of town, occupying part of the former New Jersey camp. This was done in order to guard more efficiently the quartermaster depot in that locality.[80] Batteries A and C, Alabama Field Artillery Battalion, arrived on October 10. Incidentally, Battery C, following the National Guard tradition of electing their officers, had elected a new lieutenant while on the rail journey to Douglas.[81] Battery C, New Jersey Field Artillery, which had been training at the Tobyhanna, Pennsylvania, artillery range, arrived in Douglas on October 11 and moved into Camp Funston next to the Alabama artillery, which occupied quarters previously used by Batteries A and B, New Jersey Field Artillery. From Colorado came the 1st and 2nd Battalions, Colorado Infantry, and Field Hospital Company No. 1, on October 18.[82]

The newcomers were phased into the training schedule. For example, the Colorado infantry completed their annual target practice with commendable results. There was increased emphasis on field training and experimentation. The first war-strength infantry regimental hike began on October 10 when approximately 1,975 officers and men under the command of Colonel Abner Pickering left Douglas to march to Fort Huachuca. The hike to the fort and return required ten days of actual walking, while two days were spent at the fort resting before beginning the return journey. The war-strength regiment consisted of drafts from the 11th, 18th, 22nd, and 35th U.S. Infantry regiments and the 5th New Jersey Infantry. The march was undertaken on orders from the War Department to test transport service, the object being to decide whether 27 wagons to a full company of 150 men would be sufficient.[83]

The army also engaged in experiments aimed at modernization. In a test of how well trucks stood up to the unimproved roads in Arizona, the 2nd Battalion, 18th U.S. Infantry, was dispatched in fourteen trucks from Douglas to Roosevelt Dam. The army was pleased with the trucks' performance, but before reaching its destination the battalion was recalled to Douglas. General Funston transferred the 18th Infantry, which had been stationed in Douglas for the last three years, to Yuma. The other two battalions and their equipment went by rail in thirty-six cars divided into two sections, followed by the 2nd Battalion upon its return to Douglas.[84]

The three hundred New Jersey infantrymen who participated in the provisional war-strength regiment in its hike to Fort Huachuca returned to Douglas on October 17 in twenty-two trucks so they could leave with the remainder of the 5th New Jersey for its home station. "The Jerseymen are reported to have acquitted themselves well on the march, out-hiking the Regulars. With the exception of one private who was slightly injured on the march none of the Guardsmen left the ranks."[85]

The war-strength regiment which left eleven days earlier for Fort Huachuca, seventy-five miles northwest of Douglas, returned on October 18, having satisfactorily proved to the War Department that the baggage train authorized by the recently passed defense bill was sufficient. The regiment's column included twenty-seven wagons, four ambulances, and one rolling kitchen, plus an allowance of two hundred thousand rounds of ammunition and three days' grain for the 906 animals.[86]

Although moving haltingly toward modernization, the army was also a stickler for regulations. After a period in which there was more or less laxity about the requirement for enlisted men to salute officers, the provost guard was ordered to be on the alert for such infractions of discipline. The result was that approximately one hundred men were soon arrested. However, the failure of men to salute in many instances was explained by an infantry private who said that the recent change in the regulation dress of enlisted men in the cavalry and artillery, including their adoption of leather leggings, had been confusing, for leather leggings used to be a distinctive mark of an officer. "When the cavalrymen and artillerymen first began wearing leather leggings I went down the street saluting until my hands got tired. Now, as a result of those mistakes, I am careful to see that whoever is passing is an officer before I salute him. Probably some of the men who were arrested were in the same predicament. The hat cord and insignia of rank at the collar or on the shoulders are the only things we have to go on by now."[87]

In what some troops would have considered a perverse Christmas present, on the night of December 25, a cordon of Military Police surrounded the red-light district to enforce an order of the secretary of war that no soldier, whether regular or guardsman, could enter it. Brigadier General T. F. Davis, commanding the Arizona District, published the order and the severe penalties for its infraction. Several arrests were made. Secretary Baker was said to have issued the order in response to a movement begun by General Hine, commander of the New Jersey brigade. "While stationed here Jerseymen writing home about the open district of the bright lights, caused numerous protests to be received by General Hine, who published an order forbidding any of his men to frequent it. The campaign was continued, it was stated, after the Jerseymen returned to their native state." The order was so worded that it might apply to any other part of the border, mentioning "Douglas or any other locality where such conditions obtain."[88]

Another complaint the troops had was against the merchants of Douglas for the alleged custom of charging soldiers exorbitant prices. The *Douglas Dispatch* suggested that even if true, these incidents were few and far between. The newspaper did admit that rents had doubled in the past year but added that there was enormous demand for rental homes, especially by officers.[89]

By mid-January, 1917, the incidence of sickness at Douglas was declining:

> Sickness in the Arizona Patrol District, due to changing weather, is gradually being overcome; the number of men entering the base hospital at Camp Harry J. Jones with more or less trifling ailments in most cases, was almost balanced by the number of men, Regulars and

militia, returned to duty. There were 48 Regulars entering the hospital during period, and 42 were discharged as cured, while 30 militiamen entered and 31 were discharged. At present there are 204 patients in hospital, including three cases of mumps and one of measles.[90]

There were still occasional scares of Mexican raids, such as one reported on February 26: "A rumor reaching here from Slaughter's ranch Friday to the effect that there had been a raid made across the line by Mexicans, caused two troops of the 1st Cavalry[91] to be sent eastward along the border to strengthen the patrol on duty there. The remainder of the 1st Cavalry was held in camp with baggage packed, ready to move at a few moments' notice, wherever it might be needed." However, the article continued:

> The "raid," occurred when a number of Carrancista troops under command of General Guillermo Chávez left their camp about three miles south of the international boundary and crossed the line to purchase tobacco and other small luxuries. The Mexicans were unarmed and paid cash for their purchases. They then returned to Mexico. Some excitable individual, or one with an exaggerated sense of humor, started the story of a raid.[92]

The Arizona adjutant general, Colonel Charles W. Harris, became frustrated by what he perceived as constant attacks by regular officers against the National Guard. For example, General Leonard Wood had been quoted as stating in testimony before a Senate committee that: "The portion of the militia now efficient and ready for service could be placed in the Yale bowl, and still leave room for a game of football."[93] Harris, who was quite active in National Guard affairs, "gave out one of the warmest statements ever coming from a National Guard officer."[94] He had repeatedly stated that if the War Department would "stop its hounding tactics and cease its efforts to ruin the guard in the interests of universal service, the guard as a whole would eventually prove to be the mainstay of the nation's defensive plans." Expressing a widely held view among guardsmen: he "cited order after order, made by the War Department to hinder and ruin the efficiency of the Guard. In these orders, according to the colonel, his troops have been made to come up to standards of service which the Regular army itself cannot reach."

Harris gave out a statement detailing his views, and since they were like those of many other guard officers the statement is perhaps worth quoting:

The acceptance of the figures gathered by officers of the War Department to discredit the National Guard without comment is unfair to the Guard. The statement that 71,834 Guardsmen out of a total of 163,000 had not had previous training, I have every reason to doubt. But what if the figures are true? What if 60 percent of the force were finally recruits? Had the Regular army been able to recruit to its required numbers it also would have had about 60 per cent recruits. And even of the present strength of the army a large percentage is recruits. The old soldiers are not remaining in the service as they formerly did, and these men must be replaced as far as possible with recruits. Had the Regular army been able to meet the requirements placed upon it, the necessity for calling the National Guard to do police duty for the Regular army would probably not have arisen.

Is it any fair basis for a criticism of the National Guard that it was able to meet the requirements of the new law promptly and by so doing had a large number of recruits in its ranks when the Regular army was not able to meet the requirements of the new law?

When the Arizona regiment arrived at Douglas it found depleted regiments of the Regular army there, and those regiments are still depleted. The federal authorities refused to muster in a single company of our organization unless it had 65 or more men to the company. Hardly a Regular company had that number of men or since. The army has been remarkably able in covering up their deficiencies.

The recent report of the acting chief of the Militia Bureau indicates that officer has no confidence in the National Guard. How can any organization expect to improve with officers in charge of its affairs who doubt its advisability, who are inimical to its success? Without giving the National Guard any chance to meet the requirements of the National Defense Act its militaristic enemies are condemning it.

Why the Regular army has absolutely failed to meet the requirements of that act. They are in a worse position than the Guard, they cannot even secure recruits. The army has a top heavy list of commissioned officers with no troops to train. The existence of an efficient National Guard is a menace to the success of their plan to secure enough recruits for the army by conscription. Compulsory training? The plan of our militarists is not for compulsory training so much as Germany has, under its state officers.

The plan is not to train officers and men together and return them to civil life to earn their living as the Guardsmen must do. It is a plan to compel military service under the present system of officers of the Regular army, that being the only part of the present army system that has not fallen down, as far as numbers are concerned.

When our troops went to the border many of the officers were anxious to secure commissions in the Regular army. With one exception [presumably Sidney Forrester Mashbir], I do not know of a single officer that is competent, that would accept a commission in the Regular army. The errors in the mobilization were not in the Guard, they were in a lack of any system that should have been provided by the army officers in control of militia affairs. The remarkable thing about the mobilization is not that the National Guard did not do better, it is that it did as well as it did considering the lack of system and failure of the departments at Washington that were responsible for the mobilization, and those departments were not controlled by the National Guard.[95]

Adjutant General Harris's frustration with the regular army perhaps reflected the decline of the 1st Arizona. General Funston announced that he had ordered the entire Arizona National Guard to concentrate at Fort Huachuca. The guard, constituting much less than a regiment, had been split up and stationed at the Roosevelt dam and other points doing guard duty. According to one newspaper, "It is being concentrated so it can gain advanced prestige."[96] Recruiting efforts around the state failed, and regimental strength steadily declined. By March of 1917, the muster rolls contained 180 fewer names than when the regiment was sworn into federal service ten months earlier, well below its required wartime strength of 1,915. Company I was down to three officers and thirty enlisted men.[97] The weather certainly did not help. On December 24, 1916, "a severe sand and windstorm badly damaged the camp, and heavy snows the following day made things mighty uncomfortable for the troopers."[98]

Both troop strength and morale reached new lows in January and February 1917. The entire 3rd Battalion had to be consolidated in order to have enough men to perform company drill. Frustrations spilled over on January 23, when a "go home" parade escalated in a quasi-mutiny involving about one hundred men. On February 1, eight soldiers refused to carry out a wood-cutting detail, and that same day a captain's tent mysteriously burned. On February 28, seven rifles were discovered missing from Company D. They were subsequently found hidden in Naco.[99] Several hundred residents of the town of Safford signed a petition calling for the release from the National Guard of two Safford boys on the ground that they had been minors when they enlisted. Application for their release through habeas corpus proceedings against Colonel Tuthill were also filed in U.S. district court in Tucson.[100]

General Funston, accompanied by Brigadier General Davis, arrived on January 12 to inspect the troops in Douglas. Funston reviewed the six regiments of regulars at Camp Harry J. Jones. Later some 1,500 guardsmen passed in review.[101] Marring Funston's visit was a most unfortunate incident:

> But for the imprudent conduct of several members of the First Arizona infantry, it is believed here that regiment might have been designated by Major General Frederick Funston as one of those to leave the border district and be mustered out of the Federal service. When Generals Funston and Davis arrived on January 12 to inspect the 1st Arizona, the troops virtually ignored their car as it rolled through the camp. The Arizonans failed to heed the red flag with its two stars, indicative of the rank of the occupant. At first it appeared that they simply had failed to note Funston's arrival, but suddenly, from several parts of the camp, came cries of "I want to go home." General Funston's demeanor, which had been genial, suddenly became frigid, and it was evident that he resented the cries and the implied disrespect.[102]

Those yelling at him were concealed by tents, lacking the courage to protest openly.

As anyone who has served in the army knows, it is not a good idea to infuriate the commanding general. Those acquainted with Funston felt sure that he would discipline the regiment for the conduct of some of its members, and "many weary days of service on the border lie before it."[103]

One Arizona newspaper tried to put a positive, if pathetically lame, spin on this deplorable incident:

> While all the members of the Arizona National Guard on duty at the border have been anxious for a long time to come home, something happened that will make them all proud of the privilege of remaining in the service of the United States on that border until such time

as their commanding officer, General Frederick Funston, sees fit to return them to their state. The soldiers of the First Arizona regiment (the state's National Guardsmen) are to be retained temporarily at least because they are among the best, if not the very best, state troops on the border, and General Funston, it is reliably reported, realizes, so long as he is to be very much limited in state troops, he must retain in the United States service on the border the very best state troops under his command.[104]

With the 1st Arizona Infantry going downhill, one can imagine the delirium with which the troops received the word that on March 27, 1917, the regiment would be recalled from the border. Preparations for return to civilian life included taking a physical exam, on March 12, when it snowed on the men waiting in line. On March 13, an order suspended all drills. And on March 16, regular officers supervised the paperwork for mustering out the regiment. Not only were the men paid, but they received a fifteen-day paid furlough after mustering out. On March 26, the troops struck their tents. They did not mind sleeping on the ground that night, no doubt dreaming of returning home.

The dream was shattered the next day. When the regiment assembled for the formal mustering out ceremony, a War Department telegram informed them that because of imminent war with Germany, all National Guard units still in federal service were to remain in federal service. On March 28, an unusually high number of men failed to report for morning formation. Even so, by March 29, the regiment had reassembled its encampment, and soldiers, however reluctantly, were heading back to the rifle range. But not unnaturally, the only thing most guardsmen wanted was out. Some got their wish when the War Department ordered the immediate release of all men with indigent dependents. Others just refused to take the new federal oath under the National Defense Act. Despite appeals from Governor Thomas Campbell, who had just been elected, 326 men resigned in April 1917. Although the 1st Arizona gained 114 recruits, at the end of April the regiment had only 442 enlisted men.[105] The 1st Arizona Infantry was pretty much worn out.

Governor Campbell addressed a letter to Secretary of War Baker asking that the 1st Arizona Infantry be mustered out at Phoenix. The governor pointed out that the citizens of the state had never had an opportunity to see the regiment; that it had been on the border for almost a year and had given valuable service to the state and nation; and that by mustering the men out at Phoenix the expense would be less because Phoenix was nearer to most of the home stations than any other point in the state.[106]

However, the Arizona National Guard was mustered out at Douglas on March 20, 1917.[107] The Phoenix chamber of commerce proposed presenting the guardsmen with bronze medals when they returned home, as had several of the larger states, in order to show appreciation for the sacrifices the troops had made. When the plan was presented to Adjutant General Harris, he disapproved of it unless the medals were given by the government. Nevertheless, the chamber of commerce insisted that an honor of this kind should be conferred on the soldiers by the state authorities or by some large commercial body in Phoenix. The cost would be small, and unless Governor Campbell could get a state appropriation, the chamber of commerce planned to enlist the assistance of other organizations in Phoenix to provide the medals.[108]

As of December 31, Adjutant General Harris ordered all guard officers who were currently on the unassigned or reserve list and who had not yet taken the federal oath to do so before January 30 or be dropped from the rolls. All retired officers were also required to take the oath or be dropped on February 1.[109]

Arizona's guard officers rallied to the colors in World War I. As Harris proudly reported in 1918:

> Practically every former officer of the First Arizona Infantry, National Guard, who attended an Officers' Camp was re-commissioned with the same rank that he formerly held in the National Guard. From our small organization of one regiment of infantry, with its medical detachment, we now have in the service a Brigadier General, a Colonel, two Lieutenant Colonels, eight Majors, and over a hundred line officers, and these figures do not include any officers who were not officers or members of the National Guard on the day war was declared.[110]

Chapter 18

Naco

Separated only by a narrow strip of vacant land from Naco, Sonora, the citizens of Naco, Arizona, were extremely nervous at the prospect of being attacked across the imaginary international boundary. In fact, the enterprising proprietor of the Hotel Naco proudly advertised that his establishment boasted bullet-proof rooms.[1]

The garrison at Naco as of June 18 consisted of two hundred regulars—Troops F and G, 1st U.S. Cavalry, and Company F, 14th U.S. Infantry. They began constructing breastworks of sandbags, in response to word that 1,500 Mexican troops had arrived within a few miles of Naco, Sonora. There also arrived in Naco, Arizona, a special train with some six hundred American refugees from the copper mining center of Cananea, Sonora. On the night of June 22, ethnic tensions increased when a Hispanic night watchman mistook soldiers preparing to change the guard for approaching bandits and opened fire, killing one and wounding three.[2] Naco not only organized a home guard but appealed for more soldiers.[3] The 1st Battalion, 1st Arizona Infantry, the band, medical detachment, and regimental headquarters left Douglas on July 15 for Naco, where they would be stationed for the next eight months.[4] Because it was feared that Mexicans might slip across the border and raid the copper mining center of Bisbee, the 22nd U.S. Infantry was rushed there from Douglas on June 26.

The colonel of the 1st Arizona assigned a sergeant to watch the railroad station, assisting the federal Bureau of Investigation in observing any suspicious activity. The bureau also investigated cases of liquor being supplied to American Indians in the 1st Arizona and attempts to induce Hispanic Arizona guardsmen to desert to Mexico.[5]

One officer from the 1st Arizona became involved in several intelligence operations in Mexico. Captain Sidney Forrester Mashbir, commanding Company K, in civilian life was a civil engineer, assistant city engineer of Tucson and Casa Grande as well as an architect. Mashbir related how General Frederick Funston assigned him the mission of checking out confidential reports of Japanese troops landing in Baja California, and crossing into Sonora. Two officers had tried and failed to verify these reports, but Mashbir had been recommended to the general as a man who had spent years surveying in the desert and who might succeed. According to Mashbir, Funston warned him: "Remember, if they get you, we never heard of you." In making a detailed undercover investigation of the Sonoran desert and Mexican troop dispositions, Mashbir said he found unmistakable signs that parties of about fifty Japanese troops at a time had indeed marched up to the American border. Besides copying what he said were Japanese ideographs written in charcoal at the base of cliffs, Mashbir asserted that "I discovered the first Japanese military documents ever found on this continent." He estimated that a total of as many as twelve thousand Japanese troops had crossed through Sonora and back to the Pacific coast without either the Mexicans or the American authorities being aware of their presence. He prepared a sketch map on August 29, 1916, of the Sonora-Arizona desert showing "every road, trail, and waterhole between Nogales and Yuma, from the Gila River to the Gulf of California."[6] While Mashbir's estimates appear to be exaggerated, to say the least, the whole subject of Japanese involvement in the Mexican Revolution merits further investigation.

Mashbir in 1916 also received the assignment of slipping into Mexico to tap the private telegraph line, running between Cananea and Agua Prieta, of the military governor of Sonora, General Plutarco Elías Calles. Mashbir admitted he botched the job, for the Mexicans discovered the wire he had installed. But his next attempt, with the assistance of a picked signal corps detachment and several Papago Indian spies, was successful. "Thereafter messages were intercepted and decoded as fast as they went through."[7] The army engaged rather extensively in this practice and in fact prepared a "Special Report on Tapping Telegraph Wires" in northern Mexico.[8] While stationed with his Company K at Camp Tuthill in Ajo, Mashbir was also involved in combating the smuggling of ammunition into Mexico.[9] Mashbir subsequently received a commission as a lieutenant in the 22nd U.S.

Infantry and went on to a distinguished career in Military Intelligence, becoming a Japanese specialist and retiring as a colonel. Lieutenant Fred J. Wright, intelligence officer of the 1st Arizona Infantry at Naco, collaborated with the Bureau of Investigation in compiling data and maps about the route from the border to the mining center of Cananea, Sonora.[10]

The rest of the 1st Arizona had a much less exciting time while stationed in Naco. Although the unit had been mustered into federal service by June 20 and recruiting continued, the 1st Arizona's strength declined during the period of its border service, which was characterized by heat, tedium, dust, monotony, and boredom.[11] To keep the troops occupied there was the usual round of drills and weekly inspections. The 1st Battalion was stationed at Fort Huachuca for a time, and the 2nd Battalion made a practice march from Naco to Huachuca. As of August 11, two companies of the 1st Arizona were stationed at Fort Huachuca.[12] On occasion an important visitor such as Governor Hunt arrived. Since he had shown little support for the National Guard, his visit on September 29 probably did little to improve morale. Colonel Tuthill reviewed the entire 1st Arizona on September 11, then on September 20–27, he led them on a grueling 120-mile march through the desert from Naco to Forrest Ranch and back. Considering the conditions under which this march took place, the troops performed remarkably well. Still, their duties revolved around training exercises and performing guard duty, not only in camp but also in town at the sandbagged entrance to the Wells Fargo office, where the army kept funds.[13]

Elements of the District of Columbia National Guard were also dispatched to Naco. The organization got an impressive sendoff—on June 21, President Woodrow Wilson, wearing a straw hat, and Secretary of War Newton Baker stood in a drizzling rain on the curb in front of the White House and reviewed the District of Columbia guard as it marched to its mobilization camp at Fort Myer, Virginia; the militia encampment was named Camp Ordway.[14] The guard consisted of the 1st Separate Infantry Battalion (Colored), the 3rd Infantry, Troop A Cavalry, Batteries A and B of the Field Artillery, Company A of the Signal Corps, Field Hospital No. 1, and Ambulance Company No. 1, totaling 1,731 men in peacetime.

As with some other state contingents, District of Columbia units were scattered along the border. In early July, Company A, Signal Corps, and Ambulance Company No. 1 (lacking their horses and mules, which were not issued until mid-August) arrived in Warren, a mining settlement on the outskirts of Bisbee.[15] The field hospital went first to Warren, then later to Douglas. Battery B arrived in Warren on August 12 minus its animals; the battery was subsequently transferred to Douglas, occupying the camp formerly used by the 1st New Jersey Infantry. The 3rd Infantry went to San Antonio on October 4. The cavalry troop was en route to the border in October. Battery A went to El Paso.[16]

The 1st Separate Infantry Battalion (Colored), Major James A. Walker commanding, went to Naco in early July. It had the distinction of being the only black National Guard unit stationed on the border. And it "had a long and glorious history as one of the oldest black units in existence, tracing its roots back to the first colored troops mustered from the District in 1863. They were directly descended from the Washington Cadet Corps, which had been formed in 1867 by Civil War Medal of Honor recipient Christian A. Fleetwood."[17]

The battalion was federalized on June 27, 1916, and departed for Naco on July 4.[18] They probably wondered what they had done to end up in such a godforsaken place as Naco.[19] Nevertheless, they were good soldiers, as a regular inspector reported: "This is a colored battalion, and the officers and men seem very anxious to learn. The major seems to have good control of his officers and men. The battalion needs training and proper discipline and instruction to make it efficient. A good deal of time is wasted in learning Army papers and methods, which might be taught with good results at the home station."[20]

The battalion's camp was about a mile north of the international boundary. Their schedule of guard duty and drills was curtailed by inclement weather—the Southwest monsoon season. As the *Washington Post* reported, "Some of the new men from Washington used apparently to the skillful handling of pens, typewriters and other instruments of clerical occupations found it a novel task to dig tent trenches in the rain to keep the water from raiding their cots and sleeping quarters. Not a few sore hands and sorer backs were the portion of many such at Naco."[21] The troops' main complaint was their forced inactivity, for they yearned to fight in Mexico and emulate the black 10th U.S. Cavalry, which had been stationed in Naco for many months and which had distinguished itself in the Punitive Expedition. Instead they spent considerable time at the firing range, for "some of the enlisted men in the battalion are deficient in the use of rifles."[22]

Back in Washington, the emphasis was on recruiting. For the 1st Separate Infantry Battalion, 134 recruits left for Naco to bring the battalion up to a strength of 470, 74 men less than war strength. Field Artillery Battery B, at war strength and fully equipped except for its animals and sterilizing water bags, likewise entrained for the border.[23] As a final boost to the recruiting drive, August 12 was officially designated as "Recruiting Day," and immediately following inspection all guardsmen at Camp Ordway were released to go into the city and talk up recruiting at every opportunity.[24] The men of Battery A, which was nearing the required minimum strength, were still training at Camp Ordway, and they produced a new war song, to the tune of "Down Home in Tennessee:"

> I'm so happy
> Oh, so happy,
> Don't you envy me?
> I leave today at three,
> For sunny old Bisbee.
> Dad and mother, sis and brother
> Turn to say good-by—
> But that's what makes the soldiers cry.
> *Chorus*:
> But down in old Bisbee,
> Just try and picture me
> With Batteries A and B
> And Troop A, cavalry
> Oh, we'll be there to greet them,
> With a three-inch shell we'll meet them,
> When we get there, we'll have the pep there,
> And we'll set our border free.[25]

A particular point of pride for the District of Columbia National Guard was that an additional cavalry troop, Troop B, was recruited, and it was planned to recruit two more Troops in order to complete a squadron. Moreover, another field artillery battery was to be organized.[26]

After six uncomfortable days of train travel, the 1st Separate Battalion's recruits joined their comrades in Naco, where facilities had been improving. By mid-August the battalion's camp was equipped with incinerators and latrines; mess halls and screened kitchens were under construction. The battalion experienced considerable difficulty in erecting its quota of four mess halls and kitchens because lumber had to be hauled in from a distance and because the proper tools were scarce. Even so, the men's health had been remarkably good.[27] The monsoon remained a problem. On August 5, a terrific thunderstorm flooded the Naco camp, "and but for the ideal situation of the camp it might have been washed into Mexico."[28]

The 1st Separate Battalion was responsible for safeguarding the customs house and the local water supply, taking over these duties from a detachment of the 2nd U.S. Cavalry.[29] The tedium of camp life was unexpectedly broken on the night of August 19. About a mile west of Naco the troops reportedly exchanged about one hundred rounds with Mexicans trying to cross the international boundary, taking one prisoner. The firing turned out all the troops in Naco.[30] However, an army investigation determined that when two unarmed Mexican civilians crossed the line several sentries had ordered them to halt. The Mexicans got scared and ran. The sentries opened fire on them but in the confusion ended up shooting at each other. One was extremely lucky, for his hat had a couple of bullet holes in it. The two Mexicans were captured but were released after questioning. "It was simply a case of excited and scared sentinels who shot at each other, as no shots were fired from the Mexican side."[31] Another incident occurred when the Mexican consul at Douglas on October 12 asked Brigadier General Davis to investigate the shooting of a Mexican customs guard at Naco, Sonora. The guard was not expected to live. He made a sworn statement to the Mexican consul in Naco, Arizona, saying he had noticed an American soldier in uniform, heavily armed, riding about five hundred yards south of the international boundary, and had placed him under arrest. He turned to lead the way to the customs house so the American could be investigated, and they had ridden only a few feet when the American shot him in the back, then rode back across the international boundary. The Mexicans could not learn the soldier's identity or the organization to which he belonged.[32]

Toward the end of its tour in Naco, the 1st Separate Battalion participated in field maneuvers. The battalion departed from Naco on October 23, 1916, and was mustered out of federal service in Washington, D.C., a week later.[33] By March 9, 1917, all District of Columbia units except the 3rd Infantry had been mustered out of federal service.[34]

Besides having been the only black National Guard unit stationed on the border, the 1st Separate Battalion had another distinction. On March 25, 1917, the unit assembled in front of their armory at 1200 U Street, NW, and marched to the White House. They were the first guardsmen called into federal service for the impending war with the Central Powers. During the next several months the battalion guarded vital government installations in Washington, D.C.[35]

Chapter 19

Nogales

Nogales, Arizona, and Nogales, Sonora, were nestled in a valley ringed by hills extending roughly north and south across the imaginary international boundary running at approximately right angles. East and west of the towns occasional white monuments marked the international boundary, which ran down the middle of the street in Nogales, Arizona.[1] In fact a German secret agent, Richard W. Schwierz, escaped from the deputy U.S. marshal guarding him in Nogales, Arizona, by the simple expedient of dashing across the street into Nogales, Sonora.

The U.S. Army thus had a serious tactical problem, standing virtually eyeball to eyeball with the Mexicans. The army had established a camp in Nogales on November 26, 1910, its first garrison being a detachment of Company B, 18th U.S. Infantry. By the time of the war crisis, the camp was named Camp Stephen B. Little, named for a private in the 12th U.S. Infantry who was killed on November 26, 1915, by a Mexican sniper while on guard duty.[2] In June 1916, the camp held some 1,500 regulars. The Mexicans evacuated the town of Nogales, Sonora, but a large force of Carranza troops massed some ten miles below the border.[3]

The city fathers of Nogales, Arizona, bombarded General Funston, the secretary of state, and various politicians with demands for more military protection because of reports that large Mexican contingents were massing near Nogales, Sonora. An unstated consideration was that the current monthly military payroll in Nogales was $32,000, and more troops meant more prosperity.[4] When the clash at Carrizal intensified the war crisis and resulted in the arrival of reinforcements—the 3rd Battalion, 1st Arizona Infantry, half of Arizona Field Hospital Company No. 1, and a battalion of the 14th U.S. Infantry—bringing the garrison to more than two thousand men, the mayor of Nogales petitioned President Wilson for martial law to be declared and asked for still more troops.[5] Not to be outdone, the mayor of Tucson led a delegation by special train to San Antonio to appeal directly to General Funston to station troops in Tucson, which he claimed was vulnerable to raids by Mexican bandits.

Detachments of the Arizona National Guard began patrolling the international boundary at Nogales on June 26. The 3rd battalion was in bivouac in pup tents at Camp Stephen B. Little behind a low hill and some 1,400 yards from the trenches of the Mexican troops in Nogales, Sonora. Despite the heat, the troops were reportedly delighted over their change from Douglas to Nogales.[6] Even though the Mexicans had largely evacuated Nogales, Sonora, American soldiers were kept on their toes by the occasional exchanges of fire along the international boundary. They must have envied the troops in Texas, who at least had the Rio Grande between themselves and the Mexicans.

On one occasion Colonel W. H. Sage, commanding at Nogales, Arizona, had to intercept a heavily armed filibustering expedition of eighteen Americans about to cross the border at Sasabe, seventy-five miles west of Nogales, to retrieve an automobile seized by the Mexican authorities. Given the tense atmosphere along the border, this was the last thing Sage needed. The citizens of Nogales considered themselves fortunate to have a cool-headed officer such as Colonel Sage stationed there.[7]

After being rushed to Nogales, the 3rd battalion of the 1st Arizona Infantry was redeployed, but discipline remained a problem. Companies I and K were ordered to Ajo, a hamlet in the desert between Nogales and Yuma. The captain commanding Company I refused to go, saying he would resign first. "His orders were changed to Casa Grande, which station seemed satisfactory as he reconsidered his tender of resignation. The other companies while not being particularly pleased with their different destinations obeyed orders and without the threat of resigning."[8] On July 3, Company I left by rail for Casa Grande, a farming community between Tucson and Phoenix. Company M went to Roosevelt Dam. Companies L and K entrained for Ajo. Their train stopped over in Tucson, where the local Red Cross chapter served them refreshments at the station and a crowd of friends and relatives saw them on their way.[9]

Despite all the alarms and excursions, the Mexican menace proved to be considerably overblown. A mob ransacked the American consulate in Nogales, Sonora. And an eight-man American outpost a mile west of Nogales fired about twenty rounds at a group of advancing Mexicans on the night of June 26. As American reinforcements raced to the scene, the Mexicans retreated back across the border. Another brief exchange of gunfire occurred on July 2.[10] To prevent such minor clashes from escalating into a general engagement, Colonel Sage met with his Mexican counterpart, General Norzagaray, and they sensibly agreed "that in this district there will be no battle until the word has been received from Washington and Mexico City, respectively."[11] (The wisdom of this arrangement was underscored when on August 27, 1918, there occurred a pitched battle between American and Mexican troops across the international boundary at Nogales.)[12] In July 1916, though, Mexican soldiers were too busy looting Nogales, Sonora, to pose an immediate threat to Nogales, Arizona. And in a larger sense, the Mexican Army in Sonora had its hands full trying to crush prolonged and bloody resistance on the part of the formidable Yaqui Indians, who had been wreaking havoc in Sonora for decades. General Plutarco Elías Calles, the commander in Sonora (and future president of Mexico), finally had to take personal charge of the counterinsurgency campaign, which seemed interminable. In September, Nogales, Sonora, was thrown into a panic by rumors that Yaquis were about to attack. They did not, although they raided several ranches close to Nogales. Besides the Yaquis, Calles had to worry about famine conditions and an epidemic of smallpox.[13]

It was bombastic Mexican propaganda rather than major raids that predominated in this section of the border, as exemplified by the following passage from a translated circular distributed from Hermosillo, the capital of Sonora: "No fighting will be necessary. Our brave troops will simply march northward, brushing the gringos aside until our glorious tri-color floats from the dome of the capitol at Washington. It will be a battle between the Mexican eagle and the American eagle, and we will strip the arrows from the latter's claws and use them to scratch the stars and stripes from the gringos' banner."[14]

The arrival of substantial National Guard units quickly increased the military presence in Nogales to more than eleven thousand soldiers. Work accelerated on preparations for the incoming units. Colonel Willard

Newhill arrived to establish a quartermaster depot to supply these troops. And at a cost of more than $25,000, the five-hundred-bed Base Hospital No. 5 was built, being completed in October.[15]

The National Guard camps were never given official names, post returns being included with those of the regulars at Camp Stephen D. Little. The National Guard never occupied any part of Stephen D. Little although some of their camps adjoined it.[16]

Utah provided the first out-of-state contingent, some eight hundred men in Battery A, Field Artillery, 1st and 2nd Squadrons 1st Cavalry, and Field Hospital Company No. 1. Utah adjutant general Edgar A. Wedgwood kept the state's troops at Fort Douglas, the mobilization point, until they were substantially uniformed and equipped (except for horses), physically examined, and mustered into federal service. The June 18 call-up required Utah to provide one field artillery battery, one cavalry squadron, and two troops of cavalry. After Carrizal, a second call-up required two squadrons of cavalry, a field artillery battery, and a hospital company. It should be noted that the Bureau of Militia Affairs had ordered Utah to change its five infantry companies to cavalry, a change that had been made quite recently, on May 10, 1916. These soldiers now formed part of the 2nd Utah Cavalry Squadron, which not surprisingly lacked experience.[17]

At Fort Douglas patriotism and morale were high as mobilization got under way. Some guardsmen reported for duty from places as far away as California, Gary, Indiana, Philadelphia, and Pittsburgh. And some recruits came from an unlikely place—the neighboring state of Nevada. Nevada was the only state in the Union that had no National Guard, having abolished it in 1906 for lack of funding. Now Nevada urgently set out to create one. Governor Emmet D. Boyle planned to organize a force of six hundred men.[18] In the meantime, former members of the Nevada National Guard set out in small groups, traveling mainly in freight trains, to reach Salt Lake City and enlist in the Utah National Guard. Ex-captain John R. Curry, leading the first group, stated that the entire organization was making its way on trains from Reno.[19]

As the Utah mobilization proceeded, the men underwent physical examinations. Given the rigorous federal medical standards, some 25 to 27 percent of the men were rejected for physical infirmities. The artillery battery moved its fieldpieces from the basement of the capitol, where they had been stored as per War Department directives, to the state fairgrounds for training purposes.

In sharp contrast to, say, the governor of Arizona, the governor of Utah enthusiastically supported the National Guard and called on the state's mayors to promote a recruiting campaign. The business community as a whole also supported the mobilization, promising to keep the men's jobs open until they returned from the border. Moreover, some businessmen and the governor's staff raised $10,000 for the guardsmen. They provided three trucks (one per cavalry squadron and one for the field hospital), five motorcycles (two per squadron and one for the field hospital), as well as more prosaic but essential supplies such as wire screening for mess halls and other buildings.

At an estimated cost to the federal government of $500,000, the Utah National Guard went to the border by rail. Battery A left on June 28, the 1st Squadron on July 7, and the 2nd Squadron and Field Hospital Company No. 1 on July 14. The troops departed from Salt Lake City in high spirits, some of them lustily singing songs such as "We Don't Know Where We're Going but We're on our Way."[20]

Where they were going was to Nogales, Arizona. The 148-man Battery A of the Field Artillery arrived on June 29 and claimed to be the first National Guard unit to arrive for border duty. The battery went into camp several hundred yards north of Nogales on a rocky knoll from which its guns commanded Nogales, Sonora. The artillerymen were overjoyed when they received their mounts and the horses for their guns on July 9, although many of the animals were straight off the range and had to be broken in. The artillerymen, like guardsmen elsewhere, undertook this unpleasant and often hazardous task. (A private kicked by a mule died on August 18 of a fractured skull.)[21] Then by July 24, which was Pioneer Day, a legal holiday in Utah, the battery could celebrate in style, for the rest of their uniforms had finally arrived.[22] The 1st and 2nd Squadrons of the 1st Utah Cavalry reached Nogales on June 10 and 16 and encamped on hills overlooking the Santa Cruz River, from where they could protect the town reservoir and the water system. Since they had no horses, the cavalrymen were assigned to outpost duty and to guard installations, ammunition stores, and railroad warehouses.[23] The army was unable to provide the 2nd Squadron with horses until the first week in September. The men philosophically took the attitude "better late than never" and appreciated the eight hundred horses they finally received.[24] Utah Field Hospital Company No. 1 set up shop north of the hills behind Nogales.

The Utah troops were pretty much all business. They spent considerable time improving their camps, clearing away cactus and bushes, digging trenches around their tents to drain off rainwater, installing piping for drinking water and shower baths, and building wooden mess halls and kitchens. Because of an emphasis on hygiene, including screened windows in the mess halls and kitchens, there were no cases of typhoid. The Utah guardsmen did not really enter into the social life of Nogales, their contacts being mainly with business and commercial elements. Discipline was strict, but there were cases of desertion, carrying weapons into Nogales, public intoxication, and crossing the international boundary.[25] And sometimes soldiers got into fistfights with Hispanic inhabitants of Nogales. There were relatively few complaints about camp life, but the men did protest that local businessmen took advantage of the situation to charge exorbitant prices for luxuries. The troops also complained that Arizona boasted almost every kind of "lizard, centipede, tarantula, spiders, and creeping and crawling and flying bugs of every conceivable size, shape, and color."[26] To boost morale, athletics was emphasized, with contests every Saturday night. Not only did troops benefit physically, but they were removed from the myriad temptations available in Nogales.[27]

As happened to other National Guard contingents, when the threat of war with Mexico diminished, the troops from Utah wanted to go home. By August, the adjutant general stated that only six out of the twenty-eight counties in the state had supplied men for the National Guard. Utah's authorized strength was 1,146, but currently there were only 775 guardsmen. To make matters worse, few recruits appeared, and many men with dependents were being discharged.[28]

Encamped to the south of the Utah units was the California National Guard brigade, Brigadier General Robert Wankowski commanding, consisting of the 2nd, 5th, and 7th Infantry, 1st Battalion of the Field Artillery, 1st Squadron of the Cavalry, Company A of the Signal Corps, Field Hospital Company No. 1, and Ambulance Company No. 1. The 4,600 Californians had mobilized on the state fair grounds at Sacramento, at Camp Hiram Johnson, named in honor of the governor. They had done so with exemplary speed; within twelve hours after receipt of the governor's orders to assemble at their armories immediately, all unit commanders reported their organizations prepared to entrain.[29] However, at the Oakland recruiting station, one in six applicants was rejected, mainly for less than perfect eyesight. The requirement on teeth had been somewhat relaxed. Whereas those with faulty teeth of any nature had previously been rejected, now the only requirement was that a man have at least four good molars; army dentists would attend to the rest of the teeth.[30] Some men had enlisted for social reasons. A sergeant in the 2nd California's machine gun company recalled that when the unit was organized in November 1915, the meeting was held in the University Club in Sacramento adjoining a brewery. Plenty of beer was consumed, and "Captain McClatchy stressed the social aspects to be gained. With visions of military balls, parades, and other social events (patriotism was not mentioned), by the end of the evening forty men had signed up."[31] Nevertheless, the regular inspector-instructor for California commended the mobilization camp: "During the encampment the discipline was excellent. The absence of drunkenness was remarkable; both officers and men appeared to be earnest and willing to do all that was required of them."[32] It has been said that the California National Guard was able to proceed to the border reasonably well armed and accoutered largely due to the unrelenting work of Adjutant General Charles W. Thomas.

The guardsmen began to leave Sacramento on the evening of June 29, the cavalry squadron leading the way. On July 1, the 2nd Infantry and the 1st Battalion Field Artillery entrained. The *Sacramento Bee* described their departure: "Wives marched with husbands from the camp to the place of entrainment, mothers strode valiantly along side of their sons, fathers marched with their arms across their son's backs, and pretty girls in dainty summer gowns marched with their sweethearts. When the place of entrainment was reached the escort for the three local organizations far outnumbered the tactical units."[33] A guardsman reminisced that "the first day out brought realization that we were a part of the Regular Army. The noncoms were called together and given the Army manual. The rules called for no fraternization with enlisted men. This created a dilemma as we were all personal friends. Especially galling to the enlisted men was the rule that noncoms supervised but did not perform with the labor details."[34] The element of personal friendship underlined a major weakness in the entire National Guard—the practice of electing their officers and noncoms. Someone who was popular was not necessarily competent.

After 1,171-mile rail journey, the Californians arrived at Nogales between July 3 and 6. They did move to the border quickly, but they were hardly ready to take the field.[35] For instance, the 350-man cavalry squadron came without their mounts. (The army was unable to provide the unit with horses until the first week in September, toward the end of their tour of border duty.) The cavalrymen went into camp on Cemetery Hill adjoining the regular infantry camp.[36] On July 3, "brown Sibley tents sprouted like mushrooms around Nogales" as the 2nd Infantry got settled on Cemetery Hill alongside the cavalry and field artillery from that state, being complimented for the speed and thoroughness with which they pitched camp. The 5th California began arriving on July 5, and the 7th California and Field Hospital No. 1 shortly thereafter. Not until October 17 did Ambulance Company No. 1 arrive in Nogales, but it came at war strength (the only California unit to do so), and it did not lose a man because of physical disability.[37]

Freight trains loaded with supplies from various arsenals rolled into Nogales beginning on July 4. A guardsman detailed to unload supplies recalled, "The arsenals were as unprepared as the rest of us. They sent everything they had in stock, even a couple of coastal defense guns. One of the first cars opened contained a shipment of coffins. This did nothing for morale."[38] There was also a problem with munitions. Initially the 2nd California received only enough pistol ammunition for elementary practice. The infantry companies received only ammunition for guard duty. As for the regiment's machine gun company, it was still without machine guns. The army claimed there were not enough machine guns or instructors, besides which machine guns were too delicate to be issued to inexperienced troops. The Californians resorted to their most effective weapon—political pressure:

> A Washington dispatch dated August 15th announced that Secretary of War Baker had assured Congressman C. F. Curry that a machine gun would be sent to Captain McClatchy's company. On the same date a dispatch from Nogales carried the story that the company had been provided with its full complement of guns, horses, and mules. We received the horses and mules, but no one remembers more than one gun. It was a Lewis water-cooled model.[39]

And as happened throughout the mobilization, the men were unfamiliar with horses and mules. The wild mules especially caused problems.

During July, a number of Californians were relieved from active duty and sent home, mainly because they were men with dependent families. Many of them were NCOs, and it became necessary to establish schools to train privates to take over their duties. Of those discharged, a surprisingly large number, 626, had disabilities ranging from defective vision and flat feet to acute gonorrhea. Forty-four California cavalrymen were rejected and sent home, including the popular major commanding the squadron, to the great distress of his men.[40] The California attorney general later held that it was proper for the state to pay transportation of California guardsmen from Nogales to their home stations. The California brigade suffered its first fatality when Private George K. Shiflett, 2nd Infantry, was run over by a Southern Pacific train.[41] Some of the California cavalrymen, incidentally, caused a minor flap by wandering across the Mexican border in an attempt to locate it.[42]

Living in tents, the guardsmen were extremely vulnerable when it came to thunderstorms during the summer "monsoon" season. During a storm on the night of July 17, a lightning bolt hit a tent of the California artillery, injuring eight men, four of them severely. A week later, a sergeant was badly hurt by lightning during another storm. And on July 26, the heaviest rainstorm of the year completely wrecked the National Guard camps. The storm destroyed the headquarters of the California brigade, washing away both the tents and their contents. The new YMCA tent was flattened. Two men were slightly injured when struck by lightning.[43] For the newcomers, lightning strikes took considerable getting used to.

Among the newcomers were the men from Connecticut, who had mobilized at Camp Holcomb at Niantic and who made a sizeable contribution to the National Guard presence: the 1st and 2nd Infantry, Field Hospital No. 1, Company A of the Signal Corps, and Troops A and B of the 5th Cavalry.

At the Yale graduation, seniors who were guardsmen had received the place of honor, leading the procession. They marched in uniform, something not seen since the Civil War. Some five hundred Yale undergraduates manned a battalion (four batteries) of the 10th Connecticut Field Artillery. Many of the college's best-known athletes were members, as was Professor Hiram Bingham, the prominent explorer and author. About 130 men were needed to bring the Yale batteries up to war strength, and an appeal was launched aimed at alumni and undergraduates. Not enough responded, and with one hundred men still needed the batteries were prepared to enlist "any specially qualified men," not necessarily Yaleies.[44] The Yale batteries lacked essential support personnel such as farriers and cooks, who preferred more lucrative civilian employment and refused to join the militia. Wealthy alumni in New York City raised a fund to hire them for the Yale units.

In July, the Connecticut Field Artillery was ordered to proceed to the artillery camp at Tobyhanna, Pennsylvania, for training. In Battery F, for instance, the men were in poor physical condition and poorly trained, whereas Battery B, a Yale unit, was considered a crack outfit. But on July 21, the War

Department announced that student organizations would be mustered out as soon as possible after September 1, and as soon as they were mustered out federal recognition would be withdrawn. On September 6, the War Department ordered the discharge of college units, and this included Batteries A, B, C, and D, (the Yale battalion) of the 10th Connecticut.[45]

One of the Connecticut cavalrymen recalled that his unit's journey to Nogales had begun in "three day coaches of the architecture of about 1876, flat wheeled and lopsided but cars nevertheless." Despite some guardsmen writing home complaining of inadequate rations on the trip, the Connecticut contingent was in high spirits when two trainloads of them rolled through El Paso. The Harvard and Yale men among them enlivened the railroad depot (and amused the bystanders) with their school cheers.[46] After a grueling train ride in day coaches, the Connecticut troops settled into their designated camp on Cemetery Hill in Nogales.

The chamber of commerce in Hartford, Connecticut, launched a drive to purchase Colt machine guns for the 1st Connecticut Infantry and the signal company, but the War Department advised against it and the project was abandoned.[47]

Troop A, Cavalry, left for the border on June 29 and had a particularly uncomfortable trip that lasted for nine days. At Nogales the unit established their camp atop a hill. Many of the men had no prior military experience; they also experienced considerable difficulty adjusting to the desert climate, and numerous discharges were granted for medical reasons. The troopers "learned to ride, shoot, mount guard and do kitchen police according to the steel-bound regulations of the army. They learned something of the value and meaning of discipline, learned how to care for themselves and their horses, and for the first time, as soldiers, carried loaded ammunition in their belts when they walked guard in the streets of the little border town, always in sight of the squalid, sneaky-looking Mexican sentries just across that narrow strip of neutral territory on the boundary line."[48] Troop A spent a month on border patrol, relieving a troop of regular cavalry near Lochiel, twenty-eight miles east of Nogales.

Troop B of the Connecticut cavalry, from Hartford, was only three years old but included many of the wealthiest young men of that city, being referred to by the rest of the men as the "millionaire troop." Described as a "posh outfit," each man owned his own horse, and for a time they constituted the only mounted cavalry unit in Nogales.[49] They settled in quite comfortably on the slopes of Cemetery Hill, on a small mesa, purchased a phonograph and ordered a piano from Los Angeles. Their quality of life declined appreciably when in August they were assigned to outpost duty at the dusty hamlet of Arivaca, some thirty miles west of Nogales. "We spent almost nine weeks at Arivaca encamped within the confines of a barbed wire enclosure, flanked by adobe walled store, adobe church, and adobe residences occupied by both men and chickens and cattle."[50]

As for those soldiers in the 1st Connecticut who were not lucky enough to be wealthy, a very welcome gift came in the form of "smoked and colored glasses" that a friend sent to their colonel for distribution to the troops. The glare from the Southwest sunlight was brutal, as was the searing heat. But to avoid heat prostration, the troops could always purchase "Horsford's Acid Phosphate—Excellent for the relief of exhaustion due to heat or change of climate. A teaspoonful in a glass of water makes a cooling, refreshing and invigorating beverage," according to its advertisement.[51]

Like the rest of the guardsmen, those from Connecticut lived in tents and were vulnerable to thunderstorms. As one recalled,

> The second day after our arrival, however, the rainy season began. . . . In less than an hour a deluge of rain fell which we will never forget. Luckily we were in our tents. The floods poured down from the mountain side. A veritable river of water ran through the top sergeant's tent and very nearly carried off the troop reports. Lightning cracking over our heads, struck one of the tent poles just east of our company street and sent three Idaho troopers to the hospital. In a few minutes the arroyos and river beds were filled with roaring torrents. The rainy season had begun. Within a week those hills which had looked so arid and brown at our arrival were green with abundant grass.[52]

A private nearly died from a lightning strike during the July 26 storm that devastated the National Guard camps.[53]

Besides the storms, there were the critters: "On account of being outflanked and outfought on every side by the rain gods, the First and Second Connecticut regiments decided to beat it—to higher ground, so in the near future they will be located on the sloping ground back of where the Twenty-first Infantry is camped. The boys said that they believed they could face a swarm of Mexican bullets, but when it came to facing a swarm of centipedes and poison spiders, which came with the waves rushing down the canyon—good night."[54]

The soldiers from Connecticut went through a weeding-out process. When the five hundred men rejected for physical disabilities were sent home in early August, they at least got to travel in two special trains of Pullmans. The Nogales chamber of commerce gave them stickers advertising Nogales to put on their suitcases and handed out 2,500 pesos—in worthless Pancho Villa fiat money.[55] Two sleepers with Connecticut soldiers discharged for dependent families or because their enlistments had expired left on August 11.[56] A few of these rejected soldiers bitterly denounced in hometown newspapers their experience in Nogales.[57] Many bandsmen of the two regiments were among those rejected. But these losses were being made up by the arrival on July 17 of two trains with 800 recruits fresh from Connecticut, where a campaign was under way to secure 1,250 recruits. In addition, two carloads of overcoats arrived.[58] A touch of home for the men from Connecticut was the appearance of a brief Camp Holcomb edition of the *Hartford Courant*, which was wired daily to the *Nogales Daily Herald*.[59]

Company B, Pennsylvania Engineers, arrived on July 19 from El Paso where the Pennsylvania division was stationed. The Pennsylvania Engineers were somewhat atypical in that they got along well with the regulars. When the 1st and 2nd Battalions of the 21st U.S. Infantry were transferred from Nogales to Yuma, the night before the 1st Battalion's departure the Pennsylvanians entertained them with a farewell smoker as a gesture of camaraderie.[60] The influx of guard units meant that the military presence in Nogales mushroomed to ten thousand men within a week.[61] And still they kept coming.

Even before the great call-up, Idaho had begun preparing. The state's adjutant general, Brigadier General Philip H. Crow, estimated that the 2nd Idaho Infantry could be mobilized within three days.[62] The regiment, commanded by Colonel William H. Edelblute, consisted of twelve infantry companies, a machine gun company, a supply company, and a hospital detachment.[63] On June 30, despite recruitment being hampered by civilian requests to form volunteer units, the regiment reached its required strength under the Dick Act, with 57 officers and 1,009 enlisted men. A problem developed, though, involving Adjutant General Crow. Since regulations prohibited adjutants general from federal service, he resigned his position in order to join the regiment. Governor M. Alexander announced Crow's commissioning as a lieutenant colonel in the 2nd Idaho. But by commissioning Crow, the governor allegedly violated Idaho's Militia Act, which provided that the senior major would be promoted to lieutenant colonel. Three disgruntled majors prevailed on the state attorney general to block Captain Max Garber, the federal mustering officer, from swearing Crow in. The governor, in his capacity as commander in chief of the Idaho National Guard, appealed to the secretary of war and to General Funston. Captain Garber immediately received orders to commission Crow and to use force if necessary.[64] Crow was commissioned as a lieutenant colonel on June 30.

By July 5 the regiment was fully mustered at Boise Barracks and "had a complete equipment for a war-strength regiment with the exception of animals and small arms ammunition, and bears the distinction of being the first regiment in the National Guard of the United States to have every officer and man belonging to it sworn in under the new oath required by the National Defense Act."[65] The next day General Funston telegraphed "reiterating the need to rush the soldiers to the border. Funston ordered Colonel Edelblute and Captain Garber to keep the destination and departure times secret because of a growing fear over the presence of Mexican spies." However, the press accurately predicted the regiment's destination and approximate hour of departure. The unit departed on July 7 in three trains via Salt Lake City, Las Vegas, and San Bernardino.[66]

After four days of hot and uncomfortable travel it arrived in Nogales on July 11 and encamped on the ridge behind the town cemetery. Although situated on high ground, the Idaho encampment was still exposed to storms, such as the one on July 26 that literally leveled the headquarters tents. Still, it was perhaps the best location of all the National Guard camps, and the troops went to great lengths to make it attractive, gathering up all the loose rocks and lining the walks with them, planting cactus and other ornamental plants in front of the tents and so forth. A nagging problem was the clouds of flies, which the men were convinced came from Nogales, Sonora, where sanitary conditions were primitive. A number of the men contracted dysentery but evidently developed immunity over time.[67]

The Idaho troops went through the same kind of routine as did other National Guard contingents: a rigorous schedule of drills and inspections, followed by route marches and then patrolling and manning outposts along the border.[68] What was presumably a welcome change of pace occurred when the units hiked to the milder climate of Fort Huachuca for a stint of target practice.

The National Guard contingents transformed their rocky hillside encampments into something more attractive. The improvements included leveling all available areas, laying out company streets, and lining them with excavated rocks.[69] Yet the terrain constricted large-scale movements. The 7th California Infantry, for instance, for lack of space could hold dress parade only by battalions. But in August, the California regiments were relocated to a site farther out on the road to Tucson, providing room for the entire California brigade to camp together.[70]

On the matter of machine guns, the army reported that "all the infantry regiments here, except the Idaho and Second California Regiments, have guns and are being assisted in the instruction of their personnel by the machine gun company of the Twelfth United States Infantry."[71]

An important improvement for the health of the National Guard was the screening of kitchens and mess halls, which contributed to the exceptionally low death rate among guardsmen on the border: for the week ending August 17, exactly 8 soldiers died of sickness among the 140,000 regulars and guardsmen on the border and in the Punitive Expedition.[72] Not only were all the soldiers inoculated against typhoid fever, but to avoid an epidemic the U.S. Public Health Service offered free inoculations to the citizens of Nogales.[73]

The men from California and Connecticut quickly got a taste of border service. On the night of July 6, a Connecticut infantry company relieved a California infantry company assigned to guard duty on the international boundary in downtown Nogales. They took up positions just to the rear of regulars from the 21st U.S. Infantry, who were stretched along the boundary on either side of the Southern Pacific depot. A shot rang out, and everyone went on high alert. The round apparently came from the Mexican side, but the Mexicans stoutly denied this. In any event, "The results of the shot amounted to practically nothing, excepting giving a thrill to some of the Yankee boys who were somewhat unused to being the object of pot shots like this. Anyhow it will give the boys from Company K something to talk about when they reach their homes after their work here is completed."[74] As it happened, their immediate work consisted in restoring their camp, which a storm battered the next day. These furious summer thunderstorms were another, and most unpleasant, aspect of border service.[75]

On July 17, a sentry from the 11th U.S. Infantry shot and mortally wounded a Mexican, who with a companion was headed for the international boundary carrying a rifle and who refused to halt when challenged. The sentry said he emptied his rifle at the Mexicans when they were on the American side of the line and saw both fall. He reported to his commanding officer that he had killed them. His orders were to stop any armed Mexicans he saw on this side of the line. The Mexican authorities claimed the man was unarmed and had been shot on the Mexican side of the border. General Calles sent President Carranza a telegram with an account of the incident. The Mexican ambassador also delivered a formal protest to the Department of State. However, after a thorough investigation, the army exonerated the private. The army's policy remained that no person would be permitted to cross the border except at immigration stations, and sentries had orders to shoot anyone within U.S. territory who failed to halt when commanded to do so.[76]

American sentries had hair-trigger reactions. An outpost near Nogales spotted movement in the night of July 20 and opened fire when their challenge was ignored; a burro died, riddled with bullets. Curiously, though, Mexican soldiers rushed into Nogales, Sonora, and informed their commander that they had been fired upon.[77] On the night of August 3, a Mexican sniper on the Mexican bank of the Santa Cruz River took a pot shot at a 12th U.S. Infantry sentry in Nogales, Arizona, itself, the bullet shattering the ankle of the sentry, who returned fire. A patrol of Company C, 5th California, nearby returned the sniper's fire. Both Mexican and American troops were rushed to the scene of trouble and a battle seemed imminent, but fortunately nothing happened. After the incident, Company C, 5th California, was assigned to reinforce the regulars guarding the boundary.[78]

On the night of August 8, an outpost of the 1st Connecticut spotted Mexicans slipping down a hill to attack the outpost—two men were out in front and six or eight squads were a little way behind them; all were dressed in white. One soldier ran back to camp for reinforcements. The 1st Connecticut immediately stood to arms, and one battalion was ordered to support the outpost. But before sending the reinforcements out, the battalion commander dispatched an officer to survey the scene personally. He returned and reported that he had seen nobody. The local newspaper dryly commented that "the outposts still maintain that they saw the Mexicans, but those acquainted with the surrounding hills know that a herd of Angora goats roam around that neck o' the woods."[79]

Occasional bullets from Mexico kept the troops alert. On October 1:

> Captain Wilson of the 2nd Idaho Infantry medical corps was shot in the left leg just above the knee this afternoon while standing in front of the Southern Pacific station checking his baggage to return to his home in Idaho. The bullet is believed to have come from the Mexican side of the line, and a Carranza soldier is said to have been seen to run following the shooting. Captain Wilson's condition is not serious. He is in the hospital here. Witnesses of the shooting declare it was intentional and deliberate, but the Mexican version of the affair is that a prisoner escaped from his guard and dashed across the line near the depot. The guard fired and the shot struck Wilson. The police confirm this portion of the story, saying they have in custody an escaped Mexican prisoner with a bullet hole through his clothing. It is reported tonight that the Mexican guard was executed . . . this afternoon. The shooting of Captain Wilson occurred at 1:30 this afternoon.[80]

The shooting, according to the *San Antonio Express,* produced rioting between Mexican civilians and U.S. troops: "The danger of an open clash between United States and Mexicans was so great tonight that the street dividing the two towns is filled with armed patrols."[81] Fortunately, the disturbances died down without further bloodshed. The captain recovered by October 19 and was able to leave for home.[82]

Such incidents could have escalated but for the continued good sense of the American and Mexican commanders. On July 21, Brigadier General Edward H. Plummer, who had commanded the National Guard troops at Llano Grande, replaced Colonel Sage as commander in Nogales, Plummer's rank reflecting the increased importance of Nogales, which now held almost three brigades of infantry. The local newspaper urged that Nogales make a concerted effort to be designated as a permanent army post—hopefully a division post.[83] One of Plummer's first actions was to confer with his Mexican counterpart, General Calles. They agreed to do everything possible to avoid friction between their respective commands.[84]

Besides monitoring the Mexican Army, Plummer had a challenge in maintaining discipline among his own troops.[85] Discipline in some National

Guard units could on occasion be harsh: even before the Alabama contingent arrived in Nogales and were still in their mobilization camp, a certain Private Goldberg of the 2nd Alabama alleged that he "had been tied down and gagged for five hours . . . following his refusal to do work assigned to him. Goldberg, it is alleged by officers at the camp, became abusive when ordered to work with other prisoners and made insulting remarks about the President, the United States flag, and every officer in the Alabama brigade."[86]

Most discipline was not enforced that brutally. The guardsmen, after all, were essentially civilians in uniform, and a number of them were put on report because they were walking around in the blistering heat with the top button of their shirts left open, contrary to regulations.[87] But some soldiers just refused to abide by the regulations. The newspaper reported that: "'Over the hill' is a game that is growing in popularity rapidly in the soldier camps. 'Over the hill' is soldier slang for desertion. There were sixteen who 'crossed the mound' from Nogales last night [Aug 18], according to military reports, and they represented pretty nearly every organization. There has been a good deal of complaint from soldiers that they are not getting action on their applications for discharge under the married men's ruling." Two deserters even hired a car to take them to Tucson. On the way they assaulted the driver and stole the car.[88]

The *Nogales Daily Herald* observed that: "For some time past, many soldiers have been in the habit of crossing the Mexican border at night to have a good time, as they term it, but others used that pretext to gain possession of cocaine or 'dope' as it is usually called, bringing it across to sell to other soldiers, thereby making a considerable profit out of the embargoed traffic. Now—returnees will be held up and searched, because of the rapid increase in illegal importation. If a soldier gets arrested by civilian authorities, he will be tried for disobeying the War Department order forbidding soldiers from crossing into Mexico." The penalty was six months incarceration and probably a dishonorable discharge.[89] Yet some soldiers were quite willing to take the risk. On the night of December 3, a dozen regulars of the 12th Infantry crossed into Nogales, Sonora, for a good time. Mexican authorities apprehended four of them and delivered the unlucky miscreants to the U.S. military, who clapped them in the guardhouse and began court-martial proceedings.[90]

Although decrying all the illegal activity, the newspaper did appreciate the efforts of the authorities:

A GOOD WORD FOR THE OFFICERS—The pen of many an editor has been too ready to adversely criticize those who are responsible for the conduct of the National Guardsmen and Regular soldiers, and too little comment has been made on the mandates of the officials, which have been for the good.

Orders have recently been issued which put the men under a great deal more restraint in the matter of personal pleasures. Some, who have derived benefit from the vices of the service men are grumbling, but rules which make them more temperate are for the real good of Nogales, as well as those enlisted.

Certain diseases which outgrew from illicit relations with women of the low character threatened to materially handicap military operations, but the officials have taken matters in charge and by strict enforcement of certain regulations, have reduced this menace. Many young men who are here at the call of Uncle Sam do not seem to realize the importance of a clean life, whether in the army or citizenry, but in after years, they will surely look back with thanksgiving to the commandants who insisted that dissipations be at a minimum.

Elsewhere the regulations may not be so rigidly enforced as at Nogales, but is to the credit of the authorities here that they are "on the job."[91]

But drug trafficking remained a serious problem, a problem that according to the local newspaper, arose when the troops came to town. The authorities reiterated that they were determined to get rid of "dope fiends."[92] But the "dope fiends" remained. In November the police broke up a smuggling ring and seized sixty cans of opium.[93]

There was also the problem of liquor, something by no means unique to Nogales. In mid-October, Secretary of War Newton Baker put the fear of God into the city fathers of border towns by announcing that unless the illegal sale of liquor was stopped, the troops would be withdrawn from those towns where the law was being violated. The Nogales police carried out a series of raids against bootleggers and illegal gambling and liquor establishments, arresting fifteen people.[94] Those favoring Prohibition quickly seized on Secretary Baker's threat to appeal to local self-interest, publishing an ad in the newspaper entitled: "Bootleggers or Troops?" and adopting the slogan "Swat the Bootleggers, vote for Prohibition."[95]

Sadly, police efforts were ineffective. The newspaper complained in December that "when we say that bootleggers are still doing a flourishing business in Nogales, and that houses of prostitution are being conducted with the law in abeyance, we are stating facts based on deductive reasoning. . . . Why?"[96] Furthermore, "Nogales is suffering from a wave of petty crime, the like of which has never before existed, and which threatens to be amplified as the days go on, unless something is done to stop it. There are countless robberies every week. We believe that the prevalence of this infernal bootlegged booze is a stimulating elixir of such crimes. We have, as one of our councilmen calls it, 'a million dollar police force with thirty-cent efficiency.' And what about county, special, and federal officers?"[97] In January 1917, the police raided two establishments selling illegal liquor.[98]

The vast majority of the troops engaged in more wholesome pursuits. A program of band concerts by the bands of regular and guard regiments expanded into a nightly affair as more and more guard units arrived. The concerts attracted a large and appreciative audience of civilians and soldiers. The local Roman Catholic priest likewise attracted impressive attendance whenever he said Mass at the National Guard encampments. Jewish soldiers, who were all excused from duty, and civilians met at the Masonic Hall to conduct Yom Kippur services, which were observed in camps all along the border.[99] All officers, whether regular or guard, and their ladies were cordially invited to the dances at the country club. The YMCA built four structures to provide recreation for the troops. And since the army is a strong believer in athletics, baseball and football games and boxing matches between regulars and guardsmen occurred routinely. The guardsmen could certainly puff away while watching the games, for the American Tobacco Company not only paid the salaries of their California employees in the guard but presented to every guardsman in the United States a bag of Bull Durham smoking tobacco and a package of cigarette papers. Tobacco men enjoyed a good business in Nogales, for both soldiers and civilians consumed enormous quantities of Bull Durham and Sweet Caporals and Tuxedo cigarettes. The guardsmen could even show off a little, for a movie team arrived to film scenes of National Guard life.[100] All this attention on the guard, plus the steady stream of packages from home for the men understandably made the regulars quite resentful.[101]

Entrepreneurs were ready to enhance the soldiers' quality of life. In August, a modern "hot tamale" factory, equipped with machinery imported from Italy, began operations. The demand was so great that a citywide delivery system with regular routes was inaugurated. And a pie factory increased its production from fifteen to over three hundred pies daily. Most of the customers were soldiers, and the foodstuffs were sold at nearly all the camps.[102]

Regardless of the amenities, many guardsmen were not only bored but lonely during their tour at Nogales. One of them even placed a lonely hearts ad in the newspaper:

> WANTED—A Nogales or Mexican girl to become my wife. I am a man of good habits and am well-to-do. I live in the East and am willing to live here with my future wife or take her back East with me. I belong to the C. N. G. of Hartford, Conn, and am stationed here at this city. Please give name and address. Address Clyde D. Sinclair, Co. H, 1st Conn. Inft.[103]

One who had better luck was Hugh Angleton of the Idaho National Guard, who in civilian life was a traveling representative of the Idaho Canning Company. He wooed and won the hand of Miss Carmen Moreno, a lovely and popular young woman who had worked for the past few months in the Owl drug store and the Montezuma hotel. On December 10 they were married.[104] What made this particular marriage noteworthy was that eventually it would have an impact on the national security of the United States. To the Angletons was born a son, James Jesus Angleton, who became the legendary, and controversial, counterintelligence chief of the CIA.[105] In discussing James Jesus Angleton, one clueless writer stated that Angleton's colleagues were in such awe of him that they called him "Jesus." Of course Angleton's middle name—*Jesús*—reflected the Mexican part of his heritage.

The guardsmen at Nogales spent some six weeks practicing platoon and company drill, but by mid-August they were ready for something more ambitious. On August 17, Battery A, Utah Field Artillery, made a practice march to Tucson, where they set up camp at Southside Plaza, spent three days swimming in the YMCA pool and enjoying the local hospitality, and then marched to Fort Huachuca and back to Nogales, a distance of about 150 miles. And in October the battery was invited to demonstrate artillery maneuvers at the Arizona state fair in Tucson.[106] The 1st and 2nd Connecticut conducted route marches to Fort Huachuca for ten days of target practice, an exercise planned for all National Guard units during September.

The 1st Connecticut could have done better on the march—nearly fifty men fell by the wayside and had to be picked up by ambulances.[107] After its return to Nogales the 2nd Connecticut engaged in a simulated battle near their camp. During the engagement the signal company, mounted scouts, and field artillery participated in the exercise, which ended in a draw.[108] The 2nd and 7th California were next in the rotation to Fort Huachuca, where they spent some time on the firing range. They started back for Nogales on October 7. The troops bivouacked at midnight; another overnight stop was planned at the Santa Cruz River about ten miles from Nogales, but when the column reached the dry riverbed the men began to shout, "Let's go and continue on to Nogales." A hurried council of officers decided to bow to the soldiers' wishes. On reaching Nogales the 2nd California had no stragglers and the 7th had only a few. According to a participant, "We had broken all records for forced marches by militiamen on the border, covering 70 miles in 69 hours. General Plummer, commander of the Nogales District, notified General Funston of the remarkable march, paying the troops a high compliment."[109]

Following the Californians, the 2nd Idaho Infantry marched to Fort Huachuca for fifteen days of target practice. They made an impressive showing, earning the praise of the regular observers. The regiment made a leisurely march back to Nogales, taking six days for a trip in which no one fell out and the troops felt fit and confident. To test their mettle, as they approached Nogales, they were ordered to "attack" the town in a war game in which the defenders were the 2nd California and a Utah cavalry squadron. During the first day of the exercise Idaho was declared the winner, while the second day was about even, according to the regular army referees. General Plummer was pleased with the troops' performance and planned more of these war games for the National Guard units.[110] The next maneuver was not long in coming: the 2nd Idaho was ordered on September 8 to march some twenty miles down the Patagonia Road and make camp on the Santa Cruz River. From that position they were to prevent the approaching 1st Connecticut, returning from Fort Huachuca, from "capturing" Nogales.[111]

With training going well, General Plummer decided to form a provisional cavalry regiment, now that the army had finally supplied horses. Comprising the regiment were the two Utah squadrons and the one from California, with Colonel John M. Jenkins, a veteran of the Punitive Expedition, in command. The regiment was formed on October 5. The Californians, incidentally, resented Utah's predominance and the tendency to call the outfit the "Utah Cavalry Regiment" or the "Mormon Rough Riders."[112] General Plummer held a review on September 23 of a provisional National Guard infantry brigade. Colonel Edelblute, of the 2nd Idaho commanded the brigade, composed of the 2nd Idaho and the 1st and 2nd Connecticut and their respective wagon trains. Colonel Sage, now commanding the 12th U.S. Infantry, was the reviewing officer. The troops passed in review before a large and admiring crowd of spectators, including a number of regular officers who were generally complimentary.[113]

In October, the provisional cavalry regiment made a practice march to Tucson, then to Fort Huachuca, where it conducted target practice, and back to Nogales, an exercise lasting twenty days. Not to be outdone, the California brigade, at this time composed of the 2nd and 7th California and Company B, Signal Corps, made their record march back from Fort Huachuca.[114]

During the National Guard's stay in Nogales a succession of personages arrived to inspect their state's troops. First was Adjutant General C. W. Thomas, Jr., of California, who arrived on August 8 and spent several days with the brigade.[115] On September 24, Governor Marcus H. Holcomb accompanied by Adjutant General Coles visited the Connecticut troops, keeping a promise he made to them at their mobilization camp at Niantic that he would visit them wherever they went. The officers of the 1st and 2nd Connecticut hosted a reception for the governor, at which the 12th Infantry band provided the music. And on October 24, Utah governor William Spry and his adjutant general, Brigadier General F. A. Wedgewood, arrived to inspect the Utah troops and make a courtesy call on General Plummer.[116]

By then most of the National Guard units had departed. First to go was the 5th California, which received urgent orders on August 30 to return to Sacramento for possible strike duty. The regiment left by rail on the night of September 1, its supply train following three days later.[117] Company B, Pennsylvania Engineers, returned to El Paso on September 16. The Connecticut brigade began leaving on October 4, when the 1st Infantry entrained for home. The Field Hospital Company, Signal Corps Company, Ambulance Company, and Troops A and B of the 5th Cavalry left on October 10 and 13, followed by the 2nd Infantry on October 18. The California Ambulance Company left on October 17, and the 2nd and 7th Infantry, the cavalry squadron, and the field hospital company were gone by October 26, as was the 1st Squadron of the 1st Utah Cavalry, which arrived in Salt Lake City on October 30 and paraded with their mascots, a burro and a fawn brought back from Nogales. Utah Battery A arrived in the state capital on December 16, and the field hospital on December 24.[118] The 2nd Squadron Utah Cavalry remained in Nogales until March, 1917, and was mustered out at Fort Douglas on March 8.[119] The only addition to the National Guard presence had been the arrival of Company A, California Engineers, on October 3.

The California National Guard had its troubles after returning to its home stations. Much of the trouble revolved around the requirement to take the federal oath.[120] Furthermore, the California adjutant general in January 1917 relieved twelve commanding officers for failing to submit quarterly reports. And 165 officers commissioned since the National Defense Act became effective had to pass an examination within a month or lose their commissions.[121]

The National Guard bonanza pumped impressive amounts of money into the Nogales economy. In September, salaries exceeded $250,000, while payments for rentals, supplies, and other things, were about $850,000, for a total of $1.1. million, much of it spent locally.[122] With this bonanza drying up, the business community was understandably apprehensive, although the newspaper stressed that the future of Nogales was assured: "So long as there is trouble in Mexico, a strong military force will be kept here, and business will be good. And, when peace again reigns over Mexico, Nogales as the 'key city to the west coast' will come into her own."[123] The businessmen's spirits improved markedly at the news that a second wave of guardsmen was heading their way, in the form of a brigade from Alabama.

The Alabama National Guard's stay in Nogales was relatively brief but was certainly memorable. A particular source of state pride was that of the southern states only Alabama had raised a regiment of cavalry. The state's National Guard numbered 2,612—210 officers and 2,402 enlisted men—but few of the companies or batteries had the required minimum peacetime strength of 65 men. Furthermore, "much of the Alabama National Guard's equipment was outdated, badly worn, and in disrepair."[124] Brigadier General Charles R. Bricken's command had been chafing in their mobilization camp at Vandiver Park in Montgomery since June 22, and the troops were anxious to leave the monotony of camp and go to the border.[125] By September 30, 182 officers and 3,194 enlisted men were training at the mobilization camp.[126] Enlivening the brigade's rail journey was the enthusiastic reception they received from their fellow citizens, especially in Tuscaloosa, as they passed through: pies, cakes, sandwiches, cigars, cigarettes, tobacco, and other luxuries. The Alabamans, noisy and full of enthusiasm, chalked the sides of their railroad cars with things such as "Montgomery Greys" [a famous militia unit], "Douglas or Bust," and announcements that they were going to Douglas "to scalp Mr. Villa." As the troop trains rolled through El Paso, dozens of the soldiers sat on car windows with their heads and feet outside. Moreover, some of them were convinced that they were headed straight for Mexico and that hostilities had thoughtfully been delayed until their arrival on the border.[127]

Most of the brigade went to Nogales—the 1st, 2nd, 4th Infantry, Company A of the Signal Corps, Field Hospital Company No. 1, and Ambulance Company No. 1 all rolled into town between October 22 and 29 and occupied the camp the Californians had vacated. (The 1st Alabama Cavalry went to San Antonio and later to El Paso, and Batteries A and C of the Field Artillery went to Douglas.)[128] The 4th Alabama had a proud heritage; it had been the "Old Fourth" one of the great regiments in the Army of Northern Virginia in the Civil War. One of its captains, Newman Smith, as a lieutenant colonel in World War II, would play an important role in strategic deception.[129] The Alabama officers had a distinction—each one was accompanied by a black servant.[130]

Nogales businessmen placed numerous large ads in the local newspaper welcoming the Alabamans, and the Alabamans soon made their presence felt.[131] The locals were charmed when the band of the 1st Alabama Infantry gave a concert, but two days later, on November 8, the *Nogales Daily Herald* headlined:

A SHOOTING OUTSIDE RESORT
Last night a miniature battle is reported to have taken place out near Bayze lake at the resort run by Margaret Fisher. It is said that a number of the Fourth Alabama boys had been to this place a few nights previous and had a row with the inmates. On leaving they threatened to return and shoot the place up. Last night about a half dozen well known cowboys were out for a good time and stopped at this place. A little later the Alabama boys led by a lieutenant appeared on the scene and knocked on the door. The woman who runs the place stepped out and asked what was wanted. She was answered by a gun being shoved against her person, at which she let out a scream. The

cowboys hearing the woman scream rushed to the door to see what was the matter, and immediately the soldiers began shooting, striking one of the men in the shoulder and another in the left leg. The boys began to return the fire and which lasted about five minutes. It is said that fully 50 shots were fired altogether, but only the two were hurt, neither of which is considered fatal. Only two of the cowboys were armed and it is not known how many of the soldiers had guns. The matter is deplored by all, as the participants among the local men are well known. The lieutenant it is reported will be court martialed, and is thought will lose his commission.[132]

A gunfight in a whorehouse certainly did get the locals' attention.

Some of the other Alabamans also used their weapons too readily. The local newspaper reported on December 26 that: "Serious charges are being prepared against Lt. Anderson, of the 2nd Alabama because of his conduct last night. It is said he used a weapon too promiscuously and disturbed the peace at the telephone office." And Private Rufus Patterson, of the 1st Alabama, was jailed for shooting at a black man while on guard duty. "'Fresh' talk from the negro, it is alleged, caused the guard to fire a shot." A local judge exonerated Patterson.[133] Then there was a case of desertion: Lieutenant Virgil T. Roach, 2nd Alabama Infantry, faced "serious charges" in Nogales, fled back to Alabama, was arrested, and was taken to Fort Leavenworth for court-martial.[134]

The Alabamans did their share of guard duty, such as protecting the pumping plant on the Santa Cruz River. They also went on practice marches and engaged in field exercises. In November, the 4th Alabama, in heavy marching order, went to Tucson and back, a total of 124 miles, hiking 18 miles the first day. The 2nd Alabama replicated the march to Tucson in December. The regular inspector-instructor, who accompanied the regiment, faulted the 2nd Alabama for a lack of organization and discipline.[135]

The Alabamans constituted the bulk of the guardsmen in Nogales because other units continued to depart for their home stations. Battery A of the Utah Field Artillery left on December 13, and Utah Field Hospital Company No. 1 departed on December 19. On December 20–21, the 1st Battalion, California Field Artillery, entrained for Los Angeles.

Governor Alexander had resisted appeals from his constituents to bring the boys of the 2nd Idaho home, thinking such a course seemed unpatriotic.

But an avalanche of letters finally persuaded him to telegraph General Funston on November 18 expressing his concern. On December 7, Funston designated the Idaho infantry as one of the units scheduled for early release. There developed, however, conflict between the Western Department and the Idahoans. The War Department designated Fort Douglas at Salt Lake City as the deactivation site because it "would provide ample and comfortable accommodations for the officers and men." The Fort Douglas barracks were winterized and prepared for a large number of men, but the Idahoans and their governor wanted the regiment to muster out in Idaho, at Boise Barracks, arguing that they could be made as comfortable as Fort Douglas. From the Western Department's point of view, the crucial consideration was the time—several weeks—the unit would have to stay in tents until it could formally be mustered out. On December 11, the Western Department informed Governor Alexander that "the Idaho regiment will be mustered out at Boise." The elated Idahoans paraded through the business district of Nogales and departed for Boise Barracks on December 19, arriving on December 23.[136] Unfortunately, illness in the regiment delayed their deactivation past the expected two weeks and many of the men suffered from rheumatism resulting from "exposure and lack of fuel"; four of them died of pneumonia. This led to recriminations and a legislative investigation, which concluded that all Idaho shared responsibility, including the National Guard.[137]

For those guardsmen still stationed in Nogales, several organizations tried to make Christmas a little cheerier. The Daughters of the Confederacy and the Daughters of the American Revolution back in Alabama sent money for the guardsmen to purchase Christmas treats. The Nogales YMCA had an extensive program of special events, while the Knights of Columbus held an open house with refreshments and entertainment.[138] Unfortunately, there occurred a strong storm on Christmas day, which of course dampened the festivities—except perhaps for the supply company of the 1st Alabama, which celebrated with an oyster supper at the Louisiana Restaurant. They consumed several thousand oysters and presented their commanding officer with "a handsome bathrobe and slippers."[139] The Nogales guardsmen probably needed a bit of cheering up, for there were indications that they might well be there for some time. The Southern Department began in November to spend over a million dollars to prepare winter quarters for the regulars and guardsmen on the border. All the tents would have wooden floors and partial wooden walls installed. These winterized tents would also boast wood stoves. In addition, barracks of rough lumber would be constructed.[140]

The Alabamans settled in for an indefinite stay. The 1st Alabama formed an Athletic Club and sponsored a smoker. The officers of the brigade presented a "Dixie Carnival" at the country club with costumes and everything; Miss Georgia Titcomb of Nogales was crowned queen. The *Nogales Daily Herald* began running a column entitled "News Notes from Mobile Alabama." And the enterprising manager of Nogales movie theaters recorded the Alabamans' activities in more than five thousand feet of film, to be exhibited in Alabama.[141]

The year 1917 opened with an inspection visit by General Frederick Funston. He came on January 9 in his private railroad car accompanied by his staff. During his overnight stay he inspected the troops and attended an informal reception given in his honor by the Nogales chamber of commerce at the Santa Cruz Club, the local country club. Funston then resumed his itinerary, going to Fort Huachuca, Douglas, Columbus, El Paso, and on back to his headquarters in San Antonio. During his visit Funston may have expressed displeasure at the many civilians seen wearing parts of the prescribed army uniform, for shortly thereafter General Plummer issued and publicized an order strictly prohibiting the practice.[142]

No doubt one of Funston's principal concerns was the incidence of disease in the National Guard camps in Nogales. The Alabama camps suffered a virtual epidemic of pneumonia. As of Christmas, five men had died and more than forty were in the base hospital, besides which a large number of measles cases were being treated. By December 28, nine soldiers had died of pneumonia in the last five days.[143] By January 5, 1917, four more pneumonia fatalities had occurred. "General depression and sadness prevails at the camp and many prayers are heard for the four who departed." And besides pneumonia, soldiers thronged the base hospital with tonsillitis, measles, influenza, and other diseases. The hospital's eight wards overflowed, and the YMCA made its building available as a ward. By the next day two more Alabamans had died of pneumonia. In an effort to check the spread of contagious diseases, General Plummer ordered that there be no more congregating—soldiers were barred from public places, which the Military Police enforced.[144] By January 11, a second Alabama officer died in the base hospital. All told, fifty-eight Alabamans contracted pneumonia, of whom sixteen died.[145]

Sensational reports of rampant disease and deplorable camp conditions in Nogales caused great alarm back in Alabama. Some of these reports were in published letters from soldiers. For example, Private Ben May of the 1st Alabama machine gun company wrote to his brother decrying such conditions. A newspaper in Montgomery published the letter, which not only increased public apprehension but also got May in serious trouble. He was brought up on charges of spreading false information about conditions and engaging in conduct unbecoming. A court-martial sentenced him to six months at hard labor and forfeiture of two-thirds of his pay for six months.[146]

Concern about conditions in Nogales was such that the Alabama brigade's officers asked Governor Charles Henderson to visit their camps in Nogales and assess the situation for himself. Henderson not only agreed but decided to take his wife along.[147] The Nogales newspaper's coverage of the governor's visit included the eye-catching headline "COL. SCREWS GOVERNOR'S AIDE." The article explained that Lieutenant Colonel William P. Screws, the regular officer commanding the 4th Alabama, would act as the governor's aide during the visit.[148] After Henderson's visit to Nogales, he traveled to Tucson, where he met with Governor Hunt of Arizona, then on to Douglas to visit the Alabama troops stationed there.

Governor Henderson went to great lengths to hear complaints and suggestions, interviewing enlisted men privately as well as meeting in conference with brigade officers. He promised to do his utmost to remedy any conditions that were detrimental to the health and morale of the brigade. Presumably the Alabama brigade marched with a lighter step when it passed in review before the governor on January 16. A reception for the Hendersons followed that night at the Santa Cruz Club.[149]

The governor's official report, issued two days later, stressed the fact that Alabama currently had 4,955 men on border duty, including the infantry brigade at Nogales. Henderson commented that the men at Nogales were amply supplied with clothing and their tents had wooden sides and floors besides stoves and fuel, but there was an unusual amount of sickness in the camps because of the radical variations in temperature in Nogales compared with Alabama; at present there were still twenty-nine pneumonia cases in the hospital. He added that the men were restless and dissatisfied because they'd been mobilized for six months and "almost to a man the Alabama National Guardsmen took the oath required by the army regulations. This was done at great personal sacrifice." Henderson complained that Washington, D.C., officials were unaware of and indifferent to the detrimental effect of climatic conditions in Nogales. He urged the War Department to return the troops home and demobilize them without delay.[150] In an editorial commenting on Henderson's report the local newspaper stated that this had been the worst winter in Arizona in many years.[151]

While awaiting the decision from Washington, D.C., the Alabamans treated the local citizenry to a parade, and what a parade it was! The flavor of the occasion is best conveyed by quoting the *Nogales Daily Herald*'s account:

ALABAMA OFFICERS WILL PRESENT MARDI GRAS IN CITY FRIDAY NIGHT
"Alabama Mystics" Will Follow Precedent Established Years Ago. Crowds Will Witness Affair. Parade Will Be Held on Streets Beginning at 8:30 O'clock—Will Be Grand Affair

The people of Nogales will have an opportunity Friday night of witnessing a miniature Mardi Gras parade such as has made Mobile, Alabama, famous throughout the country for nearly a hundred years as the "Mother of Mystics."

The "Alabama Mystics," an organization formed among the officers of the Alabama brigade, will make their initial appearance Friday night in a beautiful street parade and grand ball at the Santa Cruz Club.

All Nogales society is eagerly looking forward to the event as it has been whispered that the Alabama officers will stage an affair that will be startlingly novel. An air of mystery and utmost secrecy except the thirty-five mystics know who will take part or any of the details.

A number of the Alabama officers are from Mobile and are members of the famous mystic organizations there that have for nearly a century magnificently celebrated Mardi Gras. . . . Gorgeously costumed and in full mask, mounted on fiery chargers, . . . two splendid military bands (one at front, one at rear) will furnish music for the parade. . . .

The grand marshal will halt the mystics near the Santa Cruz club where they will dismount and assemble for the grand march up stairs to the ball room. . . . When the mystics enter the ball room the grand march will begin.[152]

WILL SERENADE GEN. PLUMMER. ALABAMA MYSTICS PLAN BIG TIME. COSTUMES HERE SOON.

As a special compliment to General Plummer the parade of the mystics will pass that officer's residence and the bands will serenade the commanding officer of this district while the revelers execute the intricate drill of the men they will represent.[153]

SOLDIER BAN IS OFF FRIDAY. MAY WITNESS MYSTICS' PARADE. FOR FRIDAY ONLY.
Quarantine Will Not Be Lifted until Epidemics Are under Control—
All soldiers in the Nogales district will be allowed to come into town on Friday night. They will not be allowed to attend movies nor congregate in public places. Letting them witness the parade is a courtesy through the efforts of the officers commanding the units under the ban.[154]

CHIVALROUS KLANSMEN WILL PARADE STREETS OF NOGALES
"Alabama Mystics" Are to Be Ku Klux Klansmen As Were Their Sires. Flaming Torches Will Feature. Because of Local Interest, Admission to Ball Room Will Be by Card Only.

The Ku Klux Klan, the invisible empire of the south during the terrible days of that section's reconstruction following the Civil War, has been chosen by the "Alabama Mystics" as the subject of the parade which will pass through the streets of Nogales tonight. Men whose sires rode with the klan on many a midnight dash to the succor of southern women at the mercy of the then ruling negroes will present a parade of the Ku Klux Klan mounted and clothed just as were the original klansmen. In full regalia the klansmen will assemble tonight at 8:15 o'clock at the Knights of Columbus hall, on Grand avenue. Illuminated by torches of colored fire, the mystics will proceed across the railroad to Morley avenue, and down Morley avenue to the Santa Cruz bank, across the railroad tracks to Grand avenue, thence to General Plummer's residence.

Two military bands will serenade the General while the mystics execute the intricate drill of the Ku Klux Klan as a special compliment to the commanding officer of the Nogales district. The klansmen will countermarch to the K. of C. hall where they will dismount and march in single file to the Santa Cruz club.

The grand knight of all the klansmen will take command when the maskers assemble in the Santa Cruz club ball room, and there part of the ancient ritual of the Ku Klux will be heard. A flaming southern cross, such as was used to bring the various clans together in '66, will illuminate the scene. The ritual will be a most interesting feature of the entertainment, for the men of the Alabama mystics have learned the secrets of the klan from their sires and it will be the first time probably that ears of others than klan descendants will hear the service that is so sacred to most southern men.

After the ritual, full lights will be turned on a beautifully decorated ball room and the grand march and first dance of the Alabama mystics will begin. Two bands will furnish music. . . . Nearly every soldier in the Alabama brigade will be in Nogales tonight to witness the parade of the Ku Klux Klan, as quarantine restrictions have been relieved just to give the men an opportunity of seeing the mystics. Great interest has been aroused in the parade and it is believed that the streets will be lined with thousands tonight as the pageant passes. Because of this interest, it has been necessary to limit admission to the Santa Cruz club ball room to those having cards sent out by the mystics. Evening dress is stipulated.[155]

THOUSANDS SEE KU KLUX KLAN
Alabama Mystics Please Everyone. Grand Ball at Club. Stage Highly Spectacular Illuminated Street Parade.

Clothed and mounted as were their sires who rode boot to boot with death in the sixties for white supremacy in the south. . . . Thousands lined the curbs . . . at times the applause was deafening. . . . The members of the klan were dressed in flowing robes of white and over every heart was a white cross on a crimson background. The horses too were clothed in a mantle of white. It was all highly spectacular and so weird was the effect that many children cried with the same sort of fear that drove superstitious negroes out of the southland after they had seen the Ku Klux in the dead of night. . . . Two excellent military bands (1st and 2nd Alabama) furnished music for the parade. . . . As a special compliment to General Plummer the maskers marched to his house and the bands serenaded. The General applauded from the gallery of his residence. Quarantine restrictions were raised. . . . Nearly every man in the brigade was in town.[156]

The Alabama parade overshadowed in the mind of the local public the only real firefight in which the National Guard engaged while on the border, a firefight, moreover, in which a National Guard detachment crossed the border into Mexico. After the Utah cavalry finally received horses they were given a sector of the border to patrol—roughly 100 to 150 miles east and west of Nogales. There was an outpost about every fifteen miles, and the cavalry patrolled in between. The incident occurred on January 26–27, 1917, at a spot near Arivaca called Casa [de] Piedra or Stone House, about five miles to the south of Ruby, Arizona. Carranza troops occupied some houses located on the international boundary, with outposts to the east and west. On January 26, some cowboys working for the Arivaca Land and Cattle Company, accompanied by four Utah cavalrymen, discovered Mexicans driving cattle across the border. The Mexicans opened fire, which the Americans returned. The exchange continued into the afternoon, when a lieutenant and six soldiers stationed at Ruby arrived as reinforcements. Running low on ammunition, the lieutenant asked for help, which came in the form of First Lieutenant Carl Arns and nineteen men of Troop E, Utah Cavalry, who arrived from Arivaca shortly before midnight. The Utah cavalry took up positions at the Stone House, but during the night Arns shifted his men toward the border until he occupied an adobe hut some twenty feet from the boundary. Early the next morning about twenty-five Mexicans opened fire on the hut from the Sonora side of the border. Arns then led fourteen dismounted troopers west of the Mexican position and crossed the border hoping to take the enemy in the rear. The Mexicans spotted him and retreated. Arns's detachment pursued them for a mile and a half into Mexico. Failing to catch up with the enemy, Arns wrecked and set fire to the huts the Mexicans had been using. Despite all the shooting in what came to be called the "Battle of Ruby," no casualties were reported on either side. The *Nogales Daily Herald* editorialized sarcastically: "Thirty-six hours of fighting and not a single casualty. It was truly a Mexican battle."[157]

The army's investigation substantially agreed with newspaper accounts that the Mexicans were Carranza soldiers, some of them not in uniform.[158]

General Francisco Serrano, the commander in Sonora, issued an official statement:

> As some American newspapers have published the statement that several cowboys were attacked in Stone House, Ariz., it having been necessary to ask the aid of American troops to repulse the attackers, I wish to explain that the incident was entirely different and contrary to the reports. The truth was that some American filibusters attacked our garrison at Casa de Piedra on the Mexican side of the line and were repulsed by our troops after a short exchange of shots. In that

region where the incident took place there have been heavy frequent incursions by cattle rustlers from the American side of the line, and that it why we have been compelled to redouble our vigilance on that part of the border.[159]

Once matters had returned to normal, Troops E and F of the Utah Cavalry were deployed in detachments at Arivaca, Stone House, Ruby, and Tres Bellotas, eight miles farther west to guard against further incursions.[160] The 2nd Squadron of the 1st Utah Cavalry thus had the distinction of making the only combat incursion into Mexico during the National Guard's deployment on the border.

The closest the Alabama guardsmen got to seeing action was on the night of February 6, 1917. At midnight the 1,200 men of the 1st Alabama were rousted from their cots. Believing they were needed to repel a Mexican attack on Nogales, they reacted with discipline and efficiency. They got under arms in record time, harnessed mules for the wagon train, loaded pack mules with machine guns and ammunition as well as rations and extra equipment, marched in full field equipment to the outskirts of town, and took up assigned positions near the cemetery. Not until they were ordered to pitch their shelter halves did they realize that this was only an exercise. The men ate breakfast in the field and were back in their camp by eleven o'clock that morning. That afternoon the 1st Alabama passed in review before their brigade commander.[161]

The incidence of disease having declined significantly, the quarantine of the Alabama brigade was raised on February 9, on orders from division headquarters. This proved to be premature. Because of an upsurge in pneumonia cases, quarantine was reimposed on March 8. The men had to remain in camp after seven o'clock in the evening and were ordered to wear their overcoats after nightfall. According to the newspaper, "The prevalence of hookworm among the Alabama soldiers is said to have lowered their powers of resistance to pneumonia and is blamed for many of the deaths."[162]

The Alabama National Guard's brigade commander, General Charles R. Bricken, was elected a judge of the state Court of Appeals in November 1916. He left Nogales on December 18 and formally resigned in February 1917 because he could not hold both positions.[163] One historian has stated that Bricken's departure "proved most auspicious for the continued progress of the Guard." His replacement, who assumed command of the brigade on Bricken's departure in December, Colonel John M. Jenkins, was a regular cavalry officer, and this change "gave Alabama's officers an excellent opportunity to observe firsthand the difference that experienced, qualified leaders could have on their organization."[164]

The National Guard exodus from Nogales resumed in February 1917, as rapidly as rail transportation became available. The 2nd Squadron of the 1st Utah Cavalry departed on February 27. On March 1, Company A, California Engineers, did likewise. But the big news was when the Alabama brigade entrained: 1st, 2nd, 4th Alabama, Company A of the Signal Corps, Field Hospital Company No. 1, Ambulance Company No. 1 all left between March 15 and 18.

In an editorial, the *Nogales Daily Herald* stated that "during their brief stay they [the Alabamans] have endeared themselves to us in a greater degree, perhaps, than has any other militia organization that has been assigned to this city."[165] Because of a shortage of Pullmans, the Alabamans had to travel in day coaches, two men to each double seat.[166] Presumably the men did not mind, for they were going home. The *Nogales Daily Herald* most assuredly did mind. An editorial excoriated the War Department for providing only chair cars for the Alabamans, both officers and enlisted men: "The excuse that no Pullman cars are available is ridiculous. . . . Is it any wonder that the War Department has failed to obtain sufficient men for the Army? Is it surprising that the National Guard is sick of the service? Hypocrisy and partiality can never inspire confidence."[167]

The citizens of Nogales were quite concerned at reports that two squadrons of the black 10th U.S. Cavalry, who had formed part of the Punitive Expedition, were to be stationed there. The locals were relieved when the black troopers were sent to Fort Huachuca instead. The 35th U.S. Infantry was ordered to march from Douglas to Nogales to reinforce the 12th U.S. Infantry. Trucks transported the 35th's baggage and supplies.[168] Once again Nogales belonged to the regulars.

Chapter 20

California

Compared with the rest of the Mexican border, the California border, under the jurisdiction of the Western Department, was a military backwater. The adjoining territory of Baja California was not only isolated and undeveloped but also virtually the fiefdom of Colonel Esteban Cantú, the governor, who merely paid lip service to the national government in Mexico City. He had given asylum to a number of officers and politicians opposed to the Carranza regime. Cantú's military resources were unimpressive: some five hundred soldiers and two hundred volunteers armed with Mauser and Remington rifles, 2,500 rifles in reserve and an ample supply of ammunition, four 4-inch fieldpieces, and two machine guns. Cantú's income, about $90,000 a month, came almost entirely from what Americans spent in Tijuana.[1] Accordingly, Cantú wanted no trouble with the United States, expressing his fervent friendship for the U.S. government and announcing that if hostilities broke out between the United States and Mexico, he would remain neutral. The Mexican consul in Los Angeles bitterly denounced Cantú for this unpatriotic stance.[2] Thus as far as the War Department was concerned, the California border was by far the least worrisome stretch of the whole international boundary.[3]

Of the seventeen companies of coast artillery in California, seven companies, 805 strong, were dispatched from Forts Winfield Scott, Baker, and Miley near San Francisco to patrol the California border. Two companies

BORDER SERVICE

went to San Diego and five to Calexico to reinforce Troops B and M, 1st U.S. Cavalry, and the 3rd Battalion and machine gun company of the 21st U.S. Infantry. The 2nd California National Guard Coast Artillery Company was activated to guard the San Diego water supply reservoir.[4]

National Guardsmen soon relieved the coast artillery companies on the border. Logically, these should have been California guardsmen, but as we have seen they were sent to Nogales. Therefore, it fell to the National Guard of Oregon and Washington to protect the California border.

The Oregon National Guard responded with brisk efficiency to the president's call, activating the 3rd Infantry, Battery A of the Field Artillery, and Separate Troop A of the Cavalry, a total of 1,577 men.[5] In Portland, applicants for enlistment flooded the armory, and the doctors could not examine them fast enough. Because there was no National Guard company in Pendleton, Oregon, twelve cowboys from there enlisted in the Idaho National Guard.[6]

The Oregon adjutant general, Brigadier General George A. White, oversaw the mustering of Company M, 3rd Infantry, the first unit to be accepted for federal service. White then asked permission to resign as adjutant general and go to the border as a private. However, there existed a vacancy for the commanding officer of Troop A, Cavalry, and after the entire troop importuned him, White consented temporarily to relinquish his state service and assume command in federal service with the rank of captain.[7]

The state mobilization site was the Clackamas range, some ten miles south of Portland, temporarily renamed "Camp Withycombe" in honor of the governor, James Withycombe. (The Clackamas range was permanently named Camp Withycombe after the governor's death in office in 1919.) Battery A, Field Artillery, was based in Portland but had been operating under a considerable handicap. Not only was the weather unsuitable for outdoor drill during much of the year, but the unit lacked horses and an adequate drilling pavilion. A few horses and one section of guns and caissons were maintained at the Clakamas range, and some members of Battery A had been able to drill there on Sundays.[8] Troop A, Cavalry, was also based in Portland and had been handicapped by a lack of horses and a suitable riding hall. When the call-up came, both Troop A and Battery A quickly reached their wartime strength, "for they were the only mounted organizations in the State service and for this reason proved very attractive to prospective recruits."[9]

Commanding the 3rd Oregon Infantry was the popular Colonel Clenard McLaughlin, who as a regular captain had been the federal inspector-instructor of the regiment. He had been unanimously chosen to be the regiment's new commander and had been commissioned as a National Guard colonel, his appointment dating from February 2, 1915.[10] Colonel McLaughlin was operating under great pressure. Given the urgency of the crisis with Mexico, his orders were to forget about recruiting his companies up to wartime strength at their home stations; the units were ordered to assemble at Clakamas as rapidly as possible, and, from companies exceeding the minimum strength, men were reassigned to bring other companies up to the minimum. The machine gun company had no machine guns; the men were armed with pistols.[11] The company had to remain behind in its armory in Portland because of the nonarrival of equipment. However, it joined the rest of the regiment at Clakamas on June 27, equipped with four Lewis guns and five small Ford trucks for their transportation, in place of the customary pack animals. All the men needed now was instruction in how to operate the machine guns and the motor vehicles.

An intense round of drills, physical examinations, issuing of supplies, and vaccinations for smallpox and typhoid ensued. In the midst of a heavy rainstorm on June 25, Major General J. Franklin Bell, commanding general of the Western Department, reviewed all troops in the camp except the 3rd Battalion, 3rd Infantry, who were excused because they were being mustered in. By June 27, all of the 3rd Infantry was in federal service. That same day the regiment departed by rail on the Southern Pacific for San Diego, accompanied by an authorized newspaper correspondent.[12] Oregon claimed the distinction of having the first National Guard regiment in the current call-up to leave its mobilization camp for the Mexican border.

However, "once the National Guard left the State, and the crisis in the Mexican situation appeared to have blown over, interest in military service ceased. Organized recruiting campaigns were conducted throughout the State, but these efforts scarcely provided enough recruits to make good the losses in membership which the regiment sustained while in service on the Border."[13] During its border service the regiment lost 54 men discharged for physical disability, 68 discharged because of dependent relatives, and 17 discharged for expiration of their enlistment, a total of 139. During the same time the regiment received 170 recruits, 18 of whom joined after the regiment's return to the mobilization camp. "Another difficulty which was encountered was due to the number of married men and men with relatives wholly or partially dependent upon them for support who were in the enlisted personnel of the State service. These men were in many cases among the most efficient and experienced soldiers in the State and the National Guard had urgent need of them at this critical time."[14]

The regiment gained the approval of the regular inspector: "It has been commanded by Col. McLaughlin, a Regular captain, United States Infantry, for about two years. This advantage in training is apparent. The training and instruction of the regiment was carried on under adverse conditions, as it was hurriedly mustered in and shipped to the border. Officers and men intelligent, zealous, and anxious to learn. Results under these conditions very creditable." Troop A, Cavalry, also received a positive report.[15]

To illustrate the opposite end of the scale and a great weakness of the National Guard, the regular inspector despaired of one unnamed infantry regiment inspected in August: "It is pitiful to watch their incompetency. The regiment would be of no value on the border. To be made efficient in any reasonable time it must be placed under a regular officer. The colonel stated that he did not think it possible to have good discipline in his regiment, as there were so many men in it who were his equals socially."[16]

From San Diego the 3rd Battalion of the 3rd Oregon was dispatched to San Ysidro, the gateway to Tijuana, to reinforce the 38th U.S. Coast Artillery Company.[17] The remainder of the regiment encamped at Balboa Park in San Diego. Battery A was sent directly to Calexico, California, across the border from Mexicali, Baja California, departing from Camp Withycombe on June 28. Colonel McLaughlin was assigned to command all troops on border patrol from the Pacific Ocean to Mountain Springs.[18]

The units on border patrol received their supplies from Fort Rosecrans in San Diego. The Oregon adjutant general wrote:

> Special mention should be made of the rations furnished by the Quartermaster Department through the quartermaster at Fort Rosecrans. This included fresh meat daily, fresh vegetables, choice canned goods, and such staple articles as flour, sugar, beans, rice, coffee, tea, etc., all of excellent quality and in sufficient quantity. Fresh bread was baked and distributed daily, first from the post bakery at Fort Rosecrans, and later from the field bakery established in our own camp. For the transportation of supplies to the regiment and its various outposts, five large motor trucks belonging to the Quartermaster Department were utilized. . . . By this means, even the furthest detachments, some

eighty-five miles distant, was [*sic*] supplied every other day. The regimental field trains were utilized for short hauls, and in hauling wood etc., for the camp.[19]

Good food contributed significantly to the health of the regiment. The very few cases of serious illness were immediately sent to the hospital at San Francisco or Fort Rosecrans for treatment. Most of the illness dealt with in camp was due to men eating and drinking items bought while off duty from stands and hucksters' wagons in the vicinity of camp. Remarkably few cases of venereal disease were discovered.

The 3rd Infantry's headquarters and 1st and 2nd Battalions moved to a new camp outside of Palm City, about fifteen miles from San Diego. Officers and enlisted men were ordered not to write or give out for publication any information regarding the location of units. Colonel McLaughlin's mission was to protect American settlers along the California border while preparing to occupy Tijuana and Tecate, Baja California, in the event of hostilities.

The only excitement the Oregonians experienced occurred on July 13. At two o'clock in the morning two Mexicans held up a sentry on picket duty and tried to steal two horses. As they were leading the animals away the sentry fired at them twice, whereupon they abandoned the horses and disappeared into the night. These proved to be the only two shots the regiment fired in anger while on the border.

With little to fear from the Mexicans, the Oregon troops spent their time in drill, instruction, and route marches. The 1st and 2nd Battalions marched to their new camp in Palm City, their baggage and supplies being transported by truck convoy; the 3rd Battalion subsequently joined them. The regiment rotated two companies to man the outpost at San Ysidro. In some of the route marches, as an experiment the infantry were accompanied by the five Ford trucks carrying the machine guns. The results were disappointing. Because the trucks had to travel slowly to match the pace of the infantry the engines were prone to overheating.

Thus some old-timers preferred to rely on the traditional use of animals. The regiment had ninety-eight mules and forty-eight horses from the remount station at Fort Keough. Unfortunately, most of these animals arrived unbroken, and it was up to the men to perform the distasteful—and hazardous—duty of spending several days breaking them for harness and saddle.

Besides the training schedule of drill, instruction, and inspection, the troops underwent the physical examinations for which there had not been time at their home stations; fifty-two men were disqualified and given honorable discharges. The Oregonians also spent time improving their camp at Palm City, among other things installing shower baths for both officers and enlisted men.

Troop A, Cavalry, accompanied the 3rd Infantry to San Diego and encamped at Balboa Park in July and into August. By then the unit had a full complement of horses and equipment, and it received orders to march the 146 miles to Calexico, its new station, reinforcing Battery A. One of the privates in Troop B was shot through the side on December 26 by a Mexican and was rushed to a hospital in San Francisco. His chances of recovery were slight. It was said he mistakenly knocked at the door of the wrong house, one occupied by an employee in the Mexican customs house who shot through the door.[20]

On July 25, elements of the 3rd Oregon marched to Imperial Beach, which had been selected as the regiment's permanent encampment, although detachments were maintained at Morena, Sweetwater, Otay, and San Ysidro. The leased three-hundred-acre beachfront site was a quarter mile east of the Pacific Ocean, with sandy soil affording good drainage, an ample supply of good water from the mains supplying the Coronado Hotel, and excellent telephone communications. Not the least of its attractions, the camp had "excellent facilities for surf bathing."[21] By August 4, the remainder of the regiment had settled into the Imperial Beach encampment, which boasted electric lights even in each squad tent, frame bathhouses, screened frame mess halls, a substantial frame storehouse, and a large corral for the animals. The YMCA played a prominent role in making the troops' monotonous existence more enjoyable. It built a frame structure at one corner of the camp to provide a free reading and writing room as well as a canteen for the men. In addition, the YMCA provided a variety of athletic and educational programs.

The 3rd Oregon assembled quietly on the night of August 10 for a maneuver. Colonel McLaughlin led his men two and a half miles north of camp on the Coronado Highway. After marching for forty-five minutes, the regiment rested for fifteen minutes then marched back. When they were 250 yards from camp, the battalions deployed and advanced in line of skirmishers then charged. The battalions reassembled, marched back into camp, and were dismissed. Five days later, Lieutenant Colonel Frank M.

Caldwell, of the army's Inspector General Department, arrived to conduct a detailed inspection of the regiment and the camp. Three days later, Caldwell held an inspection and review of all the troops at Imperial Beach in full field equipment. A more welcome development was the arrival on August 22 of the quartermaster from Fort Rosecrans to give the troops the first pay they had received since mobilization.

The by-now dreary routine of drill and instruction resumed, but this time at the regimental level and including instruction in marching, advance and rear guard formation, and attack. "At 8:00 P.M. a night maneuver was held involving use of these formations and application of the principles of attack and defense of rear guard."[22]

Further training was cut short on August 31, when the Western Department ordered the 3rd Oregon to return immediately to the state mobilization camp at Clackamas for possible strike duty.[23] The outposts were called in to rejoin the regiment, which assembled at Palm City. At Imperial Beach tents were struck and all tents and baggage were packed for shipment, the men pitching shelter halves for the night. Fifteen days' rations were issued. The following morning, Colonel McLaughlin telegraphed the Western Department that the first elements of his regiment were ready to depart from Palm City as soon as rail transportation arrived. That same afternoon headquarters, headquarters company, the machine gun company, the medical detachment, and the 1st Battalion left in a train consisting of three tourist sleepers, ten chair cars, two baggage cars, two flatcars, and four boxcars. On September 2, the 2nd and 3rd Battalions followed. By September 7, all Oregon troops were back at Clackamas. Governor Withycombe had boarded the first train to escort the troops back home.

At Withycombe, the training schedule resumed, and on September 13 the governor reviewed the regiment in full field equipment, complete with machine guns, field and combat trains. The following day the 3rd Oregon departed from Withycombe by rail for Portland to enjoy the homecoming ceremonies the city of Portland had prepared in their honor. The troops marched from their armory through the main streets of the city then returned to camp. While continuing to hone their military skills, the men of the 3rd Oregon were required to take the federal oath binding them to three years in the National Guard reserve after their current enlistments expired. Many men declined to do so.[24]

The climax of the 3rd Oregon's National Guard experience came on September 25, when they paraded and were officially mustered out of federal service. The units jubilantly boarded trains for their home stations. The men of Battery A and Troop A were not as fortunate; they remained in federal service until February 22, 1917, when they were mustered out at Vancouver Barracks, Washington.[25]

Guarding the eastern section of the California border was the Washington National Guard.[26] As early as 1914 during the American occupation of Veracruz, the Washington guard had begun to prepare for mobilization in the event of hostilities with Mexico. Although war was averted then, the experience gained in detailed planning proved invaluable when the guard was called up in June 1916. Even before the president's official telegram was received at ten o'clock on the night on June 18, Washington adjutant general Maurice Thompson and his staff were in action, for he had been notified unofficially at four thirty that afternoon. By ten thirty that night, mobilization orders were delivered to Western Union for transmittal to all guard officers directing them to assemble their men, begin energetic recruiting, and have all reservists report for duty.[27] Before the next morning, General Orders No. 19, containing all the details of the call-up, was printed and mailed to the officer corps. The mobilization point at American Lake, southeast of Tacoma, was designated as Camp Elmer M. Brown, in honor of a retired medical corps lieutenant colonel who had died on May 12, 1916. A force of carpenters was busy expanding the facility by constructing bathhouses, mess halls, and administrative buildings. As the Washington troops were assembling, Major General J. Franklin Bell, commanding the Western Department, inspected them as part of an extensive tour of military installations.[28]

All the mobilized units were to recruit up to war strength and then report to camp no later than June 25. The Washington National Guard performed the considerable feat of recruiting up to wartime strength and assembling at their mobilization camp in six days. The units arrived at Camp Elmer M. Brown as follows:

Troop B, Cavalry, from Tacoma on June 20
Field Company A, Signal Corps, from Seattle on June 21
Regimental Infirmary, 2nd Infantry on June 24
2nd Infantry: most arrived by June 25

The last units to arrive were the regiment's Companies H and I and Machine Gun Company, from Spokane, who reached camp at six o'clock on the morning of June 26.[29] A few guardsmen living in other states rushed back to Washington to report for duty.[30] Unlike the experience of some other states, every one of Washington's guardsmen took the oath required by sections 70 and 73 of the National Defense Act of June 3, 1916. One 2nd Infantry guardsman had refused to sign the federal muster roll despite the pleas of his comrades not to disgrace his company. They had to be restrained from ducking him in American Lake. The shaken soldier was sent to the guardhouse, where after contemplating his situation for an hour he signed.[31] By the time the troops were mustered into federal service on June 28, the Washington contingent numbered a total of 61 officers and 2,069 enlisted men.

Under federal regulations, states were required to have on hand only sufficient quantities of certain articles of uniform and equipment for the minimum peacetime strength, the balance of the equipment to be supplied at the time of mobilization by the army's quartermaster corps. There occurred a slight delay in the arrival of the balance of equipment, but by the time the men left for the border they had all of their essential equipment.

A source of particular pride was that the Washington organizations went to the border at full war strength. As the adjutant general reported, "This is the only instance in the entire United States, either in the Regular Army or the National Guard, where all the organizations called for were furnished at full strength."[32]

The Washington guardsmen were soon on their way to Calexico. Company A of the Signal Corps, Troop B of the Cavalry, and attached medical troops left by rail on June 30. In an unusual development, before the 2nd Infantry departed the officers presented Captain Harold Coburn, the regular inspector-instructor and mustering officer, with a jewel-mounted swagger stick as a token of their appreciation. The regiment, Colonel William M. Inglis commanding, followed in four sections on July 4 in twenty-one chair cars instead of the tourist sleepers ordered. But when the train reached Sacramento, California, tourist sleepers were provided, to the troops' great delight.[33] At each station crowds greeted the troop trains as they passed through, and at several cities the men received gifts of tobacco and sandwiches.

The guardsmen reached Calexico during the afternoon of July 7 and established a makeshift camp in an alfalfa field. During the next few days a more permanent encampment was constructed, although intense heat and a scarcity of water hampered the men. Bathing was out. The city sprinkler initially hauled water to the camp. Drills began on July 9, and the men began to accustom themselves to the heat—108 degrees in the shade. Because of the heat, reveille was at five forty-five in the morning, no work was performed in the middle of the day, and taps was at nine o'clock at night.[34] Adding to the troops' discomfort, an intense windstorm on the evening of July 12 blew over a number of tents. Still, the adjutant general of Washington reported proudly on July 15 that the troops at Calexico enjoyed ample tentage and all the facilities for comfort and convenience. Conditions continued to improve: a post exchange opened on July 17, and water was piped to the camp on July 21. A week later construction of mess halls began. The 2nd Infantry even began to publish a weekly newspaper, *The Washingtonian*.

The camp was located at the eastern edge of Calexico and named Camp Beacom in honor of Colonel John Henry Beacom, 6th U.S. Infantry, who died of heart failure at Colonia Dublán on September 17, 1916, while on duty with the Punitive Expedition. Beacom, age fifty-nine, a native of Wellsville, Ohio, was stricken while preparing to leave the Punitive Expedition for his new assignment as commander of the National Guard troops at Calexico.[35] In October, Major General Bell made Calexico the division headquarters of the Southern California Border District, which stretched twenty-five miles along the border.[36]

There appeared to be the prospect of action on July 26 at the news that a force of several thousand Carranza troops was on its way to Mexicali to depose Governor Cantú. Since Mexicali was just across the border from Calexico, there was the possibility that if a battle occurred at Mexicali, incoming fire could hit the Washington camp less than a quarter of a mile away.[37] But nothing that exciting happened to break the monotony of camp life.

Instead, on July 26 a series of parades and inspections culminated with the arrival of Major C. B. Blethan, representing the state of Washington. He reviewed the regiment the next day and reported its condition to Governor Ernest Lister. The report was favorable, for the regiment was taking drills and field exercises in stride. Company drills gave way to battalion and regimental drills, and route marches became routine. The men held up well on long marches under a blazing sun. Because of excellent sanitary arrangements, there were remarkably few instances of sickness, and only one death occurred among the Washington troops, a private in Company A, 2nd Infantry.

There were hangovers, however. Private Elliott Metcalf, of Troop B of the Cavalry, wrote a humorous reminiscence of border duty entitled "Troop 'B' and the Battle of Calexico" in which he referred to the beer and the swimming tank at Holtville, the arrest in Mexicali of one of his comrades, and the time members of his troop beat up an allegedly abusive Oregon artilleryman.

The month of August passed uneventfully until the evening of August 31. While the men were formed in their company streets for the Retreat ceremony a newsboy began selling papers at one end of camp. As the men read that they were to be sent home the next day they sent up a heartfelt cheer. Each company in succession took up the cheer as the news spread throughout the camp—the troops were ordered back to the mobilization camp for possible strike duty. For the most part the border duty of the Washington troops had been uneventful. They did manage to achieve the dubious distinction of having the most trials by summary court-martial of any National Guard organization—203, the next highest being the 7th California Infantry with 77.[38]

The 2nd Infantry was ordered to return to American Lake for mustering out, arriving there on September 4.[39] However, completion of records and preparations for returning to state status took until October 8, when the regiment was formally mustered out of federal service. Troop B, Cavalry, and Company A, Signal Corps, though, remained on duty in Calexico. In December, Governor Lister emphatically protested to Secretary Baker that these units had been on active duty for almost six months and that "the life work of these men is not military service." They were finally mustered out of federal service at Vancouver Barracks, Washington, on February 15, 1917.[40]

On the way there, Troop B received a signal honor—it was the only National Guard unit that a state legislature recognized by extending to it the privileges of the House of Representatives. It seems that the legislature invited the cavalry to stop off in Olympia on their way home and pay the politicians a visit. With the help of Governor Lister, the railroad schedule was changed, and when the unit rolled into the Olympia depot a large delegation of young women, matrons, and legislators was on hand to welcome them. Troop B marched in a body to the capitol, where they were ceremoniously escorted into the House of Representatives. Marching into that august body, they were seated up front and the officers were prevailed upon to give brief talks about their experiences. Afterward, the cavalrymen were escorted to the Elks Temple, where the female population of Olympia treated them to a feast. The guardsmen then hurried back to their train and proceeded on to Tacoma.

As with the Oregon National Guard, that of Washington was recalled from the border for possible strike duty. In the state of Washington there was certainly no lack of strikes, labor disputes, and civil disturbances, and in the months that followed, the National Guard was indeed called out twice to help restore order. On November 5, 1916, a serious clash occurred in Everett between a sheriff's posse and two shiploads of Industrial Workers of the World (IWW), the radical labor organization, resulting in the deaths of seven men, one a reserve National Guard lieutenant, and the wounding of numerous other persons. Four companies of the 2nd Washington Infantry, in addition to five companies of coast artillery and units of naval militia, were mobilized, and the adjutant general took personal command of the situation. It took two days to restore order. A lesser crisis occurred in July 1917, when the sheriff requested the assistance of Troop A of the Washington Cavalry in connection with the arrest of a large number of IWWs at Ellensburg. The cavalry prevented matters from getting out of hand.[41]

These incidents underlined the principal function of the National Guard, that of being a governor's last line of defense in cases of civil disturbance or natural disaster. When called into federal service, the guardsmen of Oregon performed in an exemplary manner, those of Washington somewhat less so. It is perhaps ironic that two of the better-equipped National Guard organizations were assigned to protect the most peaceful section of the Mexican border.

Conclusion

The National Guard call-up was significantly more important than the Punitive Expedition—a campaign in Mexico involving at most 12,000 regulars versus the intensive training and equipping of 150,000 National Guardsmen as the country moved toward entry into World War I. And hopefully the present work defines what the Punitive Expedition was and was not, thus clearing up the widespread misconception that the 1916 call-up was part of the Punitive Expedition. Many fewer individuals were involved in chasing Pancho Villa than has been thought. And in any case, they never caught up with Villa. He was assassinated in 1923.

The great 1916 call-up occurred because of developments emanating from the Mexican Revolution. To cite but one example of how the army reacted to the revolution, in 1910 Fort Bliss in El Paso had a garrison of about 350; by the fall of 1916, there were more than 40,000 troops stationed in and around Fort Bliss. Not only did the army vastly increase its presence on the border, it also injected millions of dollars into the economy of the Southwest. The military buildup resulted from the Mexican Revolution, and the 1916 mobilization was decisive in defusing the war crisis.

From 1903 with the passage of the Dick Act, then the 1916 National Defense Act, the National Guard was in the process of transforming itself from a collection of militia units into a viable reserve for the U.S. Army, much to the displeasure of the generals, who tried with scant success to create a separate army reserve. As of 1916 the National Guard was theoretically

The Great Call-Up

organized into twelve divisions, but the war crisis caused the army to rush many units to the border piecemeal and later organize them into provisional tactical formations.

By the time the bulk of the mobilized National Guard arrived on the border—110,000 by the end of July—the war crisis with Mexico had subsided. However, protection of the border remained a priority, and the guard was deployed accordingly. From a command standpoint, the deployment provided an unanticipated opportunity to train and equip the guard, which had many weak officers and undertrained personnel (and many raw recruits as units rapidly increased to wartime strength). The army seized the chance to improve the National Guard's capability as a fighting force. Although the regulars looked down on the National Guard, they were nevertheless instrumental in providing leadership and training during the border service.

Although the majority of guardsmen chafed at continuing on active duty—they had come to the border to whip the Mexicans and go home—the months on the border enabled commanders to gain experience in handling large formations. Furthermore, brand-new units—such as the 1st Mississippi, which was cobbled together as a regiment from three separate battalions, or the Utah cavalry, which had recently been converted from five infantry companies—became much more cohesive organizations.

What the mobilization showed was that the United States was unprepared to fight an adversary such as Germany. The army was understrength and woefully ill equipped with modern weapons such as aircraft, machine guns, and artillery, relying instead on aimed rifle fire by the infantry. Although beginning to mechanize, the army still relied heavily on cavalry. The call-up underlined the army's dependence on railroads, highlighting the necessity for the government to control and coordinate the railroads in any future mobilization. Moreover, the army's logistical system had proved incapable of supporting the 1916 mobilization. The National Guard blamed the army, who blamed Congress for not providing greater appropriations. A large part of the problem was that the call-up was conducted through the four geographic departments while logistics were highly centralized in two depots. Unfortunately, the army failed to learn one of the great lessons from the mobilization. The general staff rejected recommendations that there be permanent mobilization sites and equipment depots for each National Guard division or that periodic call-ups be held to test mobilization plans. The general staff's rationale was that sufficient facilities existed to support

Conclusion

partial call-ups and that another full mobilization was unlikely. The general staff's assessment was amply justified—until April 6, 1917, that is.

As for the National Guard, the army justifiably criticized it as a quasi-social institution, whose officers and NCOs were elected, not necessarily on their military abilities, and whose discipline was undermined by fraternization between officers and enlisted men. The 1916 call-up brought to the fore the two-tiered National Guard: the "silk stocking" units and all the rest. And the army deplored the lack of training that the guard exhibited. However, it was the army that ordered the guard to recruit immediately up to war strength and then criticized the guard for consisting largely of recruits. The army felt that most guard units required at least six months of intensive training before they were even conceivably ready to take the field. Furthermore, influential generals such as Scott and Wood had little use for the guard, emphasizing that it would take at least two years to train American troops to a European level and advocating universal military training in peacetime and compulsory military service in wartime. The army's assessment of the guard's performance has been lukewarm at best.

However, the call-up proved to be a godsend in terms of preparedness for World War I. The mobilization that occurred when the United States declared war on Germany on April 6, 1917, went more smoothly as a result of the lessons learned from the 1916 call-up. One army officer recently wrote disparaging "the painfully obvious conclusion that the National Guard was more trained and ready after the border deployment than prior. . . . Almost every writer who cited the National Guard's role on the border included this common theme. There are no military units that are less trained after a mobilization and deployment than prior, so this recurring point seems wasted and offers nothing with respect to any deeper understanding."[1] This truism notwithstanding, what is "painfully obvious" is that the whole subject of the National Guard on the Mexican border in 1916–17 has heretofore been inadequately studied, even by the army itself. That being the case, it seems perfectly justifiable to examine in detail how the National Guard improved during its border service.

By America's entry into World War I the National Guard had become much more tactically proficient with well-trained officers and NCOs. It was the guard's border veterans who provided the leadership in 1917 to expand the guard to 379,000 men. And in terms of "a deeper understanding" of what the border service meant, the National Guard 26th (New England) Division was the first full U.S. Army division to organize and deploy to

France in September–October 1917, *ahead of the regulars.* This could not have occurred as quickly without the leadership of the 1916 veterans. Of the forty-three divisions that eventually constituted the American Expeditionary Force in World War I, the National Guard provided seventeen.[2]

The army never gave the National Guard credit for its transformation from militia to the only existing army reserve. Nor, because of professional jealousy, did the regulars credit the guard's accomplishments. For example, the War Department issued a medal to the regulars in 1917 for their service in Mexico, but not until 1918, under pressure from governors and Congress, did the War Department authorize a medal for guardsmen who had served on the border.

What subsequent conflicts—down to Afghanistan today—have shown is that the U.S. Army cannot fight a war without the National Guard.

Appendix

National Guard Order of Battle

San Antonio (Camp Wilson)

2nd Texas Infantry (transferred to Rio Grande Valley, then to Corpus Christi)
3rd Texas Infantry (transferred to Rio Grande Valley, then to Corpus Christi)
4th Texas Infantry (transferred to Big Bend and back)
1st Texas Cavalry Squadron (transferred to Laredo, then to Big Bend)
Battery A 1st Texas Field Artillery (transferred to Fort Ringgold, then to Corpus Christi)
Texas Field Hospital Company No. 1 (transferred to Corpus Christi)
Companies A and H Texas Engineers

1st Illinois Infantry
2nd Illinois Infantry
3rd Illinois Infantry
4th Illinois Infantry
7th Illinois Infantry
8th Illinois Infantry
1st Illinois Field Artillery
Company A Illinois Engineers
Company A Illinois Signal Corps
Illinois Field Hospital Company No. 2

1st Wisconsin Infantry
2nd Wisconsin Infantry

Appendix

3rd Wisconsin Infantry
Troops A and B Wisconsin Cavalry
Battery A Wisconsin Field Artillery
Wisconsin Field Hospital Company No. 1

1st Kansas Infantry (transferred from Eagle Pass)
2nd Kansas Infantry (transferred from Eagle Pass)
Company K Kansas Signal Corps

1st Battalion Virginia Field Artillery
Company A Virginia Engineers
Company A Virginia Signal Corps
Virginia Field Hospital Company No. 1

3rd District of Columbia Infantry
Troop A District of Columbia Cavalry

2nd West Virginia Infantry

1st Mississippi Infantry

Battery A New Hampshire Field Artillery
Company A New Hampshire Signal Corps

Company A Missouri Signal Corps

Oklahoma Ambulance Company No. 1

Florida Field Hospital Company No. 1

New York Division Field Train (transferred from McAllen, Mission, Pharr)

1st Alabama Cavalry

1st Minnesota Infantry (transferred from Llano Grande)
2nd Minnesota Infantry (transferred from Llano Grande)

Corpus Christi (Camp Scurry)

2nd Texas Infantry (transferred from San Antonio)
3rd Texas Infantry (transferred from San Antonio)

National Guard Order of Battle

Texas Field Hospital Company No. 1 (transferred from San Antonio)
Battery A Texas Field Artillery (transferred from San Antonio)

Brownsville and Llano Grande

1st Illinois Cavalry
Illinois Field Hospital Company No. 1

1st Virginia Infantry
2nd Virginia Infantry
1st Virginia Cavalry Squadron
Virginia Field Artillery Battalion
Virginia Field Hospital Company No. 1

1st Iowa Infantry
2nd Iowa Infantry
3rd Iowa Infantry
1st Iowa Cavalry Squadron
1st Iowa Field Artillery Battalion
Iowa Ambulance Company No. 1
Iowa Field Hospital Company No. 1

4th South Dakota Infantry

1st Louisiana Infantry
Troop A Louisiana Cavalry
Battery A Louisiana Artillery
Louisiana Field Hospital Company No. 1

Troop A Kansas Cavalry

Troops A, B, C Colorado Cavalry

Troop A New Hampshire Cavalry

1st Indiana Infantry
2nd Indiana Infantry
3rd Indiana Infantry
1st Battalion Indiana Field Artillery

Appendix

4th Nebraska Infantry
5th Nebraska Infantry
Company A Nebraska Signal Corps
Nebraska Field Hospital Company No 1

1st Minnesota Infantry (transferred to San Antonio)
2nd Minnesota Infantry (transferred to San Antonio)
3rd Minnesota Infantry
1st Minnesota Field Artillery

1st North Dakota Infantry

1st Oklahoma Infantry
Troops A and B Oklahoma Cavalry
Company A Oklahoma Engineers
Oklahoma Field Hospital No. 1
Oklahoma Ambulance Company No. 1

McAllen, Mission, Pharr

New York Division Headquarters
1st Battalion Signal Corps
22nd Engineers
1st Cavalry
Cavalry Squadron A
1st Field Artillery
2nd Field Artillery
3rd Field Artillery
2nd Infantry
3rd Infantry
7th Infantry
12th Infantry
14th Infantry
23rd Infantry
69th Infantry
71st Infantry
74th Infantry

1st Field Hospital Company
2nd Field Hospital Company
3rd Field Hospital Company
4th Field Hospital Company
1st Ambulance Company
2nd Ambulance Company
3rd Ambulance Company
4th Ambulance Company
Division Field Train (transferred to Camp Wilson)
Field Bakery Detachment
2 Bakery Units

3rd Tennessee Infantry

Laredo

1st Texas Cavalry (transferred from San Antonio, then to Big Bend)

1st Missouri Infantry
2nd Missouri Infantry
3rd Missouri Infantry
4th Missouri Infantry
Troop B Missouri Cavalry
1st Battalion Missouri Field Artillery
Company A Missouri Signal Corps (transferred to San Antonio)
Missouri Field Hospital Company No. 1
Missouri Ambulance Company No. 1

2nd Maine Infantry

1st New Hampshire Infantry
Troop A New Hampshire Cavalry (transferred to Brownsville)
Battery A New Hampshire Field Artillery (transferred to San Antonio)
Company A New Hampshire Signal Corps (transferred to San Antonio)
New Hampshire Field Hospital No. 1 (transferred to Deming)

2nd Florida Infantry

Appendix

Eagle Pass

1st Maryland Infantry
4th Maryland Infantry
5th Maryland Infantry
Troop A Maryland Cavalry
Battery A Maryland Field Artillery
Maryland Field Hospital Company No. 1
Maryland Ambulance Company No. 1

1st Kansas Infantry (transferred to San Antonio)
2nd Kansas Infantry (transferred to San Antonio)
Battery A Kansas Field Artillery
Troop A Kansas Cavalry
Company A Kansas Signal Corps

1st Vermont Infantry

1st Tennessee Infantry

Big Bend

4th Texas Infantry (transferred from and to San Antonio)
1st Texas Cavalry Squadron (San Antonio, Laredo, Big Bend)

El Paso (Camps Cotton, Stewart, Pershing)

Battery A New Mexico Field Artillery (transferred from Columbus)

5th Massachusetts Infantry
8th Massachusetts Infantry
9th Massachusetts Infantry
1st Massachusetts Field Artillery
1st Massachusetts Signal Battalion
1st Squadron Massachusetts Cavalry
Massachusetts Field Hospital Company No. 1
Massachusetts Field Hospital Company No. 2
Massachusetts Ambulance Company No. 1
Massachusetts Ambulance Company No. 2

National Guard Order of Battle

Pennsylvania Division Headquarters
1st Pennsylvania Infantry
2nd Pennsylvania Infantry
3rd Pennsylvania Infantry
4th Pennsylvania Infantry
6th Pennsylvania Infantry
8th Pennsylvania Infantry
10th Pennsylvania Infantry
16th Pennsylvania Infantry
18th Pennsylvania Infantry
13th Pennsylvania Infantry (replaced 2nd Pennsylvania Infantry, which became 2nd Pennsylvania Artillery; 9th Pennsylvania Infantry became 3rd Pennsylvania Artillery)
1st Pennsylvania Field Artillery
1st Pennsylvania Cavalry
1st Battalion Pennsylvania Signal Corps
Companies A and B Pennsylvania Engineer Battalion (Co. B—to Nogales)
Pennsylvania Field Hospital Company No. 1
Pennsylvania Field Hospital Company No. 2
Pennsylvania Ambulance Company No. 1
Pennsylvania Ambulance Company No. 2

31st Michigan Infantry
32nd Michigan Infantry
33rd Michigan Infantry
Troops A and B Michigan Cavalry
Batteries A and B Michigan Field Artillery
Companies A and B Michigan Engineers
Company A Michigan Signal Corps
Michigan Field Hospital Company No. 1
Michigan Ambulance Company No. 1
Michigan Ambulance Company No. 2

Battery A Rhode Island Field Artillery
1st Rhode Island Cavalry Squadron
Rhode Island Ambulance Company No. 1

1st South Carolina Infantry
2nd South Carolina Infantry

Appendix

Troop A South Carolina Cavalry
Company A South Carolina Engineers
South Carolina Hospital Company No. 1
South Carolina Ambulance Company No. 1

2nd Ohio Infantry
3rd Ohio Infantry
4th Ohio Infantry
5th Ohio Infantry
6th Ohio Infantry
8th Ohio Infantry
Squadron A Ohio Cavalry
1st Ohio Field Artillery Battalion
1st Ohio Engineer Battalion
Company A Ohio Signal Corps
Ohio Field Hospital Company No. 1
Ohio Field Hospital Company No. 2
Ohio Field Hospital Company No. 3
Ohio Ambulance Company No. 1
Ohio Ambulance Company No. 2

1st Kentucky Infantry
2nd Kentucky Infantry
3rd Kentucky Infantry
Company A Kentucky Signal Corps
Kentucky Field Hospital Company No. 1
Kentucky Ambulance Company No. 1

Troop B 10th Tennessee Cavalry
Tennessee Field Hospital Company No. 1
Tennessee Ambulance Company No. 1

1st North Carolina Infantry
2nd North Carolina Infantry
3rd North Carolina Infantry
Troops A and B North Carolina Cavalry
Companies A and B North Carolina Engineers
North Carolina Field Hospital Company No. 1
North Carolina Field Hospital Company No. 2
North Carolina Ambulance Company No. 1

National Guard Order of Battle

1st Georgia Infantry
2nd Georgia Infantry
5th Georgia Infantry
1st Battalion Georgia Field Artillery
Troop A 1st Georgia Cavalry Squadron
2nd Georgia Cavalry Squadron
Georgia Field Hospital Company No. 1

Batteries B and C 1st Colorado Field Artillery Battalion (transferred from Deming)
Company A Colorado Signal Corps

Battery A District of Columbia Field Artillery

1st Alabama Cavalry (transferred from San Antonio)

Deming (Camp Cody)

1st Delaware Infantry

1st Arkansas Infantry
2nd Arkansas Infantry

1st Wyoming Infantry
Wyoming Field Hospital Company No. 1

New Hampshire Field Hospital Company No. 1

Batteries B and C 1st Battalion Colorado Field Artillery (transferred to El Paso)

Columbus (Camp Furlong)

1st New Mexico Infantry
New Mexico Field Hospital Company No. 1
Battery A New Mexico Field Artillery (transferred to El Paso)

2nd Massachusetts Infantry

APPENDIX

DOUGLAS

1st Arizona Infantry
Arizona Field Hospital Company No. 1

1st New Jersey Infantry
4th New Jersey Infantry
5th New Jersey Infantry
1st New Jersey Cavalry Squadron
Batteries A, B, and C New Jersey Field Artillery Battalion
New Jersey Field Hospital Company No. 1
Company A New Jersey Signal Corps
New Jersey Ambulance Company No. 1

2nd Montana Infantry
Troop A Montana Cavalry

Battery B District of Columbia Field Artillery
District of Columbia Field Hospital Company No. 1

Batteries A and C Alabama Field Artillery Battalion

1st Colorado Infantry Battalion
2nd Colorado Infantry Battalion
Colorado Field Hospital Company No. 1

NACO

1st Battalion 1st Arizona Infantry (transferred from and to Douglas)
Arizona Field Hospital Company No. 1

1st District of Columbia Separate Infantry Battalion

NOGALES

Battery A Utah Field Artillery
1st Squadron 1st Utah Cavalry
2nd Squadron 1st Utah Cavalry
Utah Field Hospital Company No. 1

National Guard Order of Battle

2nd California Infantry
5th California Infantry
7th California Infantry
1st Battalion California Field Artillery
1st Squadron California Cavalry
Company A California Engineers
Company A California Signal Corps
California Field Hospital Company No. 1
California Ambulance Company No. 1

1st Connecticut Infantry
2nd Connecticut Infantry
Troops A and B 5th Connecticut Cavalry
Company A Connecticut Signal Corps
Connecticut Field Hospital No. 1

Company B Pennsylvania Engineers (transferred from and to El Paso)

2nd Idaho Infantry

1st Alabama Infantry
2nd Alabama Infantry
4th Alabama Infantry
Company A Alabama Signal Corps
Alabama Field Hospital Company No. 1
Alabama Ambulance Company No. 1

California

3rd Oregon Infantry
Troop A Oregon Cavalry
Battery A Oregon Field Artillery

2nd Washington Infantry
Troop B Washington Cavalry
Company A Washington Signal Corps

Notes

Abbreviations

AA	*Alpine Avalanche*
ADS	*Arizona Daily Star*
AGC	Adjutant General Correspondence
AMJ	*Albuquerque Morning Journal*
AZR	*Arizona Republican*
BDFP	*Burlington Democrat Free Press*
BDH	*Brownsville Daily Herald*
BI	Bureau of Investigation
CCC	*Corpus Christi Caller*
EPH	*El Paso Herald*
EPMT	*El Paso Morning Times*
FFC	Frederick Funston Collection
LWT	*Laredo Weekly Times*
MNGM	Massachusetts National Guard Museum
NARS	National Archives and Records Service
NDH	*Nogales Daily Herald*
NMAG	New Mexico Adjutant General Correspondence
NYSMM	New York State Military Museum
NYT	*New York Times*
RAJ	Records of the Adjutant General's Office
RDS	Records of the Department of State
RG	Record Group
RGR	*Rio Grande Republican*
SAE	*San Antonio Express*
SFNM	*Santa Fe New Mexican*
TMFM	Texas Military Forces Museum

Introduction

1. *War Department Annual Reports, 1916*, 1:474.

2. Buckley, "Trucks along the Southwest Border," 217; Reilly, "The National Guard on the Mexican Border," 229.

3. See, for example, Matthews, *U.S. Army on the Mexican Border*; Cyrulik, "A Strategic Examination of the Punitive Expedition"; Tompkins, *Chasing Villa*; Braddy, *Pershing's Expedition in Mexico*; Clendenen, *Blood on the Border*; Mason, *Great Pursuit*; Welsome, *The General & the Jaguar*; Hurst, *Pancho Villa and Black Jack Pershing*. See also Salinas Carranza, *La Expedición Punitiva*; Fabela et al., eds. *Documentos Históricos*, vols. 12 and 13 deal with the Punitive Expedition.

4. Howard, "New Yorkers on the Southern Border," 12–16.

5. Dubach, "Reinforcements on the Border."

6. *SAE*, June 19, 1916.

7. Whitehorne, *The Inspectors General*, 70.

8. Harris and Sadler, *The Border and the Revolution*; *The Texas Rangers and the Mexican Revolution*; *The Secret War in El Paso*; and *The Plan de San Diego*.

Chapter 1

1. Clendenen, *Blood on the Border*, 147–49.

2. See Meyer, *Huerta*.

3. Richmond, *Venustiano Carranza's Nationalist Struggle*.

4. Quirk, *An Affair of Honor*.

5. See Katz, *The Life & Times of Pancho Villa*.

6. The plan was translated by the Immigration Service and is in E. P. Reynolds to Supervising Inspector, Jan. 30, 1915, Albert B. Fall Collection microfilm, roll 13, Archives and Special Collections, New Mexico State University, Las Cruces, New Mexico. It was also published in *Investigation of Mexican Affairs*, 2:1205–1207.

7. Harris and Sadler, "The Plan of San Diego," 381–408, and *The Plan de San Diego*; in "Borderline Failure," Orr seems unaware of the extent to which Carranza manipulated the Plan de San Diego in order to secure diplomatic recognition in 1915 and to attempt to force the recall of the Punitive Expedition in 1916.

8. For the official army report, see Commanding Officer to Commanding General, Southern Department, Mar. 11, 1916, Records of the IG Office, Entry 25, Box 17, RG 159, National Archives and Records Service, Washington, D.C., hereafter cited as NARS.

9. Link, *The Papers of Woodrow Wilson*, 36:295–96.

10. Lansing to All, Mar. 10, 1916, 812.00/19517, Records of the Department of State, RG 59: Decimal Files, Internal Affairs of Mexico, 1910–29, microcopy no. 274, NARS, hereafter cited as RDS.

11. *SAE*, May 7, 8, 1916; *EPMT*, May 8, 10, 11, 12, 14, 15, 1916; *AA*, May 11, 1916; Clendenen, *Blood on the Border*, 279–81.

12. *War Department Annual Reports, 1916*, 1:872–73.

13. *EPMT*, May 15, 22, 1916.

14. Tyler, "The Little Punitive Expedition," 271–91; Cramer, "The Punitive Expedition," 200–227.

15. Three troops and the machine gun troop of the 6th were at Sierra Blanca, one troop at Valentine, three troops at Marfa, and two troops at Marathon. *EPMT*, May 22–24, 29, 1916. In an effort to improve communications, the army had laid a telegraph line from Marathon to Boquillas, with outposts along the river tapping into this main line. However, on occasion the line along the river was cut, presumably by Mexicans. *EPMT*, May 11, 14, 16, 21, 22, 1916.

16. *SAE*, May 9, 10, 1916.
17. Clendenen, *Blood on the Border*, 279–81; Tyler, *The Big Bend*, 165–69.
18. *EPMT*, May 16–18, 1916.
19. *EPMT*, May 23, 1916.
20. *EPMT*, May 16, 1916.
21. *NDH*, Apr. 6, May 10, 12, 16, June 1, 12, 13, 1916.
22. Scott and Funston to Secretary of War, May 8, 1916, 812.00/18125, RDS.

Chapter 2

1. *Report on Mobilization*, 10.
2. Link, *The Papers of Woodrow Wilson*, 37:121–22, 138.
3. "Data Furnished by the Adjutants General."
4. Gen. Frederick Funston, Annual Report for Fiscal Year 1916, Southern Department, Records of the Adjutant General's Office 1780s–1917, RG 94, NARS.
5. *Tombstone Prospector*, June 25, 1914.
6. *Report on Mobilization*, 948; *NDH*, Mar. 21, 1916; Ellis, "Men of Taylor!," 259–61.
7. *SAE*, May 17, 1916.
8. *ADS*, May 10, 1916.
9. *NDH*, May 12, 1916.
10. Tackenberg, "'Sore as a Boil,'" 443n1; *ADS*, May 10, 1916.
11. Dumke, "Douglas," 283–98.
12. *ADS*, May 10, 11, 1916.
13. *ADS*, May 12, 13, 1916; *EPMT*, May 11, 1916.
14. *ADS*, May 13, 1916; Tackenberg, "'Sore as a Boil,'" 432.
15. *Arizona Republic*, May 9, 1956.
16. "History of Arizona's National Guard," 7, Arizona State Archives, Phoenix, Arizona.
17. *ADS*, July 6, 1916; *EPMT*, May 11, July 10, 1916.
18. Tackenberg, "'Sore as a Boil,'" 431; *ADS*, May 12, 13, 1916; Wilson, "Peoples of the Middle Gila," chapter 17: 1–4.
19. There is a photograph of the encampment in Tackenberg, "'Sore as a Boil,'" 432.
20. *ADS*, May 13, 1916.
21. *EPMT*, May 19, 1916.
22. *ADS*, May 16, 1916; see also *ADS*, May 18, 1916.
23. *ADS*, May 23, 1916; see also *ADS*, May 24, 1916.
24. *ADS*, May 27, 1916; *SAE*, May 28, 1916.
25. *EPMT*, July 2, 1916; Tackenberg, "'Sore as a Boil,'" 443n2.
26. *ADS*, May 28, 1916.
27. *ADS*, May 28, June 27, 1916.
28. For example, the Tucson newspaper reported that "Ex-Deputy Sheriff Taylor, of this county, who disappeared during the mobilization of the national guard, of which he was a member, is under arrest at Calexico, Cal., on the charge of bootlegging, according to information received by local officers," *ADS*, June 21, 1916.
29. *ADS*, June 27, 28, July 6, 7, 1916.
30. *SAE*, June 18, 1916.
31. *EPMT*, June 2, 1916.
32. *SFNM*, Mar. 11, 1916.

33. Adjutant General to Chief, Jan. 7, 1916, New Mexico Adjutant General Correspondence, 1913–17, New Mexico State Records Center and Archives, Santa Fe, New Mexico, hereafter cited as NMAG.

34. *Report of the Adjutant General . . . New Mexico . . . November 30, 1914 to November 30, 1916*, 38.

35. Comfort to Adjutant General, May 19, 1916, NMAG.

36. *Report on Mobilization*, 948; *NDH*, Mar. 21, 1916; *SAE*, May 17, 1916.

37. Herring to Governor, Apr. 10, 1916, NMAG; *SFNM*, Mar. 11, 1916.

38. Chief, Division of Militia Affairs to Adjutant General of New Mexico, May 7, 1915, NMAG; "Data for Armory Inspection Reports—Infantry—1916," NMAG; *SFNM*, Mar. 11, 1916.

39. *Report of the Adjutant General . . . New Mexico, 1914–1916*, 34; see also Herring to Martin, June 9, 1916, NMAG.

40. General Orders No. 11, May 9, 1916, NMAG; *AMJ*, May 12, 1916.

41. A roster of the New Mexico National Guard is in Busch, "Guarding the Border," 108–27.

42. *AMJ*, May 12, 1916.

43. *SFNM*, May 12, 1916.

44. ——— to O'Ryan, May 27, 1916; Heard to Adjutant General, July 19, 1916; Adjutant General to Department Adjutant, Sept. 1, 1916, NMAG.

45. *Report of the Adjutant General . . . New Mexico, 1914–1916*, 5.

46. ——— to O'Ryan, May 27, 1916, NMAG.

47. *Report on Mobilization*, 110.

48. *Report on Mobilization*, 139.

49. See, for example, Howard to Herring, May 11, 1916, NMAG.

50. *SFNM*, May 10–12, 13, 1916; Deming even observed a civic holiday when its Company I left for Columbus on May 13. *EPMT*, May 14, 1916.

51. Schrader, *United States Army Logistics*, 2:391.

52. *EPMT*, May 11, 1916.

53. *EPMT*, May 24, June 4, 1916.

54. *EPMT*, May 29, 31, 1916.

55. Schrader, *United States Army Logistics*, 2:394; King, Biggs, and Criner, *Spearhead of Logistics*, 90; *EPMT*, June 4, 1916.

56. *SAE*, May 22, 1916.

57. *SFNM*, May 19, 1916.

58. *EPMT*, July 16, 1916; regarding the campaign of eastern newspapers to denigrate the National Guard, see O'Ryan to Herring, May 20, 1916; Kelly to Brooks, May 26, 1916; Foster to Herring, May 26, 1916; Herring to Reilly, June 8, 1916, NMAG.

59. Busch, "Guarding the Border," 54.

60. *SFNM*, May 19, 1916.

61. *SFNM*, May 19, 1916.

62. *SFNM*, May 13, 15, 18, 27, 1916.

63. *SFNM*, May 18, 1916.

64. *SFNM*, May 19, 1916.

65. *Report of the Adjutant General . . . New Mexico, 1914–1916*, 9; *EPMT*, June 6, 9, 1916; *SFNM*, May 18, 1916.

66. *SFNM*, May 23, 1916.

67. *RGR*, May 12, 1916.

68. *SFNM*, May 12, 1916.
69. *Report of the Adjutant General . . . New Mexico, 1914–1916*, 8–9; *SFNM*, May 18, 20, 1916.
70. *Annual Report of the Adjutant General . . . Massachusetts . . . December 31, 1916*, 45.
71. *Report of the Adjutant General . . . New Mexico, 1914–1916*, 9; *SFNM*, May 30, 1916; *AMJ*, June 5, 1916.
72. *SFNM*, May 18, May 22, 1916; *EPMT*, May 18, 1916.
73. *SFNM*, May 24, 1916.
74. *SFNM*, May 18, 1916; see also *SFNM*, May 19, 1916.
75. *SFNM*, May 27, 30, 1916.
76. *SFNM*, May 19, 1916.
77. *SFNM*, May 20, 1916.
78. *SFNM*, May 25, 1916.
79. *SFNM*, June 5, 1916.
80. *SFNM*, May 19, 1916.
81. *SFNM*, May 19, June 5, 1916.
82. *SFNM*, May 22, 1916.
83. *SFNM*, May 24, 25, 1916.
84. *SFNM*, May 26, 1916; see also *AMJ*, May 29, 1916; Horne, *Black and Brown*, 124.
85. *SFNM*, May 27, 1916.
86. *SFNM*, May 29, 1916.
87. *SFNM*, May 29, 1916.
88. *SFNM*, May 29, 1916.
89. *SFNM*, May 29, 1916; *EPMT*, June 24, 1916.
90. ——— to O'Ryan, May 27, 1916, NMAG.
91. *SFNM*, May 30, 1916.
92. *SFNM*, June 2, 1916.
93. *SFNM*, June 8, 1916.
94. *EPMT*, Mar. 13, 1917.
95. *EPMT*, June 9, 17, 19, 1916; *SAE*, June 15, 1916.
96. *SAE*, June 10, 1916; *SFNM*, May 31, 1916.
97. *SFNM*, May 31, 1916.
98. New Mexico opened a recruiting office in El Paso. *EPMT*, June 24, 29, 1916; in August 1916, Battery A was reduced to seeking recruits in Arizona. *EPMT*, Aug. 13, 1916.
99. National Guard scandals were not limited to Texas, however. Senator Borah of Idaho, for example, had charged that some of the federal government's appropriation for the guard had been embezzled. *NDH*, Apr. 15, 1915.
100. Memorandum for the Adjutant General, Apr. 23, 1915; Adjutant General to Commanding General, Apr. 24, 1915; Assistant Attorney General to Secretary of War, Apr. 26, 1915; see also Chief, Division of Militia Affairs to Adjutant General, Apr. 28, 30, 1915, all in Records of the Adjutant General's Office 1780s–1917, RG 94, NARS (hereafter cited as RAJ).
101. Garrison to Ferguson, July 1, 1915, RAJ.
102. *Biennial Report of the Adjutant General of Texas . . . January 1, 1915 to December 31, 1916*, 53.
103. *BDH*, June 13, 1917.
104. Harris and Sadler, *Texas Rangers*, 208.

105. Harris and Sadler, *Texas Rangers*, 205–209; *SAE*, June 9, 12, 13, 1916; Milner, "An Agonizing Evolution," does not mention this affair.

106. Baker to Ferguson, May 1, 1916, "Mexican Border Service, Original Telegrams, Documents from the Texas Adjutant General's Office 1916–1917," Texas Military Forces Museum, Camp Mabry, Austin, Texas, hereafter cited as TMFM.

107. "Hulen, John Augustus," in *New Handbook of Texas*, ed. Tyler, Barnett, Barkley, 3:778–79; Henderson, *History of the 141st Infantry*, xli.

108. Baker to Ferguson, May 1, 5, 1916, TMFM; *SAE*, May 3, 4, 7, 1916.

109. [Hutchings] to Wolfe, May 9, 1916, TMFM; in commemoration, on February 3, 1966, Governor John Connally formally designated the month of May 1966 as Border Service Month.

110. *SFNM*, May 30, 1916.

111. *AA*, June 15, 1916.

112. *AA*, June 15, 1916.

113. *SAE*, May 17, 1916.

114. *Biennial Report . . . Texas . . . 1915–1916*, 104; for a photo of Governor Ferguson and his personal staff, see *SAE*, May 7, 1916.

115. *LWT*, Dec. 31, 1916; *SAE*, Jan. 13, 1917.

116. *Biennial Report . . . Texas . . . 1915–1916*, 6; *SAE*, May 17, 1916.

117. Battery B was mustered in San Antonio on June 30 and Battery C in Dallas on July 4, 1916. *Biennial Report . . . Texas . . . 1915–1916*, 139; "Swearing in the Militia," 1867–68; Chief, Militia Bureau to Adjutant General of Texas, December 9, 1916, TMFM.

118. Hutchings to Robinson, May 10, 1916; Barnum to Hutchings, May 10, 1916, TMFM.

119. Hutchings to Chief, Division of Militia Affairs, May 8, 1916, TMFM; Long to Chief, Division of Militia Affairs, May 9, 1916, TMFM.

120. Mills to Adjutant General, May 11, 1916, TMFM; *EPMT*, May 14, 1916.

121. Long to Adjutant General of Texas, May 3, 1916, Adjutant General Correspondence, Texas State Archives, Austin, Texas, hereafter cited as AGC.

122. "Camp Mabry," in *New Handbook of Texas*, ed. Tyler, Barnett, Barkley, 1:941.

123. Funston to Ferguson, May 9, 1916, TMFM.

124. *Biennial Report . . . Texas . . . 1915–1916*, 4; Milner, "An Agonizing Evolution," is inadequate on the topic of the 1916–17 Texas National Guard service on the Mexican border with one page (p.50) devoted to the mobilization and a map (p.54) that shows where the guard was stationed on the border.

125. *SAE*, May 13, 1916; *EPMT*, May 12, 1916.

126. "Fort Sam Houston," in *New Handbook of Texas*, ed. Tyler, Barnett, Barkley, 2:1117.

127. *Biennial Report . . . Texas . . . 1915–1916*, 3–5; "Swearing in the Militia," 1867–68.

128. *SAE*, May 10, 1916.

129. *SAE*, May 11, 1916.

130. *SAE*, May 12, 13, 14, 1916; *EPMT*, May 30, 1916.

131. *SAE*, May 13, 1916.

132. *SAE*, May 15, 17, 1916.

133. *SAE*, May 22, 1916.

134. *SAE*, May 23–28, 30, 1916; *EPMT*, May 9, 1916.

135. *SAE*, June 1, 6, 8, 1916; *EPMT*, Aug. 21, 1916.

136. *SAE*, June 9, 1916; *EPMT*, June 22, 1916.

137. *SAE*, May 20, 21, 1916.
138. *SAE*, May 17–20, 1916.
139. *Report on Mobilization*, 102–103; *SAE*, May 23, 1916; *EPMT*, June 6, 1916.
140. *SAE*, May 11, 17, 1916; *EPMT*, May 12, 1916.
141. *SAE*, May 14, 23, 26, 1916.
142. *SAE*, May 27, 28, 31, 1916.
143. *SAE*, June 1, 1916; "Leon Springs," in *New Handbook of Texas*, ed. Tyler, Barnett, Barkley, 4:163.
144. *EPMT*, June 3, 1916.
145. *SAE*, May 23, 1916.
146. See Elam, "Big Bend Archives," 117–22.
147. *General Funston's Annual Report for the Southern Department, 1916*, 42; RAJ, RG 94, NARS.
148. Justice, *Revolution on the Rio Grande*; Cano and Sochat, *Bandido*; Smithers, "Bandit Raids," 75–105.
149. Wilson and Taylor, *Southern Pacific*, 78–79; a photograph of the Pecos High Bridge is in Orsi, *Sunset Limited*, 23.
150. Davenport, *Soldiering at Marfa*, 21, 22, 25, 26, 60.
151. For a scholarly study see Ragsdale, *Quicksilver*.
152. *AA*, Sept. 21, 28, Oct. 19, 1916, Jan. 11, 25, Feb. 15, 1917.
153. *EPMT*, Aug. 8, 1916, Feb. 3, 1917.
154. Perry to Wilmot, May 11, 1916; Wilmot to Hutchings, May 12, 1916, AGC.
155. Glenn to Ferguson, May 12, 1916, AGC.
156. Commanding Officer, Western Texas Cavalry Patrol District to Commanding General, Southern Department, Oct. 22, 1915, No. 2332526-A, with attachments, RAJ, RG 94; a detailed discussion of the Big Bend supply system and problems is in Smithers, *Chronicles of the Big Bend*, 18–29.
157. *EPMT*, June 6, 8, 15, 1916.
158. *SAE*, May 10, 1916.
159. *SAE*, May 20, 1916; *EPMT*, June 20, 1916.
160. "Memorandum for the Chief of Staff," Tasker Bliss Papers, Library of Congress, Washington, D.C.
161. *EPMT*, June 13, 1916.
162. *EPMT*, May 25, June 4, 1916.
163. *Biennial Report . . . Texas . . . 1915–1916*, 7.
164. For example, two companies of the 4th Texas arrived at Marathon to relieve the 127th Coast Artillery Company, which was transferred on June 3 to Comstock and Dryden. A company of Texans relieved the Coast Artillery company stationed at Sanderson, and Company D, 4th Texas, relieved the 69th Coast Artillery Company at Sierra Blanca. *SAE*, May 25, 26, 28, 29, 1916; *EPMT*, May 27, 29, June 2, 1916.
165. *SAE*, June 6, 1916.
166. *SAE*, May 27, 28, 31, 1916.
167. *SAE*, May 27, 28, 31, 1916; *NYT*, June 20, 1916; *AA*, June 1, 8, July 6, 1916.
168. *EPMT*, June 5, 8, 14, 16, 1916.
169. *AA*, June 8, 1916.
170. *SAE*, June 3, 1916.
171. Harris, "Protecting the Big Bend," 292–302.
172. *Biennial Report . . . Texas . . . 1915–1916*, 7.

173. *SAE*, July 18, 1916.
174. *NYT*, June 20, 1916.
175. *SAE*, May 18, 1916.
176. "Hulen, John Augustus," in *New Handbook of Texas*, ed. Tyler, Barnett, Barkley, 3:778–79; *SAE*, May 17, 20, 21, 1916; *EPMT*, May 8, 1916.
177. *SAE*, June 3, 1916.
178. *SAE*, June 5, 1916.
179. *SAE*, June 15, 1916.
180. *SAE*, June 4, 1916.
181. *SAE*, June 1, 1916.
182. *SAE*, May 29, June 3, 1916.
183. *SAE*, June 6, 1916.
184. *SAE*, June 10, 1916.
185. *SAE*, June 18, 1916.
186. Adjutant General to Carlton, May 26, 1916, TMFM.
187. *SAE*, June 18, 1916.

Chapter 3

1. Harris and Sadler, *Texas Rangers*, 303–305.
2. Link, *Wilson*, 288.
3. Memorandum, June 8, 1916, Fierros Brigade file; Fierros to González, June 9, 1916, Esteban Fierros file, both in Pablo González Archive, Nettie Lee Benson Latin American Collection, University of Texas at Austin.
4. Robertson to Lansing, Mar. 28, 1917, 812.00/20746; Garrett to Lansing, June 8, 1916, 812.00/18352 and 812.00/18358, RDS.
5. Harris and Sadler, "Plan of San Diego," 398.
6. *SAE*, June 12, 1916.
7. *SAE*, June 14, 1912.
8. Funston to Secretary of War, June 7, 1916, 812.00/18364; Garrett to Secretary of State, June 7, 1916, 812.00/18336; Robertson to same, 812.00/20165, all in RDS.
9. Rodgers report, June 12, 1916, 812.00/18394, RDS.
10. *SAE*, June 17, 1916, has a photo of the three prisoners, the captured flag, and the Hispanic cowboy who warned ranchers of the raiders' approach.
11. Harris and Sadler, "Plan of San Diego," 394.
12. Harris and Sadler, *Plan de San Diego*, 198.
13. Link, *Wilson*, 300.
14. Stout, *Border Conflict*, xi.
15. *War Department Annual Reports, 1916*, 1:25, 26.
16. *SAE*, May 8, 9, 1916.
17. "Memorandum for the Adjutant General," May 26, 1916, and "Memorandum for the Chief of Staff," May 26, 1916, Tasker Bliss Papers, Library of Congress, Washington, D.C.
18. *SAE*, May 12, 20, 22, 1916.
19. *War Department Annual Reports, 1916*, 1:1165–66.
20. *War Department Annual Reports, 1916*, 1:185; *SAE*, May 10, 11, 1916.
21. Bliss to Chief of Staff, June 6, 22, Dec. 5, 1916; Bliss to Finley, June 24, 1916, Tasker Bliss Papers, Library of Congress, Washington, D.C.

22. *Report on Mobilization*, 150–51.
23. Lansing to Secretary of the Treasury, June 19, 1916, 812.113/4266a, RDS.
24. Link, *Papers of Woodrow Wilson*, 38:378–86.
25. Memorandum for the Adjutant General," June 25, 1916, Tasker Bliss Papers, Library of Congress, Washington, D.C.
26. Lansing to Wilson, June 21, 1916, 812.00/18533A, RDS.
27. *SAE*, June 22, 1916.
28. Link, *Papers of Woodrow Wilson*, 37:281.
29. "Memorandum for the Chief of Staff," June 22, 1916, Tasker Bliss Papers, Library of Congress, Washington, D.C; *SAE*, May 14, June 18, 23, 1916.
30. Link, *Papers of Woodrow Wilson*, 37:283–86; see also Funston to McCain, June 27, 1916, 315, Frederick Funston Collection, Kansas State Historical Society, hereafter cited as FFC.
31. *NYT*, June 19, 1916.
32. *Seattle Sunday Times*, June 20, 1916; *NYT*, June 20–22, 1916.
33. Link, *Papers of Woodrow Wilson*, 37:293–94; *SAE*, June 25, 26, 1916.
34. Link, *Papers of Woodrow Wilson*, 37:302; Gilderhus, *Diplomacy and Revolution*, 46.
35. González to Carranza, June 24, 1916, Telegrams, State of Morelos, 1916, Venustiano Carranza Archive, Centro de Estudios Históricos Carso (formerly Condumex), México, D.F.
36. Link, *Papers of Woodrow Wilson*, 38:153.

Chapter 4

1. *Report on Mobilization*, 10–11; Bruscino, "The Army and Security," 40.
2. Clendenen, *Blood on the Border*, 288–89, 297.
3. *Fifteenth Biennial Report of the Adjutant General . . . Oregon . . . November 1, 1914 to October 31, 1916*, 70.
4. Gibbons, *How the Laconia Sank*, 41–43.
5. *War Department Annual Reports, 1916*, 1:895.
6. *Report on Mobilization*, 96.
7. "Memorandum for the Adjutant General," June 25, 1916, Tasker Bliss Papers, Library of Congress, Washington, D.C.
8. Ibid.
9. *War Department Annual Reports, 1916*, 1:190; but the War Department's 1917 annual report states that as of July 31 there were 107,133 guardsmen (5,056 officers and 102,077 enlisted men) on border duty: *War Department Annual Reports, 1917*, 1:197; furthermore, it has been stated that "in all, 254,314 National Guardsmen were mobilized for duty on the Mexican border," Schrader, *United States Army Logistics*, 2:390, a figure much at odds with the official number of approximately 150,000.
10. Palmer, *Newton D. Baker*, 1:7, 11–18.
11. *War Department Annual Reports, 1916*, 1:163–67, 897–904.
12. See, for instance, George Marvin, "Marking Time with Mexico," 526–33.
13. *Report on Mobilization*, 97.
14. *War Department Annual Reports, 1917*, 1:447.
15. "Transportation of Troops," 2.
16. "Transportation of Troops," 5.

17. Gibbons, *How the Laconia Sank*, 80–81.
18. Gibbons, *How the Laconia Sank*, 82–83.
19. Gibbons, *How the Laconia Sank*, 81.
20. Cooper, *Citizens as Soldiers*, 161; *Report on Mobilization*, 25–26.
21. *Report on Mobilization*, 134.
22. Whitehorne, *Inspectors General*, 72–73.
23. *War Department Annual Reports, 1916*, 1:819, 838; *Seattle Daily Times*, July 25, 1916.
24. *Report on Mobilization*, 23–24, 134.
25. *Report on Mobilization*, 53; transporting the first 100,000 guardsmen and their equipment required 4,900 road engines, about 3,000 passenger cars, some 400 baggage cars (most equipped as kitchens), 1,300 boxcars, 2,000 stock cars, and 800 flat cars. *War Department Annual Reports, 1916*, 1:193, 379.
26. Risch, *Quartermaster Support*, 573.
27. *Report on Mobilization*, 5.
28. Whitehorne, *Inspectors General*, 73.
29. *War Department Annual Reports, 1917*, 1:254–55.
30. *Report on Mobilization*, 3, 59–64.
31. *Report on Mobilization*, 71–92.
32. Whitehorne, *Inspectors General*, 74.
33. *War Department Annual Reports, 1916*, 1:191; Whitehorne, *Inspectors General*, 74.
34. *Report on Mobilization*, 92.

Chapter 5

1. "MG Frederick Funston"; "Frederick Funston"; Coats, *Gathering at the Golden Gate*, 234, 239; Linn, *The Philippine War*, 108–109, 124; Swift, "Soldiers," 10–17.
2. "Fort Sam Houston," in *New Handbook of Texas*, ed. Tyler, Barnett, Barkley, 2:1117.
3. *SAE*, June 21, 1916.
4. Fort Worth was selected as the supply center for the U.S. Army on the border and in Mexico. *SAE*, July 2, 4, 1916.
5. *SAE*, July 1, 2, 1916.
6. *SAE*, July 2, 1916.
7. *SAE*, July 5, 10, 12, 14, 1916.
8. *SAE*, July 3, 1916.
9. *SAE*, July 4, 1916.
10. *SAE*, July 14, 1916.
11. *SAE*, July 13, 16, 1916.
12. *SAE*, July 4, 1916.
13. *The Adjutant General's Report Illinois 1916–1917 Roster*, 801. The best account of the Illinois mobilization is McCann, *With the National Guard*, 90–120.
14. *SAE*, June 25, 1916.
15. *SAE*, June 29, 1916.
16. *War Department Annual Reports, 1916*, 1:342, 344.
17. *SAE*, July 1, 2, 1916; the flavor of the various National Guard units' railroad trips to the border is captured in Meggs, *The War Train*.

18. For a history of the 1st Illinois, see McCann, *With the National Guard*, 247–71.
19. *SAE*, July 2, 1916.
20. *Blue Book of the State of Illinois 1919–1920*, 84.
21. *Report on Mobilization*, 12.
22. Gibbons, *How the Laconia Sank*, 61–62.
23. *SAE*, July 8, 1916.
24. *The Adjutant General's Report . . . 1917*, 681; *SAE*, July 9, 13, 1916.
25. Gibbons, *How the Laconia Sank*, 65–66.
26. *SAE*, July 14, 1916; *The Adjutant General's Report Illinois 1917*, viii; Lee, "Ready and Willing," 62.
27. Finnegan, "Preparedness in Wisconsin," 201.
28. *Report on Mobilization*, 131.
29. Thisted, *With the Wisconsin National Guard*, 45.
30. Thisted, *With the Wisconsin National Guard*, 40.
31. War strength was: infantry company—150 men; cavalry troop—100; field artillery battery—176; field hospital—67; regimental medical detachment—24. Thisted, *With the Wisconsin National Guard*, 12.
32. Thisted, *With the Wisconsin National Guard*, 42.
33. Small units continued to arrive: Company K, Kansas Signal Corps on July 26, transferred in from Eagle Pass, and a company of Texas Engineers, from Port Arthur, who rather melodramatically called themselves "The Devil's Own," on July 29.
34. *Report on Mobilization*, 63.
35. *SAE*, July 17, 1916.
36. *SAE*, July 18, 1916.
37. *SAE*, July 17, 18, 1916.
38. *SAE*, July 14, 15, 1916.
39. *SAE*, July 16, 1916.
40. *War Department Annual Reports, 1917*, 1:350.
41. *SAE*, July 14, 16, 1916.
42. *War Department Annual Reports, 1917*, 1:472.
43. *SAE*, July 17, 1916.
44. *SAE*, June 25, 1916.
45. *SAE*, July 16, 18, 19, 22, 1916
46. Funston to Adjutant General, Aug. 1, 1916, FFC.
47. *SAE*, July 18, 1916.
48. Thisted, *With the Wisconsin National Guard*, 39.
49. Hannah, *Manhood*, 3–4; *SAE*, July 6, 7, 8, 16, 1916; *Quincy Herald-Whig*, Feb. 19, 1984.
50. See Christian, *Black Soldiers*; Leiker, *Racial Borders*; Weaver, *The Senator*; cf. Nash, "Blacks on the Border."
51. *Muscogee Times Democrat*, July 1, 1916.
52. *SAE*, July 15, 1916; see also *SAE*, July 16, 1916.
53. *BDH*, July 26, 1916.
54. *SAE*, July 25, 26, 1916.
55. *SAE*, July 27, 1916.
56. *SAE*, Sept. 15, 1916; Texans' antipathy toward black soldiers was intensified as a result of the bloody riot in Houston in 1917, Haynes, *A Night of Violence*.
57. *SAE*, July 26, 1916.

58. *BDH*, Aug. 24, 25, 27, 28, Sept. 3, Oct. 8, Nov. 1, Dec. 1, 11, 1917; *EPMT*, Aug. 24–31, Sept. 2, 4, 28, 29, Oct. 8, 14, 21, 1917.
59. McCann, *With the National Guard*, 153 ff.
60. McCann, *With the National Guard*, 156.
61. *SAE*, July 25, 1916.
62. *SAE*, July 23, 26, 28, 1916.
63. McCann, *With the National Guard*, 156–58.
64. McCann, *With the National Guard*, 170–71.
65. McCann, *With the National Guard*, 148.
66. Thisted, *With the Wisconsin National Guard*, 15.
67. *War Department Annual Reports, 1916*, 1:60.
68. *SAE*, June 25, 1916.
69. *SAE*, July 17, 23, 1916.
70. *EPMT*, Aug. 3, Sept. 3, 1916.
71. *SAE*, July 28, 1916.
72. *SAE*, July 25, 1916.
73. *SAE*, July 27, 1916.
74. *SAE*, Dec. 18, 20, 1916, Jan. 3, 1917.
75. *Report on Mobilization*, 64–70; *War Department Annual Reports, 1917*, 1:318–19; Risch, *Quartermaster Support*, 593–95; *SAE*, July 27, 1916.
76. *SAE*, July 11, 1916.
77. *SAE*, July 27, 1916.
78. *SAE*, July 27, 29, 1916.
79. *SAE* July 31, 1916.
80. *SAE*, July 28, 1916.
81. *SAE*, July 31, 1916.
82. *SAE*, Oct. 31, Nov. 2, 10, 1916.
83. *SAE*, Sept. 11, 17, Oct. 8, 14, 21, Nov. 26, 1916.
84. *SAE*, Nov. 29, Dec. 1, 21, 25, 1916.
85. *SAE*, Sept. 7, 10, 1916.
86. *SAE*, Nov. 19, 1916.
87. *SAE*, Dec. 18, 1916.
88. Funston to Rev. E. T. Mobberly, Nov. 4, 1916, FFC.
89. See Col. Malvern Hill Barnum to Department Commander, Oct. 23, 1916, FFC.
90. *SAE*, Sept. 9, 23, 25, 28, Dec. 14, 1916.
91. *SAE*, Sept. 26, Nov. 16–18, 1916.
92. Chaplains to Funston, Dec. 13, 1916, FFC; *SAE*, Nov. 19, 26, Dec. 8, 24, 1916, Jan. 16, 1917.
93. *SAE*, Dec. 8, 1916.
94. Funston to Gambrell, Dec. 6, 1916; Ham to Funston, Jan. 8, 1917; Funston to Ham, Feb. 15, 1917, FFC; *SAE*, Dec. 10, 1916.
95. *SAE*, Dec. 10, 14, 1916.
96. *NYT*, Nov. 20, 21, Dec. 11, 1916.
97. Baker to Oliver, Jan. 12, 1917, [Judge Advocate General] to Funston, Jan. 19, 1917, FFC.
98. *SAE*, January 16, 1917.
99. Reeder to Baker, Dec. 4, 1916, FFC; *SAE*, Dec. 16, 1916.
100. Maher and Bohls, *Long Live the Longhorns*, 49; *SAE*, Oct. 14, 1916.

101. *SAE*, Oct. 30, Nov. 15–27, 30, Dec. 1, 1916.
102. *SAE*, Dec. 15–17, 1916.
103. *SAE*, Dec. 24, 28, 1916, Jan. 1, 4, 6, 7, 10, 11, 14–17, 1917.
104. *SAE*, Jan. 7, 9, 15, 18–22, 28, 1917.
105. *SAE*, July 27, 29, 30, 1916.
106. *Report on Mobilization*, 50–52.
107. *EPMT*, Nov. 12, 1916.
108. Harris and Sadler, "Bastion," 72; *EPMT*, July 15, 1916.
109. *SAE*, July 30, 1916.
110. *SAE*, Sept. 10, 1916.
111. Funston to Adjutant General, Sept. 3, 1916, and Secretary of War to A. S. Burleson, Sept. 8, 1916, both in the Roy W. Aldrich Papers, Center for American History, University of Texas, Austin.
112. *SAE*, Sept. 3, 7–10, 1916; a minor addition to the troops at Camp Wilson was the arrival on September 10 of Company H Texas Engineers, from Dallas. The unit was to receive equipment and training before being assigned to the border. *SAE*, Sept. 10, 1916.
113. *SAE*, Sept. 11, 1916.
114. *SAE*, Oct. 3, 4, 17, 1916, Dec. 31, 1916.
115. *SAE*, Oct. 10, 12, 1916.
116. *NYT*, June 20, 28, 1916; *Report of the Adjutant General of West Virginia 1915–16*, 5, 8.
117. *SAE*, Oct. 21, 1916; Bailey, "A Search for Identity," 134–41; Bailey published his dissertation as *Mountaineers Are Free*.
118. *SAE*, Oct. 22, 1916.
119. *War Department Annual Reports, 1917*, 1:475–76.
120. *SAE*, Sept. 6, 8, 1916.
121. *SAE*, Sept. 14, 1916.
122. *SAE*, Sept. 16, 18, 1916.
123. *SAE*, Sept. 16–20, 22–28, Oct. 3, 1916.
124. *SAE*, Sept. 20–24, 29, Oct. 1–5, 1916.
125. *Biennial Report of the Adjutant General . . . Mississippi . . . 1916–1917*, 9.
126. *Biennial Report of the Adjutant General . . . Mississippi . . . 1916–1917*, 21–22.
127. *Biennial Report of the Adjutant General . . . Mississippi . . . 1916–1917*, 34.
128. *SAE*, Oct. 25, Nov. 18, 1916.
129. *SAE*, Nov. 3, Dec. 3, 18, 1916.
130. *SAE*, Nov. 12, 1916.
131. D'Este, *Eisenhower*, 115–16.
132. Eisenhower, *At Ease*, 118–19.
133. *Chicago Daily News*, Dec. 28, 1943.
134. *SAE*, Nov. 17, 1916.
135. *SAE*, Nov. 4, 11, 16, 18, 19, 26, 29, 30, 1916.
136. Battery F was mustered out on Sept. 25. *SAE*, Sept. 26, 1916.
137. *SAE*, Sept. 14, 23, Oct. 13, 1916.
138. *NDH*, Oct. 16, 1916.
139. Funston to Scott, Nov. 29, 1916, FFC.
140. *NYT*, Sept. 16, 1916.
141. *SAE*, Oct. 23, 1916.

142. *SAE*, Oct. 24, 25, Nov. 2, 1916.
143. *SAE*, Oct. 28, Dec. 1, 1916.
144. *SAE*, Nov. 1, 1916.
145. *SAE*, Oct. 29, 1916.
146. *SAE*, Dec. 24, 30, 1916.
147. Hannah, *Manhood*, 213–15.
148. Peacock to Funston, Dec. 6, 1916, FFC; see also Ayres, "Democracy at Work," 211–17.
149. Funston to Peacock, Dec. 9, 1916, FFC.
150. Funston to Baker, Feb. 15, 1917, FFC.
151. *SAE*, Dec. 7, 11, 24, 1916.
152. *SAE*, Dec. 21, 23–26, 28, 1916.
153. *SAE*, Jan. 18, 22, Feb. 4, 1917.
154. Scott to Funston, Oct. 27, 1916, FFC; see also *SAE*, Dec. 8, 9, 1916.
155. *SAE*, Dec. 28, 1916, Jan. 14, 23, 1917.
156. *SAE*, Mar. 3, 8, 1917.
157. See, for example, *SAE*, Feb. 6, 10, Mar. 2, 18, 19, 1917.
158. *SAE*, Feb. 11, 13, 14, 18, 1917.
159. *SAE*, Mar. 15, 1917.
160. *SAE*, Feb. 18, 1917.
161. *SAE*, Feb. 28, Mar. 1, 9, 1917.
162. *SAE*, Mar. 11, 1917.
163. *SAE*, Mar. 18, 22, 1917.
164. *SAE*, Jan. 26, 28, 1917.
165. *SAE*, Mar. 13, 1917.
166. Bailey, "A Search for Identity," 141–42.
167. *SAE*, Feb. 20–25, 1917.
168. *SAE*, Mar. 17, 1917.
169. *SAE*, Mar. 24, 1917.
170. *SFNM*, Mar. 27, 1917.
171. *SAE*, Mar. 24, 1917.
172. *SAE*, Mar. 24, 25, 1917.
173. *SAE*, Mar. 23, 1917.
174. *Biennial Report . . . Texas . . . 1917 to . . . 1918*, 8.

Chapter 6

1. "Corpus Christi, Texas," in *New Handbook of Texas*, ed. Tyler, Barnett, Barkley, 2:332–33.
2. *CCC*, July 19, 1916; *SAE*, July 20, 1916; the dynamic Roy Miller had been elected mayor in 1913 at age twenty-nine. Walraven, *Corpus Christi*, 76.
3. *CCC*, July 20, 1916.
4. *CCC*, Aug. 31, 1916.
5. *CCC*, Aug. 31, 1916.
6. *CCC*, Aug. 31, Sept. 1–3, 20, 1916; Walraven, *Corpus Christi*, 76, 85.
7. *CCC*, Sept. 6, 8, 13, 1916.
8. *CCC*, Sept. 1, 1916.

9. *CCC*, Sept. 7, 1916.

10. "Special Orders, 2d Texas Infantry," Special Orders 100, September 27, 1916, Special Orders 120, October 9, 1916, Special Orders 135, November 3, 1916, all in TMFM.

11. Truck Company 31 was transferred to Fort Sam Houston on October 14, 1916. *SAE*, Sept. 3, 8, 1916; *CCC*, Sept. 8–10, Oct. 14, 1916.; occupying its encampment was U.S. Hospital Company No. 6, which arrived on October 27, having traveled overland from San Antonio by truck in ten hours. *SAE*, Oct. 28, 1916.

12. Givens, "Corpus Christi History."

13. *CCC*, Sept. 14, 21, 1916.

14. The district was bounded on the south by Leopard Street, on the east by Waco and Media Streets and on the north by the S.A. U. & G. Railroad tracks. *CCC*, Sept. 22, 1916.

15. *CCC*, Sept. 2, 9, 10, 15, 19, 20, 21, 1916.

16. *CCC*, Sept. 9, 14, 15, 1916.

17. *CCC*, Oct. 6, 1916.

18. *CCC*, Sept. 24, 18, 1916.

19. *CCC*, Sept. 13, 1916.

20. *CCC*, Sept. 14, 15, 29, 30, Oct. 6, 1916.

21. *CCC*, Sept. 15, Nov. 30, 1916.

22. *CCC*, Sept. 19, 15, 1916.

23. *CCC*, Sept. 17, 20, 1916.

24. *CCC*, Dec. 9, 1916.

25. *CCC*, Sept. 22, 23, 1916.

26. *CCC*, Sept. 24, 1916.

27. *CCC*, Sept. 17, 21, 28, Oct. 24, 1916.

28. *CCC*, Sept. 17, 30, Oct. 1, 4, 5, 1916; "The Best Football Team Ever"; the 3rd Texas Infantry also organized a football team, but it paled by comparison.

29. *CCC*, Sept. 21, 1916.

30. *CCC*, Sept. 26, 1916.

31. *CCC*, Sept. 24, 1916; *SAE*, Sept. 27, 1916.

32. *CCC*, Sept. 24, 27, 28, 1916.

33. Givens, "Corpus Christi History."

34. *CCC*, Sept. 28, 29, 1916.

35. *CCC*, Oct. 1, 1916.

36. *CCC*, Oct. 3, 1916.

37. *CCC*, Oct. 1, Dec. 9, 1916.

38. *CCC*, Oct. 6, 1916.

39. *CCC*, Oct. 15, 1916.

40. *CCC*, Oct. 8, 1916.

41. *CCC*, Nov. 18, 1916.

42. *CCC*, Oct. 11, 12, Dec. 9, 1916.

43. *CCC*, Oct. 12, 1916.

44. *CCC*, Oct. 14, 1916.

45. *SAE*, Nov. 9, 1916; *CCC*, Dec. 20, 1916.

46. *CCC*, Nov. 28, 1916; see also Dec. 3, 1916.

47. *CCC*, Oct. 15, 20, Nov. 5, 1916.

48. *CCC*, Oct. 18, 1916.

49. *CCC*, Oct. 22, 1916.

50. *CCC*, Nov. 28, Dec. 13–16, 1916.
51. *CCC*, Oct. 27, 1916.
52. *CCC*, Jan. 28, Feb. 11, 25, 28, 1917.
53. *CCC*, Dec. 16, 1916.
54. *CCC*, Nov. 9, 28, 1916. See also *CCC*, Dec. 10, 1916, for an account of how Sheriff Mike Wright secured a confession regarding who had started the guardhouse fire.
55. *CCC*, Oct. 19, 26, 28, Nov. 5, Jan. 30, 31, 1917.
56. *CCC*, Nov. 1, 1916.
57. *CCC*, Nov. 5, 8, 11, 15–18, 1916.
58. *CCC*, Nov. 19, 21, 1916.
59. *CCC*, Oct. 22, 1916.
60. *CCC*, Nov. 7, 8, 14, 16, 19, 21, 1916.
61. *CCC*, Nov. 23, 26, 1916.
62. *CCC*, Nov. 23, 28, 1916.
63. *SAE*, Nov. 1, 1916; *CCC*, Nov. 26, 1916.
64. *CCC*, Nov. 17, 30, Dec. 1, 3, 1916.
65. *CCC*, Nov. 28, Dec. 8, 10, 15, 1916; *SAE*, Dec. 18, 1916.
66. *SAE*, Dec. 10, 1916.
67. *CCC*, Dec. 5, 6, 1916.
68. *SAE*, Dec. 6, 10, 16, 17, 1916; *CCC*, Dec. 17, 1916.
69. *CCC*, Dec. 20, 22, 1916; *SAE*, Dec. 22, 1916.
70. *CCC*, Dec. 21, 22–24, 29, 30, 1916.
71. *CCC*, Jan. 4, 1917.
72. *CCC*, Dec. 21, 23, 28, 30, 1916, Jan. 3, 4, 14, 1917.
73. *CCC*, Dec. 30, 1916, Jan. 2, 1917; *SAE*, Jan. 2, 1917.
74. *CCC*, Jan. 6, 7, 1917; *SAE*, Jan. 6, 1917.
75. The strengths of the units at Camp Scurry were: Brigade Headquarters, 16; 2nd Infantry 1,261; 3rd Infantry 1,472; Battery A, 206; Field Hospital No. 1, 63. *CCC*, Jan. 7, 9, 13, 1917; *SAE*, Jan. 9, 1917.
76. *CCC*, Jan. 11, 26, 27, 1917.
77. *CCC*, Feb. 13, 1917.
78. See, for example, *CCC*, Jan. 30, Feb. 2, 1917.
79. Hulen to Parker, Feb. 2, 1917, FFC.
80. *SAE*, Jan. 14–17; *CCC*, Jan. 18, 1917.
81. Walraven, *Corpus Christi*, 85–86; "The Best Football Team Ever"; *CCC*, Jan. 12, 1917; *SAE*, Jan. 1, 1917.
82. *CCC*, Feb. 11, 1917; *SAE*, Jan. 22, 28, 1917.
83. *CCC*, Feb. 6, 7, 24, 28, 1917.
84. *CCC*, Jan. 18, 24, 1917; Henderson, *History of the 141st Infantry*, 44; "The Best Football Team Ever."
85. *CCC*, Feb. 4, 18, 1917.
86. *CCC*, Feb. 20, 24, 1917.
87. *SAE*, March 4, 5, 1917.
88. *CCC*, Feb. 18, 1917.
89. *CCC*, Feb. 11, 14, 15, 1917.
90. *SAE*, March 8, 12, 1917.
91. *SAE*, March 23, 24, 26, 29, 1917.

92. The supply companies of the 2nd and 3rd Texas remained at Camp Scurry temporarily to wind up the brigade's affairs. *SAE*, March 10, 12, 13, 24, 26, 1917.

93. *SAE*, Dec. 15, 1916.

Chapter 7

1. McCain to Funston, July 2, 1916, FFC.
2. *BDH*, June 20, 1916.
3. Marcum, "Fort Brown," in *New Handbook of Texas*, ed. Tyler, Barnett, Barkley, 2:1090.
4. Rozeff, "Soldiers Stationed"; see also Pattullo, "Brother Bill," 14, 37–38.
5. Bacevich, *Diplomat in Khaki*, 65–67.
6. *NYT*, June 25, 1916; *EPMT*, June 23, 1916; *BDH*, June 23, 24, 1916.
7. *NYT*, June 25, 1916; *BDH*, June 27, 1916.
8. Parker, *Old Army*, 425.
9. *War Department Annual Reports, 1916*, 1:381.
10. *SAE*, July 9, 1916.
11. *BDH*, June 27, July 1, 6, 1916.
12. *BDH*, July 7, 15, 1916; see also Peavey, *Echoes*, 137–38.
13. *BDH*, July 22, Sept. 2, 1916.
14. *BDH*, July 24, 26, Aug. 3, 4, 7, 14, 1916.
15. *BDH*, July 28, Aug. 5, 9, 12, 1916.
16. *Adjutant General's Report Illinois 1916–1917*, 577; *BDH*, July 4, 1916.
17. *BDH*, June 24, 29, July 1, 4, 5, 17, 20, Aug. 4, 22, Sept. 2, 1916.
18. *BDH*, Aug. 2, Sept. 2, 21, 1916.
19. *BDH*, Sept. 9, 1916.
20. *SAE*, Sept. 23, 1916.
21. *SAE*, June 25, 1916; *BDH*, July 4, 5, 13, 1916.
22. *BDH*, July 8, 1916.
23. Gibbons, *How the Laconia Sank*, 54–55.
24. *BDH*, July 8, 17, 26, 1916.
25. *BDH*, July 11, 12, 17, 21, 1916.
26. *BDH*, Aug. 7, 1916; Cutchins, *A Famous Command*, 223–33.
27. *Waterloo Evening Courier*, June 27, 1916.
28. Snook, "The Mexican Border (1916–1917)" and "The Building of Camp Dodge"; Bauer says next to nothing about the Iowa National Guard on the border, merely mentioning that they were there for nine months: *The Spirit of the Guard*, 6–7.
29. *BDH*, July 18, 24, 25, 28, 1916.
30. In November 1916, a sergeant in the 1st Iowa Infantry drowned while duck hunting on the Brulay ranch nine miles south of Brownsville. *SAE*, Nov. 8, 1916.
31. *BDH*, Dec. 1, 1916.
32. *BDH*, July 25–27, 29, 31, 1916.
33. *BDH*, July 7, 1916.
34. *Report on Mobilization*, 63.
35. *NYT*, June 25, 1916.
36. Millett, *The General*, 286–90.

37. *BDH*, July 21, 1916; *SAE*, June 24, 1916; Houston, "The Oklahoma National Guard," 448–49; Franks, *Citizen Soldiers*, relies heavily on Houston's article in discussing the 1916 call-up; see also Daugherty and Woods, "Oklahoma's Military Tradition," 429.

38. *BDH*, July 25, 28, 1916.
39. Gibbons, *How the Laconia Sank*, 59–60.
40. Casso, *Louisiana Legacy*, 55, 111.
41. *SAE*, Sept. 10, 1916.
42. *BDH*, Sept. 25, 1916; *SAE*, Oct. 3, 1916.
43. *SAE*, Sept. 10, 1916.
44. *BDH*, Aug. 4, 5, 1916; Gillette, "A Small War," 43–44, 47–48. This is a scholarly treatment of the subject, whereas Cropp, *The Coyotes*, devotes two pages (111–12) to the state guard's Mexican border service.
45. Gillette, "Small War," 49, 53–54.
46. *SAE*, Dec. 24, 1916; Cooper, *Citizens as Soldiers*, 166.
47. Gillette, "Small War," 54, 56, 59, 61, 62.
48. Gillette, "Small War," 59; *SAE*, Nov. 23, 1916.
49. *SAE*, July 9, 18, 1916; *NYT*, June 25, 1916; *BDH*, Aug. 4, 1916.
50. The Louisiana units were originally scheduled for Llano Grande, just west of Mercedes. *NYT*, June 25, 1916; *BDH*, July 18, 20, 1916.
51. *BDH*, July 21, 1916.
52. *NYT*, June 25, 1916.
53. *NYT*, June 25, 1916.
54. *NYT*, June 25, 1916.
55. Shortly thereafter he was transferred to Nogales. *BDH*, July 18, 1916; *SAE*, July 22, 1916.
56. Hartman, *Nebraska's Militia*, 88–89.
57. A private in Battery A 1st Indiana Field Artillery, accidentally killed himself at Point Isabel on October 10 while cleaning his pistol. *SAE*, Oct. 11, 1916.
58. *SAE*, July 19, Oct. 18, Nov. 22, 1916; *BDH*, July 26, Aug. 26, 1916.
59. Cooper, *Citizens as Soldiers*, 157–59.
60. Cooper, *Citizens as Soldiers*, 163–65; see also Stenberg, "Dakota Doughboys," 50–64.
61. *Fort Wayne Journal-Gazette*, June 24, 1916.
62. Watt and Spears, eds. *Indiana's Citizen Soldiers*, 106, 119.
63. *NYT*, June 19, July 7, 1916; *SAE*, June 24, July 12, Sept. 8, Oct. 3, 1916.
64. *Report on Mobilization*, 123.
65. *SAE*, July 18, 1916.
66. *SAE*, July 22, 1916.
67. Gibbons, *How the Laconia Sank*, 72–73.
68. Watt and Spears, *Indiana's Citizen Soldiers*, 120n25.
69. The daily schedule at Llano Grande is in *Border Memories*.
70. Gibbons, *How the Laconia Sank*, 60, 62–67.
71. *NYT*, June 25, 1916.
72. *BDH*, July 18, 20, 1916.
73. *BDH*, July 31, 1916.
74. *War Department Annual Reports, 1916*, 1:824–26; *War Department Annual Reports, 1917*, 1:813.

75. Huston, *The Sinews of War*, 297.
76. Pershing, *My Experiences*, 1:131–32.
77. *War Department Annual Reports, 1916*, 1:827; *NYT*, July 3, 1916.
78. Schrader, *United States Army Logistics*, 1:395.
79. *BDH*, July 26, 1916.
80. *War Department Annual Reports, 1916*, 1:827; *War Department Annual Reports, 1917*, 1:874; *BDH*, Sept. 8, 1916.
81. Gillette, "Small War," states that the 4th South Dakota was equipped with Colt machine guns.
82. Diebert, *A History of the Third United States Cavalry*, 92–93; *BDH*, July 26, 1916.
83. *BDH*, July 27, 28, Aug. 4, 14, 15, 1916.
84. *BDH*, July 9, Aug. 19, 1916.
85. *BDH*, Aug. 2, 1916.
86. *BDH*, Aug. 1, 4, 7, 8, 1916.
87. *BDH*, Aug. 22, 23, 1916.
88. *BDH*, Aug. 5, 1916.
89. The order of troops in line was: mounted Band 1st Illinois Cavalry; mounted detachment 1st U.S. Engineers; 2nd Squadron, 3rd U.S. Cavalry; 1st Illinois Cavalry; Battery D, 4th U.S. Field Artillery, and Battery F, 5th U.S. Field Artillery; Transportation units—U.S. motorcycle machine gun detachment; U.S. motor truck squadron; Iowa Ambulance Co. No. 1; U.S. Field Hospital No. 5; Iowa Field Hospital No. 1; Texas Field Hospital No. 1; Company D, U.S. Signal Corps; the Field Trains of the 4th and 36th U.S. Infantry; 1st and 2nd Virginia Infantry; 1st U.S. Engineers; 2nd Squadron, 3rd U.S. Cavalry; 1st Illinois Cavalry; Battery F, 5th U.S. Field Artillery; Battery D, 4th U.S. Field Artillery; 1st Iowa Field Artillery Battalion, and the pack train attached to the 3rd U.S. Cavalry. *BDH*, Aug. 7–9, 1916.
90. Parker, *Old Army*, 427.
91. The Navy Department was concerned about defending Point Isabel and ordered an expert engineer to investigate the matter. *SAE*, Sept. 15, 1916.
92. *BDH*, Aug. 10, 1916.
93. *BDH*, Aug. 12, 1916.
94. *BDH*, Aug. 17, 21–23, 29, 1916, Jan. 1, 1917. In September, a private in Company L 2nd Virginia Infantry, died in the Brownsville military hospital following an operation. *SAE*, Sept. 21, 1916; a private absent without leave from Company M of the 1st Virginia Infantry was killed by a train thirteen miles north of Brownsville on October 11. *SAE*, Oct. 13, 1916.
95. *BDH*, Aug. 14, 1916; *SAE*, July 22, Sept. 1, 11, 1916.
96. *BDH*, Feb. 9, Mar. 2, 1917.
97. *BDH*, Aug. 16, 1916.
98. *BDH*, July 13, 1916.
99. *BDH*, Aug. 15, Sept. 2, 4, 1916; *SAE*, Sept. 3, 1916.
100. *BDH*, Sept. 23, 1916, Jan. 3, Feb. 12, 1917.
101. *BDH*, Sept. 29, 30, 1916; *SAE*, Sept. 25, 28, 30, Oct. 1, 1916.
102. *BDH*, Aug. 17, 18, 1916.
103. District Commander to All Commanding Officers, August 18, 1916, quoted in Gibbons, *How the Laconia Sank*, 57–58.
104. Gibbons, *How the Laconia Sank*, 59.
105. *BDH*, Aug. 19, 21–23, 1916; *SAE*, Sept. 3, 1916.

106. *BDH*, Aug. 21–23, 1916.
107. *SAE*, Aug. 31, 1916.
108. *BDH*, Aug. 30, 1916.
109. *BDH*, Sept. 1, 1916.
110. *SAE*, July 24, 1916.
111. *BDH*, Sept. 5, 6, 9, 1916; *SAE*, Sept. 10, 1916.
112. *BDH*, Sept. 8, 1916.
113. *BDH*, Sept. 29, 1916.
114. Gibbons, *How the Laconia Sank*, 68–69.
115. *SAE*, Sept. 10, 1916.
116. *BDH*, Sept. 6, 9, 13, 18, 1916.
117. *BDH*, Sept. 19, 1916; *SAE*, Sept. 9, 19, 1916.
118. Gibbons, *How the Laconia Sank*, 69–70.
119. *BDH*, Sept. 28, 29, 1916.
120. *BDH*, Sept. 13, 18, 20, 1916.
121. *SAE*, Sept. 10, 1916.
122. *BDH*, Sept. 16, 1916.
123. *BDH*, Sept. 13, 1916; *SAE*, Sept. 14, 1916.
124. *BDH*, Sept. 18, 19, 1916.
125. *BDH*, Feb. 8, 10, 1917.
126. *BDH*, Sept. 8, 27, 1916; *SAE*, Sept. 17, 1916, Jan. 8, 9, 1917.
127. *BDH*, Sept. 12, 1916.
128. *BDH*, Sept. 23, 27, 30, Dec. 12, 1916.
129. *BDH*, Sept. 18, 1916.
130. *BDH*, Dec. 13, 1916.
131. *SAE*, Sept. 25, 1916.
132. *SAE*, Sept. 26, 1916.
133. *BDH*, Sept. 11, 16, 19, 20–22, 1916.
134. *BDH*, Sept. 23, 1916.
135. *SAE*, Sept. 30, 1916.
136. *SAE*, Oct. 6, 1916.
137. *NDH*, Oct. 16, 1916.
138. *SAE*, Oct. 15, 17, 18, 1916.
139. *SAE*, Nov. 1, 1916.
140. *SAE*, Nov. 3, 1916.
141. *SAE*, Nov. 14, 15, 1916.
142. *SAE*, Nov. 17, 1916.
143. *SAE*, Nov. 18, 1916.
144. *SAE*, Nov. 21, 1916.
145. *SAE*, Nov. 23–26, 1916.
146. *SAE*, Nov. 26, 1916.
147. *SAE*, Nov. 26, 1916.
148. *SAE*, Nov. 29, 1916.
149. *SAE*, Nov. 29, 1916.
150. *SAE*, Nov. 17, 23, 1916.
151. The infantry entrained on December 18; the artillery battalion left on December 14–16 with the troops traveling in twelve Pullmans. *BDH*, Dec. 8, 14, 18, 19, 1916.
152. Hartman, *Nebraska's Militia*, 91; *EPMT*, Jan. 6, 1917.

153. Hartman, *Nebraska's Militia*, 91.
154. *BDH*, Dec. 19, 1916.
155. *BDH*, Jan. 2, 1917.
156. *BDH*, Dec. 13, 29, 1916.
157. *War Department Annual Reports, 1916*, 832–33; *BDH*, Dec. 14, 1916.
158. *BDH*, Dec. 16, 1916, Jan. 8, 1917.
159. *BDH*, Jan. 3, 1917.
160. *BDH*, Jan. 10, 15, 1917; *SAE*, Jan. 9, 16, 1917.
161. General Orders No. 6, Jan. 10, 1917, Headquarters Thirteenth Provisional Division, New York State Military Museum and Veterans Research Center, Saratoga Springs, New York, hereafter cited as NYSMM; *BDH*, Jan. 12, 1917.
162. General Orders No. 1, Jan. 4, 1917, Headquarters Brownsville District, NYSMM; *BDH*, Jan. 5, 1917.
163. General Orders No. 3, Jan. 10, 1917, Headquarters Brownsville District, NYSMM; *BDH*, Jan. 10, 1917.
164. A private in Troop C, Colorado Cavalry, drowned in the Rio Grande in February trying to bring back from Mexico a comrade who had deserted. The Mexicans imposed a $50 fee for the return of the body. The deceased private's comrades had to be restrained from crossing the river and forcibly retrieving the body, which was visible from the American bank and was guarded by Mexican soldiers. *BDH*, Feb. 12, 13, 16, 17, 1917; *SAE*, Feb. 12, 13, 1917.
165. *BDH*, Jan. 12, 15, 23, Mar. 3, 1917; *SAE*, Jan. 13, 1917.
166. *BDH*, Dec. 12, 1916, Jan. 27, Feb. 7, 1917.
167. Parker to Funston, Jan. 18, 1917, FFC.
168. Brooks to Funston, Jan. 19, 21, 1917, FFC.
169. Parker to Funston, Jan. 18, 26, Feb. 6, 1917, FFC.
170. *BDH*, Feb. 15, 1917.
171. *BDH*, Dec. 22, 1916, Jan. 2, 1917.
172. Cooper, *Citizens as Soldiers*, 171, 173–74.
173. *BDH*, Jan. 22, Feb. 2, 1917.
174. *BDH*, Feb. 5, 9, 1917.
175. *BDH*, Feb. 11, 12, 1917.
176. Cropp, *The Coyotes*, 112.
177. *SAE*, Mar. 17, 1917.
178. *SAE*, Dec. 15, 16, 1916.
179. *SAE* Dec. 17, 1916.
180. Lopez report, Apr. 14, 1917, Records of the Federal Bureau of Investigation, Old Mex 232, roll 856, microcopy, RG 65, NARS, hereafter cited as BI.
181. *SAE*, Mar. 6, 9, 1917.

Chapter 8

1. O'Ryan, *The Story of the 27th Division* 1:15, and *History of the 27th Division*, 21.
2. *NYT*, June 19, 1916.
3. *NYT*, June 19, 21, July 15, 1916.
4. *War Department Annual Reports, 1916*, 1:895.
5. *NYT*, July 7, Aug. 5, 1916; *SAE*, Mar. 1, 1917.

6. *NYT*, June 20, 21, 1916.
7. *NYT*, June 27, 1916.
8. *Annual Report . . . New York, 1916*, 15–16; *NYT*, July 1, 1916.
9. *NYT*, June 26, 1916.
10. *SAE*, July 6, 7, 1916; *NYT*, Dec. 5, 1916.
11. There is an article about Mrs. Vanderbilt in *NYT*, July 9, 1916.
12. *NYT*, July 9, 10, 15, 16, 20, 21, 25–27, 29, Sept. 23, 1916.
13. *NYT*, June 21, 29, 1916.
14. *SAE*, Mar. 29, 1917.
15. *Annual Report . . . New York, 1916*, 17.
16. O'Ryan, *The Story*, 1:18; *Albany Times-Union*, June 19, 24, 1916.
17. *NYT*, June 22, 1916.
18. *NYT*, June 24, 1916.
19. *NYT*, June 25, 1916.
20. *SAE*, June 21, 1916.
21. *NYT*, June 25, 1916; see also article of same date listing the eight hundred state National Guard officers, among them many prominent men.
22. *NYT*, July 12, 1916; Harris, *Duffy's War*, 45, 47.
23. *EPMT*, June 28, 1916.
24. O'Ryan, *The Story*, 1:18, 19.
25. O'Ryan, *The Story*, 1:18, 19.
26. Rutherford Ireland, "History of the Twenty Third Regiment, N. G. S. N.Y. Re-designated the One Hundred and Sixth Infantry A. E. F." 2 vols. (1937), 1:235, 237, NYSMM.
27. *NYT*, June 22, 1916.
28. *NYT*, June 26, 1916.
29. *NYT*, June 20, 25, July 1, 1916; *Albany Times-Union*, June 28, 1916.
30. *NYT*, June 20, 1916.
31. *Squadron A*, 146.
32. *NYT*, July 13, 14, 1916.
33. Article on and photo of the armored car, *NYT*, June 25, 1916.
34. *NYT*, July 16, 17, 1916.
35. The basis for this statement is that the unit participated in President Wilson's inaugural parade on March 5, 1917. *NYT*, Mar. 6, 11, 1917.
36. Flynn, *The Fighting 69th*, 11.
37. *NYT*, June 24, 1916; *Albany Times-Union*, June 27, 1916.
38. See Mason, "Our Citizens in Arms," 546–49.
39. *NYT*, June 22, 1916.
40. *NYT*, July 13, 1916.
41. *NYT*, June 24, 1916.
42. *NYT*, June 25, 1916.
43. *NYT*, July 1, 1916.
44. *NYT*, June 26, 27, 1916.
45. *NYT*, June 20, 1916.
46. *NYT*, June 26, 1916.
47. *NYT*, June 28, 1916; see also *NYT*, June 25, 1916.
48. *NYT*, June 27, 1916.
49. See Todd, *New York's Historic Armories*, 102.

50. Falls, *History of the Seventh Regiment*, 180; *NYT*, June 27, 1916.
51. *SAE*, July 1, 1916.
52. Gibbons, *How the Laconia Sank*, 47.
53. *SAE*, July 2, 1916.
54. See *One Hundred Years*, 20–21.
55. *NYT*, July 6, 7, 1916.
56. *NYT*, June 30, July 1, 1916.
57. *NYT*, July 6, 7, 9, 1916.
58. *NYT*, July 10, 1916.
59. *Albany Times-Union*, July 10–15, 17–22, 25, 1916.
60. O'Ryan, *The Story*, 1:18; *NYT*, Oct. 8, 1916; Banks, *Doing My Duty*, 46–47, 50, 59, 66–67. Despite the subtitle of Banks's work (*Doing My Duty: Corporal Elmer Dewey—One National Guard Doughboy's Experiences during the Pancho Villa Punitive Campaign and World War I*), Corporal Elmer Dewey did not participate in the Punitive Expedition.
61. *NYT*, June 28, July 17, 1916.
62. McNair was included in a list of regular officers that O'Ryan requested be transferred to the New York guard. *NYT*, June 29, 1916.
63. *NYT*, June 28, 29, July 2, 1916.
64. O'Ryan, *The Story*, 1:21.
65. *NYT*, June 29, July 16, 1916.
66. *BDH*, June 27, July 1, 4, 1916.
67. Hammond, *Along the Rio Grande*, 190.
68. *NYT*, July 1, 1916.
69. *NYT*, June 28, 1916.
70. *NYT*, June 30, 1916.
71. *NYT*, June 30, July 16, 1916.
72. *NYT*, July 1, 1916.
73. *NYT*, July 1, 1916.
74. *NYT*, July 13, 1916; *BDH*, July 14, 1916.
75. *NYT*, July 14, 1916.
76. *NYT*, July 14, 15, 1916.
77. *NYT*, July 16, 1916.
78. *NYT*, July 15, 1916.
79. See, for example, *NYT*, July 16, 1916.
80. *NYT*, June 30, July 2, 1916.
81. *NYT*, July 19, 1916.
82. *NYT*, June 30, 1916.
83. *NYT*, July 10, 1916.
84. *NYT*, June 29, 1916; Pattullo, "Brother Bill on the Border," 14, 35, 38.
85. *NYT*, July 1, 1916.
86. *NYT*, July 2, 1916.
87. Harris, *Duty, Honor, Privilege*, 19.
88. Waldman, "America's Castles," 43–46.
89. Falls, *History of the Seventh Regiment*, 160, 163, 165–66.
90. Falls, *History of the Seventh Regiment*, 166.
91. Marcoux, "New Yorkers," 59; on p. 64, Marcoux has a useful map of the New York division's camps. See also his "City Slickers in the Boondocks," 14–24.

92. De Castro, Valladares, and Lotwin, *The Second New York Infantry*, 20.
93. *BDH*, July 7, 1916.
94. *NYT*, July 2, 7, 1916.
95. *NYT*, July 6, Aug. 10, 1916.
96. *NYT*, July 8, 1916.
97. *NYT*, July 8, 1916.
98. *NYT*, Dec. 4, 1916.
99. *NYT*, July 16, 1916.
100. *BDH*, June 29, 1916.
101. *NYT*, July 9, 1916; *BDH*, July 1, 1916.
102. "Life on the Border," 946–47.
103. Ireland, "History of the Twenty Third Regiment," 1:240, NYSMM.
104. *NYT*, July 18, 1916.
105. Hammond, *Along the Rio Grande*, 184.
106. *BDH*, July 6, 1916; *NYT*, July 4, 1916.
107. *NYT*, July 4, 17, 1916.
108. Besides the units moving south, on July 10 an order went out to all six thousand recruits currently in New York armories to prepare to entrain for the border. *NYT*, July 10, 1916; see also *NYT*, July 13, 1916.
109. *NYT*, June 28, 1916.
110. Grose, *Gentleman Spy*, 21.
111. Brown, *The Last Hero*, 36.
112. Persico, *Roosevelt's Secret War* 92–93.
113. Jeffery, *The Secret History of MI6*, 442.
114. Waller, *Wild Bill Donovan*, 18–19.
115. Jim Bishop and Virginia Lee Bishop, *Fighting Father Duffy*.
116. Harris, *Duffy's War*, 1, 2; see also Dunlop, *Donovan*, 47; Hourigan, "The Fighting 69th."
117. Duffy, *Father Duffy's Story*.
118. *NYT*, July 9–11, 1916; Ireland, "History of the Twenty Third Regiment," 1:238, NYSMM.
119. *NYT*, July 4, 5 1916.
120. *NYT*, July 5–8, 1916.
121. *NYT*, July 10, 11, 1916.
122. *NYT*, July 12, 14, 1916.
123. *NYT*, July 13, 1916; *Albany Times-Union*, July 12, 13, 15, 19, 1916.
124. *NYT*, July 14–18, 1916; Harris, *Duffy's War*, 6–8.
125. *NYT*, July 18–20, 22, 23, 29, 1916.
126. O'Ryan, *The Story*, 1:38; *NYT*, July 17, 18, Aug. 3, 1916; *Albany Times-Union*, July 17, 1916; "The Fighting 69th in the Mexican Border Campaign."
127. *NYT*, Aug. 13, 1916.
128. *SAE*, July 3, 1916.
129. *NYT*, July 8, 1916.
130. A table listing units' date of departure for the border, arrival on the border, and return from the border is in O'Ryan, *The Story*, 2:573; *Annual Report . . . New York 1916*, 147–49.
131. Gibbons, *How the Laconia Sank*, 67–68.
132. Gibbons, *How the Laconia Sank*, 68.
133. Gibbons, *How the Laconia Sank*, 75.

134. O'Ryan, *The Story*, 1:21.
135. *Squadron A*, 150.
136. Memorandum, Nov. 18, 1916, Headquarters 6th Division, NYSMM; *NYT*, Dec. 21, 1916.
137. The Rockefeller Foundation gave the YMCA $65,000 for work among the troops on the border, where the YMCA established thirty-six camp libraries. *NYT*, Aug. 12, 1916.
138. Ireland, "History of the Twenty Third Regiment," 1:243, NYSMM; O'Ryan, *The Story*, 1:28; *NYT*, July 23, Aug. 6, 7, 1916; *SAE*, July 21, 1916.
139. *NYT*, July 9, 1916.
140. *NYT*, July 26, 1916.
141. O'Ryan, *The Story*, 1:26–28, 2:573–74.
142. O'Ryan, *The Story*, 1:28, 2:574.
143. Funston to Baker, Feb. 15, 1917, FFC.
144. *NYT*, July 18, 23–25, 27, 28, 1916. A second lieutenant of the 69th New York Infantry died of meningitis in the base hospital at Fort Sam Houston, and a member of the signal corps died in the field hospital at McAllen. *NYT*, July 28, August 8, 1916.
145. *NYT*, July 23, 1916.
146. See, for example, *BDH*, Aug. 4, 1916; *Brooklyn Daily Eagle*, July 2, 17, Aug. 9, 1916.
147. *NYT*, July 20–23, 25, 27–28, Aug. 4, 1916; *BDH*, July 8, 1916.
148. *EPMT*, Aug. 7, 1916.
149. *NYT*, July 25, 1916.
150. *NYT*, July 30, 1916.
151. *NYT*, July 11, 12, 1916.
152. Dunlop, *Donovan*, 44–47.
153. Special Orders No. 40, Aug. 2, 1916, Headquarters 3rd Brigade, New York Division, NYSMM.
154. Sterling, *Trails and Trials* 53; *NYT*, Aug. 2, 5, 1916.
155. *NYT*, Aug. 7, 1916.
156. *NYT*, Aug. 19, 21, 1916.
157. *NYT*, Aug. 13, 1916.
158. *Annual Report . . . New York 1916*, 91–94, 163–67.
159. Ireland, "History of the Twenty Third Regiment," 1:240–41, NYSMM; *Brooklyn Daily Eagle*, Aug. 31, 1916; *NYT*, Aug. 28, 1916.
160. Ireland, "History of the Twenty Third Regiment," 1:242, NYSMM.
161. Hughes, "The Big Hike," 4–6, 24–27.
162. O'Ryan, *The Story*, 1:36; *NYT*, Aug. 12, 1916; Sterling, *Trails and Trials*, 54–56; De Castro, Valladares, and Lotwin, *Second New York Infantry*, 32, 34.
163. Marcoux, "New Yorkers," 60.
164. *NYT*, Sept. 8, 1916.
165. *NYT*, Aug. 12, 1916.
166. *NYT*, Aug. 10, 23, 28, 1916; Harris, *Duffy's War*, 43.

Chapter 9

1. *NYT*, Aug. 31, 1916.
2. *NYT*, Sept. 1–4, 8, 1916.

3. *NYT*, Aug. 18, Sept. 6, 1916.
4. Gibbons, *How the Laconia Sank*, 84–89.
5. *War Department Annual Reports, 1916*, 1:520.
6. A list of deaths from all causes is in *Annual Report . . . New York, 1916*, 107.
7. See, for example, Special Orders No. 46, Aug. 5, 1916, Headquarters, 3rd Brigade, New York Division, NYSMM.
8. *NYT*, Sept. 7, 8, 1916.
9. *NYT*, Sept. 6, 7, 1916.
10. *NYT*, Sept. 10, 1916.
11. *War Department Annual Reports, 1917*, 1:442–43; *NYT*, Sept. 13, Oct. 1, 1916.
12. *Nashville Banner*, Sept. 18, 1916.
13. *NYT*, Sept. 8, 16, 17, 1916.
14. *NYT*, Sept. 18, 21, 22, Nov. 25, 1916.
15. *NYT*, Aug. 28, 1916.
16. *NYT*, Aug. 29, 1916.
17. *NYT*, Aug. 28, 1916; three men of the 7th New York died while on border duty. Falls, *History of the Seventh Regiment*, 180.
18. *NYT*, Sept. 14, 1916; a list of those who died, their name, rank, organization, and cause of death is in O'Ryan, *The Story*, 1:32–33.
19. *NYT*, Sept. 9, 1916.
20. *NYT*, Sept. 10, 1916.
21. *NYT*, Sept. 15, Nov. 3, 12, 1916.
22. General Orders No. 1, Jan. 16, 1917, Headquarters, 1st New York Brigade, NYSMM; *NYT*, Jan. 17, 1917.
23. *NYT*, Jan. 17, 18, 21, 22, 1917.
24. *NYT*, Sept. 14, 1916.
25. *NYT*, Sept. 15, 17, 1916.
26. *NYT*, Sept. 10, 1916. As of September 11, no new cases had appeared. *NYT*, Sept. 12, 1916. However, a major in the 2nd New York Artillery, who returned in January suffering from typhoid fever, died suddenly on February 12. *NYT*, Feb. 12, 1917.
27. *NYT*, Sept. 13, 17, 1916.
28. *Annual Report 1916*, 102–106.
29. *NYT*, Sept. 10, 1916.
30. Funston to Scott, Feb. 7, 1917, FFC.
31. A feature story on the unit is in *NYT*, Oct. 8, 1916.
32. *SAE*, Dec. 13, 1916.
33. *NYT*, Oct. 15, 22, 1916; *NDH*, Sept. 18, 1916; *War Department Annual Reports, 1917*, 1:896.34. Gibbons, *How the Laconia Sank*, 64.
35. See Martin, *Three Quarters*, 103–104.
36. *NYT*, Sept. 17, Nov. 2, 1916; Nelson, *A More Unbending Battle*, and Harris, *Harlem's Hell Fighters*.
37. *NYT*, Sept. 18, 21, 1916.
38. *NYT*, Sept. 18, 21, 1916.
39. *NYT*, Sept. 21, 1916.
40. *NYT*, Sept. 21, 22, 27, 1916.
41. *NYT*, Sept. 24, 1916.
42. *NYT*, Oct. 1, 2, 8, 1916.
43. Funston to Scott, Nov. 29, 1916, FFC; Glendon Swarthout's novel *The Tin Lizzie Troop* depicts the border adventures of men from an elite guard unit from Philadelphia.

44. *NYT*, Sept. 28, 29, Oct. 1, 6, 14, 22, 1916.
45. *Annual Report . . . New York 1917*, 27.
46. *NYT*, Oct. 3, 1916.
47. *NYT*, Oct. 13, 1916; Ireland, "History of the Twenty Third Regiment," 1:242, NYSMM.
48. *NYT*, Oct. 28, 29, 1916.
49. General Orders No. 46 (Confidential), Nov. 1, 1916, Headquarters, 6th Division, NYSMM; see also Memorandum, Nov. 14, 1916, Headquarters, 6th Division, NYSMM.
50. *NYT*, Nov. 3, 24, 1916.
51. *NYT*, Oct. 15, 21, 1916.
52. *NYT*, Oct. 23, 1916.
53. *NYT*, Oct. 16, 23, 1916.
54. *NYT*, Oct. 25, 28, Nov. 4, 1916.
55. *NYT*, Nov. 17, 18, 21, 1916.
56. *NYT*, Nov. 22, 1916.
57. *NYT*, Nov. 23, 28, 29, Dec. 3, 1916.
58. *NYT*, Dec. 25, 1916.
59. Memoranda for Whitman's visit, Nov. 14, 15, 1916, Headquarters, 6th Division, NYSMM.
60. *NYT*, Nov. 17, 18, 1916, Jan. 7, 1917.
61. *NYT*, July 6, Dec. 1, 2, 1916.
62. *NYT*, Dec. 3, 5, 6, 9, 1916.
63. *NYT*, Jan. 24, 1917.
64. *NYT*, Jan. 25, 1917.
65. *NYT*, Dec. 5, 16, 23, 24, 1916.
66. *NYT*, Dec. 21, 24, 25, 1916.
67. *NYT*, Dec. 19, 28, 30, 1916, Jan. 3, 6, 7, 1917.
68. *NYT*, Jan. 10, 1917; *SAE*, Jan. 11, 1917.
69. *NYT*, Jan. 11, 13, 21, Feb. 2, 1917.
70. Nelson, *The Remains of Company D*, 61.
71. *NYT*, Jan. 12, 1917.
72. *NYT*, Dec. 8, 1916.
73. *NYT*, Dec. 25, 1916; See memoranda announcing religious services: Headquarters, 6th Division, Nov. 25, 26, 1916, NYSMM.
74. *NYT*, Dec. 28, 1916.
75. *NYT*, Jan. 2, 1917.
76. *NYT*, Jan. 3, 1917.
77. *SAE*, Jan. 12, 1917.
78. *NYT*, Jan. 21, 1917.
79. *NYT*, July 3, 1916, Jan. 22, 1917.
80. *Biennial Report . . . Tennessee . . . 1917 to . . . 1919*, 6.
81. *EPMT*, Feb. 4, 5, 1917; *NYT*, Feb. 7, 1917.
82. *NYT*, Feb. 18, 23, Mar. 6, 1917.
83. *SAE*, Mar. 1, 9, 1917.
84. *NYT*, Feb. 25, 26, 1917.
85. *NYT*, Mar. 4, 6, 11, 1917.
86. *NYT*, Mar. 7, 1917.
87. Forde, "The Sixty-Ninth Regiment," 145–58.

88. *NYT*, Mar. 1, 2, 6–8, 1917.
89. *NYT*, Mar. 15, 1917.
90. *NYT*, Mar. 7, 13–15, 1917.
91. *NYT*, Mar. 9, 17, 25, 29, 30, 1917.
92. Annual Report . . . New York . . 1917, 27–28.

Chapter 10

1. Report No. 865, House of Representatives, 53rd Cong., 2nd sess., vol. 3; "Fort McIntosh," in *New Handbook of Texas*, ed. Tyler, Barnett, Barkley, 2:1109.
2. *History of the Missouri National Guard*, 90; *SAE*, June 23, 1916.
3. *LWT*, May 7, 1916.
4. *LWT*, June 4, 11, July 16, Aug. 6, Sept. 3, 1916.
5. *LWT*, June 11, 1916.
6. *LWT*, June 11, 18, July 9, 16, 1916; *SAE*, June 19, 1916.
7. *SAE*, July 14, 1916.
8. *SAE*, June 20, 1916; *LWT*, July 2, 1916.
9. *SAE*, July 3, 1916.
10. *The Service of the Missouri National Guard*, vii-x; as an example of how the 1916 mobilization has been neglected, only parts of two pages (27 and 253) are devoted to the Missouri border experience in Westover's "The Evolution of the Missouri Militia."
11. Patrick, ed., *Guarding the Border*, 95.
12. *Service of the Missouri National Guard*, x.
13. *History of the Missouri National Guard*, 204, 31.
14. *SAE*, June 20, 1916; *LWT*, July 2, 1916.
15. The 1st Battalion was organized on Feb. 4, 1915.
16. *LWT*, July 2, 5, 7, 9, 16, 1916.
17. *SAE*, July 27, Sept. 5, 1916.
18. *SAE*, June 28, 1916.
19. *LWT*, July 9, 23, 1916.
20. *History of the Missouri National Guard*, 89.
21. *Service of the Missouri National Guard*, xi, xii.
22. Annual Report . . . Maine . . . 1916, 6–7.
23. McConville to Adjutant General, July 6, 1916; Presson to Hume, July 14, 1916; Johnson to Presson, July 10, 1916; Presson to Johnson, July 12, 1916; same to Ingraham, July 12, 1916, Maine State Archives, Augusta, Maine.
24. Hume to Presson, July 17, 1916, Maine State Archives.
25. Presson to Hume, July 14, 1916, Maine State Archives. Chief, Division of Militia Affairs to Adjutant General of Maine, June 8, 1916; Hume to Adjutant General, July 17 and 19, 1916; Cummings to same, July 24, 1916, Maine State Archives; *LWT*, July 9, 1916.
26. Cummings to Adjutant General, July 19, 1916, Maine State Archives.
27. Major, A. G. Dept., to Office of Selectmen, Aug. 11, 1916; Selectmen to Presson, Nov. 9, 1916; Adjutant General to Selectmen, Nov. 13, 1916, Maine State Archives.
28. See, for example, Ingraham to Presson, July 24, 1916; Presson to Ingraham, July 27, 1916, Maine State Archives.
29. *Seattle Daily Times*, July 6, 1916.

30. Gibbons, *How the Laconia Sank*, 90–94.
31. Presson to Hume, Sept. 12, 1916; see also same to same July 14, 27, Aug. 1, 15, 1916, Hume to Presson, July 21, 1916, Presson to Pendell, July 24, 1916; same to Drake, Aug. 3, 1916; same to Ingraham, Aug. 1, 1916; Ingraham to Presson, Aug. 4, 1916, Maine State Archives, Augusta, Maine.
32. "History Mexican Border Expedition," 27.
33. *NYT*, June 19, 1916; *SAE*, July 9, 1916.
34. "History Mexican Border Expedition," 32–34.
35. *LWT*, Aug. 6, 1916.
36. *SAE*, July 16, 1916; *LWT*, July 23, 1916.
37. "History Mexican Border Expedition," 39–40, 65–66.
38. *LWT*, Aug. 6, 1916; *SAE*, Aug. 3, 1916.
39. "History Mexican Border Expedition," 51.
40. *Report on Mobilization*, 63.
41. *History of the Missouri National Guard*, 90; "History Mexican Border Expedition," 43–46.
42. *SAE*, Aug. 20 and Sept. 14, 1916; *History of the Missouri National Guard*, 210.
43. *LWT*, Sept. 3, 1916.
44. *NYT*, July 18, 1916.
45. *LWT*, Aug. 6 and 13, 1916.
46. *LWT*, July 23, 1916.
47. *SAE*, July 9, 1916.
48. *NYT*, July 18, 1916; *EPMT*, July 18, 20, 1916.
49. *LWT*, July 23, 1916.
50. *LWT*, July 23, 1916.
51. *NYT*, July 21, 1916. *LWT*, July 23, 1916; *SAE*, July 22, 23, 25, 1916.
52. *LWT*, Oct. 8, 1916.
53. *LWT*, July 30, 1916.
54. *LWT*, July 23, 1916.
55. *LWT*, July 23, 1916.
56. *LWT*, July 23 and 30, 1916; *SAE*, July 9, 1916; *LWT*, July 23, 1916.
57. *SAE*, Dec. 23, 2916.
58. "History Mexican Border Expedition," 70–71.
59. *LWT*, Aug. 6, 1916; *SAE*, Dec. 26, 1916; *History of the Missouri National Guard*, 211–12; "History Mexican Border Expedition," 49.
60. *LWT*, Jan. 21, 1917.
61. "History Mexican Border Expedition," 75–79.
62. *SAE*, Aug. 5, 1916; *History of the Missouri National Guard*, 210–211; "History Mexican Border Expedition," 49–50, 54, 57.
63. *SAE*, July 27, 1916.
64. *Service of the Missouri National Guard*, xii–xiii.
65. See, for example, "History Mexican Border Expedition," 47–48, 54–57.
66. Patrick, *Guarding the Border*, 99, 106–14.
67. *LWT*, July 23, 1916.
68. *LWT*, Aug. 27, 1916; *History of the Missouri National Guard*, 211.
69. *LWT*, Sept. 3 and 17, 1916; *SAE*, Sept. 12, 1916.
70. *History of the Missouri National Guard*, 274–75; *SAE*, Dec. 24, 1916; *Service of the Missouri National Guard*, xiii–xiv.

71. *SAE*, Aug. 27 and 31, 1916; *LWT*, Sept. 3, 1916.
72. *LWT*, Sept. 3, 1916.
73. That same day Colonel Lyman W. V. Kennon, commander of the 9th U.S. Infantry and the 3rd U.S. Brigade, 15th Provisional Division, left for Fort Sam Houston to command a brigade composed of Kansas and Illinois troops. *SAE*, Sept. 8, 1916.
74. *LWT*, Sept. 3, 1916; *SAE*, Sept. 1 and 8, 1916.
75. *History of the Missouri National Guard*, xiv-xv.
76. *SAE*, Sept. 20, 22, 27, 1916; *LWT*, Oct. 1, 1916.
77. "History Mexican Border Expedition," 80.
78. *LWT*, Oct. 8, 1916.
79. *LWT*, Oct. 8, 1916.
80. *SAE*, July 24 and 25, 1916; *EPMT*, Oct. 8, 1916; Adjutant General of the Army to Commanding Officer, 2nd Maine Infantry, Oct. 30 and Nov. 1, 1916, Maine State Archives.
81. McCraw to Secretary of War, Oct. 15, 1916, Maine State Archives.
82. *LWT*, Oct. 8, 1916; *SAE*, Dec. 7, 1916.
83. *LWT*, Oct. 22, 1916; *SAE*, Oct. 17, 1916.
84. *SAE*, Dec. 30, 1916, Jan. 1, 1917.
85. *NYT*, Feb. 18, 1917.
86. *History of the Missouri National Guard*, 91.
87. *SAE*, Oct. 31, Nov. 8, 1916.
88. *Report of the Adjutant General . . . Florida . . . 1917*, 7.
89. *Report of the Adjutant General . . . Florida . . . 1916*, 20, 24.
90. *Report of the Adjutant General . . . Florida . . . 1916*, 22.
91. *Report of the Adjutant General . . . Florida . . . 1916*, 23, 26.
92. *Report of the Adjutant General . . . Florida . . . 1916*, 27–28.
93. *LWT*, Oct. 8, 1916.
94. Hawk, "Florida National Guard"; see also Hawk's *Florida's Army* (139–43) for photographs of the 2nd Florida on the border; *Report of the Adjutant General . . . Florida . . . 1916*, 27.
95. *LWT*, Dec. 17, 1916.
96. *History of the Missouri National Guard*, xv.
97. *SAE*, Dec. 2, 1916.
98. *History of the Missouri National Guard*, 31, 242; *SAE*, Sept. 27, 1916.
99. Colonel Philip J. Kealy, commissioned on June 29, 1916, commanded the 3rd Missouri but because of physical disability had to leave the regiment on July 1. His successor, Colonel Carl A. Martin, was a regular officer and commanded the regiment on the Mexican border. After the 3rd Missouri returned from Laredo, Colonel Kealy was again elected as commander. *History of the Missouri National Guard*, 54.
100. *SAE*, Dec. 15, 16, 19, 1916; *History of the Missouri National Guard*, 91, 159, 175, 193, 202, 212.
101. *History of the Missouri National Guard*, 256, 259; *LWT*, Dec. 31, 1916.
102. *History of the Missouri National Guard*, 75; *LWT*, Dec. 31, 1916; *SAE*, Dec. 30, 1916.
103. *LWT*, Dec. 31, 1916.
104. *LWT*, Dec. 24, 1916, Jan. 28, Feb. 4, 1917; *SAE*, Sept. 23, 1916; "History Mexican Border Expedition," 92–95.
105. "History Mexican Border Expedition," 96–97.

106. *Journal of the Honorable Senate, January Session, 1917,* 122–23, 437, 501; *Journal of the House of Representatives, January Session, 1917,* 831.
107. *NYT,* Feb. 17, 1917; *LWT,* Feb. 18, 1917; *SAE,* Feb. 16, 1917; Breniman reports, March 9, 1917, roll 861, and March 18, 1917, roll 860, Marks report, March 10, 1917, roll 861, BI; Garret to Secretary of State, Feb. 15, 1917, 812.00/20527, RDS.
108. *EPMT,* Feb. 19, 1917.
109. *LWT,* Feb. 18 and 25, Mar. 4 and 11, 1917; *SAE,* Mar. 10, 1917; *Report of the Adjutant General . . . Florida . . . 1917,* 7.
110. *LWT,* Mar. 11, 1917.
111. *Report of the Adjutant General . . . Florida . . . 1916,* 30.

Chapter 11

1. *SAE,* Aug. 18, Sept. 23, 26, Oct. 14, 21, 1916.
2. Cole, "Marylanders," 192.
3. *NYT,* June 19, 26, 1916.
4. Cole, "Marylanders," 191.
5. *SAE,* July 1 and 5, 1916; *NYT,* July 4, 1916
6. *NYT,* Aug. 20, 1916.
7. Cole, "Marylanders," 194–96.
8. *NYT,* June 19, 22, 1916; *SAE,* July 1, 4, 7, 8, 1916; Brian Dexter Fowles, *A Guard,* 54–56.
9. *SAE,* July 14, 1916.
10. Fowles, *A Guard,* 56; *EPMT,* Sept. 9, 1916.
11. *SAE,* Oct. 1, 1916; *NDH,* Mar. 2, 1917.
12. *SAE,* Jan. 20, 1917; *NDH,* Jan. 23, 1917.
13. *Biennial Report . . . Vermont . . . Ending June 30, 1916,* 3, 4; *BDFP,* June 19, 20, 1916; Cummings, "The Mobilization at Norwich," 115–22; *BDFP,* June 19, 20, 1916.
14. Reeves to W. W. Strickney, Oct. 27, 1916, Vermont Historical Society, Barre, Vermont.
15. Haraty, ed. *Put the Vermonters Ahead,* 150.
16. *NYT,* June 28, 1916.
17. Haraty, *Put the Vermonters Ahead,* 150.
18. *Biennial Report . . . Vermont . . . Ending June 30, 1916,* 16; *EPMT,* July 3, 1916.
19. Newton, "Vermonters in Texas," 33.
20. Haraty, *Put the Vermonters Ahead,* 150–51.
21. Johnson, "The Vermont Militia," 168.
22. *SAE,* July 4, 1916.
23. *Biennial Report . . . Vermont . . . Ending June 30, 1918,* 7, 9; Dwight D. Harrington, "Vermonters at the Mexican Border," Vermont Veterans Militia Museum, Camp Johnson, Colchester.
24. Reeves to Stickney, Oct. 27, 1916, and attachment, Vermont Historical Society.
25. Johnson, "Vermont Militia," 168.
26. *Report on Mobilization,* 63.
27. Haraty, *Put the Vermonters Ahead,* 154.
28. *Biennial Report . . . Vermont . . . Ending June 30, 1918,* 3.
29. *NYT,* Sept. 1, 1916; *SAE,* Sept. 1, 1916.

30. Special Orders No. 8, Jan. 25, 1917, 1st Infantry Regiment, Vermont National Guard, Special Orders, 1915–1917, Military Records Collection, Department of Buildings and General Services, Public Records Division, Middlesex, Vermont.

31. Haraty, *Put the Vermonters Ahead*, 152–54.

32. Cole, "Marylanders," 193; *Northwest Worker*, Oct. 26, 1916.

33. *SAE*, Oct. 31, Dec. 14, 1916.

34. *Biennial Report . . . Tennessee 1917 . . . to . . . 1919*, 7; Wolfe, "The Border Service," 376; *NYT*, Sept. 15, 16, 1916.

35. *Biennial Report . . . Tennessee . . . March 19, 1917*, 7.

36. *Nashville Banner*, June 19, 1916; Memphis *Commercial Appeal*, June 20, 21, 24, 26, 29, 1916.

37. *Nashville Banner*, June 22–24, 1916.

38. *Biennial Report . . . Tennessee . . . March 19, 1917*, 8.

39. *Nashville Banner*, July 8, 1916.

40. *Biennial Report . . . Tennessee . . . March 19, 1917*, 9; see also *Nashville Banner*, July 3, 6, 7, 12, Aug. 2, 12, 1916.

41. *Nashville Banner*, Aug. 23, 1916.

42. Memphis *Commercial Advertiser*, June 27, 1916.

43. Memphis *Commercial Appeal*, June 28, 1916.

44. *Nashville Banner*, July 6, 7, 10, 11, 12, 15, 18, 19, 22, 1916; Adjutant General McCain, USA, stated that "the War Department has nothing to do with the commissioning of officers for service in the state militia or national guard of the several states. These officers are appointed by the governors of these states. In the case of Capt. W. N. Hughes Jr. of Nashville, of the regular army, who is mentioned for appointment as colonel of the First Tennessee regiment, it was explained that in the event of his selection for the honor it would be necessary for the secretary of war to grant him a leave for such service in the state militia." Memphis *Commercial Appeal*, June 29, 1916.

45. *SAE*, July 22, 1916.

46. *NYT*, Mar. 30, 1917; see also *Biennial Report . . . Tennessee . . . March 19, 1917*, 28.

47. *Nashville Banner*, Aug. 24, 30, Sept. 16, 18, 1916.

48. *NYT*, Sept. 14, 15, 21, 1916; Wolfe, "The Border Service," 376, 378.

49. Wolfe, "The Border Service," 382.

50. Wolfe, "The Border Service," 383.

51. *Biennial Report . . . Tennessee . . . 1917 . . . to . . . 1919*, 7; *SAE*, Mar. 16, 25, 1917.

52. *EPMT*, Dec. 25, 1916.

53. *EPMT*, Mar. 26, April 9–10, 1916.

54. Harris and Sadler, *The Texas Rangers*, 315–16.

55. *General Funston's Annual Report*, 42.

56. *General Funston's Annual Report*, 42.

57. *NYT*, June 20, 1916; *EPMT*, June 20, July 15, 1916; *SAE*, July 15, 16, 18, Sept. 22, Oct. 13 and 28, 1916.

Chapter 12

1. *NYT*, July 9, 1916; *SAE*, July 1, 2, 11, Aug. 20, 1916; *EPMT*, July 13, 1916; for example, Company L, 4th Texas, was stationed in Alpine. *EPMT*, July 3, 1916.

2. See Ainsworth, "Boredom," 81–96.

3. Harris, "Protecting the Big Bend," 292–302; Raun, "The National Guard," 123–37; Ainsworth, "Boredom," 89, 90, 93, 94.

4. Meyer, *Hanging Sam*.

5. A private in the 10th Pennsylvania drowned while swimming at Boquillas. *NYT*, July 16, 21, 1916; *SAE*, July 20, 1916; *EPMT*, July 20, Aug. 3, 1916; *AA*, July 13, 1916.

6. *SAE*, July 12–14, 1916; *NYT*, July 13, 1916; *EPMT*, July 16, 30, 1916.

7. *EPMT*, July 15, 1916; *SAE*, July 16, 18, 21, 1916.

8. *SAE*, July 26, 1916; *EPMT*, July 27, 28, 1916.

9. *SAE*, Aug. 4, 1916; *EPMT*, Aug. 7, 1916.

10. *SAE*, Aug. 27, 28, 1916.

11. *NYT*, Aug. 30, 1916; *SAE*, Aug. 30, 1916.

12. *SAE*, Aug. 5, 1916; *EPMT*, Aug. 5, 1916.

13. *NYT*, Oct. 21, 1916; *SAE*, Oct. 21, 22, 1916; *EPMT*, Oct. 21, 31, 1916.

14. *SAE*, Sept. 24, 26, 29, 1916; *NYT*, Sept. 26, 1916; *EPMT*, Sept. 25, 1916.

15. *NYT*, July 15, 1916.

16. *SAE*, July 16, 27, 28, 1916; *EPMT*, July 27, 1916.

17. *AA*, June 22, 29, 1916.

18. *AA*, July 13, 27, 1916.

19. *EPMT*, May 15, 1916.

20. *EPMT*, Sept. 29, Oct. 9, 1916.

21. Weekly report, Mar. 13, 1915, 812.00/14659, RDS.

22. *EPMT*, June 29, 30, July 4, 1916.

23. *EPMT*, June 27, July 13, 23–25, 1916.

24. *EPMT*, July 31, 1916.

25. *EPMT*, Aug. 10, 20, Sept. 6, 1916.

26. *EPMT*, Aug. 31, 1916.

27. *EPMT*, Sept. 13, 14, 1916; *AA*, Sept. 14, 21, 1916.

28. *EPMT*, Oct. 16, 1916.

29. *SAE*, Dec. 22, 1916; see also *AA*, June 29, July 13, 1916.

30. *EPMT*, May 19, Sept. 24, 1916.

31. *EPMT*, Nov. 27, 1916.

32. *EPMT*, Dec. 10, 1916.

33. *EPMT*, Sept. 24, 1916.

34. *EPMT*, Oct. 1, 1916.

35. *SAE*, Oct. 18, 1916.

36. *EPMT*, Aug. 19, 1916.

37. *War Department Annual Reports, 1917*, 1:315; *SAE*, Nov. 4, Dec. 2, 1916; *EPMT*, Nov. 7, Dec. 4, 17, 18, 1916.

38. *EPMT*, Dec. 17, 1916.

39. *EPMT*, Dec. 18, 1916. In February 1917, the tractors were transferred to Fort Sam Houston in San Antonio for further testing, which was pronounced successful. *SAE*, Feb. 17, Mar. 14, 22, 25, Apr. 10, 1917.

40. *AA*, May 25, Oct. 5, 1916.

41. *War Department Annual Reports, 1917*, 1:468.

42. *EPMT*, June 25, Aug. 18, Sept. 24, Oct. 15, 1916; *AA*, Aug. 3, 1916.

43. *EPMT*, Aug. 28, Sept. 4, 1916.

44. *EPMT*, Sept. 16, 19, 1916.

45. *EPMT*, Aug. 25, 26, 1916.

46. *EPMT*, Oct. 26, Sept. 24, 1916, Jan. 26, 1917.
47. *SAE*, Dec. 5, 16, 1916.
48. Funston to Scott, Feb. 7, 1917, FFC.
49. *SAE*, Jan. 27, 29, 1917; *AA*, Feb. 8, 1917.
50. *EPMT*, Jan. 30, Feb. 3, 4, 1917; *AA*, Feb. 15, Apr. 12, 1917.
51. *EPMT*, Mar. 16–18, 20, 21, 1917.
52. *EPMT*, Mar. 9, 1917.

CHAPTER 13

1. "Fort Bliss," in *New Handbook of Texas*, ed. Tyler, Barnett, Barkley, 2:1089.
2. *NYT*, June 20, 1916.
3. *EPMT*, June 19, 1916.
4. *SAE*, June 19, 1916; *EPMT*, June 27, 1916.
5. *EPMT*, July 2, 3, 1916.
6. Harris and Sadler, "Bastion," 73–74.
7. *EPMT*, Aug. 27, 1916.
8. Putnam, ed., *Report of the Commission*, 56.
9. *SAE*, July 1, 1916; on December 31, 1916, the Massachusetts National Guard numbered 485 officers and 9,164 enlisted men. *Annual Report . . . Massachusetts . . . 1917*, 3.
10. *Annual Report . . . Massachusetts . . . 1916*, 4, 5, 6, 81, 83.
11. *EPMT*, Sept. 6, 1916.
12. *NYT*, June 26, 1916.
13. Batchelder, *Watching and Waiting*, 7, 10, 11, 17–20, 22–24.
14. *Report on Mobilization*, 63.
15. *EPMT*, July 13, 1916.
16. Cole to Chief, Division of Militia Affairs, June 20, 1916; Mills to Massachusetts Adjutant General, June 22, July 4, 1916; Commanding General Eastern Department to Massachusetts Adjutant General, June 24, 1916; Cole to Commanding General Eastern Department, June 24, July 6, 1916; Cole to Logan, July 13, 1916, Massachusetts National Guard Military Museum, Worcester, Massachusetts. Hereafter cited as MNGM.
17. Putnam, *Report of the Commission*, 56; *Annual Report . . . Massachusetts . . . 1916*, 25, 80.
18. Cole to Chief, Division of Militia Affairs, June 23, July 8, 24, 1916; Mills to Massachusetts Adjutant General, June 24, July 8, 1916, MNGM.
19. *NYT*, June 20, 27, July 7, 1916.
20. Batchelder, *Watching and Waiting*, 37, 38.
21. Smith, "Recollections," 6–7.
22. Batchelder, *Watching and Waiting*, 47.
23. *NYT*, June 26, 1916.
24. *EPMT*, July 4, 7, 1916.
25. Batchelder, *Watching and Waiting*, 58–59.
26. *EPMT*, July 7, 1916; Batchelder, *Watching and Waiting*, 70–71.
27. *EPMT*, July 19, 24, 25, 26, 1916.
28. *EPMT*, July 28, 1916.
29. *RGR*, June 20, Nov. 17, 1916; *SFNM*, June 24, 1916; *EPMT*, July 7, 1916.
30. *EPMT*, July 8, 1916; *RGR*, July 11, 1916.

31. *RGR*, July 21, 1916.
32. *RGR*, July 11, 14, 18, 21, 28, Aug. 1, 8, 25, 1916; *EPMT*, July 13, 28, Aug. 26, 1916.
33. *EPMT*, July 27, 1916.
34. *EPMT*, Aug. 1, 2, 1916.
35. *EPMT*, Aug. 2, 3, 1916.
36. *EPMT*, Aug. 30, 1916.
37. *EPMT*, July 4, 1916.
38. Commanding General Southern Department to Adjutant General of the Army, July 21, 1916; Adjutant General to Commanding General Southern Department, July 24, 1916, MNGM.
39. Gallup to Massachusetts Adjutant General, July 6, 1916, MNGM.
40. *EPMT*, July 8, 1916.
41. *Annual Report . . . Massachusetts . . . 1916*, 91, 92.
42. *EPMT*, Aug. 24, 1916.
43. Batchelder, *Watching and Waiting*, 76.
44. *EPMT*, July 4, 1916; *NYT*, July 5, 1916.
45. *EPMT*, July 13, 25, 26, Nov. 19, 1916, Jan. 15, 1917.
46. *Pennsylvania in the World War*, 1:120; *EPMT*, Aug. 23, 1916.
47. *Official History of the Militia*.
48. Stephen L Harris is in error when he writes that New York was "the only state to provide a whole division." *Duffy's War*, 31.
49. The commanding officers of all these units are listed in *Pennsylvania in the World War*, 1:120–21.
50. *NYT*, June 20, Aug. 11, 1916; *NDH*, July 19, 1916; *EPMT*, Aug. 1, 1916; Harris and Sadler, "Bastion," 87.
51. *EPMT*, July 10, Sept. 8, 1916.
52. *EPMT*, July 15, 1916.
53. *EPMT*, July 5, 10, 1916.
54. *EPMT*, July 13, 16, 1916; *Albany Times-Union*, July 11, 1916.
55. *EPMT*, July 7, 11, 1916.
56. George Brooks III, *With the First City Troop*, 21, 31, 103; *EPMT*, July 12, 21, 1916; see also *History of the First Troop*, 15–16.
57. *EPMT*, July 6, 7, 27, 1916.
58. *EPMT*, July 12, 19, 1916.
59. *Pennsylvania in the World War*, 1:123.
60. *EPMT*, July 21, 23, 25, 27, 29, Aug. 2, 1916.
61. *Report on Mobilization*, 63.
62. *EPH*, July 15, 1916.
63. Provisional Infantry Brigade (7th, 20th, 23rd, and 34th U.S. Infantry and Provisional Motorcycle Company—attached); 2nd Massachusetts Infantry Brigade (5th, 8th, and 9th Infantry); Michigan Infantry Brigade (31st, 32nd, and 33rd Infantry); Provisional Cavalry Brigade (8th and 17th U.S. Cavalry); Provisional Cavalry Regiment (1st Squadron Massachusetts Cavalry, 1st Squadron Rhode Island Cavalry, Troops A and B, Michigan Cavalry); Provisional Field Artillery Brigade (5th U.S. Field Artillery; 8th U.S. Field Artillery, less Batteries D and F; 1st Massachusetts Field Artillery; Battery A, New Mexico Field Artillery; Batteries A and B, Michigan Field Artillery); Signal Corps (Company B, U.S. Signal Corps: detachments, Company I, U.S. Signal Corps, and Company A, Massachusetts Signal Corps); Ambulance Companies (U.S. Ambulance

Company No. 1, Massachusetts Ambulance Company No. 1, and Michigan Ambulance Companies Nos. 1 and 2); Field Hospital Companies (U.S. Field Hospital No. 1, Massachusetts Field Hospital No. 1, and Michigan Field Hospital No. 1); Motor Truck Train (Companies 4, 16, 19, and 20); and Sanitary Trains. Harris and Sadler, "Bastion," 75–76; *EPH* July 15, 1916.

64. Private Herbert C. Day deserted from the machine gun company of the 32nd Michigan while the regiment was still at the mobilization camp. He was later arrested and court-martialed. *EPMT*, Feb. 8, 1917.

65. *SAE*, July 16, 1916.
66. Harris and Sadler, "Bastion," 85–87.
67. *EPMT*, July 12, 1916.
68. *NYT*, June 22, 1916.
69. *EPMT*, July 6, 23, 1916, Jan. 14, 1917.
70. *EPMT*, Aug. 12, 18, 1916, Jan. 5, 1917.
71. *EPMT*, July 16, 19, 23, 1916.
72. Batchelder, *Watching and Waiting*, 81.
73. *EPMT*, Sept. 26, 1916.
74. *EPMT*, July 17, 1916.
75. *EPMT*, July 22, 1916.
76. *EPMT*, July 26, 1916.
77. *EPMT*, Aug. 20, 1916.
78. Waldman, "America's Castles," 40–43.
79. *Report on Mobilization*, 124.
80. *EPMT*, July 8, 1916.
81. Stiness, ed., *Battery A*.
82. *EPMT*, July 7, 1916.
83. *EPMT*, Sept. 3, 1916.
84. Helen Roberts Coggeshall, "The Happy Invasion of 1916," 111, 113; Batchelder, *Watching and Waiting*, 65–66.
85. *EPMT*, July 30, 1916.
86. *EPMT*, Sept. 9, 12, 1916; Sherburne became a brigadier general in World War I. Carter, *The 101st Field Artillery*, frontispiece.
87. Sibley, *With the Yankee Division*, 25–26.
88. *EPMT*, July 29, 1916.
89. *EPMT*, Aug. 1, Oct. 13, 1916.
90. *EPMT*, Jan. 13, 1917.
91. Zierdt, *Narrative History*, 111–12; *EPMT*, Sept. 20, Oct. 6, 1916.
92. *EPMT*, Sept. 10, 1916.
93. *EPMT*, July 23, Aug. 26, Sept. 7, 12, 1916.
94. *EPMT*, Sept. 7, 1916.
95. *EPMT*, July 20, Aug. 1, 23, 1916; *SAE*, Aug. 24, 1916.
96. *EPMT*, Aug. 23, 24, 1916.
97. *EPMT*, Aug. 12, 1916.
98. *EPMT*, Oct. 13, Nov. 14, 16, 1916.
99. Coggeshall, "Happy Invasion," 111–12.
100. Batchelder, *Watching and Waiting*, 66–67.
101. Batchelder, *Watching and Waiting*, 93–94; *EPMT*, Aug. 26, 1916.
102. *EPMT*, Aug. 14, 1916.

103. Brooks, *With the First City Troop*, 18–19.
104. *SAE*, Jan. 3, 1917.
105. *EPMT*, Aug. 14, 22, 24, 27, 31, 1916.
106. *EPMT*, July 27, Aug. 3–5, 1916.
107. *EPMT*, Aug. 29, 30, Sept. 23, Oct. 9, 1916.
108. Batchelder, *Watching and Waiting*, 93–99; *EPMT*, July 4, 13, 20, 22, 25, 26, Aug. 6, 27, 1916.
109. *EPMT*, Aug. 1, Dec. 5, 1916.
110. *EPMT*, Aug. 6, 26, 1916.
111. *EPMT*, July 13–15, 21, 26, Aug. 6, 1916.
112. *EPMT*, July 16, 1916.
113. *EPMT*, July 19, 27, 29, Aug. 8, 10, 13, 1916.
114. *EPMT*, Aug. 11, Sept. 5, 1916.
115. See, for instance, *EPH*, July 17, 1916.
116. *EPMT*, July 16, 19, 23, 25, 31, Aug. 2, 6, 14, 20, 1916.
117. *EPMT*, Aug. 14, 1916.
118. *EPMT*, Dec. 27, 1916.
119. *EPMT*, July 19, 1916.
120. *EPMT*, July 19, 29, Aug. 2, 3, 7, 8, 1916.

Chapter 14

1. *Seattle Sunday Times*, Aug. 13, 1916.
2. *EPMT*, July 26, Aug. 8, 13, 29, 1916.
3. The 1916 South Carolina call-up rates two short paragraphs in Rhodes, *South Carolina*, 37.
4. *EPMT*, Aug. 12, 14, 1916, Feb. 23, 1917.
5. Orangeburg, South Carolina, *Times and Democrat*, Jan. 26, 1975.
6. *EPMT*, Aug. 13, 14, 1916.
7. *EPMT*, Aug. 14, 26, 1916.
8. *EPMT*, Aug. 18, 20, 21, 1916.
9. *EPMT*, Aug. 19, 31, Sept. 1, 1916; *NYT*, Sept. 1, 1916.
10. *EPMT*, Aug. 29, Sept. 3, 4, 1916.
11. *EPMT*, Aug. 10, 21, 26, 30, 1916; on the subject of sentries falling asleep, see Pattullo, "Sentinel Rheumatism," 23–28.
12. Gordon, *History of the First Regiment*, 121–25.
13. *EPMT*, Sept. 10, 1916.
14. Niedringhaus, "Dress Rehearsal," 40, 44; *NYT*, June 21, 1916; *EPMT*, Aug. 12, 1916.
15. *Harrison Times*, May 20, 1916.
16. Niedringhaus, "Dress Rehearsal," 49.
17. Leeke, "Our Late Unpleasantness," 42–44.
18. *Report on Mobilization*, 24, 134.
19. George N. Vourlojianis, *The Cleveland Grays*, 104; Leeke, "Our Late Unpleasantness," 44; *EPMT*, Feb. 23, 1917; as of February 1917, the Cleveland Grays were described as being Company F, 5th Ohio Infantry. *EPMT*, Feb. 7, 1917.
20. Niedringhaus, "Dress Rehearsal," 49–54.

21. Harris and Sadler, *Secret War in El Paso*, 285–86.
22. Vourlojianis, *Citizen Soldiers*, 38–40.
23. *A Brief History*, 97–98.
24. *A Brief History*, 99.
25. *EPMT*, Sept. 15, 1916.
26. Leeke, "Our Late Unpleasantness," 44.
27. Leeke, "Our Late Unpleasantness," 45; *EPMT*, Sept. 4, 1916.
28. *A Brief History*, 99.
29. *EPMT*, Sept. 12, 1916.
30. *EPMT*, Sept. 14, 1916.
31. *SAE*, July 14, 1916.
32. *EPMT*, Sept. 16, 17, 18, 26, 28, Oct. 6, 1916.
33. Fostoria, Ohio, *Daily Review*, Sept. 22, 1916.
34. *Military History of Kentucky*, 324–26; Le May, Trowbridge, and Canon, comps. *Kentucky's Flying Soldiers*, 11; Stone, *Kentucky Fighting Men*, has nothing to say about the 1916 National Guard mobilization.
35. *Nashville Banner*, July 19, 1916.
36. Schwarz and Milligan, *History of the First Regiment*.
37. *EPMT*, Sept. 5, 6, 24, 1916.
38. *EPMT*, Sept. 18, 1916.
39. Commanding General to Adjutant General, Sept. 29, 1916, Georgia National Guard History Office, Atlanta, Georgia; Griffith, "In Pursuit of Pancho Villa," 4.
40. *SAE*, July 14, 1916.
41. *SAE*, July 19, Aug. 26, 1916; *Tacoma Times*, Aug. 26, 1916.
42. "Condensed Fact Sheet"; *NDH*, Jan. 17, 1917.
43. Metz, *Desert Army*, 92–93.
44. Coggeshall, "The Happy Invasion," 108.
45. Smith, "Recollections," 7–9.
46. *EPMT*, Oct. 4, 30, Nov. 4, 5, 1916; Nankivell, *History of the Military Organizations*, 290–91.
47. Harris and Sadler, "Bastion," 86–87; *NYT*, June 19, 1916; *SAE*, Oct. 3, 1916; *EPMT*, Nov. 4, Dec. 24, 1916.
48. 1st Infantry Brigade (1st, 2nd, and 3rd Kentucky Infantry); 2nd Infantry Brigade (5th, 8th, and 9th Massachusetts); 3rd Infantry Brigade (1st and 2nd South Carolina Infantry); Engineers (Company A South Carolina Engineers); Cavalry (1st Squadron Massachusetts Cavalry, Troop A South Carolina Cavalry, Troop A Tennessee Cavalry); Artillery (Battery A New Mexico Field Artillery, 1st Massachusetts Field Artillery); Signal (1st Massachusetts Signal Corps Battalion); Ambulance (Massachusetts Ambulance Company No. 2, Kentucky Ambulance Company No. 1); Field Hospitals (Massachusetts Hospital Company No. 2, Kentucky Hospital Company No. 1, South Carolina Hospital No. 1, Tennessee Hospital Company No. 1); Trains (Pack Train No. 22). Harris and Sadler, "Bastion," 77; *EPMT*, Sept. 3, 1916.
49. *EPMT*, Aug. 25, Sept. 3, 1916.
50. Harris and Sadler, *Texas Rangers*, 316–17; *EPMT*, Sept. 22, 23, 25, 26, 1916.
51. *EPMT*, Nov. 9, 1916.
52. 1st Infantry Brigade (31st, 32nd, and 33rd Michigan); 2nd Infantry Brigade (2nd, 3rd, and 6th Ohio); 3rd Infantry Brigade (4th, 5th, and 8th Ohio); Engineers (1st Ohio Engineer Battalion, Company D Ohio Engineers); Cavalry (1st Squadron Ohio

Cavalry); Artillery (1st Battalion Ohio Artillery); Signal Corps (1st Ohio Signal Corps Battalion); Ambulance (Ohio Ambulance Companies Nos. 1 and 2); Field Hospitals (Ohio Hospital Companies Nos. 1, 2, 3); Trains (Pack Train No. 23). Harris and Sadler, "Bastion," 79–80.

53. Provisional Infantry Brigade (7th, 20th, 23rd, and 34th Infantry); Provisional Cavalry Brigade (8th and 17th Cavalry); Provisional Field Artillery Brigade (5th Field Artillery, less batteries D and F, 8th Field Artillery); Signal Corps (Headquarters, 1st Field Battalion, Company A); Ambulance (Ambulance Company No. 1); Field Hospital (Hospital Company No. 1); Truck Companies (Nos. 16, 20, 24, 46, 47, 48, 65, 67); Trains (Pack Trains Nos. 1 and 21); and Provisional Motorcycle Company. Harris and Sadler, "Bastion," 80–81.

54. Batchelder, *Watching and Waiting*, 136–40; *EPMT*, Sept. 14, 1916; "National Diary, Co. C, 101st Inf. Mass NG," 257, MNGM.

55. *EPMT*, Sept. 16, 1916.

56. *Pennsylvania in the World War*, 1:124.

57. *EPMT*, Sept. 18–22, 1916; "National Diary," MNGM, 265; Batchelder, *Watching and Waiting*, 151–55.

58. Harris and Sadler, "Bastion," 76; *EPMT*, Oct. 11, 1916.

59. *NDH*, Aug. 29, 1916; *EPH*, Aug. 30, 1916.

60. Brooks, *With the First City Troop*, 76.

61. *EPMT*, Sept. 26, 1916.

62. *EPMT*, Sept. 27, 28, 29, Nov. 3, 1916.

63. Fostoria, Ohio, *Daily Review*, Oct. 5, 1916.

64. Batchelder, *Watching and Waiting*, 162–198; see also the diary of Private Jack Kerns, Company H, 5th Ohio, in *EPMT*, Jan. 28, 1917.

65. Batchelder, *Watching and Waiting*, 181.

66. "National Diary," 275–85, MNGM; *EPMT*, Sept. 28, 30, Oct. 1, 2, 3, 1916.

67. Batchelder, *Watching and Waiting*, 184–85; *RGR*, Oct. 3, 1916; see also Fostoria, Ohio, *Daily Review*, Oct. 13, 1916.

68. Batchelder, *Watching and Waiting*, 187; Richard F. Mason, transcriber, "Diary and Letters of Raymond H. Franks, Corporal Machine Gun Company 4th Ohio Infantry, Mexican Border Service," in the collection of the Ohio Army National Guard (2006), 45; "National Diary," 281–82, MNGM.

69. *RGR*, Oct. 6, 1916.

70. Mason, "Diary and Letters," 45, Ohio Army National Guard; "National Diary," 283, MNGM.

71. *EPMT*, Oct. 4–8, 11, 13, 14, 1916; *Annual Report . . . Massachusetts . . . 1916*, 91.

72. Smith, "Recollections," 8–10, 17, 18.

73. *EPMT*, Aug. 8, 11, 15, Sept. 5, 16, 26, Oct. 10, 1916.

74. *EPMT*, Aug. 8, Sept. 27, 1916.

75. Harris and Sadler, *Secret War*, 283–84; *EPMT*, Jan. 19, 1917.

76. *SAE*, Dec. 26, 1916.

77. Coffin and Sanders, *A History of the Third Field Artillery*, 30; Fostoria, Ohio, *Daily Review*, Nov. 2, 17, 1916.

78. Griffith, *In Pursuit*, 4; Smith, "Recollections," 21.

79. *EPMT*, Jan. 27, 28, Feb. 18, 1917.

80. *EPMT*, Mar. 6, 7, 1917; see also *EPMT* Feb. 4, 1917.

81. *EPMT*, Sept. 14, Oct. 11, Nov. 7, 1916, Jan. 12, Mar. 14, 1917.

82. *War Department Annual Reports, 1916*, 1:60–61, 164; *EPMT*, June 29, Aug. 3, 16, 18, Sept. 2, 3, 1916.
83. *EPMT*, Aug. 3, 18, Dec. 18, 20, 21, 1916.
84. See, for example, *EPMT*, Dec. 23, 1916.
85. *EPMT*, Jan. 6, 1917.
86. *EPMT*, Jan. 30, Mar. 21, 1917.
87. *EPMT*, Mar. 2, 4, 1917.
88. *EPMT*, Feb. 28, Mar. 4, 1917.
89. *EPMT*, Mar. 4, 1917.
90. *EPMT*, Aug. 12, 1916.
91. *EPMT*, Feb. 28, 1917.
92. *EPMT*, Jan. 27, 1917.
93. Fostoria, Ohio, *Daily Review*, Dec. 15, 1916.
94. *SAE*, Jan. 15, 1917.
95. *EPMT*, Dec. 21, 1916, Jan. 14, 16, 1917.
96. *EPMT*, Feb. 17, 1917.
97. *EPMT*, Jan. 8, 1917.
98. *EPMT*, Mar. 2, 9, 1917.
99. *EPMT*, Mar. 12, 15, 1917.
100. *SAE*, Dec. 19, 24, 25, 1916; *NYT*, Dec. 20, 24, 27, 1916; *EPMT*, Dec. 20, 25, 27, 31 1916.
101. *EPMT*, Nov. 28, 1916.
102. *EPMT*, Dec. 31, 1916.
103. *EPMT*, Jan. 22, 1917.
104. A list of departures is in Harris and Sadler, "Bastion," 87–90.
105. Ohl, *Minuteman*, 20.
106. Smith, "Recollections," 23.
107. Baker to Funston, Feb. 6, 1917, Funston to Scott, Feb. 7, 1917, FFC.
108. On the erroneous reports that Pershing commanded Fort Bliss, see, for example, Metz, *Desert Army*, 85, 93. Pershing commanded the El Paso District.
109. *EPMT*, Feb. 7–11, 22–24, 1917.
110. *EPMT*, Mar. 21, 1917.
111. Harris and Sadler, "Bastion," 96–97; *EPMT*, Feb. 18, Mar. 20, 1917.
112. Harris and Sadler, "Bastion," 97; *EPMT*, Feb. 12, 1917.
113. *EPMT*, March 7–10, 1917.
114. *EPMT*, Mar. 9–11, 1917.
115. *EPMT*, Dec. 17, 1916, Jan. 3, 17, Feb. 27, Mar. 2, 1917.
116. *EPMT*, Feb. 6, 1917; "National Diary," passim, MNGM.
117. *EPMT*, Jan. 31, Feb. 2, 1917.
118. *EPMT*, Nov. 25, 1916, Jan. 6, 11, 19, 1917.
119. Funston to Baker, Feb. 15, 1917, FFC.
120. *EPMT*, Oct. 14, 1916.
121. *EPMT*, Dec. 8, 1916.
122. *EPH*, Mar. 1, 1916; *SAE*, May 20, 1916; *EPMT*, Nov. 10, Dec. 15, 16, 1916; Smith, "Recollections," 10; Exner, "Prostitution," 205–20; Sandos, "Prostitution and Drugs," 621–45; Gabbert, "Prostitution and Moral Reform," 575–604.
123. Funston to Baker, Feb. 15, 1917, FFC.
124. Boies, "The Girls on the Border," 221–28.

125. *EPMT*, Oct. 2, Dec. 20, 27, 1916.
126. Batchelder, *Watching and Waiting*, 94; *EPMT*, Sept. 26, 1916.
127. Smith, "Recollections," 20.
128. *Annual Report . . . Massachusetts . . . 1916*, 26.
129. *EPMT*, July 26, 1916.
130. *EPMT*, Aug. 18, 1916.
131. *EPMT*, Sept. 9, 1916.
132. *EPMT*, Aug. 15, 1916.
133. *EPMT*, Sept. 12, 1916.
134. *EPMT*, Oct. 10, 1916.
135. *EPMT*, Aug. 29, 1916.
136. *EPMT*, Sept. 24, 1916.
137. *EPMT*, Nov. 18, 19, 21, Dec. 13, 22, 1916.
138. *EPMT*, Nov. 21, 1916.
139. *EPMT*, Jan. 10, 1917.
140. *EPMT*, Feb. 7, 1917.
141. *EPMT*, Oct. 30, 1916.
142. *EPMT*, Dec. 14, 1916.
143. *EPMT*, Jan. 3, 1917.
144. *EPMT*, Feb. 20, 1917.
145. *EPMT*, Jan. 10, 1917.
146. *EPMT*, Jan. 14, 1917.
147. *EPMT*, Mar. 9, 1917.
148. *EPMT*, Feb. 25, 1917.
149. *EPMT*, Nov. 1, 1916.
150. *EPMT*, Dec. 21, 1916.
151. *EPMT*, Feb. 20, 1917.
152. *EPMT*, Dec. 15, 1916.
153. *EPMT*, Dec. 15, 1916.
154. *EPMT*, Dec. 17, 1916.
155. *EPMT*, Feb. 25, 1917.
156. *EPMT*, Mar. 21, 1917.
157. *EPMT*, Mar. 21, 1917.
158. *EPMT*, Feb. 4, 5, 1917.
159. *EPMT*, Sept. 22, 1916; *RGR*, Sept. 22, 1916.
160. *EPMT*, Oct. 3, 1916.
161. *EPMT*, Oct. 6, 1916.
162. *EPMT*, Dec. 2, 4, 5, 1916.
163. *EPMT*, Dec. 12, 1916.
164. *EPMT*, Dec. 19, 1916.
165. *EPMT*, Jan. 1, 2, 1917.
166. *EPMT*, Jan. 17, 1917.
167. *EPMT*, Jan. 17, 1917.
168. *EPMT*, Jan. 17, 1917.
169. *EPMT*, Jan. 30, 1917.
170. *EPMT*, Feb. 2, 1917.
171. *EPMT*, Feb. 7, 1917.
172. *EPMT*, Feb. 24–26, 1917.

173. *EPMT*, Nov. 28, 1916.
174. Funeral in *EPMT*, Dec. 12, 1916.
175. *EPMT*, Dec. 14, 1916.
176. *EPMT*, Dec. 31, 1916.
177. *EPMT*, Jan. 9, 1917.
178. *EPMT*, Jan. 10, 1917.
179. *EPMT*, Jan. 22, 1917.
180. *EPMT*, Feb. 11, 27, 1917.
181. *EPMT*, Feb. 11, 27, 1917.
182. *EPMT*, Feb. 13, 1917.
183. *EPMT*, Feb. 15, 1917.
184. *EPMT*, Feb. 17, 26, 1917.
185. *EPMT*, Feb. 20, 21, 1917.
186. *EPMT*, Feb. 20, 21, 1917.
187. Funeral in *EPMT*, Feb. 23, 1917.
188. *EPMT*, Jan. 14, 15, 1917.
189. *EPMT*, Feb. 5, 7, 1917.
190. *EPMT*, Feb. 20, 1917.
191. Funeral in *EPMT*, Feb. 23, 1917.

Chapter 15

1. *RGR*, July 21, 1916.
2. *EPMT*, July 20, 23, 25, 1916.
3. *NYT*, June 19, 1916; *EPMT*, July 30, Aug. 2, 1916.
4. *EPMT*, July 29, 30, Aug. 2, 20, 1916.
5. *EPMT*, Aug. 2, 4, 1916.
6. *EPMT*, Aug. 11, 1916.
7. *Harrison Times*, May 20, 1916.
8. *Harrison Times*, Mar. 18, 1916.
9. *Harrison Times*, June 24, July 22, Sept. 16, 1916.
10. *NYT*, June 19, July 2, 6, 1916; *SAE*, July 25, 1916.
11. *NYT*, June 23, 1916.
12. *EPMT*, Aug. 14, 1916.
13. *EPMT*, Aug. 17, 1916.
14. *EPMT*, Aug. 24, Sept. 21, 1916.
15. *EPMT*, Aug. 26, 1916.
16. *EPMT*, Aug. 27, 1916.
17. *SAE*, Sept. 6, 8, 10, 1916; *EPMT*, Sept. 9, Dec. 13, 1916.
18. *EPMT*, July 16, Dec. 2, 1916.
19. *EPMT*, Sept. 21, 28, 29, Oct. 2, 1916.
20. *SAE*, July 15, 1916.
21. *SAE* Sept. 23, 1916; *EPMT*, Sept. 30, Oct. 1, 1916.
22. Blevins, Nicholl, and Otto, eds., *The Colorado Labor Wars*; DeStefanis, "The Road to Ludlow," 341–90; *The Military Occupation*.
23. *SAE*, Nov. 11, Dec. 18, 23, 28, 1916, Jan. 1, 18, 1917; *EPMT*, Dec. 25, 26, 1916.
24. *SAE*, Oct. 14, 15, 1916.

25. *SAE*, Dec. 9, 1916.
26. *EPMT*, Jan. 2, 1917.
27. "History Mexican Border Expedition," 58–59, 80–85, 96; *EPMT*, Nov. 11, 15, 19, 1916; *SFNM*, Nov. 15, 1916.
28. *EPMT*, Nov. 24, 1916.
29. *EPMT*, Dec. 1, 24, 1916.
30. *EPMT*, Dec. 10, 1916.
31. *EPMT*, Dec. 16, 21–23, 28, 1916, Jan. 1, 2, 8, Feb. 1, 1917.
32. *EPMT*, Dec. 26, 1916.
33. *EPMT*, Dec. 26, 1916.
34. *EPMT*, Jan. 13, 14, 1917.
35. *EPMT*, Jan. 17, 1917.
36. *EPMT*, Jan. 18, 1917.
37. *EPMT*, Jan. 23, 1917.
38. *EPMT*, Jan. 25, 1917.
39. *EPMT*, Jan. 29, 1917.
40. *EPMT*, Feb. 3, 1917.
41. *EPMT*, Feb. 5, 1917.
42. *EPMT*, Feb. 20, 26, Mar. 8, 1917.
43. *EPMT*, Feb. 22, 1917.
44. *EPMT*, Feb. 26, 1917; *SAE*, Feb. 27, 1917.
45. *SAE*, Mar. 3, 1917.
46. *EPMT*, Mar. 2, 1917.

Chapter 16

1. *EPMT*, June 20, July 7, 19, 1916.
2. *SFNM*, July 10, 1916, Jan. 14, 1917; Hopper, "New Columbus," 10–11.
3. *EPMT*, Aug. 20, 1916.
4. *EPMT*, June 20, 1916.
5. *EPMT*, June 25, July 1, 1916.
6. *EPMT*, July 13, 1916.
7. *EPMT*, June 27, 1916.
8. *SFNM*, June 26, 1916.
9. *EPMT*, Sept. 9, 30, 1916.
10. *SAE*, Sept. 30, 1916.
11. For a historical sketch of Battery A, see *A History of the Sixty-Sixth Field Artillery*, 93–95.
12. *EPMT*, June 27, 1916, Jan. 7, 1917; *SFNM*, June 26, 1916.
13. *EPMT*, June 25, 1916.
14. *SFNM*, June 22, July 17, 1916; *EPMT*, June 26, 28, 29, 30, July 7, 11, 1916; this was not quite true: a dozen more musicians were needed for the band of the 1st New Mexico Infantry. The band had not yet been mustered in to federal service. *EPMT*, July 18, 1916.
15. *EPMT*, July 25, 1916.
16. *EPMT*, Aug. 3, 1916.
17. Harris, *Ghost Towns Alive*, 211.

18. *EPMT*, June 27, 28, 29, 30, July 5, 7, 21, 24, 1916; *AMJ*, June 28, 1916.
19. *EPMT*, July 1, 1916; *AMJ*, July 1, 1916.
20. *EPMT*, July 2, 1916; for a scholarly account see Hurst, *The Villista Prisoners*.
21. *EPMT*, July 2, 3, 1916.
22. *EPMT*, July 4, 1916.
23. "Diary of Lt. Colonel Charles Stewart Farnsworth March 12–June 16, 1916," Palace of the Governors History Library, Santa Fe, New Mexico, 166, 168.
24. Lt. Col. C. S. Farnsworth, "Report of Operations Base of Communications Mexican Punitive Expedition from June 19th, 1916, to February 5th, 1917," Museum of New Mexico, Santa Fe, New Mexico, 6–7.
25. *EPMT*, Oct. 8, 1916.
26. Farnsworth, "Report of Operations," Museum of New Mexico, 6–9.
27. For a sketch of the 24th U.S. Infantry's history see Hovey, "The Twenty-fourth Regiment of Infantry," 91–93.
28. Busch, "Guarding the Border," 66–70.
29. *EPMT*, July 7, 1916.
30. *SFNM*, June 29, 1916.
31. *SFNM*, July 7, 1916; *RGR*, July 11, 1916.
32. *SFNM*, July 19, 1916.
33. The lieutenants were James I. Costillo, 18th Infantry; J. Merwin, 1st Infantry; Merrill H. Nallger, 16th Infantry; Charles D. Shaw, Jr., 2nd Infantry; David M. Garrison, 10th Infantry; J. M. Rose, 3rd Infantry; Daniel S. Fressing, 4th Infantry; Walter Ettingie, 6th Infantry, and Jess Webb, 8th Infantry. *EPMT*, July 27, 1916.
34. *Seattle Daily Times*, June 20, 1916.
35. *SFNM*, July 13, 1916.
36. Jolly, "History National Guard of New Mexico 1606–1963," 34, is incorrect in stating that only the 1st New Mexico was attached to the Punitive Expedition.
37. Farnsworth, "Report of Operations," 5, Museum of New Mexico.
38. *Report on Mobilization*, 63.
39. *EPMT*, July 5, 1916.
40. *SFNM*, July 27, 1916.
41. *SFNM*, July 10, 1916.
42. *EPMT*, July 9, 1916; *SFNM*, July 14, 1916.
43. *EPMT*, July 4, 8, 1916.
44. *EPMT*, July 24, Aug. 12, 16, Sept. 9, 1916.
45. *EPMT*, July 31, 1916.
46. *SAE*, Aug. 19, 1916; *EPMT*, Aug. 18, 1916.
47. *EPMT*, July 14, 1916.
48. *EPMT*, July 18, 1916.
49. *EPMT*, Aug. 26, 1916.
50. *EPMT*, Aug. 5, 13, 1916; *SFNM*, Aug. 10, 1916.
51. *SFNM*, June 24, 1916.
52. Funston to Governor, Aug. 11, 1916, NMAG.
53. Harris and Sadler, *The Border and the Revolution*, 19–20.
54. Herring to McDonald, Aug. 23, 1916, NMAG.
55. *EPMT*, July 29, Aug. 8, 1916.
56. *EPMT*, Dec. 3, 1916.
57. *EPMT*, Dec. 14, 1916.

58. *SAE*, Aug. 4, 5, 1916.
59. *SAE*, Aug. 8, 15, 1916; *NYT*, Aug. 6, 1916.
60. The court-martial proceedings for Clark are in "Memorandum for the Secretary of War," Oct. 4, 1916, Tasker Bliss Papers, Library of Congress; see also *EPMT*, Aug. 4, 5, 15, 16, Sept. 27, 1916; *SAE*, Sept. 8, 27, 1916.
61. *EPMT*, Aug. 18, 1916.
62. *SAE*, Oct. 13, 1916.
63. *EPMT*, July 28, Sept. 9, Oct. 26, 1916.
64. *EPMT*, July 23, 26, 1916.
65. *EPMT*, July 6, 1916.
66. Busch, "Guarding the Border," 80–81; *EPMT*, Jan. 29, 1917.
67. *SFNM*, Oct. 10, 1916; *EPMT*, Oct. 11, 1916.
68. *EPMT*, Aug. 10, 1916.
69. Coggeshall, "The Happy Invasion," 112–13. The girls and matrons are listed.
70. *EPMT*, July 15, 1916; *SFNM* July 14, 1916.
71. *EPMT*, July 19, 23, 1916.
72. *EPMT*, Nov. 1, 4, 1916.
73. *EPMT*, Aug. 12, 1916.
74. *EPMT*, Aug. 22, Sept. 2, 1916.
75. *EPMT*, Jan. 16, 18, 1917.
76. *EPMT*, Sept. 4, 1916.
77. *EPMT*, Dec. 25, 1916.
78. *SFNM*, Aug. 26, 1916.
79. *AMJ*, Nov. 8, 1916.
80. *SFNM*, Nov. 13, 1916.
81. *EPMT*, Nov. 23, 1916.
82. *EPMT*, Nov. 25, 1916.
83. Ilfeld to Herring, Dec. 6, 9, 15, 1916, NMAG; Herring to Ilfeld, Dec. 7, 18, 1916; NMAG; Hurd to Herring, Dec. 23, 1916, NMAG; Herring to Editor, Dec. 11, 1916, NMAG; *SFNM*, Dec. 12, 1916.
84. Mann to Adjutant General, Nov. 14, 1916; Herring to Chief, Militia Bureau, Sept. 19, 1916, NMAG; *Report of the Adjutant General . . . New Mexico . . . 1914[–]1916*, 8.
85. *EPMT*, Feb. 6, 1917.
86. *EPMT*, Feb. 6, 18, 1917; *SFNM*, Feb. 12, 20, 1917.
87. *SFNM*, Jan. 30, 1917; *EPMT*, Feb. 4, 17, 1917.
88. *EPMT*, Feb. 6, 9, 17, 1917.
89. Farnsworth, "Report of Operations," 10–12; *EPMT*, Feb. 3, 6, 14, 18, 19, 21, 22, 27, Mar. 16, 1917; Briscoe, "Pershing's Chinese," 467–88.
90. *EPMT*, Mar. 7, 1917; see also *SFNM*, Feb. 16, 1917; *EPMT*, Feb. 20, 1917; *SAE*, Feb. 17, 1917.
91. *EPMT*, Feb. 21, 1917; *AMJ*, Feb. 14, 22, 1917.
92. *EPMT*, Feb. 24, 1917.
93. *EPMT*, Feb. 28, 1917.
94. *EPMT*, Mar. 2, 1917.
95. *EPMT*, Feb. 17, 1917.
96. *EPMT*, Feb. 14–18, 25, 1917; *AMJ*, Feb. 15, 17, 1917; *SFNM*, Feb. 16, 17, 1917.
97. *EPMT*, Mar. 12, 1917.
98. *EPMT*, Mar. 16, 1917.

99. *Report of the Adjutant General . . . New Mexico . . . 1914[–]1916*, 41.
100. *EPMT*, Dec. 5, 1916.
101. *EPMT*, Jan. 29, 1917.
102. *SFNM*, Aug. 9, 1916.
103. *AMJ*, Jan. 10, 1917.
104. *SFNM*, Feb. 17, 1917.
105. *SFNM*, Mar. 27, Apr. 2, 5, 1917.
106. *Report of the Adjutant General . . . New Mexico . . . 1916[–]1918*, 10.
107. *SFNM*, Mar. 15, 1917.
108. *EPMT*, Feb. 16, 1917.
109. *SFNM*, Feb. 15, Apr. 6, 1917.
110. McCain to Commanding General, Mar. 30, 1917, NMAG; *Report of the Adjutant General . . . New Mexico . . . 1916[–]1918*, 29.

Chapter 17

1. Dumke, "Douglas," 283–98; *EPMT*, July 16, 1916.
2. *NYT*, June 20, 1916; a new regiment, the 35th U.S. Infantry, was also being formed from cadres drafted from existing units but was proceeding slowly for lack of equipment. *EPMT*, July 13, 1916. In Arizona, the 1st U.S. Cavalry experimented with coloring their horses to make them blend with the ground and be less vulnerable to snipers. After dampening the animal's coat, dye was applied with an ordinary grooming brush or sponge, changing the horse's color from a dark chestnut to yellow dun. The experiment was proclaimed a success, for the horse was reportedly invisible at a distance of four to five hundred paces. *SAE*, Aug. 4, 11, 1916. However, the practice was not generally employed.
3. *EPMT*, Mar. 27, July 13, 1916.
4. *EPMT*, Aug. 10, 1916.
5. *EPMT*, July 2, 1916.
6. *EPMT*, June 27, 1916; *NDH*, June 21, 1916.
7. *ADS*, June 20, 1916.
8. *ADS*, June 20, 1916.
9. Tackenberg, "'Sore as a Boil,'" 433.
10. *ADS*, June 25, 1916; *EPMT*, June 25, 1916.
11. *EPMT*, June 27, 1916.
12. *ADS*, June 28, 1916.
13. *EPMT*, June 22, 1916; *NDH*, July 1, 1916.
14. Tucson sent two National Guard infantry companies and a hospital corps to the border. The Tucson Aero squadron was incorporated into Company K. Towns such as Prescott, Kingman, Bisbee, and Globe also organized home guards. *EPMT*, June 22, 26, 28, 30, July 2, 1916.
15. *EPMT*, July 5, 1916.
16. *ADS*, July 1, 2, 4, 5, 7, 12, 14, 1916.
17. *ADS*, July 2, 1916.
18. *EPMT*, July 2, 1916.
19. *ADS*, July 6, 1916.

20. *ADS*, July 14, 1916. Officers in the National Guard had to purchase their own uniforms.
21. *EPMT*, July 19, 1916.
22. Tackenberg, "'Sore as a Boil,'" 433.
23. *EPMT*, Aug. 13, 1916.
24. *ADS*, June 25, 1916.
25. Smith, *Fort Huachuca*, does not mention that various National Guard units from Douglas and Nogales used the fort in 1916.
26. *EPMT*, July 3, 15, 1916.
27. *Annual Report . . . New Jersey . . . 1916[–]1918*, 7–8.
28. *NYT*, June 19, 20, 1916.
29. *NYT*, June 23, 27, 29, 1916.
30. The *El Paso Morning Times* on Oct. 22, 1916, published a photo captioned "Off for Mexico without horses" showing raw recruits of the Essex Troop of New Jersey in civilian clothes carrying their suit cases. *EPMT*, Oct. 22, 1916.
31. *NYT*, June 20, 24–28, 1916.
32. *NYT*, Nov. 12, 1916.
33. Srodes, *Allen Dulles*, 48–49.
34. Grose, *Gentleman Spy*, 20–21.
35. *NYT*, June 21, 27, 28, 1916.
36. *NYT*, June 29, July 1, 1916.
37. *NYT*, June 29, July 1, 2, 23, Aug. 6, 1916; *EPMT*, July 19, 1916.
38. *NYT*, Sept. 3, 1916.
39. *History of the Essex Troop*, 85.
40. *NYT*, June 30, 1916.
41. *EPMT*, July 4, 1916; Tackenberg, "Call Out the Guard!," 85.
42. *EPMT*, July 3–5, 1916; *NYT*, July 4, 6, 1916.
43. Tackenberg, "Call Out the Guard!," 85–86.
44. Tackenberg, "Call Out the Guard!," 86–87.
45. Swarthout, *History Second Regiment*, 7; Lacey, *The Montana Militia*, relies very heavily on Swarthout's account; see also *EPMT*, July 6, 1916.
46. Swarthout, *History*, 9, 11; Lacey, *Montana Militia*, 40, 41.
47. Swarthout, *History*, 9, 24.
48. *EPMT*, July 19, 1916; Lacey, *Montana Militia*, 41.
49. *EPMT*, Aug. 1, 1916.
50. *EPMT*, Aug. 4, 1916.
51. Breniman report, July 28, 1916, roll 863, BI.
52. *EPMT*, Aug. 1, 1916.
53. *EPMT*, July 13, 1916.
54. Lacey, *Montana Militia*, 41.
55. *History of the Essex Troop*, 87, 89.
56. *History of the Essex Troop*, 91–92.
57. Tackenberg, "Call Out the Guard!," 87–89.
58. *ADS*, July 14, 1916; see also *AZR*, July 13, 1916.
59. Lacey, *Montana Militia*, 41, 42.
60. Lacey, *Montana Militia*, 42; *NDH*, Aug. 19, 1916.
61. *EPMT*, Sept. 14, 19, 1916.

62. *EPMT*, July 23, 1916; *SAE*, July 24, 1916; Tackenberg, "Call Out the Guard!," 87–88; *History of the Essex Troop*, 88–89.
63. Lacey, *Montana Militia*, 41; *NYT*, Aug. 18, 1916.
64. *EPMT*, July 16, Aug. 3, 1916.
65. Swarthout, *History*, 36.
66. Lacey, *Montana Militia*, 44; *NYT*, Aug. 21, 1916.
67. *EPMT*, Aug. 31, 1916; Tackenberg, "Call Out the Guard!," 89.
68. *SAE*, Sept. 2, 1916.
69. *EPMT*, Sept. 5, 1916.
70. *EPMT*, Sept. 16, 1916.
71. *EPMT*, Oct. 3, 1916; *SAE*, Oct. 3, 1916.
72. *NYT*, Oct. 12, 1916.
73. *SAE*, Oct. 12, 1916.
74. *NYT*, Oct. 2, 8, 1916.
75. *NYT*, Nov. 4, 1916.
76. *NYT*, Mar. 15, 1917.
77. Swarthout, *History*, 2.
78. Lacey, *Montana Militia*, 42.
79. *History of the Essex Troop*, 97–98; *EPMT*, Oct. 3, Nov. 17, 1916.
80. *EPMT*, Oct. 31, 1916.
81. *EPMT*, Oct. 8, 1916; a private in Battery A died on November 19 after being struck on the head with a stick by another private from the same battery while both were in the guardhouse for trivial offenses. *EPMT*, Nov. 21, 1916.
82. Nankivell, *History of the Military Organizations*, 206–10.
83. *EPMT*, Oct. 11, 1916.
84. *EPMT*, Sept. 19, 21, 1916.
85. *EPMT*, Oct. 19, 1916.
86. *EPMT*, Oct. 20, 1916.
87. *NDH*, Nov. 16, 1916.
88. *EPMT*, Dec. 26, 1916.
89. *NDH*, Jan. 16, 1917.
90. *NDH*, Jan. 16, 1917.
91. *NDH*, Feb. 26, 1917.
92. *NDH*, Feb. 28, 1917.
93. *SFNM*, July 15, 1916, quoting an article in the *St. Louis Globe-Democrat*.
94. *EPMT*, Feb. 16, 1917.
95. *NDH*, Dec. 18, 1916.
96. *EPMT*, Sept. 2, 1916.
97. Tackenberg, "'Sore as a Boil,'" 437.
98. *Arizona Republic*, May 9, 1956.
99. Tackenberg, "'Sore as a Boil,'" 438.
100. *EPMT*, Dec. 15, 1916.
101. *SAE*, Jan. 13, 1917.
102. *NDH*, Jan. 26, 1917.
103. *NDH*, Jan. 26, 1917.
104. *NDH*, Jan. 26, 1917.
105. Tackenberg, "'Sore as a Boil,'" 437–41.
106. *EPMT*, Feb. 24, 1917.

107. *NDH*, Mar. 10, 1917.
108. *NDH*, Mar. 1, 1917.
109. *EPMT*, Jan. 1, 1917.
110. *Annual Report . . . Arizona*, 2

Chapter 18

1. *Fort Wayne Weekly Sentinel*, July 21, 1916.
2. *Salt Lake Tribune*, June 21, 23, 26, 1916.
3. *EPMT*, June 22, 23, 26, 1916; *ADS*, June 22, 23, 1916.
4. Tackenberg, "'Sore as a Boil,'" 433; *AZR*, July 12, 13, 1916.
5. Hopkins reports, June 27, July 9, 12, 23, Aug. 4, 1916, roll 863, BI.
6. Mashbir, *I Was an American Spy*, 5–9, 27, 38; *Arizona Republic*, May 9, 1956.
7. Mashbir, *I Was an American Spy*, 38.
8. See Commanding General, Nogales, Arizona, to Commanding General Southern Department, May 16, 1916, in 8536–83, Office of the Chief of Staff, War College Division, RG 165, NARS.
9. Breniman to Neunhoffer, Sept. 26, 1916, and Breniman report, Sept. 27, 1916, both in roll 862, BI.
10. Hopkins to Barnes, Jan. 10, 1917, roll 862, BI.
11. Tackenberg "'Sore as a Boil,'" 430, 433, 435; *AZR*, July 12, 13, 1916.
12. *NDH*, Aug. 19, 1916; *EPMT*, Aug. 13, 1916.
13. Tackenberg, "'Sore as a Boil,'" 425–37.
14. *NYT*, June 22, July 2, 1916.
15. *Washington Post*, July 12, 18, 26, Aug. 17, 1916.
16. *NYT*, Sept. 15, 1916; *SAE*, Oct, 3, 5, 7, 1916.
17. Ball, "1st Separate Battalion, DCNG."
18. Johnson, "Military Service in World War I," 1.
19. A photo of the unit's encampment at Naco is in Taylor and Swartzwelder, "The United States Military," 4.
20. *Report on Mobilization*, 74.
21. *Washington Post*, July 12, 1916.
22. *Report on Mobilization*, 74; see also Cunningham, "Ninety-Two Days in Naco," 75–87.
23. *Washington Post*, July 18, 26, Aug. 2, 13, 1916.
24. *Washington Post*, Aug. 12, 1916.
25. *Washington Post*, Aug. 12, 1916.
26. *Washington Post*, Mar. 9, 1917.
27. *Washington Post*, Aug. 12, 1916.
28. *Washington Post*, Aug. 6, 1916.
29. Johnson, "Military Service in World War I," 1.
30. *EPMT*, Aug. 10, 21, 1916; *SAE*, Aug. 21, 1916.
31. Short report, Aug. 23, 1916, roll 862, BI.
32. *EPMT*, Oct. 13, 1916.
33. Johnson, "Military Service in World War I," 1.
34. *Washington Post*, Mar. 9, 1917.
35. Ball, "1st Separate Battalion."

Chapter 19

1. *Investigation*, 2:1812.
2. Kennedy, "Border Troubles," 14, 17–19.
3. *EPMT*, June 25, 1916.
4. *NDH*, May 4, 1916.
5. *NDH*, June 27, 1916.
6. *EPMT*, June 22, 1916; *ADS*, June 27, 28, 1916.
7. *ADS*, June 28, 1916; *NDH*, June 19, 21, 26, 1916.
8. *NDH*, July 5, 1916.
9. *ADS*, July 4, 5, 1916; Tackenberg, "'Sore as a Boil,'" 433.
10. *NDH*, June 28, 1916; *EPMT*, June 28, July 3, 1916.
11. *EPMT*, June 30, 1916.
12. Clendenen, *Blood on the Border*, 346–49; Eppinga, *Nogales*, 115–17.
13. *EPMT*, July 2, 3, 18, 22, 30, Aug. 11, 22, Sept. 23, Oct. 20, 28, Dec. 30, 1916; *NDH*, Sept. 11, 18, 1916.
14. *EPMT*, June 28, 1916; *NDH*, June 28, 1916. For additional imaginatively bombastic articles from the Mexican press, see *NDH*, July 12, 1916.
15. *NDH*, July 1, 5, 28, Oct. 11, 1916.
16. Gardiner, "The History of AZ EE: 9:109," 13. A detailed map of the National Guard camps around Nogales is on p. 15.
17. Roberts, *Legacy*, 88. This is arguably the best history of a state National Guard. It is based on Roberts's "History of the Utah National Guard"; see also his "The Utah National Guard on the Mexican Border in 1916," 262–81.
18. *EPMT*, June 20, 1916.
19. *SAE*, Aug. 19, 1916.
20. Roberts, *Legacy*, 88–91.
21. *NDH*, Aug. 19, 1916.
22. *NDH*, July 10, 17, 24, 1916; *BDH*, Sept. 8, 1916.
23. Roberts, *Legacy*, 94.
24. Dubach, "Reinforcements," 17.
25. Dubach, "Reinforcements," 25–28.
26. Roberts, *Legacy*, 92–94, 97–98.
27. Dubach, "Reinforcements," 20.
28. Dubach, "Reinforcements," 21–23.
29. Hudson, "The California National Guard, 1903–1940," 154; see also his "The California National Guard and the Mexican Border, 1914–16," 157–72.
30. *Oakland Tribune*, June 22, 1916.
31. Pickett, *The Second California Infantry*, 3.
32. *Report on Mobilization*, 123.
33. Quoted in Pickett, *Second California Infantry*, 7.
34. Pickett, *Second California Infantry*, 8.
35. Hudson, "California National Guard, 1903–1940," 157–58.
36. *NDH*, June 29, 30, July 3, Sept. 2, 7, 1916; *EPMT*, June 30, July 1, 3, 1916; *BDH*, Sept. 8, 1916. In August, each artillery battery received twelve mules, and Battery B also got ten horses. *NDH*, Aug. 19, 1916.
37. *NDH*, Oct. 17, 1916.
38. Pickett, *Second California Infantry*, 8.

39. Pickett, *Second California Infantry*, 12.
40. Hudson, "California National Guard, 1903–1940," 161–62; *NDH*, July 3, 5, 20, 24, 1916; *EPMT*, July 28, 29, 1916.
41. *NDH*, Aug. 9, Oct. 16, 18, 1916.
42. *EPMT*, July 4, 6, 1916.
43. *NDH*, July 19, 1916; *EPMT*, July 19, 28, 1916; the records of firing of nine California companies were also lost in a flood in Nogales, *War Department Annual Reports, 1917*, 1:876.
44. *NYT*, July 4, 1916.
45. *War Department Annual Reports, 1916*, 1:910; *SAE*, June 20, July 9, 1916; *NYT*, June 22, 23, 25, 27, July 4, 15, Aug. 18, 31, Sept. 1, 8, Nov. 29, 1916.
46. Howard, ed., *The Origin and Fortunes*, 190. *EPMT*, July 3, 1916; *NDH*, July 7, 14, 1916.
47. *NDH*, Aug. 3, 1916.
48. McCarthy, ed., *A History of Troop A*, 5–6.
49. Pickett, *Second California Infantry*, 16.
50. Howard, *Origin and Fortunes*, 196–98; *NDH*, July 14, 31, 1916; a private in Troop B died in the base hospital in October. *NDH*, Oct. 20, 1916.
51. *NDH*, July 22, 1916.
52. Howard, *Origin and Fortunes*, 194.
53. *NDH*, July 27, 1916.
54. *NDH*, July 14, 1916.
55. *NDH*, Aug. 2, 4, 1916; *EPMT*, Aug. 3, 1916.
56. *NDH*, Aug. 11, 1916.
57. *NDH*, Aug. 14, 1916.
58. *EPMT*, July 19, 1916; *NDH*, July 22, Aug. 8, 1916.
59. See, for example, *NDH*, July 18, 19, 21, 1916.
60. *EPMT*, July 28, 1916.
61. *NDH*, July 6, 1916.
62. Svingen, ed. *The History of the Idaho National Guard*, 49.
63. *A History of the Sixty-Sixth Field Artillery*, 90–91.
64. Svingen, *History of the Idaho National Guard*, 51–52.
65. *Report of the Adjutant General . . . Idaho 1915–1916*, 25.
66. Svingen, *History of the Idaho National Guard*, 52–53.
67. Svingen, *History of the Idaho National Guard*, 53; the Idaho regiment lost two privates—one from pneumonia and the other who died in the hospital on August 19, cause unspecified, *NDH*, July 12, 14, 27, 31, Aug. 19, 1916.
68. Svingen, *History of the Idaho National Guard*, 53–54.
69. *NDH*, July 20, 1916.
70. *NDH*, July 21, Aug. 17, 1916.
71. *Report on Mobilization*, 63.
72. *NDH*, Aug. 17, 1916.
73. *NDH*, July 20, 1916.
74. *NDH*, July 7, 1916.
75. *NDH*, July 8, 12, 1916.
76. *EPMT*, July 18, 19, 23, 30, 1916.
77. *NDH*, July 21, 1916.
78. Hudson, "California National Guard, 1903–1940," 163; *NDH*, Aug. 4, 1916.

79. *NDH*, Aug. 9, 1916.
80. *EPMT*, Oct. 2, 1916.
81. *SAE*, Oct. 3, 1916.
82. *NDH*, Oct. 19, 1916.
83. *NDH*, Aug. 16, 29, 1916.
84. *NDH*, July 21, 24, 27, 1916.
85. Truss, "Progress toward Professionalism," 118–19.
86. *Nashville Banner*, July 20, 1916.
87. *NDH*, July 24, 1916.
88. *NDH*, Aug. 19, 1916.
89. *NDH*, Oct. 21, Nov. 1, 1916.
90. *NDH*, Dec. 4, 1916.
91. *NDH*, Nov. 16, 1916.
92. *NDH*, Oct. 13, 1916.
93. *NDH*, Nov. 20, 1916.
94. *NDH*, Oct. 16, Nov. 4, 1916.
95. *NDH*, Nov. 5, 1916.
96. *NDH*, Dec. 5, 1916.
97. *NDH*, Dec. 6, 1916.
98. *NDH*, Jan. 12, 1917.
99. *NDH*, Sept. 26, 1916.
100. *NDH*, July 7, 8, 13, 14, 17, 19, 21, 24, 27, Aug. 9, 19, Sept. 23, Oct. 26, 28, Nov. 1, 7, Dec. 14, 1916.
101. *NDH*, Aug. 10, 1916.
102. *EPMT*, Aug. 31, 1916; *NDH*, Aug. 19, 26, 1916.
103. *NDH*, Aug. 25, 1916.
104. *NDH*, Dec. 19, 1916.
105. Holzman, *James Jesus Angleton*, 8–9; Winks, *Cloak & Gown*, 328–29. Both Holzman and Winks erroneously state that Hugh Angleton participated in the Punitive Expedition against Pancho Villa. So, for that matter, do Martin, *Wilderness of Mirrors*, 11, who states that James Angleton "was the firstborn son of Hugh Angleton, a man who had moved west to Idaho not long after the turn of the century and then set off for Mexico with 'Black Jack' Pershing in pursuit of Pancho Villa"; and Mangold, *Cold Warrior*, 31, who says that Hugh Angleton "had ridden into Mexico as a cavalry officer with General John J. Pershing."
106. *NDH*, Aug. 19, 24, 1916; Roberts, *Legacy*, 94.
107. *NDH*, Aug. 19, 21, 23, 24, 1916.
108. *NDH*, Aug. 26, 1916.
109. Pickett, *Second California Infantry*, 16.
110. *NDH*, Aug. 31, Sept. 5, 1916.
111. *NDH*, Sept. 5, 8, 1916.
112. *NDH*, Sept. 11, 1916; Roberts, *Legacy*, 96, 97.
113. *NDH*, Sept. 23, 1916.
114. Roberts, *Legacy*, 96–97; *NDH*, Oct. 3, 11, 1916.
115. *NDH*, Aug. 8, 1916.
116. *NDH*, Sept. 25, 27, Oct. 24, 1916.
117. *NDH*, Aug. 31, Sept. 1, 4, 5, 1916.
118. A list of the dates when the California units were mustered out of federal service is in Hudson, "California National Guard, 1903–1940," 167.

119. Roberts, *Legacy*, 98–99.
120. *NDH*, Dec. 30, 1916.
121. *NDH*, Jan. 23, Feb. 22, 1917.
122. *NDH*, Oct. 24, 1916.
123. *NDH*, Nov. 25, 1916.
124. Truss, "Progress toward Professionalism," 100, 104.
125. A detailed account of the mobilization camp is in Truss, "The Alabama National Guard," 205–23.
126. Land, "Alabama National Guard," 54.
127. *EPMT*, Oct. 23, 1916.
128. *NDH*, Oct. 21, 23, 24, 26, Nov. 1, 1916.
129. Holt, *The Deceivers*, 283, 287.
130. Pickett, *Second California Infantry*, 17.
131. *NDH*, Oct. 28, 1916.
132. *NDH*, Nov. 8, 1916.
133. *NDH*, Dec. 26, 1916, Jan. 24, 25, 1917.
134. *EPMT*, Feb. 18, 1917.
135. Truss, "Progress toward Professionalism," 111–12, 114–17.
136. As of Dec. 15, 1916, the regiment numbered 1,129 men. *Report of the Adjutant General State of Idaho*, 19.
137. Svingen, *History of the Idaho National Guard*, 54–56.
138. *NDH*, Dec. 22, 23, 27, 1916.
139. *NDH*, Dec. 26, 1916.
140. *NDH*, Oct. 27, 1916; *BDH*, Nov. 15, 1916.
141. *NDH*, Dec. 30, 1916, Jan. 6, 9, 10, 22, 1917.
142. *NDH*, Jan. 6, 9, 10, 16, 1917.
143. *NDH*, December 19, 26, 28, 1916.
144. *NDH*, January 5, 6, 1917.
145. *NDH*, January 11, 12, 16, 1917.
146. *NDH*, Feb. 7, 1917; Truss, "Progress toward Professionalism," 117–18.
147. *NDH*, Jan. 6, 13, 16, 1917.
148. *NDH*, Jan. 15, 1917; there is a photograph of Colonel Screws, who commanded the 167th U.S. (formerly Alabama) Infantry with distinction in France in 1918, on p. 77 of Ferrell, *The Question of MacArthur's Reputation*.
149. *NDH*, Jan. 16, 17, 1917.
150. *NDH*, Jan. 18, 1917; see also *EPMT*, Jan. 14, 16, 1917.
151. *NDH*, Jan. 19, 1917.
152. *NDH*, Jan. 22, 23, 1917.
153. *NDH*, Jan. 24, 1917.
154. *NDH*, Jan. 25, 1917.
155. *NDH*, Jan. 26, 1917.
156. *NDH*, Jan. 27, 1917.
157. *NDH*, Jan. 30, 1917; see also *SAE*, Jan. 27, 1917.
158. Wilson, *Islands in the Desert*, 230–31; Roberts, *Legacy*, 95–96; see also *EPMT*, Jan. 27–29, 1917; *NDH*, Jan. 27, 30, 1917.
159. *EPMT*, Jan. 30, 1917.
160. Wilson, *Islands in the Desert*, 231.
161. *NDH*, Feb. 7, 1917.
162. *NDH*, Feb. 9, Mar. 8, 1917.

163. *NDH*, Dec. 18, 1916, Feb. 6, 12, 1917.
164. Truss, "Progress toward Professionalism," 101–104.
165. *NDH*, Mar. 12, 1917; see also Sterkx, "Unlikely Conquistadores," 163–81.
166. *NDH*, Mar. 13, 15, 1917.
167. *NDH*, Mar. 15, 1917.
168. *NDH*, Jan. 29, Feb. 6, 19, Mar. 14, 1917.

Chapter 20

1. *Fifteenth Biennial Report . . . Oregon* , 61.
2. *La Prensa*, June 27, 1916.
3. "On October 4, 1916, so much of the State of California as lies south of the 33d degree North Latitude, was designated the Southern California Border Patrol District. This organization obtained at outbreak of war." *Order of Battle*, 616.
4. *EPMT*, June 26, 1916; *NDH*, June 26, 1916; *SAE*, June 26, 28, 29, 1916; *NYT*, June 19, 25, 26, 1916.
5. *Fifteenth Biennial Report . . . Oregon*, 55–56; *NYT*, June 19, 1916.
6. *Seattle Daily Times*, June 20, 23, 1916.
7. *Fifteenth Biennial Report . . . Oregon*, 47; *SAE*, July 17, 1916.
8. *Fifteenth Biennial Report . . . Oregon*, 47.
9. *Fifteenth Biennial Report . . . Oregon*, 57.
10. *Fifteenth Biennial Report . . . Oregon*, 52.
11. *Fifteenth Biennial Report . . . Oregon*, 57; "Transportation of Troops," 3.
12. *NYT*, June 26, 1916.
13. *Fifteenth Biennial Report . . . Oregon*, 57.
14. *Fifteenth Biennial Report . . . Oregon*, 57.
15. *Report on Mobilization*, 78, 83–84.
16. *Report on Mobilization*, 80.
17. The following account of the Oregon National Guard's border service is based on the "War Diary, Third Oregon Infantry," *Fifteenth Biennial Report . . . Oregon*, 58–67.
18. These were the 38th and 60th U.S. Coast Artillery Companies, the 3rd Oregon Infantry, Troop A of the Oregon Cavalry, and the 5th and 8th Companies of the California Coast Artillery Reserves. The 38th U.S. Coast Artillery Company was transferred to Tecate, California, and units of the 3rd Oregon Infantry relieved the two California reserve companies.
19. *Fifteenth Biennial Report . . . Oregon*, 67.
20. *EPMT*, Dec. 27, 1916.
21. *Fifteenth Biennial Report . . . Oregon*, 68.
22. *Fifteenth Biennial Report . . . Oregon*, 65.
23. *NDH*, Aug. 31, 1916.
24. *Fifteenth Biennial Report . . . Oregon*, 52–53.
25. *Sixteenth Biennial Report . . . Oregon*, 7.
26. Unless otherwise indicated this account of the Washington guard is based on the *Washington National Guard Pamphlet*.
27. *Report of the Adjutant General . . . [Washington] 1915–1916*, 20.
28. *Seattle Daily Times*, June 20, 23, 1916.

29. In July, a new unit, Battery A, Field Artillery, was organized, with sixty-five men, and it was anticipated that it would soon be recruited up to war strength. *Seattle Daily Times*, July 14, 1916.
30. *Seattle Daily Times*, June 23, 1916.
31. *Seattle Daily Times*, June 28, 1916.
32. *Report of the Adjutant General . . . [Washington] 1915–1916*, 22.
33. *Seattle Daily Times*, July 5, 1916.
34. *Seattle Daily Times*, July 27, 1916.
35. *EPMT*, Sept. 18, 21, 22, 27, 1916.
36. *NDH*, Oct. 10, 1916.
37. *Seattle Daily Times*, July 27, 1916.
38. *War Department Annual Reports, 1917*, 1:233.
39. *NDH*, Aug. 31, Sept. 2, 1916.
40. *Seattle Daily Times*, Dec. 15, 1916; *SAE*, Jan. 31, 1917.
41. *Report of the Adjutant General . . . [Washington] 1917–1918*, 19; *Historical and Pictorial Review*, xxiv.

Conclusion

1. Orr, "Borderline Failure," 6.
2. Reilly, "National Guard," 230.

Bibliography

Archives

Archives and Special Collections, New Mexico State University, Las Cruces, New Mexico
Arizona State Archives, Phoenix, Arizona
Center for American History, University of Texas at Austin
Centro de Estudios Históricos Carso (formerly Condumex), México, D.F.
Kansas State Historical Society, Topeka, Kansas
Library of Congress, Washington, D.C.
Maine State Archives, Augusta, Maine
Massachusetts National Guard Military Museum, Worcester, Massachusetts
Military Records Collection, Department of Buildings and General Services, Public Records Division, Middlesex, Vermont
Museum of New Mexico, Santa Fe, New Mexico
National Archives and Records Service, Washington, D.C.
Nettie Lee Benson Latin American Collection, University of Texas at Austin
New Mexico State Records Center and Archives, Santa Fe, New Mexico
New York State Military Museum and Veterans Research Center, Saratoga Springs, New York
Ohio National Guard Collection, Columbus, Ohio
Palace of the Governors History Library, Santa Fe, New Mexico
Texas Military Forces Museum, Camp Mabry, Austin, Texas
Texas State Library, Austin
Vermont Historical Society, Barre, Vermont
Vermont Veterans Militia Museum, Camp Johnson, Colchester, Vermont

Secondary Sources

The Adjutant General's Report Illinois 1917: Roster of National Guard and Naval Militia As Called for World War Service. Springfield, Ill.: n.p., 1929.
The Adjutant General's Report Illinois 1916–1917: Roster of Officers and Enlisted Men Mexican Border. Springfield: n.p., 1927.

Bibliography

Ainsworth, Troy. "Boredom, Fatigue, Illness and Death: The United States National Guard and the Texas-Mexico Border, 1916–1917." *Journal of Big Bend Studies* 19 (2007): 81–96.

Annual Report of the Adjutant General for the Year 1919. Albany: J. G. Lyon Co., 1921.

Annual Report of the Adjutant General of the Commonwealth of Massachusetts for the Year Ending December 31, 1916. Boston: Wright & Potter Printing Co., State Printers, 1917.

Annual Report of the Adjutant General of the Commonwealth of Massachusetts for the Year Ending December 31, 1917. Boston: Wright & Potter Printing Co., 1918.

Annual Report of the Adjutant General of the State of Maine for the Year Ending December 31, 1916. Augusta, Maine: By Authority of the State Legislature, 1929.

Annual Report of the Adjutant General of the State of New York, 1916. Albany: J. B. Lyon, 1917.

Annual Report of the Adjutant General of the State of New York, 1917. Albany: J. B. Lyon, 1920. Last modified May 10, 2011. dmna.ny.gov/historia/research/AG_Reports/AG_Report_1917.pdf.

Annual Report of the Adjutant General State of New Jersey, November 1, 1916–June 30, 1918. Trenton: State of New Jersey, 1919.

Annual Report of the Adjutant General to the Governor of Arizona. Phoenix: State of Arizona, 1918. April 30, 2014. Azmemory.azlibrary.gov/cdm/ref/collection/statepubs/id/11776.

Ayres, Harrol B. "Democracy at Work—San Antonio Being Reborn." *Social Hygiene* 4 (April 1918): 211–17.

Bacevich, A. J. *Diplomat in Khaki: Major General Frank Ross McCoy & American Foreign Policy, 1898–1949.* Lawrence: University Press of Kansas, 1989.

Bailey, Kenneth R. "A Search for Identity: The West Virginia National Guard, 1877–1921." Ph.D. dissertation, Ohio State University, 1976.

———. *Mountaineers Are Free: A History of the West Virginia National Guard.* St. Albans, W.Va.: n.p., 1978.

Ball, Jim. "1st Separate Battalion, DCNG." AfriGeneas Military Research Forum Archive. March 25, 2005. http://www.afrigeneas.com/forum-militaryarchive/index.cgi/md/read/id/2018/sbj/1st-separate-battalion-dcng/.

Banks, Stephen A. *Doing My Duty: Corporal Elmer Dewey—One National Guard Doughboy's Experiences during the Pancho Villa Punitive Campaign and World War I.* N.p.: Signature Books Printing, 2011.

Batchelder, Roger. *Watching and Waiting on the Border.* Boston: Houghton Mifflin, 1917.

Bauer, Richard E. *The Spirit of the Guard: The Iowa National Guard in Two Wars.* Lake Mills, Iowa: Graphic Publishing, 1980.

"The Best Football Team Ever." Texas Reader. April 27, 2014. www.texasreader.com/the-best-football-team-ever.html.

Biennial Report of the Adjutant General of the State of Mississippi: For the Years 1916–1917 to the Governor. Jackson: n.p., 1917.

Biennial Report of the Adjutant General of Texas from January 1, 1915 to December 31, 1916. Austin: Von Boeckmann-Jones, 1917.

Biennial Report of the Adjutant General of Texas from January 1, 1917 to December 31, 1918. Austin: Von Boeckmann-Jones, 1919.

Biennial Report of the Adjutant General State of Tennessee for the Period January 1, 1917 to January 1, 1919. Nashville: State of Tennessee, 1919.

Bibliography

Biennial Report of the Adjutant General State of Tennessee, Nashville, March 19, 1917. Nashville: State of Tennessee, 1917.

Biennial Report of the Adjutant, Inspector and Quartermaster General of the State of Vermont for the Two Years Ending June 30, 1916. Rutland: Tuttle, 1916.

Biennial Report of the Adjutant, Inspector and Quartermaster General of the State of Vermont for the Two Years Ending June 30, 1918. 2nd rev. ed. Rutland: Tuttle, 1919.

Bishop, Jim, and Virginia Lee Bishop. *Fighting Father Duffy.* New York: Farrar, Straus, Cudahy, 1956.

Blevins, Tim, Chris Nicholl, and Calvin P. Otto, eds. *The Colorado Labor Wars: Cripple Creek 1903–1904.* Colorado Springs: Pikes Peak Library District, 2006.

Blue Book of the State of Illinois 1919–1920. Springfield: State of Illinois, n.d.

Boies, Elizabeth. "The Girls on the Border and What They Did for the Militia." *Social Hygiene*, 3, no. 2 (April 1917): 221–28.

Border Memories 1916, Mexican Border Service Omaha Battalion Fourth Nebraska Infantry Regiment at Llano Grande, Texas. Omaha: Festner Printing, 1917.

Braddy, Haldeen. *Pershing's Expedition in Mexico.* El Paso: Texas Western College Press, 1966.

Brief History of Troop A, 107th Regiment of Cavalry Ohio National Guard, the Black Horse Troop for Many Years Known as the First City Troop of Cleveland. [Cleveland]: Veterans' Association, 1923.

Briscoe, Edward Eugene. "Pershing's Chinese Refugees in Texas." *Southwestern Historical Quarterly* 62, no. 4 (April 1959): 467–88.

Brooks, George, III. *With the First City Troop on the Mexican Border: Being the Diary of a Trooper.* Philadelphia: John C. Winston, 1917.

Brown, Anthony Cave. *The Last Hero: Wild Bill Donovan.* New York: Times Books, 1982.

Bruscino, Thomas A., Jr. "The Army and Security on the Mexican Border, 1915–1917." *Military Review* (July–August 2008): 31–44.

Buckley, Thomas C. "Trucks along the Southwest Border: Army Motorization and Highway Construction in the U.S.-Mexico Border Country, 1916–1926." *Journal of Big Bend Studies* 13 (2001): 215–34.

Busch, Rebecca Anne. "Guarding the Border: The New Mexico National Guard at Columbus, New Mexico, 1916–1917." M.A. thesis, New Mexico State University, 1997.

Cano, Tony, and Ann Sochat. *Bandido: The True Story of Chico Cano, the Last Western Bandit.* Canutillo, Tex.: Reata Publishing, 1997.

Carter, Russell Gordon. *The 101st Field Artillery A. E. F. 1917–1919.* Boston: Houghton Mifflin, 1940.

Casso, Evans J. *Louisiana Legacy: A History of the State National Guard.* Gretna, La.: Pelican Publishing, 1976.

Christian, Garna L. *Black Soldiers in Jim Crow Texas, 1899–1917.* College Station: Texas A&M University Press, 1995.

Clendenen, Clarence C. *Blood on the Border: The United States Army and the Mexican Irregulars.* New York: Macmillan, 1969.

Coats, Stephen D. *Gathering at the Golden Gate: Mobilizing for War in the Philippines, 1898.* Fort Leavenworth, Kans.: Combat Studies Institute Press, 2006.

Coffin, Louis, and Cameron H. Sanders. *A History of the Third Field Artillery Ohio National Guard Which Served through the World War 1917–1918–1919 as the 136th F. A. Regiment, U.S.A.* Cincinnati: Mounted Press, 1928.

Bibliography

Coggeshall, Helen Roberts. "The Happy Invasion of 1916." *Password* 6, no. 4 (Fall 1961): 107–14.

Cole, Merle T. "Marylanders on the Mexican Border, 1916–1917." *Maryland Historical Magazine* 86, no. 2 (Summer 1991): 190–98.

"Condensed Fact Sheet, National Guard and Organized Reserve Units Mobilized in 1916 for MEXICAN BORDER Duties." Atlanta: Georgia National Guard History Office, n.d.

Cooper, Jerry M. *Citizens as Soldiers: A History of the North Dakota National Guard.* Fargo: North Dakota Institute for Regional Studies, North Dakota State University, 1986.

Cramer, Stuart W., Jr. "The Punitive Expedition from Boquillas." *Journal of the United States Cavalry Association* 28 (November 1916): 200–227.

Cropp, Richard. *The Coyotes: A History of the South Dakota National Guard.* South Dakota Board of Military Affairs and the National Guard Officers Association. Mitchell, S.Dak.: Educator Supply, 1962.

Cummings, Charles R. "The Mobilization at Norwich." *Vermonter* 21, no. 5 (1916): 115–22.

Cunningham, Roger. "Ninety-Two Days in Naco: The District of Columbia's First Separate Battalion and the Mexican Border Mobilization of 1916." *Journal of America's Military Past* (Winter 2001): 75–87.

Cutchins, John A. *A Famous Command: The Richmond Light Infantry Blues.* Richmond, Va.: Garrett & Massie, 1934.

Cyrulik, John M. "A Strategic Examination of the Punitive Expedition into Mexico, 1916–1917." M.A. thesis, U.S. Army Command and General Staff College, Fort Leavenworth, Kansas, 2003.

"Data Furnished by Adjutants General of the States of Arizona, New Mexico, and Texas. Letter from the Secretary of War . . . Referred to the Committee on Military Affairs and ordered to be printed." 64th Cong., 2nd sess. H. R. Doc. 1468. Session vol. no. 114.

Daugherty, Fred A., and Pendleton Woods. "Oklahoma's Military Tradition." *Chronicles of Oklahoma* 57, no. 4 (Winter 1979–80): 427–45.

Davenport, B. T. *Soldiering at Marfa, Texas 1911–1945.* Kearney, Neb.: Morris Publishing, 1997.

De Castro, Vincent A., Frank Valladares, and Albert S. Lotwin. *The Second New York Infantry at the Mexican Border.* N.p., 1916.

D'Este, Carlo. *Eisenhower: A Soldier's Life.* New York: Henry Holt, 2002.

Destefanis, Anthony R. "The Road to Ludlow: Breaking the 1913–14 Southern Colorado Coal Strike." *Journal of the Historical Society* 12, no. 3 (September 2012): 341–90.

Diebert, Ralph C. *A History of the Third United States Cavalry, 1846–1933.* Harrisburg, Pa.: Telegraph Press, ca. 1933.

Dubach, Thomas Reese, Jr. "Reinforcements on the Border: The Utah National Guard's Role in the Punitive Expedition, 1916–1917." Added June 4, 2012. Digital Commons at Utah State University. http://digitalcommons.usu.edu/gradreports/137.

Duffy, Francis P. *Father Duffy's Story: A Tale of Humor and Heroism, of Life and Death with the Fighting Sixty-Ninth.* New York: George H. Doran, 1919.

Dumke, Glenn S. "Douglas, Border Town." *Pacific Historical Review* 17 (1948): 283–98.

Bibliography

Dunlop, Richard. *Donovan: America's Master Spy*. New York: Rand McNally, 1982.
Eisenhower, Dwight. *At Ease: Stories I Tell to Friends*. Garden City, N.Y.: Doubleday, 1967.
Elam, Earl H. "Big Bend Archives: The Big Bend Military District and Colonel James J. Hornbrook's Recruiting Announcement." *Journal of Big Bend Studies* 2 (1990): 117–22.
Ellis, Catherine H. "Men of Taylor! We Need Your Help: Snowflake's Company F, National Guard of Arizona, 1913–1915." *Journal of Arizona History* 47, no. 3 (Autumn 2006): 249–72.
Eppinga, Jane. *Nogales: Life and Times on the Frontier*. Charleston, S.C.: Arcadia Publishing, 2002.
Exner, M. J. "Prostitution in Its Relation to the Army on the Mexican Border." *Social Hygiene* 3, no. 2 (April 1917): 205–20.
Fabela, Isidro, et al., eds. *Documentos Históricos de la Revolución Mexicana*. 28 vols. México, D.F.: Editorial Jus, 1960–76.
Falls, Dewitt Clinton. *History of the Seventh Regiment 1889–1922*. New York: Veterans of the Seventh Regiment, 1948.
Ferrell, Robert H. *The Question of MacArthur's Reputation: Côte de Chatillôn, October 14–18, 1918*. Columbia: University of Missouri Press, 2008.
Fifteenth Biennial Report of the Adjutant General of the State of Oregon, November 1, 1914 to October 31, 1916. Salem: State Printing Department, 1917.
Finnegan, John P. "Preparedness in Wisconsin: The National Guard and the Mexican Border Incident." *Wisconsin Magazine of History* 47, no. 3 (Spring 1964): 199–213.
Flynn, Sean Michael. *The Fighting 69th: One Remarkable National Guard Unit's Journey from Ground Zero to Baghdad*. New York: Viking, 2007.
Forde, Frank. "The Sixty-Ninth Regiment of New York." *Irish Sword* 17 (1989): 145–58.
Fowles, Brian Dexter. *A Guard in Peace and War: The History of the Kansas National Guard, 1854–1987*. Manhattan, Kan.: Sunflower University Press, 1989.
Franks, Kenny A. *Citizen Soldiers: Oklahoma's National Guard*. Norman: University of Oklahoma Press, 1984.
"Frederick Funston." Wikipedia. Last modified January 13, 2014. http://en.wikipedia.org/wiki/Frederick_Funston.
Gabbert, Ann R. "Prostitution and Moral Reform in the Borderlands: El Paso, 1890–1920." *Journal of the History of Sexuality* 12, no. 4 (October 2003): 575–604.
Gardiner, Ronald. "The History of AZ EE: 9:109; A Military Camp in Nogales, Arizona, 1916 through 1918." Report prepared for Santa Cruz County Planning and Zoning Department of Public Works. Tucson: Cultural Resources Management Division, Arizona State Museum, 1987.
General Funston's Annual Report for the Southern Department, 1916. Records of the Adjutant General's Office, Record Group 94. Washington, D.C.: National Archives and Records Service, 1962.
Gibbons, Floyd P. *How the Laconia Sank: The Militia Mobilization on the Mexican Border*. Chicago: Daughaday, 1917.
Gilderhus, Mark T. *Diplomacy and Revolution: U.S.-Mexican Relations under Wilson and Carranza*. Tucson: University of Arizona Press, 1977.
Gillette, Mary Murphy. "A Small War in a Beer-Drinking Country: The South Dakota National Guard on the Mexican Border." *South Dakota History* (Spring 1986): 35–66.

Bibliography

Givens, Murphy. "Corpus Christi History." *Corpus Christi, Texas, Caller* online. November 11, 1998. http://www.caller2.com/autoconv/givensm98/givensm2.html.

Griffith, Joe. "In Pursuit of Pancho Villa 1916–1917." Historical Society of the Georgia National Guard. May 1, 2014. http://www.hsgng.org/legacy/pages/pancho.htm.

Gordon, Harmon Yerkes. *History of the First Regiment Infantry of Pennsylvania*. Philadelphia: n.p., 1961.

Grose, Peter. *Gentleman Spy: The Life of Allen Dulles*. Boston: Houghton Mifflin, 1994.

Hammond, Tracy Lewis. *Along the Rio Grande*. New York: Lewis Publishing, 1916.

Hannah, Eleanor L. *Manhood, Citizenship, and the National Guard: Illinois, 1870–1917*. Columbus: Ohio State University Press, 2007.

Haraty, Peter H., ed. *Put the Vermonters Ahead: A History of the Vermont National Guard 1764–1978*. Burlington, Vt.: Queen City Printers, 1978.

Harris, Charles H., III, and Louis R. Sadler. "Bastion on the Border: Fort Bliss, 1854–1943." Historical and Natural Resources, Report No. 6. Cultural Resources Management Branch, Directorate of Environment, U.S. Army Air Defense Artillery Center, Fort Bliss, Texas, 1993.

———. *The Border and the Revolution: Clandestine Activities of the Mexican Revolution: 1910–1920*. 2nd ed. Silver City, N.Mex.: High-Lonesome Books, 1990.

———. *The Plan de San Diego: Tejano Rebellion, Mexican Intrigue*. Lincoln: University of Nebraska Press, 2013.

———. "The Plan of San Diego and the Mexican-United States War Crisis of 1916: A Reexamination." *Hispanic American Historical Review* 58, no. 3 (August 1978): 381–408.

———. *The Secret War in El Paso: Mexican Revolutionary Intrigue, 1906–1920*. Albuquerque: University of New Mexico Press, 2009.

———. *The Texas Rangers and the Mexican Revolution: The Bloodiest Decade, 1910–1920*. Albuquerque: University of New Mexico Press, 2004.

Harris, Jodie P. "Protecting the Big Bend—A Guardsman's View." *Southwestern Historical Quarterly* 78, no. 3 (January 1975): 292–302.

Harris, Linda G. *Ghost Towns Alive: Trips to New Mexico's Past*. Albuquerque: University of New Mexico Press, 2003.

Harris, Stephen L. *Duffy's War: Fr. Francis Duffy, Wild Bill Donovan, and the Irish Fighting 69th in World War I*. Washington, D.C.: Potomac Books, 2006.

———. *Duty, Honor, Privilege: New York's Silk Stocking Regiment and the Breaking of the Hindenburg Line*. Washington, D.C.: Brassey's, 2001.

———. *Harlem's Hell Fighters: The African-American 369th Infantry in World War I*. Dulles, Va.: Potomac Books, 2003.

Hartman, Douglas R. *Nebraska's Militia: The History of the Army and Air National Guard, 1854–1991*. Marceline, Mo.: Walsworth Publishing, 1994.

Hawk, Robert. *Florida's Army: Militia/State Troops/National Guard 1565–1985*. Englewood, Fla.: Pineapple Press, 1986.

———. "Florida National Guard: Mexican Border to World War 1916–1919." March 16, 2005. http://floridaguard.net/history/print.asp?did=1315 (site discontinued).

Haynes, Robert V. *A Night of Violence: The Houston Riot of 1917*. Baton Rouge: Louisiana State University Press, 1976.

Henderson, Harry McCorry. *History of the 141st Infantry, 36th Division Texas National Guard*. San Antonio: Naylor, 1950.

Historical and Pictorial Review National Guard of the State of Washington 1939. Olympia, Wash.: Military Department of the State, 1939.

Bibliography

"History Mexican Border Expedition Compiled for State Committee on Military Records & History by W. P. A. Project No. 1435." Concord: New Hampshire Department of State, Division of Records Management and Archives, n.d.
History of the Essex Troop, 1890–1925. Newark: Essex Troop Armory, 1925.
History of the First Troop Philadelphia City Cavalry 1848–1991. Philadelphia: Winchell, 1991.
History of the Missouri National Guard. N.p.: Military Council, Missouri National Guard, 1934.
History of the Sixty-Sixth Field Artillery Brigade, American Expeditionary Forces. Denver: Smith-Brooks Printing, n.d.
Holt, Thaddeus. *The Deceivers: Allied Military Deception in the Second World War.* New York: Scribners, 2004.
Holzman, Michael. *James Jesus Angleton, the CIA and the Craft of Counterintelligence.* Amherst: University of Massachusetts Press, 2008.
Hopper, James. "New Columbus and the Expedition." *Collier's* 57 (August 5, 1916): 10–11, 35.
Horne, Gerald. *Black and Brown: African Americans and the Mexican Revolution, 1910–1920.* New York: New York University Press, 2005.
Hourigan, Joseph F. "The Fighting 69th in the Mexican Border Campaign." http://www.hourigan.com/69thny/Mexican.htm (site discontinued).
Houston, Donald E. "The Oklahoma National Guard on the Mexican Border, 1916." *Chronicles of Oklahoma* 53, no. 4 (Winter 1975–76): 447–62.
Hovey, H. W. "The Twenty-fourth Regiment of Infantry." In *The Black Military Experience in the American West*, ed. John M. Carroll. New York: Liveright, 1971.
Howard, James L., ed. *The Origin and Fortunes of Troop B: 1788, Governor's Independent Volunteer Troop of Horse Guards: 1911, Troop B Cavalry, Connecticut National Guard, 1917.* Hartford: Case, Lockwood & Brainard, 1921.
Howard, William F. "New Yorkers on the Southern Border." *New York Archives* 9, no. 3 (Winter 2010): 12–16.
Hudson, James J. "The California National Guard, 1903–1940," Ph.D. dissertation, University of California at Berkeley, 1952.
———. "The California National Guard and the Mexican Border, 1914–1916." *California Historical Society Quarterly* 34, no. 2 (1955): 157–72.
Hughes, Rupert. "The Big Hike." *Collier's* 58 (November 11, 1916): 4–6, 24–27.
Hurst, James W. *Pancho Villa and Black Jack Pershing: The Punitive Expedition in Mexico.* Westport, Conn.: Praeger, 2008.
———. *The Villista Prisoners of 1916–1917.* Las Cruces, N.Mex.: Yucca Tree Press, 2000.
Huston, James A. *The Sinews of War: Army Logistics 1775–1953.* Washington, D.C.: Office of the Chief of Military History, United States Army, 1966.
Investigation of Mexican Affairs, Report and Hearing before a Subcommittee on Foreign Relations. 66th Cong., 2nd sess. S. Doc. 285. Serial 7665. 2 vols. Washington, D.C.: Government Printing Office, 1920.
Jeffery, Keith. *The Secret History of MI6, 1909–1949.* New York: Penguin Press, 2010.
Johnson, Charles, Jr. "Military Service in World War I." In *African American Soldiers in the National Guard: Recruitment and Deployment during Peacetime and War.* Westport, Conn.: Greenwood Press, 1992. The African American Experience. Greenwood Publishing Group. May 3, 2013. http://testaae.greenwood.com/doc.aspx?fileID=JBS&chapterID=JBS-546&path=books/greenwood.

Bibliography

Johnson, Herbert T. "The Vermont Militia." *Vermonter* 29, no. 10 (1924): 154–71.

Jolly, John Parker. "History National Guard of New Mexico, 1606–1963." Santa Fe: n.p., 1964.

Journal of the Honorable Senate, January Session, 1917. Concord: State of New Hampshire, 1917.

Journal of the House of Representatives, January Session, 1917. Concord: State of New Hampshire, 1917.

Justice, Glenn. *Revolution on the Rio Grande: Mexican Raids and Army Pursuits 1916–1919.* El Paso: Texas Western Press, 1992.

Katz, Friedrich. *The Life & Times of Pancho Villa.* Stanford: Stanford University Press, 1998.

Kennedy, John W. "Border Troubles, and Camp Stephen D. Little." *Periodical* 10, no. 1 (Spring 1978): 14–25.

King, Benjamin, Richard C. Biggs, and Eric R. Criner. *Spearhead of Logistics: A History of the United States Army Transportation Corps.* Washington, D.C.: U.S. Army Transportation Center, Fort Eustis, Va., and Center of Military History, United States Army, 2001.

Lacey, Richard H. *The Montana Militia: A History of Montana's Volunteer Forces 1867–1976 (Including a History of the 163rd Regiment).* Dillon, Mo.: Dillon Tribune-Examiner Press, 1976.

Land, Frank S. "Alabama National Guard." *Alabama Historical Quarterly* 1, (Summer 1930): 51–73.

Lee, Jean C. "Ready and Willing: The 123rd Field Artillery in World War I." *Prairie Journal: The Western Illinois Story* 2, no. 1 (Fall 1984): 58–73.

Leeke, Jim. "Our Late Unpleasantness with Mexico: The Ohio National Guard on Border Service, 1916." *Timeline* 19, no. 3 (May–June 2002): 40–54.

Leiker, James N. *Racial Borders: Black Soldiers along the Rio Grande.* College Station: Texas A&M University Press, 2010.

Le May, Jason, John M. Trowbridge, and Harold Canon, comps. *Kentucky's Flying Soldiers: A History of the Kentucky Army National Guard's Fixed Wing Aviation.* Frankfort, Ky.: Office of the Adjutant General, n.d.

"Life on the Border—A Guardsman's Letter." *Outlook* 113 (August 23, 1916): 946–47.

Link, Arthur S., ed. *The Papers of Woodrow Wilson.* Vols. 36, 37, 38. Princeton, N.J.: Princeton University Press, 1981–82.

———. *Wilson: Confusions and Crises, 1915–1916.* Princeton, N.J.: Princeton University Press, 1964.

Linn, Brian McAllister. *The Philippine War, 1899–1902.* Lawrence: University of Kansas Press, 2000.

Maher, John, and Kirk Bohls. *Long Live the Longhorns: 100 Years of Texas Football.* New York: St. Martin's Press, 1993.

Mangold, Tom. *Cold Warrior: James Jesus Angleton; The CIA's Master Spy Hunter.* New York: Simon and Schuster, 1991.

Marcoux, Carl Henry. "City Slickers in the Boondocks: The Seventh Regiment, New York National Guard in the Rio Grande Valley, 1916." *Periodical: Journal of America's Military Past* 24, no. 3 (Fall 1997): 14–24.

———. "New Yorkers on the Texas Border: The Seventh Regiment New York National Guard in the Rio Grande Valley, 1916." *Rio Bravo* 3, no. 1 (Fall 1993): 51–68.

Bibliography

Marcum, Richard T. "Fort Brown, Texas: The History of a Border Post." Ph.D. dissertation, Texas Technological College, 1964.
Martin, Clarence S. *Three Quarters of a Century with the Tenth Infantry New York National Guard 1860–1935.* N.p., n.d.
Martin, David C. *Wilderness of Mirrors.* New York: Harper and Row, 1980.
Marvin, George, "Marking Time with Mexico: Why the National Guard Was Unprepared to Guard the Nation." *World's Work* 32 (September 1916): 526–33.
Mashbir, Sidney Forrester. *I Was an American Spy.* New York: Vantage Press, 1953.
Mason, Gregory. "Our Citizens in Arms." *Outlook* 93 (July 5, 1916): 546–49.
Mason, Herbert Molloy, Jr. *The Great Pursuit.* New York: Random House, 1970.
Matthews, Matt M. *The U.S. Army on the Mexican Border: A Historical Perspective.* The Long War Series Occasional Paper 22. Fort Leavenworth, Kan.: Combat Studies Institute Press, 2007.
McCann, Irving Goff. *With the National Guard on the Border. Our National Military Problem.* St. Louis: C. V. Mosby, 1917.
McCarthy, Robert John, ed. *A History of Troop A Cavalry, Connecticut National Guard and Its Service in the Great War as Co. D, 102d Machine Gun Battalion.* N.p., 1919.
Meggs, Brown. *The War Train: A Novel of 1916.* New York: Atheneum, 1981.
Metz, Leon C. *Desert Army: Fort Bliss on the Texas Border.* El Paso: Mangan Books, 1988.
Meyer, Harold J. *Hanging Sam: A Military Biography of General Samuel T. Williams. From Pancho Villa to Vietnam.* Denton: University of North Texas Press, 1990.
Meyer, Michael C. *Huerta: A Political Portrait.* Lincoln: University of Nebraska Press, 1972.
"MG Frederick Funston." Museum of the Kansas National Guard. January 24, 2011. http://www.kansasguardmuseum.org/dispmoh.php?id=2.
The Military Occupation of the Coal Strike Zone of Colorado by the Colorado National Guard 1913–1914. Denver: Press of Smith-Brooks Printing, n.d.
Military History of Kentucky, Chronologically Arranged. Frankfort: Military Department of Kentucky, 1939.
Millett, Allan R. *The General: Robert L. Bullard and Officership in the United States Army 1881–1925.* Westport, Conn.: Greenwood Press, 1975.
Milner, Elmer Ray. "An Agonizing Evolution: A History of the Texas National Guard, 1900–1945." Ph.D. dissertation, North Texas State University, 1979.
Nankivell, John Henry. *History of the Military Organizations of the State of Colorado 1860–1935.* Denver: W. H. Kistler Stationary, 1935.
Nash, Horace D. "Blacks on the Border: Columbus, New Mexico, 1916–1922." M.A. thesis, New Mexico State University, 1988.
Nelson, James Carl. *The Remains of Company D: A Story of the Great War.* New York: St. Martin's Press, 2009.
Nelson, Peter N. *A More Unbending Battle: The Harlem Hellfighters' Struggle for Freedom in WWI and Equality at Home.* New York: BasicCivitas, 2009.
Newton, Craig A. "Vermonters in Texas: A Reassessment of National Guard Duty on the Mexican Border in 1916." *Vermont History* 37 (Winter 1969): 30–38.
Niedringhaus, David A. "Dress Rehearsal for World War I: The Ohio National Guard Mobilization of 1916." *Ohio History* 100 (Winter–Spring 1991): 35–56.

Bibliography

Official History of the Militia and the National Guard of the State of Pennsylvania. Vol. 3, section 16. Harrisburg: Charles J. Hendler, 1939.

Ohl, John Kennedy. *Minuteman: The Military Career of General Robert S. Beightler*. Boulder: Lynne Rienner, 2001.

One Hundred Years 1847–1947: A Historical Sketch Twelfth Regiment New York. N.p., n.d.

Order of Battle of the United States Land Forces in the World War. Vol. 3, part 2. Washington, D.C.: Center of Military History United States Army, 1988.

Orr, Brent A. "Borderline Failure: National Guard on the Mexican Border, 1916–1917." School of Advanced Military Studies, United States Army Command and General Staff College, Fort Leavenworth, Kan., 2011.

Orsi, Richard J. *Sunset Limited: The Southern Pacific Railroad and the Development of the American West 1850–1930*. Berkeley: University of California Press, 2005.

O'Ryan, John F. *History of the 27th Division: New York's Own*. New York: Bennett & Churchill, 1919.

———. *The Story of the 27th Division*. 2 vols. New York: Wynkoop Hallenbeck Crawford, 1921.

Palmer, Frederick. *Newton D. Baker: America at War*. 2 vols. New York: Dodd, Mead, 1931.

Parker, James. *The Old Army: Memories, 1872–1918*. Philadelphia: Dorrance, 1929.

Patrick, Jeff, ed. *Guarding the Border: The Military Memoirs of Ward Schrantz, 1912–1917*. College Station: Texas A&M University Press, 2009.

Pattullo, George. "Brother Bill on the Border." *Saturday Evening Post*, August 5, 1916, 14, 35, 37–38.

———. "Sentinel Rheumatism." *Saturday Evening Post*, August 19, 1916, 23–28.

Peavey, John R. *Echoes From the Rio Grande*. Brownsville: Springman-King, 1963.

Pennsylvania in the World War: An Illustrated History of the Twenty-Eighth Division. 2 vols. Pittsburgh: States Publication Society, 1921.

Pershing, John J. *My Experiences in the World War*. 2 vols. New York: Frederick A. Stokes, 1931.

Persico, Joseph E. *Roosevelt's Secret War: FDR and World War II Espionage*. New York: Random House, 2001.

Pickett, Edwin R. *The Second California Infantry on the Border in 1916*. Sacramento: Sacramento Corral of Westerners, 1982.

Putnam, Eben, ed. *Report of the Commission on Massachusetts' Part in the World War*. Vol. 1. Boston: Commonwealth of Massachusetts, 1931.

Quirk, Robert E. *An Affair of Honor: Woodrow Wilson and the Occupation of Veracruz*. New York: Norton, 1967.

Ragsdale, Kenneth Baxter. *Quicksilver: Terlingua and the Chisos Mining Company*. College Station: Texas A&M University Press, 1976.

Raun, Gerald G. "The National Guard on the Border and One Soldier's Viewpoint." *Journal of Big Bend Studies* 6 (1994): 123–37.

Reilly, Henry J. "The National Guard on the Mexican Border." In Frank Tompkins, *Chasing Villa: The Last Campaign of the U.S. Cavalry*, 221–30. 2nd ed. Silver City, N.Mex.: High-Lonesome Books, 1996.

Report No. 865. House of Representatives, 53rd Cong, 2nd sess. Session vol. 3.

Report of the Adjutant General for the Years 1915–1916. Olympia, Wash.: Frank M. Lamborn Public Printer, 1916.

Bibliography

Report of the Adjutant General for the Years 1917–1918. Olympia, Wash.: Frank M. Lamborn Public Printer, 1918.
Report of the Adjutant General of the State of Florida for the Year 1916. Tallahassee: T. J. Appleyard, 1917.
Report of the Adjutant General of the State of Florida for the Year 1917. Tallahassee: T. J. Appleyard, 1918.
Report of the Adjutant General of the State of New Mexico from November 30, 1914 to November 30, 1916. Santa Fe: New Mexican Printing, 1916.
Report of the Adjutant General of the State of New Mexico from November 30, 1916 to November 30, 1918. Santa Fe: n.p., 1918.
Report of the Adjutant General of West Virginia 1915–16. Charleston: Tribune Printing, n.d.
Report of the Adjutant General State of Idaho 1915–1916. Boise: n.p., n.d.
Report on Mobilization of the Organized Militia and the National Guard of the United States 1916. Washington, D.C.: Government Printing Office, 1916.
Rhodes, Gwen R. *South Carolina Army National Guard*. Dallas: Taylor Publishing, 1988.
Richmond, Douglas W. *Venustiano Carranza's Nationalist Struggle, 1893–1920*. Lincoln: University of Nebraska Press, 1983.
Risch, Erna. *Quartermaster Support of the Army: A History of the Corps 1775–1939*. Washington, D.C.: Center of Military History, 1989.
Roberts, Richard C. "History of the Utah National Guard: 1894–1954." Ph.D. dissertation, University of Utah, 1973.
———. *Legacy: The History of the Utah National Guard from the Nauvoo Legion Era to Enduring Freedom*. Salt Lake City: National Guard Association of Utah, 2003.
———. "The Utah National Guard on the Mexican Border in 1916." *Utah Historical Quarterly* 46, no. 3 (Summer 1978): 262–81.
Rozeff, Norman. "Soldiers Stationed in Harlingen, 1915–1916, and Some of Their Action." June 28, 2005. http://www.cameroncountyhistoricalcommission.org/Harlingen%20History.htm (site discontinued).
Salinas Carranza, Alberto. *La Expedición Punitiva*. México, D.F.: Ediciones Botas, 1936.
Sandos, James A. "Prostitution and Drugs: The United States Army on the Mexican-American Border 1916–1917." *Pacific Historical Review* 49 (November 1980): 621–45.
Schrader, Charles R., ed. *United States Army Logistics 1775–1992*. 3 vols. Washington, D.C.: Center of Military History United States Army, 1997.
Schwarz, W. R., and J. T. Milligan. *History of the First Regiment of Infantry Kentucky National Guard from Its Organization in 1847 to the Present Day*. Louisville: Jobson Printing, 1915.
The Service of the Missouri National Guard on the Mexican Border under the President's Order of June 18, 1916. Jefferson City, Mo.: Hugh Stephens, 1919.
Sibley, Frank P. *With the Yankee Division in France*. Boston: Little Brown, 1919.
Sixteenth Biennial Report of the Adjutant General of the State of Oregon to the Governor and Commander-in-Chief for the Period November 1, 1916, to October 31, 1918. Salem: State Printing Department, 1919.
Smith, Albion. "Recollections of Camp Cotton." *Password* 6, no. 1 (Winter 1961): 5–23.

Smith, Cornelius C., Jr. *Fort Huachuca: The Story of a Frontier Post*. Fort Huachuca, Ariz.: n.p., 1976.

Smithers, W. D. "Bandit Raids in the Big Bend Country." *Sul Ross State College Bulletin* 43, no. 3 (September 1963): 75–105.

———. *Chronicles of the Big Bend: A Photographic Memoir of Life on the Border*. Austin: Madrona Press, 1976.

Snook, David L. "The Building of Camp Dodge: History of the Iowa National Guard." March 16, 2005. Iowa National Guard. http://www.iowanationalguard.com/History/History/Pages/Building-Camp-Dodge.aspx.

———. "The Mexican Border (1916–1917): History of the Iowa National Guard." March 16, 2005. Iowa National Guard. http://www.iowanationalguard.com/History/History/Pages/Mexican-Border.aspx.

Squadron A: A History of Its First Fifty Years, 1889–1939. New York: Association of Ex-Members of Squadron A, 1939.

Srodes, James. *Allen Dulles, Master of Spies*. Washington, D.C.: Regnery Publishing, 1999.

Stenberg, Richard K. "Dakota Doughboys in the Desert: The Experiences of a North Dakota National Guard Company during the Mexican Border Campaign of 1916–1917" *North Dakota History* 71, nos. 1 and 2 (2004): 50–64.

Sterkx, H. E. "Unlikely Conquistadores: Alabamians and the Mexican Border Crisis of 1916." *Alabama Review*, July 1971, 163–81.

Sterling, William Warren. *Trails and Trials of a Texas Ranger*. Norman: University of Oklahoma Press, 1959.

Stiness, Henry R. W., ed. *Battery A on the Mexican Border, 1916*. Providence, R.I.: Edward S. Jones Sons, n.d.

Stone, Richard G., Jr. *Kentucky Fighting Men, 1861–1945*. Lexington: University Press of Kentucky, 1982.

Stout, Joseph A., Jr. *Border Conflict: Villistas, Carrancistas and the Punitive Expedition, 1915–1920*. Fort Worth: Texas Christian University Press, 1999.

Svingen, Orlan J., ed. *The History of the Idaho National Guard*. [Boise]: Idaho National Guard, 1995.

Swarthout, Glendon. *The Tin Lizzie Troop*. New York: Doubleday, 1972.

Swarthout, W. N. O. *History Second Regiment Infantry National Guard*. Helena, Mont.: W. N. O. Swarthout, 1916.

"Swearing in the Militia." *Literary Digest* 13 (June 24, 1916): 1867–68.

Swift, Shippen. "Soldiers." *Military Heritage*, June 2001, 10–17.

Tackenberg, William D. "Call Out the Guard! The New Jersey National Guard on the Arizona Border, 1916–1917." *Journal of Arizona History* 40, no. 1 (Spring 1999): 83–102.

———. "'Sore as a Boil but Solid as a Rock:' The Arizona National Guard on the Mexican Border, 1916–1917." *Journal of Arizona History* 42, no. 4 (Winter 2001): 429–44.

Taylor, Tobi, and Debby Swartzwelder. "The United States Military and the Border." *Archaeology Southwest* 20, no. 4 (Fall 2006): 4.

Thisted, Moses N. *With the Wisconsin National Guard on the Mexican Border in 1916–1917*. Hemet, Calif.: Alphabet Printers, n.d.

Todd, Nancy L. *New York's Historic Armories: An Illustrated History*. Albany: State University of New York Press, 2006.

Bibliography

Tompkins, Frank. *Chasing Villa: The Last Campaign of the U.S. Cavalry*. 2nd ed. Silver City, N.Mex.: High-Lonesome Books, 1996.
"Transportation of Troops to Mexican Border. Letter from the Secretary of War, transmitting, in response to House Resolution 292, information regarding the transportation of troops to the Mexican border. July 29, 1916." 64th Cong., 1st sess. Session vol. 145. H.R. Doc. 1311.
Truss, Ruth Smith. "The Alabama National Guard from 1900 to 1920." Ph.D. dissertation, University of Alabama, 1992.
———. "Progress toward Professionalism: The Alabama National Guard on the Mexican Border, 1916–1917." *Military History of the West* 30, no. 2 (Fall 2000): 97–121.
Tyler, Ron, Douglas E. Barnett, Roy R. Barkley, eds. *The New Handbook of Texas*. 6 vols. Austin: Texas State Historical Association, 1996.
Tyler, Ronnie C. *The Big Bend: A History of the Last Texas Frontier*. Washington, D.C.: National Park Service, 1975.
———. "The Little Punitive Expedition into the Big Bend." *Southwestern Historical Quarterly* 78, no. 3 (January 1975): 271–91.
Vourlojianis, George N. *Citizen Soldiers: 107th Regiment, Ohio National Guard*. Cleveland: Cleveland Landmarks Press, 2007.
———. *The Cleveland Grays: An Urban Military Company, 1837–1919*. Kent, Ohio: Kent State University Press, 2002.
Waldman, Andrew. "America's Castles." *National Guard* 64, no. 8 (August 2010): 40–48.
Waller, Douglas. *Wild Bill Donovan: The Spymaster Who Created the OSS and Modern American Espionage*. New York: Free Press, 2011.
Walraven, Bill. *Corpus Christi: The History of a Texas Seaport*. Woodland Hills, Calif.: Windsor Publications, 1982.
War Department Annual Reports, 1916. 3 vols. Washington, D.C.: Government Printing Office, 1916.
War Department Annual Reports, 1917. 3 vols. Washington, D.C.: Government Printing Office, 1918.
Washington National Guard Pamphlet: The Official History of the Washington National Guard. Vol. 5. Tacoma: Headquarters Military Department State of Washington, Office of the Adjutant General, n.d.
Watt, William J., and James R. H. Spears, eds. *Indiana's Citizen Soldiers: The Militia and National Guard in Indiana History*. Indianapolis: Indiana State Armory Board, 1980.
Weaver, John D. *The Senator and the Sharecropper's Son: Exoneration of the Brownsville Soldiers*. College Station: Texas A&M University Press, 1997.
Welsome, Eileen. *The General & the Jaguar: Pershing's Hunt for Pancho Villa*. New York: Little Brown, 2006.
Westover, John Glendower. "The Evolution of the Missouri Militia 1804–1919." Ph.D. dissertation, University of Missouri, 1948.
Whitehorne, Joseph W. A. *The Inspectors General of the United States Army 1903–1939*. Washington, D.C.: Office of the Inspector General and Center of Military History United States Army, 1998.
Wilson, John P. *Islands in the Desert: A History of the Uplands of Southeastern Arizona*. Albuquerque: University of New Mexico Press, 1995.

Bibliography

———. "Peoples of the Middle Gila: A Documentary History of the Pimas and Maricopas, 1500's-1945." Researched and written for the Gila River Indian Community, Sacaton, Ariz., 1998. Revised July 1999, Report No. 77, Las Cruces, N.Mex.

Wilson, Neill C., and Frank J. Taylor. *Southern Pacific: The Roaring Story of a Fighting Railroad.* New York: McGraw-Hill, 1952.

Winks, Robin W. *Cloak & Gown: Scholars in the Secret War, 1939–1961.* New York: William Morrow, 1987.

Wolfe, Margaret Ripley. "The Border Service of the Tennessee National Guard, 1916–1917: A Study in Romantic Inclinations, Military Realities and Predictable Disillusionment." *Tennessee Historical Quarterly* 32, no. 4 (Winter 1973): 374–88.

Zierdt, William H. *Narrative History of the 109th Field Artillery Pennsylvania National Guard 1773–1930.* Wilkes-Barre: Special Publication Wyoming [sic] Historical and Geological Society, 1932.

Newspapers

Albany Times-Union
Albuquerque Morning Journal
Alpine Avalanche
Arizona Daily Star
Arizona Republic
Arizona Republican
Brooklyn Daily Eagle
Brownsville Daily Herald
Burlington Daily Free Press
Chicago Daily News
Corpus Christi Caller
Daily Review (Fostoria, Ohio)
El Paso Morning Times
Fort Wayne Journal-Gazette
Fort Wayne Weekly Sentinel
Harrison Times (Arkansas)
La Prensa (San Antonio)
Laredo Weekly Times
Memphis *Commercial Advertiser*
Memphis *Commercial Appeal*
Muscogee Times Democrat
Nashville Banner
New York Times
Nogales Daily Herald
Oakland Tribune
Quincy Herald-Whig
Rio Grande Republican
Salt Lake Tribune
San Antonio Express
Santa Fe New Mexican
Seattle Daily Times
Seattle Sunday Times
Tacoma Times
Times and Democrat (Orangeburg, S.C.)
Tombstone Prospector
Washington Post

Index

Page numbers in *italics* indicate illustrations.

Abbott, Edmund C., 27, 355
Acosta, Juan Antonio, 54
Active Service Auxiliary, 177
Adams, Granger, 345, 346, 347, 367
Adamson, W. M., 382
Aero Club of America, 33, 177
Aero Club of New England, 33
Aero Squadron of Tucson, 512n14
1st Aero Company, 181, 206
1st Aero Squadron, 362
African Americans: all-black units, 62, 92, 107, 112, 207, 253, 278, 317, 358, 370, 402, 438; on courts-martial panels, 94; in District of Columbia Guard, 402; as Guard officers, 93; Mexican attitudes toward, 375; in New York Guard, 207; racial tensions and, 92–94, 253–54, 278–79, 438; as servants, 428
Agua Prieta, Sonora, 374
Aguinaldo, Emilio, 78
Aker, Samuel I., 304
"Alabama Mystics," 433–35
Alabama National Guard, 115; casualties, 431; cavalry, 427; composition, 428; demobilization, 438; disruptive behavior of, 428–29; in Douglas, 390; health issues, 431–33, 437; in Ku Klux Klan parade, 433–35; mobilization, 427–28; officer elections, 390; recreation, 431; training, 437

Albany (USS), 63
Albuquerque Morning Journal, 28, 372
alcohol consumption, 88, 113, 160, 197–98, 312, 339, 365; bootlegging and, 422–23
Alexander, M., 417, 429, 430
Allen, Frank M., 86
Allen, Hubert A., 153, 164, 170
Alta Vista Army Camp, 119–20
ambulance train, 177
American Bible Society, 101, 312
American Defense Society, 199
American Expeditionary Force, 116, 183, 454
American Red Cross Society, 34, 81, 163, 178, 185–86, 219, 246, 285–86, 287, 343, 369, 377
American Revolution, 141
American Tobacco Company, 423
ammunition shortage, 190–91
ammunition smuggling, 385, 400
Anderson, A. V. P., 284
Anderson, William D. A., 190
Andrews, James M., 207
Angleton, Hugh, 424, 518n105
Angleton, James Jesus, 424
Arivaca Land and Cattle Company, 436
Arizona Daily Star, 25
Arizona District, 375, 392
Arizona National Guard: decline in troop strength, 395; deficiencies,

537

Index

Arizona National Guard (*continued*)
22, 23–24; demobilization, 397–98;
desertions, 25–26, 378; discipline, 24,
406; Indians in, 24; initial activation,
21; intelligence activities, 400–401;
mobilization, 22, 376; morale, 378–79,
395–396; in Nogales, 406; private
contributions to, 377–78; recruitment,
22–23, 25–26; route march, 401;
shooting incidents, 406; state
government's attitude toward, 25, 375;
students in, 23; in WWI service, 398
Arkansas National Guard: casualties, 347,
348–49, 350, 351, 352; demobilization,
351–52; mobilization, 345–46; physical
readiness, 346; political favoritism
in, 353; recruitment, 349; shooting
incidents, 346
Armistead, George D., 104
armored car, 167–68, 181–82, 325
armored units, 177, 181–82
Armour, J. Ogden, 140
Armour Grain Elevator Company, 140
Army Corps of the East (Mexico), 54
Army Magazine, 348
Army Post Football Tournament, 102
army regional departments, 70, 77, 82
Army War College, 63, 174
Arns, Carl, 436
Articles of War, 215
artillery review, in El Paso, 331–32
Associated Press, 90, 140
athletic activities, 102–103; baseball,
122, 133–34, 144; boxing, 350; in
Columbus, 365; in Corpus Christi,
122–23; in El Paso, 310; field day
competitions, 130, 155; football,
102–103, 122–23, 129, 130–31, 230, 269,
133134; New York Guard and, 178–79;
in Nogales, 423; polo, 155, 212
aviation and aircraft: in Columbus, 354,
361–62; of Missouri Guard, 245; of
New Mexico Guard, 33; of New York
Guard, 177, 181; in scouting activities,
338–39

Baca, James, 367
backbone drills, 95
Bacon, Robert, 366–67

Baja California, 439
Baker, Newton D., 5, 39, 41, 66, 67–68,
79, 97, 98, 102, 111, 194, 248, 319, 333,
337, 361, 392, 401, 412, 422
Baltimore and Ohio Railroad, 268, 278
Baptist General Convention of Texas, 101
Barrett, Henry S., 275
baseball games, 133–134, 144
Batchelder, Roger, 293, 328
Battle of Hart's Mill, 331
Battle of Jenkins Ferry, 120
Battle of Palo Alto, 166
Battle of Resaca de la Palma, 163, 166
Battle of Ruby, 436–37
Battle of the Crater, 41
Baylor University, 122
bayonet drill, 339
Beekman, William S., 198
Belardi, John, 122
Bell, George Jr., *232*, 290, 295, 302, 304,
325, 326, 335, 337
Bell, J. Franklin, 82, 441, 446, 448
Bender Hotel, Laredo, 258
Benet-Mercier machine gun, 97, 98, 151,
293
Berry, Harry S., 277
bible distribution, 101
Bierne, Owen, 325–26
Big Bend District, 46–48, 114–15;
Army regulars in, 289; economic
impact of Guard in, 287; friendly fire
incidents, 283; order of battle, 460;
shooting incidents in, 282–83; threat
environment in, 281–82, 284
Bigford Ranch, 257
Bingham, Hiram, 413
blanketing game, 121
Blethan, C. B., 448
Bliss, Tasker, 48, 61, 73, 149, 199, 253,
273, 345
blockade, of Mexican ports, 63
Blocker Ranch, 272
Blocksom, A. P., 152, 169
Boise Barracks, 417, 430
Bolleter, Vernon, 121
border outposts, 211, 272, 303, 331
border patrols. *See* U.S.-Mexican border
patrols
Border Virginian, The, 154

538

Index

Boston Globe, 310
Boston Post, 310
Boyd, Charles, 62
Brady, William, 172–73
Brensinger, George, 380
Bricken, Charles R., 427, 437
Brooklyn armory, 185
Brown, Anthony Cave, 192
Brown, Elmer M., 446
Brown University, 305
Browne, A. A., 137–38
Browning machine gun, 151
Brownsville Board of City Development, 138, 139, 140
Brownsville Daily Herald, 93, 139, 158, 167
Brownsville garrison, 137
Brownsville Military District, 49–50, 134; demobilization of Guard in, 171–73; economic impact of Guard in, 138, 173; hurricane impact on, 156; logistical problems in, 137; military's impact on, 160–61; order of battle, 457–58; parades and exhibitions, 162; press facilities in, 139–40; provisional brigades in, 153; regular units stationed in, 150; reorganization of Guard in, 168–70; reorganization of regular troops in, 170; scope of, 136; training cantonment in, 171–72; training program in, 127, 153–54; war game in, 163–66
Brumbaugh, M. G., 299
Buffalo (USS), 63
Bujac, E. P., 356
Bull Durham Company, 378
Bullard, Robert L., 142, 169
Bureau of Investigation, 52, 53, 54, 138, 152, 376, 385, 399–400, 401
Burnett, F. C., 351
Bush, George Herbert Walker, 320
Bush, George W., 3, 320
Bush, Harold Montford, 319
Bush, Prescott Sheldon, 319–20
Bush, Samuel Prescott, 319
Butler, Harry F., 288
Butler, M. C., 283

Cal Hirsh and Sons, 38
Caldwell, Frank M., 444–45
California border: order of battle, 465; threat environment, 439
California National Guard, *239*; casualties, 413; cavalry, 425–26; coast artillery, 440; demobilization, 426, 429, 438; mobilization, 410–11; in Nogales, 411–12, 418; physical readiness, 412; recruitment, 411; route march, 425
Calles, Plutarco Elías, 374, 407, 419
Calumet smelter, 384
Camp Ashland, 146
Camp Beacom, 448
Camp Bob Williams, 143
Camp Brooks, 343
Camp Cecil A. Lyon, 103–104
Camp Cotton, *230*, 291, 294, 295, 303, 315, 323–24, 330
Camp Deming, 343, 345. *See also* Deming concentration point
Camp Dodge, 141
Camp Douglas, 87, 88
Camp Dunne, 82–83
Camp Elmer M. Brown, 446
Camp Fielder, 379–80, 382
Camp Frederick Funston, 382, 390
Camp Furlong, 28, 357
Camp Glenn, 323
Camp Hagman, 143
Camp Harris, 323
Camp Harry Clark, 384
Camp Harry J. Jones, 22, 374, 376, 390, 392, 396
Camp Hiram Johnson, 410
Camp Holcomb, 416
Camp Keyes, 246
Camp Lincoln, 82–83
Camp Mabry, 42, 107
Camp Maine, 250
Camp Marfa, 46
Camp Missouri, 245–46, 250, 255
Camp Morehead, 146
Camp New Hampshire, 250
Camp Ord, 268, 269
Camp Ordway, 401, 403
Camp Owen Bierne, 325
Camp Parker, 141, 159, 163
Camp Perry, 317
Camp Pershing, 291, 295, 301, 310

Index

Camp Scurry, 134; athletics at, 130–31, 133; cantonment efforts, 118, 124–25, 135; crime and punishment at, 127–28; Funston visit to, 124–25; holiday observances at, 129–30, 131; morale at, 125, 126; naming of, 120; order of battle, 456–57; religious observance at, 125; tent winterization, 126; training at, 126; unit strengths, 482n75. *See also* Corpus Christi concentration point

Camp Spaulding, 248, 249

Camp Stephen A. Little, 376, 405, 406, 408

Camp Stewart, 282, 291, 301, 310

Camp Tom C. Rye, 275

Camp Travis, 104, 116

Camp Tuthill, 400

Camp Whitman, 179, 180, 185, 192

Camp Whitney, 293

Camp Willis, 317

Camp Wilson, 42, 43–44; composition of militia at, 82–83; engineer units at, 103; holiday observances at, 113; improvements to, 89; order of battle, 455–56; post office at, 104; press correspondents at, 90–91; religious observance at, 100–102; scope of build-up at, 81–82; taxi service at, 100; as tent city, 88–89; Texas Guard dispersal from, 79; trench warfare instruction at, 109. *See also* San Antonio concentration point

Camp Withycombe, 440

Campbell, Thomas, 397–98

Cano, Chico, 46, 282

canteen coupon book, 121

Cantú, Esteban, 439

Carnegie Library, 115

Carrancistas, 55, 210, 281, 297, 359, 371, 436, 448

Carranza, Venustiano, 4, 15, 16, 18; capitulation by, 64–65; demand for Punitive Expedition withdrawal, 53; on Glenn Springs raid, 19; on invasion of Texas, 54; Plan de San Diego and, 17, 52, 57, 468n7; U.S. ultimatum to, 64, 183

Carrizal engagement, 62–63, 162, 183, 406, 408

casualties: Alabama Guard, 431; Arkansas Guard, 347, 348–49, 350, 351, 352; California Guard, 413; Colorado Guard, 487n164; Delaware Guard, 352; in El Paso, 334–35, 340–42; Georgia Guard, 323, 341; horses and mules causing, 308; Illinois Guard, 112; Iowa Guard, 142, 172–73; Kentucky Guard, 342; Maryland Guard, 274–75; Massachusetts Guard, 340; Michigan Guard, 341–42; Minnesota Guard, 147; Missouri Guard, 244, 258, 263; Montana Guard, 387; New Hampshire Guard, 259–60, 350, 352; New Jersey Guard, 387; New Mexico Guard, 372; New York Guard, 188, 192, 198, 205, 208, 213, 218; North Carolina Guard, 341; Ohio Guard, 335–36, 342; Pennsylvania Guard, 301, 340–41; pneumonia deaths, 335; Rhode Island Guard, 340; South Carolina Guard, 341; South Dakota Guard, 145; Tennessee Guard, 341; Texas Guard, 132–33, 288; Utah Guard, 409; Virginia Guard, 154; Washington Guard, 448; in World War I, 225; Wyoming Guard, 351

caterpillar tractors, 332

caterpillar train, 286–87, 289

cavalry: provisional brigade, 170; provisional regiment, 425–26

cavalry charges, 162, 338

censorship of press, 185–86, 361

Central Baptist Church, 101–102

Central Department, 70, 77

Cervantes, Viviano Saldívar, 53

Chapa, Francisco, 45–46

Chase, Emory A., 178

Chattanooga (USS), 64

Chávez, Guillermo, 393

Chesterfield cigarettes, 139

Chicago Daily News, 90, 158

Chicago News, 30–31

Chicago Tribune, 129, 139, 140

Chinese refugees, 370

Chisos Mining Company, 46–47

Christmas observance, 110, 113, 130, 131, 216, 278, 286, 331, 351, 369, 430

Civil War, 41, 182

Index

Civilians' Training Camp, 104
Clackamas Range, Ore., 440
Clark, Harvey C., 244, 253, 257, 260
Clark, Hugh, 364
Clark, W. A., 383–84
Clement, Charles M., *232*, 299, 302, 325, 327
Clement, James L., 154
Cleveland Chamber of Commerce, 319
Cleveland Plain Dealer, 318
Cleveland (USS), 63
Close, Edward B., 178
Coast Artillery, 19, 20, 45, 48, 61, 243, 246, 257, 279, 439–40
Coburn, Harold, 447
Colorado National Guard, 137, *237*; casualties, 487n164; cavalry, 163; composition, 325; demobilization, 172; in Douglas, 390; mobilization, 325, 348; as strikebreakers, 348
Colorado State Agricultural College, 348
Columbus concentration point: aircraft at, 354, 361–62; economic impact of military in, 354; health and hygiene at, 372; officers' dance at, 366; order of battle, 357, 463; Pershing inspection of, 367; Punitive Expedition at, 370; as Punitive Expedition logistical base, 354; recreation in, 30, 365–66; religious observances at, 366; threat environment, 370–71; training routine at, 361
Columbus Courier, 372
Columbus News, 336
Columbus raid, 17
combat maneuvers, 123–24
Committee of Mines and Mining, 384
communications: in Big Bend region, 47, 468n15; interception of Mexican, 400; in Laredo District, 256; naval radio station, 145; New York Guard radio installation, 196–97; telephone system in Brownsville, 139
concentration points, 6, 79. *See also by city*
Conley, Lewis S., 193–94
Connecticut National Guard: camp conditions, 414–15; composition, 413; demobilization, 426; physical readiness, 416; private contributions to, 414; recruitment, 416; route march, 424–25; shooting incidents, 418; socially elite units in, 414–15
Constantine, Arthur, 136
Constitutionalist Army (Mexico), 15
Cook, Jess, 363
Copper, Arthur, 270
Copper Queen Consolidated Copper Company, 374
Cordova Island, 295, 330
Corner Ranch massacre, 371
corporal punishment, 215–16, 316, 421
Corpus Christi Caller, 120
Corpus Christi Commercial Club, 117, 124, 130
Corpus Christi concentration point: athletics at, 122–23; crime and punishment, 127–28; duck hunting at, 128; economic impact of Guard units at, 117, 120, 134; improvements to, 118–19; Military Police unit at, 120; order of battle, 456–57; parades and exhibitions at, 122; reaction to demobilization, 134; Texas Guard arrival at, 119. *See also* Camp Scurry
Corpus Christi Musketeers, 119
Costillo, James I., 510n33
counterinsurgency operations: Mexican Army in, 407; U.S. training in, 304
courts-martial proceedings: black officers on panels of, 94; for border crossing, 282–83, 421; for desertion, 26, 347, 378, 381, 386, 429; for disobeying orders, 282–83; for espionage, 114; for failure to report, 44; for false and misleading statements, 364–65, 432; for fraudulent recruitment, 355–56; for gunfight in a whorehouse, 428–29; New Mexico Guard and, 358; of newspaper reporter, 96; preceding punishment, 215; for prejudicial conduct, 198, 206, 335–36; for refusal to take federal oath, 364; for rioting, 94; for sleeping on duty, 316; states with highest number of, 449
criminal activity: ammunition smuggling, 400; burglary, 259; at Camp Scurry, 127–28; cow killing,

Index

criminal activity (*continued*) 371; drug trafficking, 340, 421; embezzlement, 288; FBI in investigating, 399–400; illegal sale of government property, 38, 263–64; murder, 154, 283, 326; smuggling, 385, 421, 422
Crow, Philip H., 416–17
Cuban insurgency, 78
Cuffier, Harry A., 184
curfews, 254–55, 298–99
Curry, C. F., 412
Curry, John R., 408
Curtis, Oakley C., 246
Curtis biplane, 177, 362
Curtis Company, 33

Daughters of the American Revolution, 430
Daughters of the Confederacy, 126, 430
Davenport, W. A., 184
Davis, Thomas F., 24, 375, 376, 382, 392, 396, 404
Day, Herbert C., 502n64
De Bremond, Charles, 37
de la Rosa, Luis, 52, 53, 54, 55, 56, 64–65, 243
de los Santos, Isabel, 58
Debord, Henry, 270
Del Rio, Tex., 278–79
Delameter, B. F., 136
Delaware National Guard, 343; casualties, 352; in Deming, 345; demobilization, 351–52
Deming concentration point: as cantonment in WWI, 353; measles outbreak, 350; order of battle, 463; preparation of camp site, 343, 345; Retreat ceremony at, 350–51
Democratic Party, 92
dengue fever, 152
Denver (USS), 64
Department of California, 78
Department of Justice, 38
Des Moines Capital, 142
Des Moines Register and Leader, 142
desertions, 286, 363, 386, 387, 421, 429
Detroit Free Press, 302
Díaz, Félix, 15

Díaz, Porfirio, 11–14
Dick Act, 44, 416, 451
District of Columbia National Guard, 105–106, 115, 325; cavalry, 403; composition, 401; demobilization, 404; in Douglas, 390; mobilization, 401; in Naco, 402; recruitment, 402–403; shooting incidents, 404; in WWI service, 404
Dixon, Richard, 335
Dockery, William, 378
Donaldson, L. S., 113
Donna concentration point, 145
Donnelly, Arthur B., 244, 253
Donohue, Dan J., 383, 386–87, 389
Donovan, William J. "Wild Bill," 192–93, 200, 201
Dougherty, Louis R., 86
Douglas concentration point: camp preparation, 376; discipline at, 392; economic impact of military at, 392; Funston inspection of, 396; health and hygiene at, 392–93; order of battle, 464; racial tensions, 23; recreation, 386; strategic position of, 374; threat environment, 393; war-strength regimental hike at, 391
Douglas Dispatch, 389, 392
Douglas garrison, 374
draft: of guardsmen, 69; New Mexico Guard and, 36, 359
Draper, Eben S., 33
Drought, Mrs. H. P., 115
Duffy, Francis P., 193, 216, 219
Dulles, Allen, 381
Dunne, Edward F., 111, 155–56

Eagle Pass concentration point: command of, 267; family housing at, 278; machine gun shortage at, 273; order of battle, 460
Easterly, Arthur H., 388
Eastern Department, 70, 77, 179
economic impact: in Big Bend District, 287; in Brownsville, 138, 160–61, 173; of call-up, 7, 79; in Columbus, 354; in Corpus Christi, 117, 118, 120, 134; in Del Rio, 279; in Douglas, 392; in El Paso, 309; in Laredo, 251; in McAllen,

Index

190; in mercury mining, 46–47; of New York Guard, 186–87; in Nogales, 405–406, 427; in San Benito, 144–45, 161
Edelblute, William H., 416, 417, 426
Edwards, H. B., 309
Eisenhower, Dwight D., 109–10, 133
El Paso and Southwestern Railroad, 301–302, 376
El Paso Chamber of Commerce, 310
El Paso concentration point: artillery review, 331–32; bid for cantonment, 339–40; camp improvement, 312–13; casualties at, 334–35, 340–42; curfew, 298–99; economic impact of Guard, 309; Guard camps at, 291–92; Guard demobilization at, 336; health and hygiene at, 334–35; horses and mules at, 307–308; living conditions at, 301–302; military parade, *233*, *234*, *235*, 326–27, 332; Ohio Guard's protest of camp conditions, 335–36; order of battle, 460–63; Punitive Expedition at, 337–38; recreational pursuits, 309–13; religious observances, 311–12; rules of engagement at, 304; shooting incidents at, 295; threat environment, 295
El Paso Morning Times, 286, 289, 301, 310, 311, 316, 335
Elephant Butte dam, 357
Elks Club of Corpus Christi, 121
Elliott, Cal O., 288
enlistment contract, 69
espionage, 114, 400–401
Ettingie, Walter, 510n33
Evans, R. K., 242
Everybody's Department Store, El Paso, 286
Exclusion Act, 370

Fall, Albert B., 296, 362
family and dependents: appropriations for, 72; discharge of men with, 361, 380, 386–87, 397, 412, 416, 441–42; recruitment of men with, 248; support for, 177–78, 247–48, 278, 285, 355
Farnsworth, Charles Stewart, 357–58, 360, 361, 367

federal Bureau of Investigation. *See* Bureau of Investigation
federal oath, 83, 87, 106, 108, 112, 183, 244, 268, 271, 292, 364, 381, 397, 398, 417, 432, 445, 447
Ferguson, James E., 38, 39, 42, 45–46, 107, 128
field day competitions, 155
field kitchens, 140
Fierros, Esteban E., 54
Fierros Brigade, 54, 55, 57, 58
filming of Guard activities, 96, 129, 139, 158, 423, 431
First National Bank of Santa Fe, 356
Fisher, Margaret, 428
Fisher, Mrs. H. H., 301
Fisk, Willard C., 189
Flagstaff Normal School, 23
Flores Magón, Ricardo, 12
Florida National Guard, 115; demobilization, 265; equipment shortages, 261–62; mobilization, 260; physical readiness, 260; shooting incident, 265
Fondern, Roy, 352
football games, 102–103, 122–23, 129, 130–31, 133, *230*, 269
Foote, W. R., 323
Foote, W. W., 323
Ford, Henry, 303
Ford Motor Company, 303
foreign duty pay, 98
foreign invasions of Mexico, 11
foreign investments in Mexico, 12
Foreman, Milton J., 139
Fort Bayard, 349
Fort Benjamin Harrison, 148, 390
Fort Bliss, *236*, 282, 290, 327, 338, 339, 451
Fort Brown, 136, 137, 139, 152, 162, 167, 168
Fort D. A. Russell, 352
Fort Douglas, 408, 430
Fort Ethan Allen, 270, 274
Fort Hancock, 296–97
Fort Huachuca, 379, 390, 401
Fort Leavenworth service schools, 61
Fort Lincoln, 148
Fort Logan H. Roots, 345
Fort McIntosh, 242, 250

543

Index

Fort Myer, 401
Fort Oglethorpe, 61
"Fort Perry," 284
Fort Riley, 61, 269
Fort Ringgold, 137, 168
Fort Sam Houston, 6, 42, 61, 77, 370; logistical preparation at, 81–82; racial tensions at, 92–94
Fort Sheridan, 111
Fort Sill, 61, 137, 143
Fort Thomas, 322
Fort William Henry Harrison, 383
Foster, J. Clifford R., 265–66
Foulois, Benjamin D., 362
France, 11
fraternization, 122, 305–306, 453
French, Francis H., 267
Fressing, Daniel S., 510n33
Frick, Henry Clay, 177
friendly fire incidents, 283
funding issues: emergency pay appropriations, 308–309; family support appropriations, 72; federal government withholding of funds, 369–70; impact on supply and logistics, 452; New Mexico Guard state appropriations, 6, 26, 27; political payoffs and, 306–307; state versus federal obligations, 276–77; Texas Guard annual federal allotment, 39
Funston, Frederick, 6, 16, 19, 54, 195, 206, 214, 251, 281, 287, 297, 309, 337, 352, 358, 363, 371, 388, 400, 417, 430; background of, 77; on Big Bend region, 46; in call-up decision, 20, 60; camp inspections by, 107, 155, 209, 221, 258, 269, 351, 367, 396, 431; death of, 115–16, 134, 353; on demobilization, 134; on El Paso as permanent post, 339; military career of, 78–79; on mobilization of Texas Guard, 42; order of route march by, 94–97; on physical standards, 35; press relations and, 91; religious observances and, 100–102; response to racial tensions, 94; on socially prominent guardsmen, 209; as Southern Department commander, 79, 82; on Texas Guard morale, 288–89; visit to Camp Scurry, 124–25, 128

Gadsden Hotel, Douglas, 23, 386
Gambrell, J. B., 101
Garber, Max, 417
Gardiner, Lewis G., 364
Garfield, James R., 319
Garner, John Nance, 124, 137–38, 251
Garrison, David M., 510n33
Garrison, Lindley M., 38
Gary, Elbert H., 177
Garza, Agustín S., 16, 54
Gaston, Joseph, 47–48, 280, 281
Georgia National Guard: casualties, 323, 341; conflict with Michigan Guard, 324; impact of call-up on, 336–37; outpost duty, 331
Germany, 217, 336, 397, 452, 453
Gibbons, Floyd, 69–70, 203
Gillespie, Hugh M., 388
Glacier (USS), 63
Glenn, Edwin F., 347–48, 349, 350
Glenn Springs raid, 18–19, 40, 47
Gómez, Félix U., 62
González, Francisco, 295, 338
González, Pablo, 54, 64–65
González, Pedro, 265
González, Tirso, 173
Goodchild, Frank M., 101–102
Goodyear Tire and Rubber Company, 320
Gorey, Frank, 206
governors' personal staff, 41
Greene, Henry A., 105, 107, 267, 279
Grose, Peter, 381
guard cartridges, 93
guerrilla raids into U.S., 57–58
Guillon, Allan, 322
Gulf Coast Exposition, 123, 128–29
Gulf Coast Lines Railroad, 119
Gutiérrez de Lara, Lázaro, 375

Hachita garrison, 362–64, 371
Hainesey, Mary, 300
Halbart, Thomas A., 277
Hall, W. P., 163
Hand, Daniel W., 185
hand grenades, 339

Hannah, Eleanor, 112
Harlingen concentration point, 145, 151
Harris, Charles W., 22, 393–95, 398
Harris, Joseph, 280
Harris, Nat E., 323
Hartford Chamber of Commerce, 414
Hartford Courant, 416
Harvard University, 133, 293, 294, 414
Haskell, William N., 195
Hatch, E. E., 153, 170
Hayes, W. C., 360, 361
Head, George J., 38
Healey, M. J., 248, 249
health and hygiene, 141; alarmist rumors concerning, 152; alcohol use and, 197–98; antityphoid serum, 270; in Columbus, 372; in Deming, 350; in Douglas, 387, 392–93; dysentery epidemic, 387; in El Paso, 334–35; food inspections, 160; in Laredo, 251, 253; in Nogales, 418, 431–33, 437; sanitary program, 89–90; smallpox outbreak, 322; snake bite serum, 216; tobacco usage and, 312; typhoid fever outbreak, 198, 204, 206; unsanitary camps and, 317–18; vaccinations, 204; water purification, 247, 253. *See also* medical support
Hebbe, Herbert G., 93
Heights Camp, 250
Henderson, Charles, 432–33
Herring, Harry T., 27, 33, 35–36, 355, 356, 357, 361, 369, 373
Hine, Edwin W., 382, 392
Hinton, Carl, 355
Hispanic uprising, 52–57
Hispanics: in border towns, 375; in Douglas, 377; in New Mexico Guard, 367; poverty of in border towns, 255; racial tensions and, 23; restrictions placed on, 294; suspected loyalty of, 284, 290–91, 296, 304, 377; in Texas Guard, 43
Hobby, William P., 108
Holcomb, Marcus H., 426
Holmdahl, Emil, 318
Hoosier Guard, The, 149
Hoover, John M., 50
Horn Palace Saloon, San Antonio, 113

horses and mules: artillery units' shortage of, 149; of California Guard, 411, 412; camouflage experimentation, 512n2; demobilization and, 110–11; in El Paso, 307–308; of Georgia Guard, 324; government purchase of, 81; of Illinois Guard, 98–99; of Kentucky Guard, 322; of Massachusetts Guard, 297–98; of New Jersey Guard, 389; of New York Guard, 195–96, 217; of Ohio Guard, 320; of Oregon Guard, 440, 443; regimental requirements for, 308; remount stations, 98–99, *236*; saddle shortage, 159; of Utah Guard, 409
hospital train, 90
hospitals. *See* medical support
Hough, Benson W., 317
House, Edward M., 41
Houston race riot, 94
Howard, William F., 5
Howard Charles W., 248
howitzers, 185
Huerta, Victoriano, 15–16
Hughes, Charles Evans, 366, 367
Hughes, Rupert, 201
Hughes, W. N., 277
Hulen, John A., 39, 43, 50, 119, 120, 124, 126, 128, 131, 132, 133, 134, 152, 170
Hume, Frank M., 246
Hunt, W. P., 25, 26, 375, 379
Hunter, George K., 147
hurricane damage, 156, 200–201
Hutchings, Henry, 39, 42, 107–108

Idaho Canning Company, 424
Idaho National Guard: casualties, 517n67; composition, 416; demobilization, 429–30; Militia Act and, 417; mobilization, 417; in Nogales, 417; Oregon guardsmen in, 440; route march, 425; sniper fire and, 420; training routine, 417–18
Ilfeld, Ludwig William, 369
Illinois Cavalryman, The, 154, 161
Illinois National Guard: in 12th Provisional Division, 115; artillery unit, 85–86, 111; athletics, 129, 130; in Brownsville District, 137, 139–40, 153; camp kitchens, 140; cavalry unit,

Index

Illinois National Guard (*continued*) 150, 158, 159, 163; composition, 82–83, 85–86; demobilization, 110–12, 163; Eisenhower training, 109–10; federal oath and, 112; filming of maneuvers, 158; governor's review of, 155–56; in hide-and-seek exercise, 159; horses and mules for, 98–99; at Landa Park resort, 99–100; machine guns and, 83, 97, 157; mock burial of Texas by, 112; physical readiness, 83–84, 94; racial tensions and, 92–94, 112; route march, 94–97; at San Benito, 155; shooting incidents, 160; in strike riot suppression, 86; supply shortages, 83; trench warfare training, 154; troop train and, 84–85; weapons training, 97–99

Imperial Beach encampment, 444

Indiana National Guard, 137, 157; artillery unit, 149; casualties, 484n57; demobilization, 166–67; at Llano Grande, 147; machine gun training, 151; mobilization, 148–49

Indians: in Arizona units, 24; in Sonora insurgency, 407

Industrial Workers of the World (IWW), 450

Inglis, William M., 447

intelligence operations, 400–401

International & Great Northern Railroad, 81, 242

International News Service, 90, 136, 140

Iowa Guardsman, The, 154

Iowa National Guard, 171, 211; in Brownsville, 137, 141–42, 153; casualties, 142, 172–73, 483n30; demobilization, 167, 172; in Donna, 145; in San Benito, 155; shooting incidents, 160

Ireland, Rutherford, 201

Irish guardsmen, 182

Japanese Army, 400
Jenkins, John M., 425, 437–38
Jewish guardsmen, 26–27, 178, 312
Johnson, Hiram, 410
Johnston, Gordon, 213
Jones, Harry J., 374

Kansas National Guard, 137; demobilization, 275; mobilization, 269; physical readiness, 269; route march, 269; transportation of by truck, 104–105

20th Kansas Infantry, 78, 95, 105

Katy Railroad. *See* Missouri, Kansas, and Texas Railroad

Kealy, Philip J., 496n99

Kellerman, Max, 215

Kennon, Lyman Walter Vere, 257, 496n73

Kentucky National Guard, 71, 327; casualties, 342; composition, 322; demobilization, 336; in large-scale exercise, 334; mobilization, 322; outpost duty, 331; physical readiness, 146–47; shooting incidents, 331

King, J. L., 125

King Ranch raid, 17

Kirk, John P., 302

Kleberg, Caesar, 128

Kleberg, Robert, 128, 134

Knights of Columbus, 311, 430

Kroog, William M., 388

Ku Klux Klan parade, 433–35

land reform, 15
Landa, Harry, 100
Landa Park resort, 99–100
Langhorne, George T., 18–19
Langon, James H., 320
Lank, W. E., 347
Lapp, Rodney, 335–36
Laredo District: curfew imposed in, 254–55; divisional review in, 257; economic impact of military in, 251; machine gun shortage in, 250; mechanization in, 250–51; medical facilities in, 253; military build-up in, 243–44; military camps in, 250; order of battle, 459; telephone communications in, 256; threat environment in, 242–43, 260; treatment of soldiers in, 264; troop recreation in, 254–55; troop strength in, 257

Laredo garrison, 242
Laredo Times, 252, 264
Laredo Weekly Times, 252, 256

Index

Las Cruces, New Mex., 296, 328–30
Lee, Robert E., 182
Lehman Ranch, 272
León de la Barra, Francisco, 14
Leon Springs military reservation, 95, 97, 109
Leon Springs remount station, 98–99
Lester, James W., 168
Lewis, Edward M., 148, 151–52, 168
Lewis, E. H., 164
Lewis machine gun, 97–98, 150, 151, 332–33
Liberating Army of Races and Peoples in America, 54
Lincoln, Abraham, 217, 218
Lind, John A., 316
Lindsey, Washington E., 373
Link, Arthur S., 53, 59
Lister, Ernest, 448
Little, Bascom, 319
Little, Stephen A., 376, 405
Llano Grande concentration point, 146–47; order of battle, 457–58; weapons training at, 149–50
Locke, F. H., 362
Lockwood, Arthur, 205
Lodge, Henry Cabot, 298
Long, John D., 42
Los Angeles Examiner, 90
Louisiana National Guard, 137, 142; in Brownsville, 153; composition, 143; demobilization, 157; machine gun training, 151
Louisiana Restaurant, Nogales, 430
Love, James M., 48, 123
Luna, Antonio J., 372
Lyon, Cecil A., 103

MacArthur, Douglas, 185
Machias (USS), 63
machine gun automobile, 333
machine gun companies, 44–45, 71, 97, 223, 333; Missouri Guard, 245; Oregon Guard, 441; South Dakota Guard, 144; transportation of, 333
machine gun school, 151
machine guns: for all Guard units, 150–51; appropriations for, 98; on armored car, 167–68; Army selection of, 150–51, 332–33; cavalry charges against, 162; of Illinois Guard, 83, 97, 140; impact on World War I, 97; of New York Guard, 175; in Nogales, 418; shortage of, 83, 97, 302, 412; training with, 97–98
Madero, Francisco I., 12–15
magonistas, 12
Maine National Guard: border patrolling, 256–57; casualties, 258–59; demobilization, 256, 258; in Laredo District, 243; mobilization, 246
Maneuver Division. *See* U.S. Army Maneuver Division
Mann, William A., 56, 242, 243, 253, 257, 260
Marietta (USS), 63
Markay, Clarence H., 178
Markay, Mrs. John W., 178
Marlin Company, 333
marriages, of guardsmen, 178
Martin, Carl A., 496n99
Martin, Hiram, 346
Martin Aviation School, 33
Maryland National Guard, 71; casualties, 274–75; composition, 267–68; demobilization, 274; mobilization, 268; in San Antonio, 81
Maryland (USS), 64
Mashbir, Sidney Forrester, 377, 395, 400–401
Massachusetts National Guard: 5th Infantry band, *231*; administrative issues, 292–93; border patrols, 296; casualties, 340; cavalry, 297–98, 305, 315; in Columbus, 360, 361, 367; demobilization, 336; in El Paso, 294; in Las Cruces, 296; mobilization, 292, 293–95; in Punitive Expedition, 5, 360; route march, 326, 328–30; shooting incidents, 295, 362; sniper fire taken by, 330–31; society elites in, 305–306; weapons issue, 293
Massachusetts Naval Militia, 33
May, Ben, 432
McAllen-Pharr-Mission triangle concentration point, 145–46, 189–90; camp preparation issues in, 196; governor's visit to, 213; inspection of, 199, 208–209; medical facilities,

547

Index

McAllen-Pharr-Mission (*continued*) 203–204; order of battle, 458–59; radio installation at, 196–97; selection of, 195
McCall, Samuel W., 294
McCormick, Robert R., 139, 156
McCraw, Bill, 259
McDonald, W. C., 355, 356
McGrath, Herb, 363
McKee, William B., 306
McLaughlin, Clenard, 66, 441, 442, 443, 444
McLaughlin, Phil, 367–68
McNair, William S., 169, 185
mechanization. *See under* transportation
Medal of Honor, 78
medical support, 60, 67; for 13th Provisional Division, 169; ambulance train, 177; in El Paso, 312, 335; hospital train, 90; for New York Guard, 178, 203–204; in Nogales, 408; in sanitary program, 89; on troop trains, 85
Mercedes concentration point, 146, 148
mercury mining operations, 46–47
Merwin, J., 510n33
Metcalf, Elliott, 449
Methodist Episcopal Church Gulf Conference, 101
Mexican-American War, 163, 211
Mexican Army, 136, 242, 297, 371, 407
Mexican Border Service medal, 219–20
Mexican Independence Day, 326
Mexican National Railroad, 242
Mexican nationalism, 12
Mexican presidential election of 1910, 13
Mexican refugees, 370
Mexican Revolution (1910–1920), 7; causes of, 12–13; Guard call-up and, 451; Japanese involvement in, 400; power struggle within, 16; U.S. influence on, 15–16; U.S. response to, 14
Mexican sovereignty, 4, 52
Mexico: blockade of ports in, 63; demand for Punitive Expedition withdrawal, 53; foreign invasion of, 11; foreign investments in, 12; government instability in, 11–12; guerrilla raids into U.S. by, 57–58; improvement in relations with, 173; land reform in, 15; planned invasion of U.S. by, 52–57; refugees from, 370, 399; rules of engagement and, 136; U.S. intelligence operations in, 400–401
Michigan National Guard, 327; autoworkers in, 303; casualties, 341–42; composition, 302; conflict with Georgia Guard, 324; demobilization, 336; discipline, 303–304; mobilization, 302; training schedule, 304
Military Day (San Antonio), 107–108
military justice. *See* courts-martial proceedings
military parade, in El Paso, 326–27
military police units, 120, 140, 298–99, 325–26
"Militia Border Patrol" (poem), 283–84
Miller, Roy, 117–18, 121, 124, 125, 128, 134
Milliken, S. A., 28
Mills, Albert L., 32, 271
Milwaukee Railroad, 87
mining interests, 46–47, 383–84
Minneapolis Symphony Orchestra, 114
Minnesota National Guard, 113–14, 115, 137, 157, 211; casualties, 147; demobilization, 166–67; health and hygiene, 152; in Llano Grande, 147; weapons training, 149
Mississippi National Guard, 108, 115, 452
Missouri, Kansas, and Texas Railroad, 79, 81
Missouri National Guard, 27, 81; athletics and, 130; border patrolling, 256; camp conditions and, 252–53; casualties, 244, 258, 263; charity of, 255; composition, 244–245; demobilization, 257, 263; fraud committed by members of, 263–64; in Laredo District, 243, 245–46; mobilization, 244; training schedule, 258
Missouri State Aeronautical Society, 245
Mitchell, Billy, 86
mobilization, phased, 183
mobilization exercises, 72, 452–53
mobilization sites: confusion concerning, 71–72; permanent, 452

548

Montana National Guard, *238*; camp preparation, 384; casualties, 387; demobilization, 389–90; desertions, 386, 387; in Douglas, 383–84; mobilization, 383; recruitment, 386–87; shooting incidents, 385; as strikebreakers, 384; training routine, 384; uniforms and, 385, 390; weapons issue, 384–85
Monticello Guard, 141
Moreno, Carmen, 424
Morgan, Gene, 90–91
Moriarity, Daniel, 109
Morín, José M., 52–53
Morton, Charles G., 325, 326
Mount Franklin, 310
Mounted Service School, 61
Munson, Edward, 253
Murray, Arthur, 163

Naco concentration point: camp conditions, 403; order of battle, 464; shooting incidents, 399; threat environment, 399
Naco garrison, 399
Nallger, Merrill H., 510n33
narcotics trafficking, 340
National Defense Act, 68, 69, 112, 266, 373, 394, 397, 417, 447, 451
National Guard: Army attitude toward, 6, 62, 298, 393–95, 453; Army request for call-up of, 20; aviation squadron, 181; in campaign plan, 63; draft and, 359; enlistment contract, 69; equipment procurement responsibilities, 275–76; family member support, 72, 177–78, 247–48, 278, 285, 355; fraternization in, 122, 305–306; general inspection of, 73; in national defense act, 68–69; officer appointments, 498n44; officer election, 277, 388, 390; organization of, 67; pay issues, 98, 120, 308–309; phased mobilization of, 183; physical condition of, 69; principal function of, 450; in Punitive Expedition, 5; railroad strike and, 203, 263, 274, 315, 336; readiness, 5–6, 73; regular officers commissioned in, 68; socially prominent guardsmen, 6, 189, 200, 209, 305–306, 318–20, 414–15; in Southern Department reorganization, 168–70; as strikebreakers, 203, 263, 274, 315, 336, 384, 445, 450; student guardsmen, 273–74, 348, 414; uncivil elements of, 264; unit strength standards and, 394; unit variations, 6; war game on Mexican border, 163–66. *See also by state*
National Guard 26th Division, 453–54
National Guard call-up: administrative confusion during, 292–93; in Army mobilization plan, 67; in border town improvement, 253; concentration points in, 6, 79; critique of, 265–66, 393–95, 453; deficiencies revealed by, 5–6; demobilization and, 215, 217; dependency on regular Army in, 70; economic impact of, 7, 79, 251–52; impact on transportation, 71–72; importance of, 451, 453–54; mobilization sites in, 71–72; mobilization total, 475n9; private contributions to, 83, 97, 140, 177–78, 181, 301, 318, 319, 320, 377–78, 380, 409, 414; rationale for, 5, 66–67; reorganization on border, 103; supply and logistics system and, 69–71; training benefits of, 336–37; unit strength standards and, 332
nationalism: Irish, 182; Mexican, 12
naval radio station, 145
Nebraska National Guard, 71, 137, 211; athletics and, 130–31; demobilization, 167, 172; equipment shortages, 147; mobilization, 146; physical readiness, 146
Nebraska state fairgrounds, 146
Nebraska (USS), 63
Nevada National Guard, 408
New Hampshire National Guard, 108, 115, 137; adoption of orphan by, 260; border patrolling, 258; casualties, 259–60, 350, 352; cavalry, 163; composition, 248; crimes by members, 259; demobilization, 172, 264–65; French Canadians in, 249; in Laredo District, 243; mobilization, 248–49; route

New Hampshire (*continued*)
march, 349–50; service recognition, 265; in urban warfare training, 256
New Jersey National Guard, *239*; artillery, 291, 390; casualties, 387; cavalry, 380, 382; composition, 379; demobilization, 388–89, 391; desertions, 386; in Douglas, 382–83; homecoming reception, 389; mobilization, 379–80, 382; morale, 381; officer elections, 388; physical readiness, 380; private contributions to, 380; in regimental route march, 391; signal corps, 389; training routine, 383
New Jersey National Guard band, 381–82
New Mexico Athletic Association of Columbus, 365
New Mexico Border Patrol District, 358
New Mexico Military Institute, 356
New Mexico National Guard, 6; aircraft support and, 33; artillery, 291; attachment to Punitive Expedition, 358–59; bill to abolish, 373; border patrolling, 362–63; casualties, 372; composition, 27, 29; deficiencies, 27–28, 357–58; demobilization, 372–73; draft and, 36; duties, 368–69; equipment readiness, 31–32, 34; government property missing from, 369–70; in Hachita, 371–72; Hispanic guardsmen in, 367; initial activation of, 21; Jewish guardsmen in, 26–27; mobilization site, 28; physical readiness, 28–29, 32, 34–36, 355, 358; political favoritism in, 356; in Punitive Expedition, 5, 360, 368; recruitment, 35–36, 355–56, 358; rejection rate, 28; shooting incidents, 357; transportation to mobilization site, 29; voting rights of, 366–67
New York 69th Infantry, 182, 195, 210
New York American, 184
New York Central Railroad, 188
New York Herald, 152
New York National Guard, 6; African American guardsmen, 207; aircraft, 177, 181; alcohol use, 197–98; ammunition shortage, 190–91; armored unit, 177, 181–82, 218; artillery, 171, 185, 201, 206, 207, 222, *227*; athletics and, 131; border patrolling, 199–200, 206, 210–11; casualties, 188, 192, 198, 205, 208, 213, 218, *225*, 491n144, 492n17, 492n26; cavalry, 171, 181, 195–96, 201, 206; commemoration of service of, 219–20; composition, 174–75, *176*; cronyism in, 193; demobilization, 203, 204, 210, 211–13, 214–15, 216–17; economic impact of, 186–87; equipment, 180; in-state duties, 217; in inaugural parade, 217–18; insult to during parade, 213–14; Irish guardsmen, 182; Jewish guardsmen, 178; machine guns and, 175, *223*; medical support, 177–78; mobilization, 178, 180–81; physical readiness, 179, 184–85, 194–95, 198; private benefactors, 177–78; railroad strike and, 203; route march, 198, 200–202, 212, *224*, *232*; as separate divisional command, 195; shooting incidents, 192, 210–11; silk stocking regiment, 6, 189, 200; supply trains of, 175, 177, 217; travel to border, 184, 186–88; "wagon wheel" punishment in, 215
New York Naval Militia, 217
New York Red Cross, 178
New York Signal Corps, 196–97
New York State Industrial Farm, 179
New York Sun, 40
New York Times, 61–62, 90, 194
New York *Tribune*, 31
New York World, 40–41, 136, 140
New York Zoological Society, 216
"New Yorkers on the Southern Border" (Howard), 5
Newhill, Willard, 407–408
Newkirk, Frank, 368
newspapers and correspondents: on border camp conditions, 252–53; censorship of, 185–86, 244, 361; denigration of Guard by, 470n58; in El Paso, 302–303, 310; fabrication of stories by, 90–91, 152; guardsmen as

Index

correspondents, 364–65; on Illinois Guard route march, 96; militia newspapers, 149, 154, 191, 197, 301, 310, 448; press facilities at Brownsville, 139–40; reporter in summary court-martial, 96; as threat to Guard security, 61–62, 110

night maneuvers, 157–58

Nogales concentration point: camp conditions, 414–15, 418, 430–31; desertions from, 421; discipline in, 420–21; economic impact of military on, 405–406, 427; equipment shortages, 412; Funston inspection of, 431; Ku Klux Klan parade in, 433–35; medical facilities in, 408; military police in, 422; order of battle, 464–65; provisional cavalry regiment at, 425–26; recreation at, 423–24; route marches, 424–25; rules of engagement at, 419; shooting incidents, 407, 418–19, 420, 435–37; state governors' inspections at, 426; threat environment, 407

Nogales Daily Herald, 416, 421, 428, 431, 433–35, 436, 438

North Carolina National Guard: casualties, 341; composition, 323

North Dakota National Guard, 103, 137; demobilization, 167, 172; at Llano Grande, 147; at Mercedes, 148; mobilization, 147–48

Norwich University, 270, 273

Nueces Hotel, Corpus Christi, 120, 121, 125, 127, 128, 134

Nuevo Laredo port of entry, 242

Obama, Barak, 3
Obregón, Alvaro, 16, 20, 54
observation balloon, 320
Office of Strategic Services, 192
Oglesby, W. R., 178
O'Gorman, James A., 194
Ohio National Guard, *234*; 8th Infantry band, *233*; casualties, 335–36, 342; cavalry, 320, 331; composition, 316–17; demobilization, 336; mobilization, 317–18; observation balloon of, 320; outpost duty, 331; physical readiness, 146, 318–19; protest of camp conditions, 335–36; silk stocking units in, 318–20

Oklahoma A&M, 102

Oklahoma National Guard, 115, 163; at Llano Grande, 147; machine gun training, 151; mobilization, 142–43

Oklahoma state fairground, 143

Oklasoda, The, 154

Operation Jump Start, 3

Order of the Eastern Star, 126

Oregon National Guard, 66, *241*; cavalry, 444; demobilization, 445–46; family-related discharges, 441–42; inspection of, 442, 445; mission, 443; mobilization, 440–42; physical readiness, 441, 444; rations, 442–43; recruitment, 440, 441; shooting incidents, 443, 444; strike duty, 445

Orozco, Pascual, 14, 15

O'Ryan, John, 168, 174, 178, 179, 182, 185, 190, 194, 195, 197–98, 199, 201, 205, 207, 209, 212, 214, 302

Packard Motor Company, 303
Packard trucks, 159
Palo Alto battlefield, 166
Parker, James, 50, 117, 132, 133, 137, 153, 154, 155, 157, 164, 165, 166, 168, 173, 195, 199, 206, 208, 212, 214, 302
Parker, William, 357
Parks, J. C., 363
Paso del Norte Hotel, El Paso, 305, 325
Pathe weekly news service, 139
Patterson, Joseph Medill, 86
Patterson, Paul, 319
Patterson, Rufus, 429
pay and pay issues: civilian truck drivers, 303; foreign duty pay, 98; monthly pay, 120; monthly payroll, 120, 134, 138, 160, 251, 405; New Mexico Guard and, 356; pay arrears, 270, 308–309
Peacock, Wesley, 113
Peacock Military Academy, 113
Pecos High Bridge, 46
Peerless trucks, 159
Penniman, P. R., 362

Index

Pennsylvania Dutch, 300
Pennsylvania National Guard, 175, *231,* 287; artillery, 307; in Big Bend District, 281; casualties, 301, 340–41; cavalry, 300–301; in Columbus, 359–60; composition, 299; demobilization, 336, 426; in El Paso, 299; engineers, 416, 426; in large unit exercises, 327–28; mobilization, 299–300; political favoritism in, 306–307; reorganization, 307
Perry, Howard E., 46–47
Pershing, John J., 3, 4, 18, 34, 62, 63, 82, 116, 134, 151, 173, 183, 192, 337–39, 338, 367, 370
Persico, Joseph E., 192
Pezzar, Norberto, 58
Pharr, Tex., *221, 222, 226. See also* McAllen-Pharr-Mission triangle concentration point
Phelan, John J., 194
Phelps Dodge Company, 374, 384
Philadelphia North American: Camp Pershing and Fort Bliss Edition, 301, 310
Philadelphia quartermaster depot, 70–71, 179, 262
Philippine insurrection, 78
Philippine Scouts, 60
Phoenix, Ariz., 377
Phoenix Chamber of Commerce, 398
Phoenix Indian School, 24
physical readiness: Arkansas Guard, 345, 346; California Guard, 410–11; Connecticut Guard, 416; dental requirements, 410–11; Florida Guard, 260; Guards' failure to meet, 21–22, 69; Illinois Guard, 83–84; Kansas Guard, 269; New Hampshire Guard, 248; New Jersey Guard, 380; New Mexico Guard, 28–29, 32, 34–36, 355, 358; New York Guard, 179, 184–85, 194–95, 198; of officers, 194–95; Ohio Guard, 318–19; Oregon Guard, 444; rejection rate, 146–47, 318; route march and, 94–97, 100; Tennessee Guard, 277; Texas Guard, 44; Utah Guard, 408; Vermont Guard, 271; war game in proving, 166
Pickering, Abner, 391

Pickering, R. R., 108
pie campaign, 110
Pittsburgh Post, 301
Pizaña, Aniceto, 52, 53
Plan de San Diego, 16–18; Carranza manipulation of, 468n7; guerrilla raids as component of, 57–58; Hispanic uprising as component of, 52–53, 54; invasion of Texas and, 53; reactivation of, 52; termination of, 64–65
Plan de San Luis Potosí, 13
Plummer, Edward H., 146, 420, 425, 426, 431
Point Isabel naval radio station, 145
political influence and cronyism: Arkansas Guard, 353; California Guard, 412; Illinois Guard, 111; Massachusetts Guard, 298; Montana Guard, 383–84; New Jersey Guard, 382; New Mexico Guard, 356; New York Guard, 193; Pennsylvania Guard, 306–307; in relaxed physical standards, 318–19; Texas Guard, 41; voting rights and, 366–67
polo matches, 310
Ponce, Victoriano, 53
pontoon outfit, 168
Porterfield, W. C., 355–56
Portland Press, 246
post exchange, *226*
Post Office Department, 104
Preparedness Day parade, 47
preparedness movement, 81, 98
presidential election of 1916, 366
presidential inauguration, 217–18
Presidio Mining Company, 47
press. *See* newspapers and correspondents
Presson, George, 248
Price, William G., 299
Princeton University, 133, 381
private contributions to Guard, 83, 140, 177–78, 181, 301, 320, 377–78, 380, 409, 414
prostitution, 90, 113, 198, 312, 339, 365
1st Provisional Brigade, 153, 158
1st Provisional Cavalry Division, 338
1st Provisional Separate Brigade, 142
2nd Provisional Brigade, 153
2nd Provisional Infantry Division, 338

Index

4th Provisional Coast Artillery Regiment, 250, 257
5th Provisional Coast Artillery Regiment, 279
10th Provisional Division, 328
12th Provisional Division: composition, 105, 108, 114, 115; tactical march, 106–107; training, 109
13th Provisional Division: cavalry, 170; composition, 168–70; demobilization of Guard units, 171; inspection of, 157
Pullman Company, 72
Punitive Expedition: background of, 3–4; in Columbus, 370; commitment of troops to Southern Department, 60–61; in El Paso District, 337–38; logistical base for, 30, 354; Mexican response to, 52–53, 59; mission of, 18; National Guard units assigned to, 5, 358–59, 360, 368; refugees accompanying, 370; scope of, 5; truck purchase for, 334
Purdue University, 148

Quartermaster Corps, 70, 72, 83, 189, 262
quartermaster depots, 70–71

race and racial tensions: black guardsmen and, 92–94, 112, 253–54, 278–79, 375; Chinese refugees and, 370; Hispanics and, 23
Railroad Corps (Mexico), 55
railroad lines: Army's dependence on, 452; in Brownsville District, 137; call-up impact on, 6, 71–72, 191; foreign investment as impetus for Mexican, 12; in Mexican invasion of Texas, 54; Punitive Expedition use of, 4; rolling stock shortage, 84–85, 183; siding construction, 81–82; through San Antonio concentration point, 79–81. *See also* troop trains
railroad strike, 203, 263, 274, 315, 336
Rains, George P., 119, 136
Ramos, Basilio, 16
Rapp, Samuel S., 179–80
Ray Consolidated Copper Company, 25
Ray Hercules Copper Company, 25

recruitment and enlistment: Arizona Guard, 22–23, 25–26; Arkansas Guard, 349; California Guard, 411; Connecticut Guard, 416; District of Columbia Guard, 402–403; fraudulent, 355, 356; guardsman contract and, 69; of men with dependents, 248; Montana Guard, 386–87; New Mexico Guard, 35–36, 355–56, 358; Oregon Guard, 441; Texas Guard, 42, 51; U.S. Army, 60, 332; Utah Guard, 409
Red Cross. *See* American Red Cross Society
Reeves, Ira L., 270, 274
refugees from Mexico, 370, 399
regionalism, 7
Reid, Henry B., 314–15
religion and religious observance: at Camp Scurry, 125; at Camp Wilson, 100–102; in Columbus, 366; in El Paso, 311–12; by New York Guard, 216; in Nogales, 423
religious revivals, 101
remount stations, 98–99, 236, 307–308
Report on Mobilization, 88
Resaca de la Palma battlefield, 163, 166
Revolutionary Congress of San Diego, 54
Reyes, Bernardo, 15
Rhode Island National Guard: artillery, 305; casualties, 340; cavalry, 305; discipline, 304–305
Ricaut, Alfredo, 56–57, 59, 243
Richardson, Lorrain Thompson, 86
Richmond Blues, 141, 163
Rio Grande ballad, 321–22
Rio Grande Rattler, 197
Roach, Virgil T., 429
Rock Island Arsenal, 71
Rock Island Railroad, 79, 81
Rockerfeller Commission for the Relief of Poland, 192
Rogers, Hopewell, 86
Rojas, José, 282, 284
Roosevelt, Theodore, 179
Roosevelt Dam, 379, 406
Rose, J. M., 510n33
Rosier, William G., 163
Rotary Club of Corpus Christi, 121

Index

Rotary Club of San Antonio, 110
route marches: 10th Provisional Division, 328–30; 12th Provisional Division, 106–107; Arizona Guard, 401; California Guard, 425; Connecticut Guard, 424–25; Illinois Guard, 94–97; Kansas Guard, 269; Massachusetts Guard, 326, 328–30; New Hampshire Guard, 349–50; New Jersey Guard, 383; New York Guard, 198, 201–202, 212, 224; at Nogales, 424–25; Oregon Guard, 443; Pennsylvania Guard, 327; supply and logistics issues on, 328–29, 391; Texas Guard, 123–24, 128–29; Utah Guard, 424; of war-strength regiment, 391; Wisconsin Guard, 100
Ruckman, John W., 260
rules of engagement, 136
Ruppe, Bernard, 356
Rye, Tom C., 275, 277

Sacramento Bee, 411
Sadler, Wilbur F. Jr., 380–81, 382
Sage, W. H., 406, 407, 420, 426
salute protocols, 391–92
Sam Fordyce concentration point, 146
San Antonio Art League, 115
San Antonio Chamber of Commerce, 113
San Antonio concentration point: athletic activities, 102–103; holiday celebrations, 110; Military Day at, 107–108; order of battle, 455–56; physical environment, 88; preparedness movement and, 81; provost guard stationed at, 94; racial tensions at, 92–94, 112; religious life at, 100–102; selection of, 79; supply shortages at, 90; troop trains through, 79, 81. *See also* Camp Wilson; Fort Sam Houston
San Antonio Express, 79, 102, 110, 112, 420
San Benito concentration point: economic impact of Guard on, 144–45, 161; entertainment program at, 154–55; field day competitions, 155; provisional 1st Separate Brigade at, 142
San Diego (USS), 64
San Francisco earthquake, 78

San Ignacio raid, 58
Sandoval, Abel, 59
Sands, W. B., 326
sanitary program, 89–90. *See also* health and hygiene
Santa Fe New Mexican, 36, 361, 368–69
Santa Fe Railroad, 312
Saturday Evening Post, 140
Savage Arms Company, 97–98
Scales, Erie C., 108
Schaick, Louis Van, 363
Scharfenberg, Paul I., 114
Scheiner, Henry, 198
School of Fire, 61
School of Musketry, 61
Schrimpser, J. E., 364
Schumnn-Heink, Ernestine, 334
Schwierz, Richard W., 405
Scott, H. B., 351
Scott, Hugh, 4, 20, 54, 63, 114, 194, 218
Scott's Ranch raid, 162–63
Screws, William P., 432
Scurry, W. R., 120
Seligman, James I., 31
Semple, William R., 289
4th Separate Brigade, 347, 349, 351, 352
Serrano, Francisco, 436–37
service schools, 61
Seventh Regiment Gazette, 191, 197, 206
Shaw, Charles D., Jr., 510n33
Sherburne, John H., 305–306
Shiflett, George K., 413
shooting incidents: Arkansas Guard, 346; in Big Bend District, 282–83; Connecticut Guard, 418; District of Columbia Guard, 404; in El Paso, 295; Florida Guard, 265; friendly fire and, 283; Illinois Guard, 160; Iowa Guard, 160; Kentucky Guard, 331; Massachusetts Guard, 295, 362; Montana Guard, 385; in Naco, 399; New Mexico Guard, 357; New York Guard, 192, 210; in Nogales, 407, 418–19, 435–37; Oregon Guard, 443; sniper fire, 90–91, 282, 295, 330–31, 374, 385, 405, 419, 420; Texas Guard, 282–83, 287–88; Utah Guard, 435–37
Sibley, Frederick W., 18, 19, 267, 279
Sickles, H. C., 357, 362

Index

"silk-stocking" units, 6, 189, 200, 209, 305–306, 318–20, 414–15
Silver City Independent, 359
Silver City Red Cross Chapter, 369
Sinclair, Clyde D., 424
Sloan, Albert B., 346
Slocum, Herbert J., 264
Smith, Albion, 324, 336–37
Smith, Newman, 428
Smyth, William, 348
sniper fire, 90–91, 282, 295, 330–31, 374, 385, 405, 419, 420
Soldiers' Comfort Club, The, 25
"Solid South," 92
Sons of the Revolution, 186
South Carolina National Guard, 327; casualties, 341; composition, 314; demobilization, 336; in large-scale exercise, 334; mobilization, 314
South Dakota National Guard, 137, 142, 163, 211, *227*; casualties, 145; demobilization, 172; mobilization of, 143–44
South Dakota (USS), 64
Southern California Border District, 448, 520n3
Southern Department, 6, 42, 51, 60, 70, 79, 116, 134, 168; in border security, 337–38; jurisdiction, 77, 82
Southern Pacific Railroad, 19, 441
Southwestern Railroad, 301–302
Southwestern Telegraph & Telephone Company, 139
Southwestern University, 122
Spain, 11, 78
Spanell, Harry J., 283
Spanish-American War, 45, 78, 179
Spaulding, Roland H., 249
"Special Report on Tapping Telegraph Wires" (U.S. Army), 400
Spratling, Edgar J., 323
Spry, William, 426
Srodes, James, 381
Standard Oil Company, 25
St. Anthony Hotel, San Antonio, 44
State Industrial Farm, 179
Sterling, William W., 201
Sterling Ranch, 201
Stewart, Sam V., 386

St. John Greble, E., 325, 331
St. Louis, Brownsville & Mexico Railroad, 191
St. Louis Globe Democrat, 252
St. Louis Post-Dispatch, 245
St. Louis quartermaster depot, 70, 71
St. Louis Republic, 245
St. Louis Star, 245
St. Louis University, 245
Stock, Arthur, 368
Stone, Edward, 378
Stone House incident, 436–37
Stout, Joseph A., 59
Stover, Willis S., 292
Stroupe, Almon, 353
Stroupe, Henry, 353
student guardsmen, 23, 273–74, 348, 413, 414
supply and logistics: administrative forms shortages, 90, 262; in Brownsville District, 137; camp preparation issues, 196; centralization of, 70, 452–53; equipment shortages, 71, 261–62, 272, 275–76, 297, 380, 412; for federalized units, 83; food shortages on troop trains, 184, 187–88; Guard call-up stress on, 69–71; illegal sale of government property, 37–39; machine guns and, 333; missing government property, 369–70; in New York Guard mobilization, 180–81; on-hand requirements for state Guard, 447; preparedness movement and, 81; private contributions to Guard and, 83, 140, 177–78, 181, 301, 320, 377–78, 380, 409, 414–15; procurement responsibilities, 276–77; for Punitive Expedition, 4, 30; route marches and, 328–29; weapons issue, 293. *See also* transportation
supply depots, 70–71
supply trains, 175, 177
surgeon general of the army, 194
Sweetser, E. Leroy, 292, 295, 306, 326, 356
Swift, Eben, 338

tactical exercises, 132
tactical march, 106–107
Taylor, Zachary, 163, 211

555

Index

Tempe Normal School, 23
Temple Sinai, El Paso, 312
Tennessee National Guard, 210, 216; casualties, 341; composition, 275, 277; election of officers, 277; equipment shortages, 275–76; mobilization, 275; physical readiness, 277
tent winterization, 126
Terlingua, Tex., 284–85
Terlingua raid, 19–20
Terrell, S. L., 286
Texas: Hispanic uprising planned in, 52–56; planned Mexican invasion of, 53
Texas Alpine Avalanche, 41
Texas A&M College, 121, 122, 129
Texas Baptist Convention, 101
Texas Cattle Raisers Association, 288
Texas National Guard, 157; in 12th Provisional Division, 115; athletics and, 122–23, 129, 130–31, 133; in Big Bend District, 46–49, 114, 280; in Brownsville District, 136–37, 153; casualties, 132–33, 288; cavalry, 45, 51, 79, *228,* 243, 281, 287; community relations, 126; in Corpus Christi, 119; criticism of, 40–41; cronyism in, 41; demobilization, 116, 132, 133, 134, 289; desertions, 286; dispersal from Camp Wilson, 79–81; engineers, 479n112; enlistments, 43; failures to report in, 44; gifts sent to, 285–86; at Harlingen, 145; illegal sale of government property and, 37–39; initial activation of, 21; inspection of, 123; in Laredo District, 243; in lower Rio Grande Valley, 49–50; in Mercedes, 146; militia ratio to total population, 41; mobilization, 39–40, 42–43; monthly pay, 120; morale, 288–89; organization as 6th Separate Brigade, 24, 41–42; in Pharr, 146; physical readiness, 44; preparation for Mexican invasion, 284–85; recruitment, 42, 51; in relief of Coast Artillery Companies, 473n164; route march by, 123–24, 128–29; in San Benito, 142; shooting incidents, 282–83, 287–88; in Terlingua, 284–85; training, 39, 50

Texas Rangers, 39, 43, 53, 279, 288, 326
Thanksgiving observance, 110, 129
Tharalson, Thomas H., 147
Thomas, Charles W., 411, 426
Thompson, Maurice, 446
threat environment: Big Bend District, 281–82, 284; California border, 439; Columbus, 371; Douglas, 393; El Paso, 295; Laredo District, 242–43, 260; Naco, 399; Nogales, 407
Thurston, Nathaniel B., 205
Tillotson, Lee O., 274
Titcomb, Georgia, 431
Toulouse, J. H., 368
training activities: benefits of, 336–37; cavalry charges, 162; combat maneuvers, 123–24; counterinsurgency, 304; field exercises, 154, 156–57, 404, 444; field maneuvers, 163–66; hide-and-seek exercise, 159; large unit exercises, 327–28, 334; night maneuvers, 157–58, 445; outpost duty as, 331; surprise attacks, 162, 199; tactical, 132; trench warfare, 109, 110, 154; urban warfare, 256; war games, 163–66, 201, 202, 207–208, 425. *See also* route marches
training cantonment, 171–72
transportation: ambulance train, 177; armored car, 167–68; in Brownsville District, 137; call-up impact on, 71–72; caterpillar train, 286–87, 289; horses and mules' importance in, 308; of Kansas Guard by truck, 104–105; of Kentucky Guard, 322–23; of machine gun companies, 98, 333; mechanization in Laredo District, 250–51; mechanization of U.S. Army, 4, 18, 30; modernization experiments in, 391; motorcycles, 177, 360; New York Division field train, 217; pontoon unit, 168; supply trains, 175, 177; tractor train, *229;* truck companies, 159; truck driver shortage, 303; truck purchases for Punitive Expedition, 334; truck shortage, 303; truck testing, 45; wagon allotment, 334. *See also* horses and mules; railroad lines; troop trains

Index

Travis, William B., 104
trench warfare, 109, 110, 154
Treviño, Jacinto, 59, 62, 66
troop trains: Alabama Guard and, 427–28, 438; California Guard and, 411; Connecticut Guard and, 414; Delaware Guard and, 345; food shortages on, 184, 187–88; hospital train, 90; Illinois Guard and, 84–85; Maine Guard and, 246; Maryland Guard and, 268; Massachusetts Guard and, 294, 360; medical support on, 85; New Jersey Guard and, 382; New York Guard and, 187–89, 193; Pennsylvania Guard and, 300–301; rolling stock requirements, 476n25; through San Antonio, 79, 81; Utah Guard and, 409; Vermont Guard and, 271–72; Virginia Guard and, 141; Washington Guard and, 447; Wisconsin Guard and, 87–88
truck companies, 159. *See also* transportation
Tucson, Ariz., 23, 26, 377–78
Tucson Aero Squadron, 512n14
Tulane University, 153
Tuthill, A. M., 24, 26, 376
typhoid fever inoculation, 270, 418
typhoid fever outbreak, 198, 204, 206

uniform shortages, 71
United Kingdom, 97–98
United States: guerrilla raids into, 3, 16, 18–19, 57, 58, 59; Hispanic fifth columnists in, 17; intelligence operations in Mexico, 400–401; invasion of Mexico by, 11; Mexico's planned invasion of, 52–57; war planning, 63–64
United Synagogues of America, 178
University of Arizona, 23
University of Indiana, 148
University of Maine band, 246, 256, 258
University of Texas, 102, 121, 122, 129
University of Vermont, 273
urban warfare training, 256
Urbansky, August, 388
U.S. 1st Cavalry, 24, 60, 209, 374, 376, 399, 512n2

U.S. 3rd Cavalry, 137, 145, 146, 150, 153, 208, 211
U.S. 3rd Field Artillery, 61, 243, 250, 257
U.S. 3rd Infantry, 279
U.S. 4th Field Artillery, 137, 153, 157
U.S. 4th Infantry, 137, 150, 153
U.S. 5th Field Artillery, 47, 61, 137, 153, 157, 291, 332
U.S. 6th Cavalry, 19, 47, 280, 282, 283, 284, 289
U.S. 6th Field Artillery, 20, 242–43, 374
U.S. 6th Infantry, 24
U.S. 7th Infantry, 47
U.S. 8th Cavalry, 18, 47, 337
U.S. 8th Field Artillery, 332
U.S. 9th Infantry, 242, 243, 250, 257
U.S. 10th Cavalry, 62, 402, 438
U.S. 11th Cavalry, 352, 369
U.S. 11th Infantry, 374, 391, 419
U.S. 12th Cavalry, 371
U.S. 12th Infantry, 20, 405, 418, 419, 421
U.S. 13th Cavalry, 352
U.S. 14th Cavalry, 18, 19, 243, 250, 257
U.S. 14th Infantry, 20, 23, 60, 374, 376, 399
U.S. 17th Cavalry, 332
U.S. 17th Infantry, 357
U.S. 18th Infantry, 348, 374, 390, 391, 405
U.S. 19th Infantry, 60, 93, 279
U.S. 20th Infantry, 47
U.S. 21st Infantry, 20, 60, 418
U.S. 22nd Infantry, 374, 376, 391, 399
U.S. 23rd Infantry, 47, 295
U.S. 24th Infantry, 278, 279, 358, 370, 371
U.S. 26th Infantry, 135, 142, 145, 146, 150, 171
U.S. 28th Infantry, 137, 145, 146, 150, 157, 211
U.S. 30th Infantry, 45
U.S. 34th Infantry, 289, 332
U.S. 35th Infantry, 391, 438, 512n2
U.S. 36th Infantry, 153, 156
U.S. 38th Coast Artillery Company, 442
U.S. Army: attitude toward National Guard, 6, 62, 298, 393–95, 453; in border security, 337–38; camp preparation, 196, 291–92; desertions, 286; in El Paso military parade,

Index

U.S. Army (*continued*)
326–27; general inspection of, 73; Guard dependence on, 70; machine gun selection, 150–51; mechanization of, 4, 18; modernization experiments in, 391; press censorship by, 185–86; recruitment drive, 332; reorganization of troops in Brownsville District, 170; request for Guard call-up, 20; salute protocols, 391–92; strength in 1916, 60; unit strength standards and, 332, 394
U.S. Army Maneuver Division, 14, 79
U.S. Border Patrol, 3
U.S. Cavalry, 4, 162
U.S. Civil War, 41, 182
U.S. Congress, 71
U.S. Engineers, 153
U.S.-Mexican border, *80, 239, 240, 344*; Japanese troops on, 400
U.S.-Mexican border patrols, 170–71; in Laredo District, 256; Massachusetts Guard, 296; New Mexico Guard, 362–63, 368–69; New York Guard, 199–200, 206, 210–11; Texas Guard, 282–83, 289; Utah Guard, 435–37
U.S.-Mexican commission, 65
U.S. Military Academy, 61
U.S. naval radio station, 145, 157
U.S. Navy, in campaign plan, 63
U.S. Signal Corps, 60
Utah, 5
Utah National Guard, 452; border patrolling, 435–37; casualties, 409; cavalry, 425–26; demobilization, 426–27, 429, 438; mobilization, 408; Nevada guardsmen enlistment in, 408; in Nogales, 409–10; physical readiness, 408; private contributions to, 409; recruitment, 409; route march, 424; shooting incidents, 435–37

Van Gent, Conrad Eugene, 102
Van Walraven, Albert A., 382, 389
Vanderbilt, Cornelius, 177, 201, 214
Vanderbilt, Mrs. Cornelius, 177–78
Variety Smoke Shop, Tucson, 378
Vaught, J. S., 363
Veracruz occupation, 16, 256

Vermont National Guard: cavalry, 273; composition, 270; equipment shortages, 272; military college cadets in, 273–74; mobilization, 270–71; outpost duty, 272; physical readiness, 271; training schedule, 273; transportation to border, 271–72
Vickers, George T., 388
Vickers-Maxim machine gun, 150, 151, 333
Villa, Francisco "Pancho," 3, 14, 15, 16, 17–18, 90, 192, 281, 284
Vincent, T. I., 366
Virginia National Guard, 105, 115, 137, 157; athletics and, 130; in Brownsville, 141, 153; casualties, 154, 485n94; cavalry, 141, 163; demobilization, 167, 172; in field exercise, 154, 156–57; machine gun training, 151; night maneuvers, 158
voting rights, 366–67

Wadsworth, James W., 178, 213
"wagon wheel" punishment, 215–16
Walker, Emmett E., 38
Walker, James A., 402
Walsh, Thomas J., 384
Wankowski, Robert, 410
war games, 334; in Brownsville, 163–66; New York Guard in, 201, 202, 207–208. *See also* training activities
Washington Cadet Corps, 402
Washington House of Representatives, 449
Washington National Guard: in Calexico, 447–48; casualties, 448; composition, 446; mobilization, 446; strike duty, 449, 450; training routine, 448; Troop B recognition, 449–50
Washington Post, 402
Washingtonian, The, 448
water system construction, 196
Waterman, J. C., 363, 371
weapons shortages, 71
weapons training: by 12th Provisional Division, 109; at Llano Grande, 149–50; machine gun, 97–99
weather conditions: drought, 200; hurricane, 156, 200–201, 250;

Index

sandstorms, 304; Texas heat, 191; Texas norther, 163; thunderstorms, 315, 387, 413, 415
Webb, Jess, 510n33
Webb Station raid, 57–58
Wedgwood, Edgar A., 408, 426
Wells, James H., 137–38
West Virginia National Guard, 71, 106, 115
Western Department, 70, 77, 82, 430
Weyrecht, C. C., 320
Wheeling (USS), 63
White, George A., 440
Whitman, Charles S., 177, 178, 183, 193, 195, 207, 211, 212, 213, 214, 218, 219
Wickersham, I. P., 348
Williams, Samuel T., 280
Willis, Frank, 316–17
Wilson, Woodrow, 3, 17–18, 39, 41, 64, 102, 194, 211, 217–18, 356, 364, 366, 401
Windmill Ranch, 269, 272
Wisconsin National Guard, 115; athletics and, 129; beer issue for, 88; composition, 86; machine gun company in, 97; preparedness, 87; route march, 100; troop train to concentration point, 87–88
Withycombe, James, 440, 445
Wood, C. R., 320, 336
Wood, Leonard, 179, 193–94, 213, 248, 271, 276–77, 332, 348, 380, 393
Wood, Worden, 295
Woon, Basil Dillon, 136

World War I, 5; call-up as preparation for, 8, 452–53; Guard demobilization and, 114, 217, 336; machine gun impact on, 97; National Guard 26th Division and, 453–54; in shaping Guard training, 109, 339; U.S. tourism and, 139
Wright, Fred J., 401
Wright, Mike, 482n54
wristwatches, 327
Wyoming National Guard: casualties, 351; demobilization, 352, 353; mobilization, 348

Yale University, 133, 413, 414
Yaqui Indians, 407
Young, Harry H., 388
Young Men's Christian Association (YMCA): in Big Bend, *229*; in Brownsville, 139, 141; in Columbus, 30; in Corpus Christi, 121, 127; in Deming, 346–47; in Douglas, 386; in El Paso, 310–11; in Imperial Beach, 444; in McAllen, 197; in Nogales, 423, 430; in San Antonio, 89, 113; scope of activities, 311; at Sterling ranch, 201; in Terlingua, 285
Young Men's Hebrew Association (YMHA), 178, 386, 423
Young Women's Christian Association (YWCA), 113, 339

Zapata, Emiliano, 14, 15, 16, 17
Zorn, P. A., 26
Zuazua, Fortunato, 55, 56

www.ingramcontent.com/pod-product-compliance
Lightning Source LLC
Chambersburg PA
CBHW020826160426
43192CB00007B/537